The Archaeology of the Spanish Civil War

The Archaeology of the Spanish Civil War offers the first comprehensive account of the Spanish Civil War from an archaeological perspective, providing an alternative narrative on one of the most important conflicts of the twentieth century, widely seen as a prelude to the Second World War.

Between 1936 and 1939, totalitarianism and democracy, fascism and revolution clashed in Spain, while the latest military technologies were being tested, including strategic bombing and combined arms warfare, and violence against civilians became widespread. Archaeology, however, complicates the picture as it brings forgotten actors into play: obsolete weapons, vernacular architecture, ancient structures (from Iron Age hillforts to sheepfolds), peasant traditions, and makeshift arms. By looking at these things, another story of the war unfolds, one that pays more attention to intimate experiences and anonymous individuals. Archaeology also helps to clarify battles, which were often chaotic and only partially documented, and to understand better the patterns of political violence, whose effects were literally buried for over 70 years. The narrative starts with the coup against the Second Spanish Republic on 18 July 1936, follows the massacres and battles that marked the path of the war, and ends in the early 1950s, when the last forced labor camps were closed and the anti-Francoist guerrillas suppressed.

The book draws on 20 years of research to bring together perspectives from battlefield archaeology, archaeologies of internment, and forensics. It will be of interest to anybody interested in historical and contemporary archaeology, human rights violations, modern military history, and negative heritage.

Alfredo González-Ruibal is a researcher with the Institute of Heritage Sciences of the Spanish National Research Council. His work focuses on the archaeology of the contemporary past and African archaeology. Among other books, he has edited *Ethics and the Archaeology of Violence* (2015, with Gabriel Moshenska) and is the author of *An Archaeology of the Contemporary Era* (2018), the latter also with Routledge. He is the managing editor of the *Journal of Contemporary Archaeology*.

The Archaeology of the Spanish Civil War

Alfredo González-Ruibal

LONDON AND NEW YORK

First published 2020
by Routledge
2 Park Square, Milton Park, Abingdon, Oxon OX14 4RN

and by Routledge
52 Vanderbilt Avenue, New York, NY 10017

Routledge is an imprint of the Taylor & Francis Group, an informa business

© 2020 Alfredo González-Ruibal

The right of Alfredo González-Ruibal to be identified as author of this work
has been asserted by them in accordance with sections 77 and 78 of the
Copyright, Designs and Patents Act 1988.

All rights reserved. No part of this book may be reprinted or reproduced or
utilised in any form or by any electronic, mechanical, or other means, now
known or hereafter invented, including photocopying and recording, or in
any information storage or retrieval system, without permission in writing
from the publishers.

Trademark notice: Product or corporate names may be trademarks or registered
trademarks, and are used only for identification and explanation without
intent to infringe.

British Library Cataloguing-in-Publication Data
A catalogue record for this book is available from the British Library

Library of Congress Cataloging-in-Publication Data
A catalog record has been requested for this book

ISBN: 978-0-367-20199-9 (hbk)
ISBN: 978-0-367-20200-2 (pbk)
ISBN: 978-0-429-26013-1 (ebk)

Typeset in Bembo
by Integra Software Services Pvt. Ltd.

"And I would discover that in war there is, apart from death, a multitude of other things: there is everything that is in our ordinary life".

Svetlana Alexievich (The unwomanly face of war)

To my mother, Mila.

Contents

List of figures	x
List of abbreviations	xvi
Acknowledgements	xvii
Dies Irae	xix

1 Introduction   1
A war too close 1
Outline of the book 3

2 Time to kill: July 1936–February 1937   9
The path to blood 9
The nature of violence 12
Patterns of murder 14
The language of the drowned 32

3 Capital of glory: October 1936–January 1937   39
Enemy at the gates 40
Crossing the gates: the fight in Casa de Campo 42
War at the university 56
They did not pass 71

4 Capital of misery: July 1936–October 1938   73
Nationalist lines at the University City 76
Republican lines at the University City 85
The underground city 91

5 The path to total war: February–October 1937   102
The last Nationalist attempts to take Madrid 103
War in the Basque Mountains 110

viii *Contents*

Belchite: beyond the ruins 121
The end of the Northern Front 135
Crumb under belt 136
The fall of Oviedo 139
Massacre of the innocents 140

6 Wait and retreat: November 1937–March 1938   143
Idle time in Extremadura 143
Killing time in Guadalajara 146
Waiting and raiding in Aragón 153
Retreat 164

7 Forgotten battles: April–July 1938   169
The offensive of Alto Tajuña 170
Death in the sheepfolds 173
The siege of La Enebrá 176
The battle of La Nava 188
The end of the offensive 193
War on the Levant 195
Lost soldiers, forgotten hills 195
XYZ: The line that stopped Franco 200
Bombers over the Levant 202

8 The Battle of the Ebro: July–November 1938   208
The archaeology of the Battle of the Ebro 210
The last day of the Battle of the Ebro 219

9 Dead men walking: November 1938–March 1939   232
Into exile 232
The trenches of the victors 236
The trenches of the vanquished 247
The last Republican offensive 258
The fall 262

10 The never-ending war: April 1939–1952   269
Guerrilla warfare 270
Spaces of punishment 279

11 Aftermath: Heritage and memory   310
Heritage and memory during war and dictatorship 310
Heritage and memory in democracy 314

Conclusions   **322**

References   326
Annex: Tables   348
Index   353

Figures

1.1	Map of Spain during the Civil War with some of the main sites mentioned in the text	4
2.1	One of the mass graves of Mount Estépar (Burgos), a typical case of a massive Nationalist *saca* from the early war period	15
2.2	Cemetery of San Rafael (Málaga): mass grave 1, layer 6. A typical case of repeated executions by firing squad in an urban context	18
2.3	One of the mass graves of the cemetery of Magallón (Zaragoza): small *paesos* in a rural area	21
2.4	The grave of Claudio Macías, dug by himself shortly before his death	22
2.5	A.M., an unknown Basque soldier murdered during Christmas of 1937. He had his hands tied behind his back before being shot and dumped into a shallow grave	28
2.6	A crucifix that was carried by one of the 59 persons killed and buried in Gumiel de Izán (Burgos). Most of those killed were railway workers	35
2.7	A high-heeled shoe carried by one of the women buried in a mass grave in Fregenal de la Sierra (Extremadura)	37
3.1	Paired pillboxes of Leganés (Madrid). Construction on these Republican pillboxes started in October 1936 but was never completed	43
3.2	The Battle of Madrid	44
3.3	Map of the trench of Casa de Vacas in the NW corner of Casa de Campo and detail of the excavated trench	47
3.4	Map of combat-related items found during surface survey in front of the trench. Inside the square, one of the two clips of an Enfield P14 found next to Firing Position 3	51
3.5	A Fifth Regiment grenade	54
3.6	The attack on the University City	57
3.7	Impact of small arms fire at the entrance of the School of Medicine. They can only be the result of the room-by-room fighting during the Battle of Madrid, as the sector later remained deep inside Republican-held territory	59

Figures xi

3.8 To the left: finds related to the November 1936 combats in the NW of the University City. In grey, second-line Republican fortifications from late 1938 (see Chapter 9). To the right: obsolete weapons employed by Republican soldiers in the defense of the University City   61

3.9 The undocumented Nationalist attack through the NW corner of the University City. Density maps of artillery shells and bullets based on surface survey   62

3.10 The University Hospital as it was immediately after the end of the war. The ruins became a pilgrimage site for war veterans. Photo by Jesús García Trevisano   66

3.11 Unexploded ordnance found at the University Hospital during survey and excavation. The number represents the actual number of complete items found in the field   67

3.12 Below: an unexploded spigot grenade found at the University Hospital. Above: a spigot grenade with the symbols of the JSU and the Communist Party   70

4.1 The city turned into a trap: map of a section of the neighborhood of Chamberí with barricades, based on documents of the period   75

4.2 Excavations at the Asylum of Santa Cristina revealed the extensive transformation of the site during the war   78

4.3 Finds from the asylum   81

4.4 Map of the mines at the University Hospital subsector   84

4.5 A labyrinth of trenches: the University City at the end of the war   86

4.6 A trench and dugout with several construction phases   87

4.7 Detail of the map of the bombing of Madrid representing the neighborhood of Argüelles and the University Hospital sector (below left)   93

4.8 A Nationalist artillery base in Casa de Campo and associated finds   94

4.9 Active and passive defense in Madrid   97

5.1 Inscriptions with the acronyms of different militias in Mojón del Lobo, near Belchite (Aragón)   103

5.2 Trenches of La Sendilla, in the Jarama frontline, and an infantry insignia found during excavations. The trench typology, with protruding firing positions and no zigzags, is typical of early fortifications   105

5.3 Above: finds from around the Palace of Ibarra   109

5.4 The Basque front in 1937 with indication of sites that have been the object of archaeological research and that are discussed in the text   111

5.5 Above: Sector 3 in Mount San Pedro, with three pillboxes. Below: the ID tag of militiaman Manuel Mogrovejo (misspelt Mogrobejo) found in San Pedro   114

xii   *Figures*

5.6   Above: Mount Lemoatx and Ganzabal. Below: the burial of
       Hilario Blanco Reguero   117
5.7   Church of Saint Augustine, which was partially destroyed
       during the Battle of Belchite. The men of the Lincoln Battalion
       entered the town through this church   122
5.8   Assault on the pillboxes of Dehesa de la Villa   125
5.9   The Carlist trench of the minor seminary of Belchite carpeted
       with shell casings and stripper clips in situ and the crucifix that
       appeared amid the ammunition   126
5.10   The fortifications around Belchite designed by captain of engineers
       Roque Adrada. The map covers the two sectors that we studied:
       1. El Saso; 2. Dehesa de la Villa—Minor seminary   128
5.11   The attack on El Saso sheepfold. Archaeological finds indicate
       that it was subjected to Republican fire coming from heavy
       artillery, mortars and small arms   129
5.12   The Parapet of Death   134
5.13   The Republican fortified hill of Castiltejón, surrounded by the
       Cantabrian mountains that separate León and Asturias. The Iron
       Age parapets of Castiltejón are clearly visible   138
6.1   The sheepfold of Alto del Molino, which was turned into a
       Republican base by the 138 Mixed Brigade. A trash pit was dug
       to the right   146
6.2   Some finds from Alto del Molino   151
6.3   Finds from surface survey near a Republican machine-gun nest
       in Mediana de Aragón   155
6.4   Fighting in no-man's-land in Mediana de Aragón   158
6.5   Bullets from no-man's-land in Mediana de Aragón   160
6.6   Possible officers' house in Mediana and some of the finds from
       the house: toothbrush, toothpaste and comb   161
6.7   Military uniform probably abandoned by deserters in a sheepfold
       in Mediana   163
6.8   Excavation of a trench and firing position defended by the
       Lincoln Battalion during the Aragón retreat. Sanctuary of El
       Pueyo (seen in the background), near Belchite (Zaragoza)   166
7.1   Map of the Abánades sector of the Offensive of the Upper
       Tajuña. All sites that appear in the map have been the object of
       archaeological research   172
7.2   R., a 25-year-old Republican soldier killed in a sheepfold
       probably during the second day of the Offensive of the Upper
       Tajuña. The careful, though shallow, burial indicates that he
       was interred by his comrades   175
7.3   The siege of La Enebrá. General distribution of finds from the
       metal-detector and surface surveys   177
7.4   Medal of Saint Joseph and Jesus child found with the remains of
       a fallen Nationalist soldier defending the outer perimeter of

Figures xiii

	La Enebrá. The medal was fixed with a safety pin to prevent loss during combat	179
7.5	Plan of a foxhole dug in the eastern part of the perimeter of La Enebrá with associated finds	181
7.6	Map of the sheepfold and enclosure of La Enebrá with distribution of combat-related finds	182
7.7	Combat-related finds inside the sheepfold of la Enebrá	183
7.8	Distribution of insignia, elements of dress and equipment and personal items found inside the sheepfold of La Enebrá, with images of some of the most prominent finds	184
7.9	Bodies of three Nationalist soldiers in the mass grave of the *corralón*, the entrance to the sheepfold	187
7.10	The Republican assault on La Nava 3	189
7.11	Map of the Levante Offensive with sites mentioned in the text	196
7.12	Map of combat-related finds in Gozalvo Hilltop, a position that saw fierce fighting during the second phase of the Levante Offensive	197
7.13	The bombing of Valencia. Dots indicate bombsites	203
7.14	The air raid shelter of Séneca square, Alicante	204
8.1	Map of the Battle of the Ebro with main sites mentioned in the text	209
8.2	Ammunition pouch full of Greek cartridges that appeared associated with the remains of a Republican soldier in the Fayón Pocket	212
8.3	Human bones and Lafitte bombs: a perfect summary of the Battle of the Ebro. Archaeologists documented the remains during surface survey	213
8.4	Underground shelter at the Republican base of Molí den Ferriol (Corbera d'Ebre)	217
8.5	Plan of Pillbox 3 upon excavation and plan of the NE wall with traces of impact of tank shells	223
8.6	Sector of the trench excavated in Hill 562 with indication of the main finds	225
8.7	Remains of a fallen Republican soldier in the trench of Raïmats	229
9.1	Refugee/concentration camps in southern France	234
9.2	One of the barracks of the internment camp of Rivesaltes, in southern France	236
9.3	The Nationalist stronghold of El Castillo, Abánades (Guadalajara)	238
9.4	Trench, dugouts and latrine in the hilltop of El Castillo with finds related to fighting activity in the position	241
9.5	Italian M1915 helmet abandoned in a covered concrete trench in El Castillo	243

xiv *Figures*

9.6 Finds of glass bottles (mostly belonging to alcoholic beverages) and animal bones in the canteen area of the Asylum of Santa Cristina in Madrid 245

9.7 Republican position of Alto de la Casilla (Abánades, Guadalajara) 249

9.8 The camp of Vallejo del Chulo, Canredondo (Guadalajara) 252

9.9 The Republican position of Casas de Murcia, that defended the south of the city of Madrid, with vitamins and medicines found at the site 255

9.10 Section through a Republican fortification in El Piul (Rivas Vaciamadrid) that watched over one of the main accesses to Madrid, the Valencia road 257

9.11 Orthogonal image produced by a drone of the Nationalist CGIS pillboxes protecting the main road leading to Brunete 259

9.12 Map of the main zone of the Republican attack on Brunete in January 1939, showing the visibility from the pillbox that we excavated. 261

9.13 Map of trench and dugouts excavated and surveyed in the NW of the University City of Madrid with ballistic evidence most likely related to the Nationalist attack on Madrid in March 1939 264

9.14 War is over, feast is over: cider bottles and Mauser clips abandoned in a Nationalist shelter at the University City of Madrid 267

10.1 Location of the guerrilla camps and Civil Guard headquarters in the Casaio area (Galicia) 274

10.2 A rural world shattered by modern war. Pottery found in the house of Cambedo (NW Portugal) destroyed by the Portuguese Army in 1946 275

10.3 Map of the attack on the guerrilla sanctuary in Repil in 1949 based on archaeological evidence and oral accounts 277

10.4 Above: Map of the concentration camp of Castuera based on historical aerial photographs and surface survey. Below: guards' barracks with traces of occupation by prisoners engaged in the dismantling of the camp 282

10.5 Latrine of the concentration camp of Castuera backfilled with garbage 287

10.6 Above: a viewshed analysis demonstrates that the latrines were perfectly visible from virtually everywhere in the camp. Below: sections of the latrines showing their irregularity and shallowness, directly contravening concentration camp regulations 289

10.7 Finds from the concentration camp of Castuera 291

10.8 Mass grave with the remains of 11 individuals killed at the cemetery of Castuera by firing squad and then dumped into the pit from the left 294

Figures xv

10.9	Objects associated with Individual 10 buried in one of the mass graves of Castuera	296
10.10	Map of the prison of Carabanchel (Madrid) as it was shortly before being demolished in 2008	298
10.11	The forced labor camp of Bustarviejo. View of the main building with railway works in the background	301
10.12	Map of the settlement of the prisoners' relatives in Bustarviejo and three huts that were excavated	303
10.13	Huts of prisoners' relatives built along the Madrid–Burgos railway in Valdemanco	306
11.1	Entrance to the basilica of the Valley of the Fallen, built 1940–1959	313

Abbreviations

Archives

AGMAV — Archivo General Militar (General Military Archive), Ávila.

AGA — Archivo General de la Administración (General Archive of the Administration), Alcalá de Henares.

IHCM — Instituto de Historia y Cultura Militar (Institute of Military and Cultural History), Madrid.

RGAPSI — Rossiiskii Gosudarstvennyi Arkhiv Sotsial'no-politicheskoi Istorii (Russian State Archive of Sociopolitical History), Moscow.

Political acronyms

CNT — Confederación Nacional del Trabajo – National Labor Confederation (Anarchist).

FAI — Federación Anarquista Ibérica – Iberian Anarchist Federation.

JONS — Juntas de Ofensiva Nacional Sindicalista - Councils of the National Syndicalist Offensive.

JSU — Juventudes Socialistas Unificadas - Unified Socialist Youth (Communist).

UHP — Uníos Hermanos Proletarios – United Proletarian Brothers (Communist).

UGT — Unión General de Trabajadores – General Workers Union (Socialist).

Acknowledgements

This work is largely based on fieldwork that I conducted between 2006 and 2019. Like any other archaeological project, it has been a collective endeavor. Therefore, my gratitude goes first to all the colleagues who had made it possible: Xurxo Ayán Vila, Álvaro Falquina Aparicio, Manuel Antonio Franco Fernández (Muros), Salvatore Garfi, Rui Gomes Coelho, Xabier Herrero Acosta, Alejandro Laíño Piñeiro, Javier Marquerie, Candela Martínez Barrio, Carlos Marín Suárez, Pedro Rodríguez Simón, Luis Antonio Ruiz Casero, Josu Santamarina Otaola, José María Señorán and Julie de Vos. Many other people (specialists, volunteers and students) collaborated in the different projects. They are simply too many to be mentioned here, but they have all my gratitude. A special thanks to the dedicated students of the Complutense University of Madrid and particularly to Gabriel Cifuentes, Bárbara Durán Bermúdez, Carla García-Mora, Pablo Gutiérrez de León and Rodrigo Paulos Bravo.

Funding for fieldwork on which this book is largely based has been provided by the Spanish National Research Council, the Ministry of Presidency, the Ruin Memories Project directed by Bjørnar Olsen (funded by the Ministry of Culture of Norway, Kulver Programme), the Complutense University of Madrid, the Regional Government of Castilla-La Mancha, the Regional Government of Madrid, the city council of Rivas-Vaciamadrid, the International Brigades Archaeology Project (IBAP), and a field school of the Institute for Field Research (IFR). I am particularly grateful to the IBAP volunteers and IFR students for contributing to fund the project, for their valuable help in the field and for their enthusiasm. Special thanks also to Isabel Baquedano at the Heritage Directorate of the Regional Government of Madrid for her staunch support of Spanish Civil War archaeology. Funding from the European-funded NEARCH project (New Scenarios for a Community-Oriented Archaeology) partly paid for three field seasons and covered the translation of two chapters of the original book in Spanish on which the present one is based. Pedro Fermín Maguire did the translation.

In every war or postwar scenario we have worked we have had the chance of collaborating with amazing people: in Guadalajara, Julián Dueñas, Luis Miguel Foguet (Domin), Ismael Gallego and Jose María Gutiérrez, as well as the inmates of the Social Integration Center "Melchor Rodríguez", who

Acknowledgements

participated in the excavation, and Pablo Jiménez Palancar, the center's educator. In Castuera, Antonio D. López Rodríguez, Guillermo León Cáceres and all the people of AMECADEC. In Catalonia Francesc Xavier Hernàndez Cardona, Mayca Rojo, Xavier Rubio, Gemma Cardona, María Yubero, Joan Sambró and the Lo Riu association. In León, the archaeological intervention was conducted by Eduardo González de Agüero and Víctor Bejega García. Several photographers have contributed generously to document and disseminate the project: Javier Durá, Jorge Fernández Bricio, Álvaro Minguito and Óscar Rodríguez.

Any errors in this book are mine alone. However, many people have helped diminish their number. Crucial advice on military history was provided by Jacinto Arévalo, José María Calvo, Ricardo Castellano, Juan Julián Elola, Rodrigo Gómez, Julián González Fraile, Javier Marquerie, Severiano Montero Barrado, Andrés Pozuelo, Ángel Sáenz and José Antonio Zarza. Other members of grassroots associations have shared their knowledge on different fields: Colectivo Guadarrama, GEFREMA, Espacios para la Memoria, ARAMA 36/37, Asociación de Amigos de las Brigadas Internacionales and Asociación Majerit. I would also like to thank all the people who visited our excavations and offered information that allowed us to interpret the sites. Our debt is particularly great with the neighbors that told us stories about the places that we excavated.

Many colleagues have generously contributed with data, illustrations, unpublished reports, theses and insightful comments. I am particularly thankful to Valentín Álvarez Martínez, Enrique Bordes, Hugo Chauton, Jorge García García, Andrés Fernández Martín, Francisco Ferrándiz, Almudena García-Rubio, Lourdes Herrasti, Jimi Jiménez, Francisco Lozano Olivares, Alberto Martí, Miguel Mezquida, Juan Montero Gutiérrez, Jorge Morín de Pablos, Gabriel Moshenska, Laura Muñoz Encinar, José Peinado Cucarella, Eduardo Penedo Cobo, Amalia Pérez-Juez, Luis Ríos, Myriam Saqqa-Carazo, Pablo Schnell, Fernando Serrulla Rech, Queralt Solé, Luis de Sobrón, and Alicia Torija. Bjørnar Olsen, Thora Petursdóttir and the rest of the Ruin Memories team deserve a special mention for several years of inspiring debates.

As always, my wife, Ana, has provided intellectual stimulus and emotional support—particularly necessary in this kind of research. I discovered the war at the same time as my late father, Constantino. Born in 1934, he was a child during the early postwar period and, as a member of a well-to-do family, was blissfully unaware of the oppressive surroundings in which he grew up. His discovery of the real nature of the war was probably more shocking for him than it was for me. During the last ten years of his life, we exchanged stories, insights and discoveries. I miss his ironic remark: "Are you still opening old wounds?" Yes, still I am. The book is dedicated to my mother, Mila, who nurtured in me a concern with human rights and a love for archaeology. It seems that I finally figured out how to bring the two together.

Dies Irae

30 October 1936. A truck full of militiamen stops in front of number 8 Avenue Queen Victoria, Madrid. Two, perhaps three militiamen armed with rifles climb the stairs or perhaps take the elevator, knock on the door, a woman—horror written all over her face—opens the door, they say, probably shout, that they are looking for Francisco and Antonio González Barros, Francisco and Antonio come forward, their wives, Rosalía and Elena, cry, children weep behind them. The brothers come out accompanied by the militiamen and now they walk down the stairs. Behind them runs Antonio's son, Paco, who is 12 years old; in the street he sees his father and his uncle being pushed into the truck, which has been requisitioned by the militias, the few pedestrians in the street look briefly and rush, the truck revs and starts, taking away the two brothers as it takes away other somber-looking, anguished men. Paco runs after the truck, runs and runs and shouts, his father stares at him, tells him to go while the truck vanishes. Paco will never see his father again. Francisco and Antonio were assassinated in the cemetery of Aravaca, outside Madrid, on the first day of November of 1936.

With them were killed Ramiro Ledesma Ramos, founder of JONS, one of Spain's fascist parties, the writer Ramiro de Maeztu, a fascist sympathizer, and several dozen people, mostly military and Falangists, but also religious people.[1] The place where the remains lie is known since the end of the war as the Cemetery of the Martyrs of Aravaca: a large white cross presides over the burials and the walls show Falangist emblems—yoke and arrows—and the dictatorship's imperial eagle. The cemetery is today a place of memory for the far right, who honor its fallen. But Francisco and Antonio were not martyrs of the Falange, Spain's main fascist party; they did not die for God and Spain, as the Francoist motto says. They were supporters of the centrist and liberal Portela Valladares, who was president of the council of ministers before the last democratic elections of 19 February 1936. They were killed for being rich bourgeois—a class enemy—in a blind, bloody revolution. Nothing remembers Francisco and Antonio as who they were in the Falangist cemetery.

On 1 April 1939, the unit in which private Francisco Rodríguez Ogallar is serving in the Popular Army of the Republic receives orders to surrender. They are stationed in Gualchos, in the southern part of the province of Granada,

xx   *Dies Irae*

a quiet front since the fall of Málaga in February 1937. Private Francisco does not know yet, but an ordeal is awaiting him, a terrible "penitentiary tourism", as it was known then. His crime: volunteering to fight for the Republic. Francisco never saw much war where he was assigned. He did not fire a single shot. Francisco and his comrades are interned in a sugar mill on the coast of Málaga, which the victorious army has transformed into a makeshift concentration camp. From there they are taken to Algeciras, in the province of Cádiz, to a larger camp, but also shabbier and colder: it is simply a barbed wire fence in the middle of a beach, beaten by the ruthless wind of the Strait of Gibraltar. Against that wind, the prisoners only have ponchos and those ponchos become homes for weeks, perhaps months. In addition to cold there is hunger. Francisco exchanges a watch, his only valuable property, a gift from his father, for a loaf of bread. And starving he builds roads. From this period of forced labor he will retain a hernia all his life and the memory of a friend who died of exhaustion, victim of a guard's sadism. Many years later, Francisco still weeps when he remembers his father's humiliation. He remembers, or rather imagines, his old father, kneeling, tears in his eyes, begging to a young, arrogant Falangist, who refuses to put his signature on a document certifying Francisco's good conduct. The only signature between Francisco and freedom. But Francisco did survive the camp and died in 2011 at 96.

Of the concentration camps there is no trace. There are maybe some ruins still of the sugar factory. Perhaps on the beach of Algeciras pieces of barbed wire and tin cans appear every once in a while, washed by the sea. In Gualchos, it is still possible to see the trenches were Francisco and his comrades lived for months.

Antonio and Francisco González Barros were builders before the war. Their brothers, Julio and Alfredo, were too. Alfredo saved his life miraculously. He was working in Madrid, but went to Galicia some time before the coup of July because her wife was about to give birth. After the war, the construction company made a fortune. In a devastated Spain, builders were meant to become rich, at least those sympathizing with the regime. They also had the invaluable help of tens of thousands of Republican prisoners redeeming their long sentences through forced labor. Many of the infrastructures still used in Spain today (roads, dams, airports) were built by businessmen like Alfredo González Barros with political prisoners like Francisco Rodríguez Ogallar. Alfredo built bridges in Tarragona and airports in Galicia. Like the one in Lavacolla. Thousands of prisoners had to prepare the terrain to construct a new runway for the airport of Santiago de Compostela. Today, the airport is used by around 2.5 million travelers every year, who know nothing about the hunger and death behind its construction. The concentration camp was installed in an old tannery. Inmates slept on the cold stone floor, infested with fleas. Today the place is a hotel and restaurant visited by pilgrims.

On 28 March 1939, Antonio Mayorgas, a lieutenant in charge of paying the troops of the 27 Mixed Brigade of the Popular Army of the Republic, finds himself with tens of thousands of *pesetas*—the Spanish currency—with no value. Every week he descended from the mountains north of Madrid to collect the soldiers' pay. But on March 28 Madrid is no longer Republican. The bank notes are not only worthless, they have also become a dangerous document—*Red* money. Antonio, however, decides to preserve it. He puts the notes in a box and hides it in his house. They were safe there while he was interned in the concentration camp of Alcalá de Henares, near Madrid. They were safe during the entire dictatorship and the transition to democracy. And there they are still today: thousands of *pesetas* from the 1930s. The salary without value of the defeated. From the Republic, Antonio Mayorgas kept one of the paramount symbols of the sovereignty of a modern State—the currency. He also kept a small medal with the effigy of the Republic and the bust of the founder of the Spanish Socialist Party, Pablo Iglesias (1850–1925). Sixty years after the end of the war, his daughter found it hiding in a bedside table. A silenced object like the memories of so many families.

***

Those are the stories of my relatives—every Spaniard has similar ones. Yet I knew virtually nothing of the Spanish Civil War when I decided to study the conflict as an archaeologist in 2005—even if my family had been deeply involved in the conflict, even if I had studied a degree in History at the university in Madrid and taken quite a few of contemporary history classes. It is not only that I knew very little about the war—less than I knew about the Second World War or even the Second Punic War. It is also that I was not interested in the least. There is a phrase for that disinterest in Spanish: *las batallitas del abuelo*. "Grandpa's little battles". Most youngsters did not want to listen to their grandparents talking about the war—those who wanted to talk, in the first place. It was simply boring. Or sad. Or both. Like many people in my generation, I discovered the conflict in my late twenties. In my case, it was in a plane to San Francisco, where I was a postdoctoral fellow at Stanford University. I used the 11-hour flight from Frankfurt to read Hugh Thomas' gripping history of the Spanish Civil War (Thomas 2001). Originally published in 1965, it is still the best history of the conflict. And it was a shock. My feeling was that I had been deceived or perhaps robbed of something valuable. How is it that nobody had told me about this fascinating story? Who had taken it away from me and why? The story of my grandfather's brothers murdered in Madrid was the only one I was ever told and not precisely by my grandfather. It was my uncle who did, the son of one of the killed. He also talked about eating potato peels during the war. But that was it. Not that I ever cared to ask, until it was too late. The war sounded as remote as the tales of the Napoleonic invasion in my home village in Galicia that were still passed on by elderly people. After reading Thomas, I felt the strong urge to know more and spent the next few months reading about the war and musing about what could be done archaeologically about the conflict, apart from digging up mass graves—what many archaeologists were already doing at the time. When I returned to Spain after getting an appointment at the Complutense University of Madrid, I started looking for traces of the conflict.

xxii *Dies Irae*

There came the second shock: they were everywhere—labor camps, trenches, pillboxes, monuments, places of execution. The familiar spaces of my childhood and youth turned out to be all of them touched by the sinister and often invisible history of the Spanish Civil War and the Franco dictatorship. When I was reading Hugh Thomas 30,000 feet over the Atlantic in 2005, I could hardly imagine that I would spend the next 14 years digging trenches, mass graves and concentration camps. Yet there are two things that I did know: first, that I wanted to excavate the war; that this was a story that had to be excavated, literally and metaphorically. Second, that I wanted to write an archaeological history of the Spanish Civil War. Not essays about this or that aspect of the conflict, but a material account of the war, a story told from things. And this is what this book is about.

Note

1 On the fascist movements in Spain see Thomàs (2011).

1 Introduction

A war too close

The Spanish Civil War broke many things apart. It shattered families and hopes. It destroyed a country physically and socially for decades. Spain has, in many ways, never recovered from the wounds. We are still fighting, by other means, some of the old battles—about national identity, religion and class. The past looms large in political discourses on the right and on the left; the remains of the conflict (mass graves and monuments) are the object of heated controversies, and war and dictatorship appear in daily conversations and in the media. The Spanish Civil War may be moving away from the present in chronological terms, but the temporality of the conflict is still the now—a non-absent past, as Domanska (2005) would put it. It is still a war too close. The growing political polarization inaugurated after the 2008 global crisis and the rise of the extreme right has contributed to bring it even nearer to the present. Yet interest in the war and in its material legacy has been high since 2000, when the first scientific exhumation of a Spanish Civil War mass grave took place (Silva and Macías 2003). The grandchildren of those who experienced the conflict—like myself—had come of age at the turn of the millennium and wanted to know more and to talk more about what had been silenced. We were free from the constraints of our parents, who suffered (or benefitted from) the dictatorship, or our grandparents, who experienced war as victims, perpetrators or bystanders. It is telling that the discovery of the traumatic past has come in the shape of archaeological excavation. Historical truth had to be unburied, literally. The memory struggle and the archaeology of the Spanish Civil War emerged at the same time and for the same reasons.

The Spanish Civil War is a crucial historical event of the twentieth century—and not just for Spaniards. The conflict, which started as a *coup d'état* staged by reactionary and fascist officers against a young democracy, is widely regarded as the prelude to the Second World War, the beginning of a cycle of violence that only finished with the end of the Greek Civil War (1946–1950): Spain became the testing ground for many of the weapons and tactics that were later used in the global conflict and witnessed the involvement of Nazi Germany, Fascist Italy

2   Introduction

and the Soviet Union. Seen by many at the time as the last opportunity to stop fascism, it provoked enthusiasm and fear all over the world—and the mobilization of tens of thousands of people who went to fight (and die) in Spain on the Republic's side. The Spanish conflict also preluded the Second World War in the scale of violence against civilians: around half of the 300,000 casualties were non-combatants, murdered by different militias or by the indiscriminate bombing of towns and villages. Unlike the Second World War, the Spanish conflict ended with the triumph of fascism: General Francisco Franco and António Oliveira de Salazar in Portugal were the only far-right dictators from interwar Europe that managed to perpetuate themselves in power until the 1970s.

The relevance of the history of the Spanish Civil War is out of the question, but why archaeology? Let me point out two reasons that are specific to the case study: first, as noted above, an important part of the history of the conflict has been buried, both literally and metaphorically. There are many aspects (mass graves, concentration camps, violence against civilians) that had been concealed or distorted, first by a dictatorship interested in erasing or downplaying its own crimes, then by a democratic transition that wanted to look only forward—out of conviction, but also out of fear. A history of political violence during the Spanish Civil War and after without archaeology can only be incomplete. Second, much of what has been written about the war in Spain falls within the realm of political, military and economic history. There has been very little academic interest about the lives of ordinary soldiers and civilians, about aspects of culture, sociality and everyday life (and death). We know comparatively little about the experiences in the trenches in Spain—compared to the First or Second World Wars. Archaeology provides extraordinary insights into all these phenomena. It makes war seem more realistic, more mundane and more culturally specific. Also more intimate. It is probably not a paradox that by putting the focus on things, we come closer to people.

Beyond Spain, the archaeology of the civil war has much to offer to the expanding fields of battlefield archaeology (Scott et al. 2009; Scott and McFeaters 2011), the archaeology of internment (Myers and Moshenska 2011) and forensic archaeology and the archaeology of crimes against humanity (Sturdy Colls 2015). These subfields have often developed independently, but they have to be understood in an integrated manner (see Theune 2018). In Spain compartmentalization is simply untenable. Unlike later civil clashes, the Spanish Civil War was a fully-fledged military conflict, with huge standing armies and neat frontlines; like later civil wars, however, it saw extreme violence against civilians—legal, paralegal and illegal—guerrilla and paramilitary actions. Being both civil conflict and total war, then, it is impossible to understand the period if we only look at the frontlines or leave aside the battlefields to focus on the concentration camps or the mass graves.

The present book differs from most publications on the archaeology of contemporary conflict in that it does not adopt a thematic approach or focus

Introduction 3

on a specific site or region. My intention has been to write an archaeological account of the Spanish Civil War, which does not mean that I will only be drawing from the archaeological record. As the reader will see, oral and written sources have been vital in my work. What it means is that things (objects, bones, ruins, landscapes) guide my narrative as much as possible. This is of necessity a fragmentary account, because there are many events and phenomena that had not yet been explored archaeologically—some of them simply cannot be. But archaeology is fragmentary by nature and this does not mean that it is not meaningful (Burström 2013). Quite the opposite. The fragments of war that I will present here, I expect, are anything but meaningless. Fragments, small details, are not just evocative: they might tell the entire truth of the war: "'Small details'," writes Svetlana Alexievich (2018: xxv), "are what is most important for me, the warmth and vividness of life: a lock left on the forehead once the braid is cut; the hot kettles of kasha and soup, which no one eats, because out of a hundred persons only seven came back from the battle…" The same can be said of archaeological finds: the bullet of a *coup de grâce*; a bottle of perfume lost in the frontline; a baby rattle in a grave; a howitzer shell that did not explode; a graffiti with the name of somebody who is going to be executed; an ammunition pouch full of smuggled cartridges… These are powerful things; things that ask to be narrated. I thus undertake the traditional work of a historian—to write a story about the past—with the sensibility and the tools of an archaeologist—a material narrative. My story starts with the bloodbath of the summer of 1936. It makes its way through the battlefields of Madrid, Guadalajara, the Basque Country, Asturias, Aragón and the Ebro—an irregular conflict transformed into total war. It then meanders through the trenches of those who were about to be defeated and those who were about to become victors for 40 years. It does not stop in 1939, but continues across concentration camps, prisons, guerrilla camps and more mass graves. Until 1952: 16 years of violence and misery (Figure 1.1). Of ruins and bones that archaeologists have been digging for the last two decades.

Outline of the book

The book follows a more or less a linear narrative that starts with the beginning of the war and ends in the early 1950s, when the last guerrillas surrendered or were exterminated and the camps closed. Chapter 2 outlines very briefly the path toward the Spanish Civil War and then addresses the unrestrained violence that followed the right-wing coup of 18 July 1936, which led to the conflict. The period of irregular political violence extended through 1936 and the beginning of 1937, after which killings generally plummeted, as expedient militia justice was replaced by formal, and usually more restrained, forms of punishment. Since 2000, scientific exhumations have produced a wealth of data on the patterns of politically motivated assassinations, mostly those perpetrated by right-wing groups. Osteological remains and artifacts associated with the bones also provide unique insight into the identity and the lives of the murdered.

4 *Introduction*

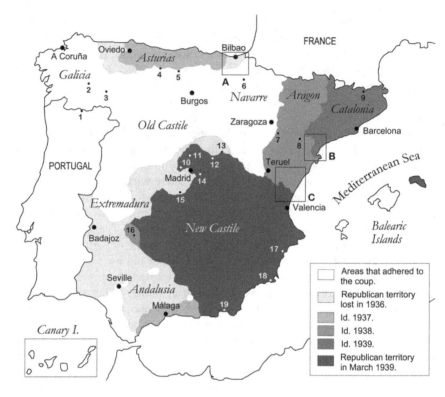

Figure 1.1 Map of Spain during the Civil War with some of the main sites mentioned in the text.

Notes: 1. Cambedo; 2. Repil; 3. Casaio; 4. Castiltejón; 5. Mount Bernorio; 6. Fort San Cristóbal; 7. Belchite and Mediana; 8. Caspe; 9. Vall de Camprodon; 10. Brunete; 11. Bustarviejo; 12. Brihuega; 13. Abánades; 14. Jarama Valley; 15. Toledo; 16. Castuera; 17. Alicante; 18. Cartagena; 19. Almería. For the sites within the squares, see the corresponding chapters: A. Chapter 5; B. Chapter 8; C. Chapter 7.
Source: © Author.

While the carnage of civilians was going on in cities and countryside, the rebels progressed fast toward Madrid from Andalusia. War was waged by highly mobile columns of the colonial army of Morocco that fought against poorly trained Republican militias, while engaging in the kind of indiscriminate violence to which they had become accustomed in Africa. The situation changed in the outskirts of Madrid. Raids muted into all-out industrialized warfare and the archaeological record changes accordingly. Chapter 3 examines the combats around the city, focusing on the Battle of Madrid (7– 23 November 1936) and its aftermath. It deals mainly with two scenarios: Casa de Campo, a large park in front of the capital where the International Brigades had their baptism of fire, and the University City, which was the furthermost point inside Madrid reached by the Nationalist

Army. In Casa de Campo, my team and I excavated one of the few intact trenches still preserved related to the combats of November 1936. The scarcity of documentary evidence associated with these combats offers an opportunity to rewrite a major episode of the Spanish Civil War from the point of view of archaeology. The same happens with the campus: most attention has been paid to the area closer to the city, but we have discovered traces of an unrecorded attack through the northern fringe of the University City, an attack that might have changed the course of the war. We also conducted excavations and surveys in one of the hotspots of the Battle of Madrid: the University Hospital, which, despite heavy modifications after the conflict, furnished astonishing material evidence of the brutal fighting—which preludes urban combats during the Second World War.

In Chapter 4 I abandon the linear narrative to look at the war in Madrid, from the end of the battles for the capital, in January 1937, to the autumn of 1938. After the hyper-eventful days of 1936, Madrid was besieged by the Nationalists and became prey to the monotony of a war of attrition, more redolent of the First World War than the Second. My team and I excavated a Nationalist base at the salient of the University Hospital and several Republican positions on the campus. Archaeology and archival documentation offer a fascinating picture of everyday life on a long-lasting urban front, which anticipated, on a smaller scale, the predicament of Leningrad or Stalingrad. This novel type of war included specific military tactics (such as mine warfare and underground combats) and terror against civilians (aerial and artillery bombings, clandestine centers of repression, murders), all of which have left material traces.

In military terms, the Battle of Madrid was a foretaste of what was to come. During 1937, the unconventional, symmetrical war of the previous months mutated into total war, with both sides deploying hundreds of thousands of soldiers in the field, backed by airplanes, tanks and artillery. The landscape of conflict and its materiality at large changed. Some of the most memorable battles of the Spanish Civil War, from Jarama to Teruel, took place or began in 1937. This was also the year in which the Northern Front collapsed, putting the Republic in a dire situation. Chapter 5 summarizes archaeological research conducted in the Jarama area, the Basque Country, Asturias and the mountains of León and Castile. War in the North is particularly interesting from an archaeological point of view, as its materiality is remarkably different from other scenarios, a phenomenon that has to do with vernacular traditions, peripheral nationalism and the military isolation of the North, which was cut off from the rest of Republican territory. The chapter also describes work that we have carried out in one of the *lieux de mémoire* of the Spanish Civil War: Belchite. The town was besieged and finally captured by the Republicans during a failed offensive against Zaragoza (one of Spain's major cities in the hand of the Nationalists). It was presented at the time as a glorious victory by the Republic and as an epic act of resistance by the Nationalists. The fact that Franco decided to preserve the town as a memorial of the war—a sort of Oradour-sûr-Glâne *avant la lettre*—

6   *Introduction*

further projected the myths into the future. We carried out our research both inside Belchite and in the surroundings, where major (and largely forgotten) battles were fought in August and September 1937.

In Chapter 6 we take a detour from the quick pace of the war to glimpse at everyday life in three fronts that remained largely static through the winter of 1938: Badajoz, Guadalajara and Zaragoza. Soldiers ate, drank, played, drew graffiti, wrote, got ill, and dug trenches, but about this historians have had little to say as a rule, concerned as they are with the large operations and political maneuvers that decided the conflict. Archaeology can counterbalance the focus on the dynamic by taking a look at quiet, secondary frontlines. Soldiers also died there: static does not mean that there was no fighting. Men stationed in the rural fronts of Extremadura and Zaragoza experienced artillery attacks, night raids and even local offensives. Through our archaeological surveys in Mediana de Aragón we were able to reconstruct with precision several small raids launched by both Republicans and Nationalists in the vast steppe between Belchite and Zaragoza. Eventually, calm was shattered to pieces in Aragón, where the Nationalists launched an offensive after winning the Battle of Teruel, which ended on 22 February 1938. The Republicans retreated *en masse*, leaving a trail of corpses behind that archaeologists have in some cases found and exhumed.

The Republicans tried to stop the Nationalist advance toward the Mediterranean that threatened to cut the government's territory into two by launching an offensive in Guadalajara, in one of those static fronts described in the previous chapter. In Chapter 7, I describe the forgotten Offensive of the Upper Tajuña River of April 1938 using a combination of archaeological and archival sources. The latter are scarce, while references in history books are virtually non-existent, despite the battle involving tens of thousands of men, tanks and aircraft. The chapter follows in the footsteps of the soldiers of the Popular Army from their departing positions to the furthermost point that they reached in a war landscape that has been preserved largely unaltered. The Offensive of the Upper Tajuña was not the only forgotten battle of 1938. Another was the Levante Offensive, which took place immediately afterwards in the hills near the Mediterranean coast in the Valencia region. Here the Nationalists launched an attack to capture the Republican wartime capital. It was a total failure, which explains the oblivion into which the battle has fallen. Archaeological research in the area has explored battlefields, soldiers' graves and the formidable belts of fortifications that largely thwarted the Nationalist offensive. Also the relentless bombing to which Mediterranean cities and towns were subjected by the rebels.

Chapter 8 examines the most famous battle of the Spanish Civil War: the Battle of the Ebro. Unlike the offensives described in the previous chapter, the Ebro was the largest and most decisive battle of the conflict and for this reason the most prominent in Spanish collective memory. It raged during most of the second half of 1938, consumed staggering quantities of men and *matériel* (around 80,000 casualties), and ended with a crushing defeat for the Popular Army. After the Ebro, the Republic would not be able to recover

Introduction   7

and their chances to win the war vanished forever. The first part of the chapter summarizes research conducted on the different scenarios of the Ebro, from the Fayón salient, where Republican soldiers were besieged and exterminated, to the rearguard airfields and boot camps. It also tackles the problem of the ubiquitous human remains still littering the landscape. The second half of the chapter describes the last Republican stronghold in the Ebro, where we found powerful traces of the last day of combats.

The last months of the conflict were of painful agony for the Republic. Chapter 9 takes the reader from the scenarios of the Republican retreat in the Pyrenees and the refugee camps of southern France to the last trenches of the war. Excavations by my team in both Republican and Nationalist positions dated from late 1938 to early 1939 furnish a moving image of the wildly differing experiences of soldiers combatting in the Nationalist and Republican armies. The poverty of the Republic is painfully obvious in the trenches of Madrid, Jarama and Guadalajara, as is the overabundance of material resources of the Nationalists. These differences are particularly clear in the kind and amount of food that combatants had at their disposal, in the different patterns and rates of recycling in both armies and in the medicines they were consuming. Our team also had the chance to excavate one of the last attacks of the Popular Army, which was launched on 13 January 1939. It took place in Brunete, 30 km away from Madrid and the scenario of a legendary battle in 1937. The war landscape had changed dramatically since 1937: it was by then heavily fortified with concrete pillboxes and this sealed the fate of the Republicans. The conflict finished two months later, with the surrender of Madrid to the Nationalists—but not before a last, failed Nationalist attack on the capital. We were able to find the exact location of the surrender took place and discovered many remains related to the last day of the war.

The conflict, however, did not really end in April 1939. Violence continued in many other ways and, in fact, the state of war was only called off in 1948. This book takes the perspective that the armed conflict in Spain actually lasted from 1936 to 1952, a perspective that is backed by the archaeological record. Chapter 10 deals with two of the forms that violence adopted after 1 April 1939: the guerrilla war and the spaces of repression. In recent years, studies of partisan camps and battle sites have been developed in Galicia, in the northwest of Spain, one of the regions where anti-Franco fighters were more active. However, it is the exhumation of mass graves with the bodies of executed guerrillas that tell more eloquently about the brutal nature of the conflict. The second part of the chapter is devoted to the *universe concentrationnaire* that shaped Franco's Spain from before the official end of the symmetrical war to the early 1950s: concentration camps, prisons and forced labor camps. Three paradigmatic sites where I have conducted archaeological research are described: Castuera, a camp in Extremadura built *ex novo*, used for one year and then abandoned; the prison of Carabanchel, the largest in Europe at the time, which housed political prisoners (and homosexuals) until 1978, and the forced labor camp of Bustarviejo, where the fate of the prisoners' relatives could be investigated. The chapter ends with the voices of the vanquished through the graffiti they left on the walls of prisons and camps.

The final chapter of the book addresses the afterlife of the war: the ways in which the conflict was memorialized, transformed into heritage, appropriated and disowned in battles of memory and counter-memory that persist to our days, unabated.

2 Time to kill

July 1936–February 1937

The path to blood

The genealogy of almost any war is long, a winding road of mounting tensions, troubles, passions and misunderstandings. It is even longer in civil conflicts. They usually stem from protracted periods of instability and deep structural problems. In the case of Spain, we could go back to the Late Middle Ages, when the country was divided into several independent kingdoms.[1] Only four survived by the end of the fifteenth century, Castile, Aragon, Navarre and Granada—the latter a Muslim polity that was conquered in 1492, the same year the Jews were expelled from Spain. The war against the Islamic polities in the Iberian Peninsula produced a peculiar ideology, in which military violence and religious identity played a central role. It also led to the emergence of extensive estates in the south, bestowed to military orders and nobles that participated in the conquest. A large part of the lands in the south was still in the hands of a few landlords in the early twentieth century; rural property in the north was more evenly distributed among farmers. The geography of the Spanish Civil War has much to do with this medieval legacy. It would be a class war between those who had much and those who had very little or nothing.

The country was unified as a single kingdom in 1492, but this was just the result of a dynastic alliance. It did not suddenly create a homogeneous country with a common identity: a diversity of languages and cultural traditions persisted and some regions preserved a high degree of autonomy. They only came under attack during the second half of the nineteenth century, which saw also the birth of peripheral nationalisms—Catalan, Basque and, with less intensity, Galician. An idea of a common Spanish nationality only developed, as elsewhere in Europe, during the last two centuries, and particularly as a result of the Napoleonic invasion of 1808, which saw wide popular mobilization. However, regional identities remained strong and their incorporation into the Spanish State complicated. The Spanish Civil War would be a war of nationalisms: between Spanish centralists and peripheral nationalists; but also between different ideas of what it is to be (or not to be) "Spanish".

The dismantling of the Ancien Regime took longer in Spain than in other European countries and met strong resistance. The landed nobility

10 *Time to kill*

remained powerful. The situation was somewhat different in the Basque Country, Catalonia and Madrid, which were industrialized and received many immigrants from the poorer areas of the country. Throughout the convulsed nineteenth century, the tensions between liberalism and conservatism were manifested in a myriad of *coups d'état* enacted by (usually liberal) military officers, in revolutions and civil wars. Three internecine conflicts were fought between 1833 and 1876, between Carlists and liberals. The Carlists defended the Ancien Regime, absolutism and the untrammeled power of the Catholic Church. They also supported alternative heirs to the throne (all named Carlos, thus their name). The liberals won every single time. The Spanish Civil War would be a war between modernity and tradition (or anti-modernism).

Along with aristocracy, the Church also held enormous economic, social and symbolic power. Education was almost entirely in its hands. It owned large estates and received high revenues from peasants cultivating its lands. The Catholic Church resisted modernity twice: first through the Counterreformation in the sixteenth century; then by adopting an active anti-modernism in the nineteenth century. This anti-modernism was particularly acute in Spain, where the local Church took sides with the powerful and alienated the popular classes, who gradually abandoned the institution and often the faith. The Spanish Civil War would be a war of religion and of ways of understanding religious belief.

In 1868, a six-year revolutionary period opened in which first a constitutional monarch and then a Republic were established. The First Spanish Republic only lasted two years (1873–1874), in which period there were five different presidents and a third Carlist War (started in 1872). During the period comprised between 1874 and 1931, known as the Restoration, conservatives and liberals alternated in government under a reinstated Bourbon monarchy. Economic development outside the Basque Country and Catalonia remained limited. Spain was still an agrarian country, but something was changing: during the early twentieth century there was an increase in social unrest, as both industrial workers and agricultural laborers engaged in political struggles to improve their conditions of living. They also protested against the colonial conflicts in Morocco, in which the lower classes bore the brunt, while the economic benefits were for the royal family, the aristocracy and the high bourgeoisie (who were able to bail out of military service). Growing tensions led to the proclamation of a dictatorship in 1923, with General Miguel Primo de Rivera as its leader and the complicity of the king Alphonse XIII. Primo de Rivera stepped down in 1930 and was succeeded by a short period of *dictablanda*, "soft dictatorship", which did little to stop the decreasing prestige of the monarchy. In the municipal elections of 14 April 1931, Republican parties obtained a large majority of the vote and the king abdicated and went into exile.

The Republic was greeted with hope by a large part of the Spanish population. It brought important changes to the country, including true universal suffrage for the first time in the country's history, secular education, the modernization of the army, and an ambitious program of social reforms and land redistribution aimed at reducing staunch socioeconomic inequalities. However, both the global and the national situation would make things extremely difficult for the young Republic. The global crisis of 1929 damaged the economy, while the representatives of the old order conspired from day one to overthrow the new regime. The first (failed) coup came in August 1932. At the same time, anarchists and communists were soon dissatisfied with the pace of progress of the young Republic, which failed to bring rapid improvement to the lower classes, while the security forces behaved very much as they had in the monarchic period. Communism mobilized a very small percentage of the population, but the socialist party was split between social-democrats and those who defended revolutionary options. Anarchists, in turn, had always been very numerous, particularly in southern Spain and Catalonia. During the first three years of the Republic around 400 people were killed in clashes with the police and other armed forces, something that convinced many in the radical Left that the new regime was not essentially different from the previous one.

Dissatisfaction increased between 1933 and 1936, when right-wing parties, then in power, started to dismantle the social legislation introduced by the earlier progressive government. Some in the Left feared that the Republic was heading towards a corporatist system similar to the one already existing in Austria since 1933. Revolutionary rhetoric escalated and on 5 October 1934, sectors of the socialist party and unions, along with anarchist and communist elements, staged an insurrection against the government. The insurrection took a nationalist character in Catalonia, where a Catalonian State was proclaimed (but within a Federal Republic of Spain). The revolution was short-lived. Only in Asturias, a mining area in northern Spain, did the revolutionaries manage to sustain the challenge for two weeks. The national government decided to throw in the colonial Army of Africa, led by General Francisco Franco, against the revolutionaries. The quenching of the revolt resulted in between 1,500 and 2,000 people dead, mostly workers and their families (around 250 members of the armed forces were also killed, as well as 34 priests) and 30,000 detainees all over Spain. Some of the violence against non-combatants that would characterize the Spanish Civil War was already present during the October revolution.

In the elections of February 1936, left-wing parties avoided the mistake of 1933 and formed a coalition: the Popular Front. This allowed them to obtain a majority of seats in the parliament (with only a slight majority of the votes) and tilt the Republican government back to the Left. The ensuing months saw further instability with violent incidents involving fascist and revolutionary groups, strikes and killings. The leftist triumph in the February elections convinced those who had been conspiring to overthrow the Republic to act as soon as possible. They were mostly military officers who had been fighting in Morocco, like Francisco Franco himself, and who embraced a diversity of right-wing ideologies. They found allegiance on a range of extreme-right groups, including Falangists (the Spanish version of fascism) and Carlists—the stubborn defenders of the Ancien Régime. Despite their

12 *Time to kill*

ideological differences, they were united by a strong anticommunism, ultranationalism and radical Catholicism. The coordinator of the coup was General Emilio Mola, a veteran of the colonial wars, while the would-be dictator, Francisco Franco, with characteristic cautiousness, only decided to join the rebellion a few days before the coup. He was to lead the insurrection of the Army of Africa. The coup started first in Morocco, on July 17. The following day it spread to the Peninsula, when army units rose up in Madrid, Barcelona, Seville and other major cities. The coup was quenched in some of the major cities, such as Madrid, Barcelona and Valencia. The rebels (or Nationalists) also failed in their main objective: to topple the government. Spain was divided. The bloodbath started.

The nature of violence

The coup of July was extremely bloody from the start. Unlike previous military insurrections from the beginning of the nineteenth century, this one showed no pity for those who did not join the cause immediately. Whoever opposed the rebels, military or civilian, was more often than not immediately executed. The coup also unleashed precisely that which it had purportedly come to suppress: a revolution—and a particularly violent one. The collapse of the Republican government left a void in power that was filled by a variety of armed groups, militias, unions and members or sections of political parties that took justice into their own hands. A period of hot, unrestrained violence opened that made the second half of 1936 probably the bloodiest in Spanish history. Although the situation started to cool down by the beginning of 1937, when violence took more institutional channels, by the end of the war at least 150,000 had been killed in the rearguard, around the same number as in the frontline—with the difference that military casualties grew as civilian casualties diminished. The total number of political killings ascends to 185,000 if we take 1948 as the end year, which is when the state of war was officially canceled. Most of the violence took place in 1936, during the first five months of the conflict, in which 80% of the total political murders were committed (Ledesma 2010: 240). During these five months, the Nationalists killed 52,800 people versus 38,000 assassinated in Republican territory. Considering that the Nationalists occupied less of Spain than the Republic during the beginning of the war, this means that right-wing killings almost doubled left-wing ones. Wherever pre-war Republican authorities resisted, violence was curtailed. In Nationalist-held territory, there were no such limits, as the authorities either encouraged political violence or turned a blind eye. The great majority of the top political representatives with the Republic (president, prime minister, ministers and leaders of political parties) condemned rearguard violence, whereas neither Franco nor his clique regretted or tried to put an end to the assassinations committed by their sympathizers. It was usually less prominent Nationalists who were appalled by the massacre and expressed their concern, seldom in public.

Time to kill 13

The rebels had planned systematic violence from the beginning, as is clear from the secret instructions issued by the mastermind of the coup, General Emilio Mola. These contemplated the assassination of an important number of politicians, military officers and trade unionists, but it is not necessarily obvious that they were targeting 150,000 people, the actual number killed. On the Republican side, violence was never planned from the top—rather the opposite—and therefore there was never a Republican master plan for extermination, but this does not mean that Republican authorities in lesser echelons and specific members of the Popular Front were not deeply involved in planning and conducting political violence: they certainly were (Ledesma 2010; Ruiz 2014). Most prominent Republican politicians, however, were radically opposed to revolutionary violence out of moral conviction and political principle, including President Manuel Azaña, but also for practical reasons: they were painfully aware of the diplomatic problem that political assassinations implied for the Republic. Thus, many people involved in the crimes of the early war period were brought to court and exhumations conducted by judicial order. By November 1937, 2,037 individuals had been exhumed in Republican Catalonia and 175 individuals had been prosecuted for the assassinations (Ledesma 2010: 240; Etxeberria and Solé 2019: 407). Nothing of the sort can be found in Nationalist Spain. At the beginning of the conflict, however, forensic doctors still conducted autopsies in areas occupied by the Nationalists, following standard legal procedures, and traces of such autopsies have been observed in contemporary exhumations (Ríos et al. 2013a; García-Rubio 2017: 191–197). As extrajudicial killings kept growing, Nationalist authorities issued orders stopping forensic work.

After the end of the hostilities, those who were killed in territory under Republican control were almost always exhumed or remembered with memorials and public ceremonies (Ledesma and Rodrigo 2006: 237–243). Those who were killed by the Nationalists were forgotten and mourning was banned in practice (Silva and Macías 2003; Ferrándiz 2006; Renshaw 2011). Scientific exhumations of Republican victims were only carried out after 2000. Between that year and 2018, the remains of 10,000 individuals from 700 unmarked graves have been recovered. Many of the interventions have not been properly published and reports are not always easy to find. However, since 2014 information has increased exponentially and we now have an important amount of data at our disposal that casts light onto the patterns of political violence during the war and after. It is important to remember that the information is partial. We know much more about right-wing violence from an archaeological and anthropological point of view than we know about left-wing crimes. Paradoxically, the fast and systematic exhumation and memorialization campaign undertaken by the Franco regime after the war has deprived us of very valuable information on revolutionary violence. Yet there is a plethora of forensic reports in archives that await a careful examination by historians, anthropologists and archaeologists. In this chapter, I will be looking at the archaeological evidence provided by the

14   *Time to kill*

recent exhumations of mass graves, with a particular emphasis on the period of hot extrajudicial violence (from the summer of 1936 to early 1937). I am interested in what mass graves, bodies and artifacts associated with them tell us about patterns of violence. The campaign of exhumations as a social phenomenon has been the object of much research and the interested reader can refer to the excellent work of Layla Renshaw (2011) and Francisco Ferrándiz (2013, 2014, 2016) (see also Chapter 11). A synthesis from the point of view of forensic science can be found in Ríos and Etxeberría (2016).

Patterns of murder

A recent PhD thesis by Fernando Serrulla (2018) offers an excellent introduction to the phenomenon of political violence from the point of view of mass graves. Serrulla, a forensic doctor, examined reports for 200 mass graves exhumed between 2000 and 2015, in which the bodies of 1,762 individuals were recovered. The number has statistical significance. The problem is that he includes in his statistics both victims of right-wing and left-wing violence and soldiers fallen in the battlefields. Nevertheless, victims of revolutionary violence and soldiers represent a small percentage of the total (1.5%), so we can take the numbers as generally illustrative of right-wing violence. According to Serrulla's data, 86% of the victims in which biological sex could be identified were men and 7% women; only 1.5% were minors and 7.5% senile adults (that is, over 50). The brunt of the repression, thus, was borne by men aged between 18 and 50 (70% of the victims), which coincides with the more politicized sectors of the population. Forty-five per cent of the graves have between one and three individuals, 70% ten or less, and only 26% ten or more. The graves with over 45 individuals represent only 3% of the total. This is a general overview: there are differences, as we will see, in the way people were murdered in different parts of Spain, in cities and rural areas; differences in the way in which men and women were killed, in which people were killed at the beginning and end of the war.

I have said above that the great majority of the killings occurred during the first six months of the war. This is generally true, but there are other moments in which there are peaks of assassinations. In the case of the Republic, this is when the troops withdrew before a Nationalist advance— most notably in the case of Catalonia, where hundreds were killed in prisons by retreating Republicans. In the case of the Nationalists, murders increased whenever they captured new cities or towns.

Large graves, small graves

There is a wide variety in the size of mass graves and the number of individuals that they contain and there are different factors to take into consideration. In the case of Burgos, one of the most thoroughly researched provinces, it has been proved that the larger mass graves are related to *sacas*.

The name refers to the taking of prisoners from jail, often under pretext of being moved to another prison, in order to be killed and buried in the open countryside. This strategy was used by both revolutionaries and right-wing militias. Instead, smaller graves, containing an average of seven people, are associated with *paseos* (Ríos 2011: 259). The term, widely used during the Spanish Civil War, describes the operation of kidnapping people from their homes to kill them in the outskirts of a village or town. It was ironically said that victims were just "taken for a walk" (*paseo*). The term *paseado* became thus synonymous with murdered. The word itself, and the strategy of killing, were copied from Hollywood gangster movies, which were popular in Spain at the time (Ruiz 2014: 137–138). Like *sacas*, *paseos* were common in both Republican and Nationalist Spain. The largest mass graves in Burgos associated with *sacas* contained great number of individuals: 81 in Costaján, 85 in La Andaya, 96 in Mount Estépar and 135 in La Pedraja (Figure 2.1)

Figure 2.1 One of the mass graves of Mount Estépar (Burgos), a typical case of a massive Nationalist *saca* from the early war period.

Source: © Juan Montero Gutiérrez.

16 *Time to kill*

(Montero Gutiérrez 2009; Montero Gutiérrez et al. 2017). The extreme violence unleashed in this province, which took the lives of 3,000 people, is particularly striking, as Burgos was immediately occupied by the Nationalists (the city became the rebel wartime capital) and there was neither armed opposition nor revolutionary crimes that had to be avenged.

Large *sacas* were not unknown in Republican-held territory. Indeed, the largest *sacas* of the war were perpetrated by revolutionaries in Madrid (Ruiz 2014). Between 7 November and 4 December 1936, in the middle of the Battle of Madrid (see Chapter 3), around 2,500 people were taken from prison and shot near the villages of Torrejón de Ardoz and Paracuellos, east of the capital. Neighbors of Paracuellos were forced to dig six large mass graves in which the corpses were thrown. The official plan was to move the captives to the Republican rearguard to avoid them being liberated by the Nationalists in case they captured Madrid, but a local committee made up of communists, anarchists and socialists decided to assassinate most of them before reaching their destiny. The modus operandi was extremely similar to Stalinist killings of the time and it has long been argued that the massacre was, if not orchestrated, at least encouraged by Soviet advisors. A document found a few years ago proves that the operation was mostly a Spanish affair, agreed between the communist Unified Socialist Youth (JSU) and the anarchists of CNT-FAI (Reverte 2007: 673–679), but the inspiration seems to be ultimately Soviet. After the war, most corpses were exhumed and reburied with honors (Rodrigo 2008: figures 21–23) and today those landing in Madrid airport can see a huge cross near Paracuellos, commemorating the massacre.

As noted above, the campaign of exhumations sponsored by the Franco regime means that there is very little archaeological information on revolutionary mass graves. There are just half a dozen examples of interventions on sites of massacres perpetrated by left-wing militias and they were usually promoted by the Church in their canonization campaign (Mezquida 2017: 174). Reports have never been published. One of the burial places is the mine of Camuñas (Sociedad Aranzadi 2008). The site had already been evaluated by a commission in 1962, but they ruled out the possibility of an exhumation due to the enormous technical difficulties. In 2008, a team was able to retrieve human remains inside the mine shaft at a depth of 20 meters. In later interventions, they recovered 41 corpses. The investigation corroborated what was known from oral sources: the mass grave was not the result of a single episode of violence, but of multiple killings through time—different *paseos*. After dropping the bodies, the killers threw quicklime to facilitate the decomposition of the corpses. Some bones were also burnt. There were remains of both men and women and it is calculated that the total number of victims exceeds one hundred—a small part of the 3,152 people assassinated in Republican Toledo.[2]

Differences can be found in the practice of right-wing assassinations in urban and rural environments. In the case of cities there were two modus operandi: either they were taken outside the city and killed and buried in some unpopulated area, as in the case of Burgos mentioned above (Gutiérrez et al. 2017),[3] or people were killed and buried in urban cemeteries, which usually filled throughout extended periods of time. The latter scenario has been documented in Seville, Palencia, Málaga and Paterna. In the two latter cases, most of the killed were victims of judicial violence. Surprisingly, those who were killed after a court sentence were often thrown into unmarked graves all the same. Chilling examples of this practice come from the cemeteries of San Rafael, Málaga, and Paterna, near Valencia. Málaga was captured during a Nationalist offensive in February 1937, whereas Paterna only fell at the end of the war, after which it became the execution place for hundreds of people who had been taken prisoner in the wartime Republican capital and other places on the Mediterranean coast. Both cemeteries have been the object of large-scale excavations and those of Málaga have been recently published (Fernández Martín and Espinosa 2019).

In San Rafael, archaeologists have exhumed the remains of 2,840 people. Around 3% of them were women. To this figure we have to add 1,350 individuals who were buried individually in marked graves as their relatives were informed of the execution and paid the pertinent fees, and 400 more corpses that were removed from the mass graves and taken to the mausoleum of the Valley of the Fallen in the late 1950s (see Chapter 11). The estimated number of murdered adults buried in San Rafael is 4,250 (Fernández Martín and Espinosa 2019: 328), which coincides with the figure furnished by archival documents. The human remains were found in nine mass graves, the largest of which contained 237 individuals (Figure 2.2). Corpses were placed in layers, following the order of execution, between four and seven per layer and down to two meters in depth. Quicklime was then added to speed up the process of decomposition. According to archival documentation, the victims were executed by firing squad in an esplanade near the cemetery. However, the abundance of spent shell casings in the mass graves indicates that some batches of people were probably killed in front of the grave so as to save time and energy.

The highest number of victims coincides with the first months of 1937 (February to March), but the killings continued, both by firing squad and by *garrote vil* (garrotte). In its modern form, this was a device used for executions in Spain between 1820 and 1974. It consisted of an iron ring attached to a wooden pole that killed the convict by breaking his or her neck. Although theoretically a quick method of killing, it required a strong and skilled executioner and when this was not the case, the victim could spend up to 25 minutes in terrible agony. In Málaga, people sentenced to garrotte were buried in individual wooden coffins and can thus be distinguished from those killed by bullets. Archaeologists also found the remains of 300 children and newborns in the mass graves (representing 11% of the skeletons). They were the sons and daughters of women who were imprisoned for their political ideology and activities or for being relatives of prominent Republican

18 *Time to kill*

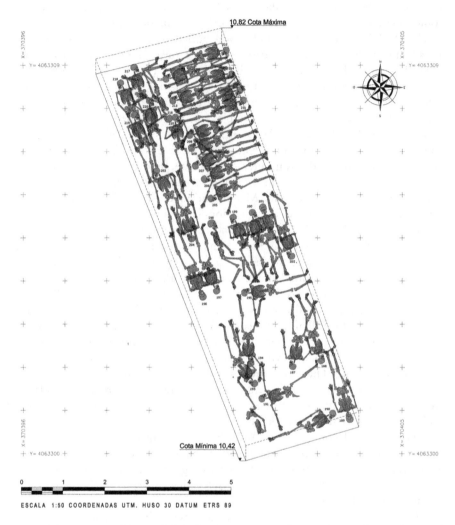

Figure 2.2 Cemetery of San Rafael (Málaga): mass grave 1, layer 6. A typical case of repeated executions by firing squad in an urban context.
Source: © Andrés Fernández Martín.

politicians. The appalling conditions in jail, with lack of food and medicines, explain the high death rate. Those buried in San Rafael covered all the spectrum of the regime's ideological enemies: from communists to people accused of Freemasonry. In October 1937, for example, 81 alleged masons were shot (Preston 2012a: 530). Revolutionary violence was also massive in Málaga: up to 1,110 people were killed in the seven months it remained in Republican hands (Preston 2012a: 289). However, most of those who carried out or instigated the killings escaped the city before the Nationalist advance, often grounding civilian evacuees and taking their means of transportation (Fernández Martínez and Espinosa 2019: 98). As would happen in other places, the people who suffered the brunt of the repression were often those who thought they had nothing to fear for not being involved in the crimes.

In Paterna, the estimated number of mass graves is 135. At the time of writing, 427 individuals have been already exhumed (Miguel Mezquida, pers. comm. 2019). They come from graves containing from 33 to 107 individuals. The shape of the grave is indicative of the nature of the killing. In the case of extrajudicial violence, large groups of people killed simultaneously are buried in wide (or long) mass graves. In the case of Paterna, the graves are narrow and very deep—in one case six meters deep. This is incontrovertible proof that the authorities were expecting to kill a huge number of people. As in the case of Málaga, the corpses were dumped after each execution into the open grave, they were covered with a layer of soil and quicklime, and the space was left open for the next batch of victims. In Paterna, archaeologists have also documented wood and concrete separating layers of bodies. The conditions of preservation in the cemetery are extraordinary: many corpses experienced saponification, which has preserved soft tissue. The same happens with clothes, some with initials embroidered (that will facilitate identifications) and even bullet holes and blood stains.[4] Saponification has been attested in other mass graves and viscera have been preserved in exceptional cases, most notably brains (Serrulla et al. 2017): in La Pedraja (Burgos), 45 brains were exhumed in a mass grave with 101 individuals (Serrulla et al. 2016).

Burials of victims of political killings in cemeteries make forensic research extremely difficult. Researchers have to distinguish between victims of repression and other people buried in the same place and individual identifications are usually very complicated. An extraordinary work was carried out in La Carcavilla, Palencia (García-Rubio 2017), where the combined efforts of archaeologists, anthropologists and historians managed to disentangle an extremely complex burial ground, in which victims from different phases of the war as well as dead unrelated to the conflict shared the same space. Research revealed movements of corpses and the lack of fit between documents and facts, which was not so much related to a strategy of concealment as to a total disrespect for the killed and their families. Unlike in Málaga and Paterna, the large majority of the graves in La Carcavilla were small and had between one and four individuals. The archaeologists were able to reconstruct the sequence of interment by studying the spatial arrangement and the chronology of killings and succeeded in identifying some of the killed. Meaningfully, the area of the cemetery chosen for the victims of judicial and extrajudicial killings in La Carcavilla was the one destined for people who had committed suicide, homeless people, the poor and those without known relatives or with mental disabilities. They all have in common their having been expelled from society: persons without rights in

20   Time to kill

death or life. Inhumation of political victims with social pariahs reinforced the equation between "Reds" and outcasts and contributed to the stigmatization of their living relatives. Besides, the areas of the cemeteries reserved for the poor were more likely to be destroyed to make place for "normal" people, as has often happened (Barragán and Castro 2004: 159). To top it all, relatives were sometimes cheated by the local authorities. In La Carcavilla, archaeological research detected a fraud: people were paying for the rental of the graves where their murdered relatives had been buried … but the truth is that they were no longer there. A particularly outrageous case is that of a woman, Felisa Díaz Barrasa, mother of three youngsters who were killed and buried in the cemetery. She asked the authorities for permission to pay for the grave rental in installments, as she was *pobre de solemnidad* (extremely poor). The authorities acceded and Felisa paid, but DNA analyses revealed that they were not Felisa's children (García Rubio 2017: 131).

People from rural areas during the period of hot violence were often taken to the killing site without passing through prison. Mass graves were dug in the place of murder, along roadsides and in empty places in-between villages or small towns. The pattern, however, varies from region to region. In Castile or Extremadura there are hundreds of these graves (Muñoz Encinar 2016; Montero Gutiérrez 2017), whereas in Galicia—where right-wing violence ended the life of around 10,000 people—there are very few, as the corpses were first exposed and then buried in cemeteries. Rural cemeteries were also used as execution places and sites of mass burial—typically in Andalusia (Baquero 2016, 2018). Victims were at times interred outside rather than inside, as a way of signifying the expulsion of the killed from the community. Mass graves in or near rural cemeteries can represent one moment of killing or several *sacas* and *paseos*. In Magallón (Zaragoza), archaeologists exhumed the remains of 81 individuals from 30 graves, with one, two, three or four individuals (Ríos et al. 2013b: 625) (Figure 2.3). This village centralized the killing activities of the local militias, who went to the villages around the locality in search for "Reds". They were kidnapped, taken to the cemetery, killed and buried there.

The size of mass graves varies from region to region. Thus, individual graves are more common in the Basque Country and Navarre, whereas massive graves, with 45 or more individuals have been documented mainly in Andalusia and in the province of Burgos (Castile). Very few graves with more than 10 victims have been found in the Basque Country (cf. Serrulla 2018: Graph 1). In Navarre, 87% of the exhumed graves to 2017 had fewer than 10 individuals (Etxeberria and Herrasti 2017: 20). The Basque Country suffered right-wing political violence to a lesser degree than other parts of Spain, in relative and absolute terms. This might have to do with the fact that, although Basque nationalism was strong in the region and therefore opposed to the Spanish nationalism of the rebels, the movement was largely conservative. Andalusia, instead, was sociologically dominated by large masses of impoverished day laborers with

Figure 2.3 One of the mass graves of the cemetery of Magallón (Zaragoza): small *paesos* in a rural area.
Source: © Álmudena García Rubio/Sociedad Aranzadi.

leftist ideas. The region suffered from both the violence of right-wing militias and the actions of the Army of Africa, whose soldiers practiced colonial warfare during the early months of the war and during their advance toward Madrid (Espinosa 2003).

Beyond patterns, every mass grave conceals a unique tragedy. Two examples illustrate the abject brutality of the political violence. In Mass Grave I of La Granja (Quintanilla de las Viñas, Burgos), archaeologists found the remains of Julián Santamaría Carretero. He was shot but managed to escape, severely wounded. He took refuge in a neighbor's home, who cured his wounds but eventually denounced him. He was again executed, this time properly: his skull was found fractured by a bullet (Montero Gutiérrez and Valdivieso 2011: 485). Yet no story surpasses in horror that of Claudio Macías. Claudio was a neighbor of Villalibre de la Jurisdicción (León) (Figure 2.4). He fought with the Republicans in Asturias and returned to his village after the fall of the Northern Front in October 1937. He went into hiding in the cellar of his house to escape the Falangists. Since they were unable to find him, they took his 16-year-old brother and killed him as a reprisal. Claudio, ill with pneumonia, began to dig his own grave in the basement of his house. His sister

Figure 2.4 The grave of Claudio Macías, dug by himself shortly before his death.
Source: © Óscar Rodríguez.

buried him there when he died and there he was found by the archaeologists of the Association for the Recovery of Historical Memory (ARMH): a home turned into a prison, turned into a grave.[5]

Gender violence

"My mother was taken away in front of me. They grabbed her from the arms and dragged her legs through the stairs. They were pointing a pistol at her, as if she were a beast. My mother only cried 'my children, my children!'... We were left as a nest hit by a broom." These are the words of Luis Vega Sevillano. He was seven years old when he saw his mother being snatched from home to be shot. His brother was not yet two. His father was captured and murdered the following day (Baquero 2016: 17–25). This happened in Paterna de Rivera (Cádiz), but it could have happened in many other villages of Spain in the summer of 1936.

In a conflict where no distinctions were made between combatants and non-combatants, it is only logical that women became victims of political violence behind the lines. However, they represent a small percentage of the killed. I have mentioned 7% from a large sample of mass graves (Serrulla 2018), but other studies suggest that they can be as little as 2–3% (Herrasti et al. 2018b: 56). This means, in any case, that the remains of around 300 bodies of women have been recovered from mass graves already. If we extrapolate the data to the total of 100,000 victims of right-wing violence during the war-period, the number would approach 3,000. It was at the beginning of the conflict that women were more likely to be killed and they were more frequently murdered by right-wing militias than by revolutionaries. One of the reasons is that the Republic marked the beginning of emancipation for women, as part of wider advances in social justice. To understand Nationalist violence against the female population, it is important to bear in mind that their propaganda stereotyped leftist women as prostitutes, which in the patriarchal mentality of the period legitimized abuses (Sánchez 2009). Wherever the Nationalists prevailed, leftist women had their hair shaven and were forced to drink castor oil, which provoked vomits and diarrhea, while they were paraded through the streets (Sánchez 2009: 20; Renshaw 2011: 67). That women's bodies were targeted had to do with Catholic notions of the sinful female body and patriarchal ideas more generally. Yet they were also punished because they were the wives, girlfriends, sisters or daughters of Republicans. They were imprisoned, tortured and killed to cause more pain and humiliation to men and sometimes simply in their place. This, again, is reflective of a strong patriarchal ideology, in which women were but an appendix of men (Solé 2016).

Female remains have appeared in many graves, mostly in the south—another clear pattern in the geography of death: around 70% of the mass graves with remains of women have been found in Andalusia and Extremadura (see Table 1 in annex). Furthermore, 88% of female remains have appeared in these two regions—the percentage is somewhat skewed by the 85 retrieved in the cemetery of San Rafael alone. Some mass graves had only female remains or they were the majority by far, clear proof that they were being targeted as a group. In fact, in some cases we know of paralegal processes affecting only women (Baquero 2016: 18). Violence against them was often carried out by the colonial army, whose members were accustomed to commit atrocities against civilians. After the atrocities committed by the Berbers in the Battle of Annual (22 July–9 August 1921), during the Rif War (1920–1927), in which 13,000 Spanish soldiers were killed and many bodies emasculated, Franco allowed his troops to murder civilians, rape women and mutilate corpses in Morocco—all of which he recognized without embarrassment in his memoirs (Bennasar 1996: 54). These practices were transferred to the metropolis during the Civil War (Richards 1998: 30, 55; Preston 2012a). But this is only part of the story: many of the killings were committed by right-wing militia (mostly Falangists), not by professional soldiers.

Examples of female mass graves in Andalusia include the cases of Grazalema (Cádiz), with 16 people of which 14 women (López Jiménez et al. 2008), and Gerena (Seville), with 17 women, all of them from another village, Guillena. This is an atypical case, as the murders took place as late as November 1937, after the period of hot violence (Ferrándiz 2014: 175). In

24 *Time to kill*

the north of Spain, women's mass graves are known, but they have often eluded researchers: in Villamediana (Palencia, Castile) they could only find three of the 13 women supposedly buried there. The grave with female remains of La Pedraja (Burgos, Castile), has never been found. In other cases, women are not in the majority, but they still represent a large percentage of the total killed. Thus, in Arroyo del Romanzal (Llerena, Badajoz), out of 40 individuals that were exhumed, anthropologists could ascertain the biological sex of 29: 15 men and 14 women (Figuero Maynar et al. 2010).

More frequently, there are fewer women than men—this is the case when they were killed in the place of absent relatives or husbands. In general, as the size of the mass grave increases, the presence of women decreases. Thus, in the cemetery of Teba (Málaga) out of 151 individuals, only six or seven were women (Fernández Martín n.d.: 13) and in Puerto Real (Cádiz), there were only two out of 185 (Baquero 2018: 178). In San Rafael, women's bodies are 3.21% of the total (Fernández Martín and Espinosa 2019: 328). The smaller percentage of women in large cemeteries, which were often used for longer periods of time, indicates that the female population was less likely to be killed in urban environments and that as the war progressed they had more chances to survive.

Proof of the savage violence during the first months of the war is the killing of pregnant women and the tortures and physical abuses of women. Although we know through oral or written accounts of many women who were killed while pregnant, the presence of fetuses in mass graves is uncommon, because the frailty of their bones works against their preservation. There are four published cases of fetal remains. In Fregenal de la Sierra, one of the female victims was in the last stages of pregnancy at the moment of the assassination and remains of the fetus were found in her pelvis (Muñoz Encinar 2016: 239). In the cemetery of San Rafael, in the pelvic area of another woman a fetus was found in an advanced stage of development. She was killed in a batch of 36 people in which she was one of the two women (Fernández Martín and Espinosa 2019: 273). Two other fetuses were found in the mass grave of Gerena, mentioned above,[6] and another one in La Campana (Carrasco 2019), in this latter case in the ninth month of gestation. It is probably not a coincidence that all fetuses have been documented in graves of southern Spain.

As for sexual violence and torture, evidence is also elusive. In some cases, as in Llerena and Fregenal de la Sierra, women and men have been found buried in different graves or women were the last to be deposited in the grave. Laura Muñoz Encinar (2019: 494) interprets this as evincing the practice of sexual violence before the killing of women, for which there are abundant oral testimonies. The same pattern of differential burial was attested in Espinosa de los Monteros.[7] In Aguilar de la Frontera, the two women in Mass Grave 5 were deposited together in a group with 16 men, but they were the first to be thrown into the pit (Espino Navarro et al. 2019). Torture or extreme cruelty is notoriously difficult to identify osteologically, but some examples have been identified. Examples are a mature woman found in Puerto Real (Cádiz), with broken arms and wrists and shots to the knees (Baquero 2018: 180), and another one in Guadalcanal (Seville) with six shots to the head (Baquero 2018: 73. This kind violence is redolent of current gendered crimes.

The large majority of women were victims of irregular violence, but not all. Catalina Muñoz was executed by firing squad on 22 September 1936 in Palencia (García-Rubio 2017: 65–66, 163–164). She was sentenced by a military court for her leftist activities. None of them implied physical violence: only her husband had been involved in a homicide and that was before the war. When she was assassinated, she was 37 and a mother of four. Her youngest child, Martín, was only nine months old. With the body of Catalina, archaeologists found a baby rattle, the only object she brought with her to the place of execution. At the time of writing, Martín is 83. He cannot even picture his mother, as there is not a single photograph of Catalina Muñoz, who was also illiterate. If she had not been prosecuted and murdered, she may have left no trace in this world. Martín's sister, Lucía, who is 94, remembers the day when her mother was taken away. She was wearing a black apron. The same apron where she would have carried Martín's rattle the last day of her life.[8]

Another woman executed after trial was Amanda García Rodríguez. Although detained shortly after the coup, she was killed as late as January 1938. She was condemned to death for her leftist activities, which included embroidering a Republican flag, but no crimes. Because she was pregnant at the time, they waited for her to give birth and three months after delivering a baby in jail she was executed by firing squad. The body of Amanda has not been exhumed, but the scenario of the killing has been the object of archaeological investigation. She was imprisoned and murdered in the castle of San Felipe, near Ferrol, in Galicia—Franco's birthplace. This is where most Republicans from the province of A Coruña were killed— amounting to 710 people between 1936 and 1939. During excavations in the ditch surrounding the late-sixteenth-century castle, archaeologists documented multiple bullet impacts on the castle's wall and 7 and 7.92 mm ammunition, of the kind used by the Mauser rifles employed in the executions (Blanco Rotea 2009).

Judicial executions of women continued well into the postwar period. The most famous case is that of the Thirteen Roses, a group of women (actually 14) aged between 18 and 29 and mostly socialist who were shot after trial in Madrid in 1939–1940. Other women were condemned to death and executed by firing squad during the early Franco regime. The body of one of them, a primary school teacher called Genara Fernández García, was exhumed in the cemetery of León. Genara first lost her job in a school for her leftist ideology and then was accused of distributing communist propaganda. She was murdered on 4 April 1941.[9]

26 *Time to kill*

Hiding the massacre?

The mass graves of the Spanish Civil War occupy an ambiguous space, in-between the visible and the invisible. They were not unknown by the neighbors, as shown by the fact that the great majority of graves have been found thanks to information provided by local people, who witnessed the events, saw the fresh burials or were told about their location by witnesses or perpetrators. The mass grave, then, was not just a way of disposing of the bodies of the killed. Even less a mechanism to erase the memory of the events. Rather, it was a technology aimed at producing a lasting and paralyzing memory of violence, which was quite successful (Renshaw 2011). This is what Ferrándiz (2009: 73) has called the "terror-inspiring efficacy" of mass graves. The semi-secrecy of the assassinations, their undefined status between the visible and invisible, the known and the unknown, made the places of assassination and interment particularly effective in creating an atmosphere of terror. They occupy a middle ground between the public performances of baroque punishment described by Foucault (1975) and the technologies of disappearance deployed by Stalinism, Nazism and the Latin American dictatorships of the 1960s–1980s. This hybrid or transitory nature is structurally coherent with a society still traditional and Catholic, but on a traumatic path of modernization. The ambiguous location of the mass graves is aptly captured by Francisco Ferrándiz (2009: 86), who describes them as a "public secret". Ambiguity is not only ontological, but also geographical: the interments appear in liminal spaces: non-places (roadsides), marginal areas (those set apart for indigents and suicide victims in cemeteries, for instance), and boundaries (the border between different villages or towns or between the rural and the urban).

In some instances there are practices that seem at first sight consistent with a strategy of disappearance. Thus, following the mass killings of surrendered Republicans in Badajoz, in August 1936, heaps of bodies were incinerated (Preston 2012a: 353–356). It was ordered by Falangist colonel Juan Yagüe, one of the commanders of the colonial army whose units were advancing toward Madrid. As many as 2,000 people may have been killed in the city. The reason for burning the corpses, however, is not necessarily related to a desire for concealment of a war crime. After all, Yagüe spoke matter-of-factly about shooting the prisoners, so it is possible that the point was simply to do away with the piles of corpses rotting under the sun in the scorching Extremaduran summer. In a traditionally Catholic country like Spain, burning the deceased was also a way of defiling them and humiliating both the dead and their living relatives. Direct archaeological traces of the disposal of bodies is lacking in Badajoz (we do have photographs), but there is interesting evidence from Mérida, another city in the same province. Here, Nationalist violence took the lives of around 300 people during the same month of August (Muñoz Encinar 2019: 488). After the massacre, the bodies were thrown into large mass graves and then burnt. The exhumation of four of the mass graves found out that most of the human remains had been

Time to kill   27

transferred elsewhere, but archaeologists could still retrieve fragments of burnt or cremated bones and objects (Muñoz Encinar 2016: 157–158). The striation and whitish color of some of the bones indicated that they were subjected to temperatures of 650°C or higher. As in Badajoz, the reasons could have been purely practical in 1936, but the removal of the bones decades later might have been inspired by a desire to conceal the traces of the crime, at a time when Nationalist violence during the war would have been uncomfortable even for those who backed the dictatorship. Destruction of burials has been actually more common in the postwar period than before, either to erase the past or to humiliate the victims. In El Coronil (Seville) a local landlord built his mausoleum on top of a mass grave "to show who was in command", according to neighbors (Baquero 2018: 127). Other examples of incineration of corpses are known. A good example comes from La Campana (Seville), where 131 people, including 16 women, were killed on 2 August 1936. The exhumation of a multi-layered mass grave retrieved the remains of 16 individuals, with traces of carbonization, who were probably killed during this repressive episode. The analysis of charred remains through Energy-dispersive X-ray spectroscopy (EDS) hinted at the use of straw in the combustion process—also attested by elderly neighbors (Carrasco 2019: 153–154). In addition, the presence of lead isotopes might be indicative of the use of gasoline to accelerate the fire. The use of quicklime to help in the decomposition of corpses or for hygienic purposes has been documented in several contexts (Schotsmans et al. 2017), some of which are mentioned above.

Mine shafts and caves were often used to dispose of the bodies: they make up 5% of all the burial sites of victims of violence during the Spanish Civil War in the sample studied by Fernando Serrulla (2017: 148). Again, this is not necessarily related with occultation, but rather a way of dealing with the corpses easily. It also made their recovery virtually impossible. In some areas where natural caves are abundant, as in the Canary Islands, they were employed as mass graves very often. One of the most sinister cases was the Sima de Jinámar (Silva and Macías 2003: 185–195), where hundreds of corpses were thrown during the first months of the war. In the karstic regions of northern Spain caves became also a preferential location for the disposal of the bodies (Etxeberria et al. 2014). As in the case of incineration, the use of caves and mine shafts can be a way not so much of concealing the massacre itself, as of inflicting further damage to the dead and to the living. It made mourning more difficult, insofar as relatives were unable to recover the corpses, and made both the person and his or her memory disappear more thoroughly, as if she or he had never existed in the first place—a typical strategy of totalitarianism (Arendt 2004: 528). Actions for making the dead disappear, therefore, were intended to annihilate their existence, not so much to erase proofs of the crime

The situation might be different in Republican territory, as the killers here could eventually be taken to justice. We have seen how revolutionaries also used a mine shaft to dump the bodies of the killed in Camuñas. In Barcelona, the original modus operandi of anarchists, consisting in leaving the corpses lying on the street or the roadside, changed when leaders became afraid of the implications of their crimes. According to the diaries of a FAI assassin, the bodies started to be sent to a factory with kilns at a certain point to cremate them and thus avoid leaving incriminating traces (Mir 2006: 112).

Ways to kill

Archaeology and physical anthropology furnish important data regarding the ways in which people were dealt with before, during and after the assassination. As noted above, torture is difficult to document, because it seldom leaves osteological traces. There are a few cases of perimortem trauma that have been interpreted as severe beatings, although it is necessary to exercise caution. In the case of one of the killed in La Guijarrosa (Córdoba), fractures in the jaw and teeth (which are less likely to fracture due to postdepositional processes) have been interpreted as provoked by a blow with the rifle butt (Steadman et al. 2007: 19). A broken face has also been explained as the result of a beating in Aguilar de la Frontera (Córdoba) (Espino Navarro et al. 2019).

Well attested in many graves, instead, is the tying of hands with wire or cable (e.g. Bores et al. 2007; Congram, Flavel and Maeyama 2014: 54; Muñoz Encinar 2016: 492–493; Espino Navarro et al. 2019; Fernández Martín and Espinosa 2019, etc.) (Figure 2.5). In most cases, this ought to have caused severe pain to the prisoners, particularly when they were tied to each other. The procedure was used by both Nationalists and revolutionaries.

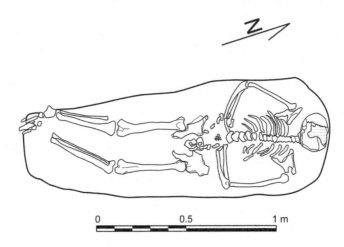

Figure 2.5 A.M., an unknown Basque soldier murdered during Christmas of 1937. He had his hands tied behind his back before being shot and dumped into a shallow grave.

Source: © Álvaro Falquina and author.

In Castuera (Badajoz), Republican prisoners were tied in pairs, the elbow of one of the prisoners to the wrist of another one and in one case to the neck. The tight wire surely caused wounds (Muñoz Encinar 2016: 484). A desire to punish and humiliate also explains the ankle fastened to the hands of one of the victims from the mass graves of Aguilar de la Frontera (Espino Navarro et al. 2019).

Punishment did not end with the death of the victims. The deposition of the corpses indicates symbolic violence in the form of bodies thrown as if they were animal carcasses or rubbish or simply buried in contravention of widely accepted Catholic norms (Congram, Favel and Maeyama 2014: 60–61). Thus, victims were frequently buried with the face to the ground: the soldier murdered in Villanueva del Duque (Guadalajara) that we exhumed had his hands tied to the back and was dropped in the shallow pit face down, with obvious disrespect. People often refer to these improper forms of burial with phrases like "they were thrown out like rubbish" or "thrown away like the body of a dog" (Renshaw 2011: 143). The way in which they were disposed of is also revealing of the speed of the executioners or the available space. The archaeological excavation of San Rafael cemetery in Málaga revealed different ways of laying the bodies: the days in which killings were few, the corpses were dropped haphazardly; those in which the executed were numerous, the gravediggers had to make the most of the pit and organize the corpses as if they were putting together a jigsaw puzzle (Fernández Martín and Espinosa 2019: 322). Except in the case of cemeteries, where graves are often deep and multilayered, the burials tend to be shallow, again evincing the speed with which these operations were conducted.

The need to end the business quickly is understandable. We are talking mostly about non-professional killers, especially during the first months of the war. Murder is not easy and first-time assassins usually experience the bloodbath as a traumatic event. When he was 16 years old, José Luis de Vilallonga, better known as an aristocrat and socialite, was recommended for a firing squad by his father. He wanted him to fight for Nationalist Spain, but considered that the boy needed some experience before going to the front and thus Vilallonga ended up shooting people at the execution wall. The first day he was totally inebriated after drinking cognac for several hours in preparation for the killing (Aguilar and Payne 2016: 153). Witness reports gathered on the murders of Monte Costaján (Burgos) reveal that the killers were

> not in normal mental and physical conditions. Several testimonies describe them as drunk, brainwashed by their superiors who provided alcohol so that they obeyed their orders unquestioningly. That explains the notoriously inaccurate shooting... Firing was not accurate, producing a long and agonizing death.
>
> (Fernández de Mata 2004: 2531)

30   *Time to kill*

Among the revolutionaries, the use of alcohol to facilitate work was also very common (Mir 2006). There are some oral testimonies of imperfect killings, such as the one of Julián Santamaría mentioned above, and perimortem traumas indicate that the shooting was often imprecise. Material witness to the state in which some killings were conducted is a smashed bottle of sherry on the bottom of a mass grave in Castuera (Muñoz Encinar 2013: 104).

We know about the way in which people were murdered through the bullets and shell casings that appear associated with the corpses, as well as through perimortem traumas. Traces of bullet impacts in the sample studied by Serrulla (2018) indicated that 59% had shots to the head, the great majority a single shot, but a remarkable 18% had two or more impacts in the skull, in four cases over four shots, unambiguous proof of vicious violence. Only 40% had shots to the head exclusively. The rest had either shots to the head and to other parts of the body or in other parts of the body but the head. The high percentage of subadults with skull trauma is intriguing: almost 70% or eleven points higher than the average—perhaps a desire to end the business quickly. Young adults (18–35) are those who received proportionately a higher number of shots to the head (that is more than one shot per individual), a fact that may indicate particular violence against this group—which is again consistent with their greater political mobilization (also most killers came from this age cohort).

The two most common calibers of the bullets found associated with the killed are 7 mm (23%) and 9 mm (51%). 9x23 mm was the caliber of the standard pistol used by the armed forces in Spain, the Astra 400, and 7x57 mm that of the service rifle, the Spanish or Oviedo Mauser. The presence of 9x23 mm ammunition only is usually indicative of assassination by the security forces (most often the Guardia Civil, a paramilitary police that played a prominent role in right-wing violence) or the military. It appears systematically associated with shots to the head. In Quintanilla de las Viñas (Burgos), for instance, the six exhumed individuals had skull traumas provoked by the impact of 9 mm bullets (Montero Gutiérrez and Valdivieso 2011: 495). Exactly the same pattern was documented in another region, Navarre, in the mass grave of Fustiñana, where seven skeletons were found with bullet wounds in the skull. They were made, again, with 9 mm pistols and had a posterior-anterior trajectory (Herrasti and Etxeberria 2017). A diversity of projectiles is invariably linked to killing by militias. In one of the mass graves of Castuera, six different types of pistol and revolver bullets were found and none belonging to a rifle (see Chapter 10). We can thus identify the act as committed by local right-wing militia and also estimate the minimum number of people involved in the killing (Muñoz Encinar 2013). Rifles and pistols were the main killing tools, although there are reported instances of machine guns (as in Paracuellos by the Republicans and Badajoz by the Nationalists). Other weapons, such as shotguns, were rarer. An example is the case of Altable (Burgos), where one of the victims had pellet injuries in two left ribs (Ríos et al. 2013a: 890).

Time to kill   31

A study on perimortem trauma based on 363 individuals identified remarkable differences between judicial and extrajudicial violence (Ríos et al. 2013b). The authors of the study distinguished three types of killing and burial: extrajudicial executions in the open countryside (208 individuals), which took place mostly during the first three months of the war and in which individuals were killed next to the mass grave; extrajudicial executions in cemeteries (81 individuals), in which people were killed at cemetery walls and then buried inside; and judicial executions, after which the killed were taken to the cemetery and buried there (74 individuals). In the case of extrajudicial murders in the countryside, 70% of the gunshots presented a trajectory from back to front, as opposed to judicial murders, in which the trajectory was from front to back (70%). The pattern of judicial killings can be easily explained, as they were by firing squad. In extrajudicial killings in the countryside, the entrance was mainly through the occipital bone (42%), whereas in judicial executions it was the frontal, mandible and temporal bones (59%). It has been argued that shooting from the back might be consistent with violence that is known to be illegal and in which people might know each other (Congram, Passalacqua and Ríos 2014). It is also probably related to the fact that killers were new to the trade.

Ríos et al. (2013b) also noticed important variability between different contexts: thus, in an instance of rural extrajudicial violence that took the lives of 29 people, the skeletons had from zero (three cases) to three (six cases) bullets in the head, whereas in another case with five victims each had a shot to the head. Variation has to do with the fact that different killing squads were at work and their level of sadism varied as well as their relationship to the victims. In general, judicial executions, as can be expected, are more standardized, although this is not universally true. In fact, a study carried with another set of graves concluded that there was important variability within judicial executions as well, with a higher number of individuals with posterior-anterior gunshot trauma than anticipated (indeed, equal to anterior-posterior) (Congram, Passalacqua and Ríos 2014). This is probably related to the fact that the site used for comparison, the cemetery of Uclés (Cuenca), belonged to a concentration camp (see also Chapter 10), which operated between January 1940 and autumn 1942, and prisons and camps in the early postwar period were known for their brutality. A "clean" execution was more likely in Madrid or Barcelona than in any of the camps, and improvised prisons established in smaller and often remote localities. Congram, Passalacqua and Ríos (2014) also obtain different results in postcranial wounds—higher in extrajudicial executions in their sample, lower in Ríos et al. (2013b). Again, this might have to do with the contexts under examination. Postcranial wounds mean very different things: executioners participating in a firing squad aim both at the heart and at the head. In extrajudicial violence, which was often conducted at short range, postcranial traumas are more probably indicative of brutality, inexperience or both. Congram et al. (2014) have also suggested that patterns evolved through the war. People, after all, learnt how to kill.

32 Time to kill

Not all people who were going to be killed remained passive. Shots to the arms evince the reflex gesture of trying to stop the bullets. In one case at least we know that the victims resisted. In one of the mass graves of Costaján (Burgos), three of the killed who were handcuffed like the rest had their legs tied as well. The perpetrators used their victims' belts to immobilize them, probably because of a thwarted escaping attempt (Bores et al. 2007).

The language of the drowned

Primo Levi (1986) famously said that the real witnesses to the Nazi camps were those who did not return or who returned mute or speaking an incomprehensible language: the language of the drowned, the non-language of those who are alone and about to die. This language is not only made of broken words, but also of things and bodies.

Bones as witnesses

Human remains, in fact, are more than just witnesses to the massacre. They are also an extremely valuable source to know about the conditions of living of large parts of the Spanish population in the 1930s. In fact, it is a unique record for the lower classes that no available documentary record can match. In the sample studied by Serrulla (2018) average height is 162 cm: Today is 174 cm for males. These twelve centimeters of difference are signs of malnutrition and heavy physical labor. In fact, 41% of the individuals studied by Serrulla (2018) show traces of having experienced harsh life conditions. These are reflected in periodontal disease, enamel hypoplasia, periostitis, hyperostosis, vertebral tuberculosis, polyarthrosis, spondyloarthrosis (arthrosis of the spine) and short stature (under 152 cm). The two most common pathologies are hypoplasia (15% of the individuals in the sample) and spondyloarthrosis (13%). People suffering from hypoplasia have teeth with less enamel: it is a typical indicator of malnutrition. In the 1930s, few had the money to pay for dental surgery and this explains the many individuals with infections and abscesses. Whenever a prosthesis or gold teeth appear (very rarely), it is usually associated with persons of some status. It is thus very telling that in the forensic record for the exhumations carried out in the mass graves of Aravaca—a product of revolutionary terror—the presence of gold teeth and dental prostheses is very common (Miriam Saqqa-Carazo pers. comm.). Good teeth, in 1930s Spain, were a marker of class. Another one was work-associated stress. Spondyloarthrosis, the second most common pathology found in exhumations, is associated with excessive physical labor. Young adults are overrepresented in both malnutrition and physical stress, which might be indicative of a worsening of living conditions among the popular classes during the 1920s and 1930s. In Burgos, comparison with anthropometric data available for the province show that people found in mass graves had lower biological living standards than the rest of the population (Ríos 2011: 130). Apart from the spine, damage in other bones also evinces physical stress. In a mass grave in Éibar (Navarre), one of the four skeletons showed intense wear on the elbow bones, typical of heavy manual labor (Etxeberria et al. 2012). Marks of insertion of the muscles in the bones (arms and back of the neck), which are common in mass graves, also inform of continuous exertion (e.g. Herrasti et al. 2012). In the burials of Costaján (Burgos), the majority of the victims had stress marks in arms and spine. Many were doubtless suffering from backache and several had vertebral injuries and dislocations (Bores et al. 2007). These bones with traces of hunger, disease and extenuating labor are a unique testimony of Spanish history, which allows us to understand why so many workers and peasants embraced leftist ideologies. They promised a life without hunger, disease and exploitation.

What makes us human

Yet archaeologists not only document bones in exhumations. They also recover objects, which are as part of us as the bones themselves, if not more (Webmoor and Witmore 2008). Things are what make us human and we are humans because we make things. Recovering artifacts, then, is an indirect way of arriving at the subjectivity, the personhood, of those who were deprived of them. This is why objects are so important, the more so in Spain, where it is so often impossible to retrieve the individual identity of the killed. We might not recover personal names, but we can recover something of their humanity—the one that their executioners tried to snatch from them. Furthermore, through things we recover collective identities, which are as important as individual ones if not more. The people whose bodies we recover, after all, were killed for belonging to specific groups. It was their ideals and solidarity that their murderers were trying to kill and it is those ideals and solidarity that are materialized in the graves that we exhume.

Artifacts, in fact, define us as members of different collectivities (Montero Gutiérrez 2016). Some objects tell us about the political identity of the killed: membership cards, medals, pins, rings with the insignia of a particular party. One of the murdered in the mass graves of Costaján (Burgos) had among his belongings a coin of Alphonse XIII on which somebody had stamped a hammer and sickle and the legend "Vote the Communist Party". Another individual was carrying a small metallic box with the image of the Statue of Liberty in New York and the legend "Universal Peace" (Bores et al. 2007). Political identity is relevant: it is the reason people were killed in the first place. This identity was exterminated thrice: through the murder of politicized individuals, the banning of those ideologies during the dictatorship, and by the repression of political memories among relatives and neighbors. Many of the killed were tagged as simple criminals who deserved their fate. Some families erased the political credentials of the victims,

34 Time to kill

insisting in that they were not involved in politics—a criminalization of the political that marked the Franco dictatorship. "My father was NOT a communist, he was a good man!" objected a woman at an exhumation (Renshaw 2011: 91)—even when one of the few mementos that survived from him was his Communist Party membership card.

Political and work identities were strongly linked together. Members of some professions were massively associated with a specific political party or ideology. Thus, many religious men and women were conservative. In Camuñas (Toledo), we can identify priests because remains of their cassocks were found.[10] In the Left, there was a strong association between particular jobs and specific parties. It is not coincidental that when the war arrived in Madrid, with the Republican Army still in disarray, the militias that defended the capital were organized based on guild: bread-makers, railway workers, typographers, metallurgists, hairdressers… (Reverte 2007: 203, 254, 271, 277, 301, 415, 645). These labor identities are often materialized in mass graves. In Matallana de Valmadrigal (León), archaeologists exhumed the bodies of eight railway workers, most of them still dressing as such: they could be identified by the buttons with the inscription *OESTE* and the image of a locomotive, which corresponds with *Compañía de Ferrocarriles del Oeste* (Western Railway Company). In this company and in León province alone 129 were purged.[11] Other mass graves with railway workers include La Lobera in Aranda de Duero and Carcedo de Bureba, both in Burgos (Montero Gutiérrez 2016: 207). In the first mass grave, archaeologists located an insignia representing a locomotive and two documents with the legend *Carnet Ferroviario* ("Railway ID"). In the second, two of the victims had buttons with the acronym FCSM, which stands for *Ferrocarril Santander-Mediterráneo* (Santander-Mediterranean Railway Line). Many railway workers, who had a strong class-consciousness, were affiliated to the Socialist Party and paid dearly for their political allegiance. It is important to take into consideration the role of material culture in the creation of such consciousness. Railways in the nineteenth and early twentieth centuries were complex infrastructures that required many logistical bases. Workers lived in company towns associated with communication hubs. Political ideas traveled fast in this context and solidarities were reinforced through cohabitation.

Other objects denoting profession are the tramway driver's buttons found in the cemetery of San Rafael (Fernández Martín and Espinosa 2019: 342); the buttons of the uniform of a road worker ("peón caminero") in Teba (Fernández Martín n.d.: 9); 40 different buttons and a thistle that may have belonged to two tailors buried in Costaján (Bores et al. 2007); the combs of a hairdresser in the same site (Bores et al. 2007), and the pencils, rubber, pencil sharpener and ruler belonging to a cabinetmaker killed and buried in Sedano, also in Burgos (Montero Gutiérrez 2016: 206). Another group that suffered right-wing repression were miners. Although mass graves of miners have been found (Baquero 2018: 104), it is less likely that tools linked to their job will be found for obvious reasons. The largest majority of victims of right-wing killings, however, were agricultural laborers, peasants and non-qualified workers. They can be materially identified, as noted above, through their strained bones, but also through their poor attire, particularly the ubiquitous espadrilles.

One of the groups that were targeted by both Republicans and Nationalists were the armed forces, which were crucial for the triumph of the coup, the revolution, or the status quo. Soldiers murdered at the beginning of the war have been found in several places: in San Fernando (Cádiz), archaeologists exhumed a mass grave containing the remains of 48 soldiers loyal to the Republic (Baquero 2018: 108). In the cemetery of San Rafael in Málaga, many items can be associated with the military that were executed there, including belt buckles with regimental numbers (Fernández Martín and Espinosa 2019: 341–342). In the disturbed mass graves of Mérida, archaeologists found a plethora of military items, including insignias, clasps, and buttons. Insignias belonged to members of the municipal police, to *Guardias de Asalto* ("Assault Guards", a body created by the Republic and faithful to it), and the artillery corps (Muñoz Encinar 2016: figs. 4.56–59).

Religious identities are strikingly present in mass graves with victims of right-wing violence (Figure 2.6). A systematic study is still to be done, but there are probably more mass graves with religious elements than without. This goes against the Nationalist account of the war, which depicted the

Figure 2.6 A crucifix that was carried by one of the 59 persons killed and buried in Gumiel de Izán (Burgos). Most of the killed were railway workers.
Source: © Óscar Rodríguez.

36 *Time to kill*

enemy as bloodthirsty atheists and the war as a Crusade "for God and for Spain" (Pérez Bowie 1988). This was of course not pure propaganda: it was largely motivated by the brutal carnage against the clergy: 6,832 people were killed by revolutionaries, including priests, monks and nuns. However, objects found in the graves problematize the idea of the war as a fight between religion and atheism. In the mass graves of Costaján at least seven individuals (of the 81 exhumed) were carrying religious symbols with them at the time of death (Bores et al. 2007). In Castuera, two crucifixes, a medal of the Virgin of Guadeloupe and a reliquary were found (Muñoz Encinar 2013). In the cemetery of San Rafael in Málaga, archaeologists collected many crucifixes and religious medals (Fernández Martín and Espinosa 2019: 343) and among the skeletons of Teba, in the same province, there were several medals of the Virgin of Carmen, patron-saint of the town (Fernández Martín n.d). This goes against the idea, repeated by both Francoist authorities and relatives of people killed by revolutionaries, that the victims were killed "just because they were Christians". Faith alone was seldom a reason to kill somebody: people were murdered either because they were members of the Church or on class and ideological grounds. Richer people and right-wing affiliates usually happened to be more devout Catholics, although women were religious as a norm irrespective of political ideas. Meaningfully, protestants did not suffer violence during the war (except at the hands of Nationalists), which again excludes the "hatred for the faith" as the main reason for the murders.

Objects also speak about gender identities, how masculinity and femaleness was played out in Spain in the 1930s. Masculinity was strongly associated with smoking. Lighters of different kinds are extremely common in mass graves, perhaps one of the most ubiquitous elements: in the mass grave of Teba alone, archaeologists found 34 associated with 151 individuals (Fernández Martín n.d.). Matches, although rarer, have also been documented (Herrasti et al. 2012: 62). In a still quite traditional society, to be a real man meant to be married and wedding rings have been found in many killing sites. As for female identities, these can be seen in adornments such as earrings, combs and elements of attire (buttons, shoes). Among the objects associated with the women from Arroyo Romanzal (Llerena, Badajoz) there were hairpins, ornamental combs (*peinetas*), thimbles and a sewing box (Figuero Maynar et al. 2010). In the two mass graves of Espinosa de los Monteros (Burgos) (Herrasti et al. 2018a), women still had their ornamental combs attached to their heads.[12] A *peineta* made of celluloid imitating tortoiseshell also appeared in La Tejera (Álava, Basque Country) (Herrasti et al. 2018b: 47). The wide distribution of this kind of comb throughout Spain makes it a shared symbol of female identity. Other, less common objects associated with women have been found, as the baleen of a corset (Herrasti and Jiménez 2012: 40). In Fregenal de la Sierra (Badajoz), six women were exhumed in a mass grave, one of them with high-heeled shoes (Figure 2.7).

Figure 2.7 A high-heeled shoe carried by one of the women buried in a mass grave in Fregenal de la Sierra (Extremadura).
Source: © Laura Muñoz Encinar.

The two women assassinated and buried in Guadalcanal (Seville) were also wearing elegant shoes (Baquero 2018: 73). This conspicuous footwear was probably at odds with the sobriety that was expected from women in the rural areas of southern Spain. They can be regarded as a symbol of independence— and independence that many men were not willing to tolerate. The objects that appeared with the dead tell us what the murderers were killing, apart from people. They were trying to erase ideas, values and identities.

Notes

1 For the more proximate causes of the war and an overview of the conflict, the reader is directed to the classic works of Hugh Thomas (2001, original from 1965) and Paul Preston (1994).
2 Another example of victims of Republican violence is the exhumation carried out in Sarrià, near Barcelona. Archaeologists unearthed the bodies of two young people, one of them with a shot to the head, and sealed with quicklime. The burial was next to the Voroshilov Barracks of the JSU. In May 1937, several anarchists were tortured to death in those barracks, so it is possible that the

38 *Time to kill*

human remains correspond to the Stalinist purges unleashed in Barcelona and about which George Orwell (1980) left powerful testimony: https://www.lavan guardia.com/local/barcelona/20190606/462709858934/fosa-guerra-civil-barce lona-sarria-sant-gervasi.html.

3 Although many of the jailed had actually been captured in the countryside.

4 Information provided by Miguel Mezquida, the director of the exhumations.

5 https://www.diariodeleon.es/noticias/bierzo/claudio-cavo-tumba_927495.html.

6 https://www.cgtandalucia.org/blog/3457-De-las-17-mujeres-de-Guillena-Sevilla-una-estaba-embarazada-de-7-meses.html.

7 https://cronicasapiedefosa.wordpress.com/2016/11/14/las-fosas-comunes-de-espi nosa-de-los-monteros-burgos/.

8 https://elpais.com/elpais/2019/05/07/ciencia/1557240719_368278.html.

9 https://www.20minutos.es/noticia/3658814/0/armh-culmina-exhumacion-genara-fernandez-pasionaria-omana-cementerio-leon/.

10 http://www.intereconomia.com/noticias-gaceta/politica/indignacion-camunas-las-mentiras-publicadas-pais.

11 https://memoriahistorica.org.es/tag/ferroviarios/.

12 http://lasmerindadesenlamemoria.wordpress.com/2012/04/25/fosas-espinosa-de-los-monteros-13-desaparecidos/.

3 Capital of glory
October 1936–January 1937

Capital of glory is the name of a collection of poems written by one of Spain's greatest twentieth-century poets, Rafael Alberti, between 1936 and 1938. The capital in question was, of course, Madrid, the first to present armed resistance to fascism. This chapter will focus mainly on the archaeological evidence for the Battle of Madrid, which took place between the 7 and 23 November 1936. The city became the first large battlefield of the Spanish Civil War and one that resonated well beyond the country. It is difficult today to imagine with how much anxiety the world followed the news about the combats in Madrid at the time. It was experienced as a crucial moment in history, the place where the universal fight between fascism and democracy was being played out. Perhaps nothing illustrates more the importance of the encounter than the long life of the Republican slogan: *No pasarán!* "They shall not pass!" Although originally referring to the Germans in Verdún in 1916, it was actually the Spanish *No Pasarán* that was impressed on the world's collective imagination, probably because it did not refer to any nation in particular but to a set of values of universal appeal, such as solidarity without borders, democracy and the struggle against oppression. That it was something crucial for the world that was at stake in Madrid is also seen in the multinational character of the battle, shaped by the presence of the International Brigades and a plethora of foreign journalists, including legendary photographer Robert Capa (Preston 2012b). The enormous interest in the fighting explains the overabundance of publications about the topic. Many memoirs by soldiers, journalists, politicians and military advisors came out during the war or soon afterwards and some have gone through several reprints and translations (e.g. Cox 2005; Colodny 2005; Koltsov 1978; Renn 2016). We also have the detailed narrative offered by historian and Nationalist army officer Martínez Bande (1982, 1984), the hefty volume by Jorge M. Reverte (2004), and accounts of specific sectors within the Madrid front (Calvo González-Regueral 2012). Still, there is much that archaeology can contribute, as I will try to show in this chapter.

40 *Capital of glory*

Enemy at the gates

The Army of Africa had been advancing very fast from the south of Spain from late July, after a sizeable number of troops had been airlifted from Morocco to the Iberian Peninsula (Espinosa 2003). It was made up of Spanish professional soldiers (legionnaires) and Moroccan mercenaries ("regulars"), shock troops that played a crucial role in the early stages of the war and in the conflict more generally. The first combats in southern Spain, in western Andalusia and Extremadura, during the summer of 1936, were asymmetrical encounters between ruthless professional soldiers, on the Nationalist side, and untrained and poorly armed militias, on the Republican. No archaeological work has been conducted on these early battles, which were quite insubstantial and ephemeral in material terms: the units involved were small and highly mobile and they did not dig in or build concrete structures. The only phenomenon that is substantial is the mass graves that the legionaries and the right-wing militias left in their wake and to which I have referred in the previous chapter.

If Madrid had not fallen in Nationalists' hands already in 1936 it was largely because Franco failed to seize the opportunity to advance into the defenseless city and instead decided to liberate Toledo, a historic city 60 km south of the capital. The pro-Nationalist garrison had been defending the Alcázar—the castle that presided the old city—from the very beginning of the war (Ruiz Casero and Vega 2019). Their feat became part of the Nationalist epic: liberating them would surely be a huge propaganda coup and a boost of morale for the rebels. The move was absurd in military terms, but it served Franco well: he was elected Chief of State the same day that Toledo fell, the 28 September. By then, however, the Nationalists had lost precious time that the Republicans employed in fortifying the capital and bringing in reinforcements. We have traces of the combats in Toledo in the shape of bombing and bullet impacts on the heavily restored castle and in other buildings. Many impacts have been documented in the Hospital Tavera, where dozens of Republican prisoners were murdered by the colonial troops. The impacts are testimony to the desperate defense (Ruiz Casero and Vega 2019: 100). On the roof of the hospital, a 75 mm shell with shrapnel still inside was found, probably fired by the Republicans during the assault on the Alcázar—a useless weapon against the sturdy walls of the fortress. The most dramatic document, however, is a graffiti left by one of the militias defending Toledo's Catholic seminary during the last day of the attack. It reads:

> Manuel Gómez Cota, militiaman of Izquierda Republicana[1] of Madrid, undertook the defense of this Seminary. [After] heavy fighting against the enemy and after moving to a safe place the women, the elderly and the children and the rest of the [employees?] and civilian staff, burn it down. It is 5 pm, this is burning, only those who sign remain: Manuel Gómez, [illegible name[2]], Eduardo Ruiz, ¡Long live Azaña! ¡Long live the Republic!.

Capital of glory 41

Around 30 Republican fighters resisted in the Seminary for three days after the fall of Toledo. By the time the legionaries entered the building only seven were alive. They committed suicide or died in the fray.[3]

During the first three months of the war, the militias disbanded and retreated quickly, as they were afraid of being surrounded, captured and then murdered. But after Toledo there were signs of stronger resistance against the Army of Africa. Archaeological evidence of this was found in a hill occupied by Republican troops near Torrejón de Velasco, a village south of Madrid, bordering the province of Toledo (López Fraile et al. 2008: 48–49). An artillery crater was excavated here which was transformed into an improvised foxhole by a Republican soldier. We know because abundant ammunition was found inside: 13 stripper clips (which hold five cartridges each) and 45 shell casings shot by the 7 mm M1893 Mauser, the standard rifle of the Spanish Army at the time. The stamps indicate that the ammunition is Spanish, Mexican and Austrian and some as old as 1918. The first large shipment of Mexican ammunition arrived in Spain on September 2. It comprised 20,000 rifles and 20 million cartridges, sent as a gift by the president of Mexico, Lázaro Cárdenas, and although they were old, at least were compatible with the Spanish standard weapons (Howson 2000: 151).

Considering the location of the site, the shooting must have taken place at some point between October 27, when the Nationalists arrived in Torrejón de Velasco and November 3, when the last Republican counterattack failed (Martínez Bande 1982: 239–249). While the remains are a material testimony of a stronger spirit of resistance in the Republican Army, they are also indicative of its inexperienced troops, which tended to waste enormous amounts of cartridges—a "crazy use of ammunition", according to Martínez Bande (1982: 301)—due to the lack of training and the fear of being overrun. But then we have to imagine in that crater a youngster, perhaps a teenager, who just a few weeks before was a waiter or a shopkeeper in Madrid. Suddenly, he is thrown into a hole, with a rifle he has just learned to use and before him a well-seasoned professional soldier, known for his penchant for killing those who surrender.

While our anonymous militiaman defended himself as best as he could in Torrejón de Velasco, Madrid was being fortified. The construction of pillboxes and trenches had been carried out so far in quite a haphazard manner, but this was going to change. The communist Fifth Regiment, with its characteristic discipline, started to fortify the mountain ranges to the west of Madrid, where the Nationalists had been stopped during the summer. The Fifth Regiment was a volunteer unit created immediately after the coup of July 18 by the Communist Party and the Unified Socialist Youth (JSU) and had its origin in a prewar militia (Blanco Rodríguez 1993). It was dissolved in January 1937, in the process that transformed the irregular units into the Popular Army of the Republic, in which it had a founding role. Between the last months of 1936 and January 1937, the Fifth Regiment erected 70 pillboxes of a specific typology near Madrid: round in plan, made with local

42   *Capital of glory*

granite, and with two rows of loopholes: wide embrasures for machine guns on top and 18 to 20 holes for riflemen below (Schnell and Baltuille 2017: 184–185). The government also began to organize the defensive efforts closer to the capital from the beginning of October, shortly after the fall of Toledo. The fortification plan has been traditionally assigned to an old Republican officer, General Masquelet (Martínez Bande 1982: 230–231), apparently without much ground. New research has discovered that the defensive system could have been devised as far back in time as 1934, during the right-wing Republican government and after the failed October revolution, and this would explain both the careful planning and the use of massively armored, isolated structures that are redolent of the colonial *blocaos* ("blockhaus") employed by the Spanish Army in Morocco (Arévalo 2008a). The coexistence of two wildly different types of fortification—the communist and the government's—is eloquent proof of the heterarchical situation within the Republic during the first six months of the war, with different powers acting more or less autonomously.

Four defensive belts were designed by the Republican command, the outer line linking the southernmost towns of the Madrid province and the inner line the villages and neighborhoods in the outskirts of the capital. The fortifications ranged from mere foxholes to well-made pillboxes of reinforced concrete (Figure 3.1) (Schnell and Baltuille 2017: 179–181). Despite their obvious quality, most of the pillboxes were never used. The military and constructors did not exchange information and many combatants were unaware of their whereabouts. Some still survive, quite miraculously, in-between highways and urban sprawls. They are easy to identify, since they have a characteristic square plan, are systematically built in pairs and set in a fan layout which provided the widest possible coverage with the machine guns. The quality of the work and the construction materials is high, unlike later Republican fortifications. Some pillboxes had inscriptions indicating the trade unions (communist, socialist and anarchist) in charge of the construction. The speed of the Nationalist advance prevented some of the forts from being finished, as happened with those of Getafe and Leganés, both villages around 15 km south of Madrid, which fell on November 4 (Martínez Bande 1982: 250). The enemy was at the gates and the gates were about to be crossed.

Crossing the gates: the fight in Casa de Campo

War arrived in the city on November 7, when the Nationalist columns occupied the outskirts of Casa de Campo ("Country House"), south of Madrid (Figure 3.2). This is a large estate—five times bigger than New York's Central Park—whose origins can be traced back to the times of King Philip II (1527–1598). The place is completely surrounded by a brick and stone wall with several gates giving access to the enclosure. After putting down Republican resistance south of the park, the Nationalist troops managed to break in on November 8. Of the four columns that had been advancing toward Madrid under the command of Colonel Juan Yagüe,

Capital of glory 43

Figure 3.1 Paired pillboxes of Leganés (Madrid). Construction on these Republican pillboxes started in October 1936 but was never completed.
Source: © Eduardo Penedo Cobo.

the "Butcher of Badajoz", three took part in the attack through Casa de Campo (Martínez Bande 1982: 299–300). Column 4, under the command of majors Castejón and Bartomeu (responsible for systematic violence against civilians during the advance toward Madrid) progressed rapidly and reached Mount Garabitas that same day, the park's main elevation, which is close to its northern limit. The fierce resistance of the Republican 3 Brigade, however, forced Column 1 to assist the advancing troops and fixed the Nationalists to the ground.

Also on November 8, the XI International Brigade arrived in the capital and was cheered by masses of Madrilenians, as they paraded through the city center marching toward the frontline. The International Brigades had been organized by the Comintern in September (Castells 2006). They established recruiting centers in different countries and the first volunteers arrived at the main headquarters in Albacete on October 14. They had citizens from 50 different countries, with a large majority of French nationals (10,000), and large contingents of German, Italian, Polish, Yugoslavian, British and North American volunteers. There were also people from Uruguay, Indochina, Australia, Palestine and even

44 *Capital of glory*

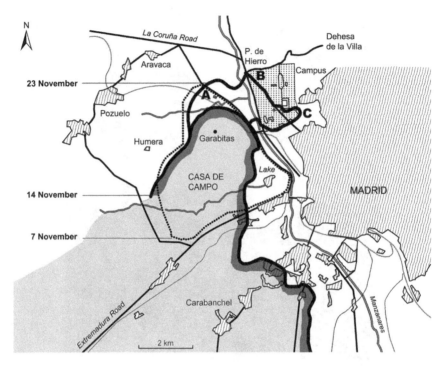

Figure 3.2 The Battle of Madrid.

Notes: In grey, Nationalist-occupied territory. The dates indicate the location of the frontline during the battle. Capital letters indicate places where archaeological research has been conducted: A: Casa de Vacas; B. Puerta de Hierro-University City; C. University Hospital.

Source: © Author.

Mongolia. At the end of the war, almost 60,000 internationals had fought for the Republic, of whom 15,000 died. Despite its communist origin, the initiative attracted people from the entire left-wing political spectrum: there were many socialists, anarchists and even liberals who just wanted to participate in the struggle against fascism. Of their stay in Albacete we have interesting archaeological evidence in the nearby castle of Almansa, were the brigaders were also stationed: archaeologists have recorded 800 graffiti from the sixteenth century to the 1940s, some of which were left by international volunteers during the war (Gil Hernández 2019: 85–87). Those who wrote on the walls came from Bulgaria, Macedonia, Denmark, the United States, Canada, Italy and Austria. The latter, a certain Fritz Freylag from Vienna, might have belonged to the XI Brigade: the Edgar André Battalion was composed mainly of German and Austrian nationals. While the French and Belgian Battalion, Commune de Paris, was sent to the strategic Puente de los Franceses—the railway bridge giving access to downtown Madrid from the west—the Edgar André arrived in the northern sector of Casa de

Capital of glory 45

Campo during the night of 8–9 November. During the next month, the battalion would sustain 192 casualties, of which 52 were dead.

Casa de Campo was heavily transformed during the war by the Nationalist troops, but it is still possible to find traces of the fighting in 1936. During our survey east of the park, in La Torrecilla, which was one of the park's farms, we found bullets and grenade fragments related to the combats of November or December, as well as a fragment of a human bone. In this same area, the remains of three individuals were found in 1984 while digging a ditch.[4] The forensic examination determined that the younger individual was between 25 and 30 years of age. The older was in his forties and the third was younger than 35. They were killed by a mortar grenade that caused them lethal wounds to the skulls. Near the bones, there were underwear shell buttons, leather buttons belonging to military jackets and several 7.92 mm Mauser cartridges of Czech manufacture.[5] The forensic doctor concluded that the remains belonged to members of the XI International Brigade that fell at some point between 7 and 14 November. We can be more precise perhaps: Francoist general Carlos Iniesta Cano, who had been a young officer at the time of the attacks in Casa de Campo, offers a vivid description of the assault of La Torrecilla farm on November 9:[6]

> Two enemy companies were able to occupy two buildings on our left flank, where they organized themselves, opposed a remarkable resistance and caused us around 14 casualties, among dead and wounded. The bandera[7]... dashed against the enemy positions, storming the houses with hand grenades and knives. The enemy, who suffered heavy casualties, was dislodged and our bandera was established in the building. The enemy attacked us with all kinds of weapons—artillery, mortars, automatic weapons and hand grenades—and tried several times to storm the positions that we were occupying—without success. They were repelled every time, leaving a high number of casualties on the undulating ground.
>
> (Iniesta Cano 1984: 96)

They were buried in unmarked graves where most still lie.

The last stand in Casa de Vacas

Our own survey focused mainly on the northern fringe of Casa de Campo, which was far less known than other parts of the park (González-Ruibal et al. 2019). Actually, with the available published information, it was impossible to ascertain when the Nationalists reached the limit of Casa de Campo in that subsector and whether there were any relevant combats in the area (apart from Mount Garabitas). The area that we surveyed was known as Casa de Vacas ("Cow House"). This was another of the farming premises that existed in the park. It was opened in 1831 as a dairy and after several periods of abandonment and refurbishment, it was transformed into a hunting pavilion in 1874, under Alphonse XII.[8] We did find evidence of royal hunting: two

46 *Capital of glory*

brass heads of central-fire shotgun cartridges and two other of the pinfire (or Lefaucheux) type, which was widely used between the mid-nineteenth century and the early twentieth century in shotguns and revolvers.[9] Two pieces, which can be dated between 1890 and 1910, bore headstamps from Eley Brothers, a London company: kings and aristocrats often consumed British products as a mark of distinction.

In Casa de Vacas, we discovered a 250-meter trench, visible on the surface, which departed from the ruins and headed northwest toward the park's wall. We hypothesized that this was a Republican trench from the Battle of Madrid, because it seemed to be facing southwards, that is, toward the Nationalist lines in November 1936. To test the hypothesis we dug a 30-meter sondage along the trench and conducted an intensive metal detector survey in front and behind the line. The results were positive: the trench was indeed Republican, it had been used during the early days of the Battle of Madrid, and, to our surprise, it had been the scenario of heavy fighting about which apparently no known documentary evidence existed. Everything seemed to indicate that the trench (originally 700 meters long) was delimiting the last chunk of terrain that the Republicans held inside Casa de Campo.

One of our collaborators found archival material that had hitherto passed unnoticed and helped to clarify who exactly had put up that last stand: three drafts for newspaper articles written by international volunteers to be published in Spanish newspapers were located at RGASPI, a Russian archive whose documents have recently been made available online.[10] The drafts refer to the participation of the Edgar André Battalion in the defense of the northern part of Casa de Campo, on the night of 8 to 9 November. One of the drafts indicates that at the beginning it was two companies of the Edgar André Battalion that were sent to the sector, but the third company, made up of Hungarians and Yugoslavians, had eventually to be deployed as well.[11] The most detailed description and the only one that explicitly mentions Casa de Vacas by name appears in a newspaper article published by Philipp Schuh, commander of the first company of the Edgar André Battalion:[12]

> Again we change positions. This time we occupy them in Casa de Vacas of Casa de Campo, where the fascists launched a massive attack. From morning to night the mortar and artillery fire over our positions did not stop for a single moment.

According to Schuh, the unit fought in the area for eight days before retreating on a Sunday. This would mean that they abandoned it in November 15, which was Sunday and the day on which the Nationalists launched the second assault on Madrid, through the University City. The strong resistance put up by the internationals in the northern tip of Casa de Campo has not made it into history books. But this does not mean that it was not decisive, as we will see.

Capital of glory 47

The archaeological excavation and survey confirmed that the occupants of the trench were international brigaders. We know because the ammunition that we found mostly belongs to the 0.303 caliber of the Enfield Pattern 14, the rifle that was typically used by international volunteers fighting in Casa de Campo in November—Robert Capa's photographs show the brigaders in the park armed with these rifles (Capa 1999: 88–89, 93). We even found the sights of a P14 in a firebay.

The trench is peculiar, quite unlike any we have excavated so far. It is not the typical zigzagging ditch, but a rather straight line only slightly undulating and with few changes in orientation (Figure 3.3), which makes it quite

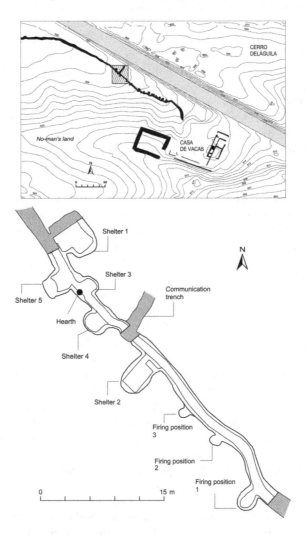

Figure 3.3 Map of the trench of Casa de Vacas in the NW corner of Casa de Campo and detail of the excavated trench.

Source: © Manuel Antonio Franco and author.

48 *Capital of glory*

vulnerable. Linear or slightly undulating trenches are very typical of the beginning of the war (Arévalo 2005: 214, 219, Annex II). There were other unusual traits: the trench had firing positions protruding from the main ditch at regular intervals, from which individual soldiers could shoot, and vanguard shelters. All trenches that we have excavated, both Nationalist and Republican, had rearguard shelters. Firing positions and vanguard dugouts, instead, are typical features of First World War trenches (particularly of the first year of the conflict). The structure of the trench is consistent with the fact that some of the members of the XI International Brigade were veterans of the Great War, including its most prominent members, such as the brigade's commander, Manfred Stern (who went by the nickname "Kleber"). Another archaic characteristic that is uncommon in later fortification is the presence of a hearth in a niche dug in the trench's wall. Opposite the hearth, another niche was dug in the wall and a piece of a concrete pipe put on the floor as a bench, so that a soldier could sit on it facing the fire. This kind of hearth is typical of early trench systems, like those of the American Civil War (Kuttruff 2009: 304), but is seldom documented in Spain.

Archaeological evidence indicates that the trench was used at least for a few days. The dugouts were covered with fiber cement roofs, which could not stop the enemy fire—one plaque appeared perforated by a 7 mm bullet. The soldiers also reused bricks from the bombed Casa de Vacas to make their fortification sturdier and more comfortable. The trench was communicated through a telephone line, of which we found cable, wire, iron hooks and porcelain insulators near the evacuation trench. Digging occurred at night, according to Philipp Schuh. The 700 hundred-meter ditch could have been excavated quite fast. One of the Republican manuals of fortification calculates that soft terrains (such as the sandy soil of Casa de Campo) allow for an excavation of 0.8 m^3 per person per hour (Capdevila 1938: 35). This means that the 700 meters of the trench in Casa de Vacas could have been dug in less than two hours by 300 men (two companies).

Only one of the dugouts that we excavated, Shelter 1, lay behind the trench, instead of in the vanguard, and it was the one that yielded more finds. The shelter had two levels of occupation: one can be dated to the period of the Battle of Madrid and the other belongs to a later Nationalist reoccupation. To the latter belong parts of fuel barrels placed around a hearth, shell buttons, legging clasps and some ammunition, including a 7.92 mm Mauser cartridge of Nazi manufacture dated 1935 (typically Nationalist) and a Spanish 7 mm cartridge dated 1937 (after the Battle of Madrid). Under this level, an earlier occupation floor yielded sardine tin cans, the cup of a military canteen, and both used and unused ammunition, all in situ lying on the floor: Spanish 7 mm and Czech 7.92 mm cartridges, as well as spent 0.303 and 7.62 mm Soviet casings and Mauser and Enfield stripper clips. The Czech markings, from the Sellier & Bellot factory in Prague, are identical to those found with the remains of the brigaders exhumed in La Torrecilla. On 29 October 6,000 German and Polish

Capital of glory 49

7.92 mm Mausers with 500 rounds each arrived in Spain, in one of the first shipments from the USSR (Howson 2000: 197–198). After France and the United Kingdom refused to supply the Republic and an arms embargo was established, the Republic had to resort to the Soviet Union as its main provider, which charged high prices and began by sending ancient stocks (Howson 2000). Shelter 2 was similar in size and shape to Shelter 1, but was excavated in the vanguard. Finds were scant. They include a 0.25 caliber cartridge, which means that a brigader was carrying a Baby Browning or similar gun as a personal side arm. The use of personal weapons was very common during the Spanish Civil War, judging from archaeological finds, and it reveals the climate of violence of the 1930s and the ease with which guns were purchased and used. The most remarkable find, however, was a silver-alloy spoon, stamped C. Meneses. This was the name of the jeweler who was the official provider of the royal house since 1856.[13] The brigaders probably helped themselves in Casa de Vacas and carried away all the useful stuff they could find, including furniture and massive bricks that they reused in the fortification.

The other shelters that we excavated were simple holes made in the trench's wall. First World War soldiers often "scooped out a hollow in the front or back of the ditch. Here, wrapped in their groundsheets, they would snatch their brief periods of sleep, curled up parallel to the trench or with their feet sticking out into it" (Ellis 1989: 16). This seems to have been the case in Casa de Vacas, too. The hollows typically yielded ammunition, tin cans, buttons and clasps. Some notable finds associated with these niches include a Soviet ammunition box which had been stuck repeatedly with a bayonet, and a military boot. The latter is further indication of the trench being occupied by international brigaders, who were well equipped: militias usually wore civilian shoes or espadrilles. Sheep or goat bones with cut marks were very abundant in the area of the shelters, which means that the soldiers were served hot meals instead of tin cans—thus confirming the relatively long occupation of the trench. A peculiar find is the fuse of a KT-1 45 mm shell, the type fired by the Soviet T-26 tank, which were among the first weapons exported to Republican Spain during the war. On November 9, the T-26s entered Casa de Campo through the gate of Aravaca (Martínez Bande 1982: 304), which lies only a few hundred meters from our trench, and crossed the railway bridge in front to launch a (failed) offensive in this sector.

Traces of combat

Several fighting positions were identified in the southern part of the trench. Inside and around these firing positions we found a huge amount of spent ammunition (mostly stripper clips, but also shell casings), predominately British 0.303, followed by Soviet 7.62 mm with traces of percussion by automatic weapon (that is, they were fired by a machine gun, not a rifle). Based on the location and the density of finds, we believe that a machine

50 *Capital of glory*

gun, probably an M1910 Maxim (a Soviet heavy machine gun), was placed in-between Firing Positions 2 and 3—there are images of brigaders operating Maxims in Casa de Campo.[14] Over the parapet, near Firing Position 3, we found two complete 0.303 clips, ready to be used and still with bits of fabric from the ammunition pouches. Many of the spent casings were found in situ, lying on the trench's floor. The part of the trench where the shelters were located also saw action. Here, evidence of combat appears mixed with glass shards, tin cans and mutton bones. Eating and fighting in the same place is not incompatible. Immediately after describing a combat in Casa de Vacas in which a comrade was wounded, Philipp Schuh writes:

> I am hungry and would like to eat. In that precise moment, a mortar shell explodes in our parapet. One of our boys shouts, wounded. I took him to the infirmary and return to the positions to continue my meal. A new whistle and a second mortar explosion. My sausage flies to the right and my bread to the left.

Heavy fighting in and around the trench was also documented through a metal detector survey. We covered an area of 125 x 20 meters and found 476 war-related items, mainly bullets (N=129) and fragments of artillery and mortar shells (over three hundred), which offer an eloquent picture of the intensity of the combats (Figure 3.4). Shell fragments belong to mortar and artillery rounds. We also discovered a complete, unexploded 105 mm shell a few meters in front of the trench; a fuse for the 77 mm grenade fired by the German Feldkanone 96; grapeshot delivered by the 75 mm shrapnel shell, and a large chunk of a 155 mm shell. Apart from heavy artillery, the Nationalists were using the standard 81 mm Valero M1933 mortar, of which we found several fragments both during survey and inside the trench. The Republicans did not enjoy an equivalent artillery support. Survey along the Nationalist lines only furnished a few fragments of artillery shells, which cannot be unambiguously assigned to any particular army. The most notable find associated with the Republicans was the fin of an 81 mm Stokes-Brandt mortar. The Stokes was the first modern transportable trench mortar; it was designed in 1915 and used during the First World War. After the conflict, its accuracy and range were improved by the French Army leading to the Stokes-Brandt Mle 27/31: it could deliver a 3 kg grenade at a distance of 10 to 3,000 meters (Lachèvre 1932). The Republic received 44,000 rounds in September 1936, just in time to participate in the Battle of Madrid (Howson 2000: 394).

The storm of steel delivered by the Nationalists was accompanied by a shower of bullets: 68% of all the small arms munitions correspond to the 7 mm caliber—a remarkable homogeneity, quite unlike that found among the Republicans. If we discount the bullets shot by Republicans, we can infer that the Nationalists were massively armed with the standard 7 mm Spanish Mauser, with only a fraction carrying 7.92 mm Mausers. The diversity of munitions employed by the government troops, instead, is quite astonishing:from old Vetterlis to

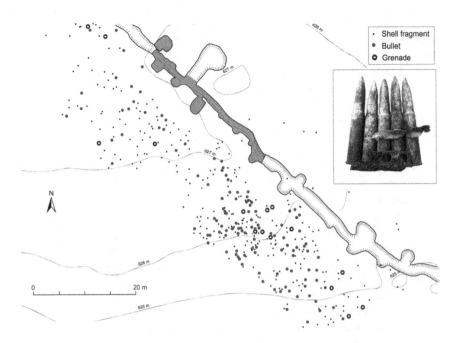

Figure 3.4 Map of combat-related items found during surface survey in front of the trench. Inside the square, one of the two clips of an Enfield P14 found next to Firing Position 3.

Source: © Manuel Antonio Franco and author.

Enfields (see Table 2 in annex). Not all were used by the international brigaders, who seem to have been primarily armed with Pattern 1914 Enfields. Other weapons, as we will see, were most likely employed by the militias and Spanish troops also operating in the area. Fieldwork in Casa de Vacas yielded 189 shell casings and cartridges, representing 57% of the total ammunition retrieve. The percentage is even higher if we look at the stripper clips, which are of British and Canadian type: 324 items (89% of the total). Indeed, the trench's floor was literally covered with them, which tells us about the intensity of the fighting and the dense occupation of the fortification with soldiers—a situation typical of the first moments of the war (Arévalo 2005: 214, 219, Annex II). The context was sealed in November 1936 as confirmed by the thin muddy layer in which the munitions were found embedded. The rains of November and the soil of Casa de Campo, which combines sand and clay, helped preserve the materials in situ. Archival documentation informs that 21,000 Enfield rifles and 29 million cartridges arrived in Spain on October 21 (Howson 2000: 379). With a few exceptions, the great majority of the casings are marked US 16 VII and thus belonged to the same lot. Their story is fascinating. They were produced by the United States Cartridge Company at Lowell, Massachusetts, on commission for the British Army during

52 *Capital of glory*

the First World War. After the conflict, Great Britain sent 200,000 Enfields and 300 million rounds to General Denikin, the leader of one of the White Armies fighting in the Russian Civil War (Moore 2002). They were then captured by the Bolsheviks, who stored them for 15 years. The USSR clearly saw the Spanish Civil War as an outlet to get rid of all the stocks of obsolete weapons and ammunition incompatible with their own that they still had in reserve. This is why the first shipments to Spain include much non-Russian material.

The presence inside the trench of Mauser stripper clips (N=40, 11%) shows that these rifles were being used by the brigaders as well. Shell casings and cartridges were found of both the 7 and 7.92 mm versions. Vetterli bullets, which were also found near the trench, are diagnostic of the combats in and around the capital in November 1936. The M1870/87 Vetterli, an Italian high-caliber single-shot rifle, was already obsolete during the Great War. They arrived in Spain with 185 cartridges each and once they were spent, the rifles were discarded (Howson 2000: 194). Given the volume of fire during the combats in the capital, we can imagine that this happened soon. We have not found a single Vetterli casing in the trench or during survey and the bullet we found was probably shot by one of the militias that also fought in this area: the Enciso Column active in Casa de Campo had 56 rifles described as "11 mm (Italian)" (de Vicente Gonzalez 2016: 6,325–6,341).

Soviet 7.62 mm ammunition represents 19% of all the cartridges and shell casings. I have mentioned above that these were likely shot by an M1910 Maxim machine gun, considering the percussion marks, but also the fact that Mosin Nagant rifles, of the same caliber, only started arriving in significant numbers from February 1937 onwards. However, we also found a Mosin stripper clip. How could that be? The answer is the Winchester M1895, a version of the famous repeating rifle made for Russia, which used a Mosin Nagant clip. Almost 200,000 rifles were produced in 1915–1916 and were first deployed in the First World War (Mercaldo et al. 2011: 77–78). Many arrived in Spain with the first shipments of Soviet weapons. We know that the militias commanded by legendary anarchist leader Buenaventura Durruti, who came to Madrid on November 8, were armed with Russian Winchesters (Radosh et al. 2001: 82) and some of them were photographed near the walls of Casa de Campo.[15]

We found 363 stripper clips in total, 330 shell casings and 258 bullets. The number of casings is low: the clips correspond to 1,815 cartridges, meaning that we only found 18% of the casings corresponding to the clips, but this difference is common in every Spanish Civil War battlefield and can be explained by war and postwar recycling. All the ammunition appeared in just 2,500 square meters. The vast majority of stripper clips were collected in the excavation of a 30 m tract of trench. If we extrapolate this to the entire line in Casa de Vacas (700 m), it would mean that around 40,000 cartridges were fired by the Republicans—over 130 cartridges per soldier (26 clips or 3 clips per soldier per day of combat), considering two companies or 300 men. Of course, not all the trench necessarily witnessed the same intensity of fighting, but then, it is impossible that we have recovered all stripper clips originally

Capital of glory 53

used in combat. The conservation bias is less pronounced than with shell casings, however, because they were not recycled and are more easily overlooked by collectors. Incoming fire was seven times less intense than outgoing fire. This can be interpreted as indiscriminate shooting on the side of the brigaders who often had little training and were undergoing their baptism of fire in difficult circumstances. Their enemies, instead, were a professional army of veterans, who had been fighting for their way to Madrid for four months (and had seen action in Morocco before). The Nationalists were probably relying more on sharpshooters, artillery, and raids. "The fascist *pacos* [snipers] shoot fiercely and well", wrote Philipp Schuh. In fact, the massive Republican fire might be the result of an excessive reaction to those raids, in which the attackers typically attract more fire than they produce.

Evidence for such raids can be documented in two places. The highest concentration of bullets appeared in the southeast zone of the survey, near the firing positions, which is also the area of the highest density of artillery and mortar shell fragments. This indicates that at least one of the attacks followed a SE-NW axis and was likely preceded by a mortar attack. It makes sense in tactical terms, because there is a slight depression on the southeast descending toward the nearby Antequina River. Nationalist troops probably advanced under the cover of the creek and then ascended in the direction of the trench through the fold in the terrain. They reached the fortification near Firing Position 1. Traces of the assault are four 9 mm pistol casings found inside the position, a 9 mm bullet outside, and fragments of both Republican and Nationalist grenades. Both pistols and grenades can only be used effectively at short range— 30 meters for a grenade, 50 meters for a pistol—so their presence is good indication of close quarters combat. More evidence of a raid that came very near the trench was found in the area around Shelter 5, which was probably used both as a dugout and a fire bay. Here we found evidence of intense rifle fire, spent pistol ammunition and grenades—one anarchist, one communist.

These peculiar artifacts deserve a few words. The anarchist grenade is of the FAI type, called after the Iberian Anarchist Federation (*Federación Anarquista Ibérica*) that originally produced it. The artifact was designed by Ramón Franco probably in the 1920s. Ramón Franco, the brother of the dictator, was a peculiar character. He became a legend after crossing the Atlantic in a hydroplane in 1926, staged a pro-Republican coup against the king in 1930, backed the leftist and Catalan nationalist party ERC, but then joined the rebels in 1936 before being killed in an airplane crash in 1938. He passed the grenade's design to an anarchist ideologue and it ended up in the hands of the FAI, which started to produce it in 1935 (Amonio et al. no date). It did not have a time delay mechanism but worked through impact; its heavy weight (around one kilo) limited its range to 15 or 20 meters and exposed the person who was throwing it to its lethal effects—thus the nickname *La Imparcial*, "Impartial". Given the location of the fragments, near the fortification, and the fact that it was a defensive grenade, it is reasonable to think that it was thrown from the trench.

54 *Capital of glory*

The communist grenade, which appeared complete, was of the Fifth Regiment type (Antonio A.R. et al. no date) (Figure 3.5). The name refers to the elite communist unit to which I have referred above. The bomb had to be improvised with the Nationalist troops already advancing toward Madrid: grenades were essential in urban and trench warfare. The artifact was basically a section of an iron or steel pipe with horizontal grooves to facilitate fragmentation. The tube was filled with explosive, paper and all sorts of materials used as shrapnel (bullets, screws, pieces of metal and even stones). The explosive was ignited with a wick that had to be lighted manually. At the beginning, the pipes came from train heating systems, but the grenades were also produced with ad hoc materials after the first months of war and despite its crudeness, they were very common in the fronts of central Spain throughout the war.

The grenades speak volumes about the times. The crudely made artifacts attest both to a tradition of do-it-yourself, that had characterized revolutionary movements in Spain from the beginning, and to the skills of industrial workers, who were able to build easily improvised explosives and tanks (Manrique and Molina 2006: 298–299). Also, and paradoxically, they attest to a preindustrial society in which common people (peasants, day laborers and artisans) were used to producing their own material culture in peaceful times. In the 1930s, rural homes were still largely autarkic in Spain. The grenades also evince the great autonomy of parties and unions within the Republic and its political

Figure 3.5 A Fifth Regiment grenade.

Notes: It is identical to the one found in front of the trench of Casa de Vacas. This one was found during surface survey in Brunete (see Chapter 10) in a much later context, evincing the protracted employment in combat of this crude, improvised bomb.

Source: © Javier Marquerie.

Capital of glory 55

fragmentation, a phenomenon that would always be its Achilles heel. The Nationalists were strongly unified: there were no Falangist or Monarchist grenades. The easiness with which weapons were produced (and used) before the war is also a reminder of the widespread social and political violence that plagued interwar Europe, with right-wing and left-wing militias fighting between themselves and against the police.

A forgotten battlefield

Fieldwork in Casa de Vacas showed that this sector saw much more action and for more days than had been usually assumed. The Republicans managed to cling to the northern tip of Casa de Campo for at least eight days after the Nationalists broke into the park. If Philipp Schuh's narrative is reliable, the brigaders retreated in neat order the same day the Nationalists launched the second phase of their offensive against Madrid on November 15. He wrote with pride that they did not abandon anything behind. The trench is, indeed, quite clean, except for the usual war debris. Was the Edgar André Battalion the last Republican unit to fight in this sector? Probably not. The Enciso Column launched an assault inside Casa de Campo from the Casa de Vacas area on November 21. They had a high number of casualties and failed to reach their objectives.[16] It is possible that the trench, once abandoned, became a no-man's land crossed back and forth by Republican soldiers in their failed attempts to recapture the park. However, the fact that the traces of the brigaders are so numerous and well-preserved indicates that the trench itself—at least the part that we excavated—was not reused after the internationals left.

The question is: Why did the Republicans hold so fiercely to this small patch of ground? Most likely, the reason was that losing Casa de Vacas would open the way for the Nationalists to the crucial La Coruña road, one of the main entrances to the capital, and enable the penetration of Madrid through the Puente de San Fernando, the main motorable bridge crossing the city's river, the Manzanares, from the west. Indeed, the Nationalists planned a pincer attack on the capital, with one flank in Puente de los Franceses to the east, and another one in San Fernando Bridge to the west. The Republicans knew that through a strike of luck. On 6 November, the day before the offensive on Madrid, Republican soldiers destroyed an Italian tank whose officer was carrying with him the plans of the Nationalist attack. It is telling that the Republican command decided to send the well-armed internationals precisely to the two key sectors of the offensive. It is obvious that Republican commanders considered international volunteers more reliable than the Spanish militias—and rightly so, as we will see.

If we agree that the position was of strategic relevance, then the question remains of why the combats in Casa de Vacas were forgotten. There seems to be a variety of reasons for this: all attention was focused on the Puente de los

56   *Capital of glory*

Franceses sector, which was closer to the city center and easier to reach by civilians and journalists (even in tramway!), including Robert Capa. Puente de los Franceses became a popular icon of resistance in the collective memory of Madrilenians, and one of the most famous war songs refers to this bridge, in whose surroundings combats continued during several months. Those who fought in Casa de Vacas were Germans, whose memoirs, when they were published in Eastern Germany, did not circulate widely. Yet neither the memoirs nor oral testimonies help much, to tell the truth. They offer very little detail about the combats and their location and they are so generic that could be applied to virtually any other military encounter during the conflict. We have to remember that this was the brigaders' first contact with Madrid and with the war. They were thrown into an alien environment, in the middle of the fray and at night. There is a lot of confusion in their testimonies: place names, dates and events are mixed up. This confusion is remembered by most of the brigaders: "One man described how disorientated volunteers, newly arrived in Spain and immediately dispatched to the Madrid front, were thrown into panic by the arrival of their evening meal, mistaking the sound of the food van for that of a fascist tank" (McLellan 2006: 298). Philipp Schuh also mistook the motors of airplanes for those of attacking tanks. The information that was reaching the officers in the rearguard had to be similarly chaotic and erroneous and this is clearly manifested in military reports. Spanish fighters, who were also active in the area, were mostly militiamen who were not likely to leave written record of their actions: only the leaders typically did. But then the commander of the Enciso Column was captured in Aragón by the Nationalists in 1938 and executed for his loyalty to the Republic.

Fighting in Madrid was actually confusing for both sides. Colonel Martínez Bande (1982), who had access to all available documentation, seems at times as if he were describing a battle from another century, because of all the gaps and hesitations in his narrative. While this scenario might look like a historian's nightmare, it offers a unique opportunity to show archaeology's worth. Here, it is the archaeological record, rather than documents and oral accounts, that provides the most accurate picture of the war.

War at the university

So far the war that I have described has little of the urban, but this was soon to change. The Nationalists planned to launch an assault between the University City, to the west of Madrid, and the Plaza de España, one of the city's main squares, in the south. The construction of the University City, modeled on American campuses, had started in 1929 in what were then the outskirts of the capital (Chías 1986). After the proclamation of the Republic in 1931, it came to represent the aspirations of a modern and progressive Spain. But by 1939 it was just a field of rubble.

November 15 was drenched in blood. The Nationalists broke through the wall of Casa de Campo and tried to cross the Manzanares River three times, with heavy casualties (Martínez Bande 1982: 323–330; Calvo Gonzalez-Regueral

2012: 40–46). Their Panzer I tanks got stuck in the sandy riverbed and the soldiers had to advance unprotected under heavy enemy fire. They finally managed to cross at night, move forward across the University City and occupy the School of Architecture, which would become their headquarters throughout the war (Figure 3.6). The militias in charge of this sector, the communist López Tienda Column, abandoned their positions and facilitated the Nationalist advance. The Durruti Column, commanded by the legendary anarchist leader, was to launch a counterattack from the University Hospital the following day, but they failed to evict the enemy from the campus. Instead, the Nationalists continued to expand the wedge inside the university and occupied many of its buildings. The arrival of the XI International Brigade (the one that had been fighting in Casa de Campo) helped balance the situation. They expelled the Nationalists from their newly held positions in the School of Philosophy and Letters and the building became their headquarters in the campus. The brigaders used its extraordinary library to make parapets: several books still have bullet holes and even bullets inside.

While the internationals were holding the line, Durruti's anarchists, despite their strenuous efforts, were faring rather worse. On November 17, they lost

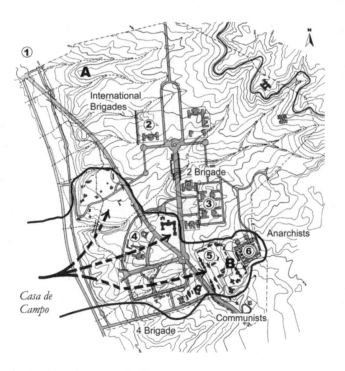

Figure 3.6 The attack on the University City.

Notes: The thick black line represents the maximum extent of the Nationalist advance. Capital letters represent the sites that have been the object of archaeological research: A. Puerta de Hierro-Dehesa de la Villa subsector. B. University Hospital.

Source: © Author.

58 *Capital of glory*

the ground in front of the University Hospital, occupied at the time by the premises of a hospice (the Asylum of Santa Cristina) and withdrew into the hospital. During the next few days, combats took place inside the building, located on the most prominent elevation of the campus. This was a massive modern building with sturdy concrete foundations which was still under construction in 1936. The fight, room by room, floor by floor, with grenades and bayonets, was ferocious—a prelude to the combats in Stalingrad during World War II, where buildings as "layered cakes" (Germans in one floor, Russians above or below) became familiar (Beevor 2011: 156). Soldiers opened holes in the walls with a pick and then shot with automatic weapons or fired flamethrowers through them (Kurzman 2006: 461), dug tunnels under the building, set up mines and, according to some testimonies, even used the elevators to send explosive charges to the floors occupied by the enemy. Fighting inside (and underneath) the hospital continued for one week after the end of the Battle of Madrid (on November 23). Durruti was not to see it: he was wounded by a bullet in mysterious circumstances near the hospital on the 19th and died the following day.

Casualties on both sides were horrendous but difficult to gauge. We know that 2,000 Nationalist troops (legionnaires and regulars) had penetrated into the campus and that one single column of the three participating in the attack had sustained 250 casualties in the first two days of combat. Considering this figure, it is likely that the Nationalists lost over 50% of their effectives during the battle. The Republicans had around 11,000 soldiers engaged in the defense (Martínez Bande 1982: 335), but the number of casualties is unknown. It had to be high, as the city's mayor asked permission to bury the dead in mass graves and the hospitals were crowded beyond their capacity. In the Nationalist case, casualties at the University City had to evacuated through a flimsy makeshift bridge over the Manzanares (known as the Death Walkway), which was under constant enemy fire, and many died before they could be transported to the rearguard. When the battle ended, three fourths of the campus were under Nationalist control. The Nationalist bulge inside Madrid would remain, just as they were unable to occupy a single inch of the city for the remainder of the conflict.

Our fieldwork focused on the parks where archaeological remains could still be found. These were located in the northwestern part of the campus, not far from San Fernando Bridge mentioned above, and around the University Hospital. To our surprise, remains of the war turned out to be plentiful in both locations. And not only that: as we will now see, we still could find traces of the Battle of Madrid.

Fighting at the Iron Gate

There is no lack of information about the war at the University City (Calvo González-Regueral 2012). In fact, the Battle of Madrid is often equated with the combats that took place on the campus. The situation, however, resembles that

Capital of glory 59

of Casa de Campo where, as we saw, all attention focused on a specific sector. In the case of the University City several buildings, which played a decisive role in the combats, are very present in historical narratives and memoirs: the University Hospital, the School of Philosophy and Letters or the School of Medicine. The violence of the combats is reflected in the many bullet and artillery impacts that can be seen today on the buildings' facades. We documented some of the facades of the School of Medicine and could relate some of the traces to the combats that took place in November 1936, when soldiers where fighting room by room (González Ruibal et al. 2010) (Figure 3.7). That the bulk of the attack was carried out through the central part of the University City, however, does not mean that this was the only relevant sector in the battle.

We know that the northwest limit of the university was also the scenario of intense fighting. Information about this area is confusing, in part because it is identified with two places which actually lie outside the campus: Puente de San Fernando, the motorable bridge over the Manzanares, and Puerta de Hierro (Iron Gate), a monumental stone arch constructed during the eighteenth century to signal the city limit. This sector simply does not appear in any of the published maps of the battle at the University City and only

Figure 3.7 Impact of small arms fire at the entrance of the School of Medicine. They can only be the result of the room-by-room fighting during the Battle of Madrid, as the sector later remained deep inside Republican-held territory.

Source: © Author.

60 *Capital of glory*

passing reference is given in the main historical narratives. Yet it can be argued that this was no irrelevant area. One argument is that the XI and XII International Brigades were sent there to stop the enemy. The problem is that we do not know exactly where, because the information is very imprecise—"Between the university city and the river", according to one historian (Castells 2006: 110). The sector occupies several square kilometers, but texts seem to indicate that combats developed near the Manzanares River, that is, around 800 meters from the campus, and historians tend to assume that the Nationalists were halted there.

Archaeology, however, tells a different story. We conducted an intensive metal detector survey, along with excavations, in a wide area of the northwestern part of the university that was supposed to have remained in Republican hands for the entire duration of the war. The first surprise was to find that the place was still crisscrossed with well-preserved trenches. Maps found at the archive indicated that most were actually dug between December 1937 and late 1938 and the materials that we found in the occupation layers during excavation confirm a later date. The second surprise came with the surface survey, which yielded a high number of finds, some of them unambiguously associated with the combats of November 1936.

The remains linked to the Battle of Madrid spread along the Dehesa de la Villa road, which was one of the entrances to Madrid from the northwest (Figure 3.8), and include nineteenth-century ammunition for two old rifles, the Vetterli Vitali M1870 (10.4 mm) and the Remington (11.4 mm).We found two shell casings of each type and one Remington and five Vetterli bullets. The Vetterli Vitali we have already met in Casa de Campo. At the University City, they were given to some of the soldiers of the XI International Brigade: Sam Lesser, a British veteran, who was deployed with the Edgar André Battalion, remembers that when they opened their ammunition boxes they found that "they contained rifles that had been used by the Austrian army in the 1870s, which had been very carefully packed and, to avoid rusting, were covered in grease" (Arthur 2009: 217). Although already obsolete by the First World War, munitions for this weapon were still produced then: our shell casing is dated 1916. As for the Remington, it was originally designed in 1864, during the American Civil War, but was employed mostly in the later wars against indigenous communities. It was also present in the campaigns of extermination of the native populations of Argentina (Landa et al. 2009: 194), where it was copied under the name *Patria* ("Fatherland"), but was known by the more explicit nickname *Mataindios* ("Indian killer"). The Spanish Army adopted the Remington as its standard rifle in 1871. It participated in the last of the nineteenth-century civil wars, the Third Carlist War (1872–1876) and in the colonial conflicts of Cuba and the Philippines (1896–1898), but by then the Spanish Mauser M1893 had already been officially adopted. Both Vetterli and Remington were archaic weapons that had to be loaded after each shot. The Remington, which was considered very fast at the time, could shoot six or seven bullets per minute (Landa et al. 2009: 193), whereas the bolt-action rifles of the

Capital of glory 61

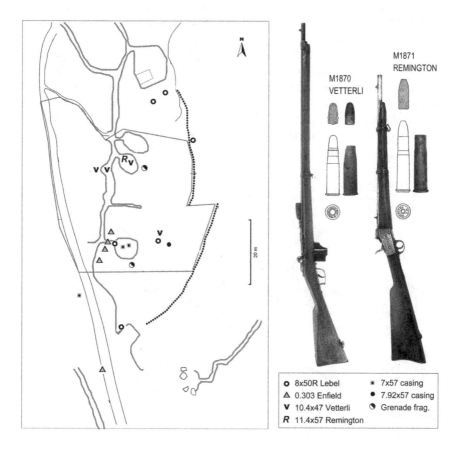

Figure 3.8 To the left: finds related to the November 1936 combats in the NW of the University City. In grey, second-line Republican fortifications from late 1938 (see Chapter 9). To the right: obsolete weapons employed by Republican soldiers in the defense of the University City.

Source: © Author.

1930s typically had a rate of fire of 15 to 20 shots per minute. The firepower of a military unit armed with Mausers was therefore between two and three times higher than another equipped with Vetterlis or Remingtons.

Nevertheless, the archaic ammunition makes up for a very small percentage of the bullets, cartridges and shell casings that we found during fieldwork. Regarding bullets, we collected a total of 328 items, of which the majority (213 bullets, 65% of the total) belong to the 7 mm Mauser, the standard weapon of the Nationalists. These were surely not all fired during the Battle of Madrid. The area remained in the frontline from November 1936 to the end of the war and, as we will see (Chapter 9), some can be related to the later

62 *Capital of glory*

stages of the conflict. It is important here to distinguish two different zones. The one we named Sector 1 is close to the Puerta de Hierro and lies in front of the enemy lines and was totally exposed to incoming fire. Sector 2, instead, is around 100 meters east of Sector 1 and occupies a fold in the terrain produced by a small elevation and a creek. It was not in enfilade from the Nationalist positions after the lines stabilized, when it remained over one kilometer inside Republican positions. This means that the bullets in Sector 2 should have arrived during the combats of 1936 (Figure 3.9). In that area we found 45 bullets of the 0.303 caliber shot likely by Enfield rifles (20% of the total)

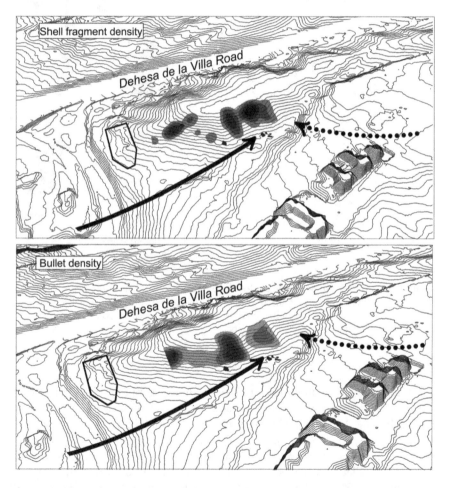

Figure 3.9 The undocumented Nationalist attack through the NW corner of the University City. Density maps of artillery shells and bullets based on surface survey.

Notes: Black lines indicate the direction of the Nationalist attack, dotted lines, the Republican counterattack.

Source: © Pedro Rodríguez Simón and author.

which, as we saw, was massively used by brigaders during the Battle of Madrid. The number is much lower in Sector 1: only 6 Enfield bullets (5% of the total). One of the Vetterli projectiles also appeared in Sector 2. The 0.303 bullets were clearly meant to stop enemies that had penetrated deep into the University City and were heading toward Madrid. We also found the fin and fuse of a 50 mm Valero mortar. Its typical range is just 600 meters and based on the orientation and location of the pieces, everything seems to indicate that the round or rounds were fired from the esplanade behind the School of Philosophy and Letters, which was occupied at the time of the combats by the Commune de Paris Battalion of the XI Brigade. Rifle fire also comes from the same area. But not all: an Enfield stripper clip was found in Sector 2, meaning that a Republican soldier had shot from there—again, something that would only have made sense in the autumn of 1936, before the stabilization of the frontline pushed the Republican first line far away from this place.

Other evidence suggests that the Nationalists were not stopped from a distance: grenades, shell casings, an Enfield stripper clip, and pistol ammunition are all indicative of fighting in the area. In Sector 1, we found four 0.303 shell casings and one of an 8 mm Lebel rifle, all typical weapons used by the Republicans during the Battle of Madrid and with percussion marks. In this same sector we recovered a 7.92 mm case with German markings, dated 1936. Although the Nazis sold weapons to the Republic, double-crossing their own allies (Heiberg and Mogens 2005), it makes sense —considering the overall context—that the cartridge was shot by an advancing Nationalist soldier. In fact, several 7.92 mm bullets were found in Sector 2 that could have been fired from this position.

Four grenade elements were recovered: two small pieces of fragmentation grenades in Sector 1, likely used by Republicans defending the zone, and two safety plaques of the Lafitte bomb, the offensive grenade of choice of the Nationalists, in Sector 2. As we saw in Casa de Campo, grenades inform us with some precision about the location of a combat, because they cannot be thrown at more than 30 meters (although fragments can spread up to 150 meters). Offensive bombs, such as the Lafitte, produce few fragments and they hardly disperse, to avoid wounding the attacker. Therefore, they offer solid evidence for the presence of Nationalists deep into this part of the campus, around one kilometer further inside Madrid than previously thought. This might not seem much in terms of distance, but it means more than it seems in strategic terms. I will return to this in a moment.

The survey covered the entire northwest part of the campus, but the finds appear concentrated in just the two sectors mentioned above. It is intriguing that we found evidence for combats along the small seasonal creek that flows parallel to the Dehesa de la Villa road, but not along the road itself. Yet trying to advance through the road was dangerous, because the soldiers would be much more exposed to enemy fire from the flanks. The creek

64 *Capital of glory*

probably looked like a safer option for the attackers, but it turned out to be a trap: it is short, funnel-like and ends abruptly.

When did this attempt at breaking into the city occur? The first days of the Battle of Madrid saw much movement of troops and the area north of the campus was a particularly chaotic scenario. What is clear is that on November 16 the situation there was difficult enough for the XI International Brigade under Emilio Kléber (*nom de guerre* of Manfred Stern, a former Austro-Hungarian officer) to transfer its headquarters to the Real Club Puerta de Hierro, a very exclusive club that is still situated to the other side of the Dehesa de la Villa road. From there, he deployed the Edgar André and Dabrowski Battalions to stop the enemy's penetration (Renn 2016: 196). The combats were so intense that the XI Brigade had to be replaced by the XII only three days later, on the 19th. The Garibaldi and Thaelmann Battalions of the XII International Brigade took positions near San Fernando Bridge and they managed to prevent the enemy from crossing the river, but not before losing 20% of their effectives in only two days (Longo 1966: 91–100).

Based on the archaeological evidence, it seems that the Nationalists were trying to penetrate into the northern part of Madrid through Puerta de Hierro and then the Dehesa de la Villa road. This was a smart move, because the area, if conquered, would provide easy access to the center of the city. The neighborhoods here were less densely built and had long avenues communicating with the heart of the capital. There was a real danger that the enemy occupied the crucial point of Cuatro Caminos (Montoliú 2000: 207), a crossroads (as the Spanish name indicates) leading to the city's strategic spots. It is obvious that the Republican high command saw the danger; otherwise, as pointed out, they would not have sent the International Brigades. This was not improvised: as we saw, the Republicans knew since November 6 that the Nationalists were planning a two-pronged attack on Madrid and that one of the pincers aimed at San Fernando Bridge and Puerta de Hierro.

As with Casa de Campo it is legitimate to ask why we know so little about this sector, if it actually was so important. The reasons are largely the same. To start with, there was chaos. Calvo González-Regueral (2012: 45) notes that the situation was evolving so fast during the first days of fighting at the University City that bureaucracy started to lag behind and reports, if written at all, became obsolete even before they reached the rearguard. Confusion was even greater in the periphery of the campus for at least two reasons: on the one hand, because of the peripheral location itself, far from the city and from observers, as happened with Casa de Vacas; on the other hand, because of the obscure and limited information that we have for the brigaders. Both Calvo González-Regueral (2012) and Manuel de Vicente Gonzalez (2014, 2016), who have worked with Spanish archival material and memoirs, stress the role of Spanish units to the detriment of the International Brigades, whose role was amplified by Republican propaganda. De Vicente Gonzalez goes as far as to argue that the internationals played an irrelevant role in the battle. Yet there is no question that the brigaders fought fiercely at the University City and paid dearly: the entire Dabrowski

Capital of glory 65

Battalion, for instance, was virtually wiped out in the defense of Casa de Velázquez, the French cultural center on campus. Even if we admit that their role in the central part of the battlefield might have been exaggerated, the same cannot be said for those fighting in the north. The scarcity of written evidence for that subsector, which can be mistaken for proof of the irrelevance of the International Brigades, which were deployed there, has political and military motives. On the Nationalist side, it makes sense that no publicity was given to a sector where they utterly failed. On the Republican side, we have to consider the peculiar status of the international units. Historian Andreu Castells (2006: note 11) notes that

> Tracing the first combats of the brigaders means penetrating a rather confusing terrain... The problem is that above the [Republican] command there was a superior one directed by the Soviet Pavlov-Koltsov-Goriev group [a group of prominent Soviet advisors]. Of this Soviet command, one of the most solid buttresses in the defense of Madrid, there are no specific data, perhaps because it always operated in the shadows.

It is in this realm of shadows, however, where archaeology can make its most relevant contribution.

Storming the Clínico

At the other side of the campus, the situation could not be more different. The fight at the University Hospital, popularly known as "El Clínico" (short for Hospital Clínico Universitario), became one of the icons of the war in Madrid and even Spain (Figure 3.10). It was transformed into a place of memory even before the end of the conflict, due to the tenacity of the Nationalist defense and the horrific casualties that they endured. The construction of the University Hospital began on a hilltop next to the city in 1932 and was not yet finished when the war broke out (Chías 1986: 139). Along the slope facing the Manzanares River a hospice was established in 1895, the Asylum of Santa Cristina. The legionnaires snatched the place away from Durruti's anarchists on November 17. Throughout the war, most of the buildings were destroyed, either by artillery fire or, more frequently, by mines. After the conflict, the hospice was thoroughly demolished, the trenches backfilled and the entire terrain landscaped and reforested. Not a promising place for a survey. Yet the results were surprisingly positive.

It is not always possible to pinpoint a specific moment in which the many bullets and grenade fragments that we found might have been used. But there are some hints. Regarding bullets, the high percentage of 0.303 munitions and the scarcity of Soviet 7.62 is surprising—the proportion is six to one. The 0.303 Enfields were first used by the brigaders, as we saw, but then remained at the Republican positions of the University City. However, by mid-1937 Soviet Mosin Nagants had largely replaced the old Enfields and these, although

Figure 3.10 The University Hospital as it was immediately after the end of the war. The ruins became a pilgrimage site for war veterans. Photo by Jesús García Trevisano.
Source: © Jorge García García.

still deployed, were rarely used in offensive operations. Thus, albeit some 0.303 bullets may come from harassing fire at any moment, it is quite likely that most were fired during the first six months of war in Madrid, which is also the period that saw more attacks on the University Hospital (see below). On the other hand, several remains of fragmentation grenades that appeared south of the hospice could only have been used during the Battle of Madrid, since the area remained deep inside Nationalist territory from November 1936 onwards and therefore off limits for Republican raiders.

The most impressive remains come from a strip of land situated northeast of the hospice, on the Nationalist frontline trenches. For some reason, this area of around 2,000 square meters was not covered in tons of rubble and sediment. The war-time surface lay untouched only a few centimeters under the present ground and yielded a plethora of finds, including a surprising amount of unexploded ordnance—artillery, mortar and hand grenades (Figure 3.11 and Table 3 in annex). Considering that the sector was carefully combed by the Service for Recuperation of War Material after the conflict, the intensity of the combats in this position must have been outstanding if so much was left. Not all can be assigned to the Battle of Madrid: most of the destruction undergone by the hospital actually occurred after the battle, mainly due to mine warfare (which we will see in the next chapter).

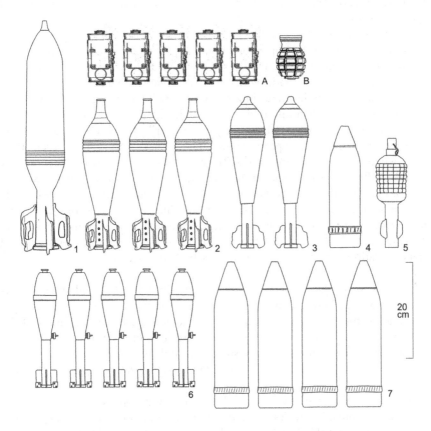

Figure 3.11 Unexploded ordnance found at the University Hospital during survey and excavation. The number represents the actual number of complete items found in the field.

Notes: A. Lafitte grenade; B. Tonelete grenade.1. Stokes-Brandt 81 mm "trench buster" mortar grenade; 2. Stokes-Brandt 81 mm mortar grenades; 3. 81 mm Valero mortar grenades; 4. 77 mm Erhardt Minenwerfer grenade; 5. Spanish Granatenwerfer grenade; 6. 50 mm Valero grenades; 77 mm Feldkanone shells.

Source: © Author.

We found four complete artillery shells during our survey, of which three appeared in the area mentioned above. However, mortar grenades were far more common. Mortars and bomb launchers were light and versatile, could be deployed anywhere and attain any point in and around the hospital. Nationalists feared them more than high-caliber guns, because they were silent and could fall in the most unsuspected places (Calvo González-Regueral 2012: 383). Grenades were even more lavishly used during the combats for the Clínico during the months of November and December 1936, but they were also the weapon of choice in the many raids and counter-raids launched by

68   *Capital of glory*

Nationalists and Republicans until the end of the war: the consumption of grenades in these raids was staggering.

If we look at the combats at the asylum and the hospital during November 1936, it is impossible not to see in them, on a small scale, a forerunner of those in Stalingrad, Warsaw or Berlin a few years later. But as the war wore on, the situation started to resemble more and more that of the First World War: endless raids in a fixed front, which were costly in lives and did not alter the situation in the least. Indeed, urban warfare was actually a return to the "aberration in the art of war" that was fighting in the trenches and that European commanders feared so much after their experience in the Western Front (Beevor 2011: 156). During the first six months following the Battle of Madrid, the University City saw 25 attacks, half of them during the first two months after the end of the battle (see Table 4 in annex) and most of them affecting the Clínico. Raids were often costly in men and *matériel* and always worthless. Referring to a Nationalist attack on 13 January 1937 that left 239 casualties in exchange for a worthless vanguard trench, Nationalist officer and historian Salas Larrázabal writes:

> This was to be the routine at the University City. Unproductive assaults with acts of heroic bravery proliferated on both sides, in which the fight was for the possession or loss of a minuscule objective which most of the time lacked any relevance. It was more a fight of amour propre than a military encounter. All heroism was completely gratuitous.
>
> (cited in Calvo González-Regueral 2012: 82)

The iteration of trench warfare is obvious in the panoply of weapons that we have documented. Grenades were the basic weapon of trench raiding parties during the First World War. Once inside the enemy trench, soldiers bombed their way through it. Indeed, although bayonets occupy a more prominent role in the collective imaginary of the conflict, grenades were responsible for far more casualties (Ellis 1989: 78–79). The weapons of the Clínico were largely offspring of the Great War, if not more archaic. Two of the grenades, the *Tonelete* and the Fifth Regiment, had a wick instead of a fuse, like the improvised jam tin grenades used by the ANZACs. We have already met the Fifth Regiment in Casa de Campo. The *Tonelete* ("small barrel") was the standard fragmentation grenade with the Spanish Army since 1918 and was a cumbersome artifact, weighing 750 grams. The Lafitte bomb, although lighter at 415 grams, was also an unwieldy contraption. It was based on a French grenade of the First World War (*pétard Thevenot-Lafitte*, from 1915[17]) and adopted by the Spanish Army in 1921. They were loaded with almost 200 grams of nitroamine, a highly sensitive explosive, and, albeit theoretically offensive, they were often used for defensive purposes, where they proved safer. To ignite the charge, the soldier had to remove a piece of bandage that fastened the safety plaque of the grenade. It is these plaques that we find more often during fieldwork. However, it is not uncommon to retrieve remains of the fabric. In fact, one of the fragments of Lafitte that we dug up at the

Capital of glory 69

Clínico still had a piece of cloth attached: a rag from a civilian striped shirt. The grenade was perhaps produced with recycled cloth, as tin can sheet was often used in the production of Lafittes (see Chapter 7). Another possibility is that the original cloth deteriorated and the soldier replaced it with a rag. In the master military narrative of the Spanish Civil War, there is little room for the makeshift and the do-it-yourself, which were instead a common occurrence on the ground.

The artillery employed against the hospital was either directly First World War surplus or weapons inspired in those used during the conflict. To the first group belong the German 77 mm gun and the Erhardt *Minenwerfer*. On 9 October 1936, a shipment of 15,000 shells and four FK16 (*Feldkanone* model 1916) firing 77 mm shells arrived in Republican Spain from the Soviet Union (Howson 2000: 364). Considering the location and orientation, the shells that we found at the Clínico were fired by Republican howitzers, although the Nationalists were the main users of the *Feldkanone* from January 1937 onwards (Manrique and Molina 2006: 204–206). They were a version of the older FK96, that had been adapted to trench warfare by extending its firing range (from 5.5 to 10 km). The *leichter Minenwerfer* ("light mine thrower") was actually a 75.8 mm mortar capable of throwing a 4.46 kg grenade at a distance of 1,300 meters. It was designed before the First World War, based on the experiences of the Russo-Japanese War (1905) and widely employed in the former conflict (Reibert 2014: 46–65). It was initially conceived for siege warfare against modern fortifications and it was in this role that it was deployed at the University City.

Modern mortars also made their appearance in the context of trench warfare during the First World War. Some of the grenades that we found were directly Great War surplus. This was the case with the 77 mm Erhardt minethrower; a shipment of 126 with 6,290 rounds arrived in the Republican zone on 2 February 1937 (Howson 2000: 369), too late to participate in the Battle of Madrid. Others were evolved versions of First World War models, such as the Stokes-Brandt that we had already found in Casa de Campo. One of the pieces that we dug up at the University Hospital was of the high-capacity type and its purpose is made clear by its nickname: "trench buster". It weighed around 7 kilos.[18] Spain devised their own mortars, the 50 and 81 mm Valeros (both of which have been found at the University Hospital), in 1933, but one of the pieces found during survey is of the so-called "reformed" type, designed by the Nationalists in January 1937 to speed up mass production and lower costs.[19] Like the Erhard, it could not have participated in the Battle of Madrid, but was probably used in one of the many later attacks.

Another Great War technology adapted to trench warfare was the bomb launcher, of whose grenades we found many remains during survey and excavation around the Clínico. During the Spanish Civil War, combatants used both the *Granatenwerfer* 16 and a local copy. The former was designed by the Austro-Hungarians and deployed by the Central Powers from 1916 onwards (Reibert 2014: 138–143). The history of the Spanish spigot mortar is directly associated with the Fifth Regiment grenade that we encountered earlier.

70 Capital of glory

According to one of its commanders, Juan Modesto (1978: 99), the unit—which produced many of its own weapons, as we have seen—started mortar production under the guidance of a certain "Lieutenant Frick, a German antifascist". Frick obviously found inspiration in the First World War weapon. The Spanish copy, like its German counterpart, was light (around 40 kg), it had a spigot instead of a tube (thus its name) and could throw a 2 kg fragmentation grenade at a distance of 50 to 300 meters, specifications which made it an ideal weapon at the University City (Figure 3.12). Grenades were in a few cases devised as a work of art with a political message: one had the acronyms of the Communist Party and the JSU. Instead of the typical waffle-like surface, their shells fragmented into five-point stars. The habit of writing graffiti on bombs was already widespread during the First World War, but the JSU workers took it a step further. In fact, trench art on recycled artillery shells is well known (Saunders 2000), but the elaborate decoration of grenades at the factory is quite unique. It can be understood in a context

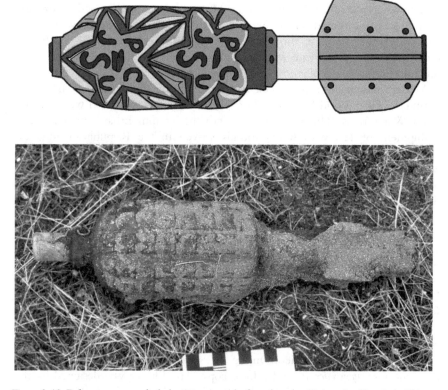

Figure 3.12 Below: an unexploded spigot grenade found at the University Hospital. Above: a spigot grenade with the symbols of the JSU and the Communist Party.
Source: © Author.

in which factories had been collectivized and were in the hands of political parties and trade unions, a situation which often led to quite impressive but often unpractical weapons.

The only complete spigot grenade that we found near the hospital did not explode for a simple reason: the safety pin was not removed. One can speculate about the reasons. Was it because in the confusion of the combat a soldier forgot to take it out? Was it because of inexperience? Sabotage? Photos of the period show teenage soldiers handling these weapons, so nerves and inexperience are probably to blame.

They did not pass

By November 23, both Nationalists and Republicans were exhausted. The Nationalist offensive had come to a halt and the Republicans did not reply with a counterattack. The rebels launched a new offensive six days later, but the strategy had changed: they abandoned the idea of a frontal attack and instead opted for entering the city through the northwest, through the La Coruña road (Martínez Bande 1982). Three battles ensued in this sector until 15 January 1937. The Republic had lost terrain, but Madrid was saved. Republican soldiers and international brigaders had indeed been up to the *No Pasarán!* The Nationalists did not pass. In this chapter we have seen how this was achieved: often using obsolete or old weapons, which were extraordinarily heterogeneous. The battlefield itself was a strange hybrid of mobile, combined warfare, in which infantry, tanks, artillery and airplanes participated, and a return to the static frontlines of the First World War, in which trenches, grenades and mortars prevailed. This is seldom considered in the main historical narratives of the battle—and the war more generally—which tend to emphasize the novelty rather than the archaic. Archaeological evidence, instead, shows eloquently the persistence of old modes of war in Madrid: from the First World War trench at Casa de Vacas to the nineteenth-century Remingtons used at the University City. At the same time, there was something radically new about the Battle of Madrid. While soldiers were killing each other with bayonets and grenades in the rooms of the University Hospital, the denizens of Madrid were going to the cinemas, filled the bars and went shopping only a few hundred meters away. Violence was incorporated into the social and material fabric of the city, as it would be later in Leningrad, Lebanon or Sarajevo.

I have also tried to show in this chapter that archaeology can change the master narrative of a military encounter as well known as the Battle of Madrid. Although the frontline had 22 kilometers (Reverte 2007: 296), all attention has been placed on the 1.5 kilometers between Puente de los Franceses and the School of Philosophy and Letters. By exploring the margins of the battlefield, it has been possible to revalue the role of the International Brigades and retrieve evidence of combats that might have changed the history of the Spanish Civil War. Madrid was perhaps

72　*Capital of glory*

closer to falling than usually assumed, but the Republican defense worked and the capital resisted. It did so for two years and five months. For its determination to fight fascism, Madrid in 1936 deserves the title of Capital of Glory bestowed by Rafael Alberti. But it was also the Capital of Misery: of rearguard killings, bombing of civilians and soon also of starvation and attrition. To these I will refer in the next chapter.

Notes

1 Republican Left: the party of Manuel Azaña, the president of the Republic during the war.
2 Originally it read Tomás Parques, a sergeant. Eduardo Ruiz was a socialist.
3 https://toledogce.blogspot.com/2019/01/los-combates-en-el-seminario-de-toledo. html.
4 J.M. Reverte Coma: http://www.gorgas.gob.pa/museoafc/loscriminales/crimino logia/esqueletos.html.
5 They are marked SB 1936 VII y SB 1935 X (Sellier & Bellot, Prague).
6 I would like to thank Severiano Montero Barrado, president of the Association of Friends of the International Brigades in Spain for providing this reference.
7 *Bandera* is the name of a unit of 300 to 1000 soldiers of the Spanish Legion.
8 http://www.memoriademadrid.es/buscador.php?accion=VerFicha&id=12020& num_id=6&num_total=90.
9 They were patented in 1835 by Cassimir Lefaucheux and became widespread in 1860. The cartridge had its own ignition system, in which the priming compound was ignited by striking a small pin which protruded radially from the base of the cartridge. The first cartridges of this type were made of cardboard with a metal base. Later, the whole casing was made of metallic alloys" (Landa et al. 2009: 192). Lefaucheaux cartridges were no longer produced after the 1920s.
10 http://rgaspi.org/ I thank Julián Dueñas for locating the documents.
11 "El contraataque en la Ciudad Universitaria". AGMAV, 545, 2.D.171.
12 "La Casa de Vacas". The text, kept in the RGASPI archive, was originally published in Spanish in an unknown newspaper during the war and afterwards in German in an issue of the journal *Sinn und Form: Beiträge zur Literatur*, a journal founded in the German Democratic Republic in 1949.
13 http://www.cmeneses.com/nuestra-historia/.
14 AGMAV, 77, 1266, 3, 1.
15 AGA, F, 04046, 53891, 001, 01.
16 AGMAV, 97, 966, 8, 2.
17 http://titus2h.e-monsite.com/pages/premiere-guerre/14-les-grenades-percutantes-offensives.html.
18 http://www.amonio.es/mortero_brandt_gran_capacidad.htm.
19 http://www.amonio.es/mortero_valero_ref_81_mono.htm.

4 Capital of misery

July 1936–October 1938

"Murder has changed the city's shape", wrote Syrian poet Adonis (2010: 200). Contemporary conflict does leave a deep imprint in urban landscapes. After the brutality of the Thirty Years War (1618–1648), warfare in towns and cities had become a rare sight in Europe. Few cities were besieged and stormed during the Napoleonic era and, a hundred years later, the Great War still saw very little urban combat as such (Beevor 2011: 151–152). Instead, cities turned battlefields would be one of the main characteristics of total war from 1941 onwards. Thus, some of the fiercest encounters of the Second World War happened inside Berlin, Stalingrad and Manila. In this, as in other (bad) things, Spain was ahead of its time in the 1930s. Madrid, a large city with one million inhabitants, was the first capital to experience modern warfare. Its transformation into a battleground in November 1936 was a prelude to what was to come: aerial bombings, people taking shelter in the metro, massacres of unarmed civilians, barricades, trenches and pillboxes dug in gardens and parks, artillery batteries in the middle of the street, hunger, disease, siege psychosis. Urban warfare, writes Antony Beevor referring to Stalingrad, "represented a new form of warfare, concentrated in the ruins of civilian life. The detritus of war—burnt out tanks, shell cases, signal wire and grenade boxes—was mixed with the wreckage of family homes—iron bedsteads, lamps and household utensils" (Beevor 2011: 154).

This was a familiar landscape for the people of Madrid between 1936 and 1939. Yet the detritus of war is more than just the backdrop of armed conflict, it is an essential part of it, when waged as a form of urbicide (Graham 2004a). Purposive city killing has been a characteristic of twentieth and twenty-first century warfare and this was also the case in Spain. A not negligible role in the Nationalist decision to bomb urban centers was probably played by the imaginary of the city in Spanish conservative thinking, in which cities were seen as places of sin of corruption. All that was evil was born there: revolutionary ideologies, feminism, modern art, new forms of leisure and sociability, atheism and secularization, etc. Nationalists were, first and foremost, anti-modern and cities like Madrid and Barcelona represented the epitome of the modern civilization they hated so much. This

74 *Capital of misery*

was even more evident in the case of the colonial officers, *africanistas*, who had eulogized the experience of fighting in the solitude of the steppes, outside civilization (Nerín 2005: 72). Life in the barracks and the isolated *blocaos* (blockhaus) of Morocco were seen as shaping superior human beings, far from the degrading effects of the urban. There is some obvious pleasure in the memoirs and testimonies of legionnaires in establishing camp at the gates of Madrid, in the University City: bringing rugged military life, with its small pleasures, rigid discipline and indulgent violence, to the heart of decadent bourgeois life.

Cities and civilians became objectives, but cities also became war machines and their inhabitants, warriors and assassins. They were not mere victims and this, again, is something that can be clearly seen in Madrid: the capital was the scenario of strategic bombing and urban combats, but ruins and narrow streets also turned into formidable defenses and the city itself into a death trap for Nationalist sympathizers. The natural affordances offered by the urban environment were extended further through the construction of shelters, tunnels, mines, pillboxes, walls of sandbags and the placement of anti-aircraft guns, machine guns and howitzers. Architect Gerardo Hernández Perdomo (2015) carried out the fascinating task of reconstructing the city turned fortress using documentary and photographic evidence. What emerges from his maps is the picture of a deadly labyrinth (Figure 4.1): trenches and barricades, antitank ditches and mine fields cut across the streets and block off bridges. Most fortifications were never used: only those south of the Manzanares River (Carabanchel, Usera) and to a certain extent in Argüelles and the western part of Chamberí saw any action. One can imagine the mixture of terror and exhilaration with which these defenses were erected in October and November 1936. Yet once violence set into the city and the assault mutated into a war of attrition, the barricades became a sort of archaeological remnant, a sad reminder of a short moment of glory transformed into a long nightmare.

Since October 1936, the civilian in the etymological root of "city" (*cives*) became indistinguishable from the military (*miles*). This was a process that had started in Madrid before the Spanish Civil War. Throughout the nineteenth century, the capital was progressively militarized with many headquarters and barracks constructed inside and around the city. This was the result of the three Carlist Wars that raged between 1833 and 1876. Madrid concentrated a huge number of troops to defend it against a potential Carlist siege (Díez de Baldeón 1993: 235), a situation that set it apart from other European capitals, where, by the late nineteenth century, troops used to be stationed outside the urban center. This military presence, in turn, favored the military coup of 18 July 1936: the main focus of the uprising, the Montaña barracks, was only a few hundred meters from the main centers of Republican power.

The strong relationship between war and city can be traced back deep in time and beyond any specific conjuncture. Paul Virilio has defended that the idea of the city is inseparable from war. *Real* war, in his view, only arises with urban civilization and is characterized by three different epochs: tactical,

Capital of misery 75

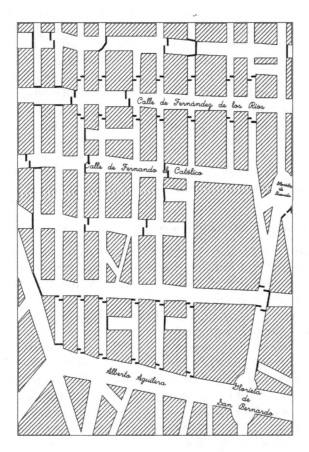

Figure 4.1 The city turned into a trap: map of a section of the neighborhood of Chamberí with barricades, based on documents of the period.
Source: © Gerardo Hernández Perdomo.

strategic and logistical (Virilio 2002: 48–49). Tactical warfare saw limited violence, the siege as its specific type of confrontation, and fortified rings around the city as the mode of deterrence. This is the kind of institutional violence that prevailed, according to Virilio, before the appearance of artillery, which would lead to the strategic epoch of weapons of destruction at a distance (from cannons to missiles), and eventually to the logistical epoch of weapons of communication. Things, however, are not so clear-cut and a unilinear narrative fails to account for the actual messiness of contemporary warfare—Virilio (2002: 12) himself saw in the contemporary politics of blockade and embargo a return to the stage of siege. Madrid was transformed—socially, psychologically and materially—by two and a half years of military encirclement, in what amounted, in many respects, to a return to premodern violence. The fate of Madrilenians (starved, prey of diseases and rumors) was

76 *Capital of misery*

not different from those who suffered medieval and early modern sieges. The ring of trenches that surrounded the capital was at the same time a First World War *déjà-vu* and an iteration of older preindustrial warfare. Both soldiers and civilians were forced to develop new and at the same time ancient skills, some of which were not totally lost in 1930s Spain: the art of foraging, of mending and improvising artifacts, of self-construction and of living underground. Everything under the constant threat of cutting-edge industrial weaponry: Madrid as a battlefield was simultaneously archaic and supermodern. In this chapter, I will be examining the war of attrition in the capital during the first two and a half years of the conflict, that is, until the autumn of 1938. We will take a glimpse first at the Nationalist lines and then at the Popular Army. Finally, the last section will delve into urban war as experienced by civilians.

Nationalist lines at the University City

While the Battle of Madrid has attracted much attention, the two and a half years that followed have been often overlooked, as if the war had vacated the capital (but see Gómez Bravo 2018). Until recently, historians have tended to focus all their attention on the main episodes of the conflict. They follow a linear narrative, jumping from one battle to the next and forgetting about a battlefield as soon as an offensive starts elsewhere. But in static fronts, battlefields do not simply vanish: hundreds of thousands of soldiers get stuck in them and they construct new fortifications, rectify the lines, fall ill, launch raids, set up mines and barbed wire, kill and are killed. Archaeology is a way of approaching post-battle scenarios. In the case of Madrid, the Capital of Misery that followed the days of glory.

Archaeological evidence for the Nationalist occupation of the University City after November 1936 is limited. Most of the area occupied by Franco's troops south of La Coruña road was heavily developed after the war and the only places where an excavation can be conducted are the green areas within the university dormitories—not a realistic option. However, during construction works near one of the colleges in the 1990s, a Nationalist position was dug up, with remains of trench and machine-gun positions (probably fire bays or foxholes). Unfortunately, the intervention focused on the large Late Roman dump that stood in the same spot and little more is known about the Civil War context (Guiral Pelegrín 1997). As we saw in the previous chapter, our work focused on the area of the University Hospital, which has the second largest park on campus. I have already mentioned that the survey was extremely successful, but the excavation was no less productive (González-Ruibal 2018a). It focused on the remains of the Asylum of Santa Cristina that, as mentioned in the preceding chapter, was established at the feet of the University Hospital in 1895. The institution was built during the regency of María Cristina of Habsburg, the mother of Alphonse XIII (thus its name), and hosted a variety of people: orphans, abandoned women, elderly people, and homeless people, among others. One

Capital of misery 77

of the many pavilions that were part of the complex was located in a fold in the terrain which made it difficult to be attained by enemy fire. With the University Hospital, they became the most advanced positions of the Nationalists in Madrid. This subsector was garrisoned, in May 1937, by the 9 "Franco" *Bandera* of the Spanish Legion (their flag had the name of the dictator embroidered), the 8 Gerona Battalion, and other minor units, totaling around 1,500 men and eight mules (Calvo González-Regueral 2012: 140).

From asylum to fortress

In the previous chapter, I noted that the area around the University Hospital in Madrid was severely bombed and mined during the war and demolished, backfilled, terraced and reforested in the postwar period. Most of the Asylum of Santa Cristina was destroyed down to the foundations or covered under several meters of rubble and soil. Yet photographs of the period showed a building that survived almost intact until the end of the war. We conducted test pits along the terrace where we expected it to be and found walls, floors and foundations of two different structures: one was a 70-m-long pavilion, one of the many that made up the asylum, and the other, a laundry. The pavilion had been razed below the floor level. Demolition works had been thorough: the walls and even most of the pavement itself had been removed. Only one of the test pits furnished some two square meters of the original encaustic cement tile pavement. In fact, the purpose of the postwar demolition was not so much to tear down a ruin (the building was in relatively good shape), but to recycle the materials in the reconstruction of the hospital and the nearby bombed houses.

That only the foundations were preserved proved not to be a problem, because the aboveground was never very important during the war after all. It was the underground that was relevant: soldiers had to dig in to survive in such an exposed position. And they dug a lot: tunnels, trenches and shelters that completely transformed the old asylum (Figure 4.2). In the photographs of the period that have been preserved, it is impossible to get an accurate idea of how much the civilian structures had been converted into something completely alien: simultaneously a fortification and a subterranean city. There is something of a sci-fi dystopia about this place during the war, a sort of steampunk scenario, about this place during the war. Because the asylum was not just a space for living (or surviving): it was also a fortification, whose intricacies the excavation began to reveal.

The laundry features already in the early maps of the asylum, so it was probably one of the first structures to be erected. It was a square building made of brick with a concrete pavement and four cement-lined basins in the middle. In a 1910 map of Madrid we can see different spaces around the building: a pond fed by a natural spring, a hencoop, and a pigeon loft, and—where the pavilion that we excavated should be—a *vaquería*,

78 *Capital of misery*

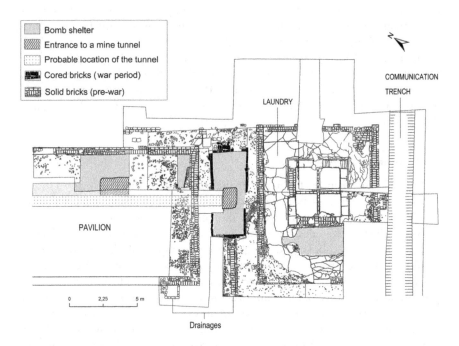

Figure 4.2 Excavations at the Asylum of Santa Cristina revealed the extensive transformation of the site during the war.
Source: © Manuel Antonio Franco Fernández, Pedro Rodríguez Simón and author.

a cowshed. The *vaquería* provided meat and milk to the hospice and also to Madrilenians. At some point it was dismantled and the pavilion constructed on top of it, but the former structure did not vanish without a trace. When we excavated the pavilion's foundations, we reached a flat level with lots of charcoal, small fragments of brick and many animal bones. They belonged mostly to cattle, with some sheep. Several bones had cut marks and one a fragment of a knife edge embedded. We also found a typical ossobuco cut and a solitary cockle (*Cerastoderma edule*). These were the remains of the cowshed and an eloquent manifestation of the asylum's self-sufficiency, at least in its early days.

The pavilion was probably built at some point during the 1910s. It was made of massive bricks and covered in Marseilles tiles—flat tiles with grooves so that they can be interlocked. They were first produced in French factories in the 1870s and became popular during the last two decades of the nineteenth century. Those from the asylum were produced in different Spanish cities (Alicante, Segovia). The building had thin brick walls and the roof was supported by forged iron columns, common in nineteenth and early twentieth-century buildings, such as covered markets. The floor was paved with beautiful encaustic cement tiles with different designs. Electricity and running water were available inside the premises (we found water pipes, wiring, porcelain

Capital of misery 79

insulators and even a light switch). It was a very modern building by Spanish standards of the time, clearly a showcase for the wealth and generosity of the rich families that funded the institution.

It is quite likely that the pavilion that we excavated was a refectory before the war. Although very little information about the asylum has been published, there is at least a picture showing a dining hall resembling in size and shape the structure that we excavated. The problem is that all pavilions were identical. The asylum reproduced the factory/military camp layout that is so typical of late nineteenth-century institutions, so it is difficult to relate the photos with specific structures. However, on the 1910 map, that is, before the construction of the pavilion, the refectory was located very close to the laundry. That building was later demolished, but it is likely that its functions were taken over by the new, more spacious structure. Furthermore, a large amount of crockery turned up around the pavilion, which surely belonged to the hospice. We know that the legionnaires found the asylum's appurtenances in pristine condition when they took it over on November 1936—to their surprise, because it had been previously occupied by anarchists! Father Urra, a military chaplain with the Nationalists who entered the place on November 17 wrote: "In the Asylum of Santa Cristina there was a strange situation: every department and the church itself were intact and without any profanation" (cit. in Chías 1986: 157).

The excavation and survey yielded much material from the prewar period. Most appeared in the area between the two structures, as well as in the laundry itself, mixed with the soil and rubble used to fill and level the terrain in the postwar period. Apart from the abundant crockery already mentioned, we also found a large quantity of glass (drinking glasses, wine glasses, jugs), including some high-quality pieces. Some of the finest material turned up in the laundry: two cut-glass droplets from a chandelier, a delicate hand-painted porcelain decorated with mythological motifs (perhaps the Judgement of Paris) and some late nineteenth-century transferware. Two tea cups depict children playing different games and were probably used by the orphans at the institution. Other notable finds from the prewar period are two biscuit figurines, one in the shape of the Divine Sheperdess and the other of a swan. All this fine material, from chandeliers to tureens, was in all likelihood gifts from the well-to-do Madrilenian families who funded the asylum. The scene during the war could not have been more surreal: the rugged Nationalist soldiers, eaten by fleas and lice and surrounded by mine and bomb craters, trenches, explosives and the ruins of bourgeois life—a life most of them had probably never experienced themselves.

Men spent most of the time underground, either in the basement of the nearby hospital or in the dugouts that they excavated amid the rubble or inside the old buildings. We located four dugouts and a communication trench, which evince the extent to which the built environment was modified. Interestingly, only the trench appears in the maps, documents and

80 *Capital of misery*

images of the period. Of the two dugouts inside the pavilion, one yielded little in the way of artifacts, but the other one was a treasure trove: it was filled in its entirety with prewar and war materials. Among the latter there were three plastic toothbrushes, cutlery, several complete inkbottles, alcoholic drinks, a rare Republican coin from 1934 and Mauser ammunition. Both this dugout and the one in-between pavilion and laundry were more than mere bomb shelters. They provided entrances to mining tunnels to which I will refer in the next section.

The soldiers discarded or lost many things during their stay at the asylum. Some were quite valuable: two wedding rings, one in silver and one in gold. The latter has the date inscribed: 1926. Considering the average age of marriage for men in Spain at that time (28 years), the owner must have been in his late thirties or early forties during the war. It could have been an officer, but then old soldiers were not an oddity in the Legion (not so likely that they were married, though). It is possible that the laundry kept something of its original use and was employed by the soldiers for washing. This would explain the high number of buttons that we have found, and also the insignias—easy to lose when dressing and undressing. We have found three in the laundry, which speak of the ideology of the Nationalist troops (Figure 4.3). They include an insignia from Falange with the yoke and arrows, another one with the Spanish and Falange flags and the motto *Viva España* ("Long live Spain") and a symbol of the Spanish Legion, which was the unit most strongly associated with the Clínico and which sustained the heaviest casualties. While the Legion is not strictly political, the truth is that it was (and still is) a notoriously right-wing military unit and their members often volunteered for political reasons: in fact, it was founded by one of the officers who participated in the conspiracy against the Republic, Millán Astray. Another political symbol appeared not in the laundry but in a sewer: a swastika. This is intriguing, because swastikas were very uncommon among Nationalist soldiers during the Spanish Civil War. However, this is not a proper insignia and definitely not an official item. It was hand-made, an example of trench art using a sheet of pewter or zinc of the kind found in ammunition boxes. The Nationalists were not unfamiliar with swastikas: they were the symbol that represented one of their staunchest allies. In a position defended by highly motivated soldiers, it is not strange that one decided to make one. Some prominent Falangists, in fact, sympathized with the Nazi ideology, starting with Franco's brother-in-law and minister, Serrano Suñer (Thomàs 2011), and the fascist component of the Nationalist side grew during the war and immediately afterwards. Surprisingly, only one religious element has been found: a beautiful crucifix that appeared in the pavilion.

Solid waste management surely was a serious problem, but it goes unmentioned in the archival record. If discarded in situ, garbage became a health hazard, given the lack of hygiene, overcrowding and limited available space. Dumping it far from the lines would require an important logistical effort and was dangerous. It seems that the soldiers used the drainage system of

Capital of misery 81

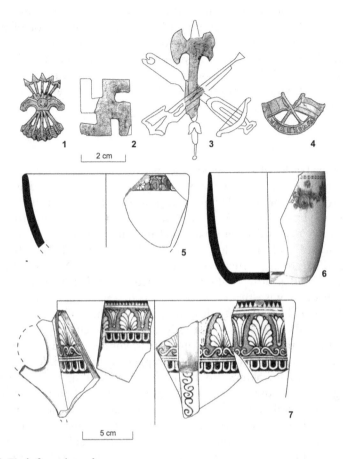

Figure 4.3 Finds from the asylum.

Notes: 1. Insignia of Spanish Falange; 2. Makeshift Nazi insignia; 3. Insignia of the Spanish Legion; 4. Insignia with the flag of the Falange (red and black) and the Spanish flag; 5–7. Coffee and teacups from the hospice that were likely reused by the Nationalist soldiers.

Source: © Author and Incipit-CSIC.

the asylum to get rid of as much of the rubbish as possible. There we found bottles, tin cans, remains of clothing, nails, ammunition and animal bones. The nails are exceedingly common and their presence is probably related to the burning of the hospice's furniture, beams and frames as firewood (Madrid's winters were notoriously cold): "Firewood was the one thing that really mattered", wrote George Orwell (1980: 30) speaking of his experiences in the front. The largest deposit of rubbish appeared in one of the entrances to the sewer system that we located by chance with one of our first test pits. It was a five-meter-deep shaft that connected with the pavilion's main drain. The predominant finds were nails and animal bones, not all of which were of domesticates: many belonged to rats and mice, which also appeared in some

82 *Capital of misery*

quantity in two other drains and other spaces. There is nothing surprising about it: 1,500 men with little opportunity for washing, a lot of tunneling and digging, garbage lying around and even a few human corpses—it was only natural for rats to thrive. They were there before the war, for sure, but their numbers likely increased in the new circumstances. Waste management, however, was probably the least of the Nationalists' worries in this dangerous frontline.

Rattenkrieg

During the Battle of Stalingrad, German soldiers who were fighting in ruined buildings, cellars and sewers soon called this modality of war *Rattenkrieg*, "rat warfare". Despite the novelty of the environment, it was a return to First World War tactics, as the Germans reintroduced the assault groups that had been established in January 1918. They consisted in 10 men armed with a machine gun, a light mortar and flamethrowers for clearing underground structures (Beevor 2011: 156). Most of the attacks consisted in "lethal little conflicts" in which half a dozen men on each side killed each other with spades, knives, grenades and submachine guns. Well before Stalingrad, *Rattenkrieg* had been run-of-the-mill at the University City of Madrid, where it was mostly a collateral effect of mine warfare. Mining and countermining developed in its modern form during the First World War (Leonard 2017). In Spain, sappers tunneled under enemy lines, set large explosive charges (four to ten tons) and detonated them after returning to their own positions (Sagarra et al. 2016: 116–118). Mines blew up entire buildings with all their defenders inside. Sometimes miners and counterminers (called *topos* in Spanish, "moles") met each other in the tunnels and horrendous combats ensued. Special units were created to wage this kind of warfare in which Republicans always had the upper hand. They did in part because they had experienced miners who knew how to dig tunnels and handle dynamite. Republican underground operations started as soon as 11 December 1936, when an explosion killed 39 legionnaires at the University Hospital (Estado Mayor Central del Ejército 1948: 60) and continued virtually unopposed through 1937. On August 27, five mines killed 70 soldiers at the Hospital again. Not until December 1937 did a specialized Nationalist unit arrive in Madrid, which had been created during the Republican siege of Oviedo, and started to balance the situation (Estado Mayor Central del Ejército 1948: 62–63). At that time, galleries were excavated mainly by Republican prisoners, especially Basques (Calvo González-Regueral 2012: 298).

Despite Nationalist efforts, Republicans never lost the initiative. In fact, the mission of rebel sappers consisted in setting up countermines, rather than in mining the enemy lines, and one of their priorities was to avoid subterranean attacks to the University Hospital, which had already cost hundreds of victims: by the end of the war, over 200 mines had been detonated at the

Capital of misery 83

University City and surroundings which had cost around 900 casualties to the Nationalists, of which 314 were dead (Sagarra et al. 2016). The explosions reduced the hospital and the Asylum of Santa Cristina to rubble and obliterated the School of Agricultural Engineering. One can grasp the magnitude of the explosions in two places. One of them is the School of Odontology, which was mined by the Nationalists as a reprisal for a previous Republican attack and had an entire aisle collapsed. It was rebuilt after the war, but reusing bricks of different color and shape which render the outcome of the explosion visible. More obvious is the crater that still exists near the University Hospital, which was the result of a Nationalist countermine blown in December 1937. At present, it is 16 meters in diameter and a three meters deep—and this was provoked by a comparatively small charge. We conducted a sondage inside and found the bottom at 1.6 meters from the present surface. The test excavation yielded bullets, barbed wire and fragments of Fifth Regiment and Lafitte grenades, which were used in any of the raids that took place in the sector. Soldiers, in fact, regularly took cover in the craters during the assaults. On the rim we retrieved two unexploded mortar grenades.

The Republican sappers both dug tunnels and used the sewage system, which connected the university with downtown Madrid. One of the main sewers, which was the object of fierce combats, went from the hospital to the building currently occupied by the University administration, a few hundred meters away, which remained in the hands of the Popular Army. Tunnels were used not only for mining and countermining, but also to listen to enemy activity. The obsession was with identifying the picks at work. In the psychotic atmosphere favored by this kind of warfare, some legionnaires and regulars are said to have developed their own geophones: they stuck a heating pipe or a canteen in the ground and applied the ear (Iniesta Cano 1984: 100). Special underground units were typically equipped with grenades, pistols, bayonets and spades in anticipation of an encounter with the enemy. Also with gas masks, an essential implement, because the explosions unleashed toxic gases. The usual Republican procedure was to detonate a mine, then bomb with mortars and finally launch a raid:

> "They met the enemy in the freshly disturbed dirt and fought like beasts, blowing machetes, biting. Rifles, used as sledgehammers against skulls, broke up in splinters and crushed bones creaked".
> (Pedro García Suárez, cited in Calvo González-Regueral 2012: 381)

In a map drawn by the Francoist Army after the war depicting all explosions at the University Hospital and the Asylum of Santa Cristina, craters from mainly Republican explosions cover virtually all the existing terrain (Estado Mayor Central del Ejército 1948) (Figure 4.4). They also offer relevant details to interpret our excavation: the pavilion that we uncovered was perforated from one side to the other by a countermining tunnel that connected the

84 *Capital of misery*

Figure 4.4 Map of the mines at the University Hospital subsector.

Notes: A. Crater still visible on the surface; B. Excavated pavilion. White circles indicate Republican mines; dashed circles, Nationalist countermines. The dotted line represents the main tunnel connecting the asylum and the hospital with its countermining galleries. Dots represent the entrance to the tunnel that we found during excavation.

Source: Work by author based on a map by the Estado Mayor Central del Ejército (1948).

hospital and the hospice. This gallery had to have entrances somewhere, although they were not marked on the map.

We were lucky enough to discover two of them in our excavations. One was located in the shelter in-between pavilion and laundry and might explain its spaciousness and the investment made in its construction. Indeed, it seems that the tunnels and their accesses were used both for mining and as bomb shelters. When we reached the floor level we identified a wooden frame of approximately one square meter. As the excavation proceeded, we realized that the frame was part of a trap door leading to a deep shaft. Unfortunately, we were unable to proceed for security reasons, but we discovered some telling materials in the one-meter-deep backfill that we did excavate. These include one complete Lafitte grenade and fragments of at least another, and

Capital of misery 85

spent Mauser ammunition. Around the trap door there were many Mauser cartridges and several complete clips and not far from the assemblage, a chamber pot. The grenades, as I have mentioned, were part of the sappers' toolkit: the Lafittes were particularly useful in underground warfare, because they had a powerful concussion effect and delivered few lethal fragments. The chamber pot was an equally indispensable item, as the soldiers had to spend long and anxious hours underground, both before entering and after leaving the hole.

One entrance to the gallery was not enough, because it could collapse due to enemy action. The other access that we documented was inside the pavilion, again in one of the shelters that we found with our test pits. This entrance was wider than the one just described and had steps hewn in the compacted natural sand. Finds associated with this tunnel were a Mauser clip on one of the steps and parts of a wz. gr. 31 percussion fuse and a lever. The wz. gr. 31 was of Polish manufacture and could be mounted in either defensive (wz. 24) or offensive (wz. 33) grenades. Republicans were the main users, but the Nationalists employed them, too. There were also two shell casings that had been disassembled and stuck through their mouths, a reminder of the many hours of boredom spent by the sentinels waiting by the shaft.

The life of soldiers in a sector undergoing mine warfare was extremely stressful from a psychological point of view. But that of sappers was even worse: hundreds of hours passed underground, in the asphyxiating atmosphere of a tunnel, several meters under the surface, entire days without seeing the daylight and under the constant fear of being blown up to pieces or buried alive... Understandably, these troops received extra food rations and much alcohol. In both shelters we found large quantities of alcoholic bottles (mostly sherry or brandy). In one of them, the label is partly legible: we could make out the word "LEGIÓN". It is probably a commemorative wine for the legionnaires—something that is still done today. The smell of fear in mine warfare was a mixture of trinitrotoluene, gunpowder, sweat, urine and alcohol. Food remains in this sector (that I will discuss in Chapter 9) struck us as particularly abundant and diverse. But then, they were the last meal of death row inmates.

Republican lines at the University City

After the Battle of Madrid, the part of the University City that remained in Republican hands was divided into two sectors, defended by two different units of the 7 Division of the Army of the Center. Its 40 Mixed Brigade was in charge of the sector around the University Hospital, whereas the 53 covered the area extending between the School of Medicine and Puerta de Hierro. In August 1938, 85% of the troop were either peasants or workers, in accordance with the official name of the Republican forces at the time: the Popular Army of the Republic. Archival research and archaeological fieldwork

86 *Capital of misery*

provide insight into the life of these anonymous soldiers (González-Ruibal et al. 2010; González-Ruibal, Rodríguez Simón and Franco Fernández 2017).

Digging trenches while hungry

Constructing fortifications was the main activity of Republican soldiers during the war. Archaeological evidence of construction and maintenance work includes a shovel, a drill, a saw, two chisels and an iron wedge found in our excavations. Trench-digging transformed the University City into a labyrinth (Figure 4.5), whose intricacy worried the high command: a report noted that "due to the diversity of communication trenches and the absence of signs, in case of combat a great confusion would ensue".[1] This had already

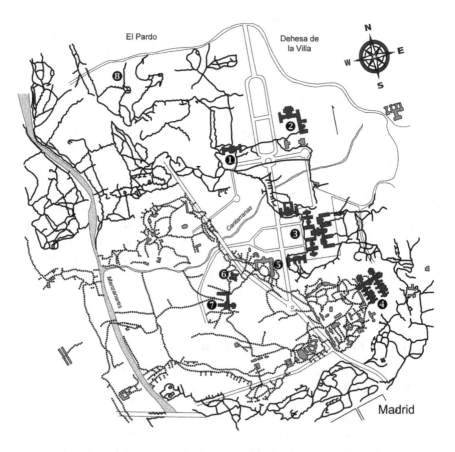

Figure 4.5 A labyrinth of trenches: the University City at the end of the war.

Notes: Solid lines: Republicans; Dotted lines: Nationalists. 1. Philosophy; 2. Sciences; 3. Medicine; 4. Hospital; 5. Agronomy; 6. French House; 7. Architecture. 8. Puerta de Hierro sector.

Source: © Author, based on a map of the period.

Capital of misery 87

occurred during the First World War, when entire units got lost in a mesh of fortifications, extending for kilometers (Keegan 2000: 177).

Fortifications were cut through earlier works: one of the complexes that we excavated revealed three construction phases between 1936 and 1939 (Figure 4.6). Archival documents inform us about the continuous improvement and expansion of the trenches. We know that during the summer of 1938 there were at least 140 Republican sappers working exclusively in the fortification of the University City. It was probably around that time when the trenches and shelters that we excavated in the northwestern part of the campus were dug (see Figure 3.8). Despite the good preservation of some parts of the trench system, it is difficult today to picture the complexity of the defenses, because there were not only fire, communication and evacuation trenches, but also concrete pillboxes, dugouts, underground shelters, covered ways, antitank ditches, barbed wire meshwork and, as we saw in the previous section, mining tunnels, most of which have disappeared today or are invisible.

The long occupation of the frontline ended up with the relaxation of the soldiers' habits. Some officers complained that well-designed pillboxes became useless because men transformed them into homes, placing beds inside and

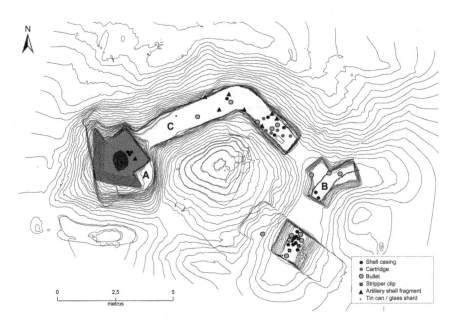

Figure 4.6 A trench and dugout with several construction phases.

Notes: A. Signal for airplanes probably dug in 1936 or early 1937; B. Communication trench, first half of 1937; C. Dugout with communication trench, summer–autumn 1938. The finds from the later occupation level are represented.

Source: © Pedro Rodríguez Simón and author.

88 *Capital of misery*

sealing embrasures. A report concludes that "materials are used in the construction of shacks (*chabolas*) and in unnecessary comforts given the necessities of the first lines".[2] Archaeology allows us to complete this picture of "domestication". In one of the shelters that we excavated we found three keyholes and a decorative element in bronze and another keyhole appeared in a nearby dugout. They belong to furniture that was probably salvaged from abandoned or bombed houses and reused in the trenches. Soldiers also recycled bricks and tiles. Springs from mattresses were also found, but in this case the purpose was not necessarily greater comfort, but a defense against mortars: the grenades bounced on the mattresses and did not explode.[3]

Considering their appearance, it is not strange that refuges were known as *chabolas*, "shacks", "shanties". In the shelter mentioned above, we can imagine men surrounded by rickety furniture, gathering around a hearth on the compacted sand floor and eating, drinking, smoking and chatting. We found a sardine tin can abandoned amid the ashes of the hearth. Near the entrance, the walls were lined with metal sheet. This might have actually extended to the entire dugout, but was salvaged after the war. The roof was likely made of trunks, planks and sandbags. A nearby, smaller shelter had a canvas roof and the sand floor lined with oilcloth. A hearth in the middle still had a tin of horse grease in situ, used to lubricate the weapons. The strangest find here was the hinge of a manual Elma ice cream-maker. Elma is a popular Basque producer of food processing machines that opened in 1924 and is still active today.[4]. It is quite unlikely that soldiers were making ice cream in the trenches, so they might have used the ice cream maker as an ordinary bucket.

Despite improvements to the trenches, the geology of the University City made life complicated. As happened in most of the Western Front during the Great War, the ditches were dug in the soft and easy to flood terrain of the University City (which was built on the Quaternary terraces of the Manzanares River). This provoked technical problems, as the rifles of the soldiers were often clogged and stopped working. Thus, on 18 January 1937 an officer lamented "the deterioration and interruptions experienced by rifles due to the large amount of mud" and emphasized the difficulties of digging trenches in "sand and earth that absorbs water easily".[5] Fortifications required constant care, because rain made them collapse: a few days later, another officer noted that "a battalion has had to abandon their trenches because they have sunk—only 60 meters in front of the enemy".[6]. He also reiterated the problem with weapons.

The other problem of flood-prone terrain is disease: stalled water is an ideal breeding ground for mosquitos and bacteria. Casualties due to illness became more common than those caused by enemy fire. The 40 Brigade lost 800 soldiers in a single month. Trench disease went from typhus and scabies to malaria. While today we tend to identify the latter illness with tropical countries, it was common in Spain until the 1950s—though not in large cities. There were foci of malaria in the School of Philosophy and Letters and the School of Odontology (next to the University Hospital).[7] To these health problems derived from the environment we have to add those of the digestive system and psychological maladies. Another problem was venereal infections, which in the case of Madrid were very common due to the proximity of brothels. About the health of soldiers we do not have much information: some fragments of medicine bottles, a pair of medical scissors and two tubes of ointment, one of them with the legend "sterilized"— probably Vaseline.

In the Republican positions and its surroundings we found a remarkable number of personal objects, elements of dress and equipment and other items. The finds reveal that soldiers did not have a very martial look. Of the five shoes we dug up, three were civilian, one of them an elegant gentleman's shoe that looked misplaced in the muddy trench. It was not the only unlikely garment: we found the button of a pea coat with the insignia of the merchant marine. While the nearest coast lies 500 kilometers away from Madrid, marine coats were warm and tough and therefore highly valued by the troops. Soldiers' belongings include a lighter made with a shell casing, coins and religious objects. Regarding currency, we found a Republican *peseta* (Spain's currency unit from 1868 to 2002) dated 1937 and a 10-cents coin from the time of Alphonse XII, dated 1879. As we will see throughout the book, pre-Republican currency is considerably more abundant than that of the 1931–1939 period. Coins of one peseta, however, are frequent in Republican lines and evince the different fates of the economy in the Republican and National sector: in the latter, it is mostly cent coins that we find. This is because the depreciation of the peseta did not stop in government-held territory and by 1939 the value of a Republican peseta was one sixth of a Nationalist one: this, however, had more of a psychological impact than an economic one, according to historian Ángel Viñas (2006: 309–310). Religious elements are paradoxically more abundant in the Republican lines of the University City than in the Nationalist. In the latter we found only one crucifix, whereas in the Republican trenches we recovered two medals and a crucifix, which shows that Catholics, despite Nationalist propaganda, were common among the Republican lines and that they did not hide their beliefs—at least after the revolutionary moment of 1936. One of the medals represents Our Lady of the Pillar, in Zaragoza, and the other Saint Anthony of Padua with a child. The latter looks like the typical gift from a mother or grandmother. We have seen in the previous section that political insignias were common in the Nationalist base at the Asylum of Santa Cristina. It is quite surprising that the only ideological elements in the Republican sector are Christian symbols.

All quiet on the University front?

According to a 1937 document, the soldiers of the 40 Mixed Brigade complained of "the poor condition of the weapons and their lack of homogeneity, which often causes problems when loading, and the bad

90   *Capital of misery*

quality of reloaded ammunition, which provokes injuries when the rifles explode".[8] The situation seems to have improved throughout the war, if we are to judge from the archaeological record, because in those places of the University City where we have found Republican occupation levels of the last months of the conflict, all ammunition belongs to Soviet 7.62 mm cartridges. Shell casings are generally scarce. This is probably related to systematic recycling policies: on 13 May 1937, an order of the 7 Division to the 40 Brigade urged soldiers to collect all spent casings. The two lines of Republican trenches that we have excavated and surveyed are riddled with bullets and artillery shell fragments: we found some 200 fragments of artillery shells and 300 bullets, only a fraction of which can be related to the Battle of Madrid in 1936 (see Chapter 3). Violence at the University City continued unabated for the entire duration of the conflict, even in those subsectors that were considered quiet.

Some of the bullets and shell fragments that we documented during our survey might be related to the offensive against Mount Garabitas in Casa de Campo, in April 1937, which ended in total disaster for the Republic (de Vicente Montoya 2016). One of the main lines communicating the rearguard and the frontline passed through the area that we surveyed and excavated. It petered out in front of a concrete bridge under La Coruña road, which is still in use today. The space under the bridge, which was very wide, was used as an improvised field hospital during the Garabitas offensive. A veteran gave a harrowing testimony:

> "There were stretchers there with over a hundred wounded and as many half-seated. I suppose that among those lying on the cots some were already dead, and the trucks and ambulances with the dead and wounded did not stop loading. Our spirits sank before such sight, also because we were hearing the roar of the fighting not far from there. We cross the bridge in a single line and pass near Puerta de Hierro, which was around 500 meters away, and then advance through a one-meter wide and two-meter deep evacuation trench... The ditch's width did not allow us to pass by comfortably and sometimes we were stained with the blood of the wounded. In the meanwhile, the roar did not stop—a constant boiling of automatic machines and huge explosions that we felt closer and closer..."
>
> (Ramón Parra Gallego, 69 Mixed Brigade, testimony
> gathered by Luis de Vicente Montoya[9])

Some artillery impacts could still be seen on the bridge before it was remodeled a few years ago. But there were other cases of shooting and shelling at the University City: on 13 October 1938, for example, a report informs that the Nationalist artillery fired 20 rounds over Puerta de Hierro (the sector of the Republican trenches that we excavated),[10] and only a few days before the end of the war, the diary of the 7 Division still records

Capital of misery 91

"relieving of sentries, blowing of countermines, little activity, enemy shots".[11].Historians might have forgotten the campus after December 1936. But the war—a dull, sordid war—continued taking lives and wounding soldiers until the end.

The underground city

Misery was definitely not an exclusive military experience. In fact, it was civilians who suffered it more acutely. The number of non-combatants who died as a result of the conflict is far greater than those in the military. In Madrid, the victims of political violence alone include over 12,000 on both sides (including Republicans executed as late as the mid-1940s). To these we have to add people killed in bombings—1,500 until April 1937 (Solé i Sabaté and Villarroya 2003: 60)—and the more difficult to calculate victims of disease and starvation provoked by the war. Considering the high number of casualties that diseases were inflicting in the better-fed military population, the numbers among civilians were surely very high. It would probably not be an exaggeration to hypothesize 20,000 to 30,000 civilian dead including all causes, which is perhaps four or five times the number of people killed in the Battle of Madrid and the subsequent war of attrition in the city. In this section I would like to examine two phenomena of violence against non-combatants: artillery and aerial bombing and the extrajudicial executions committed under the cloak of revolutionary or popular justice in the capital.

City in flames

On 30 October 1936, seven days before the beginning of the Battle of Madrid, the Condor Legion bombed Getafe, some 20 km south of the city, and destroyed a school, killing 60 children (Reverte 2007: 196). It was a gruesome prelude to what was awaiting Madrid. In fact, the capital had experienced air raids before: the first took place in the night of the 27 to 28 August and was carried out by Italian planes. Madrid would become the first metropolis to suffer a strategic bombing campaign and although the figures pale in comparison with cities razed during the Second World War, the truth is that entire neighborhoods, most notably Argüelles, near the University City, were devastated by raids (Moreno Aurioles and García Amodia 2018). The aerial campaign, which developed in relation to the Battle of Madrid, lasted for about three weeks. From early 1937 onwards, bombing was less intense and erratic and it was carried out basically by the artillery batteries located in Casa de Campo, as bombers were transferred to more active fronts (de Vicente González 2015). There is a diversity of archaeological traces of the attacks on the city: the bombs themselves, which are routinely discovered during construction works (artillery shells much more commonly than aviation bombs); traces of bomb impacts, which are still ubiquitous, particularly in the district of Argüelles and Centro; artillery

92 Capital of misery

bases, and bomb shelters. Our archaeological knowledge of them is disparate. Unfortunately, there is not a precise record of the places where unexploded ordnance has been retrieved, although the number of explosives destroyed or deactivated by the police is known. The official number is 2,277 in the region of Madrid from 1985 to 2018, of which 306 are in the city itself, according to a recent investigation conducted by two journalists.[12] However, only one is an aviation bomb and artillery shells account for 38 of the findings, the rest being hand grenades (238), mortar projectiles (22) and other elements. The numbers are a gross underestimation, considering what I know from other sources (including members of the police and my own experience). The official record for the entire country is 35,000 unexploded ordnance recorded by the police since 1985.

Traces of impacts on facades of buildings that were far from any site of military relevance offer clear proof of the indiscriminate character of the attacks. That the bombing was not only motivated by strictly military reasons is nowhere better seen than in the powerful map produced by architects Enrique Bordes and Luis de Sobrón. Drawing on archival documentation produced by the city authorities (and particularly the firefighter squads), they have been able to locate every building impacted by bombs.[13] The map shows that Argüelles was the most affected part of the city, with 84% of the buildings damaged by the beginning of 1937 (Figure 4.7). The neighborhood was considered part of the frontline and it was the area through which the Nationalist forces were supposed to be advancing into the city. Extensive bombing in two other points can be linked to military operations as well: the neighborhoods south of the Manzanares River, around the bridges of Segovia and Toledo, which were two of the main access points to downtown Madrid. Yet the map also shows very intensive bombing in the city center, in the area of Puerta del Sol and Gran Vía, as well as damage to buildings in virtually any other neighborhood. The Nationalist command had divided the capital into two sectors: a war zone and a non-war zone, including a neutral sector that was not to be bombed. The neutral zone was located in the eastern part of the city and comprised, very conveniently, the high-class Salamanca neighborhood. The non-war category did not mean that the area was not to be bombed—this was the prerogative of the neutral zone only. It meant that attacks there did not have an explicit military purpose.

Aerial raids, however, account only for a fraction of the explosives dropped in Madrid during the war. According to calculations by Pablo Schell (personal communication, April 2019), less than 8% of all the bombings in Madrid were carried out by airplanes. They had a great psychological impact, but as the war of attrition set in, it was an earlier weapon—the cannon—that took the initiative. In total, Madrid was bombed 75% of the days that lasted the siege and most of the attacks against the non-war zone were purely retaliatory in nature. They were the response to a Republican raid or the explosion of a mine in the frontline.

Capital of misery 93

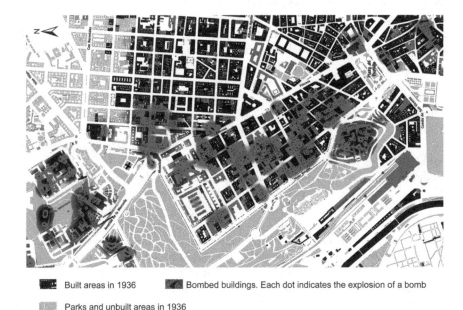

Figure 4.7 Detail of the map of the bombing of Madrid representing the neighborhood of Argüelles and the University Hospital sector (below left).
Notes: The original in color has been modified for reproduction in grey scale. The full map is available here: https://www.madridbombardeado.es
Source: © Enrique Bordes and Luis de Sobrón.

Artillery bases were located mainly in Casa de Campo. Within this park, the so called "Guns of Garabitas" became a sort of mythological monster feared and hated by the citizens of Madrid—but also seen as a symbol of hope among Nationalist sympathizers. Madrilenians believed that the Nationalists bombed the city from Mount Garabitas, which looked like a perfect place, because it dominated the entire skyline of the city. Thus, a pro-Nationalist living in Madrid at the time described it as a "defiant hill, smoky with guns" (Borrás 1963: 164). Instead, Luigi Longo (1956: 132), a communist leader with the International Brigades, wrote: "From the heights of Garabitas, powerful guns, turning on steel platforms, methodically drop on Madrid a rain of grenades over the houses, squares and streets of the city". One of the popular poems (*romances*) that proliferated during the war went: "From Garabitas come/black shells filled with sorrow/because they destroy the houses/that are the oldest and meanest" (Salaún 1982: 132).[14]

Despite its prominent role in the collective imagination, the truth is that there were never guns in the hill. It is a matter of common sense. Artillery pieces are not placed on elevations in modern warfare because they are an easy target for counter-battery fire and aerial bombing. Instead, they can be located in foothills or slopes, in places where they can be easily moved and camouflaged. Mount Garabitas was actually involved in the bombing, but as an observatory, connected with the batteries at its feet. A survey of the hill documented a belt of trenches surrounding the hilltop with many fire bays, dugouts and two concrete pillboxes for antitank guns (Garfi 2019a: 30). It was inexpugnable, as the Republicans that tried to capture it knew well.

One of the battery sites was pointed out to us by an amateur metal detectorist. It is located almost one kilometer away to the west of the hilltop. The function of the place was obvious: we documented six large dugouts of the size of a howitzer and a little further to the south, a long berm which could have been used to place a few more guns (Figure 4.8). The base is naturally defended by a hillock, on whose slope the dugouts were excavated. The metal detector survey of the site delivered plenty of evidence related to the artillery battery. In front of one of the dugouts we found dozens of sheaths used to wrap the Garrido fuses before they were set up on the artillery shells. The Garrido M1924, designed by Colonel Antonio Garrido Valdivia, was the standard fuse with the Spanish Army and could be used with many of the standard shells of the period (70, 75, 105 and 155 mm).[15]. We also retrieved some transport plugs, which are screwed in place of the fuse when the shells are moved. In another dugout we recovered more plugs and a primer, which is a small cylinder with an explosive charge used for initiating the propellant combustion that will push the grenade out of the howitzer. It was produced by the arms factory of Seville (Pirotécnica Sevillana) and dated in 1937.

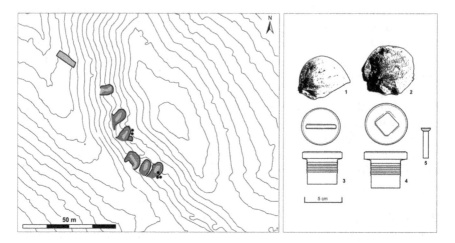

Figure 4.8 A Nationalist artillery base in Casa de Campo and associated finds.
Notes: 1–2. Fuse sheaths; 3–4. Transport plugs; 5. Primer.
Source: © Manuel Antonio Franco Fernández and author.

Capital of misery 95

If we trace lines following the axes of the dugouts, we can see that five of the guns were aiming at the northwest of Madrid and could not have hit the city, except perhaps Tetuán, a working-class neighborhood in the north which was actually bombed. Two of the structures are in enfilade with the Republican positions north of the University City, precisely the area where we conducted our survey and excavations. Three others could have hit the area around the strategic San Fernando Bridge and the Republican base at Club Puerta de Hierro behind. Finally, a sixth dugout is oriented towards the central part of the University City (the School of Medicine, which was an important Republican position) and the middle-class neighborhood of Chamberí, which was also shelled during the war. Both Tetuán and Chamberí are located within a 6 km radius from the battery, that is, well within the range of the typical 155 mm howitzer of the kind deployed by the Nationalists in Casa de Campo.

Archaeology helps provide a different perspective on the myth of Garabitas. It shows the actual location of the guns, but this is not the most interesting point. What archaeology makes more clearly visible is the *chaîne operatoire* of bombing. A grenade that explodes in a house in Madrid requires somebody transporting the shells to the battery and unboxing them, another one unloading the shells, unscrewing the transport plug, unwrapping the fuse and screwing the fuse in the shell; somebody has to load the grenade in the howitzer and set up the primer and somebody else fire the load that will travel six kilometers to the city. There it will kill somebody in the street, perhaps a woman or a child, or mutilate a soldier in his trench.

Modern weapons are sophisticated. Their working depends on lengthy technical processes with many steps that require full attention and involve several persons. This is essential to dissolve the feeling of guilt after a military action. Historian Sönke Neitzel and sociologist Harald Weltzer in their analysis of the conversations among German soldiers recorded in secrecy by the Allies during the Second World War conclude that to perpetrate an atrocity or to participate enthusiastically in the German war machine it was not necessary to be a convinced Nazi (Neitzel and Weltzer 2012): it sufficed to be willing to fulfill military obligations. This was not just about obeying orders or not disappointing officers and comrades, it was also about the satisfaction that came out of completing entrusted tasks successfully. The same happens in any army: "The immediate social environment, the modern work ethic, and fascination with technology may indeed yield something like a 'universal soldier'", argue Neitzel and Weltzer (2012: 339–340). The soldiers' attention is primarily focused on things at hand, things as banal as unwrapping a fuse, unscrewing a plug, setting up a primer… Why should the soldier responsible for firing the shell feel more responsible than those in the observatory who located the target or the officers who decided which target had to be hit? In this complex technical sequence, everybody is guilty, which is the same as saying nobody.

96 *Capital of misery*

Apart from technical aloofness there is also physical distance. The servicemen who were mounting shells at the feet of Garabitas did not see children running in panic through the streets of Madrid and did not hear soldiers screaming while bleeding to death. They only saw the fuse, the transport plug, the primer, the shell, the gunpowder. Zygmunt Bauman (1989) has argued that twentieth-century mass violence cannot be understood if we do not consider the production of distance—both spatial and emotional. A shell fired in Casa de Campo has to travel six kilometers to Tetuán to kill. It is not like shooting somebody in the head—but it is. Distance is created in three ways. Technically—through artifacts that separate executioners and victims; geographically—when we displace violence or exploitation far from our homes (as with sweatshops or the ecological devastation brought up by capitalist predation), and discursively—through concepts that deprive others of their humanity (reds, Jews, bourgeois, priests).

Madrid could be defended against bombs in different ways. In military parlance, we talk about passive and active defense. Passive defense, according to the US military includes "Measures taken to reduce the probability of and to minimize the effects of damage caused by hostile action without the intention of taking the initiative"—such as air raid shelters. Active defense, instead, implies "limited offensive action"—like anti-aircraft or counterbattery fire (Naval Education and Training Command 1993: 5–7, AI5). We found archaeological traces of active defense during our survey of the University City (González-Ruibal et al. 2019). The most intriguing element appeared underneath a dugout. The shelter had probably been built in 1938, when large fortification works were undertaken in the sector, and soldiers reused a previous structure excavated in the ground. It formed a perfect arrow and it was pointing toward the enemy lines (see Figure 4.6). Given its size (2x2.5 m), it could have been seen by an airplane flying at low altitude, especially if it was painted or lighted in some way. These kind of earthen signals were used during the Spanish Civil War to transmit information about the location of the enemy as well as other relevant details (such as the presence of anti-aircraft guns), but no information about them has been published. Aviation signals were particularly needed in Madrid, where the situation was chaotic in 1936 and many pilots were Russian and therefore unacquainted with the city. The Polikarpovs I-16, one of the most advanced fighters of the time, had arrived in Spain on October 27 (Viñas 2006: 356) and on November 13 they had their baptism of fire over Madrid, successfully intercepting a bombing raid.

Republicans could also rely on anti-aircraft guns to make life difficult for enemy airplanes. During our surveys, we found the cone that contained the fuse of a 76.2 mm shell fired by the Soviet M-1931 gun (Figure 4.9). The M-1931 shot two kinds of shells, one with iron segments that scattered after explosion and the other one filled with shrapnel (lead bullets). It is to this second kind of shell that our cone belongs. The first documented cargo of 76.2 mm guns arrived on 6 January 1937 (Howson 2000: 391). We also found

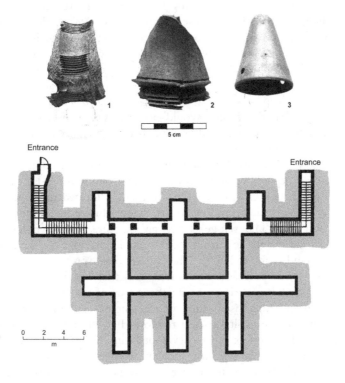

Figure 4.9 Active and passive defense in Madrid.

Notes: Above: 1–2. Fuses from anti-aircraft gun Flak 18, used by the Nationalists; 3. Cone from a 76.2 mm Soviet anti-aircraft gun, used by the Republicans. Below: map of the underground shelter of the Artillery Workshop.

Source: © Author (map modified after Álvaro Valdés, n.d.).

evidence of Nationalist anti-aircraft fire in the same place, more specifically, two fuses of the legendary German 88 mm Flak 18. One of the iconic weapons of the Second World War, the Flak 18 was widely used in Spain, both as an antitank and an anti-aircraft gun, its original role. In the case of the University City, it was used as an anti-aircraft gun, but it was not during the Battle of Madrid: Germany sent 71 Flak-18s to the Condor Legion, 24 of which went to Spanish troops between January and March 1937 (Manrique and Molina 2006: 198–199).

Material testimonies of passive defense—bomb shelters—are both abundant and understudied in the capital. In fact, going underground would be the general trend in modern warfare from the Battle of Madrid onwards. It is what geographer Stephen Graham (2004b) has called "vertical geopolitics". Against the horizontal dimension of geopolitics (battlefields, borders, alliances between nation-states), the vertical axis extends from the deepest antinuclear shelters to the satellites of the exosphere. The underground world belongs to

98 *Capital of misery*

partisans, terrorists and civilians fleeing from a war that respects nobody; the air is for the powerful. During the Spanish Civil War underground cities grew under the pavement. This happened near the frontline in Madrid and neighboring cities—Alcalá de Henares and Guadalajara (Schnell and Moreno 2010)—but also in other places, sometimes very far away from the line of fire, such as Barcelona and Cartagena on the Mediterranean coast (see Chapter 8). In the capital, construction work started in January 1937, once it became obvious that the capital would not fall into Nationalists' hands but they were not leaving either, and continued throughout the war (Castellano Ruiz de la Torre 2007: 109).

Unfortunately, very few of them have been systematically studied and none is open to the public. As far as I am aware, only two shelters have been the object of archaeological work. One of them is located in El Retiro Park in the center of Madrid, very close to the Prado Museum—where incendiary bombs fell in 1936. The refuge is a large structure with two levels, three entrances and a capacity for around 200 people. It was dug at a depth of eight meters and had toilets.[16] The other one was under an artillery workshop that made precision instruments and that had been built between 1899 and 1905 in Chamberí, in the northern part of the city (Valdés n.d.). It was a fine building that used some of the engineering innovations of the period (the first in the capital to use reinforced steel) and it was part of the military-industrial complex that developed in Madrid during the late nineteenth century. This did not prevent its demolition in 2017, which unveiled the Civil War shelter under the foundations (Madrid Ciudadanía y Patrimonio 2016; Cano and Mendoza 2017). The structure was constructed in 1938 and with a surface of 218 square meters had capacity for up to 872 people, if we use the calculations of the Commission for Passive Defense in Alicante of four people per square meter (Lozano and Lumbreras 2015: 375) or half that figure with the numbers of Barcelona's Commission—two to three people per square meter (Miró and Ramos 2010: 61). Other shelters that have been found in Madrid had a similar capacity. Test pits conducted inside the shelter of the artillery workshop were unable to find traces related to the Civil War. However, part of the original electric system that provided light to the structure was visible on the walls. Its users in this case were not civilians, but the personnel of the artillery workshop, which remained active throughout the war producing explosives.

Shelters adopted different layouts, but the basic structure was an L-plan, to prevent shell fragments, rubble or the blast from hurting the people inside. More common, however, was the U-plan. Different elements could then be added, such as perpendicular galleries or rooms, as in the artillery workshop. All spaces were for collective use and shared similar features: the entrance (of which there were at least two, in case one collapsed) was through a hatchway with double-shutter steel doors that gave access to the stairs; the refuges were made of exposed brick and had vaulted roofs. They had electricity and often toilets and brick-and-concrete benches attached to the walls. Shelters in

Madrid were typically built at a depth of eight to ten meters and the brick roofs were simply covered with dirt and not with concrete. This, however, was enough to stop the impacts of 100 kg aviation bombs (the kind most commonly used against the city) and more than enough against the 155 mm artillery shells. In 1937, shelters took two months to be completed, but the time increased as construction material became scarcer (Morcillo 2007). The quality of the construction is outstanding, considering the difficulties and the haste in which they had to be built and evinces a real concern for the safety of the civilian population.

Even greater care was taken to protect politicians, high-ranking officers and diplomats. In Madrid, the military command, led by General José Miaja, had its refuge outside Madrid, in El Capricho Park—known by its codename Posición Jaca (Morcillo 2007). This was a gas-proof, bomb-proof complex with thick reinforced concrete roofs and bullet-proof doors. It had electric generators, a water reservoir and pipe system and an advance ventilation system, latrines, septic tank, telegraph and telephone. Inside, 200 people could live inside isolated for two weeks in a prelude to the asphyxiating total war atmosphere typical of the years to come.

Extermination

Another subterranean city emerged after the coup of July 18: the city of mass graves and torture centers. The city of revolutionary violence. There is very little we can say archaeologically about it, because mass graves were either exhumed, memorialized or both after the war—although, as noted in Chapter 2, forensic reports of the 1940s offer a fascinating insight that deserves to be explored in detail. Regarding centers of detention, they were popularly known as *checas* (from the Soviet Cheka) and were lodged in preexisting buildings (train stations, cinemas, convents). Once they were closed, they reverted to their original use and all traces of their brutal past were erased. Still, there is something of the atmosphere of the war that seems to have survived in some of these places. This is the case, for instance, with the *checa* of Fomento Street, number 9, one of the most feared centers (Preston 2012a: 332, 400), which was active between August 26 and November 9. The *checa* was, officially, a Provincial Committee of Public Investigation, where representatives from the different parties of the Popular Front delivered revolutionary justice. The truth, however, is that the *checas* were sites of brutal and arbitrary violence. The one in Fomento Street was established in a palace in the center of Madrid that has seen virtually no changes since 1939. Despite being very close to Gran Vía—the busiest avenue in Madrid—Fomento is usually empty of people and cars, very much as it was during the war. Unlike most other streets, it is still cobbled and silent. The atmosphere of the place (its sound and texture) has changed little in 80 years. Many people were tortured here, some until they died; many were taken from the building to the outskirts of Madrid and killed, among

100 *Capital of misery*

other places to the cemetery of Aravaca. Others died in detention, due to the beatings or, in one documented case, out of pure fear. It became again a place of horror in 1939–1940, when the new regime used it as an interrogation center by the Brigada Político-Social, Franco's secret police (Ruiz 2014: 330). Today, there is no memorial or plaque to commemorate the victims – neither those who suffered revolutionary violence nor Francoist reprisals.

Although it is difficult to document much of the ephemeral materiality of political repression in wartime Madrid, it is indeed possible to study the landscapes and itineraries of violence, that is, the places through which the victims passed through their ordeal: detention, seclusion, torture, execution, burial. There were around 200 *checas* in Madrid during the early months of the war (Preston 2011: 357). As pointed out above, the reutilization of buildings was the norm and would also characterize Francoist terror and later political violence in Latin America. It means that any space can be converted into a space of torture and therefore that terror is everywhere. It is a particularly perverse and effective microphysics of power, in which violence permeates the entire urban fabric. During the nineteenth and early twentieth century, the prison was clearly demarcated, jails were built in specific places of the city—usually the margins— and their function was manifest in its peculiar architecture. Everything changed during the Spanish Civil War: every building could be a prison and imprisonment was no longer something that happened in the urban fringe, but at the very heart of the city. A similar phenomenon was independently taking place at the same time in Stalinist Moscow. In both cases, violence was seen as foundational by the revolutionaries. Consequences were of the first order: in the same way that any building could be a detention center, anybody could be an executioner—or a victim. In this ambiguity lay the effectivity of terror.

While detention occurred at the center, illegal and para-legal executions occurred in the urban periphery: roadsides and parks filled with corpses. For the criminals, Madrid offered the advantage of being surrounded by parks: the murders and the disposal of corpses took place in the large parks of El Pardo, Casa de Campo, Dehesa de la Villa and Pradera de San Isidro, that form an arch from the south to the west of the capital. Unlike what was the rule in the Nationalist zone, however, Republican authorities documented the corpses, took photographs of the crime scenes, opened forms with all relevant data to facilitate identifications and the relatives were contacted whenever possible (Ledesma 2010: 191–192). The geography of terror in Madrid, therefore, was divided into three zones. In the first place, a central core, in which we find the *checas* and detention centers. This is the urban area proper: streets are put at the service of the perpetrators, who move swiftly around in cars or trucks looking for victims. In this same zone there is another kind of underground city: the hideouts where right-wing people tried to pass unnoticed, including penthouses, basements, boiler rooms and even elevator shafts (Montoliú 1998: 86). Around this central core we have the green belt of individual or small-group executions, which worked as an exhibitor for corpses. Here, we can include the cemeteries that surround Madrid. The third ring was that of the large mass graves with hundreds or thousands of victims, conveniently removed from the city: around seven kilometers to the northwest, Aravaca. Twenty kilometers to the northeast, Paracuellos. In Republican Madrid, 8,815 people were assassinated by revolutionaries, mostly during the first few months of the war (Espinosa 2010: 78). For many, the city of misery became a graveyard.

Notes

1 AGMAV, C.474, Cp.7, D.1.
2 AGMAV, A.474, Cp.7, D.1.
3 A description of such heterodox use of mattresses during the Battle of Belchite can be found in Izquierdo (2006): 21–22.
4 http://avpiop.com/es/patrimonio/elma_s-a-/18.
5 AGMAV, A.72, L.1.132/R.182/Cp. 15–16/Cj. 959.
6 AGMAV, C.792/Cp. 11, D.1.
7 AGMAV, A.70, L. 1051–1054, R. 155–156, CJ. 881–884.
8 AGMAV, A.74, L.1.185/R. 193/Cp. 1–17/Cj. 1012.
9 http://frentedebatalla-gerion.blogspot.com/2010/09/operacion-garabitas-testimo nios-la.html.
10 AGMAV, A.70/L. 1051–1054/R. 155–156/Cj. 881–884.
11 AGMAV, A.70/L. 1051–1054/R. 155–156/Cj. 881–884.
12 https://elpais.com/politica/2019/03/29/actualidad/1553889697_864651.html.
13 www.madridbombardeado.es.
14 Desde Garabitas vienen/obuses negros de pena/porque destrozan las casas/más ruines y más viejas.
15 http://amonio.es/espoleta_garrido_mod24.htm.
16 https://www.publico.es/politica/madrid-redescubre-refugio-guerra-civil.html.

5 The path to total war

February–October 1937

The nature of war in Spain changed in 1937. The symmetrical non-conventional conflict of 1936, characterized by a "primitive" form of warfare, in which small units (columns and militias) fought against each other with little heavy weaponry, came to an end during the early months of the year. The conflict then morphed into symmetrical conventional war, with large battles fought by two regular armies with the massive support of aviation and artillery. The transition occurred in Madrid in the autumn of 1936, as we saw in the previous chapter, but the shift was not complete until February 1937. The story of the Spanish Civil War during this year is the story of its massive offensives, both Republican and Nationalist: Jarama, Guadalajara, Vizcaya, Brunete, Zaragoza, Asturias and Teruel. The Battle of Teruel, which started on December 15, marked the apex of large-scale military operations: the first actual example of total war in Spain according to historian David Alegre (2018). In a sense, then, the year was a long and bloody path toward total war. This can be seen in the tens of thousands of casualties, enormous material losses and mass mobilization of men and means that characterized each of the battles fought between Jarama and Teruel.

A change in the nature of war meant a change in its materiality as well. War in 1937 became heavier and more solid: shallow trenches and improvised barricades gave way to complex systems of fortifications in which reinforced concrete was frequently used; war-related infrastructures, such as air-raid shelters and airfields proliferated; the volume of war debris increased exponentially, and military artifacts became more standardized and modern. Archaeological visibility, therefore, increased with conventional warfare. Strongly related to the transformation of non-conventional to conventional war is the greater control exercised by the Republic over its own territory. The militias were replaced by the new Popular Army, which was able to muster 750,000 men and hundreds of tanks and airplanes, and there was a drastic decline in murders and other forms of violence behind the lines. Of those vanishing militias we have some extraordinary testimonies in Aragón, where we have recorded graffiti of anarchist and communist units, which were still active in the area during the early months of 1937 (Figure 5.1). The repetition of the

Figure 5.1 Inscriptions with the acronyms of different militias in Mojón del Lobo, near Belchite (Aragón).
Source: © Author.

acronyms, usually with little other information, was a performative act of self-assertion: those who have never had a voice now shout. And they shout their collective identity to the world: Unite Proletarian Brothers (UHP), Iberian Anarchist Confederation (CNT), Iberian Federation of the Libertarian Youth (FIJL), Anarchist Iberian Federation (FAI). The revolutionary dream ended between May 1937—when communist-backed Republican authorities crushed the anarchists and other revolutionary factions, as masterfully described by Orwell (1980)—and August 1937, when the libertarian Council of Aragón was dissolved. With the revolution over, revolutionary violence also stopped. It had left almost 4,000 dead in Aragón alone (Espinosa 2010: 78).

In this chapter, we will follow the development of the war in 1937 through some of the scenarios that have benefitted from archaeological research: the Jarama valley, Guadalajara, Aragón and the Northern Front (the Basque Country, Asturias and León). Although archaeological information is still limited and fragmentary, it provides an accurate and often moving picture of this eventful year.

The last Nationalist attempts to take Madrid

As we saw in Chapter 3, the Nationalist command eventually gave up direct attempts at conquering Madrid after a series of battles on La Coruña road, which ended on 15 January 1937. The rebels then decided to try their hand

104 *The path to total war*

from other directions, with bids to surround the capital and cut off its communications with the rest of the Republican territory. The first such attempt was the Battle of Jarama, between the 6 and 27 of February (Beevor 2006: 290–297). The fighting ended in stalemate. Both sides suffered great losses (18,000 casualties in total) and the rebels failed to enter the capital. The battle would remain in the collective memory not just of Spaniards, but also of many British and Americans, since it was the baptism of fire for the XV Brigade, made up of the British and Abraham Lincoln Battalions. Archaeological research has been conducted on the Jarama front (Penedo et al. 2008; Penedo et al. 2009; Crespo Fraguas et al. 2019), Guadalajara and further south in Toledo (Carrobles and Morín 2014; Ruiz Casero 2015, 2017; Ruiz Casero and Vega 2019). I will review here the evidence for the battles of Jarama and Guadalajara, as the combats of Toledo were independent of the attempts to capture Madrid, despite its proximity to the capital.

The archaeology of the Battle of Jarama

Between 2002 and 2006 the Jarama area, southeast of Madrid, suffered another wave of devastation, this time brought about by a construction boom in and around the city. Construction was usually preceded by surveys and excavations in areas with archaeological potential, including many scenarios of the Battle of Jarama (Penedo et al. 2008). Of all the towns where excavations were carried out, Ciempozuelos yielded the most interesting data that have been published to date. This municipality suffered Nationalist attacks from the first day of the fighting. The 5 Brigade, supported by artillery and tanks, enveloped the village and defeated the 18 Republican Mixed Brigade, which suffered a great number of losses (around 1,300 men, almost half of its members) and was forced to surrender the position.

Excavations at the Republican stronghold of La Sendilla revealed a complex system of trenches, foxholes, underground galleries and a dugout, in which archaeologists found inkpots, an artillery shell and Lafitte grenades that were probably left by the Nationalists after capturing the place, which seems to have been abandoned hastily (Penedo et al. 2008) (Figure 5.2). There was abundant unspent Mauser ammunition and even an intact Ferrobellum, a Republican stick grenade which, unlike the iconic German *Stielhandgranate*, was a fragmentation—and therefore defensive—bomb. They were built in great quantities by the collectivized company Ferrobellum (hence the name) in Madrid (Manrique and Molina 2006: 117). The most surprising finding, however, were six sealed bottles still containing water. The fortification had a very interesting structure: trenches were regularly interrupted by "roundabouts" to facilitate the circulation of soldiers. A similar design is found in First World War trenches, which obviously served as a model. From both these roundabouts and trenches emerge foxholes, with bricks laid at their base to prevent soldiers from sinking into the sandy floor.

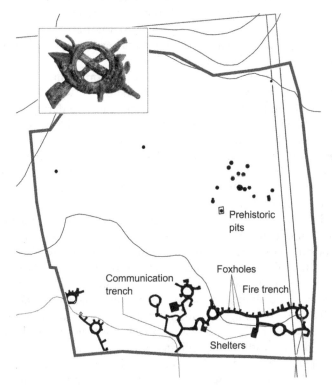

Figure 5.2 Trenches of La Sendilla, in the Jarama frontline, and an infantry insignia found during excavations. The trench typology, with protruding firing positions and no zigzags, is typical of early fortifications.

Source: © Eduardo Penedo Cobo.

Another part of the defensive system surrounding Ciempozuelos was located in Buzanca, a position of great strategic value, as it had visual control over the route that connected the Spanish Levant with the Peninsula's central plateau. On the line of the excavated trenches, which yielded the usual traces of combat, the remains of two soldiers were exhumed: one under 20 years of age at the time; the other, under 25 (Penedo et al. 2009). Amid their bones there were spent ammunition and Mosin Nagant and Mauser stripper clips, witness to the intense shooting delivered from the position before the soldiers fell. The Mosin rifle was first used in great numbers during the Battle of Jarama: around 75,000 arrived in Spain between January 15 and February 7 (Manrique and Molina 2006: 96). A bullet killed the youngest soldier. It went right through his head from front to back, meaning that he was not trying to escape but remained in his position, facing the enemy. Elsewhere, archaeologists found an individual grave with the remains of another soldier, a man under 30, around 1.60 m tall, and whose life was taken by a bullet

106 *The path to total war*

that perforated his jaw. Next to his body there were several spent Mosin Nagant shell casings. His hand was clasping a cartridge: a combatant ritual indicating that the soldier had died fighting. At the time of the excavation, some elderly people in Ciempozuelos could still remember many Republican soldiers retreating from their positions.

My team and I had the chance to work in the northernmost fringe of the battle of Jarama in the village of Vaciamadrid, in the alluvial plain of the Jarama river. The entire place was wiped out of existence during the combats and it was replaced by a new settlement built in the 1950s at some distance from the original location. Virtually nothing can be seen on the surface, except heaps of overgrown rubble. What remained of the ruins was bulldozed in the 1980s. We conducted a sondage in the vestiges of what had been the town council—an early twentieth-century building with massive brick walls that survived the war despite heavy damage. In fact, members of an extended family of 12 lived as squatters there from 1939 and until they were given a house in the new village in 1959. The excavations yielded a mixture of finds covering virtually the entire history of the place from the Iron Age to the mid-twentieth century. The most abundant remains were of the nineteenth and early twentieth centuries and showed a good standard of living, including fine domestic wares and perfume, alcoholic and medicine bottles. A 0.303 shell casing was found amid the ruins whereas the survey yielded stray Mauser bullets and many artillery and mortar shell fragments. Although in theory within Republican lines, Vaciamadrid was completely exposed to enemy fire from higher positions. It was intensely destroyed by Nationalist artillery fire and sparsely occupied by Republican troops. The rubble is now the home of a thriving community of poppies—an enduring legacy of the war.

Guadalajara is not Abyssinia: the first fascist defeat

After the Jarama offensive failed, the Nationalists tried another route to Madrid, this time from the northeast, across the vast and rural region of Guadalajara. The main road between Barcelona and Madrid (National II or N-II) runs through this province. It looked like an ideal scenario to put in practice the concept of *guerra celere*, "fast war", the Italian equivalent of the German Blitzkrieg, as the mechanized fascist troops could use the road for a quick advance into the capital. It was the Corpo di Truppe Volontarie (CTV) that was to spearhead the offensive. The CTV had been sent by Mussolini to help the Nationalists "liberate Spain" and contribute to the construction of a new fascist Europe (Rodrigo 2016). Up to 35,000 Italian soldiers, supported by four companies of Fiat Ansaldo miniature tanks, 1,500 lorries, 160 field guns and four squadrons of Fiat CR 32 fighters, participated in the attack, with the backup of 15,000 Nationalist soldiers of the Soria Division (Beevor 2006: 299). It started on March 8, but it was slowed down due to snow and fog, which allowed the rather mediocre Republican troops holding the line to retreat in good order. The following day, the International Brigades arrived in the area and stopped the attackers. The brigaders resisted for three days around the small town of Brihuega, which was the furthermost point reached by the CTV—100 kilometers away from Madrid. While the offensive faltered, the rain and the snow rendered the terrain around the N-II into a quagmire, impracticable for the war machinery, which was stuck in the middle of the road and bombed at will by the Republicans. On March 12, the government initiated a counteroffensive that led them, by the 23rd, near their original positions. The CTV had lost 5,000 men and an enormous amount of weapons and vehicles (Beevor 2006: 303). It was a great blow to fascist pride, widely exploited by Republican propaganda. Some of the Italians were veterans from the Italo-Ethiopian War (1935–1936), but, as the Republican song went, "Guadalajara is not Abyssinia, the Reds here throw grenades like pinecones", which was sung to the music of *Faccetta nera*, a Fascist anthem in the Abyssinian Campaign..

The fortifications of the Spanish Civil War in Guadalajara have been the object of thorough surveys and systematically catalogued (Castellano Ruiz de la Torre 2008; 2014), but the great majority postdate the battle itself. The only archaeological project that specifically focuses on the combats of March 1937 was conducted by archaeologist and historian Luis Antonio Ruiz Casero (2019) on the Brihuega sector. Ruiz Casero combined surface survey, the study of materials in local collections, archival sources, memoirs, photographs, aerial imagery and films to produce an accurate reconstruction of one of the iconic episodes of the battle: the combats at the Palace of Ibarra. This was not a minor event, at least in the collective imaginary of the time. It was visited by Ernst Hemingway, written about by André Malraux and mentioned by Mussolini in one of his discourses. It became part of the fascist and antifascist myths.

The Palace of Ibarra was an eighteenth-century manor house near the town of Brihuega and the most advanced position that the Italians would conquer during the offensive. It was surrounded by a thick scrub oak forest, where the CTV dug foxholes and trenches, some of which can still be seen today. On March 14, units of the XII International Brigade backed by T-26 tanks launched an attack through this sector, evicted the Italians from their positions in the forest and surrounded them in the palace. After 20 hours of fighting, most of the fascist combatants had either died or been taken prisoners. Only a handful managed to escape the siege.

The battle of the Palace of Ibarra has been described as a fascist epic, a slaughterhouse, a minor encounter and a perfectly devised Republican operation. As Ruiz Casero (2019) shows, none of this is accurate. The palace itself was destroyed and later demolished and only a few annex buildings survive with war scars. Thus, in order to clarify the events, he had to adopt a forensic architecture approach (Forensic Architecture 2014) and use the extensive corpus of photographs from the palace and written information. In this way, he could discard the most exaggerated estimates of troops and

108   *The path to total war*

casualties, which suggest up to 500 soldiers for the CTV in the palace and 300 dead. Ruiz Casero notes than such overcrowding was physically impossible and by calculating its size and structure and cross-checking with written evidence, he reaches the conclusion that the actual number of defenders in the palace was around 138, of which around a hundred were casualties (43 dead and 59 prisoners). The number of casualties among the Republicans was similar and the soldiers who participated in the assault were only slightly more numerous than the defenders (in a proportion of 1.5:1). The taking of the compound, which required three assaults, was carried out mainly by members of the Franco-Belgian André Marty Battalion of the XII International Brigade, although there were also Italians from the Garibaldi Battalion.

A careful examination of the photographs of the main facade allowed Ruiz Casero to identify 658 small arms impacts and 10 artillery impacts (four from mortars, six from T-26 tanks). The total impacts are probably closer to 1,000, with an obvious concentration around the openings (doors and windows), as not all images allow for a precise identification of bullet traces (Figure 5.3). The dense concentration of fire on the buildings contradicts historians who minimize the intensity of the combats. Fire came from a perimeter wall surrounding the palace at a distance of 50 to 100 meters. Around this perimeter wall, many artifacts have been retrieved, including a large number of Soviet 7.62 mm shell casings, stripper clips and a complete clip. Grenades played a prominent role in the fights in the forest, in the assault on the palace and in the counterattacks that were launched from inside. Two complete grenades discovered in the woods are of the *Tonelete* type and the defensive Polish wz. 33 grenade. Both were used by Republican combatants, as the Italians employed their own equipment only. The support of the Republican T-26 tanks is well attested through the KT-1 fuses. The amount of impacts on the facades of the buildings indicates that soldiers were armed with both rifles and Maxim machine guns. Soviet aid was not limited to armament, though: a 250 g can of pork foie gras was found that had been produced in the factory of Petropavlovsk (Kamchatka), in the Russian far east—10,000 km from Guadalajara.

As for the Italians, they were bringing their own food all the way down from Italy: the tin cans that the Regio Esercito (the Italian military) sent to Spain by the millions are still a common sight in the fields of Guadalajara. They are stamped with the initials of the military administration (AM: *Amministrazione Militare*) and the year (1936). Italian soldiers jokingly read the acronym as *Asino Morto* ("dead donkey"). Italian military remains in the Palace of Ibarra include one clip from a Mannlicher M1895 rifle and another one belonging to the Mannlicher-Carcano M1891. Both were standard weapons with the Regio Esercito widely employed in the First World War and the colonial conflicts (González-Ruibal 2010: 561–562). The CTV soldiers were also armed with Breda M1930 light machine guns, which employed the same ammunition as the Mannlicher-Carcano rifle loaded in magazines of 20 cartridges, and Brixia M1935 mortars, that fired a 45 mm grenade. Elements of both weapons appeared in the forest and near the palace. The fascist troops were generally well armed with the latest weaponry

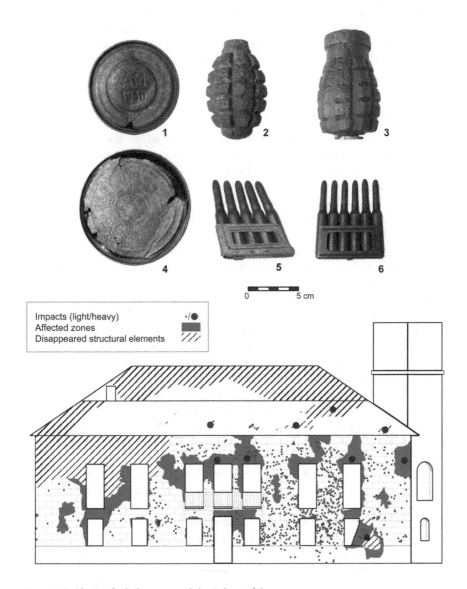

Figure 5.3 Above: finds from around the Palace of Ibarra.

Notes: 1. Italian meat can with the acronym AM (Amministrazione Militare); 2. Polish fragmentation grenade; 3. *Tonelete* fragmentation grenade; 4. Foie gras can from the USSR; 5. Mannlicher 8x56R clip; 6. Mannlicher-Carcano 6.5x52 clip.

Source: © Luis Antonio Ruiz Casero and Esther Garrido Plaza, with modifications.

110   *The path to total war*

delivered by Italian factories. At the same time, the standardized equipment of the CTV exposed them as what they were: not a simple group of volunteers, but a full-fledged corps of the Italian Army illegally fighting a war in Spain. Indeed, Italian weapons, uniforms and war machinery were much publicized by the Republic to depict the conflict as an external aggression.

War in the Basque Mountains

My narrative has focused thus far on Central Spain, where the majority of the most crucial military encounters of the first year of the war took place. The north of the country had remained largely loyal to the Republic and was in a difficult situation: isolated from the rest of the territory and surrounded by Nationalist troops from three sides and by the sea. This created important political, logistical, economic and military problems to the Republic, who had to accept a large measure of autonomy from the authorities (military and civilian) in the Northern Front: the Nationalists, instead, benefitted from a continuous territory. The coup failed in most of Asturias, Cantabria and the larger part of the Basque Country and not by chance: Asturias, a mining region, had a strong Leftist tradition and the Basque Country was ruled by the Basque Nationalist Party (PNV) that, while center-right in its ideology, was strongly opposed to the reactionary Spanish nationalism of the rebels. In the Basque Country, the coup of July 1936 only succeeded in the conservative province of Álava, in the southern plains. The Nationalists managed to occupy almost the entire province of Guipúzcoa by the month of October thanks to the thrust of the bellicose Carlist columns from Navarre. The Carlists, as we saw in Chapter 1, were an ultra-traditionalist group that defended a return to the Ancien Regime. Basque authorities tried to conquer Álava's capital, Vitoria, in December 1936, using the Euzko Gudarostea, the Basque Army recently created by the PNV. The offensive, also known as Battle of Villareal, ended in failure (Beevor 2006: 309).

From that point onwards, the front stabilized and the Basque authorities started the construction of strongholds along the mountains of Vizcaya. The main line of fortifications was built around Bilbao, the largest Basque city, an important industrial hub and an international harbor, from which Republicans received supplies. Work on the line, known as the Steel Belt, started in November 1936 and involved thousands of workers, engineers and architects. Like other similar complexes in interwar Europe, such as the Siegfried and Maginot lines, it turned out to be useless. In this case, the blame has to be pinned not just on the concept, but also on the betrayal of one of its designers, engineer Alejandro Goicoechea, who deserted to the Nationalists with the maps of the fortifications. The Steel Belt is now protected as heritage by the government of the Basque Country and the remains have been systematically inventoried, mainly by the amateur association Sancho de Beurko.[1] At the time of writing, however, no published archaeological work exists. Research, instead, has been conducted on other strongholds of the Basque front that saw heavy action during the Nationalist offensive of spring 1937 (Figure 5.4).

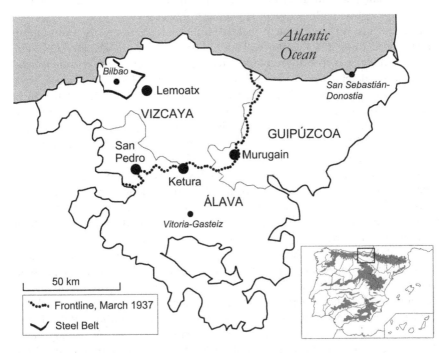

Figure 5.4 The Basque front in 1937 with indication of sites that have been the object of archaeological research and that are discussed in the text.
Source: © Author.

The hills that fell in April

During the first months of 1937, the frontline remained static and Republican soldiers spent their time improving the fortifications. But then, on March 31, the Nationalists launched an offensive on Vizcaya, which started with the carpet bombing of the entire town of Durango, perhaps the first such case in history (Solé i Sabaté and Villarroya 2003: 79). The attack was spearheaded by the fearsome Navarre Brigades, made up mostly of Carlist soldiers. The Republican strongholds began to fall. One of the first was Mount Murugain (Mondragón) (Telleria 2011). In November 1936 the place had become the headquarters of a Dragons Battalion of the Euzko Gudarostea, consisting of members of the communist JSU and the socialist UGT, and they were stationed there until pressure from the Navarre Brigades and their massive artillery support drove them out in the spring of 1937. The Navarre Brigades seized Murugain on April 4 after causing 450 casualties to the enemy, 150 of them fatal. Among the killed was probably soldier number 78539, whose identification tag appeared in front of a trench (Herrasti et al. 2014: 370). Republicans here reused an Iron Age hillfort: the main trench was dug parallel to the prehistoric wall, which made an excellent parapet, but

112 *The path to total war*

a rather inadequate linear fortification. If taken at the right angle, a single hit could do away with all the men defending the sector.

The bottom of the trench yielded hundreds of items of ammunition in situ, something that, as we will see, is typical of most Basque sites. The empty shell casings that archaeologists recovered are related to the end of the Republican defense and are mostly 7.92x57 mm. These cartridges were employed in the ZB vz. 24, a Czech Mauser, which was one of the most advanced bolt-action rifles of the time. They were the first rifles to arrive at the Northern Front and became the standard weapon of the Euzko Gudarostea. Most of the casings are only marked "M". We are not sure about the factory or country that produced them, because the contractor seems to have tried to avoid responsibility under the international arms embargo to Spain. Mexico, Standard Electric (Madrid) and Hirtenberg (Austria) have been suggested. It is not likely, however, that ammunitions made in Madrid during the war would have reached the isolated northern front in any numbers—and Madrid needed every bullet it could muster at least until March 1937. According to oral repots, the cartridges could have been produced in Austria, marked M as if they had been manufactured in Mexico and then put into boxes labeled in French and Spanish, all to fool the embargo.[2] Other cartridges, however, do present well-known markings showing that they were produced in the Czech Republic, Poland and Germany. Most of the German 7.92 mm cartridges were from ageing Great War surpluses and dated to 1917 and 1918. It is likely that they reached the Basque Country through smugglers, although the Nazis did sell some weapons to the Republic in secret—while supporting the Nationalists (Heiberg and Mogens 2005).

Thirty kilometers southeast of Murugain, and near the limit between Álava and Guipúzcoa as well, archaeologists have explored the Republican fortifications of Ketura (Zigoitia) (Santamarina et al. 2018). Like Murugain, they fell in April 1937, but remains of the combats are less abundant—a few shell casings. More interesting are the many graffiti that the soldiers defending the position left on the walls of concrete pillboxes. There are many references to a "Madrid Battalion"; political symbols (the communist hammer and sickle); acronyms (UGT), and slogans ("Long live the Red Army") and dates (10 March 1937). Male personal names are also abundant and varied and often include last names (José Luis Garai, Pablo Mendieta) and rank (Capitán Álvarez), something quite unusual. Particularly mysterious, amid so many male names is a certain Katalina, whose identity could not be ascertained. Male names present in Ketura, instead, have been found in documents and newspapers. We know the fate of three and it was harsh: Pablo Mendieta, for instance, spent six years in concentration camps and prisons before being released in 1943 (Santamarina Otaola et al. 2018: 200). Other soldiers in the sector were less lucky: between 12 and 15 individuals were exhumed from a mass grave in nearby Etxaguen. They were probably communist militiamen from UHP and, according to oral testimonies, they were killed by a direct hit to the house in which they were sheltered (Herrasti et al. 2014: 298).

The Madrid Battalion was a socialist unit within the Basque Army formed in September 1936. The name was given in January 1937 as homage to the resistance of the capital against fascism and the many "Madrid" graffiti in Ketura evince the central place of this city in Republican wartime imaginary. References to communism, in turn, exemplify its strong influence in many socialist organizations during the war. Members of the battalion were also responsible for paintings depicting scenes of bullfighting and flamenco in a nearby church. The researchers note how archaeology problematizes simplistic visions of the Civil War—also those that idealize the vanquished (Santamarina Otaola et al. 2018: 205–206). In the case of the Basque Country, Republican fighters are invariably presented as *gudaris*, Basque Nationalist warriors, but the glorification of Madrid and the Andalusian scenes oddly fit with this perception.

From San Pedro to Mauthausen

Mount San Pedro, in the limit between Álava and Vizcaya, had been captured by the Basque Army during the Battle of Villarreal in December 1936. The hilltop was then heavily fortified with trenches hewn in the limestone and pillboxes, and acted as an effective deterrence against the Nationalists until the end of May 1937. Archaeological work developed in three different sectors (Ayán Vila et al. 2017; Santamarina Otaola et al. 2017; Santamarina Otaola 2019). Sector 1 had a concrete pillbox and was linked through a long communication trench with the other two sectors. Sector 2 had a fire trench with several firing positions—an archaic type of fortification that resembles the one we excavated in Casa de Campo (see Chapter 3)—and Sector 3 three concrete pillboxes connected by a trench (Figure 5.5). Traces of the combats of May were ubiquitous. As in Lemoatx, to which I will refer later, after Republicans lost the position, they launched several counterattacks to retake it, in the last of which (May 31) they managed to hold the mount for a few hours.

In the pillbox of Sector 1 and its immediate surroundings, archaeologists found 138 spent shell casings, over half of them of 7.92 mm caliber and likely shot by Czech Mausers (Ayán Vila et al. 2017: 138–139). The great majority of the ammunition that could be identified came from the Czech Republic (32%) and Germany (25%), followed by France (7%), the US (6%) and Poland (4%). Spanish (4%) and Soviet (1%) casings represent a small fraction of the total. Two of the pillboxes in Sector 3 (3a and 3d) yielded a similar amount of spent ammunition, around 130 casings each, but the type of cartridge indicates that there were different types of weapons in each firing position. Thus, in pillbox 3a and its communication trench, soldiers were armed primarily with either Spanish Mausers or a Hotchkiss machine gun (both firing 7 mm bullets) and Czech Mausers. In pillbox 3d, instead, there was probably a Maxim machine gun, as 42% of the spent shell casings were Soviet 7.62 mm. A third pillbox (3c) did not yield so many finds, but these appeared in its communication trench: a huge number of spent cartridges,

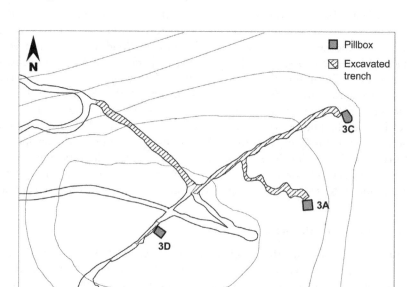

Figure 5.5 Above: Sector 3 in Mount San Pedro, with three pillboxes. Below: the ID tag of militiaman Manuel Mogrovejo (misspelt Manoel Mogrobejo) found in San Pedro.
Source: © Author, based on Santamarina Otaola et al. (2019).

with Czech Mausers again dominating the assemblage (55%). Yet the star find was an ammunition box complete with 281 unused cartridges. They are of the 7 mm type with the mysterious "M" stamp referred above and were ready to be used with a Hotchkiss M1914 machine gun, mounted on 24-cartridge feeding strips. The Hotchkiss was the standard medium machine gun of the French Army during the First World War and was produced under license in Oviedo (in the western part of the Northern Front, but in Nationalist hands). Republicans were also using old Berthier and Lebel rifles, both of which employed 8x50 R mm cartridges, and a few Enfields. As in Sector 1, the geographical provenance of the ammunitions in Sector 2 and 3 is astonishing: Austria, Czechoslovakia, Germany, Poland, United States, Mexico, United Kingdom, the Soviet Union and Spain.

The path to total war   115

Mount San Pedro furnished other relevant finds: one of the pillboxes contained fragments of the newspaper *Euzkadi*, which was the official publication of the Basque Nationalist Party (PNV) between 1913 and 1937. They were from the 5 May 1937 issue and the news that day referred, among other things, to the destruction of Gernika (April 26), the bombing of a town that shocked the world and inspired Picasso's most famous painting, and the evacuation of children through the port of Bilbao (Santamarina Otaola 2019: 49–50). The newspaper contextualizes the drama of the moment: the soldiers who were defending San Pedro were seeing their world falling into pieces: the Basque towns razed to the ground, families torn apart. The soldiers themselves were also torn apart—literally: in one of the trenches appeared two fragments of a skull, doubtless a soldier shattered by the explosion of an artillery shell. Shrapnel was found everywhere in the trenches.

The most poignant find, however, is a hand-made identification tag worn by a Republican soldier (Santamarina Otaola et al. 2019). The plaque reads "Miliciano Manoel Mogrobejo". This allowed the researchers to identify the man and reconstruct his story: Manuel Mogrovejo (his name misspelt on the tag) was born in 1918 and joined a communist militia, the Leandro Carro Battalion in 1936, when he was only seventeen. He lost his tag, but survived the war. We know that he crossed the border with France from Catalonia in April 1939, with the retreating Republican Army. He spent time in the concentration camp of Gurs in southern France (see Chapter 10), which he left to join the French Foreign Legion. In 1940, with the surrender of France, he was captured by the Nazis and sent to a prisoner of war camp in Austria and then to the concentration camp of Mauthausen. At least 7,200 Spaniards were interned there, with the connivance of the Franco regime, and over 5,000 died, but not Manuel. He was liberated by American troops and returned to Spain. He was living in Barcelona, in 1959, still chased by the Franco police—for a minor crime in 1942 that he could not have possibly committed (he was in Mauthausen)— and died in Paris in 1993.

Taken and retaken: Mount Lemoatx

To the other side of the front, very close to Bilbao, another mount was witness to desperate fighting: the Republican stronghold of Mount Lemoatx. Excavations and surveys have uncovered here fascinating archaeological remains related to the combats of late May and early June, a period during which the position was taken and retaken several times by Nationalists and Republicans (Diego 2018). Before the first Nationalist assault, the place was subjected to heavy bombing by the German, Italian and Spanish aviation. The bombs caused many casualties and devastated the fortifications, which had to be repaired. On May 29, the 2 Navarre Brigade stormed and conquered the hilltop after 12 hours of combat. The next day, the Republicans launched the first of several assaults aimed to retake the position. The names of the battalions that charged time and again against the doomed

116 *The path to total war*

mountain speak eloquently of the political diversity within the Republican Army: Gorki, Russia and Rosa Luxemburg (communist), Malatesta and Saco Vanzetti (anarchist) and Simón Bolívar (Nationalist, liberal). The fighting was savage and involved close quarters combat and the massive use of hand grenades. All raids failed until June 2, when Republicans deployed tanks and captured the hilltop. But it was a short-lived victory: three days later Mount Lemoatx was again in the hands of the Navarre Brigade.

As in all the other cases described so far, Republican soldiers fortified the mountaintop. In this case, the structures were not as elaborate as in San Pedro: they were just trenches with machine-gun nests, advanced firing positions and shelters and they were surrounded by barbed wire, but there was no concrete. The trenches were linear, adapted to the terrain, and vulnerable to bombing (Figure 5.6). Archaeologists here excavated over 300 meters of the trench system, which yielded an extraordinary volume of ammunition, much lying in situ on the bottom of the trench. In the NW sector alone, 1,452 cartridges or casings were dug up (Peña et al. 2018a: 125). It is again the stripper clips, rather than the shell casings, that attest to the intensity of the combats: in a six-m^2 unit, the number of Mauser stripper clips was 22, equivalent to 110 shots (Peña Muñoz et al. 2018a: 133). The heterogeneity of the armament is similar to the sites mentioned above, but here 7.92 mm Mausers clearly dominate the assemblage (almost 90% of the finds). In one of the machine-gun nests or firing positions, archaeologists found a carton box with thirty-six 7.92 mm clips. In this case, 75% of the ammunitions came from Germany and were likely used by Franco's troops, as the NW sector, where the casings were found, suffered several Republican counterattacks. The provenance of the rest of the ammunition covers all the countries mentioned so far plus a new one: Hungary. As in San Pedro, cartridges attest to the presence of not just Mausers, but also Lebels or Berthiers, Mannlichers and Enfields (Sampedro et al. 2018: 186–187). An MG08/15 was also used, the German standard machine gun during the First World War, of which part of the feeding belt was found. Like the Mauser, it fired 7.92 mm bullets. Twenty of these weapons were sold by the Germans to the rebel army at the beginning of the war (Manrique and Molina 2006: 128).

The NE sector also yielded much spent and unspent ammunition in situ. The most striking find, however, was the complete carrying equipment of a soldier inside a dugout, including shoulder straps, ammunition pouches, one of them still full of cartridges, and a bayonet scabbard with the bayonet inside (Peña Muñoz et al. 2018a: 141). It seems that the equipment was abandoned in the middle of the fray. It was not the only thing lost: archaeologists retrieved a complete Mauser (except for the wooden parts) in the same sector. Reports on the combats in Lemoatx mention the massive use of grenades in the repeated assaults. Archaeological excavations and surveys have found many parts, belonging to a variety of types (Sampedro et al. 2018: 188–189). They include the common Lafitte and Polish wz. 33 grenades used

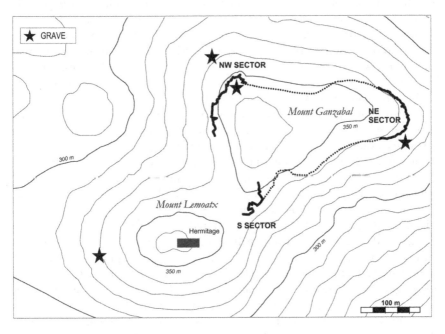

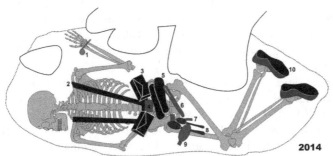

Figure 5.6 Above: Mount Lemoatx and Ganzabal.* Below: the burial of Hilario Blanco Reguero.**

Notes: *The dotted line indicates the trench, thick black line the parts of the trench that have been excavated. Map by author based on Peña Muñoz et al. (2018a). **1. ID tag; 2. Straps; 3. "Garay" ammunition pouches; 4. Buckle with the symbols of the Basque Army; 5. Rubber soles from cloth shoes; 6. Fountain pen; 7. Razors; 8. Spoons; 9. Grenade; 10. Boots.

Source: © Lourdes Herrasti, with modifications by author.

by Nationalists and Republicans, respectively, the French or Russian F-1, a fragmentation grenade from the First World War; the OTO M35 Italian offensive grenade, and two locally made bombs: the so-called "Bilbao" and "Pera Asturiana" (*Asturian pear*). Both were fragmentation grenades, the first manufactured in Derio, close to Lemoatx, which explains its ubiquity at the

118 *The path to total war*

site, and the second—as the name implies—in Asturias. The Bilbao grenade mounted the same kind of fuse as the Polish grenades, but the other had a simple wick. In Asturias, militias made a wide range of improvised bombs and commonly used dynamite: as a mining region, it had plenty of supplies and miners knew well how to handle it: the *dinamiteros* ("dynamite-men") become a true icon of workers' resistance against fascism, which was widely used by the Republic (Álvarez Martínez 2010).

The diversity of light arms ammunition is not just matched, but even surpassed by the heterogeneity of artillery shells that have been recorded during excavations or metal detecting: 14 different guns from 65 to 155 mm produced in Spain, Germany, France, Austria and Italy (Sampedro et al. 2018: 191–192). The variety and quantity of finds gives an idea of what the defenders of the mountain (either Nationalist or Republican) had to endure. The bombs came from howitzers and airplanes. Spanish bombs included the Hispania A6 (50 kg); Germans contributed the SD10 (10 kg) and SD50 (50 kg), and a single piece from an Italian 50 or 100 kg bomb was found. As befits the military scenario, all were filled with high explosive, rather than with flammable material—as happened in Madrid, Durango, Gernika and other cities razed by the Nationalist aviation. It comes as no surprise that many graffiti left by Republican prisoners from the Northern Front in prisons and concentration camps represent bombers and aerial bombing. In the case of the camp of Camposancos, they appear with obsessive repetition and with extraordinary attention to detail: bombs drawn one by one falling from the airplane's belly (Ballesta and Rodríguez Gallardo 2008: 205–206). These graffiti are a chilling testimony of what we would call today post-traumatic stress disorder.

The fortifications of Lemoatx were generally rich in finds—not only ammunition and explosives—ranging from elements of attire to medicines (Peña Muñoz et al. 2018b). Related to attire is a metallic plaque with the coat of arms of the region of Castile and León, of the kind that was worn on the *ros*— a military hat similar to the kepi and used between 1860 and 1933. Typically Basque were a leather coat and a black beret, which could be restored. The attire of the Republicans was a hodge-podge of civilian and military cloth which is well known from historical photographs. Shoes and boots were common—in contrast to the espadrilles frequent in central and southern Spain. Food-related items were surprisingly scarce, but spoons turned up in considerable numbers. Drink was well attested: many bottles of Pedro Domecq sherry, the Nationalists' drink of choice (Peña Muñoz et al. 2018b: 157–158). A peculiar and very Spanish find was the spout of a wineskin (*bota de vino*). Artifacts related to hygiene were represented by plastic toothbrushes, combs, shaving razors, and two rare objects: a can of talcum powder and a shaving brush. Well-preserved medical items include a professional thermometer of the London-based company J. Hicks, several vials still containing medical substances, probably morphine, and a flask of Sloan's liniment. Writing equipment (inkbottles, pencils and mines) was common, as well as newspaper fragments. One of them could be identified

The path to total war 119

as the issue of 18 April 1937 of *El Liberal*, published in Bilbao. This was a center-left publication, associated with the moderate branch of socialism. In fact, the Basque socialist Indalecio Prieto, who led this line within the party, was the director of the newspaper for some time. After *Euzkadi*, it was the second most-read periodical in the Basque Country.

Republicans paid a high toll during the combats: 178 died, for 41 Nationalists (Diego 2018: 75–80). It tells of the politics of reconciliation of the victors that a huge cross commemorated for decades the Nationalist dead, but nothing remembered the fallen Republicans. The bodies of many of them lay buried in improvised graves until very recently (Herrasti and Etxeberria 2018). The archaeological investigation located four graves with the remains of six individuals. In one of the graves lay the body of a member of the Euzko Gudarostea, who was interred with his equipment and personal belongings: ammunition pouches, grenades, shoulder straps, uniform, boots, fountain pen, razors and pocketknife (see Figure 5.6, below). The carrying equipment is of a Basque type called Garay, made of vulcanized fabric and produced in Vizcaya. He also had a belt buckle with the symbols of the Basque Army and an identification tag, which allowed the investigators to find his name: Hilario Blanco Reguero, a Basque militiaman fighting in the Socialist Battalion 28 from the town of Barakaldo. A grenade killed him and many fragments appeared around the skeleton. In the only mass grave found in the area, researchers recovered the remains of three soldiers, one also in the attire of the Euzko Gudarostea. The others did not have any element that could identify them, and were most probably Asturian militias. They may all have fallen victim to artillery fire: they were buried in a crater left by a bomb and one of them had the back of the skull perforated by a shell fragment. He was not yet 20. Neither was one of his other dead comrades. The member of the Euzko Gudarostea was younger than 27 and was carrying a silver crucifix around his neck. Members of the Basque Nationalist Party were usually fervent Catholics and a chaplain was present to assist the wounded and dying during the fighting in Lemoatx. The remains of another young soldier, between 18 and 20 years of age, were found lying in an individual grave. Near his skull appeared his bayonet and Mauser clips. He was also carrying with him a knife and two lighters. Around 12% of all soldiers mobilized by the Republicans in the Basque Country died—7,000 men (Herrasti et al. 2014: 298). The city of Bilbao fell into Nationalist hands on June 19, only one week after the last Republican attempt at recovering Lemoatx. The situation in the Northern Front became desperate for the Republicans.

War: Basque style

The Basque sites have several elements in common: to start with, the heterogeneity of the ammunition and the even greater heterogeneity of its provenance. The panorama in this theater as late as May 1937 is redolent of Madrid in November 1936. The reason is that central Spain could be

120 *The path to total war*

supplied easily from the Mediterranean ports by the USSR, whereas the North remained isolated. Cut off from the rest of loyal territory, but also from the main provider of the legal government, the Basques relied on purchases in the black market. The diversity of the weapons is an eloquent testimony to the difficulties met by Republican authorities in the north to obtain military supplies and their dire situation facing an army massively supported by Italians and Germans and with a high degree of uniformity. While some weapons were modern and efficient (the Czech Mausers), others were old (the Mannlichers or Berthiers) and even modern rifles were often loaded with ammunition that was decades old, as seen in Murugain. Apart from the problems of employing ageing weapons, the diversity of calibers was a challenge during combats, as soldiers could not exchange cartridges and ammunition officers had to have stocks ready for a variety of guns.

Another common characteristic of the Basque sites is the extraordinary volume of spent ammunition recovered in situ. This reflects the intensity of the combats during the spring of 1937 and offers eloquent testimony to the fierce resistance that the northern soldiers put up against the Nationalists, but also, perhaps, to a trigger-happy attitude derived from a lack of proper training, discipline and military experience. In this, again, the Basque positions resemble Madrid in November 1936. There are two further reasons for the abundant finds: on the one hand, once the Nationalists overran the Republican positions, they continued their march toward Bilbao. They did not spend much time in the newly captured fortifications. On the other hand, the rainy spring favored the sedimentation of the trenches, whose floor was covered under a thick layer of mud. Much *matériel*, thus, escaped the attention of the recovery services of the Nationalist army and scrap dealers.

The trenches furnished other artifacts that distinguish the Basque theaters. There is a Basque material culture that was manifested in civilian and military dress (berets, checkered shirts, leather coats, boots) and insignias and symbols (the buckles of the Euzko Gudarostea). The persistence of militias late into the war, which had disappeared from other theaters, is very characteristic and has a material dimension. Their political and military identity was obvious, among other things, in graffiti—as in the repeated mentions to the Madrid Battalion in Ketura. The Basque case shows that many combatants were strongly political and that their beliefs were reinforced through symbolic acts, including writing and wearing insignia. Yet collective identities were not the only relevant ones. The Basque case is unique in the number of identification tags that have been retrieved among Republican forces (Herrasti et al. 2014), far superior to any other region. The reasons for these are manifold and include the interest of the Basque Nationalist government in having a modern and efficient military, equal to other European nations. There might have been a concern for the soldiers as individuals too and valuable members of the community, something that might also be related to (Basque) nationalist ideals. The fact that we have both ID tags and detailed lists with the names of fallen soldiers (Diego 2018: 76–79), which are so often absent

The path to total war   121

in other scenarios, would corroborate this. Individuality could also be related to political consciousness: after all, political awareness implies the development of self-consciousness. Thus the makeshift tag of "miliciano Mogrobejo" and similar badges (Herrasti et al. 2014): there is a desire of being identified in case of death, but also a pride in being a militiaman.

In terms of landscape, there are also similarities across sites. Soldiers tended to fortify hilltops, which exposed them to the enemy's massive firepower, as they were an easy target for both artillery and aviation. The overabundant remains of artillery fragments in Lemoatx or San Pedro attest to the hell into which the Basque mountains were turned. In addition, most Basque sites tend to have linear, rather than zigzag trenches. This is in part related to topography—the ditches were adapted to the contour lines of the hills—or previous fortifications (prehistoric, medieval or Carlist), but it rendered the positions extremely vulnerable to artillery barrages. Again, the trenches of the Basque mountains in the spring of 1937 are similar to those of Madrid half a year before, but different to those that were being dug in central Spain during the time of the offensive on Vizcaya. The isolation of the Northern Front might have to do with this asynchrony. The peculiar materiality of war in the Basque Country is unequivocal testimony both to the autonomy of the Northern Front and the cultural and political diversity of Spain in the 1930s—a diversity that the rebels were eager to annihilate.

Belchite: beyond the ruins

To alleviate the pressure in what remained of the Republican north, the Popular Army launched two offensives during the summer of 1937. The first was in Brunete, near Madrid. After three weeks of heavy fighting, the battle finished on July 25 and put an end to each side's respective bids to either conquer the capital or break the siege (Beevor 2006: 384–398). The offensive failed to slow down the rebel advance in the Northern Front, it did not compromise the Nationalist lines in Madrid, and caused the Republic enormous losses: the occupation of 50 km^2 of irrelevant territory was at the price of 25,000 casualties and 80% of the armored force. The Nationalists suffered 15,000 casualties. Santander fell only one day after the Brunete offensive. A second offensive was then devised by the Republicans, this time against Zaragoza, the largest city in the Aragón front (Martínez Bande 1973). The plan was again to draw attention away from the north, as well as to capture a major provincial capital in Nationalist hands. The Popular Army launched a general attack on several points along a 100-km sector. The Eastern Army was put in charge of the attack, with the support of the XI and XV International Brigades. Some 80,000 soldiers were mobilized, with over 100 tanks and 90 airplanes. The results, however, were again disappointing. Government troops were caught up in useless combats and missed the opportunity to seize control of the provincial capital, encroaching only on uninhabited terrain and small towns and villages without strategic value.

The most famous of these towns is Belchite. Its ruins were turned into a metaphor of the Spanish Civil War after Franco decided to leave the village untouched as testimony to the fighting, and to build a new Belchite next to it (Michonneau 2017) (Figure 5.7). The ruins we can see today are nonetheless more the result of natural weathering processes and pillaging than of the war itself. Traces of war are, nevertheless, abundant: the brick churches of Belchite display bullet holes, shrapnel marks and, in at least one case, an unexploded artillery shell still stuck in one of its towers. Walking among bullet-ridden convents and shaking walls one has the feeling of being

Figure 5.7 Church of Saint Augustine, which was partially destroyed during the Battle of Belchite. The men of the Lincoln Battalion entered the town through this church.

Source: © Author.

The path to total war   123

thrown back in time. The ruins' lure should not distract us from the fact that Belchite was merely a small part of the battle. In fact, the very part that Franco wanted us to remember. To better comprehend the conflict in the region, we explored the war landscape surrounding the old town, which had largely fallen into oblivion (González-Ruibal, Rodríguez Simón and Garfi 2015; Rodríguez Simón et al. 2017; Garfi 2019a, b).

Warriors of Christ

Five hundred meters south of Belchite there is an impressive ruin that is seldom visited by tourists. It is an eighteenth-century brick building whose walls bear conspicuous traces of combat. Before the war, it was a minor seminary—a Catholic school for children who wanted (or were forced by their families) to become priests. The minor seminary of Belchite was a large building, only a fraction of which (the church) is still standing. One may get the wrong impression that the ruins and rubble are the effect of devastating industrial war. The building was certainly affected by bombing and bullets, but it was far from being in irreparable condition. There were plans, in fact, for restoration, but these never came to fruition. Instead, authorities decided to demolish everything but the church in the early 1940s. Corruption might have something to do with this, as most of the building materials were sold.

I have said that the place is rarely visited, but it does receive a special kind of visitor in a particular time of the year. Since the end of the war, the minor seminary became a place of pilgrimage for extreme-right militants, Carlist veterans, and their families. Carlists, as we saw in Chapter 2, were fundamentalist Catholics who wanted to abolish virtually everything that modernity and liberalism had brought to Spain during the previous hundred years (Aróstegui et al. 2003): their motto was "God, King and Fatherland". They were particularly strong in the north (the Basque Country, Navarre and parts of Aragon and Catalonia) and in rural areas. It was Carlist soldiers, known as requetés, who fought in this sector during the Battle of Belchite, more specifically the Tercio de Almogávares,[3] who held the seminary from August 24 to September 3, when they were forced to retreat. Requetés wore conspicuous red berets and often went into battle singing religious hymns, carrying huge processional crosses, and with many crucifixes and religious medals attached to their uniforms. They believed that those medals were able to stop enemy bullets. Carlists were known for their bravery, but also for committing atrocious crimes behind the lines. In the province of Navarra, it has been calculated that they killed over 15% of all men voting for left-wing parties before the war (Mikelarena 2016: 31).

In the seminar, we excavated the latrines outside the building. The place had been used as a concentration camp by the Nationalists during the last stages of the war and we hypothesized that the privies could belong to that period. This and the other concentration camp in New Belchite, one of whose barracks is still standing, are examples of what the selective memory of the war has done in

124   *The path to total war*

the town, as they have been completely erased from public memory. The same fate was experienced, until very recently, by the barracks built for civilians with Republican sympathies who had lost or were expelled from their houses in Belchite. The place, known as Russia (because it housed the "Reds"), is now abandoned and often confused by visitors with a concentration camp (not surprisingly, considering the architecture and layout).

The latrines, however, were not built for the camp, but before: impacts of grenades fired by trench mortars showed that the building existed before the battle. Under and around the structure, we found the remains of a prewar garden, including stumps of fruit trees and brick rows delimiting flowerbeds. There was also a fountain and a grotto imitating the cave of the Virgin of Lourdes, a typical late nineteenth-century religious landscape. But one destroyed by industrial war: the fountain was riddled with bullets and the grotto was empty and crumbling. The excavation of the latrines furnished some war-time objects related to hygiene, such as a comb, a toothbrush, toothpaste and a basin.

In front of the seminary, a field known as Dehesa de la Villa had been strongly fortified with several pillboxes and well-designed trenches months before the beginning of the battle. We excavated one of the pillboxes and a trench that defended the southern flank of the seminar, which was the most exposed. The excavation of the pillbox and the metal detector survey of the surroundings yielded eloquent evidence of close-quarters combat, including two pistol shell casings inside the structure and bullet holes on its walls (Figure 5.8). This shows that the defenders did not surrender and the attackers—*Guardias de Asalto* or Assault Guards, an elite unit loyal to the Republic—had to storm the fortifications and shoot the people inside. Before the final assault, the *guardias* attacked the place with machine guns, rifle fire and trench mortars. The latter are not effective against reinforced concrete, but are lethal against enemies retreating in open land. The pillboxes were isolated from each other, so they could not be easily evacuated. In a way, they resembled the solitary *blocaos* (blockhaus) built by the colonial army in Morocco (and before that in Cuba) to control vast expanses of hostile territory.

Once the pillboxes fell, there was only the trench in front of the seminary and the seminary itself. The excavation of the trench revealed that the position had been defended fiercely but briefly. We documented many shell casings and stripper clips from 7 mm Mauser rifles, but very few tin cans and glass shards that would indicate a protracted resistance. In total, we recovered a minimum number of 75 Mauser stripper clips (equivalent to 375 shots) and 94 shell casings, of which 53 were of 7 mm Mauser, 34 Soviet 7.62 mm—used by the attackers—the remaining belonging to the 8 mm Lebel caliber. The distribution and density of shells and stripper clips indicates that the Carlist soldiers were shooting massively toward the southwest, that is, toward the pillbox that had just been captured by the Republicans. Once the assault guards occupied the trench, they used it against the *requetés*, as shown by both the Mosin Nagant ammunition and 7 mm Mauser shell casings produced by Republican factories. These can be

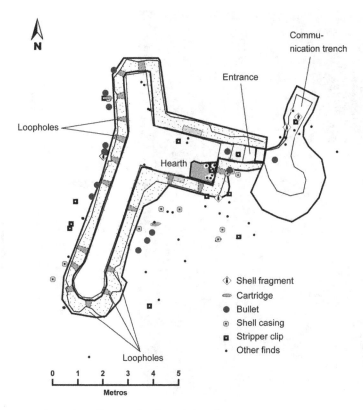

Figure 5.8 Assault on the pillboxes of Dehesa de la Villa.
Source: © Pedro Rodríguez Simón and author.

recognized because they bear stamps from factories in Girona (Catalonia) and Alicante. This ammunition was poor quality: we found five cartridges that had percussion marks but the bullet still intact. We can imagine the despair and frustration of the Republican soldier shooting round after round to no effect. Malfunction or sabotage? The surviving *requetés* retreated toward Belchite: only 70 of the original 270 men that made up the unit were capable of reaching the town (Michonneau 2017: 32–33) and over half of them would still die or be taken prisoner during the siege.

The excavation of the trench was exciting and monotonous at the same time. It was exciting because one could feel the battle in the well-preserved trench floor, carpeted with shell casings, bullets, cartridges and stripper clips (Figure 5.9); it was monotonous because it was just that: loads of spent ammunition. Or almost: we found a singular artifact among the heaps of shell casings: a crucifix. This was surely worn by a *requeté* around his neck. Did he

126 *The path to total war*

Figure 5.9 The Carlist trench of the minor seminary of Belchite carpeted with shell casings and stripper clips in situ and the crucifix that appeared amid the ammunition.
Source: © Author.

lose it in the fray of the battle or was he killed? We will never know. But it is difficult to imagine a better metaphor for Carlism: a Christian cross over a heap of bullets.

Vile treason or fierce fight?

El Saso was a strongly fortified plateau located some two kilometers east of Belchite. Yet whereas the combats around the seminary were much publicized as an act of heroic resistance by the Nationalists, those in El Saso only deserved a line in the detailed history of Colonel Martínez Bande: "The sheepfold at El Saso was also lost because an NCO rebelled against his superior" (Martínez Bande 1973: 135). Months before the battle began, the rebel army decided to construct a defensive system in the plateau, which incorporated an old sheepfold. Corrals are the unsung heroes of the Civil

The path to total war 127

War: a lot has been said about tanks and bombers, but the conflict would have been completely different without their ubiquitous presence. The sheepfold of El Saso was located in a strategic point, with wide visual control over the surrounding landscape and overlooking the road to Zaragoza. This persuaded engineers to turn it into a stronghold: they built trenches around it, concrete galleries for shooters, two underground shelters and a concrete machine-gun nest. In charge of the works was Roque Adrada, a captain of engineers, who not only erected the fortifications, but also described them in a handbook for sappers (Adrada Fernandez 1939). Adrada devised an in-depth defense system in El Saso, equipped with advanced defense posts built in reinforced concrete, heavy-artillery-proof armored nests, a thick mesh of barbed wire and an antitank minefield. Behind the line stood pillboxes for riflemen, shelters and dugouts for squads and platoons and even an anti-gas shelter (Figure 5.10). Yet the entire complex collapsed relatively quickly. Martínez Bande's brief note suggests that it was all due to treason. So, was there little or no fighting in El Saso? Other sources, including contemporary documents and witness accounts, both Republican and Nationalist, suggest that things were different, but there is a great confusion surrounding this episode (González-Ruibal, Rodríguez Simón and Garfi 2015: 69–71).

Our excavations and surveys at the sheepfold and neighboring structures, yielded an enormous amount of war materials: the position was bombed with high explosive and shrapnel shells, 81 mm mortars and trench mortars. An accurate impact on one of the sheepfold's central pillars caused the roof to collapse, spreading shell fragments throughout the building. The careful mapping of each shell fragment and the processing of the data using GIS provided a very accurate picture of the event (Figure 5.11). There was nobody inside when the explosion occurred, because they had all fled to the trenches or sheltered in the underground galleries. As for the shrapnel shell, this fell some 20 meters away from the sheepfold. This explosive artifact is an early nineteenth-century invention by a military of the same name that became widespread as a way of sweeping away crowds in no-man's-land (Marshall 1920). The shell, provided with a time fuse and loaded with lead bullets, was made to detonate above the enemy's heads: hundreds of projectiles then shot out, killing, wounding and mutilating everyone within its reach. The head wounds of those not wearing a helmet were gruesome: the bullets tore apart noses and ears, destroyed jaws and ripped open skulls. Although shrapnel shells were considered obsolete after the Great War experience, where high explosive prevailed, it was widely employed during the Spanish Civil War, where their effectiveness increased with soldiers usually lacking helmets and battles in open field more frequent. Both shrapnel shells and trench mortars were likely used in Belchite to wipe out soldiers in the trenches or retreating from them.

After bombing the position, Republicans attacked with rifle and machine-gun fire, as evinced by bullets riddling the sheepfold and pillbox—some very close to the embrasures, surely because soldiers were trying to shoot through

128 *The path to total war*

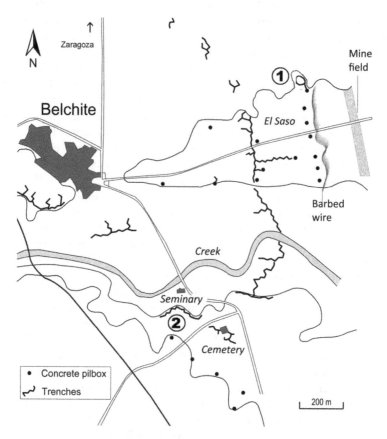

Figure 5.10 The fortifications around Belchite designed by captain of engineers Roque Adrada. The map covers the two sectors that we studied: 1. El Saso; 2. Dehesa de la Villa—Minor seminary.
Source: © Author.

them. The results of our research suggest that Nationalist soldiers did not surrender straight away: neither after the artillery storm nor after the hail of bullets: the fighting continued along the trench communicating the machine-gun nest with the rest of the fortification. Inside the nest we found many remains of the assault: shell casings, bullets and cartridges of both Nationalist and Republican rifles and machine guns. We documented manifold Lebel casings and cartridges, which almost without doubt fed the 25-cartridge magazines of a heavy Saint-Etienne M-1907 French machine gun placed inside the pillbox. The mechanically complex Saint Etienne was a French weapon, veteran of the Great War, where it jammed easily in the muddy conditions of the Western Front and was soon replaced by the more effective Hotchkiss. After the conflict, some were sent to the colonies, others to Italy.

The path to total war 129

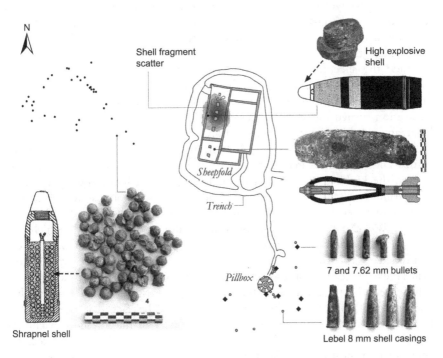

Figure 5.11 The attack on El Saso sheepfold. Archaeological finds indicate that it was subjected to Republican fire coming from heavy artillery, mortars and small arms.
Source: © Author.

Some would end up used by the Germans in the Atlantic Wall, where one example has been dug by archaeologists (Carpentier and Marcigny 2014: 43). When the Spanish Civil War broke out, these guns were bought by both the government and the rebels.

Inside the communication trench, we found fuses from the grenades employed by the Republicans to clear out the fortifications. Other materials were lost in combat, such as a six-point star, which was an officer insignia—the rank indicated by the number of stars. It might possibly have belonged to sub-lieutenant (*alférez*) Jesús Moreno Corella, who was in command of the position and who, according to historian Martínez Bande, was killed by a subordinate. We cannot tell exactly what happened to Jesús Moreno, but we can deduce that *something* happened to him. The star appeared immediately next to what must have been a pair of trousers (we found the buckles and a button) and a military canteen. The remains were mixed up with spent shell casings and the grenade fuses mentioned above. The sub-lieutenant might have been killed at the pillbox entrance, as he directed the defense against the Republican attack—either by his own men or by the

130   *The path to total war*

attackers. Whatever the case, we can speculate that the Nationalist command found quite embarrassing losing the supposedly inexpugnable El Saso to the Republicans and this might explain why treason was emphasized rather than the combat itself.

Inside the sheepfold, we found traces of the everyday life of Nationalist soldiers. The collapse of the roof provoked by the explosion sealed the occupation level from 1937. The traditional appearance of the corral prior to excavation turned out to be misleading. The engineers transformed what had been an ordinary sheepfold into a fully fledged combat shelter, for which they dug 30 cm into the original floor; reinforced the walls with rammed earth walls and excavated a perimeter trench for fast and safe circulation around the building. Access was through a deep trench communicating with the perimeter ditch. We found several hearths on the floor, as well as a large amount of sheep bones cut into small pieces, which must have been part of a stew. We also found the fishbones and scales of a conger eel, which was dried on the coast and shipped to central Spain. In Aragon it was widely consumed, particularly in the town of Calatayud, where fishermen from Galicia exchanged it for esparto grass cords, which they used for making fishing nets. More surprising is the presence of mussel shells, because, unlike conger eel, they have to be consumed fresh. The fact that they reached Belchite is a measure of the sophisticated character of the logistical machinery of Franco's army (Seidman 2011). The food was neither bad nor scarce: the abundance of meat must in fact have been quite a novelty for many soldiers, as animal protein was a rare occurrence in the diet of the pre-war popular classes.

Neither were troops short of drink: inside the sheepfold we retrieved thousands of glass shards, belonging to various bottles of wine, brandy, beer and soda. Coffee-time, however, was a different matter. Unlike lamb or wine, coffee had to be imported from overseas, a difficult operation in the war context. Therefore, soldiers and civilians alike were forced to make do with all kinds of surrogates, such as chicory and barley. Toasted grains of the latter cereal appeared in great numbers, undoubtedly for making infusions. We also found artifacts related to writing: inkbottles, a pencil and a pencil sharpener. Soldiers spent much time writing letters for their relatives and girlfriends or for other comrades who were illiterate. A piece of a compass, instead, can be associated with an officer working with maps (perhaps the ill-fated Jesús Moreno). Copper coins were common: we found ten lying on the sheepfold's floor. It might seem surprising that not even one belongs to the period of the Spanish Civil War. Most coins date to the Six-Year Revolutionary period (1868–1873), followed by a few coins of Alphonse XII (1874–1886), and one from that of Alphonse XIII, who ruled until the advent of the Republic in 1931. They mostly belong to the types popularly known as "fat bitches" and "small bitches" (*perra gorda* and *perra chica*), five and ten cents coins respectively, named after the rampant lion stamped on their reverse. They were not taken out of circulation until 1941. Nationalists only started minting their own coins in April 1937. But why so

The path to total war   131

many? Simply because they slipped out of the soldiers' pockets, when they were sitting with their backs to the pillars: exactly the spot where we have found them.

Once El Saso and the seminary fell, the siege of Belchite was complete. Between August 31 and September 6, Republicans and Nationalists engaged in house-by-house, room-by-room combats.

Life under the rubble

The tenacity of the Falangist and Carlist fighters in Belchite made the town become the epicenter of the doomed Republican offensive. We conducted a survey in different parts of the town that had not been cleared of rubble. One of them was the surroundings of the church of Saint Augustine, the way through which the Americans of the XV Brigade entered Belchite. There we found several artillery shell fragments and fuses and fragments from aviation bombs. The area that furnished more finds was situated along an irrigation canal that surrounds the town and passes next to the church of Saint Augustine. Here we found spent Mauser shells, fired by the Nationalists, a clasp of a Mosin Nagant's strap, the rifle used by the brigaders, a Nationalist 25-cents coin dated 1937 and, quite surprisingly, an undetonated *Tonelete* grenade—the standard hand grenade of the Spanish army. This particular type was of the kind produced by the Nationalists during the war. Grenades played a paramount role in the house-to-house fighting in Belchite. In the same area, we also found large amounts of medicines. Although it is hard to tell whether they predate the war, it is quite likely that they were used by the combatants: there were several field hospitals operating in the village during the battle. Whatever the case, they are a wonderful collection of 1930s medicines: we have corn-removers that may have been used by soldiers to cure the wounds caused by wearing espadrilles; *Bulgarol* for intestinal problems (which were very frequent in the trenches); *Lasa*, a codeine-based type of cough syrup; *Doctor Moliner*, another brand of cough syrup... Lung-disease drugs were in fact the most common on the front, given the number of hours soldiers spent outdoors, exposed to inclement weather.

Our survey also put us in touch with what we might call the deep history of the place. Because old Belchite is more than a war ruin: it is a millenary village whose life was forever interrupted by Franco's orders. Not by war, as commonly thought, since the place could easily have been rebuilt. The objects amid the rubble speak about this community's evolution for almost two thousand years—indeed, we found some *terra sigillata* which revealed a hitherto undocumented early Roman occupation. From the seventeenth and eighteenth centuries, we have beautiful pottery of Islamic tradition, wares painted and glazed in manganese green, cobalt blue and turquoise. Well into the twentieth century, Belchite's inhabitants still acquired hand-made ceramics to prepare and serve food and to store oil and water. Slowly, however, modernity began to leave its mark: electric porcelain insulators, taps

132 *The path to total war*

for running water, industrial wares replacing artisanal potteries. Such is at least the material culture of the wealthier houses, the same ones that must have owned a few pieces of fine glass (drinking glasses, decorative bottles and flowerpots). And also an unusual object of refinement: a porcelain stand for soft-boiled eggs. All of these artifacts appear broken and scrambled amid bricks, shrapnel and shell casings. By forcing us to remember the war, the Franco regime made us forget that in Belchite there is life under the rubble.

Parapet of Death

The Nationalists tried to relieve Belchite's besieged garrison by sending troops from Zaragoza, the main target of the Republican offensive. On August 30, the British Battalion of the XV International Brigade went to Mediana, midway between Belchite and Zaragoza, to stop the Nationalist advance. Between the besieged town and Mediana lie 20 kilometers of pure desert, not a single tree or river in sight, only dry land and sparse shrubs. A British fighter described it as "a terrible and depressing landscape which seems to eat one from the inside and crush one's spirits" (Walter Gregory, quoted in Baxell 2012: 266). British soldiers had been decimated—the battalion had lost 75% of its numbers in the combats around Quinto, close to Belchite—and initially refused to obey orders. They eventually bucked up their strength, marched to the front and succeeded in stopping the Nationalist forces. Rebel troops had to retreat to the village of Mediana and the battalion of volunteers began digging themselves into the high land south of the village (Baxell 2012: 269). The rebels then sent their 13th Division to the area, an elite unit hardened in the Battle of Brunete that had ended only one month before. Yet the Republican trenches resisted their thrust.

The bloodiest sector in the Mediana frontline was known as the Parapet of Death, which we had the opportunity to survey (Rodríguez Simón et al. 2017; Garfi 2019a, b). It lay next to the road communicating Zaragoza and Belchite and was therefore of strategic relevance. The heights to both sides of the road, overlooking Mediana, were in Republican hands, but the Nationalists managed to climb the hills and establish an advanced position very close to the Republican soldiers. Several units fought in this position, including the aforementioned XV International Brigade and the XI. According to military maps, the XI Brigade was deployed in the Parapet of Death until September 3, whereas the British were deployed in the same sector during the next four days. About the encounter between Nationalists and British in Mediana we have an exceptional document that has been recently located in the RGASPI archive, a report called "The XV Brigade in the Aragon Offensive":[4]

> "Both groups [British and Nationalists] made contact at 3; the fascists, surprised, ran back. The British quickly took possession of the hills that the fascists had conquered from the XI Brigade. These heights presided over the village of Mediana that was the 'no-man's land'... For three days and

The path to total war 133

nights, the fascists repeated their attempts to break the Republican line in the sector, employing a large amount of artillery and airplanes... The fourth day the fascist attacks diminished in intensity. The battalion fortified the positions and, for this reason, casualties were not many... The battalion remained in these positions until after the conquest of Belchite".

The Republican trenches are very visible today in the dry landscape. They are consistent with the harsh circumstances in which they were dug. Those that are closer to the enemy lines were short fighting positions with parapets or siege-work like ditches, not continuous trenches (Garfi 2019a, b). These works were connected to the road through a long and deep trench, still conserving almost its original depth. The Nationalists did have proper fire trenches, perhaps because they were in an advantageous position (in higher terrain). They did not need communication trenches, as they could use the naturally protected valleys descending from the heights. The finds in and around the Republican communication trenches consisted in bottles of alcoholic drinks, tin cans, ammunition boxes, medicines, inkbottles and the odd lost cartridge. Instead, near the Republican and Nationalist fire trenches and the space in-between, the most common finds were grenade parts. No-man's-land is littered with offensive and defensive grenades, Spanish and foreign-made, Lafitte, *Tonelete*, Polish, Ferrobellum.... We recorded with a GPS only those items visible on the surface and still documented 1,800 (Rodríguez Simón et al. 2017: 675): scatter maps offer an accurate picture of the intensity of the battle (Figure 5.12). Apart from hand grenades, there were also artillery shell fragments and mortar rounds, belonging to 50 and 81 mm Valeros: we even discovered a complete and unexploded 81 mm grenade fired by the Nationalists. Mortars were more lavishly used than howitzers, because of the risk of friendly fire. Rife and machine-gun bullets turned out to be relatively few, if compared with grenades, but this is probably again because of the proximity of the lines. Pistol bullets were comparatively common for the same reason. The density of grenades was higher in those areas where trenches were closer: it seems that soldiers were throwing grenades from one parapet to the other. The report mentioned above confirms this point:

> The British and fascist battalions had advanced positions in those hills. In one of the places the separation was of only 40 meters—they often threw hand grenades from one group to the other.

In the sector where the density of grenade fragments was higher the distance between the Nationalist and Republican trench was exactly 41 meters, and a Republican sapper's ditch came as close as 32 meters (Garfi 2019a). There are military, sensorial and moral implications to combat at short distance. According to an experiment carried out by Fábrega-Álvarez and Parcero Oubiña (2019: 61) specific bodily features can be identified at 29 to 36

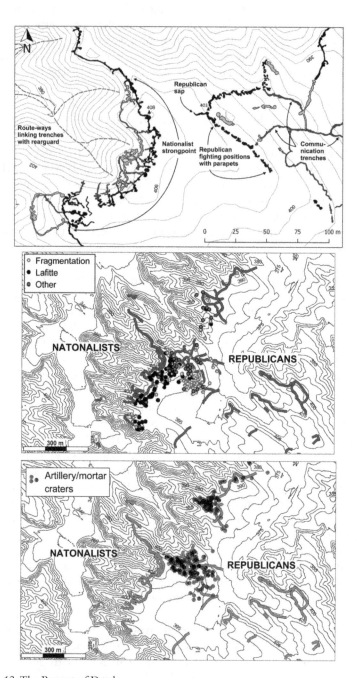

Figure 5.12 The Parapet of Death.

Notes: Above: map of the Nationalist and Republican trenches in the area that saw the fiercest fighting.*
Below: scatter maps of grenades and artillery craters in the wider sector. The concentration in the area where the trenches are nearer to each other is obvious.**

Sources: *© Salvatore Garfi, with modifications by author; **© Pedro Rodríguez Simón and author.

meters (depending on the environment) (Fábregas-Álvarez and Parcero-Oubiña 2019: 61). This means that in the Mediana trenches that were closer soldiers could almost identify their enemies as specific individuals. They could also hear them talking, praying or crying when wounded or about to die.

Next to the point where the trenches almost touched we found an odd object, odd at least in this context: a bottle of perfume. Why should a soldier carry with him cologne to the very first line? It seems absurd. Yet it is not really so, if we consider that the combats in Mediana took place in the summer and in a semi-desert environment. Under the pitiless sun and high temperatures, the corpses stank as they rotted in no-man's land. "I have not seen any dead", wrote Wilfred Owen in a letter to his mother after three weeks in the Western Front, "I have done worse. In the dank air, I have perceived it, and in the darkness, felt." (cit. in Saunders 2009: 41).

The end of the Northern Front

After the conquest of Bilbao on June 19, the Basque Country fell in Nationalist hands and Franco's troops marched toward the west: first to Cantabria and then Asturias, which had been fortified during the preceding months. In the former, probably due to the scarcity of troops to defend the territory, Republicans built several separate and unconnected nodes of resistance, rather than a continuous line, as in Bilbao (Bolado del Castillo et al, 2010; Blanco Gómez et al. 2013)—a system more redolent of Nationalist fortification. The strongholds were reinforced with concrete trench works and pillboxes for machine guns. Some of the defenses were used to try to contain the rebel offensive known as the Battle of Santander (August 14–September 17). As had happened in Madrid the previous autumn, the advance was often so swift that some of the structures remained unused. While they have not been excavated, we do have some eloquent testimony from graffiti (Bolado del Castillo et al. 2010). In the Tolío Mountains, where 23 machine-gun nests were built, a picturesque inscription reads:

> Segunda República 1937/CNT FAI/UGT/Viban todos los/conpañeros/ mueran todos/los facistas/Muera Franco/y/Aranda y el/peinaovejas de/ Mola/el ijoputa de Queipo/de Llano 1937.
> "Second Republic 1937/CNT FAI/UGT/long live all/comrades/death to all/facists (sic)/death to Franco/and/Aranda and/sheep-comber (sic) Mola/and sonfabitch/Queipo de Llano 1937".[5]

The text clearly makes up for its spelling mistakes with plenty of enthusiasm. Not enough, however, to stop the *facist* offensive. Which indeed it was (fascist), as it involved 25,000 of Mussolini's soldiers. The Italians suffered a great number of casualties (almost 500 dead and three times as many disappeared). The Duce had a great pyramid built to honor their memory in the mountain pass of El Escudo, although the fallen Italians are no longer

136   *The path to total war*

buried in it: now they rest in the *Sacraio Militare Italiano* in the church of
Saint Anthony of Padua (Zaragoza). The fascist pyramid, however, continues
to preside like a specter over the mountains.

Crumb under belt

The attack against the Republican stronghold in the north came not only
from the west, but also from the east (Galicia) and south (León and Palencia).
The southern frontline was particularly arduous, because it coincided with
one of the highest ranges in Iberia, the Cantabrian Mountains. Here,
industrial war became preindustrial again: fortifications made of dry stone
were almost indistinguishable from shepherd huts and corrals (Alonso
González 2008: 304–311), which, in fact, were often reutilized. The well-
made walls and parapets reveal the skilled work of peasants and stonemasons
who were just engaging in their craft. Two sites from the Spanish Civil War
have been excavated in the mountain range: Mount Bernorio (Palencia) and
Castiltejón (León). Both had been Iron Age settlements and for good reasons:
hillforts were established in prominent, naturally defended places and their
fortifications, as we saw in Murugain, could be put back into service.

Mount Bernorio was located at a strategic point along a route
communicating the landlocked Castilian plains with the port city of
Santander. Such location explains its decisive role during the Cantabrian
Wars (29–26 BC). Europe's largest Roman legionary camp, which lies
opposite the hillfort, attests to the fighting, as do the countless arrowheads
and Roman artillery projectiles found in the walls that once protected the
Iron Age settlement (Torres Martínez et al. 2011, 2013). Two thousand years
later, all the north of Castile had been occupied by the Nationalist army—all
but Mount Bernorio, which became a Republican salient. On
17 October 1936, the Nationalists captured the position and fortified it,
taking advantage of the sector's relative calm. As this was a secondary front,
they mobilized the least possible number of troops to defend it, and this
meant building a strong defensive system to compensate for the lack of men.
An artillery battery was very appropriately placed upon Emperor Augustus'
camp and the kitchen was set up in its parapets. On 14 August 1937, the
Nationalists launched their great offensive towards Santander. With the fall of
the city, the old hillfort lost all its strategic value. Civil War remains are thus
from a specific time window: the year between July 1936 and August 1937.

Most of the vestiges preserved today come from the phase of the
Nationalist occupation—trenches, foxholes, shelters, a fort and a pillbox
(Torres-Martínez and Domínguez Solera 2008). The surface is also
punctuated by the craters of artillery grenades. Soldiers found faithful allies in
the prehistoric ruins: the rubble from ancient towers was transformed into
firing positions and—as in the hillfort of Murugain—the perimeter trench
reused the wall as a parapet. Present and past were united in even more
surprising ways: a bullet was found perforating the shoulder-blade of an Iron

Age bovid. Archaeologists have found the usual battlefield materials: rubber soles, the grommets of capes and awnings used by soldiers to protect themselves against the region's harsh climate. Also abundant Czech ammunition that, by the summer of 1937, had already passed from Republican into Nationalist hands.

The Republican fortifications of Cueto de Castiltejón lie in the limit between Asturias and León (González Gómez de Agüero and Bejega 2015; González Gómez de Agüero et al. 2017). They also occupy an Iron Age hillfort, where a beautiful bronze brooch, a spearhead and a cauldron's handle were found during fieldwork. The hilltop is located 1,400 meters above the sea level and watches over the entrance to Asturias, the last stronghold of the Popular Army in the Northern Front. This explains why the place was fortified so intensively. Control of the road was crucial and Republicans did not spare any of their dwindling resources in defending the pass: a monumental bunker with loopholes for a dozen riflemen was built in Arboleya, near Castiltejón. There are graffiti with personal names (Dimas Serra, Marsel, Alfredo Gómez) and a date indicating the completion of the work: 20 August 1937, which is only ten days before the final Nationalist offensive in the North.

Castiltejón was an advanced vanguard position in front of Arboleya, with perfect visual control over the valley and the road leading to Oviedo, Asturias' capital. Republican soldiers constructed two dugouts, one on the hilltop and one on the foothill, and several trenches (Figure 5.13). In the hilltop, there is also a cave that was used as a shelter and observation post: a narrow slit was cut in the rock to watch over the road. Several graffiti were found there in pencil with personal names (Salvador, Pascual) and numeric codes that are hard to decipher but might be coordinates. The excavations yielded few remains, as local people probably took as much as they could at the end of the war and the soldiers probably did not have much in the first place. Inside the lower dugout, a piece of tire was found which had been reused to make a rubber sole. The use of recycled tires to make sandals or espadrilles was already common before the war. Establishing its origin poses no challenge in this case because the Firestone logo has been preserved. Espadrilles are inadequate footwear in a war in all cases, but much more so in the high mountains, where they do not afford any protection against the cold and the rocky surfaces. The shelter on the hilltop provided more materials: around the remains of a bonfire, glass shards were found, belonging to bottles of wine and soda water, a can of condensed milk "La Rosita", buttons, stockpot handles and animal bones. Faunal remains belong mostly to cattle (95%), followed by caprines and chicken. Beef was rare in Spanish trenches, but cows were abundant in the green and rainy North—not so much during the war, if we are to judge by the tiny pieces of bone that appeared at the site. The type of cuts and the absence of de-fleshing marks suggest that they were used to cook stews—very little meat to feed many.

Figure 5.13 The Republican fortified hill of Castiltejón, surrounded by the Cantabrian mountains that separate León and Asturias. The Iron Age parapets of Castiltejón are clearly visible.
Source: © Author.

A series of spent 8 mm shell casings were found outside the shelter. They were fired by old Mannlicher and Lebel rifles. Mannlicher casings bear stamps of the Austro-Hungarian Empire (1918) and of independent Hungary (1920). The Lebel munitions, in turn, were inscribed "Western 1918". These were poor-quality cartridges manufactured at the end of the First World War in the United States for the French Army. More spent ammunition appeared in a trench overlooking the road: there were eight Lebel casings, all marked Western 1918, which reveal the position of a rifleman covering the road. Surface survey in neighboring positions also yielded this type of ammunition. During fieldwork, neighbors brought a Czech M1930 helmet to the dig, which probably came with the rifles and munitions from that provenance. The Republic was in desperate need of head protection at the beginning of the war and was forced to import large numbers of Czech and French Adrian helmets. The former, made of thick steel sheet, were superior to the Adrians. In the mountains, helmets were badly needed, as the effectiveness of artillery increased substantially its lethal effects. Explosions in rocky areas, as Austrians and Italians had the chance to experience in the Alps, burst rocks into fragments that multiply the effect of shrapnel and cause the most gruesome wounds (Keegan 2000: 228).

The path to total war 139

Archaeology eloquently attests to the state of the Republican Army in the North by the end of the campaign: military apparel was virtually non-existent; clothes were predominantly civilian, tins scarce, weapons old and obsolete. Nobody captured the essence of the Northern Front as Peruvian poet César Vallejo in these verses: "Potential warriors/without socks to cannon thunder,/satanic, numerical,/crumb under belt,/double-caliber rifle: blood and blood" (Vallejo 2007).

The fall of Oviedo

In Asturias, the last stronghold of the Nothern Front, the most solid line was around the city of Oviedo. The frontline had stabilized there a year before, on 16 October 1936, when the Nationalists managed to break a three-month Republican siege to the city. One of the sectors that we know best from an archaeological point of view is located between Las Matas and Fitoria, in the outskirts of the city (Álvarez Martínez et al. 2009). The fortifications at Las Matas were built in the summer of 1937 by soldiers and civilians drafted specifically to this end: all men between 16 and 45 were mobilized to participate in the war effort. Some of them left graffiti, like Eugenio, who signed on 26 July 1937, or Avelino, just a few days later.

Archaeologists also had the chance to excavate one of the structures: a round pillbox built to house a machine gun in Fitoria (Álvarez Martínez and Requejo Pagés 2008). They were fortunate enough to find a context sealed as it had been left in October 1937, when Republicans surrendered. The state of preservation of the war level was excellent due to the pillbox's lack of an adequate draining system, which caused layers of soil and rain-washed waste to accumulate inside. Under the sediments and over the original floor, four shells casings, two defensive grenades and two fuses were found and a fifth grenade was recovered by the door. The nest had two slits and was very narrow: only 2.34 meters on its widest side. We have to imagine two or three soldiers crammed there with a bulky Hotchkiss with its tripod, weighing 18 kg, ammunition boxes and grenades. The grenades appeared without their fuses. This is because they were usually stored separately to avoid accidents. In this case, however, grenades and fuses correspond to different typologies. The fuses are Polish wz. 31s, a model that we have already encountered (and will encounter again). The grenades' bodies, instead, correspond to the *Pera asturiana* type, that we saw in Lemoatx. These had a wick, so the Polish fuses could not be used in them. The pillbox of Fitoria was abandoned without a fight.

Neither the strong fortifications of Asturias nor the equally strong determination of many Republican soldiers were enough to prevent the advance of the Nationalists, backed by overwhelming firepower and with absolute air supremacy. The attackers, however, suffered great losses. This was particularly the case with the *regulares*, the Moroccan soldiers, used as both shock troops and cannon fodder. In Asturias, they left a traumatic

140   *The path to total war*

memory of looting and raping, which overlapped with the previous memories of crimes already committed during their quenching of the October 1934 Revolution. A series of "Moorish cemeteries" were built in the North for the fallen colonial soldiers. One of them is the cemetery of Barcia, an eerie and overgrown ruin, built in Orientalist style with a monumental entrance in the shape of a horseshoe arch (Álvarez Martínez et al. 2006). Between 400 and 500 soldiers were buried inside and soon forgotten.

The Northern Front collapsed on 21 October 1937 and Republican soldiers started a long and painful pilgrimage through a newly established network of concentration camps (Costas and Santos 2008). Some people, however, escaped and took refuge in the many caves that exist in Asturias and spent many years in hiding. In Santo Adriano, next to Oviedo, several have been surveyed (Fernández Fernández and Moshenska 2017). One was used temporarily by a group of communist militiamen. We know because they drew the flag of the Spanish chapter of the Communist International. They also wrote down their date of entry and departure. The latter is illegible, but the arrival was on October 21—the very same day of the Republican surrender in Asturias. Another of the caverns became the home of a lonely militiaman who left an inscription reading: "Republic. Liberty. Culture. Education". The Franco regime demonized its enemies as bloody Reds trying to impose a communist dictatorship. The graffiti of Santo Adriano reminds us of the diversity of people who actually backed the Republic and the strong liberal element that was always part of the project. At least one of the people who went underground in the area committed suicide but others did not fare badly, as they were able to reintegrate in their communities after a partial amnesty in 1938. Others were not so lucky.

Massacre of the innocents

On October 22, only one day after the victorious Nationalist offensive in Asturias, the 4 Mountain Battalion of Arapiles, number 7 of the 6 Navarre Brigade arrived in the village of Valdediós, well-known for its extraordinary Asturian pre-Romanesque church. Next to the church is a Cistercian monastery, abandoned in the mid-nineteenth century in the process of church confiscations carried out by the liberal regime of the time. It was re-occupied during the Civil War: this time, by the patients and clinical staff of the psychiatric hospital of La Cadellada (Oviedo) that had been evacuated for its proximity to the front. For a whole year, it fulfilled its functions, mainly providing healthcare for mental patients, as well as some wounded soldiers. Until the fall of Asturias.

Then the Nationalist troops arrived. Their arrival did not scare the hospital workers, who were after all civilian staff in charge of the ill and wounded— mostly civilians as well. But things started on a bad note: shortly after their arrival, the men of the Arapiles Battalion made several arrests and sent various people to Gijón. We now know that most of them were shot—and they

The path to total war   141

were not the worse off. The soldiers then decided to have a party at the monastery. They forced the female staff of the hospital to prepare food and then dance with them. Soldiers drank, danced and started harassing the women. The party turned violent, things became savage. No one stood up for the nurses of the hospital. Not even the unit's chaplain. The party degenerated into gang rape. After torturing them at will, the soldiers dragged the women to a chestnut wood, where they made them dig their own grave, ordered them to lie inside, and shot them. The men also executed four wards, the kitchen hand and the teenage daughter of one of the nurses. The unit chaplain witnessed the massacre. He just gave absolution to the victims.

In the year 2003 Sociedad Aranzadi carried out preliminary surveys in the area where witnesses placed the massacre (Etxeberria, Herrasti and Ortiz, n.d.; De la Rubia and Landera. n.d.). The result was positive, and a large L-shaped grave was found with 19 skeletons. 11 of them belonging to women, all aged between 20 and 40, except a younger one of 19. Her name was Luz Álvarez Flórez and she was a kitchen assistant. Only one more woman could be identified: Rosa Flórez Martínez, the 35-year-old head nurse. Luz was her oldest daughter; the youngest was sent to work as a maid at a house in Gijón following her mother's assassination. The women were still wearing their nurse uniforms, as can be deduced from the presence of certain items of clothing and professional symbols. One of them was wearing her hair in a clasp, which preserved a lock of brown hair. The soldiers could not have been that drunk: out of 17 victims, 14 had their skull fractured by a rifle shot in the immediate surroundings of the ear. Two of the men also present concussions in other parts of their bodies: the clavicle in one case, the leg in the other. The man who was shot in the clavicle is 18-year-old nurse Urbano Menéndez Amado. He was Luz's boyfriend. The shot in the leg was received by Antonio Piedrafita García, who was 31. A medal of the Virgin Mary was found next to his body. Of the other six men and five women who were part of the hospital's staff no identification could be made.

On 28 October 1937, the 4 Mountain Battalion of Arapiles number 7 of the 6 Navarre Brigade departed from Valdediós. They left behind a beautiful place, with an extraordinary pre-Romanesque church and a collective grave with 19 corpses. To this day, the Arapiles Battalion is an integral part of the Spanish Army. In 2014 an exhibition about this unit was organized, without any mention whatsoever of the atrocities committed during the war. But as the government delegate put it, "in 250 years of history we all go through different phases, some better than others".[6] These others, it seems, we had better forget.

Notes

1 https://www.cinturondehierro.net/es-es/.
2 http://www.municion.org/7mm/7mm2.htm.

142 The path to total war

3 The *almogávares* were shock troops from the Late Middle Ages. The *tercios*, in turn, refer to the military units of the Spanish Empire of the sixteenth and seventeenth centuries. Both terms are evidence of the imperialist and nationalist ideology of the rebels.

4 F.545. Op.3. D.474. We thank Julián Dueñas for locating this document for us.

5 Aranda, Mola and Queipo de Llano were all rebel commanders.

6 http://www.20minutos.es/noticia/2147989/0/.

6 Wait and retreat

November 1937–March 1938

In his book *Passing time: An essay in waiting*, Andrea Köhler (2017) reminds us that life means waiting and the wait, joyful or terrible, long or short, is interwoven not just with boredom, but also with emotions—fear, anxiety, love or desire. Archaeologists know about the topic, because our work consists largely in waiting: we wait for things to emerge slowly from the soil, we wait for them to take shape and make sense. We wait and we document the act of waiting, the slow, idle time of life.

It is meaningful that in Spanish, Catalan and Galician-Portuguese there is only one word to refer to two very different things: to hope and to wait. *Esperar* means at the same time to look forward to and to wait for somebody or something or for something to happen. Emotion is part of the wait. Instead, in German, English, French, Italian and many other languages, the spatio-temporal experience is separated from the emotional (warten/hoffen, attendre/espérer, aspettare/sperare).

War means waiting. It is easy to forget, when war narratives are full of action—military operations, political maneuvers, biographic drama. But dead time is more frequent than killing time. Death typically occurs in monstrous bursts punctuating long spans of downtime. War means waiting but of a special kind that is better captured by the Romance languages of Iberia. Because it is a wait filled with expectation, with fear or hope, anxiety or desire. What we find in our work are the ruins of *la espera*. What is a shelter, but a place to wait and to expect (a letter to arrive, a bombing to stop)? Or the execution wall or the edge of a mass grave: the place where *esperar* only means waiting: the end to come. In this chapter I will describe three scenarios of waiting during the very harsh winter of 1938, in Guadalajara, Aragón and Extremadura.

Idle time in Extremadura

Most of Extremadura had been occupied by the colonial Army of Africa during the summer of 1936. Only a small Republican territory remained in the eastern part of the region. One of the headquarters was located in an old

144 *Wait and retreat*

farm known as Casa de la Sierra, in a mountain range south of the town of Don Benito (Badajoz). Miguel Hernández, one of Spain's great twentieth-century poets, a communist and a future victim of the dictatorship, spent some time there and harangued the troops from the stairs of the main building, which, after decades of abandonment, is collapsing. Its mudbrick walls were originally covered in inscriptions and graffiti, only a handful of which survived by the time I visited the place in 2012. Most were personal names (*Antonio Capilla García*), place names (*Don Benito*), indications (*proibido la entrada*, "entrance forbidden", misspelt in Spanish), humorous sentences ("Pedro is a rascal, a good friend says") and political slogans: *aviso: todo el que proboque palabras de desmoralizacion sera considerado como fazioso* ("warning, whoever provokes words of demoralization will be considered a rebel", with plenty of orthographic errors). The most spectacular graffiti covers an entire wall. It represents a bullfighter, identified as *Juan España* ("John Spain"), armed with a rapier and charging against the enormous horny head of Hitler, next to which we can read *Hitler el Hijo de Puta* ("Hitler, the son of a bitch"). The man is holding with his right hand the bullfighting cape, which is the map of Spain. The two Republican capitals are marked: Madrid and Valencia. The iconography and the message are curiously nationalistic, but the Republic often resorted to the nationalist imaginary that had typically belonged to the right (and still does): bullfighting, the Peninsular War, the idea of a foreign invasion (Núñez Seixas 2006).

Casa de la Sierra was in a better condition a decade before I visited. Two amateur researchers documented more graffiti and published them (Cerrato et al. 2002). Based on the large corpus of inscriptions that they were able to document, they propose several interpretations. Thus, most of the writers on the walls had very little education and the orthographic and calligraphic errors make the understanding of the text often difficult. The limited literacy probably explains (here as in other places) that it is mostly personal names that were written. Illiterates in Spain were often taught to write their own name, so that they could sign documents. This was the case of Máximo Vizuete, who starts to write correctly under the sample provided by a literate person. However, at some point, one letter falls (Viuete), and he continues copying the misspelled name. Communist slogans are common ("long live the USSR; long live the Army of the People, Partit Socialist Unificat de Catalunya"), more than Republican ("long live the Spanish Republic"), a fact that might be influenced by the commanders, as the region had been socialist, not communist, before the war, or simply by the growing sway of communism during the war. Some slogans have to do with the proper order in the base. One of the most original reads: "It is strictly forbidden to piss on the stairs for hygienic reasons and I certify it for the general public interest and whoever disobeys these orders will be considered comrade pig".[1] Finally, the fact that some graffiti are lists of military units, ballistic problems and tactic exercises seems to indicate that the walls were used as a blackboard or paper. The base remained in Republican hands until the summer of 1938 and witnessed no combat.

This was not the case of Sierra de Argallén, a mountain range only 30 km south of Casa de la Sierra (Domínguez et al. 2017). The area, a bulge into Nationalist territory, was attacked by the rebels in June 1937 and again in the winter of 1938. During the latter attack, which began on January 30, the rebels occupied several towns, villages and positions held by the Republicans, who in turn launched a counteroffensive on the night of 15–16 February, with contingents of the XII International Brigade and two battalions of the 106 Mixed Brigade. Colonial troops, however, stopped their advance. By the end of the combats, the positions had barely changed and so remained until the offensive on La Serena Pocket during the summer of 1938. The losses were high nonetheless: 650 among the Republicans in just 15 hours of combat, of which 250 were dead or missing. During excavations in an Islamic castle at Sierra de Argallén, archaeologists found the improvised burial of a soldier, who seems to have been hit by one bullet, perhaps two—he had perimortem traumas in the jaw and left humerus. He was between 25 and 30 years of age, around 1.70 m tall, and had occupational stress markers (for example, in the area of the right shoulder), revealing a physically demanding job before the war. The body appeared inside a foxhole that partly reused a medieval wall. In the same context, archaeologists found spent 7 mm shell casings, produced in Mexico and Austria and probably fired by the soldier, and a grenade pull ring. The provenance of the casings indicates that the deceased was most likely Republican.

Nationalist troops that fell in this and other combats in the area were more fortunate than the unknown soldier of Argallén. In June 1937, after the first offensive, the Nationalist authorities established a cemetery in Campillo de Llerena to bury their dead. It is known as the "Cemetery of the Italians", because some of the fascist troops, the Blue and Black Arrows,[2] that participated in the first attack were buried there and a monument honored them (Aguado Benítez 2004). However, most of the interred bodies belonged to Spanish troops killed in the operations that took place in the sector between June 1937 and February 1939, including two captains, one lieutenant, three *alféreces* (sub-lieutenants), two sergeants, four corporals and 52 privates from the February 1938 combats. The few Italian bodies in the cemetery were transferred after the war to the Italian *Sacraio Militare* in Zaragoza (see Chapter 5). Only the Spaniards remained in Campillo de Llerena. During the restoration of the cemetery, archaeologists mapped the cemetery and exhumed several graves.[3] Among the finds, we can note four identification tags of the type usually worn by Nationalist troops (Herrasti et al. 2014: 296), crucifixes and religious medals, a sewing kit (perhaps belonging to a military tailor), and, in a few cases, glass bottles containing identification documents. The whereabouts of most Republican soldiers killed in action, like the one in the castle of Argallén, remain unknown.

Killing time in Guadalajara

Five hundred kilometers east of the Extremadura front, soldiers were experiencing a particularly harsh winter. It is not rare for temperatures to drop below minus 10 degrees Celsius in Guadalajara and snowy blizzards are an integral part of the winter landscape. But the winter of 1938 was marked by the arrival of a polar continental air mass that plunged temperatures below minus 20 degrees in central Spain. Snow fell even in the Mediterranean coast, in Barcelona. The cold was harder to bear in the rocky landscape of La Alcarria, a deeply rural area in central Guadalajara. Outcrops are so ubiquitous that, in many places, it is simply impossible to excavate a trench. Or, perhaps more appropriately, we might speak of hewing a trench in stone, as this is what combatants on both sides were forced to do. Soldiers cut into the limestone with picks and hammers, and then used those same stones to construct parapets. Such was the work of the 549 Battalion of the 138 Mixed Brigade of the Popular Army during the months of January and February 1938. The traces of their work (and of thousands of their comrades) are visible in the dozens of kilometers of ditches and walls cutting into and dividing the terrain. The battalion was garrisoned at Alto del Molino ("Mill Hill"). The place that we excavated was on the frontline when the soldiers turned it into their base (González-Ruibal 2012a). The Nationalists had occupied the village of Abánades, two kilometers north, and all the surrounding hills during the Battle of Guadalajara (8–23 March 1937).[4] The sheer proximity of the enemy explains Republican efforts to fortify: during the winter of 1938 they built numerous trenches, machine-gun nests and artillery positions. It also explains the large amount of ammunition that we found. Most, however, appeared in a surprising spot: a trash pit, next to the sheepfold that the soldiers had turned into their temporary home (Figure 6.1). The soldiers at Abánades allowed themselves

Figure 6.1 The sheepfold of Alto del Molino, which was turned into a Republican base by the 138 Mixed Brigade. A trash pit was dug to the right.
Source: © Author.

Wait and retreat 147

not only to throw away hundreds of shell casings, but even full cartridges in perfect condition. No less than 34 cartridges and 85 shells were collected. Most of the latter had not even been fired, meaning that their bullets had simply fallen off or been extracted. Therefore, at least 70 perfectly usable cartridges were thrown away, or, in other words, the equivalent to 12 full magazines. A considerable amount if we think of the Republic's dire situation. Also, in this case we are not talking about a mobile position or a retreat that might justify a hasty disposal. Had this been peacetime and if the rubbish were of a different type (clothes or pens) it would definitely represent a case of wasteful consumerism. In fact, mass consumption is closely connected to industrial war or vice versa. The culture of disposability was probably born inside a trench.

The ammunition is almost entirely Soviet 7.62 mm (98%) which is proof of the great standardization achieved by the Popular Army by the beginning of 1938. Gone were the days of the old Vetterlis and Mannlichers. Inscriptions on the cartridges' bases indicate that they were produced between 1922 and 1936 at the factories of Podolsk, Frunze and Tula. The latter is the most frequent origin of Soviet ammunition in Republican positions. Tula had been one of Russia's most important steel industry centers from the eighteenth century, housing an important ammunition factory since 1883, which continued to play a key role in the Second World War—and later (Trapeznik 2009). Some of the cartridges must have been used to feed one or more Maxim machine guns, as we found an aluminum plate with the inscription *Cia. ametralladoras*, that is, "Machine-gun co. (company)". Inside the sheepfold turned shelter for the troops, we found three shell casings belonging to pistols: 9 mm, 7 mm and 0.22. The former two belong to personal weapons carried by the soldiers, further proof of the wide availability of guns in prewar Spain. The 7 mm shell is an interesting specimen of a Lefaucheux pin-fire cartridge. I have already referred to this kind of ammunition in relation to a shotgun cartridge that appeared in Casa de Campo (see Chapter 3). The Lefaucheux was also used in revolvers since 1854 and, in fact, both Union and Confederate soldiers carried Lefaucheux pistols with them during the American Civil War (1861–1865) as personal weapons: they were never a service firearm in any army (Lord 2013).

In the previous chapter, I mentioned the relevance of sheepfolds during the Spanish Civil War: they went from keeping animals to housing troops, supplies, weapons, and even field hospitals (Albir Herrero and Mezquida Fernández 2014). But pens had seen turbulent times before. In Alto del Molino, for example, we discovered that the Republicans had not been the first troops to use the corral: a group of guerrillas had also found shelter there during the Peninsular War (1808–1812). They left a bronze button with a bust of King Ferdinand VII, then called "patriotic" because it was worn by those who fought for the Bourbon restoration and to expel the Napoleonic troops.

148 Wait and retreat

When Republican soldiers arrived, the sheepfold was in disrepair, with its roof collapsed. The excavation of the structure yielded over 500 items, from underpants buttons to empty ammunition boxes. Life conditions were not easy in Alto del Molino, especially during the harsh winter of 1938: soldiers huddled around the many hearths that we documented on the floor to warm themselves up. They probably covered their bodies with as many clothes and blankets as they could lay their hands on. There is no trace of the blankets, but plenty of remains of clothing: dozens of mother-of-pearl buttons for underwear (underpants and undershirts). Another highly useful element to warm up was alcohol, which acts as a vasodilator. The problem is that after a while the effect gives way to its opposite—following the initial warm-up, body temperature drops. Alcohol was, in fact, an essential element in the armies of the twentieth century: the full load of a French soldier on campaign during the First World War included enough tinned food for four days and two liters of wine (Ellis 1989: 36). A major legal drug, wine has allowed soldiers to maintain morale in many fronts. One of the most frequent finds in German trenches of the First World War are beer and spirits (Schnitzler and Landölt 2013: 189–194); bottles of alcoholic beverages were also the most common artifact by far in the Italian forts on the remote Ethiopian border between 1935 and 1941 (González-Ruibal 2010). The Republican soldiers of Guadalajara drank a cheap cognac, of the brand Peinado. This is a liquor distilled since the early nineteenth century in the town of Tomelloso (Ciudad Real), where it is still produced today. We also found a great number fragments of anisette and wine bottles, other unidentified spirits, the precinct of a liquor produced in Barcelona (Salvador Claros), and even two small bottles of champagne![5] Considering that Alto del Molino was occupied in January of 1938, the troops might have possibly drunk this at a Christmas celebration. It may also have been a present sent by relatives or friends from the rearguard: the 138 Brigade was, as we will see, recruited in Catalonia, the largest champagne-producing area in Spain (where it is called *cava*). The taste of *cava* surely transported the combatants home for a few moments.

A better way than alcohol to stave off the cold were the calories provided by food. An army logistics document from the period of the Republican offensive on the upper Tajuña river (April of 1938, see Chapter 7) informs us about the diet on the frontline.[6] There were two types of rations: the normal ration, for troops stationed in stable positions, and the backpack ration when the troops were mobile (as in attacks, for example). Normal rations included bread (400 grams), condensed milk, coffee, legumes (250 grams), frozen meat (100 grams), salt, paprika, onion, garlic, tomato, cod, cognac, wine and fruit. The backpack menu was poorer, but not bad either: bread (same amount), tinned meat (250 grams), marmalade, chocolate, liquor, wine and fruit. Since the position in Alto del Molino was stable, the remains that we found fit quite nicely the "normal" diet. Thus, most of the tins were of condensed milk (44 items), instead of the sardine and tuna that we so often find in battlefields. Since one can of milk was shared between every five soldiers, the vessels at the Alto del Molino would represent almost 250 rations, that is, the equivalent to a platoon's 10-day consumption or a couple of days in the life of a single company.

Roughly the other half of the tins corresponds to tomato or legumes. Only 6% of the vessels contained sardines. A peculiar find were four anchovy tins (two from France). As one might expect, these were not a frequent element in army logistics. The presence of these delicatessen might be due to extraordinary or festive circumstances—like the champagne. Another rare can is the olive oil container that we found inside the trash pit. The colors (red and yellow) and design indicate that it might have been canned by the brand Carbonell (still popular today). Ironically, this had been the official provider of the Royal House...

The trash pit also yielded many cod fish bones. Dry cod was common in the front, for its easy transportation. It was consumed as a stew with potatoes, just like cow, sheep, or goat, of which we also have many bones. Bovid bones deserve specific attention. Local people at Abánades remember an episode that took place at some point prior to the spring offensive (see Chapter 7). Nationalist troops were stationed in the village, where their kitchens and several warehouses and logistic services were established at the time. One day, the Nationalists seized a cow and set out to slaughter it. The animal, sensing what was coming, decided to escape. It ran off southwards, toward the Republican trenches. Soldiers ran after her before she vanished in no man's land. They then shot at the cow, so that her meat could not be used to feed their enemies—without success. The animal dodged the bullets and made its way toward Alto del Molino, where the Republicans did what their enemies were expecting to do. The cow was slaughtered and eaten. According to some old neighbors, the feast was broadcast with loudspeakers to infuriate the Nationalists. A full cow was not a common delicacy in 1938 and least of all in Abánades, a dry region unfit for grazing cattle. It was actually so unusual, that it is not totally unfounded to suppose that our cattle bones belonged to the runaway cow.

In terms of food, the situation in Alto del Molino was far more favorable than in other Republican sites. We know, for instance, the menu in the trenches of the University City in Madrid for 1937, and it was less varied and meager in comparison. Fruit, which was present in Guadalajara, was completely absent in Madrid. Meat portions were of 20 grams (Seidman 1999), ten times smaller than in Abánades. The military situation in Guadalajara in December 1937 probably has to do with the menu. The Nationalists were organizing an attack on Madrid through Guadalajara, but the Republicans found out and the operation was canceled. The Popular Army then launched its own attack on the area and mustered troops for a larger offensive that came to fruition, after several delays, on March 30 (see Chapter 7). The abundance of food and supplies in the sector could be connected with the preparations for the attack.

150   *Wait and retreat*

Many of our finds appeared in the trash pit that I have already mentioned. Waste management is of paramount importance at war. Where great human agglomerations occur, illnesses can become more dangerous than enemy bullets. We have already seen how many of the casualties at the University City were caused by epidemics (see Chapter 4). Digging a trash pit was the most basic hygienic measure to avoid them, but did not guarantee a parasite-free environment. Nits and fleas were in fact ever-present in all static fronts. The unpublished diaries of musician Buenaventura Leris, who served in Guadalajara during the war, mention them on numerous occasions. During his stay at the trenches of Torrecuadradilla (a village next to Abánades) in November of 1937, he wrote: "These youngsters have an immense amount of parasites which give them a very bad time, no matter how used to them they have become". Just a few days after this entry, he writes in his diary: "Most of the battalion has symptoms of scabies".[7] It should come as no surprise that Republican propaganda claimed that "all nits are fascists". Fascists, in turn, must have found nits to be quite communist. The fight against such peculiar forms of fascism left us a black plastic nit comb with the inscription "[Pat] ent 1933". Also related to hygiene are shaving razors (Figure 6.2).

Chances to wash were scarce and it must have been quite difficult to get rid of bodily odors. Cologne was a way of fighting it. We have found two bottles at Alto del Molino. One was a tiny art-deco bottle of the brand Myrurgia. Myrurgia is a perfume and soap factory established in Barcelona in 1916 and still active. Back then, their essences used exotic names (Hindustan, Oriental Woods) or names referring to Spanish folklore (Goyesca, Maja,[8] Sighs of Granada)—a stark contrast to the realities of the trench. It is highly unlikely, in any case, that there were any women on the frontline. A possible explanation is that the perfume might have been a souvenir given by a wife or girlfriend to a soldier: psychological studies point to smell as the most evocative of all senses. It is not only more intensely linked to memories, but it also causes recollections to be more pleasurable (Mohr et al. 2001).

Hygiene does not grant immunity from diseases. The abundance of medicines collected in Alto del Molino speaks volumes about the army's (poor) health conditions. This was not exclusive to rural fronts: in the autumn of 1937, over 70% of soldiers hospitalized in Madrid were ill, not wounded (Matthews 2012: 105–106). The fact that medicines in the dump were broken indicates that they were used, and therefore, that illness was rife among the troops. Some bottles have inscriptions allowing us to identify the drug. The most abundant is Urodonal Etach, of which we found four items. It was usually administered to combat uric acid, a typical symptom of obesity and of high consumption of protein and alcohol. Its consumption in this case had more to do with treating arthritis and other rheumatic diseases. Contrary to what we might think, conditions of cold and humidity in the trenches were not the direct cause of rheumatic problems. Joint and muscle pain was provoked in most cases by trench fever, a disease transmitted by parasites

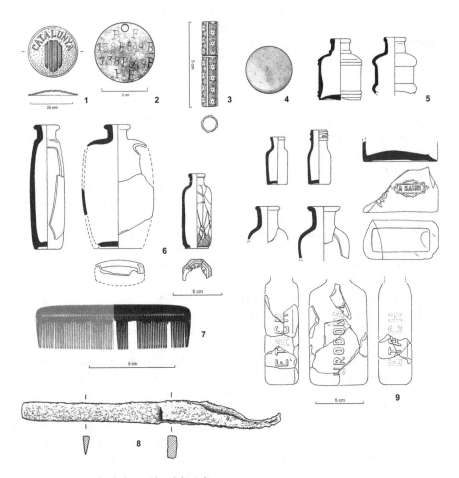

Figure 6.2 Some finds from Alto del Molino.

Notes: 1. Insignia with the coat of arms of Catalonia; 2. ID Tag; 3. Lighter; 4. Checkers piece; 5. Inkbottles; 6. Cologne and perfume; 7. Comb with nit comb; 8. Razor; 9. Medicines.

Source: Drawing by Anxo Rodríguez Paz for the author.

(Glover 1946). Parasites often caused skin diseases. Aurelio Gamir's Bardanol, of which we found a cap, treated eczema and dermatosis.[9] It was made of a plant—burdock (*Arctium lappa*)—often found in the Valencia region, where this medicine was made. Bronchopulmonary diseases were particularly prevalent. As mentioned above, the winter of 1938 in Spain was one of the coldest in recent history: in January of that year temperatures of minus 20 degrees Celsius caused as many victims on the Teruel front as the bullets and explosives: Nationalists suffered 14,000 deadly casualties, 16,000 wounded and 17,000 illness-related casualties (Thomas 1994: 794). To cure lung diseases, the Republicans relied on cough syrup made by Cavacases, also

152 *Wait and retreat*

produced in Valencia, and Juanola cough pills. A tin of these pills appeared during surface survey in a Republican position near Alto de Molino. The inscription reads "Juanola pills cure cough. 8 Montseny Street, Barcelona". They were invented in 1906 by a local pharmacist, Manuel Juanola, and are still available.[10]

Life in a static position meant mostly boredom, which soldiers fought by playing games and writing letters. In Alto del Molino we have found a piece of a checkers game and plenty of writing material: two quills, mechanical pencil leads (a nineteenth-century invention in its present form) and a dozen inkbottles and inkbottle caps of the brands Milan and Waterman. Milan had been producing stationery in Catalonia since 1918, while Waterman had been founded in New York in 1883. Excavations at Republican sites have furnished a significantly higher number of inkbottles than Nationalist positions: this is coherent with the Republic's project of promoting literacy, and with the emphasis placed on education as a tool for emancipation. Soldiers wrote millions of letters, but very few have been preserved (Matthews 2012: 138). Inkbottles are the reminders of what we have lost.

Other objects forgotten in the sheepfold include a brass lighter decorated with stars, a padlock, a great number of buckles and clasps (from belts, fasteners and bags) suggesting the heterogeneous character of their uniforms. Thus, we have found elements belonging to the Carniago load-carrying equipment, standard with most units of the Spanish Army before the war, but also clasps of the Mills webbing equipment—a version of the British Pattern 1908, adopted by the Spanish Legion during the Rif War (1920–1926). We also recovered some insignia. Two of the badges show the Catalan flag and the inscription *Catalunya*. The soldiers of the 138 Mixed Brigade arrived from Catalonia to Guadalajara in June 1937 and stayed there until the end of the war. Among the men who fought in Guadalajara was Joaquim Soms (1914–2012), who composed a *sardana* (a musical piece typical of Catalonia) called "Catalans a l'Alcarria"—the region where Alto del Molino is located. The piece, which was to cost him a year in prison under Franco, became the war-time anthem for all Catalan combatants on the Guadalajara front. Soms was the conductor of a band that went around the trenches playing music in order to raise the spirits of the soldiers. The neighboring camp of Canredondo (Chapter 9) yielded several more badges of this type: soldiers must have either been quite careless about them or decided to get rid of them hastily after the war, for fear of retaliation.

Much rarer than the Catalan insignia is an identification tag with information about the unit (138 B, 549 B) and possibly about the person carrying it (the initials PF). Tags had begun to be used systematically during the First World War. Spain introduced replicas of the German ones during the colonial conflict in the Rif in the1920s, but massive conscription at the onset of the Spanish Civil War caused most soldiers to leave for the front without any kind of personal identification. This was particularly the case with the Republican Army, since most of the badges remained in the hands of the professional army in Africa. The Republicans often improvised their own tags: the one that we found in the Alto del Molino is one of the most frequent types and could therefore almost be considered official (Herrasti et al. 2014). Still, the practice of improvising identity tags was not as widespread in Spain as it became among combatants of the First World War, which might reflect a lower degree of individualization on the part of Spanish soldiers in comparison with Germany or the United Kingdom (Robertshaw and Kenyon 2008: 155): after all, many came from rural areas, from traditional communities where illiteracy prevailed and the modern concept of the individual self was not developed. The soldiers of Alto del Molino led a relatively calm existence until the end of March. There was some shooting and some shelling, for sure, there was bitter cold, but, all in all, they were probably better off than their comrades in Aragón.

Waiting and raiding in Aragón

In the winter of 1938, the fate of the war was being decided in the southern part of Aragón, in the province of Teruel which, as we saw, was the scenario of one of the largest battles of the Spanish Civil War. While the Battle of Teruel was raging, most of the Aragón frontline, however, remained calm—perhaps precisely because of that. This was the case in the lands of the province of Zaragoza that had experienced the ravages of war during the summer of 1937. In the previous chapter, we saw how the Popular Army managed to stop the Nationalist units in Mediana de Aragón that came to the rescue of Belchite. After September 1937 the front did not move and the soldiers of both armies dug in and waited. They waited but were neither safe nor idle. Raids, some of them of considerable proportions, were common currency in this sector until March 1938, when the Nationalist offensive forced the Republicans to withdraw. In Chapter 5, we saw that the war landscape in Mediana had remained exceptionally well preserved. There is no need to excavate, or even to carry out surveys with a metal detector to record the remains. The scarce sedimentation and the sparse vegetation have left most of the artifacts visible on the surface.

Our research focused not so much on what was inside the fortifications as on the space in between them: that is, on the no-man's-land (González-Ruibal, Rodríguez Simón and Garfi 2015). Despite its name, this land of nobody is the scenario of many dramas. Soldiers cross it on their way to a surprise attack, to spy on the enemy's lines, to desert or to move forth toward the enemy's trenches in a large offensive. The space in-between lines acquired both epic and sinister dimensions during the First World War: its lunar landscapes witnessing the deaths of millions of human beings in pointless attacks. Walking across no-man's-land in Mediana, one feels transported to the time of the Spanish Civil War. Among other reasons, because our survey follows in the exact footsteps of the soldiers who crossed

154   *Wait and retreat*

this nothingness 80 years ago: we jump across the parapets of the Republican trenches, we walk down the steep hillsides, in the shadow of the dales, and up the hillsides on the opposite line. Protected by the gypsum outcrops, we find the Nationalist trenches in front of us. Today, we can approach and even cross them oblivious of any danger. Our only enemies here are the sun and the wind, as implacable today as they were then. Field walking is a sensorial experience, for sure, but it is also a way of reading the landscape. This is nowhere as evident as in the desolate fields of Mediana: every step is full of evidence of what happened. Suddenly, the landscape is no longer a bare and empty desert, but a place full of history—and stories.

Our work in the area began with an advanced Republican post that had a large amount of ammunition on the surface. The excavation revealed a dugout for a machine gun, which yielded a rather homogeneous assemblage: one hundred Soviet 7.62 mm shell casings and a stack of empty ammunition boxes. In all likelihood, this was the position of a Maxim machine gun. From this prominent place, it was easy to harass the enemy, who occupied lower altitudes. Nationalist soldiers were surely tormented by the machine gun, and would do anything to destroy it. Artillery, mortars and rifle and machine-gun fire tried to silence it: we found dozens of incoming bullets stuck in the parapet, as well as artillery and mortar craters and shrapnel in the surroundings. As action at a distance proved useless, the Nationalists decided to try a riskier operation: a surprise attack. This probably took place at night: soldiers crept up the foothills, which were not exposed to the enemy's visual control; yet no sooner had they started making their way up the spur that they were heard by a sentinel nestled in his listening-post at the top of the hill; he fired, they fired back and a full-blown battle broke out: attackers threw Lafitte bombs, Republicans responded with rifle and machine-gun fire and Polish grenades. The ground today shows traces of unexploded Lafittes, grenade rings and safety levers, mortar shell fragments, casings and lost cartridges (Figure 6.3). The machine gun—well-protected inside its earthen nest and surrounded by barbed wire—could not be neutralized. Seventy-seven years later, we could still record the traces of combat on the naked surface with our GPS. We know that the Nationalists made similar bids at other neighboring spurs, probably to drain their enemies' forces through attrition, take prisoners and destroy their listening posts. The result was very similar in all cases: a grenade combat in no-man's-land and the Nationalist retreat without having made it close enough to the Republican parapets—although the sentinels might have been killed. These surprise attacks undoubtedly had the effect of undermining troop morale by creating a constant state of tension. How many sleepless nights did the soldiers go through? A coffee pot lying next to the machine-gun nest reminds us of the fuel that kept night battles going.

Soldiers of the Popular Army dreaded these unexpected (or perhaps over-expected) blows, but perhaps they feared the ordeal of mortars even more. Republican positions were systematically bombed with 81 mm Valero

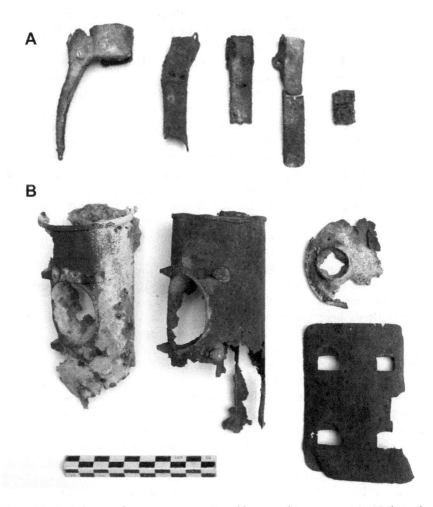

Figure 6.3 Finds from surface survey near a Republican machine-gun nest in Mediana de Aragón.

Notes: A. pieces from Polish grenades used by the Republicans to repel a Nationalist raid; B. Lafitte grenades used by the Nationalists during the raid.

Source: © Author.

mortars, of which there is plenty of evidence: on the one hand, the entire surface is pierced with craters, many of them with grenade fragments still embedded; on the other, not all projectiles exploded: we found three complete grenades stuck in the ground. The 81 mm Valero, which we have often met, shot a 4-kilogram projectile (containing 550 grams of high explosive trinitrotoluene) at a range of over two kilometers. Rebel troops made massive use of this mortar and of other similar trench weapons. One of them was the Italian Brixia or Breda, which we found in the attacks on the

156 *Wait and retreat*

Palace of Ibarra (see Chapter 5). The Republican artillery proved to be more effective in this case than the Nationalist: the craters produced by Republican fire are closer to the rebel parapets—some even impacted the parapets and shelters themselves—while the mortar impacts on Republican lines appear at a certain distance from the lines and do not actually seem to have been lethal. This is due to the fact that the Republicans were better placed than their opponents, but also because they placed residential zones in naturally protected areas, on the hillsides, whereas the Nationalists insisted on erecting their fortifications upon elevations (like the blockhouses they made in Morocco), making them easy targets for enemy artillery.

The Republican troops also launched their own, and seemingly more successful, attacks on enemy trenches. In fact, taking advantage of their more favorable topographic position, the Republicans attacked on several occasions. Without adequate listening posts, the Nationalists were more easily caught off guard and their lines were hit at different points. At one of these points we found enough material to paint a picture of what might have happened. Here we found an advanced foxhole connected to the main resistance trench through a long and narrow ditch. The foxhole is circular, 1.5-meters deep (originally increased by sandbags). Inside there was a soldier, armed with an M1930 Breda light machine gun and a German Mauser rifle. The sentinel was also equipped with Lafitte bombs. The work of a sentinel was hard. Isolated in his pit, surrounded by an eerily silent landscape, the only companion was the relentless wind, which swept the steppes and froze one to the bone. Nothing usually happened.

But then suddenly it does: first, Republicans appear by surprise and attack with grenades. The sentinel is forced to crouch while the attackers cut the barbed wire with pliers. After the explosions come the shots. The Breda replies to the Mosin's fire. But the Republicans keep coming closer and closer. They throw grenades, they advance. The sentinel throws his Lafittes, which explode at a close range, but he is unable to stop the attackers, who fall upon him and shoot from the top of the parapet. How does the story end?

We do not know. But several Mosin shell casings around the foxhole and the trench indicate that Republicans made it that far. They might possibly have penetrated the trench, killed or wounded its occupants and then returned to their positions, perhaps after taking some prisoners and weapons: a typical night raid of the kind that were so abundant during the Spanish Civil War, and of which so little has been written. A few more spots along the sector show similar episodes; they all invariably leave the same marks on the terrain: mortar craters, rifle and machine gun ammunition, a few pistol bullets and cartridges and great amounts of Lafitte fragments (safety pins, springs, weights, metal sheet). The Republicans never succeeded in seizing enemy fortifications. Perhaps they did not mean to either. What is patently clear is that, at least in this area, they penetrated enemy lines further than the Nationalists did into Republican ones. The surprise attacks we have recorded archaeologically might also have ended badly. Like the one described by Mexican brigader Néstor Sánchez, for example. Sánchez was barely 19 years of age when he fought in the Mediana trenches, although he was already a veteran after having participated in the Mexican Cristero War at 14.[11] His unit was sent to Mediana to attack a trench in a nearby village held by the Nationalists, Fuentes de Ebro:

> "It was already dark as we approached the enemy lines, which surrounded a fortified hilltop and it was there that we began to attack more consistently, trying to make the most of the surprise factor; we threw ourselves into the fray, trying to destroy all obstacles with our hand bombs and to force the fascists back into their trenches as we cut through their barbed wire with pliers. But our enemy, probably aware of our offensive,–or rather surprise attack–was prepared and expecting us, and let us come closer, our soldiers already cutting through the fences of their parapets when the horrific sound of their machine-guns began to roar (...) Next came the bombing of hand grenades between ourselves and the enemy, lighting up the night with blasts that covered up the screams of our wounded as they begged to be saved".
>
> (Sánchez Hernández 1997: 148)

The presence of Republican shell casings on the Nationalist parapets suggests that surprise attacks were probably more successful in Mediana. In any case, the most frequent find in no-man's-land are bullets, hundreds of bullets. So many that they allow us to create density maps that provide an accurate picture of where shots were coming from, and where they were aiming at (Figure 6.4). Thanks to this we have a better understanding of the battlefield's dynamics. If few documents speak of this frontline, the bullets do in their stead. They also provide other types of information, if we look at the way they impacted.

Contrary to what many of us would think, the science of so-called terminal ballistics is anything but precise. Terminal ballistics studies the effect of a bullet on a human organism. The issue is of enormous importance, not only from a military perspective, but also politically and ethically (Cornish 2013). Since 1868, several conventions have been held with the aim of limiting the unnecessary injuries of military projectiles. The problem is that, on one hand, efforts to limit such harm are quite ineffective. Until the 1880s, rifles fired bullets of 11mm or similar calibers, like those of the Vetterli which, as we have seen, was still used in the Spanish Civil War. Because of their great caliber, these bullets caused horrendous wounds and mutilations. Did the situation improve with smaller calibers? It did partly, but not always. Intuitively, we tend to think that modern bullets simply go through bodies or remain lodged inside them. Although this is partly true, according to a study made prior to the First World War, 63% of projectiles of the then new 0.303 caliber did not cause clean linear wounds. This is due to two phenomena: fragmentation and tumbling. The effect of the first is easy to understand. As

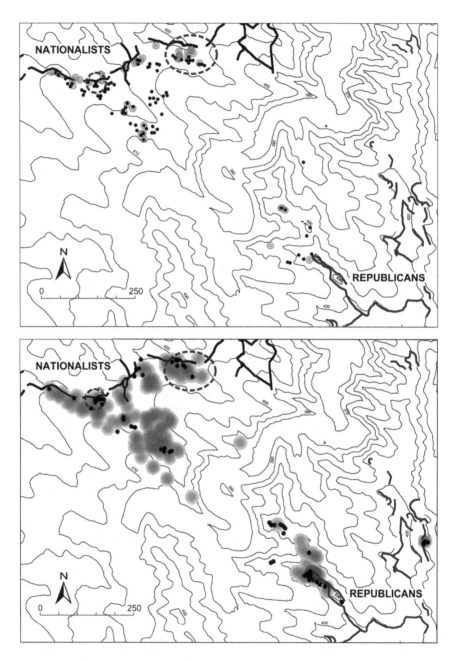

Figure 6.4 Fighting in no-man's-land in Mediana de Aragón.

Notes: Above: location of artillery shell fragments, including mortar (dots) and of artillery craters (grey circles). Below: density of bullets (shaded) and shell casings (dots). The maps show that the Republicans clearly had the upper hand in this sector.

Source: © Author.

for the second, it means that the asymmetry in the weight of the bullet caused it to flip around in the air (while maintaining a linear trajectory), because the center of gravity was often placed at the base. Many bullets thus ended up impacting on their back or, what is worse, continued to tumble inside the human body. This produces what is known as "cavitation" (Cornish 2013: 15). The phenomenon consists in the formation of cavities inside the tissue of an organ. It can either be temporary (as they receive an impact, organs move to later return to their original position) or permanent (when organic or muscular mass is lost and expelled through the wound's opening). A small 7 mm bullet can therefore make a several centimeters-wide tunnel inside a body (up to 12.5 times the projectile's width) and since there are limits to our organs' elasticity, it can cause irrecovcrable tear. Understandably then, several nations have accused each other of using explosive bullets. In the Spanish Civil War too: a Nationalist newspaper, for example, spoke of the capture of explosive bullets from the "Reds".[12]

Having documented thousands of bullets on the battlefield, we have verified the existence of clear impact patterns which might be related to different patterns of trauma. The strongest differences are to be found between Spanish bullets and the rest. Spanish 7 mm bullets with their rounded points belonged to a relatively old-fashioned model of small-caliber ammunition which soon adopted the familiar pointed projectile. The advantage of rounded bullets is that they have a more balanced gravitational center and tend to flip less in midair. The problem is that they fragment upon impact causing the lead from the bullet's core to drip down the base (an effect called "lead snowstorm"), similar to that of an explosive bullet. Most of the 7 mm Mauser bullets that we have recorded at Mediana only preserve their metal jacket, which either burst open in a flower shape or was simply empty, as if they were hollow-point projectiles (Figure 6.5). Instead, Soviet 7.62 mm and German 7.92 mm bullets, which were pointed, nearly always appear complete, sometimes with their point folded from the impact, but only rarely do we find empty or fragmented jackets. The materials employed also make a difference: German bullets were made of iron, as copper was scarce in the 1930s. This lack of fragmentation is beneficial (for whoever receives the shot), but the problem here is cavitation: both projectiles tend to flip in the air, producing disproportionate-sized wounds. In fact, some of the bullets we have recorded, especially the German ones (whose weight is particularly unbalanced) show bases deformed by impact. Soviet ones are more unlikely to have flipped because of the cavity they have at the base, which favors a linear trajectory.

We can conclude that there is no such thing as a good bullet. One might possibly receive a clean wound from a projectile that does not fragment, expand or flip. But the impact is also likely to cause the destruction of vital organs, or extensive damage to tissues, without this necessarily provoking instant death (as was often the case with nineteenth-century calibers). Small calibers are more likely to cause a slow and painful death or traumas

160 *Wait and retreat*

Figure 6.5 Bullets from no-man's-land in Mediana de Aragón.
Notes: 1, 2, 3 and 5: 7 mm bullets showing different kinds of impact. 4. Italian 6.5 mm bullet; 6. Soviet 7.62 mm bullets.
Source: © Author.

requiring a long recovery period. And even if one does survive a shot, one can die or lose a limb from bacterial infection.

When they were not fighting, soldiers on both sides used to either build fortifications or simply get bored. On one of the foothills, Republicans built the greatest dwelling area in this sector. We were able to record no less than 80 structures (Garfi 2019b). They are small square or rectangular-shaped shelters, semi-excavated into the hillside and closed by walls made of local gypsum blocks. They were originally covered with brush, metal sheet from old ammunition boxes and the odd tile salvaged from a sheepfold. The available space is quite limited, some four or five square meters: enough, however, for a pair of combatants to huddle to sleep and exchange fleas.

An exception to this is an approximately 10-square-meter hut at the south end of the complex (Figure 6.6). This was possibly the officers' residence. The excavation exposed several rooms at different heights: the higher and more isolated ones were probably used as dormitories. We found the remains of a hearth and plenty of artifacts in the exact place where they had been

Figure 6.6 Possible officers' house in Mediana and some of the finds from the house: toothbrush, toothpaste and comb.
Source: © Author.

abandoned, most of them related to personal hygiene: a shaving basin, fragments of a mirror, a toothbrush, toothpaste and a flea-comb (*liendrera*). The flea-comb might appear as rather primitive to us, but recent studies have proven it to be more effective against parasites than shampoo. The brush has the French words *qualité superieure* written on it. The first industrially produced brush dates back to 1885 and the first nylon-bristle one is from 1938 (Miller et al. 2000: 16). The production of plastics was still in its infancy in Spain and this explains that combs and toothbrushes often came from more industrialized countries such as Germany, France, the United States or even Japan. The Spanish Army contributed greatly to popularize hygienic habits among the population. It did so for practical purposes: losing a combatant due to illness could often be prevented through basic hygienic measures –such as teeth-washing.

The most surprising finding was a newspaper. Due to its small size, we thought that it was one of the newspapers printed by unions and parties. The cleaning confirmed this point. A few words preserved here and there allowed us to identify a discourse delivered by the secretary of the Communist Party. We could made out "política" (*politics*), "firmes" (*firm*), "fuerzas antifascistas" (*antifascist forces*), "abarca a todas las" (*comprises all*), "debe desarrollarse sin límites" (*has to be developed without limits*), "nuestro Frente Popular" (*our Popular Front*) and "su función" (*its function*). Thanks to Google Books, it was possible to trace these few words to a discourse by the communist leader José Díaz (1885–1942), which reads:

> "It is the first time that all the political forces of the people are united on the base of a common program of demands, which comprises all the layers of the industrious people and that can be developed without limits.

162   *Wait and retreat*

> This is our Popular Front: the organization that fights against fascism, against traditional oppressors and invaders. Its function has not ended and cannot end in a very long time".

Díaz was a prominent member of the Spanish Communist Party, a staunch defender of a democratic republic and an enemy of the revolutionary experiments of Trotskyists and anarchists. He was evacuated to Russia at the end of 1938 to receive cancer treatment and committed suicide in 1942 before the disease put an end to his life. His sister was assassinated by the Nationalists in Seville as a reprisal for his brother's political activities. Díaz pronounced the discourse at the Central Committee of the Communist Party in Valencia between 13 and 16 November 1937. It seems that the document we found has to be dated around those days. The publication allows us to infer that the occupants of the trench were sympathizers of the Communist Party. It also provides a date around which the hut was occupied. Other shacks yielded more fragments of printed papers, where it is possible to make out some broken words in Catalan, a cinema program, and a piece of sports news mentioning the London Wembley stadium.

Mediana had yet another surprise in store for us. Behind the Nationalist trenches extends a desolate landscape only interrupted by the occasional sheepfold. Over the past few years the tiles covering these constructions have become valuable pieces, as building materials for vintage homes, and they are being systematically looted. In one case, the looting uncovered what looked like a stack of old clothes lying in the wattle-and-daub structure under the roof of a sheepfold. And indeed it was, but when one of our collaborators walked past the ruins and saw them, these clothes captured his attention and he decided to take a closer look.[13] As he sorted out the rags, he realized that he was holding nothing other than Spanish Civil War uniforms. He took the best-preserved ones and left the rest, which we were able to collect ourselves a few months later.

In total there were three pairs of trousers, two civilian shirts, two military shirts and a long winter coat (Figure 6.7). Some could be of Republican make, based on the collar design, but most were of the type produced by the Spanish Army before the war. A Mauser M-1893 in good condition was also found under the roof. Who were these soldiers? To which army did they belong? It is difficult to say, but it is quite likely that they were Nationalists. Although the Mauser was used by both sides, it was less common in frontline troops of the Popular Army, particularly at this stage of the war, when government soldiers were mostly armed with Mosin Nagant rifles. Besides, the sheepfold is within Nationalist territory, while close to the Republican lines.

What were they doing in this sheepfold? Why were they getting rid of their weapons and uniforms? One possibility is that they were deserters trying to go over to the Republican side. In retrospect, a bad move, but at the time it might have seemed logical. The Zaragoza offensive was a large Republican attack that seemed to be quite successful. If the soldiers were leftist, it would have made all the more sense to try to switch sides. Or if their families were

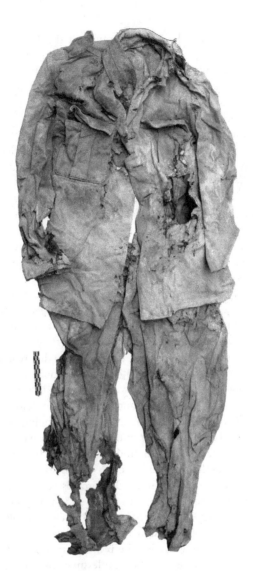

Figure 6.7 Military uniform probably abandoned by deserters in a sheepfold in Mediana.
Source: © Author.

in Republican territory. Or they were simply deserting, to join no side. To go home. Interestingly, none of the garments show any kind of identification, either of unit, rank, or army. In fact, even the buttons were taken out, as if to eliminate all possible information regarding the owners. What happened with those soldiers? Did they reach Republican lines? Their towns? Their families? Did they survive the war? We will probably never know.

164 *Wait and retreat*

Retreat

While soldiers idled or launched raids throughout the 1,200-km-long frontline, troops in Teruel were experiencing a very different kind of combat. This was all-out industrialized warfare at its worst. The battle had started on 15 December 1937, when the Popular Army launched a massive offensive and eventually captured this small provincial capital (but an important communications hub) in Nationalist hands since the beginning of the war. The Nationalists sent their own counteroffensive in December 29, which raged until 22 February 1938 (Alegre 2018). Teruel was retaken by Franco's armies and the operations cost over 100,000 casualties on both sides, including at least 37,000 dead. The losses in *matériel* were enormous for the Republic, which had 35% of their tanks and airplanes destroyed. The Popular Army, which suffered more casualties, also had more problems replacing its soldiers than the Nationalists. This explains the ruthless behavior of some Republican commanders, who ordered the shooting of soldiers for desertion or refusing to continue fighting. A particularly tragic case is the fate of the 84 Mixed Brigade (Corral 2004).

The unit had fought bravely during the battle of Teruel. The combats developed under terrible conditions, with temperatures dropping below minus 20 degrees. Almost a third of the members of the brigade, 600 men, lost their lives in the fray, but the 84 Brigade kept fighting and had a key role in the conquest of the town. Due to their heroic efforts, they were granted leave for one week. However, as soon as they arrived to the rearguard, they were ordered to return to the frontline to stop the Nationalist counteroffensive on Teruel. Around 300 refused. Forty-six of them, probably chosen at random, were executed without a proper trial and buried in the fields of Piedras Gordas, near Rubielos de Mora (Teruel). They passed from being heroes to villains to corpses in a matter of days. In 2009 and 2010 surveys were conducted, at the request of their relatives, to try to find the burials (Etxeberria, Herrasti and Jiménez 2011). The results were different to what had been expected. No mass grave was found, but two small, unmarked graves with two and three bodies respectively. They were soldiers, because at least two had military buckles with the infantry symbol. They were killed by rifle bullets. It is plausible that not all soldiers were executed at the same time and that in Piedras Gordas, or elsewhere, there are still graves with the remaining bodies. The case of the 84 Brigade is somewhat unique for the ruthlessness of the punishment. More serious cases of insubordination had been dealt with in a more lenient way before. The summary executions can be explained in the context of mass violence, destruction and demoralization that was the Battle of Teruel. The killing of deserters, in fact, would become more common from January 1938 onwards, as the situation of the Republic deteriorated and morale collapsed.

The Nationalist offensive in Teruel led to the withdrawal of the Republican forces along the entire Aragón front. The retreat that ensued was painfully experienced by the international volunteers who suffered much during the combats. The great Aragón retreat, in fact, became part of the mystique of the International Brigades, particularly the British and North American (Baxell 2012: 306–323). The Aragón Offensive started on 7 March 1938, only two weeks after the end of the Battle of Teruel, and on April 15 the Nationalists reached the Mediterranean in Vinaroz (Castellón), thus cutting the Republican territory into two and isolating Catalonia.

Only two days after the beginning of the offensive, the XV International Brigade was sent to Belchite, which the brigaders had captured only a few months before, this time to resist the Nationalist advance. The Lincoln-Washington Battalion was deployed in El Pueyo Hill to reinforce a unit of marines of the 95 Mixed Brigade, with very little fighting experience. El Pueyo was a sanctuary of the sixteenth to eighteenth century, itself built on top of a Roman town. There are several references to the combats in and around Belchite during the Aragón Offensive. Authors agree that Belchite was quickly overwhelmed and that the brigaders had little opportunity to return the enemy fire (Baxell 2012: 307). This was due to the massive Nationalist firepower and particularly aviation, that enjoyed total control of the sky (Eby 2007: 291). We have a unique witness account, the powerful narrative of Fausto Villar, a Spaniard with the Lincoln Battalion in El Pueyo.[14] He noted that on Wednesday, March 9, a great concentration of German and Italian planes appeared over Belchite. He counted 120. Then explosives started falling on El Pueyo: "The battle is no longer a battle. Heavy artillery and enemy tanks, with their rapid fire, force our brigaders to take shelter as best as they can". When Fausto leaves the underground shelter he finds a chilling scene:

> "Commissar Parker is lying on the ground while part of his encephalic mass is protruding from a side of his head. There are four or five corpses of dead officers as well, next to the commissar's body. And there is also the commander, lieutenant Dave Reiss, lying on a blanket, with a very pale face, his eyes glazed, and part of the intestines coming out of the abdomen…"

An artillery shell had hit the place where the battalion's staff was hiding. Around 30 men were killed and wounded in this position by artillery and aviation bombing before they retreated toward Belchite (Baxell 2012: 308).

The trenches in El Pueyo cut through the layers of the Roman town and were exposed during archaeological works to uncover the ancient remains.[15] In 2014, archaeologist Pedro Rodríguez Simón excavated and documented a trench held by the Lincolns while documenting the ruins of a Roman bath complex. The trench, which was not visible on the surface, unlike other fortifications, was part of a complex that connected the first line and the buildings of the sanctuary. It was backfilled soon after the combats, thus sealing the context of March 1938. In the 10-meter long tract that was excavated, remains of tin cans, shoes and fabric were found, along with 69 Soviet 7.62 mm spent casings. Since the ditch was a communications trench, Pedro Rodríguez Simón believes that it might indicate fierce fighting while retreating, as the soldiers were using elements that were not originally conceived for combat. Firing was surely at short distance, as it was not possible to fire on the plain or the lower part of the hill from that position. A GIS analysis confirmed its limited visibility: the soldiers could only shoot effectively at a range of 50 meters around the trench. The excavations that we conducted in a nearby fire trench in 2015 furnished more shell casings and an empty Soviet ammunition box, thus indicating that fighting was generalized (Figure 6.8). The combats in El Pueyo may not have lasted long, but archaeological evidence makes it clear that the Americans did defend the position against overwhelming enemy fire. Belchite fell on March 10, only one day after the XV Brigade arrived at El Pueyo.

The Republicans put up some serious resistance in a few places. One of them was Caspe, 70 km east of Belchite. Reinforcements arrived here to stop the Nationalist offensive on March 13 (Melguizo Aísa 2018: 15–20). The situation was desperate. Alcañiz, Teruel's second largest town situated only 28 km south of Caspe, fell on the 14th, and thousands of soldiers of the Popular Army were captured. Caspe itself fell on the 17th, after heavy fighting in its surroundings, but the brigaders held the line along the river Guadalope, east of the town, and dug in. The sector was defended mainly by the XIV International Brigade (made up of French and Belgians) and the XII (Italians). A new phase of the Nationalist attack began on March 26. With

Figure 6.8 Excavation of a trench and firing position defended by the Lincoln Battalion during the Aragón retreat. Sanctuary of El Pueyo (seen in the background), near Belchite (Zaragoza).

Source: © Author.

massive artillery and tank support again, Carlist and colonial troops initiated an assault on the brigaders, whose first line was overrun despite fierce resistance. The XIV International Brigade managed to hold the sector for three days, but the line eventually collapsed and the Republicans fled on the 29th. The casualties were high on both sides. A Nationalist commander admits 350 casualties among his own troops in a single day and Nationalist reports inform of 250 dead found and 100 prisoners taken in the hills east of Caspe.

Archaeologists have exhumed the remains of four Republican soldiers who fell during the Battle of Caspe. Three of them appeared in a single mass grave in Hill 238, which was held by the XIV International Brigade until March 28. The soldiers were probably buried by the Nationalists, since they were thrown in the mass grave in a haphazard manner. It is possible to infer the cause of death in two cases: Soldier 1 has the skull fractured by a bullet that went from the left temporal bone to the occipital. Soldier 2 had a large fragment of artillery shell lodged between the cervical vertebrae and a foot missing. Several objects appeared associated with the bones. Soldier 1 had the insignia of a machine-gun company, while in the zone of the upper right pocket of his jacket he was carrying a signet ring with the emblems of the Communist Party, a utility knife, a handkerchief, two pencils and a mechanical pencil. In the documents of the XV International Brigade, mechanical pencils and utility knives are mentioned as gifts presented to soldiers who excelled in combat (Melguizo Aísa 2018: 24). The soldier had a leather belt and two ammunition pouches, which were carrying Soviet 7.62 mm cartridges still wrapped in paper.

Soldier 3 also had a leather belt and two ammunition pouches with 15 Mosin Nagant full clips. On his back he was carrying a bandolier with two more ammunition pouches, one with 10 clips and the other one with two Spanish grenades, of the type nicknamed *saleret* ("small salt shaker" in Catalan),[16] a Republican version of the French F1 grenade of the First World War, but with a wick, instead of a fuse. Part of the jacket was preserved and in one of the pockets there were five cigarette papers of the brands Pay Pay and Bambú, a gasoline lighter and 18 copper coins, mostly *perras gordas* and *chicas* from the 1870s. The soldier was wearing as an adornment an Argentinean silver coin dated 1883. The reason for wearing it may be that the coin displays an effigy of the Republic. Also, some Argentinean volunteers were fighting with the XII International Brigade in the area.

A single boot (all soldiers were wearing them) and a piece of printed paper is all that was found with Soldier 2. The paper seems to be a page of a dictionary, which would make sense if he was an international brigader.

The soldiers likely fell during the combats of March 26–27 and belonged to either the XII or XIV International Brigades—or both. Around half the members of the brigades were Spaniards at the time. The lack of systematic documentation of casualties, in part due to the chaos of the combats during the great retreat, and of ID tags has made their identification impossible so far.

The remains of a fourth individual appeared in another hill further south (Melguizo Aísa 2018: 40–42). The burial had been disturbed by a bulldozer, but

168   *Wait and retreat*

several human bones could be found belonging to a single individual, as well as different artifacts associated with the deceased, such as a Mosin Nagant ammunition clip, lenses from eyeglasses and a Republican grenade of the *biberón* (baby bottle) type.[17] The weapons indicate that the fallen soldier was Republican and the bones that he was closer to his forties than to his thirties, an age consistent with an international volunteer. Considering the location of the grave, researchers consider quite likely that the fallen soldier belonged to the XIV International Brigade. The brigade, which retained only 40% of foreign members by March 1938, lost half its men during the Aragón Offensive: 2,565.

While the Republicans were catastrophically losing ground on the Aragón front, they launched an offensive in another part of Spain. It was in Guadalajara, the static frontline that I have described earlier in this chapter. Unlike the Aragón offensive of the Nationalists, very little has been written about this one. So little, that we have called it the Forgotten Battle and used archaeology to reconstruct it.

Notes

1 "se proive terminantemente mease en la escalera por causa de la yngiene lo que cetifico para el conocimiento de los ynteresados y el que desovedezca esta ordenes sera considerado como camarada cerdo".
2 The Blue Arrows were a mixed brigade (Spanish and Italian). The Black Arrows were only Italian.
3 www.campillodellerena.es/documentos/20140407091751.pdf.
4 The Republicans had taken Abánades on 2 January 1937.
5 Called *Benjamín* in Spanish, they refer to 20 cl. bottles of *cava* (Spanish-made champagne).
6 IV Cuerpo de Ejército. Informe de los servicios de Intendencia: AGMA C,761,3,3, hoja 9 (IV Army Corps report from the logistics services).
7 Unpublished diaries of Buenaventura Leris, deposited at the Museum of Abánades.
8 The term Goyesca refers to the painter Francisco Goya, whose works included picturesque depictions of Spanish popular types, including *majos* and *majas*. These terms, used to refer to the aesthetics and attitudes of the Spanish lower classes depicted them in opposition to the more cosmopolitan and French-inspired elites.
9 http://blog.uchceu.es/eponimos-cientificos/files/2011/10/gamir.pdf.
10 https://juanola.es/.
11 The Mexican Cristero War (1926–1929) was waged as a Catholic reaction to the secularist measures of the 1917 constitution, implemented by President Plutarco Elías Calles.
12 *ABC/Doble diario de la Guerra Civil: 1936-1939*, Volume 2, p. 18.
13 This incredible find is owed to Jonatan Querol, who we are truly grateful to for the information.
14 While the memoir has not been published, excerpts of it have been made available through the Internet: https://sites.google.com/site/gceformulario/4-km-en-belchite.
15 https://guerraenlauniversidad.blogspot.com/search?q=el+pueyo.
16 http://amonio.es/grana_saleret.htm.
17 Like the *saleret* grenade, this was a bomb produced by the Republic around Valencia. http://amonio.es/biberon.htm.

7 Forgotten battles
April–July 1938

Soviet tanks advance slowly over the bare land, crushing bushes and barbed wire in their way. The infantry marches a short distance behind. A sudden explosion shakes the T-26 that leads the attack, propelling stones and shell fragments around; there are no casualties, but the tanks stop. This first explosion is followed by one more, and yet another one. And then there is silence: nothing to be heard but the humming of the idling motors. The hatch opens, and the tank commander emerges and announces that they have to stop, because the machine guns are not working properly and there is no ammunition left. The battalion's commissar is not convinced, so he leaps into the tank and verifies that there is no problem with the armament. The officer insists on withdrawing. A short argument follows, then the commissar draws his gun and shoots the officer point blank. Problem solved. The tanks are back in motion.

This scene did not take place in Stalingrad or Kursk, but in Sotodosos, a tiny village in the province of Guadalajara. A small battle by Second World War standards, but in the context of the Spanish Civil War the Offensive on the Upper Tajuña River was no minor event, either in terms of the number of forces mobilized (tens of thousands of soldiers, airplanes, tanks, and much artillery) or casualties (around 8,000 counting the dead and the wounded). But the battle is absent in both the collective memory of Spaniards and the work of historians and for quite simple reasons: the operation was conceived as a secondary maneuver to distract units away from the main front in Aragón, the Republican offensive did not alter the course of the war in any way, and it took place in a year of many decisive battles. In comparison with other military encounters of the Spanish Civil War, the amount of archival evidence is limited: archaeology was here crucial to reconstruct the battle, including several events that have left no written traces (González-Ruibal 2013, 2014, 2016a).

Although we decided to call it "The Forgotten Battle", it is not the only one to have fallen into collective oblivion. The term has also been used for the Levante Offensive, which successfully stopped the Nationalist advance toward Valencia and caused over 10,000 casualties to Franco's troops (Fuertes Palasí and Mallench Sanz 2013) and whose archaeological traces I will also describe in this chapter.

170   *Forgotten battles*

The offensive of Alto Tajuña

With Julián Dueñas Méndez.[1]

It is often said that war is 99% boredom and 1% action. On 30 March 1938 soldiers were about to run out of their 99% share of boredom. Many of them forever. Spring had not started well for the Republic. As we saw, the Nationalists were smashing the Popular Army in Aragón. The easiest way to relieve pressure from a certain area is to organize an offensive elsewhere, slowing down the enemy's advance by forcing them to send troops to a different front. The province of Guadalajara, and particularly the Abánades-Sotodosos sector, was a good option for this counteroffensive: with a bit of luck, the Republicans might not only attract a considerable Nationalist contingent, but also take over the main road connecting Madrid and Barcelona. It was not, however, an easy objective: the road was some 18 kilometers away from Republican lines, and the Nationalists had deep fortifications and a rugged territory to their advantage. In the worst of cases, simply by relieving the pressure from the Aragón front, the offensive in Guadalajara would already be contributing to the war effort.

For the attack, an army corps was created with the 5, 6 and 14 Divisions, under charismatic anarchist leader Cipriano Mera, a mason by trade and with no formal military training. The 5 Division was to be deployed in Abánades, the 6 would remain in the reserve and the 14 would attack the neighboring village of Sotodosos. The front covered some 19 kilometers from east to west. Within the 5 Division, the attacking units would be the 2 and 39 Mixed Brigades. The Republicans had in front the 75 Division, which was aware of an imminent offensive but not of its magnitude. The plan consisted in a surprise night attack by the infantry to the less fortified sections of the frontline, with the support of cavalry and tanks, which would also provide cover to a second wave of forces in reserve. The plan was to be carried out on the night between the 30 and 31 March at 2:00 a.m. However, things started to go wrong from the first minute. In fact, even before the first minute.

Over the previous months—while the Catalans dug trenches in Alto del Molino (see Chapter 6)—minor attacks had been carried out in the area. The Nationalists reacted by filling the frontline with watch posts: any Republican movement was unlikely to go unnoticed. Also, important modifications had been made to the access routes leading to the rebel lines and to the positions themselves, which in some cases made them unassailable. In addition, the troops that were to take part in the attack had been arriving in the area the days before the attack, apparently not too discreetly. They traveled from Madrid on requisitioned buses and trucks, many of them driven by civilians, some of whom used the opportunity to desert or sabotage the vehicles. This provoked traffic jams in the sector, which were carefully recorded by the Nationalists. As if all this were not enough, soldiers started making fires at night, and testing their newly acquired weapons, which caused the Nationalists to send both reconnaissance planes and some bombers.

Forgotten battles 171

The Republicans still managed to launch their attack on the 31st, but with a very serious delay. The reason for the delay is astonishing. The advance was to be led by the 39 Mixed Brigade, with the 2 operating as a reserve, at 3:00 a.m. But as the clock hit 4:00 a.m., there was still no sign of the 39.[2] At 5:00 a.m, the commanders asked the 2 Brigade to replace the other unit. With one thing and another, the attack only began at six o'clock (Spanish punctuality: fortunately this was not D-Day). Half an hour later they found their comrades from the 39 who, as it turned out, *were* at their designated positions—they had simply not begun to move yet: the brigade's commander had been missing for 24 hours and was later found sleeping in his car some 20 km away from his troops (Mera 1976: 245). Even so, the division leader ordered the units to advance (by then it was already 7:00 a.m). Barely an hour later they came under the attack— with no casualties—by the Nationalist aviation, something which would never have happened had the attack started at night, as planned. But problems did not end there. In trench war, infantry advances must be preceded by an artillery barrage that destroys barbed wire fences and forces the enemy underground. But the Republican artillery only came into action at midday! Apparently, no one had shown them the objectives they were expected to destroy... More waiting around, as the artillery attack is yet to be prepared. The officers are rearranged, new orders arrive at 2 p.m. and the assault finally starts at 3 p.m. (12 hours later than planned): the 2 Mixed Brigade inaugurates the offensive (Figure 7.1).

Now comes the truly inexplicable part of the story: although at this point every Nationalist soldier was well aware of the offensive, the Republicans swiftly seized the two key fortified elevations in the sector: Majada Alta, which fell at 3:30 p.m., and Vértice Cerro, an hour later (military reports refer to them as Cerro Rojo—"Red Hill"—and Cerro Blanco—"White Hill"). It took the Nationalists the rest of the war to reconquer these positions, which were captured in just minutes. The rapid Republican advance was made possible by the fact that the troops of the 1st Gerona Battalion number 18, who were numerically inferior to their attackers, took to their heels. Clearly infuriated, the commissar of the 2 Mixed Brigade describes the operation as follows: "Such a brilliant performance on the part of the 2nd Brigade aroused certain feelings among the officers in command of the 39, who, without any orders to that effect, or any need for it on our part, placed about two companies in the recently conquered positions, next to our men, no doubt trying to justify or cover up for their previous passivity." The commissar returned to the rearguard at night and talked to his superiors, so that they would withdraw the 39 and put an end to the confusion. The officers acquiesced, but the 39 only withdrew after two days. The whole operation looked more like a schoolyard game than an offensive—but with people dying.

There is little we can tell archaeologically from these first moments of the attack. We have a striking testimony of the departing positions of 39 Brigade: an anarchist soldier left a graffiti on a rock shelter on his way to the front: 39

172 *Forgotten battles*

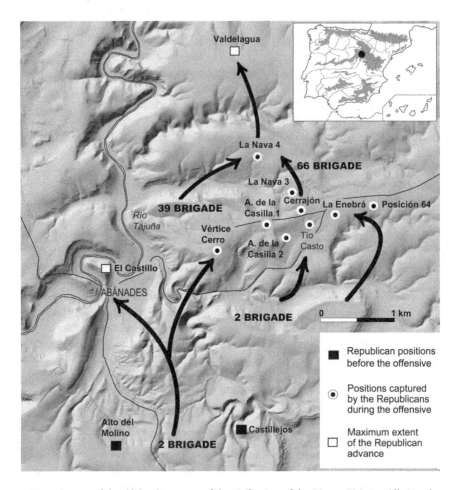

Figure 7.1 Map of the Abánades sector of the Offensive of the Upper Tajuña. All sites that appear in the map have been the object of archaeological research.
Source: © Author.

BM CNT, that is 39 Mixed Brigade, National Confederation of Work (*Confederación Nacional del Trabajo*). The CNT, as we have seen in previous chapters, was Spain's main anarchist trade union, to which Cipriano Mera was affiliated. Although most of the traces of the first day of combat have been erased by later military occupations, there is at least one place where these have been preserved: a concrete pillbox situated in the Vértice Cerro. The fort was well known in Abánades. The aim of the excavation was in fact to try to confirm a story often told in the village, according to which the pillbox became the grave of a certain Lieutenant Mateo and his men, when a direct impact of the Republican artillery pulverized the bunker, burying them all inside. The unfortunate lieutenant was nowhere to be found. But we did find materials related to the Republican offensive of March 31: inside the pillbox we found many empty shell casings fired by the defenders of the Vértice Cerro, which prove that the attack here was easy but not altogether unopposed.

The initial progression in the Abánades subsector was surprisingly successful considering the Republicans' poor coordination. We could wonder what might have happened if everyone had set out at the designated time and according to the original combat plans. On the other subsector (Sotodosos-Saelices) the first day of fighting turned out to be far bloodier. Since the information available to the Republicans was wrong and the tanks had not been deployed, the infantry collided over and over again against the Nationalist strongholds of Puntal del Abejar and Alto de la Mocasilla, two heights that were much better fortified than expected. Also, nearby Nationalist reserves were promptly carried to the front to assist the defenders, making the Republican advance even harder. The 70 Mixed Brigade sustained up to 70% casualties in a single day, among them many officers and commissars. Most of the soldiers and officers died trying to cut through the barbed wire fences.

Death in the sheepfolds

Republican advances continued throughout 1 April in the Abánades sector: the village itself fell into the hands of the 2 Mixed Brigade. So did El Rondal, a heavily fortified hill immediately to the south of the village—the position, by the way, from which Nationalists had shot at the fleeing cow just a few weeks earlier. Now they were shooting at men instead—perhaps more successfully: in the cultivated lands at the feet of El Rondal farmers plow up human remains from time to time. The bones, before we asked neighbors to preserve them, were routinely thrown into pits or burned.

Having abandoned the more exposed trench lines after the first day of the offensive, Nationalist troops regroup and defend themselves from makeshift positions, where they resist sometimes for a few hours, sometimes an entire day. They soon received reinforcements who managed to contain the Republican advance. Among them were hardened and experienced ones like the 152 Moroccan Division, whose Moroccan soldiers were still vividly remembered by the older people of Abánades. The defenders also had the support of aviation, which, taking advantage of their air supremacy, bombed Republican positions at will—also, by mistake, its own infantry marching to reinforce the front.

Archaeology allows us to follow the Republicans' advance step by step. We found the most eloquent testimonies, again, in sheepfolds, the points of resistance where Nationalists tried to stop, or forestall, the offensive. Here, Republican casualties began to rise. Neighbors of Abánades have often found human remains along the lines of advance and the occasional bone can still

174 *Forgotten battles*

be seen on the surface. We cannot generally tell which army the fallen belonged to, when we only have scattered remains, but neighbors in the postwar period found belongings that identified the dead: a watch, a wallet, a ring or an insignia—they were looted without moral considerations. According to one neighbor, a corpse still had a ring on his finger of the anarchist CNT. Based on their location, probably all the human remains we know belong to soldiers fallen within the first two or three days of the offensive, between the attack on the Red and White Hill and the scenario of the "Battle of La Nava", further north, to which I will refer below.

We encountered one of the fallen from the first two days of the fighting quite unexpectedly, as we were digging a sheepfold that had been briefly occupied by the Nationalists (Martínez Barrio and Alonso Muela 2014a). The sheepfold of Tío Casto, as it is known, is located in a strategic position: next to the main track leading to the dirt road that communicated the two sectors of the front (Abánades and Sotodosos). The Republicans necessarily had to make their way up this route to cut the Nationalist link with Sotodosos. It could be expected that the rebels had turned the corrals along the line of advance into points of resistance. The roof of Tío Casto's sheepfold had collapsed, so we decided to excavate the access, which is called *corralón* ("large corral") and, as it was originally uncovered, was mostly clear of rubble.

The *corralón* indeed provided quite a few findings. We can confidently date them during the first two days of the offensive. A few Soviet bullets are indicative of the Republican attack, but, once they took over the position, they themselves came under fire from the retreating Nationalists, as evinced by eight Spanish Mauser bullets. We also found three 9 mm pistol shell casings and a piece of fragmentation grenade, revealing combat at close range. Since the shell casings bear stamps from the Santa Barbara Factory, in Toledo (in Nationalist hands since September 1936), it is likely that the shooter was Nationalist. We have also recorded two elements of 81 mm mortar grenades, which were probably fired by Nationalists after they lost the position.

Once the surface layer was removed, we metal-detected the *corralón* systematically to make sure that we were not missing any objects. Near the entrance, the detector started beeping intensely: as we dug the area, bones began to appear almost on the surface. They belonged to an individual buried in supine position (Figure 7.2). His hands were carefully placed on his belly and the overall disposition of the burial indicated a concern about the fallen, which suggests that it had been his comrades who had buried him (cf. Spars 2013: 111). Inside the soldier's pocket we found some copper coins from the Republic and from Alphonse XIII. He wore his trousers fastened with a civilian Art Deco enameled bronze belt, which probably means that he was wearing a mixture of military and civilian clothes. The mother-of -pearl buttons of his underwear were still in place. His comrades seemingly took all the gear with them (pouches, ammunition, etc.) and buried him only with his clothes and boots. We did not find either feet or

Figure 7.2 R., a 25-year-old Republican soldier killed in a sheepfold probably during the second day of the Offensive of the Upper Tajuña. The careful, though shallow, burial indicates that he was interred by his comrades.

Source: © Author.

cranium, because the corpse was buried very superficially. Fighting a battle leaves little time to excavate deep pits. That the owner of the corral knew of the existence of a shallow grave (he remembered the boots protruding from the tomb) and cohabited with it quite naturally speaks volumes about the neighbors' relation to mass death and the peculiar politics of memory in the country after the war.

Our anthropologists inferred from the remains that this was a tall individual for the time (Martínez Barrio and Alonso Muela 2014a): 1.72 m. He must have been about 25 years of age. And we know what killed him: a 7 mm Mauser bullet that went through his first left rib and broke several others. The dead soldier was wearing a gold wedding ring—the ring of a young husband whose wife was unable to bury him, to mourn him properly. There is little we can tell about this man's identity. The ring has the inscription "R", but listings of the fallen are lacking and therefore there is very little we can contrast the archaeological and osteological information with. We cannot even tell for certain whether he was from the 2 Mixed Brigade, given the widespread confusion of units.

Two more corrals stand near the Tío Casto sheep pen, one to the north and another to the west. The one to the west barely yielded any findings at all, which indicates that it was not used as a parapet. But the structure located

176 *Forgotten battles*

further north, the sheepfold of Martín, did provide some information confirming the Republicans' direction of advance, from south to north. The Nationalists were shooting at the advancing Republicans from the *corralón*, which is oriented toward the south and which yielded rifle and pistol ammunition. Rifle casings (7.92 mm Mauser) are different from Vértice Cerro and Tío Casto, where the predominant caliber is 7 mm. We can infer from this that the soldiers in this position might have belonged to another Nationalist unit, perhaps one of those that came to reinforce the front the day after the beginning of the offensive. As in the case of the sheepfold of Tío Casto, soldiers ended up fighting at close range: we collected five pistol shell casings. Three of them belong to the 9x23 mm caliber, which corresponds to the official pistol of the Spanish Army, the Astra 400, and two are 7.62 mm casings perhaps from a personal weapon.

The remains inside the sheepfold were visible on the surface: many tin cans, whose distribution indicates the location where soldiers sat down to eat—toward the back, as far as possible from the door. The 27 tins can be related to the single meal of a platoon (15 to 30 men) who did not spend more than one day at the place. They are nearly all of sardines (backpack menu) and some dated in 1937. We also found a condensed milk of the brand Nuria—a factory established in Barcelona in 1919. As Barcelona lay deep inside Republican territory, it is possible that the soldiers eating sardines were government troops in a recess of the battle, perhaps after capturing the sheepfold. As we removed the top layer, we discovered a crater left by the impact of a Republican mortar round—the sheepfold, thus, was unroofed already during the war. The direction of the impact indicates that it was used to storm the sheepfold when it was still occupied by the Nationalists. Inside the crater, we found the head of the partly unexploded 50 mm grenade and a scatter of shell fragments.

Nationalist soldiers likely abandoned the sheepfold toward the end of April 1, because we know that the next day Republican soldiers were already attacking La Nava, a position immediately to the north. They were forced to run through the field behind the pen, while being shot at with machine guns, rifles and mortars (remains of all of which we have found in the area). The field is known as Cerrada del Cerrajón. *Cerradas* are small plots surrounded by stone walls, for planting wheat and grazing lambs, but in 1938 the walls became improvised parapets and the plots, killing fields. Not all the Nationalists managed to cross the Cerrajón: Martín, the owner of the land, told us that he discovered several corpses as he plowed the land. Before we follow the advance of the Republicans toward La Nava, let us take a small detour to visit another sheepfold under fire.

The siege of La Enebrá

There was a sheepfold that did not fall as easily in Republican hands: La Enebrá Socarrá (Figure 7.3). For several field seasons, we studied this forgotten battle inside the forgotten battle: we could not find any explicit

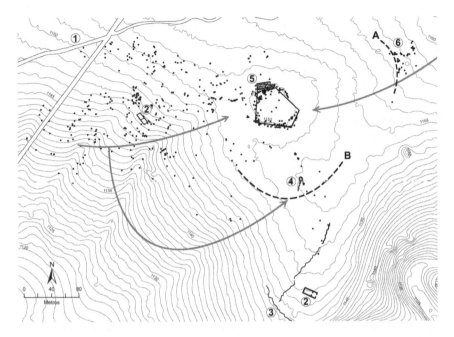

Figure 7.3 The siege of La Enebrá. General distribution of finds from the metal-detector and surface surveys.

Notes: Grey arrows indicate the most likely routes of advance of the Popular Army. A. Eastern defensive perimeter of the Nationalists; B. Southern defensive perimeter; 1. Abánades-Sotodosos road; 2. Sheepfolds; 3. Nationalist first line trenches before the attack; 4. Republican foxhole dug after the fall of the defensive perimeter; 5. Sheepfold of La Enebrá; 6. Nationalists foxholes and graves.

Source: © Manuel Antonio Franco Fernández and author.

mention of it in contemporary documents. History here necessarily has to be archaeological. We have to go back to the beginning of the offensive. Just like it happened at the Red and White Hill, the Nationalist soldiers in the Valdecaleras area abandon the first-line trenches and retreat toward the plateau. The Republicans move forward from the south and east, in a pincer maneuver that encircles the Nationalists in a place known as La Enebrá, presided by a sheepfold and its *cerrada*. This was back then a flat area devoid of vegetation, where the only natural shelters were a few rocky outcrops, some 30–40 centimeters high, located a couple of hundred meters from the sheepfold to the south and east. Here, the rebels improvised a first defensive perimeter.

The soldiers at la Enebrá were almost totally besieged: their position was a salient with Republicans on all sides but the north. We are not completely sure about the exact identity of the Nationalist fighters. Some were likely troops already stationed in the area before the Republican offensive began, more specifically, the 20 Battalion of the 25 San Quintín Regiment number 25. But

178   *Forgotten battles*

they were also probably accompanied by reinforcements, the soldiers of the 267 Cazadores de San Fernando Battalion number 1, who arrived on the very first day of the offensive. We have a singular piece of evidence that can be related to the soldiers of San Quintín: inside the sheepfold we recovered the identification tag of a Falangist. It reads: *F.E. de las JON.S 7570 Valladolid.* It belonged to the member 7,570 of the fascist party "Falange Española de las Juntas de Ofensiva Nacional-Sindicalista" in the province of Valladolid. The party in question had been dissolved on 19 April 1937, when Franco ordered its unification with the Carlists and a "T" was added to the acronym, standing for *tradicionalist,* "tradicionalista" (FET de las JONS) (Thomàs 1999), so our unknown soldier had been a Falangist for a year or more before arriving in Abánades. The city of Valladolid was the base of the San Quintín regiments, which sent as many soldiers to the frontline as it issued death sentences: inside the army barracks, a military court decided over the future of hundreds of Republicans, many of whom were eventually executed (Palomares 2000: 262). The Cazadores de San Fernando Regiment, in turn, were a colonial army unit. In fact, its original name was *Cazadores Africanos,* "African Hunters". We also have material evidence pointing to their presence in La Enebrá. According to the meager documentary sources at our disposal, theirs was the only battalion armed with both Mauser and Lebel rifles[3] and we did find Lebel cartridges and shell casings during the survey of La Enebrá. Facing the colonial troops and the Falangists was the 2 Mixed Brigade, who had hitherto borne the brunt of the offensive. It originally consisted of railway workers from Madrid and militiamen from Extremadura—two groups with strong leftist sympathies— but by the spring of 1938 not many of the original combatants were probably still fighting.

Defending the perimeter

We will return to the soldiers' identities again further below. For now, let us take a look at the siege. From the south, the place was protected by a trench, located some 200 meters south of the sheepfold, and some foxholes, where we found Mauser ammunition, including a lost clip. The situation was worse for the besieged on the east side, as there was no proper fortification, only shallow pits.

One of the soldiers defending the eastern perimeter—let us call him Juan— prepares his foxhole as best as he can. The soil is incredibly hard, and his entrenching tool keeps bouncing back. He digs the ditch pointing toward the enemy, trying to cover the widest possible range, but exposing as little of his body as possible to enemy bullets. When he has finished, he places a few stones in front for further protection. When the "Reds" fall upon him, he will have little time to open his cartridge bag, so he decides to take out several clips for his 7.92 mm Mauser and places them behind him: when the assault starts all he will have to do is to reach out and recover his cartridges. To his right there is a spare ammunition box.

To his left, his comrade—we can call him Pedro—is ensconced in a slight elevation of the ground. He is wearing Mills webbing equipment. His rifle is also a German Mauser. He has pinned onto his jacket a silver medal of Saint Joseph that his mother gave him on leaving for the front. He hopes that the medal will work as a "stopper" (*detente*) against enemy bullets (Figure 7.4). To the right of Juan, along a rocky outcrop, two other comrades are sheltered, who could be called Francisco and Alfonso. Francisco is very tall for the time. In front of the parapet they dig a foxhole. And where digging is made impossible by the ever-present rock, they simply make a low parapet of limestone blocks. They have barely finished digging themselves in when the first shots and explosions are heard. Soviet bullets fly around. The Nationalists reply and the enemy hesitates to advance. Perhaps the defensive perimeter is working. Perhaps more reinforcements will arrive, or artillery might disperse the Republicans. Silence returns. Juan pulls out a pair of sardine cans and a spoon from his pouch and eats, if the tight knot he probably has in his stomach allows him to. Francisco and Alfonso share

Figure 7.4 Medal of Saint Joseph and Jesus child found with the remains of a fallen Nationalist soldier defending the outer perimeter of La Enebrá. The medal was fixed with a safety pin to prevent loss during combat.

Source: © Author.

180 *Forgotten battles*

canned meat and tuna. Cannon and gunshot fire reverberate in the distance: the Republicans advance, but not in La Enebrá. Not for now.

The soldiers' meal is interrupted by a new and thicker hail of bullets. An artillery grenade falls 30 meters away from their positions and shell fragments shower the ground. These bullets are more accurate. Francisco, to the right, is hit by bullets or shrapnel; Alfonso runs towards the sheepfold of La Enebrá, but is killed almost as soon as he abandons his parapet. Juan retreats from his position too, leaving behind most of his ammunition and the spoon with which he was eating just a few minutes ago: he is luckier than his comrades and makes it to the enclosure, dodging bullets and shell fragments. Pedro is covering them with his Mauser and retreats as best he can, shooting, loading, losing cartridges on the way. Finally, he falls, his body perforated by bullets. In the south, the Nationalists throw a volley of Lafitte from the trench, but they are also forced to abandon it. The Republicans have broken the perimeter; the only obstacle left now between attackers and defenders is the stone wall of the *cerrada*, the enclosure where the survivors of San Quintín and San Fernando are huddled together.

Let us leave the Nationalist soldiers regrouping inside the corral. What is the scene I have just described based on? Except for the invented names, the rest comes from archaeological evidence. We first found the bones of the soldier I have named Pedro, which were disarticulated, many missing, and inside a shallow grave, in which we also found boot eyelets, jacket and underwear buttons, the muzzle cover of a German Mauser and fragments of the Mills web equipment. The human remains belonged to a man less than 30 years old and 1.55 m tall—only 30 centimeters taller than his rifle. The anthropologists detected plausible perimortem trauma in ribs and thoracic vertebrae (Martínez Barrio and Muela Alonso 2014b), which might have been caused by bullets, as we found no shell fragments in or near the grave. A meter away from the burial we also discovered a 7.92 mm ammunition clip, more eyelets and the Saint Joseph medal. More remains came from two negative structures: one was the foxhole with ammunition where the soldier I called Juan took shelter. The ditch contained tins, a spoon, stripper clips, shell casings, and ammunition clips as described above (Figure 7.5). The mixture of cans and cartridges indicating a lunch in the middle of the fray we have already seen in Casa de Campo (see Chapter 3) and there are written references: "We shoot while we eat. Eating and shooting are both necessary to survive and we combine them in a chillingly mechanical way", remembers a Falangist veteran from Belchite (Izquierdo 2006: 43).

A few meters to the right of Juan's foxhole there was another pit, possibly another firing position: inside, we collected different war materials (spent and unspent 7.92 mm ammunition, trench coat buttons and can openers). In this second foxhole human remains were dumped: we found two leg bones belonging to two different individuals, one of them of a rather tall individual. Along La Enebrá we also retrieved a skull fragment, a femur, a vertebra, a phalanx and a coxal bone, all probably from different individuals (Martínez

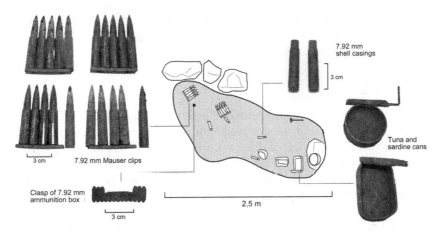

Figure 7.5 Plan of a foxhole dug in the eastern part of the perimeter of La Enebrá with associated finds.
Source: © Author.

Barrio and Alonso Muela 2014b). All human remains appeared disassembled and scattered due to the action of scavengers. In the postwar period, writer Ricardo Fernández de la Reguera published a novel about a Nationalist soldier during the Spanish Civil War. Although it is a fictional account, the author interviewed veterans, whose experiences he included in the work. Among the places visited by the fictional soldiers is Abánades. Here the main character, Augusto, wanders through a battlefield full of junk and corpses:

> But the unhomely plain saw no spring whatsoever. It is nothing but a stony desert of rotting corpses. Many are the unburied bodies. The atmosphere is almost unbreathable, it stinks. The graves are soon found. They are everywhere. It is a shocking sight. Legs and arms, hips, chests, skulls can all be seen poking out (…) The floor is sown with landmines, with shell fragments, with cannon and mortar grenades. (…) Augusto stands still before the graves (…). He is particularly obsessed with those piles of stones. Next to some are empty rifle shells. Others do not even have that. It is a heartbreaking scene. Augusto thinks about the men who laid down the stones to protect their heads.
>
> (Fernández de la Reguera 1955: 98)

During our survey with the metal detector between the defensive perimeter and the sheepfold of La Enebrá we recorded craters, shell fragments of different calibers, and remains of Valero mortar grenades. A landscape similar to the one described by Fernández de la Reguera. The most remarkable findings are a pair of complete grenades that the Nationalists must have thrown as they retreated: a Lafitte and a model 35 Breda. The Breda, a peculiar Italian offensive grenade made of aluminum and painted bright-red, has been labeled "the most inefficacious grenade ever adopted" (Manrique and Molina 2006: 111).

Fighting in the corral

As the soldiers abandoned the defensive perimeter, they sheltered behind the enclosure's southern wall, where we found many traces of fighting. In fact, 85% of the materials recovered there are combat-related: stripper clips, German Mauser shell casings, Soviet 7.62 mm bullets, clasps from ammunition boxes, artillery shell fragments and pieces of Lafitte and Roma grenades—the latter, also known as SCRM 1935, were another type of Italian offensive grenade. We found 19 stripper clips along this wall alone, the equivalent to almost a hundred rifle shots. Artillery shell fragments—mostly belonging to shells fired by T-26 tanks—were also concentrated along the southern wall (Figure 7.6). Pressure from the Popular Army troops forced the Nationalist to a new retreat. The survivors sheltered inside the sheepfold. They must have left many dead or badly wounded comrades in the *cerrada*: neighbors from Abánades described the enclosure to us as full of corpses at the end of the war.

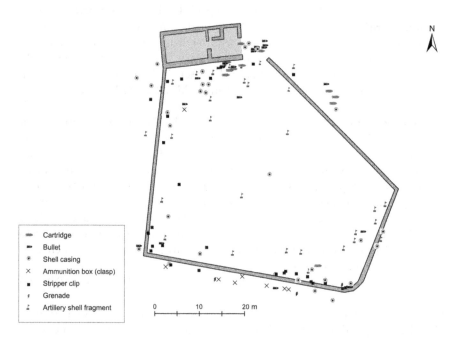

Figure 7.6 Map of the sheepfold and enclosure of La Enebrá with distribution of combat-related finds.

Source: © Manuel Antoni Fernández and author

Inside the corral, the situation must have been truly dramatic. Remnants from diverse units crammed inside, with some of the soldiers wounded. Everyone had seen their comrades fall and the prospects were disheartening. The Nationalists were heterogeneously armed: although most had German Mauser rifles (77% of the ammunition belonged to this weapon), there was some 6.5 mm Mannlicher-Carcano, 8 mm Lebel and 7 mm Spanish Mauser ammunition, which reinforces the idea that there were members from different units sheltering inside the sheepfold. We found 60 stripper clips, the equivalent to 300 cartridges inside the sheepfold alone. The defenders also had at their disposal an 81 mm Valero mortar, of which we documented a number of transport plugs, propellant rings, safety pins and 16 caliber cartridges (identical to those employed by shotguns) to fire the grenades (Figure 7.7). The propellant rings or augmentation charges are nitrocellulose packets filled with powder which were used to increase the speed, and thus the range, of the round. They do not seem to have been necessary in this case: the enemy was just a few dozen meters away. In fact, as in other sheepfolds, the pistol shell casings we found reveal the short distance

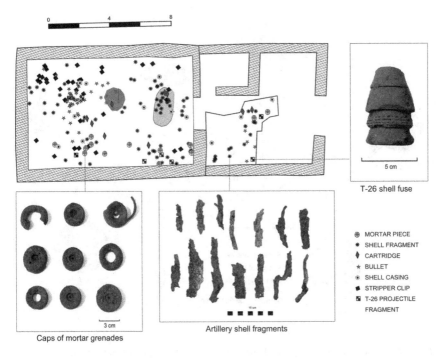

Figure 7.7 Combat-related finds inside the sheepfold of la Enebrá.
Source: © Manuel Antoni Fernández and author.

separating the besiegers and the besieged: we found six of these, of two different calibers (9 mm and 7.62 mm), as in the sheepfold of Martín. A fuse of a Polish grenade (probably thrown by a Republican) and some pieces of a Lafitte grenade also confirm that there was short-range combat.

On the floor of the sheepfold and the enclosure we recovered a large number of buttons, shoes, buckles, cans, glass, medicines and personal objects, including a Japanese-made toothbrush (Figure 7.8). A standard Infantry insignia—worn by both sides—also turned up. In terms of gear, the soldiers used both the Carniago and Mills webbing equipment, which can again be related to the presence of two different units. We found a number of bag eyelets and clasps. Spanish soldiers at the time did not use rucksacks: they carried all their belongings in shoulder bags or hanging from the straps and belt, and the blanket was simply rolled around the torso. Other pieces of military equipment are a Mauser muzzle cover, which was used to prevent mud from entering the rifle and jamming it, and two tins of gun grease. A fragment of a French Adrian helmet, widely used by Republican soldiers, probably belonged to the attackers.

Nationalist soldiers must have resisted for one or two days at La Enebrá. Based on the space available and the number of cans, we can calculate that 20 men resisted in the sheepfold until the end. We found 80 food cans,

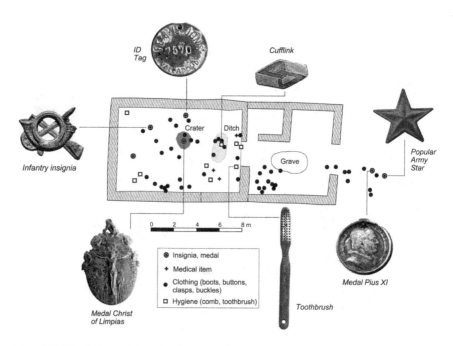

Figure 7.8 Distribution of insignia, elements of dress and equipment and personal items found inside the sheepfold of La Enebrá, with images of some of the most prominent finds.

Source: © Manuel Antonio Fernández and author.

which amount to two cans per person a day for two days. Seventy-seven percent of these are of sardines, followed by tuna (17%) and condensed milk (6%)—a typical backpack menu. If La Enebrá had been occupied as a stable base before the battle, it would have yielded different materials—similar to those we found in Alto del Molino. Combatants took their cutlery to the slaughterhouse: we collected three spoons and two forks. Alcoholic beverages were abundant: in war, they are vital under any circumstances, but more so in the middle of a battle. We found the remains of three Pedro Domecq sherry bottles, the Nationalists' preferred drink. The cans were scattered on the floor: toward the end of the battle the place must have looked like a rubbish dump.

Despite the Republicans' numerical superiority, seizing La Enebrá from its defenders was not an easy task: they were well dug-in and had plenty of ammunition. We know nothing about the fallen on the Republican side but there is no question that the assault caused deaths: Popular Army casualties during the first day of the Upper Tajuña offensive are counted in the hundreds. Since a direct attack against the corral could not be attempted without great sacrifice, the Republicans requested help, which came in two forms: artillery and tanks. We have evidence of both. A T-26 tank (or tanks) showered 45 mm KT-1 fuses and shell fragments. Their dispersal indicates that the T-26 attacked from the southeast. As if this was not enough, Republican howitzers fired several rounds, at least one of which fell inside the sheepfold. Evidence of the hit are a crater of an explosion and over a hundred shell fragments.

The fallen

Inside the crater we found many fragments of artillery shell and human remains, destroyed and dismembered. We thought that the impact killed a soldier, but we were wrong: there were two (Martínez Barrio and Alonso Muela 2014a). The state of the remains was not so much due to an explosion (they were not splintered, broken or scarred), but to postdepositional processes—again, the burial was very shallow—and therefore we cannot tell with certainty that they were both killed by an explosion. The best preserved part was the lower part of a leg with the foot still inside a boot. We know that the dead were young: between 16 and 20 years of age. One of them was about 1.58 m tall and the other 1.67 m. We can also ascertain that one of them had a rib infection before he died, and that the other—perhaps the same person—had a job that entailed great physical exertion, because his muscles left a deep mark in his bones. At least one of them was wearing the standard Carniago gear. One of the leather ammunition pouches was found complete, though empty. And they were wearing leather boots, considered a luxury by many (especially the espadrille-wearing Republicans). Not far from the crater, some civilian cuff links were found, perhaps belonging to an officer, as they are evidence of certain social standing.

186 *Forgotten battles*

One of the dead from the crater may have come from Cantabria or thereabouts: he was wearing a medal from the Sanctuary of Santísimo Cristo de la Agonía (Holy Christ of Agony) in the village of Limpias (Cantabria), which became famous in the 1920s for a series of miraculous healings. According to believers, the image of Christ moves his eyes, opens his mouth, perspires and sighs, and blood drops fall from his wounds (Carrandi 2004). Catholic soldiers, steeped in a religious imagery of sacrifice, suffering and bleeding bodies, surely experienced modern warfare in a particular way.

Outside the access to the sheepfold, we found yet another medal, which commemorates the Holy Year of 1933. The find is sadly ironical at multiple levels: to start with, the medal appeared next to the red star of a Popular Army uniform. Then, the year 1933 saw the celebrations of the Extraordinary Jubilee of Human Redemption (the same year that the Nazis came to power, another irony). The medal's reverse shows Jesus Christ crucified, the obverse, Pius XI, the pope that asked Spanish Nationalists to love their enemies: "Love these dear sons and brothers of yours, love them with a peculiar love, made of compassion and mercy" (Raguer 2001: 119–122). Near the crater was the Falange party identification tag that I have mentioned above. We cannot be positively certain that it belonged to the soldiers in the crater, but it is likely. The death of these two men was probably quick.

The same cannot be said of three of their comrades. We found them inside the entrance to the sheepfold, the *corralón*, inside a shallow pit, carelessly tossed one on top of each other (Figure 7.9). The first soldier was buried in lateral decubitus, with his legs flexed so he would take up less space inside the pit. The next corpse was laid down next to it in dorsal supine position; the third was facing downwards, in prone position. They were surely buried by the Republicans, hastily and without much care, yet nobody took the trouble to take away their gear. They were buried with almost everything they had on them. This is particularly obvious in the case of the second soldier, who was still wearing his straps and ammunition pouches full of cartridges. He was carrying a Mills webbing equipment identical to the one worn by the comrade who died in the defensive perimeter. But in this case, the ammunition pouches and the belt belonged to the type used by the Browning M1918 machine-gunners. The M1918 was designed to be the light machine gun of the US Infantry during the First World War, although it was mainly used during the Second. A few saw action during the Spanish Civil War. However, the soldier who fell at La Enebrá was not carrying an automatic rifle, but a 7.92 mm Mauser. We know because the pouches had nine full clips of this weapon. If all his pouches were originally fully loaded, this means that he had time to shoot only three clips before he was killed. Inside his pocket were three coins: one peseta of Alphonse XII dated 1876 and another one of his son, Alphonse XIII, dated 1904. The soldier buried at the bottom of the pit only had one ammunition clip. He was carrying a gas lighter and various leads from a mechanical pencil. All that we found of the

Figure 7.9 Bodies of three Nationalist soldiers in the mass grave of the *corralón*, the entrance to the sheepfold.
Source: © Author.

third individual were buttons and remains of clothes. He was the last to be buried, so part of the gear we found dispersed on the surface may have belonged to him. All three soldiers were wearing cloth shoes with rubber soles which, as in other cases, came from reused tires. Inside the sheepfold there was also a heel with the "F" for Firestone.

The soldiers seem to have been victims of an artillery grenade: amid their bones there were scores of shell fragments. The individual buried at the bottom of the pit was hit by fragments on his shoulder, his vertebrae, forearm, hip, and the upper part of the leg, and the shock wave fractured some of his left ribs. The second soldier was pierced by 11 shell fragments. These cut into most of his body parts, cervical vertebrae included: a 15-cm piece of shell fragment was stuck into what had been his neck. Part of his left-side ribs and forearm were fractured. The only individual with no associated fragments was the third, although skull and femoral concussions indicate that he was also reached by the blast. The explosion that wounded the soldiers inside the corral might possibly have been the same one that killed his comrades inside the sheepfold. I say wounded and not killed, because two of them survived.

At least they did for a few minutes. We can tell because both show traces of bullet impacts. Among the bones of the first soldier was a pistol round, completely deformed by impact. In the second case (the soldier with a shell

188   *Forgotten battles*

fragment stuck in his neck), we recorded two impacted pistol bullets, one next to the right scapula and another by the eighth thoracic vertebra: that is, the heart region. They were most likely killed by the Republicans who captured the sheepfold. They found two soldiers in agony and killed them with a *coup de grâce*—out of pity or rage or both.

The shrapnel-ridden skeletons belong to young men between 17 and 19 years of age, barely adults. This might have been their first day of fighting. It is not difficult to imagine them: hundreds of kilometers away from home, thrown in the middle of an incomprehensible battle, perhaps trying to appear manly in the eyes of other, possibly older, soldiers (that ostentatious gas lighter...), but probably scared to death as they carried rifles almost their own size (the soldiers were both around 1.60 m tall). They feel the sudden flash of an explosion and then there is total darkness. As they come back to their senses, they find themselves surrounded by the remains of the comrades who had been shouting and shooting with them just a few minutes before, covered in their blood and their own. If their shock allows, they will feel the insufferable pain of their pierced bodies and hear the agonizing screams of their surviving comrades. Time passes slowly as they bleed to death. And then the enemy appears. The last face they will ever see in their lives is their enemy's. Not their friends', their relatives' or their girlfriends', but the face of the Republican who draws his gun and shoots them pointblank.

The battle of La Nava

(with Julián Dueñas Méndez).

By the 2 April the Popular Army had managed to consolidate its positions and resisted successfully several counterattacks. But the situation became complicated at this point. Before them, there was an open plateau known as La Nava. It was solidly fortified with the characteristic Nationalist strongholds: isolated trench systems, whose shooting ranges covered the entire terrain. This type of stronghold had been developed by the Germans at the end of the First World War to control a vast expanse of land with limited means, as opposed to the continuous linear trenches of the Allies—the latter still typical of many Republican positions in Spain (Arévalo 2008b 286–287). In La Nava, these fortified isles were also reinforced with concrete machine-gun nests, strategically disposed to turn any frontal attack into suicide.

In the Abánades sector, as we have seen, the 2 and 39 Mixed Brigades were leading the offensive. Although two brigades may look like many soldiers (between 6,000 and 8,000), they are not that many if we consider that they had to defend much newly acquired terrain. The Republicans thus decided to bring the 66 Mixed Brigade from the reserve, to help out in the advance toward La Nava. The 66 was put in charge of the frontal attack, while forces of the 39 and the 2 Brigades progressed along the flanks: the former, through the west, parallel to the river Tajuña, and the second through the east. Before them, two units that we have already met were defending the sector: the 20 San Quintín Battalion and the 267 Cazadores de San Fernando Battalion, reinforced by the 266 Serrallo Battalion number 8.[4]

Between stone walls and concrete pillboxes

The fortifications of La Nava begin immediately behind Cerrada del Cerrajón, the enclosed field where we left a group of Nationalist soldiers running away from the Republican advance. Those who did not fall in the enclosure managed to barricade themselves behind the stone wall on the other side. Traces of combat are abundant: Mauser stripper clips, many spent shell casings and remains of Lafitte grenades. In order to neutralize the Nationalists, the Republicans resorted to mortars, which left a path of shell fragments and craters behind them, still visible on the surface as shallow depressions (Figure 7.10). According to local accounts, at least one Republican soldier fell in the attack and his body was found abandoned next to the wall after the war. We searched for it in vain: the remains did not appear, but we recovered much Soviet 7.62 mm ammunition. One soldier

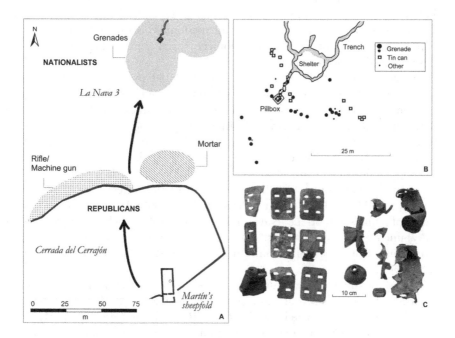

Figure 7.10 The Republican assault on La Nava 3.

Notes: A. General map of Cerrada del Cerrajón and La Nava 3 with traces of fighting; B. The Nationalist stronghold with finds from surface survey; C. Lafitte grenades found during surface survey.

Source: © Author.

190 *Forgotten battles*

left something more behind: a full Mosin Nagant clip, a belt buckle and a Swiss-style pocket knife. They appeared together in the same place. They probably fell from the side bag of a soldier while he was crouching near the wall—or perhaps after being hit.

For the Republicans the worst was yet to come. Behind the enclosure lay the stronghold known as La Nava 3, with its machine-gun nest pointing straight to Cerrada del Cerrajón. Nationalist soldiers were sheltered by a reinforced-concrete pillbox, a deep dugout blasted into the bedrock and trenches bristling with firing positions and protected by a thick mesh of barbed wire. The Republicans charging against La Nava 3 had to face a hail of bullets, grenades and mortar rounds, as the Nationalists were armed with 7.92 mm Mausers, an M1930 Breda machine gun, and an 81 mm mortar—based on our finds.

The pillbox defending the Nationalist stronghold protruded from the rest of the fortifications and communicated with the main complex through a 20 m-long trench. One of the walls has a graffiti reading "LONG LIVE FRANCO". There are more words which we have not been able to decipher, except one: "VALENCIA", which might refer to the Republican wartime capital, the Nationalist's ultimate objective. The filling of the communication trench yielded the greatest amount of materials: 70% of the finds correspond to ammunition or grenades. We also found, among other things, some 30 cans of sardines, condensed milk, meat and tuna (in this order), two more bottles of Pedro Domecq sherry and, surprisingly, a well-preserved roll of cloth tape.

Grenade fragments dominate the assemblage: 44 pieces of Lafitte, which came from at least 21 artifacts. The rebels used them to defend the position against the Republicans and they bear witness to the end of the Nationalist defense of La Nava 3. Interestingly, one of the Lafitte safety plaques was made out of a sardine can. The shortage of raw materials forced the Nationalists to use scrap metal to make their grenades; the canning industries from Galicia and Cádiz had their tin reserves confiscated, and some Galician canned fish industries began to build Lafittes in 1938 (Vilar Rodriguez and Lindoso 2009: 163). There were no traces of tank shells in La Nava and few of artillery. This, coupled with the abundant grenades, suggest that the Republicans took the position by assault and that Nationalists must have abandoned it as soon as they ran out of bombs.

The assault on La Nava—unlike La Enebrá—does feature in Republican papers, so we can follow it quite precisely, almost by the hour. We know that the attack was carried out by three Republican battalions (261, 262 and 264). The 261 Battalion was ordered to advance through the central, and therefore most dangerous, sector. Some 300 men began the assault at 10:00 a.m. The fire of automatic weapons from La Nava, joined by the Nationalist artillery, produced many casualties, including the three captains leading the attack. The Republicans, however, managed to move forth,

Forgotten battles   191

albeit very slowly. At three in the afternoon, when the 261 battalion was some 150 meters away from a machine-gun nest, the documents describe an episode that we might connect with our own archaeological findings: "the defenders"—the report says—"make an exit carrying a great amount of [Lafitte] bombs and are pushed back into the pillbox, with some casualties on the part of the defenders themselves".[5]

The troubles of the men in the Popular Army were not yet over, as one hour and a half later, 34 Junkers JU-52 bombed all the positions captured since the start of the offensive, including, of course, La Nava. On April 2 alone, the 261 battalion sustained 80 casualties, that is, almost 25% of its men. The attack on the forts of La Nava 2 and 3 was tremendously costly. Attacks continued from both sides. The 152 Moroccan Division (the "Moors") arrived to reinforce the Nationalists and the Junkers continued to drop their load over the attackers. After retreating, the Nationalists defended themselves in La Nava 2. They were finally expelled with a bayonet charge on April 4, but only after the T-26 tanks had come to their assistance one more time. Lying on the land there were 200 corpses, mostly Nationalists according to Republican documents, many of them Moroccans. But Republican losses were also high: by the time the offensive finished on April 6, the 261 battalion's losses amounted to 190: over half of all the men involved in the attack in La Nava.

The Nationalists who managed to escape first from La Nava 3 and then from La Nava 2 found refuge in some corrals to the northeast. They were attacked by the 66 Mixed Brigade on April 4 and 5. On the afternoon of the 5th, two Republican tanks opened fire against this last position and the infantry charged. Forty-eight Nationalist soldiers died in the fray, including several officers, while 23 of them were captured. Republican prisoners were not as lucky as the Nationalists: the attackers found them dead. Documents do not say much about this: they might have been hit by friendly fire.

While the 66 Mixed Brigade engaged in bloody fighting in La Nava, the 39 was luckier. The same unit that had played a dishonorable role on the first day of the offensive behaved in an exemplary way: they advanced rapidly through the left flank and crossed the limit between the municipalities of Abánades and Cortes de Tajuña, over a kilometer north of the position where the 2 Mixed Brigade ground to a halt. We have archaeological traces of their actions in two sites: the pillboxes of La Nava 4 and a sheepfold in Valdelagua, the northernmost point reached by the Republicans during the Offensive of the Upper Tajuña.

In La Nava 4, we excavated two pillboxes identical to that of La Nava 3. The finds are also similar: lots of ammunition and Lafitte grenades, which evince similar tactics of attack and defense. We also found a pair of gas masks on the surface: the possibility that the enemy might have used toxic gas was never completely ruled out, although it never actually materialized (Manrique and Molina 2006: 532–535). These masks, however, could still be useful. After the battle of Belchite, the stench from the rotting corpses was so strong

192 *Forgotten battles*

that Republican soldiers were forced to use masks to bury the bodies (Beevor 2006: 413). At least one of the pillboxes was armed with a Hotchkiss machine gun: apart from related ammunition, graffiti on one of the walls clearly depicts one of these machines with its tripod. And there was more writing and drawing: the castle that identified the engineering corps, the unit numbers and *Arriba España* ("Long Live Spain") next to the yoke and arrows that symbolizes the Falange, and the name of one of the soldiers who served at the pillbox (or who helped in its construction): Paulino. The soldiers of the 39 Mixed Brigade captured the position on April 2, the same day as the assault on La Nava 2, and continued forward to the north, chasing the disbanded Nationalists.

A sheepfold too far

Republicans progressed until Valdelagua, where the 154 Battalion of the 39 Mixed Brigade engaged in close-quarters combat against the 1st Bandera of the Spanish Legion. Here we excavated a large sheepfold where Nationalist soldiers took shelter as they retreated from La Nava. They must have spent quite a few days there, judging from the large amount and wide range of materials that we collected. As in all battlefields, the elements related to ammunition are plentiful, but less than elsewhere: they make up for 20% of all remains (including several parts of ammunition boxes). The war materials are once again very similar to those we have found elsewhere: 7.92 mm Mauser cartridges of German and Czech provenance. There had evidently been fighting around the pen: not only had some of the casings been fired, but we also found Soviet 7.62 bullets. The surroundings also yielded bullets and shell casings. The Nationalists relied on a mortar and two machine-guns for their defense, from which we collected three empty magazines. One of them belonged to a Hotchkiss, the same that defended La Nava 4. The other two magazines fed a Saint Étienne, the obsolete machine gun whose traces we already found in Belchite. Faced with the Republican offensive, the Nationalists had to mobilize all kinds of weapons, since first-class material was probably on the main front at the time—Aragón. We also documented hinges and handles from ammunition boxes: the pen was used to store the growing supplies reaching Nationalist troops.

Like all the sheepfolds where soldiers spent some time, this one yielded buttons from uniform and underwear, buckles and fasteners of the Carniago field gear, shoe remains and even the odd Infantry insignia. But the most abundant elements by far were food cans, of which we retrieved around 90, suggesting a stay of several days. Food and drink represent 54% of the assemblage, a higher percentage than any of the sites discussed above. Valdelagua probably became a logistical center until the end of the battle. As well as the typical backpack food (sardines, which predominate), we have large meat cans coming from Mérida (Extremadura), tomato, vegetables and

Forgotten battles 193

legume cans and condensed milk of the brands *La Lechera* ("The Milkmaid") and *El Niño* ("The Kid"). Both companies were based in Cantabria, which fell into the Nationalists' hands in August 1937. With the conquest of Asturias two months later, Nationalists controlled all the main milk-producing areas in Spain. It was not only Republican soldiers who would be deprived of this source of proteins and calcium, but, more tragically, children (see Chapter 9). Of course soldiers were not just drinking milk. We dug up several caps from alcoholic bottles, the majority with the name *García Gómez - Segovia*. This refers to Nicomedes García Gómez (1901–1989), owner and founder of the anisette brand *Anís La Castellana*, and whiskey brand *Whisky DYC*. The bottles we found are of anisette, not whiskey, whose distillation was only allowed in 1958. *La Castellana* has an alcohol per volume content of between 35% and 45% (depending on whether it is sweet or dry), similar to the Republicans' *Peinado* brandy (40 percent). The presence of drinks with high alcoholic content, rather than wine, as in many static fronts, is surely related to the combats: strong alcohol for heavy fighting.

Among the typical lost objects we can mention a mercury thermometer, doubtless forgotten by medical staff, coins, an inkbottle and a Swiss-army-type knife with several functions (including a corkscrew). These knives have a relatively long history (Shackleford 2009: 129–131): they were designed in Switzerland in 1891 as a strictly army tool. Their appearance makes sense in the military context of the late nineteenth century. It is related, on the one hand, with the appearance of modern bolt-action rifles, as one of the knife's functions was to disassemble such rifles. On the other hand, this was also the time when canning became the predominant form of food supply in Western armies. The possibility of manufacturing cans automatically from 1883 greatly contributed to their popularization and caused production to peak from six containers an hour to 2,500 (Busch 1981: 96–97). Swiss-Army knives provided soldiers with a tool that could open tins easily: the first models had a screwdriver, a borer and a tin-opener. Despite their modesty, they can perhaps be seen an early example of the military-industrial complex.

The 39 Mixed Brigade, the timid combatants who had failed to participate in the initial attack, had eventually progressed more into the enemy lines than anyone else in the entire Abánades sector. But it was in vain: they were forced to retreat as enemy reinforcements arrived. The Popular Army had fallen too far short of their original aims: the Barcelona road still lay 15 kilometers ahead.

The end of the offensive

The Republican offensive ran out of steam: casualties were high, the original objectives too remote. The men of the 39 Mixed Brigade abandoned Valdelagua and retreated. From April 6, the Nationalists tried to recover lost

194 *Forgotten battles*

terrain and resorted to shock troops: the 1st Bandera del Tercio, the 3rd Arapiles Battalion and the 3rd Tabor de Regulares de Alhucemas.[6] They also resorted to the constant and massive use of artillery.[7] The 66 Mixed Brigade had also to withdraw to the fortified positions of La Nava. La Nava 2, which cost so much blood, soon fell back into Nationalist hands, but La Nava 3 resisted for a while, before constant mortar fire (of which we have abundant proof, including a complete round) forced the Popular Army soldiers to return to Vértice Cerro and Alto de la Casilla: the first elevations captured during the beginning of the offensive. In Vértice Cerro, the Republicans of the 138 Mixed Brigade (the Catalans) and the 39 Brigade, who had retreated from Valdelagua, managed to stop the Nationalists. On April 16 the Nationalists launched a counteroffensive. The main aim was to recover the lost positions in Sotodosos and, only secondarily, those of Abánades. They used Moroccan shock troops and a formidable artillery preparation: they fired 15,000 rounds of all calibers in a few hours. The attack, however, was unsuccessful. They occupied La Molatilla, but not Puntal del Abejar, whose barbed wire fences had caused hundreds of Republican casualties in the first few days of fighting. We carried out a short survey in La Molatilla. Human remains had been uncovered in this hill by metal detectorists and we went to document the context. The place of the find was a fire trench that had been severely hit by artillery fire: shell fragments, fuses and craters were visible everywhere. There was barely a square meter not devastated by bombs. As we excavated the trench we found the human remains, barely half a dozen bones. But these few bones belonged to no fewer than three combatants. They were probably shattered by artillery fire. It is possible that one of them—or all—might have been Nationalist, because the metal detectorists found a pouch for a Lafitte grenade, typical of the rebel army. It is difficult to tell, because the remains were in secondary position and mixed up. During the excavation, another surprise awaited us: we found an intact, unexploded artillery shell on the trench wall. It was so well preserved that it still had the original orange and yellow paint. This was an Italian 75 mm high explosive shell, filled with trinitrotoluene. One of the many that fell in La Molatilla. It seems that human remains and explosives that were lying around were dumped inside the trench after the war.

In Abánades, the line that communicated Vértice Cerro and La Enebrá resisted and it would to do so until the end of the war. Combats ground on with less intensity until April 24. By then, the battle was an unequal fight in which the Republicans were entrenched and the Nationalists bombed at will. On a single day, they fired 500 artillery shells against Vértice Cerro. Little wonder then that its surface is a lunar landscape of craters today, with shell fragments appearing everywhere—and even unexploded ordnance, including 155 mm grenades, weighing 45 kilos. The Offensive of the Upper Tajuña was a fight amid trenches and barbed wire, where advances and retreats were not counted in hundreds of kilometers, but in thousands of meters. Not so different from the Western Front, 20 years before.

War on the Levant

When the Nationalists arrived in the Spanish Levant on 15 April 1938 and cut Republican territory in two, they had two options: they could head north and advance into Barcelona or march south and try to capture Valencia, the Republican wartime capital. General Franco chose to move south. The decision was a controversial one, because it was not the most logical: Barcelona was deprived of any serious defenses and it could have been taken quite easily. After the war, some interpreted Franco's decision as yet another proof of his desire to extend the conflict, consolidate his power and annihilate the enemy. More likely, it was the result of the general's very mediocre skills as a military strategist. Whatever the reason for a southern offensive, it was catastrophic for the rebels. It comes as no surprise, then, that the Levante Offensive (23 April–25 July) became yet another forgotten battle of the Spanish Civil War (Fuertes Palasí and Mallench Sanz 2013), since the Nationalists had every reason to cross it out from public memory and history books. It was a tremendous defensive victory for the Republicans, superior to the Battle of Guadalajara (Beevor 2006: 347) and it is striking that the government did not exploit it more for propaganda purposes.

The attack was through one of the most rugged areas of the Spanish Levantine coast, the Maestrazgo, which lies in-between the provinces of Teruel and Castellón and had already been an important theater of the Carlist Wars in the nineteenth century. The Nationalists had to neutralize line after line of Republican fortifications, which made the most of the mountainous terrain and whose defenders demonstrated a surprising tenacity. In one sector alone, the rebels were forced to overcome 14 defensive belts in some 65 km, for which they employed almost 37,000 artillery shells and four million cartridges in three weeks (González García 2014: 192). The Nationalist Army managed to capture most of the province of Castellón, north of Valencia, but it took them four long months and failed to achieve any of its main goals, did not inflict any relevant damage on the Popular Army and suffered a horrific number of casualties—around 20,000. Their advance was stopped by the formidable defenses constructed by the Republic, which shattered wave after the wave of Nationalist attacks between July 18 and 25.

Archaeological research on the battle has focused on two areas: the mountains of Teruel and Castellón and the fortifications north of Valencia—the XYZ and other lines (Figure 7.11).

Lost soldiers, forgotten hills

The Maestrazgo and surrounding areas are a region of imposing beauty, a typical Mediterranean landscape that seems to have come to a standstill at some point in the sixteenth or seventeenth century: its dense villages clustered on hilltops and crowned by castles and churches convey this impression, as do its markedly rural character and low population density. It

196 *Forgotten battles*

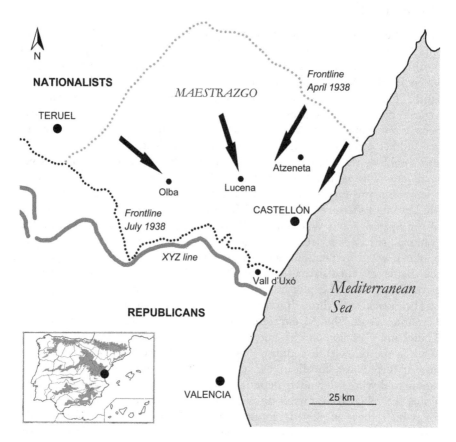

Figure 7.11 Map of the Levante Offensive with sites mentioned in the text.
Source: © Author.

is hard to believe that total war wreaked havoc here 80 years ago and that every inch of the dry and rocky landscape was sprayed with shell fragments and bullets. Yet a careful look at the terrain reveals the traces of the war: hundreds of kilometers of trenches and uncountable pillboxes can still be seen (Rodríguez Simón and Pérez Esteban 2011).

Intensive surveys have been carried out between Olba (Teruel) and Atzeneta del Maestrat, north of the city of Castellón (Mezquida 2014; González García 2015, 2017). The pattern is, by now, well-known: Nationalists storm Republican-held hilltop positions that fall quickly and then the same Republicans try to recapture them with high human and material losses. We have seen it in Lemoatx, in the Basque Country, a year before (see Chapter 5). The novelty here is that the intensive survey, which documented 3,500 artifacts, has enabled a very detailed reconstruction of the combats. Gozalvo Hill (Lucena del Cid), which witnessed intense fighting during two days

(June 10–12), provides eloquent illustration (González García 2015). Here it was possible to identify the location of the Nationalist riflemen who occupied the position after evicting the Republicans by tracing the Mauser stripper clips and Lafitte pieces and the route of advance of a Republican night raid through the spent Mosin Nagant ammunition and Republican grenades (Figure 7.12). The main accumulation of artifacts is on the southern side of the hilltop, which is from where the main Republican counterattack came. The soldiers of the Popular Army almost made it to the summit, but they failed to retake the position. The mixture of grenades and Soviet shell casings indicates that the fighting was savage: the Nationalists threw a myriad of Lafitte bombs and the Republicans fired on them from a very short distance with Mosin rifles, while covered from neighboring hills by a Degtyarev DP1928 light machine gun—its location revealed by a 7.62 mm casing scatter with no stripper clips. Considering that the assault took place at night, we can imagine the chaos in which the combats developed. If there were no victims to friendly fire, it was nothing short of miraculous.

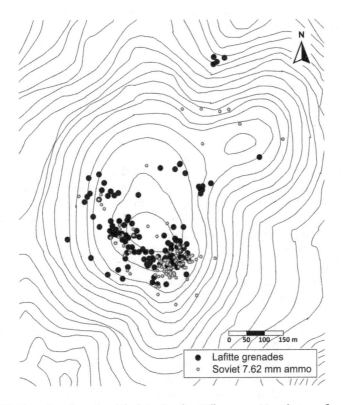

Figure 7.12 Map of combat-related finds in Gozalvo Hilltop, a position that saw fierce fighting during the second phase of the Levante Offensive.

Source: © Author's work based on González García (2015).

198   *Forgotten battles*

While the Nationalists advanced through Castellón with heavy casualties, there was no advance in the province of Teruel, the westernmost part of the front, at least until a new offensive was launched on July 13 with reinforcements from the CTV. Although the attack was successful, the rebel troops failed to isolate and capture the Republican troops who were still resisting in the Teruel salient. The salient was eventually lost, but the soldiers were able to retreat in an orderly way, while putting up a fierce resistance that severely slowed down the Nationalist attack and thwarted their plans to capture Valencia. One of the places in Teruel where the Republicans resisted for a few days was Olba. Here, archaeologists have documented several positions that were involved in the July combats (Mezquida 2014). As in other rural areas, *parideras* (sheepfolds) were used as strongholds and resting places. One of them, in Loma del Morrón, was occupied by a unit of Carabineros. This was an armed police established in 1829 with the purpose of patrolling the borders and coasts. It was one of the corps most loyal to the government: two thirds remained with the Republican government, a fact that explains its dissolution after the war. We know that the *paridera* was defended by Carabineros, because one of their insignias appeared inside, along with elements of equipment, gear and tin cans. Munitions were abundant and reveal that the soldiers were heterogeneously armed with Mosin Nagants and Spanish Mausers and perhaps also captured German Mausers. Three grenade pull rings and a complete Universal grenade (typical of the Levant) indicate that there was close-quarter combats in the sheepfold, a situation that was common along the sector, judging from archaeological finds. In one of the excavated trenches, archaeologists found a 7.63x25 cartridge, used by the famous Mauser C-96 pistol. This was one of the earliest automatic pistols ever produced and saw military action for the first time in the Boer War (1899–1902). Its beautiful and iconic design, however, conceals an unwieldy and technically complex weapon. It enjoyed great popularity in Spain, where it was copied both under license and illegally and used by anarchist gunmen in some high-profile terrorist attacks before the war. The heaviest fighting was documented in the hermitage of San Cristóbal, which was protected by a trench and several foxholes. A sondage in one of the trenches yielded over a hundred spent Soviet 7.62 mm casings fired by rifles and automatic weapons, whereas the materials found in a foxhole evinced the presence of a Maxim machine gun and an unexploded Universal grenade.

In the battlefields of the Levant, munitions indicate the increased involvement of the Axis and the Soviet Union in the Spanish Civil War. On the Nationalist side, the support of the Axis forces is apparent in the massive presence of German-made 7.92 mm ammunition which shows that the rebels employed German Mausers massively, whereas the remains of Brixia 45 mm mortars is indicative of the steady Italian supply. Among the Republicans, the panorama diverges from one sector to another. Thus, in the frontlines of Castellón, Republicans seem to have been homogeneously armed with Soviet weapons and munitions, whereas in the Teruel salient they still used a variety of weapons and employed a large amount of black-market ammunition (from Austria and Greece). This might be related to the fact that it was former police units (Carabineros) that were fighting there. However, automatic weapons (Maxim and Degtyarev) are clearly more abundant with the Popular Army by this stage of the war and this might also be related to higher Nationalist casualties. The massive presence of Soviet guns and munitions in the summer of 1938 should not deceive us as to the chances of Republican fighters. On the one hand, the artillery and air superiority of Franco's army was overwhelming. On the other hand, the cartridges that the Republicans were receiving from the Soviet Union still came from old stocks. Gozalvo Hill yielded a high number of legible stamped shell casings, which provides the opportunity for comparison with the German materials. Thus, 181 Soviet shells are dated between 1900 and 1929 versus 252 dated 1930–1937 (58% of the 1930s). Instead, 553 German cartridges are dated 1930–1937 versus 10 of 1900–1929 (90% of the 1930s) (González García 2015: 244–245). Soviet ammunition from the Teruel sector with legible markings are also from the 1910s and 1920s (Mezquida 2014). This is evidence that could only have been reached through the archaeological record, since shipment documentation never specifies the dates of the cartridges.

One of the characteristics of the archaeological record of the Levante Offensive is the high density of artillery finds, which would again be replicated in the Ebro. In Gozalvo Hill alone, González García (2015: 242) found 47 fuses, which is eloquent testimony of the storm of steel that the defendants—in this case probably the Nationalists who had occupied the position—had to endure. In another area, in the Santa Creu mountain range, almost 200 shrapnel bullets were recorded in a single hilltop. They were dispensed by the 75 mm shells fired by the Republicans against the Nationalist machine guns that were showering their retreating soldiers (González García 2017: 235). The effect of shrapnel and high explosive in the open hills of the Levant, where there is virtually no available cover, had to be devastating.

The Levante Offensive left the mountains of Teruel and Castellón filled with corpses. Many of them were hastily buried in shallow graves, others simply left around: in Atzeneta del Maestrat (Castellón) the graves of three soldiers were found almost on the surface, the bodies just covered with some stones and their equipment and bones protruding amid them (González García 2017: 240–241). Here, the graves of men fallen in 1938 are interspersed with others who were killed a century before, in 1839, during the First Carlist War. An archaeological team has exhumed the bodies of several soldiers in both Teruel and Castellón, most of them Republicans as they often appear associated with Soviet ammunition. In the mountain range of Serra del Toro (Castellón), systematic surveys have located 76 graves between 2012 and 2018, of which 18 have been exhumed. Thirteen of the burials yielded the remains of 17 individuals,[8] a minuscule percentage of the

200 *Forgotten battles*

1,500 missing soldiers in the sector. Unfortunately few data have been published to date (Domínguez et al. 2017: 317–318; Mezquida 2017: 188–190). We know that perimortem traumas were caused by impacts of shell fragments, bullets and even knives or bayonets. Among the deceased, there were teenagers and men in their forties—often family men—who tended to desert at the first opportunity. In Teruel, archaeologists found several improvised graves around Olba (Mezquida 2014). One of them hid the remains of a soldier killed by an explosion which caused him multiple fractures in limbs, pelvis and cranium and left many fragments embedded in his flesh and bones. Like most other soldiers he was short (1.60–65 m) and young (18–25). From another, older individual (25–30), only a few remains could be retrieved. Those killed in the hills of the Levant, like those in the forgotten battle of Guadalajara, were either buried in shallow graves or covered with a few stones. The bodies thus suffered the action of scavengers and rain, visible in scarred bones. In the same province of Teruel, in the hills of Peña Salada (Abejuela), a mass grave was discovered near a trench with two 15-year-olds and one even younger.[9] This is highly unusual. We know that by the summer of 1938, many of the most seasoned Republican soldiers had been killed and the government was forced to recruit 17 and 18-year-olds, who were not supposed to be drafted until 1941. But no individuals under 17 had been officially in the frontline since the transformation of the militias in the Popular Army early in 1937. How can we explain the existence of these child-soldiers? Maybe they volunteered and recruiters turned a blind eye, desperate as they were for replacements. Maybe some unit drafted them illegally and against their will. We will never know. Another young soldier was found in Hoya de Ramos, near Olba. He was not yet 20 and had bullet holes in the right shoulder blade and the skull—a *coup de grâce*. Oral testimonies revealed that the execution had been ordered by the Republican command, probably for attempting desertion. This was the nastiest side of the Republican resistance in the Levant: teenage recruits, the killing of deserters. In that, too, the Spanish Civil War preluded the brutality of the Second World War.

It was not only the mountains, however, that became anonymous grave fields. The cemeteries themselves filled with corpses of fallen soldiers. While searching for two people murdered in 1938 in Borriol (Castellón) after the Nationalists occupied the town, archaeologists found a mass grave in the local cemetery with the remains of 72 Nationalist soldiers who were buried there between 5 and 17 September 1938. Ironically, the victors and the vanquished ended up sharing a similar fate: oblivion and anonymity.[10]

XYZ: The line that stopped Franco

The Levante Offensive ended with a nasty surprise for the Nationalists. On July 13 they launched what they believed was going to be the decisive assault that would bring Valencia to its knees, but their hopes were shattered both by the tenacious defense of the Republicans and the inexpugnable

Forgotten battles 201

fortifications of the XYZ line, a complex of several defensive belts that surrounded the wartime Republican capital (Galdón Casanoves 2010; Gil Hernández and Galdón Casanoves 2006). The rebel soldiers launched assault after assault against the fortifications, but were torn to pieces by crossfire from carefully placed pillboxes, which survived the massive artillery fire and aerial bombing of the German and Italian aviation.

The name XYZ is evocative of the desperate nature of the complex: it was devised as the last stand of the Republic, a way of either preventing the rebels from capturing the capital or giving enough time to the authorities and troops to retreat further south. The works were carried out by both civilian workers and prisoners of war and supervised by military engineers. The line was in fact only one part of the dense networks of fortifications that deeply transformed the Levantine landscape: Almansa, Portitxol and Puig-Carassols lines and the coastal defenses with their hinterland (Gil Hernández 2017). Many of the works have been surveyed and inventoried during the last few years and analyses have been conducted to assess the efficaciousness of the fortifications, by calculating the firing ranges of the pillboxes (e.g. Frasquet Carrera 2015; Durbán and Clemente 2016). The quality of the constructions (pillboxes and concrete-reinforced trenches) was state-of-the-art, as was the planning: crossfire from different positions made enemy penetration virtually impossible wherever the fortifications were deployed. The XYZ line was a feat of engineering, for which the Republic was able to mobilize enormous resources, in spite of its critical situation (citizens starving, teenagers sent to the front, frontlines collapsing), and to complete it in record time. Around 5,500 men participated in the construction. It is commonly accepted that the linear defensive works of the 1930s and 1940s were a huge strategic failure, as they did not manage to prevent enemy invasions: that was the case with the Maginot and Siegfried lines, the Atlantikwall or even the Steel Belt in the Basque Country. Yet the XYZ was indeed effective: one of the few such complexes that actually worked. But it came with a price. As Gil Hernández (2017: 89) notes, the militarization of the landscape in Valencia made the war present at all levels, in every farm, village and town. The entire territory and society was permeated by institutional violence. It was the materialization of total war.

One of the municipalities that was transformed by war was La Vall d'Uixó (Castellón), whose territory was heavily militarized with the construction of the XYZ and with the garrisoning of a large number of Republican troops. They reused many civilian spaces, among others, Finca Gil, an agricultural estate whose main building was converted into a hospital in 1938. The walls were decorated with very elaborate propaganda graffiti, that replicate war-era posters (Vicent Cavaller and Lengua 2007): "Capacity building is the fundamental ground to achieve victory", reads one, next to the image of a soldier reading a book. Another one shows a man handling a pick with energy and the slogan: "Each meter of trench represents the life of a comrade". Others encourage soldiers never to retreat: "Soldiers, make a vow never to retreat a single step when command orders to nail yourselves

202 *Forgotten battles*

to the ground". This order had sinister implications, as many soldiers were executed for leaving the frontline, deserting or refusing to combat, as we have seen (see also Chapter 6 and Corral 2006). A similar graffiti reads: "Without discipline, there is no army, without army there is no victory". These slogans are indicative of the increasing stress to which the soldiers of the Popular Army were subjected and the growing number of deserters among its ranks. Other inscriptions express support for the Republic: "Long live the Republic!", "We have faith in Victory" and "Long Live the Republican Aviation" (this last one with two beautiful pictures of airplanes). Next to Finca Gil there is another house with graffiti, Villa Dolores, but these seem more spontaneous (and have more spelling mistakes): "against capitalism", "Long live CNT", "Long Live the 36 B[rigade]", "Long Live the 5th", "Spain will never be for the invaders, because there are hearts ready to defend it". In their enthusiasm, however, the slogans seem to be betraying the anxieties of an army in constant retreat.

Bombers over the Levant

Another materialization of total war and an unequivocal sign of the dissolution of the civilian/military divide was the destruction of the rearguard through aerial bombing, which increased in intensity during the Aragón and Levante offensives. Archaeological evidence of the bombings comprises anti-aircraft positions, air-raid shelters and buildings with traces of impacts. By the spring of 1938, most Mediterranean cities and towns had been provided with underground shelters, which saved many lives. In recent years, many refuges have been discovered and reopened to the public in towns that were the target of aerial (and sometimes naval) bombing: Almería and Jaén (Andalusia), Cartagena (Murcia), Alicante, Alcoi, Valencia, Gandía, Castellón de la Plana (Valencia), Valls, La Canonja, Reus, Cambrils, Benissanet, Barcelona, Terrassa, Gavà, Roses and Lleida (Catalonia). In fact, bomb shelters are the archaeological phenomenon of the Spanish Civil War that has received greater attention, second only to mass graves (Besolí 2004; Trias 2006; Moreno et al. 2006; Morcillo 2007; Besolí and Peinado 2008; Díaz i Ortells et al. 2008; Ferrer 2009; Schnell and Moreno 2010; Miró and Ramos 2011; Moreno Martín and Muñoz Ballester 2011; Grup Búnkers Arenys 2012; Peinado 2019; Lozano and Lumbreras 2015; Jaén 2016).

During the Levante Offensive, the Mediterranean coast suffered both tactical and strategic bombing. The former was aimed at ports and communication hubs; the latter, at demoralizing the enemy. The difference between tactical and strategic bombing was not always clear-cut: in the packed Mediterranean cities, port facilities, train stations and houses were often close together. Yet this does not mean that the Nationalists were not targeting civilian areas. A study of Valencia by archaeologist José Peinado (2019) shows that civilian quarters were attacked indiscriminately. Using the detailed documentary evidence produced by the city authorities, he mapped the place of each of the buildings bombed during the war (Figure 7.13). The resulting map shows a concentration of impacts in the port area (which went through 550 raids), but also in the inner city, in areas of no military value (Peinado 2019: 103–105, fig. 33). Yet even in the harbor area, many of the bombs fell in the civilian quarter, where working-class people lived. The bombings peaked in June and July 1938, that is, coinciding with the Levante Offensive, with 52 bombings in just two months (Peinado 2019: 97).

Other port cities suffered greatly: Cartagena (Murcia), from which tons of military supplies arrived for the Republic, was raided by the Condor Legion already on 25 November 1936. This attack prompted the construction of a large underground complex for 5,000 people which could not be completed before the end of the war (Besolí and Peinado 2008). In another Mediterranean city, Almería, local authorities developed an ambitious plan to protect the entire population against bombing: they built shelters for 40,000 people (war-time population was slightly over 50,000). The biggest of all, which is now open to the public, appeared in 2001 during construction works. Further inland, the city of Jaén constructed 35 shelters between mid-1937 and early 1939 with capacity for 15,200 people, that is 38.25% of the total population (Jaén 2016: 13). Alicante suffered 83 aerial and naval attacks

Figure 7.13 The bombing of Valencia. Dots indicate bombsites.
Source: © José Peinado Cucarella.

from November 1936 to the end of the war, which killed 480 people and destroyed 740 buildings (Lozano and Lumbreras 2015: 365). The bombing of the central market, on 25 May 1938, caused at least 230 dead (Solé i Sabaté and Villaarroya 2003: 191–193). The response to the raids was the construction of 81 refuges.

Two have been excavated (Lozano and Lumbreras 2015). The shelter of Plaza de Séneca consists in a 43 m long corridor that connects several cubicles (Figure 7.14). The walls are not made of brick, as in Madrid, but of reused ashlars and masonry. Available space is 214 square meters; a maximum of 856 people could fit inside. The roof is a 1.40 m-thick slab of reinforced

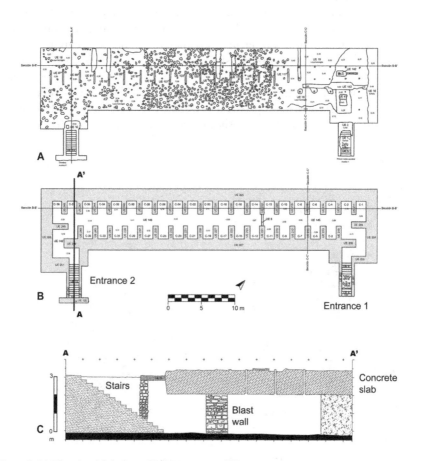

Figure 7.14 The air raid shelter of Séneca square, Alicante.

Notes: A. Plan of the concrete roof; B. Plan of the galleries; C. Section through the second access. The shelter had another concrete slab, which is visible in aerial photographs of the war, but was demolished in the 1940s.

Source: © Francisco Lozano Olivares with modifications by the author.

concrete with pebbles, cobbles and boulders, which was in turn covered with earth to absorb the impact of the bombs. Sixty-four air vents provided ventilation. Many graffiti were documented with the usual personal names (both male and female) written in pencil, charcoal or simply incised. There were also numerous trade union acronyms made with the smoke of a candle: CNT, UGT and AIT. About CNT and UGT we have talked before. The AIT was the Spanish chapter of the anarchist International Working People's Association (IWPA). Some graffiti are indications on how to use the shelter: "Give up your seat to children and the elderly", "Keep silent during the alarm", "Respect the refuge: It is everybody's property", "Do not stop on the stairs", "Do not smoke", etc. At both entrances there were signs depicting a large ear and the legend "Spies are listening". This warning was common in the newspapers and posters of the time and would become famous during the Second World War.

The excavation of the shelters yielded 10 coins, lost by the users during the alarms. Contrary to what we see in other Civil War contexts, Republican coins are more frequent than pre-Republican ones: archaeologists found only three pieces from the 1870s but five from 1937–1938. The explanation is simple: currency was minted during the war in the Valencia region, in Castellón and Caspe (Lozano and Lumbreras 2015: 382), and gallego vila thus easily available in Alicante. Two items stand out in the assemblage: a 1937 Nationalist coin and a Chinese piece from Emperor Guangxu, coined in Guangdong (1890–1908). The Nationalist coin, if not lost after the war, would indicate some permeability across the frontlines. As for the Chinese, Alicante was a sea port receiving vessels from around the world. Ammunition was also found in the shelter and, alongside the expected Mauser, there was a rare 8 mm Lebel casing produced in Hungary and a 6.5 mm Carcano, perhaps captured during the Levante Offensive. It makes sense that military personnel in the rearguard were armed with old stocks and heterogeneous weapons.

Barcelona was one of the cities that suffered more from air raids, if not the most. In only three days (16–18 March 1938), the Italian *Aviazone Legionaria* killed almost a thousand people and left 2,000 wounded (Solé i Sabaté and Villarroya 2003: 180–181). The traces of the raids left in many buildings have been documented archaeologically through detailed maps (Gallego Vila and Solé 2018). In the case of the Church of Saint Felipe Neri, the analysis of the facade provides uncontroversial evidence of the bombing of the church and contradicts popular interpretations, that circulated until recently, which took the marks to be bullet holes left by the execution of priests during the war. Barcelona had a weak active defense, but a strong passive one. The central point of the active defense was the complex of Turó de la Rovira, which has been the object of archaeological interventions (Miró 2009: 37–41; Ramos 2018: 145–148). This was an anti-aircraft position built between the end of 1937 and the beginning of 1938 and situated in a hill that provided a 360° view over the city. It had four platforms for anti-aircraft guns (105 mm Vickers), a dormitory for the troops and underground shelters.

206 *Forgotten battles*

Regarding the passive defense, a commission was already organized in September 1936 and throughout the war it supervised the construction of 1,400 underground shelters, about which we have quite a lot of documentary and archaeological information (Besolí 2004; Miró and Ramos 2010). Many were built by collectives, unions and private individuals and neighbors who contributed to the construction had a space reserved on the common bench. To speed up construction, it was common to reuse former underground structures. The commission calculated two-three people per square meter (versus four people in Alicante). In general, construction standards were high and some of the structures were extremely strong: the one in Plaza de Tetuán, which had 300 square meters, was entirely covered with a thick reinforced concrete roof that could withstand the impact of 500 kg bombs (Besolí 2004: 195), five times more than the average shelter in Madrid. Some spaces were actually quite comfortable, considering the circumstances, and at the beginning, even had the brick walls plastered and painted—something unheard of in Madrid, but not uncommon in other places (Grup Búnquers Arenys 2012). Many had electricity provided by generators, running water, shelves, an infirmary, latrines and even a kitchen. Different toilets for men and women were common in the larger shelters. They were often provided with in-built benches, but not always: in some cases neighbors had to bring their own chairs from home, in others, they removed benches from the churches burnt by revolutionaries at the beginning of the war. Archaeological excavations in one of the subterranean structures of Barcelona, Plaça de Diamant, yielded numerous finds, such as tin cans, kitchen utensils and even sterile gauzes and newspapers (Besolí 2004: 192–193). Well-preserved newspapers have also appeared in one of the shelters of Arenys de Mar, north of Barcelona: they were adhered to the walls during construction and thus date the building: 4 September 1937 (Grup Búnquers Arenys 2012: 3). In the same refuge it was possible to document many graffiti with drawings, slogans and dates. Some of the latter refer to the days in which the town was bombed, a phenomenon observed in other places. The last raid was on 6 January 1939. Among the drawings there is a tank and an anthropomorphized crescent moon, probably done by a child. As for the slogans, one is repeated five times: *Viva el Refugio!* ("Long live the Shelter!"), which is a surprising replica of the most common *Viva la República!*

Passive defense in Republican Spain was one of the most advanced in Europe. Not only big cities, like Madrid or Barcelona, but also smaller towns and villages like Alcoi, Gavá and Arenys de Mar had high-quality buildings capable of accommodating a large percentage of the civilian population. The huge material investment in the shelters, even during the hardest times for the Republic, indicates the strong commitment of the authorities to protect civilians. The diversity of plans, materials and constructive solutions employed in passive defense evinces a high degree of autonomy of the local commissions. It is not surprising that other countries took good note of the Spanish experience. The British, for instance, sent experts to Barcelona to study the effects of bombing on the city and its inhabitants, as well as the structures designed to protect them. Surprisingly enough, the lessons were not taken (Moshenska 2013: 129–131). The reasons were purely ideological: there was the impression that providing underground refuge to the population would create a "deep shelter mentality" that would make the population reluctant to work or fight (Moshenska 2013: 131). The conservative British government was also afraid that underground refuges could reinforce class solidarity and eventually bring revolution. Thus, authorities promoted the construction of individual structures—the famous Anderson shelters—against sturdy collective refuges, which were both more effective and cheaper. As Gabriel Moshenska (2013: 131) notes, "the British population entered the war with a generally lower standard of air protection than Barcelona had achieved years before". It was not indiscriminate air raids against civilians that provoked defeatism, but, as we will see in Chapter 10, an age-old problem related to war: hunger.

Notes

1 This section has been written in collaboration with Julián Dueñas Méndez, who did all the archival research.
2 This account is based on the report by the Commissar of the 2 Mixed Brigade: AGMAV, C. 955, 6, 1.
3 AGMAV, A. 72, C.1810, L.7, D. 1/56.
4 The 152 Moroccan Division reports on the fighting that took place between April 1 and 7, both included: AGMAV, 1819, 7, 2. 80, 81 Y 82; Bon 267 Caz. San Fernando AGMAV, 1819, 7, 1.
5 Operations diary of the 261 Battalion AGMAV, C. 1034, 6.2.
6 *Tabor* was the name given to Moroccan battalions.
7 General Rada's number 152 Moroccan Division. Report of the fighting taken place between April and 7, both included: AGMAV 1819, 7, 2. 80, 81, 82- Operations diary of the 261 Battalion: AGMAV C. 1034, 6, 2.
8 Miguel Mezquida (director of the project), personal communication, 10 April 2019.
9 https://elpais.com/ccaa/2014/09/12/valencia/1410535521_886399.html.
10 https://elpais.com/ccaa/2014/07/18/valencia/1405708991_424402.html.

8 The Battle of the Ebro

July–November 1938

While the Nationalist offensive on the Levante was still raging, the Republicans were preparing their own attack. The operation was risky, as it involved re-crossing the Ebro (Spain's second largest river), and had two main goals: to alleviate the pressure on Valencia and to demonstrate to the world that the Republic was not yet defeated. In the best-case scenario, the Republicans could stitch their two territories back together. What followed was the largest and most decisive confrontation of the Spanish Civil War. Indeed, it sealed the fate of the Republic. It was a true *Materialschlacht* ("battle of material") that again is reminiscent of those of the First World War, due to the number of troops and equipment involved (300,000 men, 800 artillery pieces, 500 airplanes), the storms of steel that pounded the combatants, the horrific losses (over 80,000 dead and wounded) and the long duration: it started on July 25 and lasted 115 days until November 16 (Besolí et al. 2005; Reverte 2006).

The frontline in the Ebro was very long: the Republicans crossed the river between Mequinenza (Zaragoza) and Amposta (Tarragona), where the Ebro flows into the Mediterranean Sea: a hundred kilometers separated both points. During the first day, the Popular Army was nowhere able to break more than 20 km into enemy territory—which was already a feat, considering the difficulty of wading the Ebro with boats and the very limited mechanical means at their disposal. In some cases, their situation ended up tragically. At both extremes of the frontline, at Fayón and Amposta, the crossing of the river was a disaster and the Republicans barely managed to establish bridgeheads, which were soon destroyed by the rebels. Even in the sectors where the Popular Army penetrated more deeply, the battle soon became a defensive business for the Republicans—a story that had repeated itself many times by then: Brunete, Zaragoza, Teruel…

On August 3, scarcely a week after the beginning of the offensive, the Popular Army stopped the attack and took defensive positions. The rebels also dug in. In the Terra Alta ("High Land"), seven Nationalist counteroffensives ensued, the first on August 6 (Reverte 2006). Each of them was characterized by horrendous losses, close-quarter combats and the overwhelming material superiority of the Nationalists. The rocky terrain allied with the artillery to multiply the number of casualties while thirst tortured frontline troops. As in the Levant, many of the Republican soldiers were 17 and 18-year-olds, who were mobilized three years ahead of time to replace the growing casualties. The combats that we saw in the previous chapter were forgotten battles, but this is definitely not the case with the Ebro. It was the battle par excellence of the Spanish Civil War, the one that has been more deeply imprinted into the collective memory of Spaniards—a sort of Spanish Verdun, but one with losers and victors of the same nation.

This chapter has two parts: in the first one, I will review the existing archaeological literature on the Battle of the Ebro, which does not allow for a coherent historical narrative, but illuminates different aspects of the combats (Figure 8.1). In the second part, I will describe in detail the results of fieldwork that we conducted in La Fatarella, in the last line of Republican defenses (González-Ruibal 2012b; Rubio-Campillo and Hernàndez 2015).

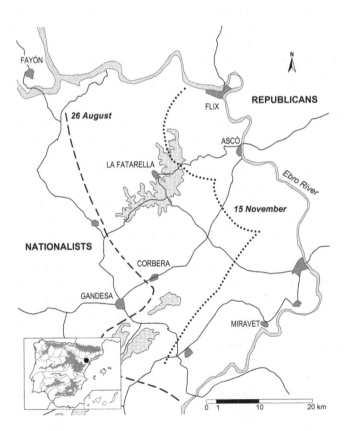

Figure 8.1 Map of the Battle of the Ebro with main sites mentioned in the text.
Source: © Author.

210   The Battle of the Ebro

The archaeology of the Battle of the Ebro

The remains of the battle are massive, because, by then, the Spanish Civil War was well into its total war stage. Archaeological research, however, is still limited, and many of the interventions, most of which take place as impact assessment and mitigation projects, have not yet been published and the reports, when they exist, provide little information (Busquets et al. 2015; Kelly 2018; Ramos 2018). Worse than this is the fact that most materials retrieved in the Ebro battlefields are the result of metal detecting and collecting. In fact, this was perhaps the earliest battlefield to be combed by collectors, who devastated some key sites of the battle and looted graves to strip soldiers of their belongings, some of which had ended up in local museums (Piñol 2011).

Fayón: the doomed salient

The Fayón-Mequinenza sector was the westernmost limit of the Republican offensive. It was also catastrophic for the Popular Army. The 42 Division, which had been decimated during the Battle of Teruel, was reconstructed with Catalan recruits in the months before the attack on the Ebro and tasked with the advance through Fayón. However, lacking artillery support and with reinforcements arriving very slowly across the river, they failed to penetrate deeply enough or to connect with the main Republican wave of advance further to the south. They were able to occupy Les Auts—the highest elevation near the river—on July 26, and captured 400 prisoners and an artillery battery, with no casualties. But then, instead of continuing the progression, they stopped and dug in (Reverte 2006: 112). They were soon surrounded by the Nationalists on three sides, with the Ebro on their back, and holding some 20 km^2 of bare hills that provided little cover. The Spanish Legion and the 102 Division proceeded to exterminate the defenders. The 102 was led by Colonel Castejón, who had led a fierce repression in Extremadura during the summer of 1936 and commanded one of the columns that failed to enter Madrid in November. He would be more fortunate in the Ebro. His troops began offensive operations as early as August 1 and the Republican defenses were shattered five days later: once the stronghold of Els Auts fell, the soldiers of the Popular Army did not have the slightest opportunity (Reverte 2006: 205–207). The Republicans had suffered great losses (800 killed and 1,500 prisoners) and the 42 Division was again in disarray, but they had fought valiantly and inflicted 1,500 casualties on the enemy, of which 135 were killed, according to Nationalist records (Reverte 2006: 215), which might underestimate their own dead and inflate those of the enemy.

Archaeological research has been conducted in various sites within the Fayón Pocket. One of them was a Nationalist position ("loma atrincherada") held by the 17 Burgos Battalion and saw heavy action during the combats of July and August (Piedrafita Soler 2010). It was a fortification typical of the rebel army: an isolated stronghold composed of a fire trench with many foxholes connected by communication ditches. One of the foxholes yielded

The Battle of the Ebro 211

37 stripper clips, revealing the position of a soldier who fired at least 200 shots with his Mauser. Another foxhole was defended by a machine-gunner, armed with a Breda M1930 machine gun, of which some ammunition and four empty magazines were found. Archaeologists also found hundreds of shell casings and stripper clips scattered inside a place in the trench, where a Republican artillery shell hit an ammunition dump. All over the fortification, hundreds of clips, shell casings and cartridges were documented bearing witness to the intensity of the combats. Crossfire from the many foxholes made any attempt at taking the redoubt suicidal, yet this did not stop the Republicans. Their failed assaults can be identified in the shape of the many *Tonelete* and Lafitte grenades employed by the Nationalists to repel them. The attacks most likely took place between July 26 and August 3—the last time the Republicans went on the offensive in the sector.

Another hill that witnessed fierce fighting in the Fayón-Mequinenza sector was the Loma de las Ametralladoras ("Machine-gun Hill") (Chauton 2017: 165–166). On August 3, the Republicans stormed the position and occupied it, but they were dislodged later that day by the Nationalists (Cabrera Castillo 2002: 302). Both sides suffered heavy casualties. The survey of the site helped locate the body of a young soldier, almost on the surface. He was lying on his back, with his right arm stretched perpendicular to the body and the left arm lying along his trunk. His left leg was slightly flexed. He was carrying a pencil and a leather wallet. The rest of his equipment was looted by metal detectorists. In his right hand, however, he was still clasping a lighter. We can reconstruct the last moments of the soldier: he was wounded while attacking the hill; he walked disoriented amid the fray; drained of force, he dropped on the ground; he lay on his back, bleeding, lit his last cigarette and died.

The bodies of other soldiers were found during surveys carried out in 2011 and 2012 in the Fayón Pocket. In Els Auts, the prominence where the Republicans had dug in and then endured continuous bombing and wave after wave of Nationalist assaults, archaeologists recovered the remains of several men. One of them was carrying 7 mm Mauser cartridges with the stamp EK (Chauton 2016: 137–138), which corresponds with Greek Powder & Cartridge Co. This factory produced ammunition for the Republic in 1938 using cryptic codes to dodge the arms embargo.[1] Surprisingly enough, the cartridges were sold by Hermann Göring for personal profit: through his interests in Rheinmetall (a munitions factory that supplied the Nationalists), he had dealings with the owner of the Greek company (Grant 2018: 205). Another Republican soldier appeared inside a trench, where he had been killed by an explosion (Chauton 2016: 137–139). He was a member of the 226 Mixed Brigade that had been created in Catalonia in 1937 and incorporated into the 42 Division in April 1938. He was wearing an insignia with the Catalonian flag and the motto *Per Catalunya*, "for Catalonia". Like his fallen comrade, he was carrying ammunition pouches brimming with Greek cartridges (Figure 8.2). Next to his body, there was an unexploded grenade and a bayonet.

Figure 8.2 Ammunition pouch full of Greek cartridges that appeared associated with the remains of a Republican soldier in the Fayón Pocket.
Source: © Hugo Chauton.

Fields of bones

The human remains of Els Auts appeared in the context of archaeological excavations. But the fields of the Ebro are filled with bones and they are often found by neighbors during agricultural works or simply during a promenade. Thousands of combatants were never properly buried and their remains have been systematically retrieved only during the last decade: a minimum number of 195 individuals have been recovered in the context of archaeological projects between 2008 and 2018 (see Table 6 in annex). The area where more bones have been documented is around Corbera d'Ebre (Ramos 2017: 62–75). This village was a strategic crossroads, was heavily bombed during the battle and, as happened with Belchite, its ruins were never reconstructed. The hills around Corbera saw innumerable combats during the months of August and September which left thousands dead on both sides. In 2008, when a surface survey was conducted in the ranges of Mas de la Pila, archaeologists recovered 397 bones, belonging to 35 individuals, with ages comprised between 18 and 45 years. Most of the elements are long bones and skulls that appeared in heaps, as if neighbors had piled them to make them visible. Archaeologists also found many Lafitte bombs in the area,[2] evidence of continuous attacks and counterattacks and close-quarters combat. Scatters of human bones and grenades have also appeared in other places, usually associated with fortifications, as in Coll del Coso or Vallfogones (Figure 8.3). Trenches, dugouts and bomb craters were often used to bury the remains of soldiers after a position was overrun by one

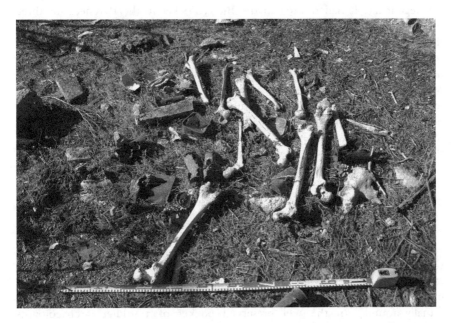

Figure 8.3 Human bones and Lafitte bombs: a perfect summary of the Battle of the Ebro. Archaeologists documented the remains during surface survey.

Source: © ATICS S.L. (Assosiació de tecnics d'investigacions culturals i socials, S.L.).

army or the other. Elements related to the cause of death have seldom been identified in improvised burials or surface finds. Among the few examples that have been published we have the shell fragments in the thorax and abdomen of an individual buried in a shelter near Corbera d'Ebre (Ramos 2017: 68), the skull perforated by a bullet in Vallfogones and the perimortem traumas consistent with bullet wounds in the bones of two Republican soldiers in Pou del Baró (Ramos 2017: 75). Age estimates are rarely precise, with the large majority of the remains belonging to individuals within the 18–45 age range. More concrete estimates have been obtained for one individual in Barranc de les Vimenoses (20 years old) and Lo Mollò (21 years old) (Ramos 2017: 63, 72).

Mass graves were also used to dispose of the bodies of the fallen in the battlefield. One was exhumed with the remains of ten Republican soldiers who fell during the attacks on Gandesa, the main town in the Ebro front that the Popular Army failed to capture, despite thousands of casualties.[3] The most numerous mass graves in the Ebro, however, have been exhumed in the rearguard. In Pernafeites (Miravet), a total of 51 burials have been excavated, of which 25 are collective and the rest individual. They had the remains of 106 soldiers killed during the Battle of the Ebro, who belonged mostly to the 43 Division, with some members of the 11.[4] The 43 Division

214   *The Battle of the Ebro*

was legendary. It had resisted in the Bielsa Pocket in the Pyrenees for three months after the Aragon Offensive. When they finally retreated to France, the French government offered them the opportunity to choose between returning to Republican territory or going to Nationalist Spain: 94% of its members (almost 7,000 soldiers) opted for the Republic (Beevor 2006: 656). Many would perish in the Ebro, painful, anonymous deaths. The soldiers seem to have died in a nearby medical facility, probably the divisional field hospital, as many of them bear marks of amputations, splints, tourniquets and stitches and broken limbs are very common—a horrifying reminder that those who suffered most were not those killed on the battlefield, but the wounded who lived enough to be carried back to a hospital. During the first half of the twentieth century, amputations were conducted even in the case of lighter wounds for fear of gangrene, something that has been attested archaeologically for the First World War.[5]

The graves of Pernafeites were an expansion of the original cemetery, which was closer to the medical facility. The arrival of more and more wounded soldiers from the frontline overwhelmed its capacity. The exhumations did not yield many objects, as they were removed from the men during the surgical operations or before the burial, but some were actually found.[6] In the well-preserved pocket of a soldier, archaeologists found rolling paper, a lighter and a wick. Another man was still wearing a leather belt with a spoon hanging from it. A spoon was precious in the frontline: it was a way of remaining reasonably clean while eating and thus a step above animals. One of the soldiers had a beautiful signet ring with an enameled red star and engraved hammer and sickle. It might have been the property of a commissar. Among the deceased was a boy aged between 14 and 16. He had perimortem trauma in the coccyx and shell fragments in the abdomen.[7] As in the case of the teenagers of the Levante Offensive, discussed in Chapter 7, the boy of Miravet raises questions. Who was he? Was he a local civilian killed in the fray? Was he a very young volunteer whose age passed unnoticed to recruiters?

Other military mass graves have been recently exhumed in Catalonia related to a forgotten, but very active front that partially coincided in time with the Battle of the Ebro: the Battle of the Segre, which took place from 9 April 1938 to 3 January 1939 in Catalonia's easternmost province, Lleida. Despite the fact that it involved the participation of almost 400,000 soldiers between both armies and resulted in heavy casualties, it has been overshadowed by the much more famous and decisive Battle of the Ebro. Pressure on isolated Catalonia came from both fronts during the second half of 1938: the Ebro on the south and the Segre on the east. A mass grave in Figuerola d'Orcau yielded the remains of 17 Nationalist soldiers—here Franco's army lost 3,500 men during the last week of May. The dead had been disposed in an orderly manner, but they were still wearing their boots and carrying ammunition pouches full of cartridges, meaning that they were buried in the middle of the fray.[8] In Soleràs, another village in Lleida, the exhumations revealed eight mass graves containing the remains of 155 men, the large majority Republican soldiers, but also 25 Nationalists and a few civilians. As in Miravet, the dead came from a nearby medical facility.[9] There were two military hospitals in Soleràs which received the wounded from both the Segre and the Ebro, as the village lies in-between the two fronts.[10] The absence of identification tags in the cemeteries is in marked contrasts with those of the Western Front: in the German cemetery of Boult-sur-Suippe, 130 tags out of 530 individuals have been documented. Those who fell in the Ebro, as in other Spanish fronts, were condemned to anonymity and oblivion. But not all: among the civilians recovered in Soleràs, a man over 60 years of age could be identified through DNA: Leandro Preixens Torebadella.[11] He had several perimortem traumas and shell fragments associated with skull and ribs. Civilians living close to the frontline were often wounded or killed during the combats, even when they were not specifically targeted. Ironically, Leandro Preixens survived as a youngster the Cuban War of Independence (1895–1898) only to be killed in the Spanish Civil War as an older man. And he died on Christmas day of 1938, a few weeks before the end of the war in Catalonia.

Behind the lines: camps, airfields and downed planes

The normal functioning of the armies fighting in the Ebro required the construction of a large network of infrastructures, from hospitals to airfields, often located very far away from the frontline. Both sides established headquarters in the rearguard. Franco himself established his base in Coll del Moro (Gandesa). It was built on top of one of the most important Early Iron Age necropolises in Catalonia. Today, the visitor can see a curious landscape with three levels of ruins: the funerary cairns of 2,500 years ago; the trenches of the Spanish Civil War, and the monuments commemorating the battle. The latter are as ruined as the earlier ruins. In the most recent monument, an ugly, but modest, modernist structure, there was a political battle of graffiti going on when I visited in 2011: Neo-nazi, Catalan nationalist and leftist messages struggling for space and memory. It is a wonderful metaphor of the end of the monolithic memory regime of the dictatorship. As in other cases, the monuments that remember the battle are inconspicuous, with no central point of remembrance. This might be related to the fact that the Battle of the Ebro spoke more eloquently of Republican resilience and bravery than of military genius on the side of Franco, who basically repeated the same operation seven times until superior firepower shattered the enemy. There has been no archaeological work on the Civil War at Coll del Moro, but during a survey looking for Prehistoric remains, archaeologists found several Moroccan falus (Jaume Nogueras, pers. comm.). These were copper coins minted between 1672 and 1901. They have a Star of David in the obverse and the Islamic date on the reverse. Most of those found in Spain are from the second half of the nineteenth century and may have come either as amulets or to conduct small transactions among Moroccan soldiers. They have been found in other fronts where the *regulares* fought.[12]

216 *The Battle of the Ebro*

The headquarters of the XV Army Corps of the Republican Army was established in the municipality of La Fatarella (Tarragona). The XV Army Corps was commanded by Manuel Tagüeña, who was a brilliant student of Physics and Mathematics at the University of Madrid before the war. In 1938, he was only 25 but an outstanding strategist, to which his mathematical background surely contributed. Up to 5,000 soldiers were garrisoned in La Fatarella. They lived in small dry-stone huts and underground shelters constructed on a steep slope, which was terraced, descending toward the river Ebro. Apart from serving as a command center, the base worked as an intermediate station for the wounded leaving the frontline in the direction of the rearguard hospitals. The topography helped the Republicans avert the worst of artillery and aviation attacks, but also made their life harder, as they had to climb and descend the slope. Unlike in Coll del Moro, nothing commemorated the headquarters here until the early 2000s. An archaeological intervention carried out at the site during heritage works produced abundant remains related to daily life, such as food items, bottles and pieces of clothing, which are yet to be properly published (Tormo Benavent 2015). Military elements were scarce. Bottles of alcoholic drinks were numerous and include two bottles of cava (the Catalan version of champagne), two bottles of anisette (Anís del Mono and Anís Molero Seco Dulce) and a bottle of sherry Pedro Domecq (Kelly 2018: 35–36). Anís del Mono was produced in Badalona, near Barcelona, and therefore in Republican territory, but Molero and Pedro Domecq were Andalusian brands and therefore came from Nationalist Spain. They could either have been stored in Catalonia from before the outbreak of the war or, perhaps more likely, were captured by the Republicans advancing on the Ebro. The Popular Army caught the Nationalists by surprise at the beginning and took hold of many supplies: several units were armed with the weapons captured to the 50 Division of the Moroccan Army Corps which was guarding the Ebro on July 25.

Another commanding post was excavated in Molí den Ferriol, near Corbera d'Ebre, which was occupied first by the 52 Palafox Battalion of the XIII International Brigade and then by the British Battalion of the XV Brigade in September 1938. Here archaeologists excavated an underground shelter with several rooms that might have been used by the unit's staff (Romero Serra 2018). The shelter was made of several interconnected galleries, whose walls had niches hewn in the rock that were used as shelves to store personal belongings and supplies (Figure 8.4). Only a few objects from the war period were found, as the space had been visited after the war: a tin can, a spoon, an aluminum mess tin, a buckle, a piece of cutlery, buttons, and paper. The most remarkable find is a 25 Remington cartridge, a unicum in the archaeology of the Spanish Civil War. This cartridge was produced between 1906 and 1942 for the semiautomatic Model 8 and was later employed in other Remington rifles, such as the Model 14 and 30, all of them used for hunting or sports.[13] It might have been the property of an international volunteer who carried it to Spain.

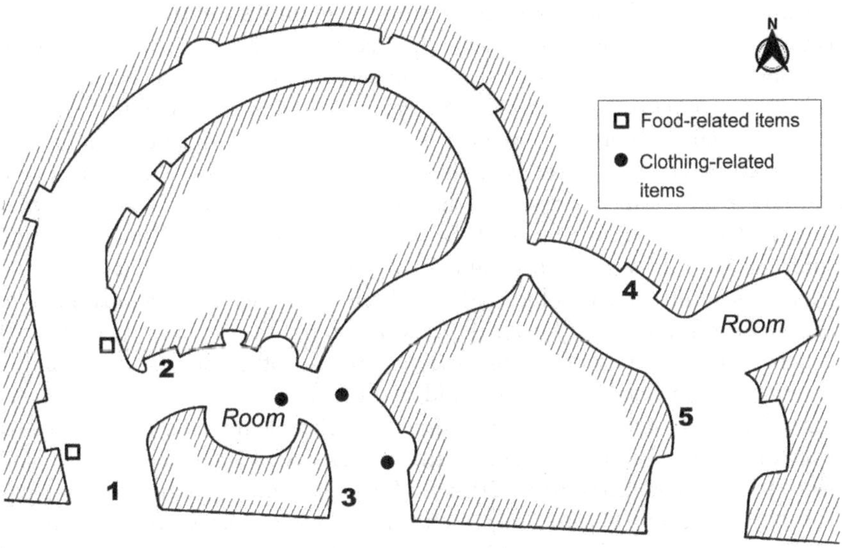

Figure 8.4 Underground shelter at the Republican base of Molí den Ferriol (Corbera d'Ebre).

Notes: 1. 0.25 Remington cartridge; 2. Anthropomorphic bas-relief; 3. Pick; 4. Letter or pamphlet; 5. Metallic box.

Source: Redrawn after Romero Serra (2018).

To the other side of the Ebro River, the Republicans established training camps and aerodromes. Among the former we have the camp of Pujalt (Barcelona), which came into existence in March 1938, as a reaction to the Nationalist advance during the Aragon Offensive. It became the boot camp for the XVIII Army Corps and remained in use until January 1939 (Pascual García 2010: 148–152). Many of the soldiers who fought and died in the Ebro were undoubtedly trained in those grounds. The camp had shooting ranges, an ammunition dump, a soccer field, kitchens, latrines, dormitories and several defensive elements (machine-gun nests, anti-aircraft positions and underground shelters). Archaeological fieldwork at the site unearthed both defensive and residential structures. Residential structures include several rectangular barracks for the troops, with dry-stone foundations, wooden walls painted olive green that have disappeared and fiber cement roofs. There are also bases for a dozen conical tents, of the so-called "Swiss-type". These were similar to the British Bell tent model, which was in use between the Crimean War and First World War. The kitchen could be easily identified by its hearths, ovens and chimneys. Alongside the official dormitories there were also makeshift homes: dugouts of different shapes and sizes, usually with a hearth. Even in a space as regimented as a military camp there was space for improvisation.

The excavations at Pujalt furnished an interesting collection of artifacts related to everyday life: hygiene, as often, occupied a prominent place (mirrors, razors,

218 *The Battle of the Ebro*

toothpaste, cologne), as well as writing material (inkbottles, fountain pen) and medicines. Among the latter, the most remarkable find is a pillbox of Cerebrino Mandri. The "cerebrino" had caffeine and acetylsalicylic acid and was used to treat "nervous and rheumatic pains", neuralgias and headaches and has been available for purchase until 2008.[14] Several insignias were also found, one of them of the railway corps and two others with the coat of arms of Catalonia and the legends *Preparem-nos* ("Let us be ready") and *Per Catalunya* ("For Catalonia"), identical to the one carried by the Republican soldier killed in Fayón, mentioned above. As in the case of the Basque Country, many Catalans saw the conflict as a war of aggression against the region and the material culture of the period—including military objects—helped reinforce a sense of national identity as separate from the rest of Spain. If we bear in mind the Spanish nationalism of the rebels, they were not wrong: the occupation of Catalonia would imply a direct attack on Catalonian culture and institutions.

Airfields have received some attention by archaeologists and in the last few years some have been transformed into heritage sites (Coma Quintana and Rojo Ariza 2010; Rojo Ariza 2013). Most aerodromes during the Spanish Civil War were small, with few structures and even fewer permanent ones— and they were short lived. In most cases, airstrips returned to their original agricultural use or were destroyed by industrial parks from the 1960s onwards. Still, some remnants persist. The aviation camp of L'Aranyó (Lleida), for instance, still conserves an air-raid shelter, a water deposit and a small building with kitchen and dining room, all of which were subject to archaeological excavation. The site had a brief life between 1937 and the spring of 1938, when the Aragón Offensive made it redundant, as it was too close to the front. In Alfés, in the same province, it is still possible to see the ammunition dump and the anti-aircraft defense system, which comprises a machine-gun emplacement and a trench. In this case, the base was established in 1936, but also disappeared with the Aragón Offensive. The airfields serving the Ebro battlefields were located in the province of Tarragona and Barcelona. In the latter, archaeologists were able to find maintenance areas, as revealed by the presence of tools (like a wrench) and duraluminum shreds, one of the first types of aluminum alloy that was widely used in aeronautic engineering in the 1930s. Ammunition is sometimes also found, either belonging to the airplanes or the soldiers guarding the bases. The aircraft ammunition is easy to identify (Rojo 2013: 102). Both the Polikarpov I-15, a biplane nicknamed *Chato* ("flat-nosed") in Spain, and the I-16, a monoplane locally known as *Mosca* ("fly"), use 7.62 mm cartridges. However, only the I-16 uses the rapid-fire ShKas machine gun, capable of shooting 1,800 bullets per minute. The ShKas requires a specific kind of ammunition, which is marked SH and can only be used with this machine gun. The shell casings also differ: the I-15 uses shells made of copper or steel, whereas the I-16 cartridges are made of copper-iron alloy. The *Chato* cartridges found in aerodromes had legible stamps that show them to be

The Battle of the Ebro   219

remarkably new and coming from the factories of Volodarskogo and Podolsk, both in the outskirts of Moscow.

Many planes were downed during the Battle of the Ebro, but only one has been excavated with some care—even if not by an archaeologist (Rojo Ariza 2013: 92–94). The remains of the plane in question were found by Isaac Montoya Salamó between 1988 and 1994, who left a detailed account of his work.[15] It had crashed in El Molar, only six kilometers from the Ebro River, in the Republican rearguard. The site had been looted, but Montoya could still find enough evidence to identify the type of aircraft involved and even the name of the pilot. The survey with metal detector located many non-disintegrating metallic links from the machine-gun belts. These were used with the 7.62 mm ammunition, of which many remains were also found, most of which had burst with the crash. There were both explosive and tracing bullets. The cartridges from El Molar had the SH markings, meaning that they were shot by the ShKAS machine gun and that the downed plane was an I-16. The Polikarpov I-16 was a revolutionary Soviet fighter, which played a prominent role during the Battle of Madrid, as it gave the Republicans air supremacy at a very delicate moment. Many more pieces of the aircraft were found, including the altimeter, variometer, compass, the chamber of one of the machine guns, and a plaque with the assemblage date (25 March 1938) and with the number of the factory (21). The Zavod ("factory") 21 was located in Gorki, where the engineer Nikolai Polikarpov had his office. The downed I-16 belonged to the newest 10 series, which started production only in January 1938. Thus, whereas the Soviet Union was still sending surplus munitions to Spain, it was also shipping its more modern war machinery. There is an explanation for this: Stalin wanted to check their performance in war conditions. The researcher who located the remains of the airplane even found out the name of the pilot: Fernando Paredes. We know that his plane was hit and crashed in El Molar on 2 November 1938, a few days before the end of the Battle of the Ebro, because a comrade referred to it in his diary. He also wrote that Paredes survived the crash and was taken to a hospital with a fractured skull. No further details are known. Two other planes were downed in El Molar during the Battle of the Ebro, but the aircraft were not I-16, which is the one flown by Paredes. The survey of one of the crash sites yielded 12.70 mm ammunition with Italian markings (SMI 1936) and links of the Breda machine gun, belonging to an Italian Fiat CR32. The other site furnished 7.62 mm and its corresponding links, but it was of the kind used by the I-15 ("Chato").

The last day of the Battle of the Ebro

On 14 November 1938, Lieutenant Gustav Trippe, from Dortmund (Germany), progresses with his tank in front of the last Republican pocket in the Ebro, near the village of La Fatarella. Despite the proximity of the enemy trenches, Trippe has half his body protruding through the turret (Proctor 1983: 235). Fatal mistake: a precise bullet shoots through his heart. When he

220 *The Battle of the Ebro*

died, Gustav Trippe was only 29 years old. If he had not died at La Fatarella, he would have surely continued fighting in the Second World War. We know the exact point where Trippe fell, because there is a monolith remembering him, with the sinister insignia of the skull and crossbones on it. Those who killed Trippe were the soldiers of the XV Brigade, who were deeply entrenched only 600 meters from the road through which the tank was moving. As we know, the XV had been originally an international brigade made up of Americans, Britons and Canadians, who had fought in some of the most memorable scenarios of the war: Jarama, Brunete and Belchite. But not in La Fatarella. The brigaders left the frontline on October 29 in a vain attempt, by President Negrín, to ingratiate the democracies (Beevor 2006: 489). They still refused to help the Republic. The brigaders went, but not the Italians or the Germans, like Trippe, who were fighting with the Nationalists. International volunteers left behind 9,934 dead, 7,686 missing and had suffered 37,541 wounded (Beevor 2006: 485–489), which means that 15% of the international volunteers who fought in Spain died there and 40% became casualties—figures above those experienced by the countries that suffered most during the First World War. The Anglo-Saxons of the XV were replaced by Spaniards, mostly local Catalans, as the region was isolated from the rest of Republican Spain. The XV, like the other international brigades, was part of the 35 Division, one of the first to enter combat in the Ebro, the one that advanced furthest and that withdrew the latest.

The new brigaders had to defend the central sector of the line protecting the last pocket of Republican soldiers to this side of the Ebro. They were helped by troops of another former international brigade, the XI, whose steps we retraced in Casa de Campo, during the now remote month of November of 1936 (see Chapter 3). The line made an arch connecting Riba-roja in the north and Ascó in the south. The central sector coincided with the place of Raïmats, which was of key strategic importance, as the main road connecting the bridgehead of Ascó with the Republican pocket ran through it. If Raïmats fell too early, the salient would be divided and the entire XV Army Corps of Tagüeña, with its 18,000 soldiers, would become easy prey for the Nationalists. It is thus not surprising that the center of the line was solidly fortified with reinforced-concrete pillboxes. These massive square structures resemble somewhat those erected around Madrid in October 1936 to cut the Nationalist offensive on the capital. In this case, however, they did fulfill their function, which was not so much stopping the enemy, but slowing them down, so that the troops had time to retreat. Behind the belt of pillboxes there were several lines of trenches excavated in the soft chalky soil.

The attack against the line was the responsibility of several divisions commanded by General Yagüe: the 4 Navarre Division; the 50, which had been disbanded during the early days of the Ebro by the Republican assault, and the 152 Moroccan Division—which had participated in the fighting in Abánades a few months before (see Chapter 7). The 82 Division took La

Fatarella on November 14 (Besolí et al. 2005: 292–293). Between the Nationalists and the Ebro the only serious obstacle was the line of Raïmats, defended by soldiers of the XV Brigade, who knew that they had to sacrifice their lives to facilitate the retreat of thousands of their comrades.

The Aviazione Legionaria and the Condor Legion pounded the Republican positions before the assault of the infantry. Our research focused on one of the key points of the Republican defense: Hill 562. Around a hundred planes bombed the area during the last three days of the siege, including 27 aircraft of the Condor Legion that razed the hill and its surroundings. There are many visible traces of the bombing. Although today, unlike in the Civil War, the hilltop is covered by a pine-tree grove, it is possible to see many craters left by bombs. In the nearby fields, a *Kopfring* was found. This is a metal ring, triangular in section, stuck in the nose of the bomb, whose purpose was to avoid the artifact penetrating into the ground, as it was most effective when it exploded above ground, scattering thick steel fragments that killed enemy soldiers and destroyed enemy vehicles. The ring in question was part of a German SD 50, a bomb that weighed as many kilos and that was filled with TNT. The acronym refers to its German name *Sprengbombe dickwandig*, "thick-walled explosive bomb". The thick walls assured lethal enough fragments. Members of the CTV who participated in the operations recorded carefully the effects of the bombing. Thanks to their work we have a rich collection of aerial photographs where the Italians annotated the kinds of craters left by different types of bombs.[16] Despite the intensity of the attack, neither the trenches nor the pillboxes seem to have suffered in the least. This is because they were not built in the hilltop—as the Basques did, in the spring of 1937 (see Chapter 5)—but on the slope.

Bombers were just one of the problems the Republicans were facing before the final assault. Another one was artillery. The 82 Division had six batteries, half of the 75 mm and the other half of 105. In the fields around Hill 562 an unexploded 105 appeared during agricultural works, as well as many shell fragments and rotating bands from a diversity of howitzer grenades. Unfortunately, there is not much information about the last two days of fighting in the Ebro. Colonel Tagüeña, the commander of the XV Army Corps, only wrote in his memoirs that the rests of the XV Brigade finally crossed the Ebro on the night of November 15, after having resisted the Nationalist onslaught for two days (Tagüeña 1974: 258–262). Republican Colonel Pedro Mateo Merino, commander of the 35 Division and, like Tagüeña, another 25-year-old and university graduate in sciences, provided a bit more information about the Raïmats sector:

> No sooner the day started on November 15, than the enemy began the attack from the southern flank in two directions: a) Ascó-Flix, bordering the river; b) along La Fatarella mountain range, with steep slopes on the eastern side, inaccessible for the Republican tanks... Later in the morning, they took Ascó... and progressed toward Flix. Hour after hour the

222 *The Battle of the Ebro*

situation became critical; until four in the afternoon combats did not stop in the left flank of the 35 Division, hanging from La Fatarella range.

(Mateo Merino 1982: 382)

Hill 562, then, fell before four in the afternoon on 15 November 1938.

Fighting in the pillboxes

The first line to fall was the belt of pillboxes running along the lower part of the slope in Hill 562. We know quite a lot about the pillboxes, because Italian officers documented the place in great detail immediately after the battle, taking photos of each structure (Martínez Bande 1978: 263, 304). They offer us an exceptional picture of the pillboxes and of the damage they sustained during the attack: we can see the damage from artillery, rifle and machine-gun fire, and the sturdy construction of the pillboxes, with a 1 meter thick concrete slab as a roof and sandbags protecting the entrances. Of the two structures that could still be seen near Hill 562 we decided to excavate the one identified as number 3 on Italian documents. It was not easy. Only a corner protruded from the agricultural terrace that sealed the fortifications after the war. We had to dismantle it with a bulldozer while taking care not to allow the underground galleries to collapse. Far from complaining, the owner of the field was happy with the excavation and he later supported the reconstruction of the pillbox to transform the place into a heritage site (Sospedra et al. 2018).

As soon as we removed the rubble we could confirm that the pillbox had been severely damaged and not only by the combats. The roof, which had been demolished in the postwar period, was a very thick block of reinforced concrete (around one meter tall), designed to bear direct artillery impacts and even aviation bombs. The pillboxes were reinforced with sandbags and corrugated metal sheet, as can be seen in the Italian photographs and the negatives imprinted on the concrete. Archaeology offers some insight that cannot be easily discovered in the photographs or available written evidence. We know that these pillboxes improved those of 1936 in a smart and inexpensive way: the embrasures were lined with wooden planks, the same used for formwork. The purpose was simple: the planks were to absorb the bullet and fragment impacts, preventing them from ricocheting on the hard concrete surfaces and entering inside. We have evidence of the efficaciousness of the technique, because the plank remains on one of the embrasures had two Nationalist bullets embedded.

However, the bunkers could not stand the massive firepower of the Nationalists for long. The interior of Pillbox 3 was riddled with bullets and shrapnel. The heaviest damage came from two artillery impacts, each facing one of the two embrasures. It is virtually impossible that a grenade fired by a howitzer can go through a loophole, but it is not so in the case of a tank. Considering the location of the impacts, we believe that a tank moved around the pillbox aiming at the embrasures (Figure 8.5). The testimony of Pedro Mateo Merino confirms this interpretation:

> The concrete fortifications, devoid of antitank weapons, were very vulnerable to the attack with armored machines and the action of artillery fire. Approaching the machine-gun nests unmolested, the fascist tanks fired their guns and machine guns point blank annihilating the garrison.
> (Mateo Merino 1982: 382)

The tanks were driven by Nationalist soldiers, but they were not strictly speaking "fascist": neither the German Panzer I nor the Italian L3, the tanks deployed in Spain by the Axis, had artillery, only machine guns. Most likely, it was Soviet T-26 that attacked Hill 562. They had been captured from the Republicans and painted with the colors and insignias of the Nationalists. There is proof, in fact, of their intervention in the combats at Raïmats: we found a KT-1 fuse of the type used by the T-26.

Once the tanks cleared the way, the infantry stormed the positions. They threw Lafitte bombs inside the pillbox (we found a firing pin), whereas the Republicans who might have survived responded with Universal grenades: a complete grenade of this type, which failed to burst properly, appeared just in front of the bunkers. As we saw in Chapter 7, the Universal is a model of fragmentation grenade common in the frontlines of the Levant and was probably produced in Valencia. It was armed with fuses of the Polish wz.

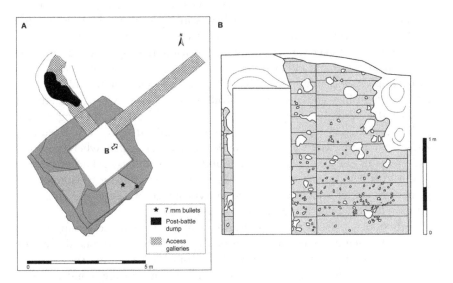

Figure 8.5 Plan of Pillbox 3 upon excavation and plan of the NE wall with traces of impact of tank shells.

Source: © Manuel Antonio Franco Fernández and author.

224 *The Battle of the Ebro*

31 type (Manrique and Molina 2006: 121). Nationalist soldiers had both 7 and 7.92 mm Mausers. The 7.92 ammunition is strikingly diverse: German, Austrian, Czech and Polish. The most abundant cartridges (67%), however, were those of 7 mm produced in Spain, mostly in Seville—one as recently as 1938. The great majority of the Nationalist ammunition appeared in the communication trench that gave access to the structure from the north. The shell casings and cartridges were mixed with tuna and sardine cans, faunal remains, charcoal and ashes, as well as a large medicine bottle. Amid the rubbish also appeared a complete Polish wz. 24 offensive grenade and a pull ring from another grenade. The wz. 24 was typically used by the Republic, but in this case was associated with Nationalist materials. It did not have the lever, which means that maybe the grenade was thrown during the combats in the pillboxes, but never exploded. The access was conserved to a depth of 1.70 m and was backfilled soon after the combats, which helped preserve the original context. The other access was through an underground gallery. The unstable terrain, made up of mixed layers of chalk and clay, prevented us from continuing the excavation: we only dug the entrance to the tunnel, which yielded much Soviet 7.62 mm ammunition and the iron butt of a Mosin Nagant. The Republican soldiers defending the pillbox probably evacuated it through this gallery—if they survived the tank attack.

Defending the trench

When we arrived at the old battlefield, we were rather disappointed. Around 30 years before, a drainage ditch had destroyed most of the zigzag trench that surrounded Hill 562. In fact, the trench was invisible on the surface, because it had been backfilled soon after the end of the combats. The owner of the camp, however, picked up many of the artifacts that appeared during the excavation of the drain and therefore not all was lost. The collection allows us to complete the story of the last Nationalist attack in the Ebro. After clearing the profiles and the surface around the drainage we realized that it had only damaged the central part of the trench, but not the angles. We could excavate six: three outward, three inward. It was very fortunate, because it is in the outward-facing angles of a firing trench where combat-related remains are more likely to be found—as was the case. The interesting thing, in this case, is that each of the angles furnished different materials. All together, they offer a picture of the battle which is as precise as it is dramatic. Let us see the evidence angle by angle (Figure 8.6).

The first of all, from south to north, was hewn in the outcrop of Hill 562 and is oriented opposite the frontline. It is thus understandable that we did not find spent ammunition here: only a 7.62 mm shell casing. Instead, we did find five 7.62 mm cartridges in pristine condition—so pristine they could be fired today: they were not even rusty. The casing was still golden and the bullet silver-colored. Even more surprising was to find a complete packet of 15 cartridges wrapped in the original paper in

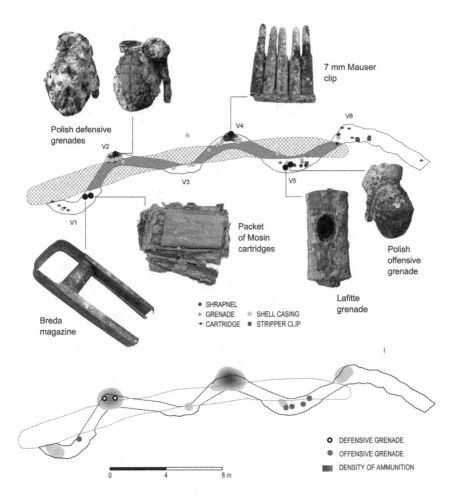

Figure 8.6 Sector of the trench excavated in Hill 562 with indication of the main finds.
Source: © Manuel Antonio Franco Fernández and author.

which they left the Soviet Union. Republican soldiers did not have the time to open the packet and even less to insert the cartridges in the clips. In the same angle we found the fuse of a grenade, which was thrown by the Nationalists storming the trench. We also retrieved an empty magazine of the Italian Breda machine gun, perhaps abandoned by the Nationalists after they occupied the position. A Republican use is not impossible, because, as noted above, they got hold of great quantities of weapons after defeating the 50 Division during the initial advance on the Ebro, but we have not found any spent casings that might indicate that the Republicans were actually firing the Breda.

226   *The Battle of the Ebro*

Angle 2, facing the enemy, is where we made the most exceptional discovery, to which I will refer in the next section. For now, suffice it to say that lying on the floor we found more evidence of intense fighting in the shape of many spent shell casings and fragmentation grenades. Angle 3, opposite the enemy, was severely affected by the drainage and only yielded three spent 7.62 mm casings. Angle 4, again oriented toward the frontline, provided abundant finds: in the small space that had not been affected by the drainage, we recovered 21 shell casings of the 7.62 mm caliber and 31 complete cartridges that were never used—some of them still had traces of wrapping. There were also a dozen iron fragments, most likely from an exploded grenade, and a Mauser clip with its five 7 mm cartridges, likely lost by some of the Nationalist soldiers who captured the position. Cartridges and shell casings appeared in situ in most cases, embedded in the trench's floor. It is quite surprising that, given the imminence of the Nationalist attack, the defenders had not unwrapped all the ammunition and mounted them in clips (for rifles), belts or magazines (for machine guns). Was it because they did not have enough clips and were expecting a lull in the combats to reload? Ammunition concentrates in the angle itself, particularly the cartridges, and indicates the place where a soldier was standing. Shell casings were more scattered, which is logical, because they are expelled from the gun with some force. As we did not find a single stripper clip, it can be hypothesized that the soldier was operating a machine gun, possibly a Degtyarev DP1928. The volume of fire from the trench was quite high. Apart from our finds, the owner of the field collected 64 shell casings from the drainage ditch and others might have been retrieved after the combats.

Angle 5 was oriented opposite the enemy and therefore did not furnish much ammunition. Instead, the small space that had not been affected by the drainage provided yet another surprise: three unexploded Lafitte bombs and a wz. 24. The Lafittes did not have the safety plaque, so they might have been thrown and simply did not burst. The Polish grenade, instead, is complete with lever and pull ring; it was therefore abandoned, perhaps by the retreating Republican troops. We also collected the fuse of a Polish grenade that did explode.

In total, the excavation of the trench yielded a minimum number of seven grenades. To this we have to add five wz. 31 fuses found by the owner of the field in the trench that could have been used in Polish or Universal grenades. Twelve grenades in total: not bad for 30 linear meters. The Battle of the Ebro was, in fact, a fight of hand grenades and knives. The 115 days were replete with bloody raids, bombs in hand and bayonets fixed. The positions lost under an avalanche of Lafittes were recovered hours later under a wave of Universal grenades. There are accounts of the battlefield after the combats that describe the ground littered with unexploded grenades, some of which keep causing casualties after the fray (Reverte 2006: 149). The battlefields described earlier, with scatters of Lafitte and human bones are the most tragic and faithful archaeological evidence of the fights. Once again, the landscape had more to do with the Western Front than with the Second World War: it was in the former conflict that grenades played a paramount role for the first time since the seventeenth century (Ellis 1989: 77–78).

Angle 6, the last one that we excavated, was the best preserved, as the agricultural ditch did not affect it. However, the finds were scarce. Although soldiers also fired from this position, the fire was not so intense: we only found a spent 7.62 mm shell casing, a couple of stripper clips and six cartridges. The fact that fewer shots were made from this angle has to do with the fact that the bulk of the attack seems to have come from the south, which is in turn consistent with the dense casing scatters in the other parts of the trench. It seems as if the men were firing toward the southeast. This also tallies well with the traces of combat from Pillbox 3: the shooting, both from tanks and infantry, came from the south or southwest. For this reason, we believe that the Nationalists were progressing from the area around the road linking La Fatarella and Ascó, the last Republican bridgehead on the Ebro.

While intense, the fighting did not last long, otherwise the number of clips and shell casings should have been higher (and we would not have found so much unused ammunition). There were not many Republican soldiers, either: considering the concentration of the finds, it seems that there was no more than one man per angle. This is not striking, for the reason that the defenders only had to hold the line enough to enable the withdrawal of their comrades. It would have been absurd to sacrifice a great number of troops in a battle that was lost beforehand. The picture offered by the trench of Raïmats contrasts with the one we dug in Casa de Campo (see Chapter 3). Things had changed dramatically in the two years that elapsed from the Battle of Madrid. So much so, that an archaeologist who dug both trenches without further information would have thought that they belonged to different conflicts. The Republicans had learnt to fight. The linear trench had been replaced by a more efficient zigzag. Soldiers were not crowded, but evenly spaced to prevent casualties, spare ammunition and increase effectivity. The weapons were more standardized and modern. Fire was more selective. Soldiers more determined. Their enemies had improved their fighting skills, too: the attack on Hill 562 is an excellent example of combined arms warfare, with aviation, tanks, artillery and infantry acting in unison (Rubio-Campillo and Hernàndez 2015). In that, it is already a battle of the Second World War.

The immense majority of the remains that we found in both the pillbox and the trench are military. However, an almost complete Waterman inkbottle, a bottle of vitamins and several tin cans turned up in Angle 6. In the entire trench we only found eight tins: one of sardines and the rest of condensed milk. The vitamin bottle reads "Clavitam", a complex that included vitamins A, B and D. At this time of the war, it was synthetic vitamins, rather than fresh fruit, meat and vegetables, that kept soldiers healthy. Clavitam was produced by Andrómaco Laboratories in Barcelona, a company established in 1923 and now based in Mexico: the preferred exile for most Republican refugees.[17] Ironically, its publicity in times of peace

228   *The Battle of the Ebro*

read: "Rather than force one to eat better to stimulate his appetite". One of the most striking artifacts appeared on the surface near Angle 1: it was a tube of toothpaste with the picture of a militiaman holding a rifle in his right hand, in typical revolutionary gait, closely resembling pictures in propaganda posters. It shows that every surface was adequate to raise the spirits of the troop and that every object, especially the most ordinary, was mobilized in the ideological struggle.

Last man standing

In the narrative above I have only mentioned Angle 2 very briefly. Not because it is not important, but rather the opposite: the first strike of the hoe revealed a rubber sole and then the presence of bones. The excavation turned into an exhumation: little by little, the remains of a human being were revealed (Figure 8.7). Also his belongings: buttons, clasps, cartridges. It was a Republican soldier. My colleague Xurxo Ayán, who was doing the digging, felt the desire to humanize the skeleton and called him Charlie—because the position had been held by the former XV International Brigade. It would have been better to call him Carles or Carlos, because by November 15, as we saw, there were no Americans left in the XV Brigade. However, the name stuck and would soon be all over the place when the media picked it up. Charlie, once named, became closer to us, more human. As we kept clearing the bones and artifacts, we deciphered his story or, rather, the end of his story.

Everything seems to indicate that we found Charlie in the same spot where he fell, inside the trench, in the same angle of the zigzag that he was defending. When the Nationalists occupied the position they simply took his rifle and then backfilled the trench with Charlie inside. Similar instances have been found in other Spanish Civil War scenarios, including in Els Auts of Fayón (Chauton 2016: 137–139). Charlie's perfectly preserved skeleton reminds us of the body casts of Pompeii that capture the instant of death. He fell on his back, his arms flexed, the left one upwards, the right one downwards, as if he had been pushed violently. The right hand was stretched and the left one flexed under the right one in a forced posture. That he died where he fell is indicated also by the objects associated with the skeleton. Charlie was carrying a side bag, which was still hanging from his left shoulder at the time of his death. If it was hanging from his left shoulder, this means that he was right-handed: in that way, he could easily pick up whatever he had inside the bag. Of this, two clasps appeared near the shoulder. Parts of the fabric, a woolen sweater, underpants and corduroy trousers were preserved by lying under Charlie's body. He was not wearing a shirt, because we found no buttons. Those that we found belonged to the underpants and the military jacket he was wearing over his sweater. In the same land where the soldiers had suffered from terrible heat during the summer, the temperatures were falling to as little as 3° degrees Celsius at night. Charlie fastened his trousers with a corduroy belt, of which we found the buckle. He was also wearing thick woolen socks. We know, because they left an imprint on the rubber soles of

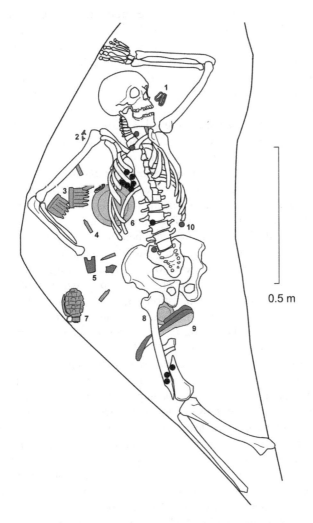

Figure 8.7 Remains of a fallen Republican soldier in the trench of Raïmats.

Notes: 1. Clasps of a shoulder bag; 2. Jacket brackets; 3. Mosin Nagant clips; 4. Loose cartridges; 5. Bottle of medicine; 6. Mess tin; 7. Polish fragmentation grenade; 8. Shaving basin; 9. Shoe; 10. Buttons. Black dots indicate grenade fragments.

Source: © Author.

his shoes, which were size 42. They were manufactured by J. Martínez Hermanos, in Elche (Alicante), a town still known for its footwear industry.

As we found it, Charlie did not have ammunition pouches, shoulder straps or helmet. Perhaps they took them away from him, but it is more likely that he was simply not carrying them. Few Republican soldiers had the full military accoutrement in the Ebro, if we are to judge from historical photographs. In fact, it seems that Charlie was carrying all his ammunition

230 *The Battle of the Ebro*

and belongings in his side bag: inside we found three Mosin Nagant clips. Like his comrades, Charlie was also carrying wrapped ammunition: eight cartridges with traces of wrapping paper. He made at least 12 shots, which is the number of spent shell casings we found under his body. He surely fired more. Some of the shell casings that the owner of the field found while digging the ditch probably belonged to him. And then others were probably lying around on the parapet and disappeared. Inside the bag, there were also two Polish wz. 33 fragmentation grenades with wz. 31 fuses. It is possible that he had already thrown some to the enemy, because if the soldiers were provided with something, that was grenades.

Apart from munitions, Charlie was carrying everyday objects: a mess tin to eat meals; a knife; a shaving basin; an unidentified object made of calamine; a toothbrush made by Foramen, a company from Barcelona; a tube of toothpaste of the Myrurgia brand; a small medicine bottle of green glass, still sealed with a cork, which reveals that Charlie was ill when he died; a military leaflet where only a few words can be made out ("medal"); a small white sheet folded carefully, perhaps a letter that he never wrote or that he might have written but whose words have been erased forever, or perhaps a paper with his name—a futile attempt to replace an identification tag. Nothing that allows us to say "Charlie was named...", "he resided in...", "he was born in". His bones, however, tell something about him. In his late forties, he was a very old fighter. Older soldiers did not have a strong morale and would rarely volunteer for a suicide mission; many of them had wives and children. Charlie probably did not. Or he did not care. He was 1.75 meters tall, very tall for the period, when the average Spaniard was 1.60. It is not impossible that he was an international brigader who had continued fighting under another name, perhaps a German or a Polish who had nothing to fear, nothing to hope for, because he had no country to return to in the first place. Over half the volunteers were given Spanish nationality and re-joined the Popular Army and the international military commission, which supervised the withdrawal of the brigaders, was struck by their age: Swedish Colonel Ribbing noted that many of his countrymen were around their forties (Beevor 2006: 487).

We also know how Charlie died. We know it with forensic precision, although it is not necessary for a forensic scientist to explain it, because it is obvious. Charlie was killed by a grenade. The grenade exploded in his right hand, which volatilized. The explosion sectioned his ulna and radius. Fragments from the grenade perforated his thorax. Some went to his right lung: we found pieces amid the ribs or stuck to the ribs themselves. Another fragment we found embedded in his lumbar vertebrae. Others went to his right leg, with such violence that they sectioned his femur in two. He must have died immediately. Why did a grenade explode in Charlie's hand? There are two potential scenarios. In one scenario, a Nationalist threw a grenade into the trench, Charlie picked it up, but it was too late: the grenade exploded as he was trying to throw it back. In another scenario, Charlie was throwing a grenade against the Nationalists who were about to storm the trench, but the grenade exploded in his hand. Maybe he miscalculated the time and waited for too long, or the grenade was defective. In support of the second hypothesis is the fact that it was a fragmentation grenade, like the ones Charlie was carrying, not an offensive one (like the Lafittes), which would be the kind most likely used by the Nationalists during the assault. Also, it is more likely that one is wounded or killed trying to throw one's grenade than returning an enemy's.[18] What we know for sure is that the Nationalists were very close.

For 73 years nobody remembered Charlie. He was killed twice, physically and in memory, like so many Republican soldiers. It was only Gustav Trippe who was honored with a monument, the officer sent by Nazi Germany to fight the Spanish Republic. But today Trippe has a competitor. In 2013, a monument was inaugurated to the memory of the XV Brigade. The plaque reads in Catalan: "XV BI – 15 BM, to the memory of the combatants of the Fifteenth Brigade, defenders of freedom". On the plaque, there is a bas-relief representing Charlie, shooting his Mosin Nagant against the advancing enemy, in the same trench that saw him die, in the same trench that we excavated.

Notes

1. http://www.municion.org/7mm/7mm.htm.
2. http://www.catpatrimoni.com/treballs%20realitzats/arqueologia/corberaebre (Arq).htm.
3. http://www.catpatrimoni.com/treballs%20realitzats/guerra%20civil/Fossa%20Mas%20den%20Grau%20-%20GC.htm.
4. https://www.diaridetarragona.com/ebre/Fotos-ineditas-Hallan-99-soldados-muertos-en-la-fosa-de-Miravet-20180722-0013.html.
5. https://www.inrap.fr/le-cimetiere-allemand-de-boult-sur-suippe-10845.
6. https://www.diaridetarragona.com/ebre/Un-anillo-comunista-papel-de-fumar-mecheros-y-torniquetes-entre-los-objetos-encontrados-en-la-fosa-de-Miravet-20180722-0017.html.
7. https://www.diaridetarragona.com/ebre/Identifican-el-primero-de-los-250-cadaveres-de-la-Guerra-Civil-hallados-en-fosas-de-Miravet-y-El-Solers–20180721-0038.html.
8. https://www.eldiario.es/catalunya/politica/Generalitat-primera-Guerra-Civil-intervendra_0_656884394.html.
9. http://www.rtve.es/noticias/20180722/recuperan-restos-246-soldados-guerra-civil-fosas-del-ebro/1767860.shtml.
10. http://fossesirepressio.gencat.cat/es/soleras-cementiri.
11. https://www.inrap.fr/le-cimetiere-allemand-de-boult-sur-suippe-10845.
12. https://guadalajaraenguerra.blogspot.com/2016/11/la-estrella-de-salomon-en-muduex-la_2.html.
13. http://www.municion.org/25Rem/25Rem.htm.
14. http://www.20minutos.es/noticia/409752/0/cerebrino/mandri/eliminado/.
15. https://www.nojubilemlamemoria.cat/pdf/Polikarpov_Molar.pdf.
16. Copies of the photographs were deposited in the Archivo General Militar de Madrid, 7/377/11, 1-16.
17. http://www.andromaco.com.mx/historia.html.
18. I would like to thank Jean-Loup Gassend for this information.

9 Dead men walking

November 1938–March 1939

After the Battle of the Ebro, the fate of the war was decided. The four and a half months that remained would be of painful agony for the Republic, for its demoralized soldiers and starving civilians. The Offensive of Catalonia, launched by the Nationalists at the end of December 1938 was quick and ended with their arrival at the French border on February 10. On their way, Franco's troops bombed villages and towns and, in turn, many Republican soldiers murdered prisoners, civilian and military alike, as they withdrew, filling up the mass graves again.

Into exile

The Catalonia Offensive is not very impressive from an archaeological point of view: it was brief, saw little action and fortifications were not as elaborate as in other fronts and were scarcely used. In April 1938, Vicente Rojo, Chief of Staff of the Republican Army, had designed an ambitious plan to defend the region with six defensive lines (L1 to L6), extending from Catalonia's boundary with Aragón to the border with France. These lines were much less spectacular than documents make us believe, because the resources to build them were simply lacking. Archaeologists have documented their remains in several places. Thus, in Agramunt (Lleida) they have catalogued numerous vestiges belonging to the L2 line, going from Tarragona on Catalonia's southern coast, to the Pyrenees. Remains consisted of trenches, dugouts and pillboxes made of masonry (Mazuque López 2009). In the same region, several traces of the L2 were found in Vallbona (Urgell) during archaeological excavations. In this case remains are more monumental and include a gallery made of stone and concrete, inside which archaeogists found an oil lamp (Pascual García 2010: 155–156). The weak, flickering light and the rancid smell of fat burning would have been the companions of the soldiers every night, but then the experience would not have been different to most Spanish villages of the time: remote rural areas were not electrified until the 1970s. L3 has been documented in Sant Pau d'Ordal (Alt Penedès, Barcelona), in a strategic point of the N-340, one of the main roads leading to Barcelona, where a battle took place on January 22–23. The excavations

Dead men walking 233

unearthed a trench and a stone wall that served as a machine-gun nest. The scarce materials found in test pits and during surface survey indicate that there was little combat. Nonetheless, these small points of resistance enabled the ordered retreat of hundreds of thousands of Republican soldiers and civilians, who could arrive safely in France (Rojo Ariza et al. 2010: 205).

Around 465,000 people crossed the border in February 1939, of which 170,000 were civilians who were escaping Francoist revenge (Alted 2012). Of this episode we have two major scenarios which have only been cursorily explored from an archaeological point of view: the mountain passes in the Pyrenees and the concentration camps in France (Legendre 2018). Work on the retreat through the Pyrenees had already been conducted by a group of amateurs, who surveyed the area of Vall de Camprodon in search for traces of the Republican exodus. Today, their spectacular finds can be seen in a museum (Centre d'Estudis la Retirada) or virtually through their webpage.[1] Unfortunately, the research was not carried out with archaeological methodology and important information was lost in the process. Still, the finds are outstanding and the museum project praiseworthy. They retrieved dozens of weapons of all kinds (rifles, machine guns, pistols, mortars, grenades) that were discarded by the soldiers before entering France. Although Soviet weapons prevail, there is a wide variety of artifacts, which remind us that the Popular Army never achieved standardization. The heterogeneous assemblage ranges from C-96 Mauser pistols to heavy machine guns—Russian and German Maxims and their Czech copies (ZB-26). Among the rifles there are some Enfields, like those that defended Madrid in November 1936. There are also Winchesters M1892s, perhaps veterans from the now remote Battle of Madrid, where they were employed by the Republican forces. Pistol finds are particularly interesting because there is very little documentary evidence about them (Legendre 2018: 58). Russians exported few handguns and many of the semiautomatic pistols and revolvers were privately owned by soldiers, as we have seen throughout the book. An Italian Beretta M1934 was in all likelihood captured from the enemy—perhaps during the Battle of Guadalajara (see Chapter 5)—and the soldier who discarded it was throwing away more than a gun: it was a souvenir of a victory over the fascists, now a bitter reminder of a broken hope.

Taken togeter, the finds are witness to the many ways in which people killed and were killed during the war, to the obscene expenditure in tools of destruction that sank the Spanish economy for decades, and to the vanquished Republic. What had started with euphoria on 14 April 1931, ended on 10 February 1939, as a trail of rusty weapons. They were abandoned by soldiers heading to an exile that we know was terrible: concentration camps in France, marginalization, further migration and further fighting, this time against the Nazis, more tortures, killings and exile. Republican veterans excelled as partisans, but paid a high toll. Many were tortured and killed by the Germans, even more sent to concentration camps in Germany and Austria, where 4,427 died in Mauthausen and Gusen alone.[2] Archaeological work has been conducted in many of the labor and concentration camps where Republicans were interned: Mauthausen and its subcamps (Dachau, Buchenwald, Gusen) and Sachsenhausen (Theune 2018). This is also, in a way, the archaeology of the Spanish Civil War—and another reminder that the War of Spain was never about Spain only. In British soil, too, Spaniards suffered the violence of the Nazi regime. On the island of Jersey, they were originally interned in a place they nicknamed Lager Franco, before being transferred to Lager Wick in February 1942 (Carr 2016). Spanish and North African prisoners worked in a nearby stone quarry. The excavations at the camp yielded many Nazi-era finds but none that can be unambiguosly pinpointed to the Spanish inmates.

The camps in southern France have yielded more conclusive evidence (Legendre 2018). We have to distinguish two types of camps: those established between February 1939 and June 1940 for Spanish refugees, and those in use from June 1940 onwards, in which Spaniards shared space with Jews, Gypsies and other groups earmarked for extermination. In the first group we have the camps of Argelés, Le Barcarés, Saint-Cyprien, Le Vernet, Brens, Bram, Septfonds, Agde, Gurs and Rieucros (Figure 9.1). Camp population started to decline in April 1939, and two years later there were only 3,000 Spaniards in them, although 167,000 refugees remained in the country. After January 1941

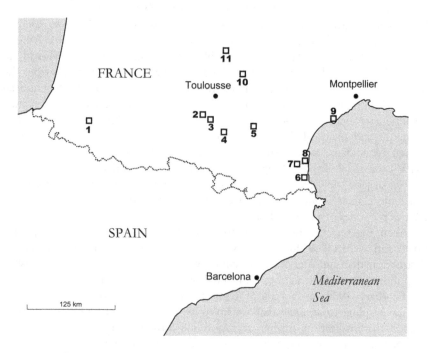

Figure 9.1 Refugee/concentration camps in southern France.

Notes: 1. Gurs; 2. Le Récébédou; 3. Noé; 4. Le Vernet; 5. Bram; 6. Saint Cyprien; 7. Le Barcarés; 8. Rivesaltes; 9. Agde; 10. Brens; 11. Septfonds.

Source: © Author.

new camps were established: Rivesaltes, Noé and Le Récébédou and several of the old sites continued in use. With a surface area comprising between 17 and 80 hectares, early internment centers were extensive, but Rivesaltes was simply colossal: 600 hectares. There is very little to be seen of the old camps, as the barracks were made of wood and soon disassembled and reused. Only one of them survives in the camp of Brens, of the so-called Adrian model, which had a surface of 150 square meters. Considering the number of internees, there were 1.5 to 2.5 square meters per person in each barrack, a situation comparable to that of the worse concentration camps in Franco's Spain (see Chapter 10). The barracks were dark and thin-walled and afforded little protection against cold. Sanitary facilities were generally deplorable. In the factory of Arandon, wich was reused as a camp and survives in ruins today, there were four showers for 1,300 inmates. Not surprisingly, malnourished refugees, especially the elderly, children and the infirm, died in scores. In Bram, 37 children below three years of age died between July 1940 and January 1941 (Legendre 2018: 67). Spaniards and Jews were buried side by side, proof that Republican Spaniards had joined the ranks of expendable people.

Among the later sites, the best preserved and most impressive is Rivesaltes, which was originally inaugurated as a military camp in 1938 (Boitel 2001). Here the barracks were made of brick and concrete, but they were not heated and cold and dampness were pervasive. In 1941 there were 6,500 internees, of which half were Spaniards and the rest Jews and Gypsies. Different barracks were provided for men and women and children and families were unmade. Conditions worsened from 1942, when the camp housed 21,000 people and interns began to die in scores. Virtually all Jewish people interned in Rivesaltes perished in extermination camps. The camp later hosted German and Italian soldiers and people from the French colonies until it closed in 1994. Its layout did not change substantially in decades, although it kept growing: it was a prototypical camp with long barracks laid in parallel rows with rectangular courtyards that organize space (Figure 9.2). There are seven units which worked as small camps, each with several structures that provided services: mess hall, workshops and warehouses. The entire space was surrounded with a barbed wire fence.

Some artifacts associated with the Spaniards have been found during surface survey (Legendre 2018: 64–65). Le Barcarés yielded several dishes and cooking ware of the period and two elements that are directly linked to the Republicans: a tube of toothpaste produced in Barcelona and an identity tag of a man named Manuel Lorenzo. In Rivesaltes, a calendar dated June 1941 has the name of the month written in Spanish (*junio*). In this latter camp, a large number of artifacts was recovered during survey, some of them dated to the 1940s, but it is impossible to tell if they belong to Spaniards, Jews or Roma. The most moving finds are dozens of suitcase handles, which speak of a shared experience of exile and uprootedness.

French camps bear important connections with the present: the Spanish refugees, like the Syrians and many others fleeing war and dictatorship in

Figure 9.2 One of the barracks of the internment camp of Rivesaltes, in southern France. *Source*: © Author.

their countries these days, were seen as potential criminals and as a burden to the national economy and they were dealt with accordingly. Refugee camps have not changed much in 80 years. They are still the same device for herding and controlling desperate human beings, but also for stereotyping them: the Other as a menace, the barbarian that has to be stopped at the gates of civilization. The famished, vanquished Spaniards in rags behind barbed wire were an anonymous mass that looked (were made to look) scarcely human and that reinforced French stereotypes as to the savagery of their southern neighbors. Camps then, like today, were not a mere container of human beings. They created a special category of human being, a *homo sacer* expelled from the realm of moral responsibility (Agamben 1995).

The trenches of the victors

We have to step a little back in time to continue with our story. Because in February 1939 the Republic was lethally wounded but not yet dead. The war went on in many other parts of Spain: from Andalusia to Madrid. The Nationalist territory kept expanding after July 1936, adding more food, factories and soldiers to the rebel side. Not surprisingly, the Nationalist trenches at the end of the conflict do not show scarcity, but rather the

Dead men walking 237

opposite. In the following sections we will take a look at two frontlines that we have visited already: Guadalajara and Madrid, first from the Nationalist trenches, then the Republican. They allow us to explore living (and fighting) conditions in a rural and urban theater respectively.

Guarding the castle in Guadalajara

Perhaps the place that we know best from an archaeological point of view is a late Nationalist fortification built on top of a steep hill near the village of Abánades, in Guadalajara (González-Ruibal 2011a, 2014). The place is called El Castillo, "The Castle". It refers to an old medieval fortification of which there is no trace on the surface. However, when Nationalist soldiers (or rather, Republican prisoners) dug the trenches, they came across pottery, bones and ashes from the early medieval period, which seem to belong to a frontier outpost around the eleventh century—the border between Christian and Muslim Iberia passed through this region. El Castillo was occupied in other historical periods. Like the sheepfolds, it was visited during the Peninsular War (1808–1812), of which we found a button of the First Regiment of Line Infantry Volunteers of Madrid. The regiment was formed in August 1808[3] and four months later, its first battalion was annihilated during the Battle of Tudela (Navarre), where a 30,000-strong Spanish army suffered 4,000 dead. The survivors retreated into Cuenca, south of Guadalajara and—thanks to the button—we know that they did it through Abánades. The excavation of the trenches also cut through Iron Age deposits (fifth–second century BC). This multilayered history shows that the hill was repeatedly chosen during the last two and a half millennia for its defensive qualities and strategic location.

After the April 1938 offensive (see Chapter 7), El Castillo became the most advanced stronghold of the Nationalists in this sector. It is, in fact, a salient surrounded by Republican positions located on higher ground. At first sight, it seems as if the life of the soldiers defending the hill was not easy. Archaeology, however, tells a different story. The hill of El Castillo has two levels: the hilltop proper and a lower terrace. Both were defended by perimeter trenches, pillboxes and covered trenches made of stone and concrete and had several dugouts for the troops (Figure 9.3). Based on existing documents, we know that the fortifications do not predate the summer of 1938—one of the covered concrete trenches has "1938" inscribed in the fresh concrete. The solidity and monumentality of the structures contrasts with those the Republicans were erecting around the same time (and that we will describe in the next section). They also had electricity and telephonic communication, as revealed by cables and wire.

The stronghold, however, was built, rather inadequately, on a hilltop and was therefore vulnerable to artillery fire and aerial bombing. We have seen other examples of fortified summits, in Aragón and the Basque Country (see Chapters 5 and 7). In the case of the rebels, the choice was probably inspired by the Moroccan experience, where building *blocaos* on hilltops was

238 *Dead men walking*

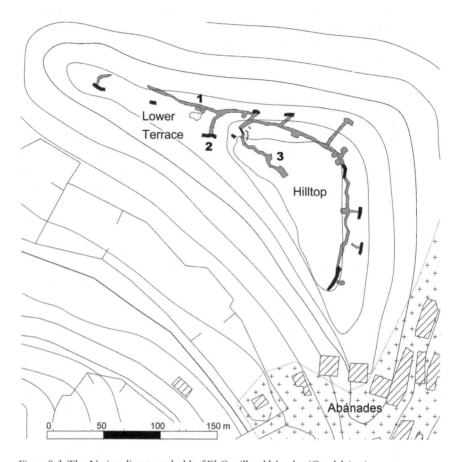

Figure 9.3 The Nationalist stronghold of El Castillo, Abánades (Guadalajara).
Notes: Numbers refer to excavated areas. Structures in black are made in concrete; structures in grey are dug.
Source: © Author.

a reasonable choice for the surveillance of wide territories with small contingents and the enemy lacked planes and had little artillery. Also, isolated outposts in the Rif mountains communicated with light signals and therefore had to be within visual range (Blanco Vázquez and Sierra 2011). The fortifications of El Castillo give the impression of a landscape of colonial war in Africa. Yet, in this case, as we will see, it does not seem that the election had negative repercussions for the defenders.

As elsewhere, soldiers spent most of their time in undeground shelters, which were covered with metal sheet or corrugated fiber cement, whose imprint can still be seen on the concrete. The metal sheet was salvaged by local farmers after the war and today can be found in fences, pigsties and hencoops. Some shelters had doors, which were inserted in grooves hewn in the rock. They were, as can be expected, cold in the winter and very dark.

Some hearths were quite elaborate: one was built with bricks and concrete with a clear aesthetic intention. We also found a latrine strangely facing the enemy in the higher part of the hilltop.

Due to the numerous finds, it is possible to interpret the function of the different structures. In the lower terrace we excavated two adjacent shelters. The smaller one, which had the brick and cement hearth to which I have referred, was used for warming up food and eating: we found a fork and a large number of tin cans inside. These were originally dumped out of the shelter, but when it was backfilled after the war they ended up back inside. The neighboring structure was a resting area and it was illuminated with candles, of which we found one—candles are listed among the five important things in trench warfare by Orwell (1980: 23). Soldiers kept their clothes, equipment and personal belongings here, of which we recovered many remains: two clasps, a button, a complete shoe and fragments of others, a makeshift hanger and two coins of 10 cents dated 1870. We also found several elements associated with personal hygiene: a razor, a fragment of mirror and a plastic comb imitating turtle shell. A surprising find in this same shelter was an earring, a cheap alloy piece with glass cabochons. There is a possible explanation for it. Like the tiny bottle of female perfume, this was probably a souvenir given by a wife or a girlfriend to a man in the front. In both cases, they acted as mnemonic aids capable of evoking a familiar sensorial world. They were perhaps seen also as charms, devices that extended the protective agency of the beloved ones.

The largest dugout was located in the upper part of the hilltop, facing the enemy. This is striking, but common in Spanish Civil War sites. Refuges were, as a rule, built in the rear of the trench and therefore with their entrances toward the frontline. This made them vulnerable from incoming fire, particularly in the first line, as in El Castillo. This did not seem to have prevented the soldiers from enjoying food, brushing their teeth or writing letters, based on our finds. The structure yielded many animal bones (of sheep or goat and chicken), sardine cans and wine bottles, most of which appeared concentrated in and around a hearth. The shelter had been improved with civilian furniture, of which we found nails and keyholes. We know that the soldiers of El Castillo brought to their trenches many things from the village houses, which had been abandoned by the neighbors as a result of the spring offensive of 1938 (see Chapter 7). In the same structure we retrieved remains of uniforms, clothes and shoes, writing material (an inkbottle and pencil leads), two coins and a pocket knife. This shelter was clearly a multifunctional space. In the trench in front of the shelter, we also found a tube of toothpaste of the La Toja brand, a famous spa on the coast of Galicia, which is still active and commercializes soaps and shampoos. The tube from El Castillo reads: "Toothpaste La Toja. Unique in the world". Advertisements of La Toja, like those of all major companies in Francoist Spain, aligned themselves with Nationalist propaganda:

240   *Dead men walking*

The factories of La Toja have contributed with its economic and moral support to the cause of Spain and its production develops in total normality. Consuming products from industries located in army-occupied territory means promoting work and serving the Fatherland.

(cit. in Rodríguez Mateos 2009)

El Castillo has furnished important data about the Nationalist frontline menu at the end of the war—and it was not bad. We recovered a minimum number of 110 tin cans. The consumption of canned food is atypical in a static front, but in this case might be related to the abundance of available supplies and perhaps to the difficulty of climbing the steep hill with the ranch every day. The tins are well preserved and in some cases it is possible to make out the factory, provenance and content. As for the latter, we have sardines in oil, marinated sardines, marinated tuna, corned beef, tomato, legumes or vegetables and condensed milk. The most abundant cans are from tuna (38%) and sardines (36%). The high percentage of tuna is surprising. In the memoirs and oral testimonies of war veterans sardines are omnipresent: it seems as if the daily menu was composed of sardines and bread alone, which is far from being true. Instead, I was unable to find mentions of tuna in Spanish war or postwar memoirs. They do appear, however, in the recollections of soldiers from other nationalities, like the Moroccans (Sánchez Ruano 2004: 239). There seems to be something cultural in this oblivion, because sardines play an important role in Spanish cultural traditions: *sardiñadas* (collective meals based on sardines) are typical of Galicia; the "burial of the sardine" traditionally marks the end of Carnival, and sardines were the first industrially processed foodstuff in the country. Tuna, although important in southwestern Spain, has never been so relevant in economic or cultural terms.

The tins from El Castillo also inform us about the development of certain fortunes during the conflict. The case of the Massó Brothers is paradigmatic. We have found many meat cans from Mérida's slaughterhouse in this and other Nationalist positions in Guadalajara. The factory, albeit located in Extremadura, was owned by Massó Brothers in Vigo (Galicia), originally a fish canning business (Martín Aceña and Martín Ruiz 2006: 459): we found Massó fish cans in Abánades. The company fared well with the Nationalists. The demand for fish and meat by the army granted the Massó large revenues, which they employed in expanding the business—they also produced munitions for the Nationalists (Vilar-Rodríguez and Lindoso-Tato 2009: 161). At the same time, they benefitted from Falangist violence, which suppressed workers' protest (Seidman 2011: 109). By the end of the war, Massó was one of the leading canning factories in the world.

Some sardines in olive oil were produced by José Barreras, also a Galician industry, but the most common are Augusto Sacco & Co (sardines) and Palacio de Oriente (tuna). Like the Massó, these companies made a fortune with the war business. Sacco & Co was in decline in the immediate pre-war period, but the conflict gave it a tremendous boost: by 1939 it was the second company in Galicia in terms of capital (Vilar-Rodríguez and Lindoso-Tato 2009: 160). Such a boom allowed Augusto Sacco to invest in strategic industries, such as mining. Palacio de Oriente also achieved extraordinary profits during the conflict. Its webpage says that the factory went from 50 workers in 1873 to over 1,000 in 1937,[4] but it does not say anything about how this exponential growth occurred.

War materials were abundant in El Castillo as well, more than in any Republican position of the time that we have documented. All soldiers were armed with Spanish or German Mausers, of which we have found around 200 cartridges and shell casings, two complete clips and even a bayonet. Spanish ammunition is the most abundant and it is only the 7 mm casings that had been fired—mostly by a Hotchkiss machine gun. We found an empty magazine belonging to this weapon on the floor of the large shelter located on the hilltop, whereas the nearby latrine was filled with spent 7 mm ammunition (Figure 9.4). The other spot that furnished a large number of shell casings (a total of 73) was the concrete parapet of the lower terrace. What we have likely documented is harassing fire over Republican troops, made from the two places that had better visual control over the enemy lines. The Hotchkiss had an effective range of over two kilometers and the Republican positions in front of El Castillo were located at a distance of 450 to 600 meters.

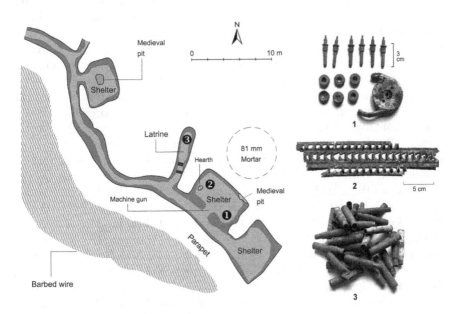

Figure 9.4 Trench, dugouts and latrine in the hilltop of El Castillo with finds related to fighting activity in the position.

Notes: 1. Pieces of 81 mm Valero mortar grenades; 2. Empty magazine of the Hotchkiss machine gun; 3. Spent 7 mm ammunition, fired by the Hotchkiss.

Source: © Manuel Antonio Franco Fernández and the author.

242 *Dead men walking*

The Nationalists were also armed with Valero 81 mm mortars. We have found dozens of related pieces, which tend to concentrate in two positions: one in the lower terrace and one in the hilltop. Maybe there was a single mortar that was moved up and down, according to necessity. Mortar elements include shotgun cartridges used to propel the grenades, safety plugs, fins, propelling charges, caps and transport cans. Many of the projectiles never actually exploded: an intact 81 mm grenade appeared in the no-man's-land in front of El Castillo and another one in the Republican stronghold of El Rondal, a hill in front of the Nationalist fortifications. There was probably a howitzer in El Castillo at some point, because we found an artillery primer and several mechanisms from time fuses. The primer is dated in 1937 and was produced by Laguna de Rins, an Aragonese company established in 1880 and specializing in high-precision topographic material.[5]

The considerable amount of spent ammunition is not matched by similar traces of incoming fire. In fact, there are virtually no impacted bullets in the Nationalist parapets or elsewhere. In the hilltop we only found a single bullet and two small artillery shell fragments and nothing in the lower terrace. There is no better proof of the tranquility enjoyed by the soldiers in El Castillo than the coffee cups, coffee grinder and liquor glasses that we found in one of the concrete parapets amid a load of shell casings. Soldiers were drinking coffee and liquor (or both things at the same time: *carajillo* in Spanish) in what is the most exposed position of the fortifications. They were shooting and drinking, but nobody seems to have been firing at them. There were also tin cans and remains of goat or sheep, evidence that the soldiers were eating in the parapet as well. The lack of response evinces the dire situation in which the Popular Army was by the end of the war. Every bullet was spared.

The provenance of the *matériel* is mostly Spanish and German. Almost all ammunition was produced during the war or shortly before: half of the Spanish cartridges (produced in Seville and Toledo) were made during the conflict. By the beginning of 1939, the Nationalists had taken hold of large Republican supplies and this explains the presence of cartridges produced in Madrid and Barcelona or in countries that had supplied weapons to the Republic in 1936, such as Mexico, Austria and Czechoslovakia. As for the German ammunition, it is all dated, as usual, in the 1930s, mostly 1935 and 1936. We also have plenty of evidence for the Italian support. The most striking are two complete M1915/16 helmets. This model imitates the famous French Adrian and was used by Italy during the First World War. They arrived in Spain with the Corpo di Truppe Volontarie, who used it in the Battle of Guadalajara. It is in fact, a rather mediocre helmet made of thin metal sheet—indeed, quite a lot thinner than the Spanish M1926 helmet (Figure 9.5). Other Italian-made objects include stylish motorbike goggles (the Italians had excelled in goggle design since the 1910s); a 25 mm flare shell casing produced by Camocini & Co (Como) in 1935, and part of a Breda M35 grenade that appeared with one of the helmets inside the latrine. The most singular object, however, was hidden in a house in

Figure 9.5 Italian M1915 helmet abandoned in a covered concrete trench in El Castillo.
Source: © Author.

Abánades. It is a mess tin engraved with the name of an Italian soldier: Armando Stellani. Many Italian objects made it into Spanish hands through informal exchanges with members of the CTV. The novelist Ricardo Fernández de la Reguera, to whom I have referred in Chapter 7, describes the bartering between Spanish and Italian soldiers:

> They lived several days with the Italians they came to replace. They got along immediately. The Italians were warm-hearted, generous and a bit naive. They got carried away by the most incredible objects. As they had lots of equipment, it was possible to get amazing bargains. In exchange for a lighter, a filthy flask or any other trinket, they gave away trousers, combat jackets, ponchos, boots, caps…
>
> (Fernández de la Reguera 1955: 123)

It is interesting that Spaniards were giving objects that they have manufactured themselves in exchange for industrial items. Spaniards were fascinated by modernity, Italians by local handicrafts. Nevertheless, the soldiers of El Castillo were well uniformed. The clasps and buckles that we found indicate that they were all carrying the standard Carniago equipment and the footwear remains belong to shoes and hobnail-studded boots. Footprints of studded soles were

244   *Dead men walking*

stamped in the fresh concrete of a machine-gun nest and, behind the boots, a dog track: the regiment's pet?

One of the most remarkable historical testimonies of El Castillo are its graffiti. We have documented 16 items, of either personal or political nature. The former are soldiers' names (Germán Ruiz, Antonio Navarro), perhaps place names (Leiva, Fraga) and a woman's name (Teresa), probably the wife or girlfriend of one of the combatants. Half of the graffiti appeared in the concrete parapet mentioned above where soldiers drank coffee and liquor. In some cases, they imitate letters but cannot be read. It is possible that somebody who was illiterate still wanted to express himself. Or perhaps he was learning to write, like the Republican of Casa de la Sierra (see Chapter 6). Thus, one of the graffiti reads VIVA and then follows with other nonsensical strokes. *Viva* ("long life!") surely was something he had seen many times, including in El Castillo itself. Three of the political graffiti, located in different places, mention General Franco: *Franco Caudillo*, *Vi[va Fran]nco* and *Franco*. The last one appears in a machine-gun nest with an *Arriba España* and the yoke and arrows symbolizing the Falange. Similar graffiti have been found in many late Nationalist fortifications throughout Spain, again showing that many soldiers were strongly ideologized and that this ideologization, at least in the Francoist side, probably increased as the war progressed, boosted by Nationalist victories and propaganda.

Eating and drinking in Madrid

As we have been seen throughout the book, alcoholic bottles are some of the most common finds in Spanish Civil War sites—and in most other conflict contexts for that matter. Yet while digging up bottles is a run-of-the-mill experience for any battlefield researcher, excavating a bar in a military context is much less so. An example is the canteen of the prisoner-of-war camp of Quedlinburg in Germany, from the First World War. The structure could be identified because the associated cesspits contained numerous beer bottles and beer drinking glasses, as well as whiteware and faunal remains (Demuth 2009: 175). If bars are rare, a canteen in the line of fire is truly exceptional. But this is what we excavated at the University City in Madrid (González-Ruibal 2018a). In Chapter 4, I mentioned a pavilion of the Asylum of Santa Cristina that had been transformed into a military structure with shelters and tunnels. We know the function of the place during the war thanks to a combination of archaeological and documentary sources. In a wartime map, the building is identified as a canteen. It is not clear whether it refers to the pre-war use of the place as a refectory or to its new function. What we know for sure is that there was a bar there during the war, because we found an extraordinary number of bottles of alcoholic drinks and because there is a specific mention of a bar in this area. According to this source, it was inaugurated late in the war, on 14 October 1938. Father Caballero, a military chaplain, tells us that the place was called *Bar de la Bandera* (*bandera* being "flag" and the term for a military company in the Legion) and was "a bar excavated underground, spacious, with shelves full of bottles, pine tables, stools" and even a piano (cit. in Calvo González-Regueral 2012: 301).

The bar was well supplied indeed: in the 2017 field season and in the area of the laundry alone, we recovered a minimum number of 18 bottles of wine, sherry or brandy produced by the Andalusian sherry barons (Pedro Domecq and González Byass). Other bottles contained anisette, spirits, beer (El Águila) and rarer products such as Kina San Clemente, a sweet wine (with supposed therapeutic properties), and Martini Rosso. We even found the porcelain head of a soda syphon—a true bar indeed (Figure 9.6). Soldiers had plenty to drink and were well-fed, in striking contrast with the starving Madrilenians and even their military counterparts. Tin cans are scarce, as befits a static frontline, but faunal remains are overabundant and evince a diverse and rich diet. In two field seasons (2017–2018), we collected 2,627 bones.[6] The most common animals in terms of minimum number of individuals were sheep or goats, with a total of 61 individuals (45% of the assemblage), followed by cattle, with 29 inviduals (22%), 26 chicken (10%), 10 pigs (7%) and 9 rabbits (7%). If we look at meat volume, however, cattle contributed more to the diet, followed by sheep and pigs. It is not only the variety of meats that is surprising and unique in Spanish Civil War contexts, the percentage of infantile animals is equally astonishing: 42% of the sheep, 27% of the cattle and 25% of the pigs were young specimens. Egg shell has also been found: bringing eggs to the first line without breaking them

Figure 9.6 Finds of glass bottles (mostly belonging to alcoholic beverages) and animal bones in the canteen area of the Asylum of Santa Cristina in Madrid.

Source: © Pedro Rodríguez Simón, Manuel Antonio Franco Fernández and the author.

246 *Dead men walking*

through the narrow trenches was nothing short of miraculous. Clams (*Chamelea gallina*) are exceedingly common and appear virtually everywhere. They were probably part of soups or stews, as was the fish of which we have retrieved 32 bones. They belong to cod (*Gadus morhua*)—a staple of the diet in central Spain for several centuries in its dry version and that has the advantage of easy transportation. The soldiers in the Clínico salient were clearly receiving special treatment.

The positions at the University City were held by legionnaires, infantry and colonial troops (*regulares*). The latter were Muslim and therefore could not (or should not) drink alcohol. They had hashish, instead, and tea. Of the latter we have evidence in the shape of a strainer found during the survey of the park in front of the University Hospital. The consumption of tea on the campus' trenches was described by Bobby Deglané, a Chilean journalist and peculiar character (he worked variously as circus performer and Nationalist spy), who visited the university during the war. In a piece entitled "Moorish tea at the University City", he tells (in a characteristic orientalizing style) of an expedition to the University Hospital. After crossing the Manzanares and a labyrinth of trenches he arrives at what he calls the "headquarters" and sits in the basement with a group of Moroccan soldiers:

> The details, suggestions and influence of the environment adhered to my spirit, intoxicating it with their exotic beauty as if this were the scenario of a legend. While the moors ate their spice-scented meals and drank the golden Moorish brew, I traveled with my imagination—at that moment galloping vertiginously—around the scary places where the war sizzled like a remote Apocalypse, but in fact only a few meters away. There they were the Moors that night, with their peaceful conversations. Outside death is lurking. They would sleep as one sleeps at the University City, with the rifle under the arm, to wake up, perhaps, before the sun announces the arrival of the day, hurried by the alarm of a surprise attack or the classic explosion of one of these shocking underground mines.
>
> (cited in Barchino 2013: 205)

Tea, among the Moors, played a role similar to alcohol among Christians. It helped them socialize, chill out and forget about the war. Despite its imaginative colonial bias, Deglané's text points to something relevant about the tea ceremony: it helped reconstruct something of the sensory environment of one's home in extremely harsh circumstances. It was not only the social act of drinking tea, but also its phenomenology. The taste and smell of the infusion, the bodily gestures involved in its preparation and serving surely had a soothing effect in the colonial troops fighting in a doubly hostile environment—in a war and in a foreign country, in which they remained always subalterns. For Deglané, the smell of tea and spices evoked sensuality and exoticism. For the Moroccans, tea-drinking was a way of restoring the routines of daily life.

The trenches of the vanquished

Republican soldiers would not have minded tasting the Nationalist menu. Their lives at the end of the war were miserable: their diet was poorer; they were more affected by diseases; had inferior equipment, and were less frequently supplied (Matthews 2012: 159–166). Demoralization is difficult to gauge, because very few letters have survived. The best source is the censorship service of the Army of Andalusia, whose collection of letters has been studied by James Matthews. References to the lack of food are plentiful. Thus, a soldier writing late in the war says:

> W]e are suffering from severe hunger in this village. We cannot resist because more than half [of our number] are hospitalized because of lack of food. I tell you, the food that we are given is nothing more than four chickpeas and that to eat them we have to grind them with a mortar and that is the only way that we eat them…
>
> (Matthews 2012: 161)

Internal political repression did not help to lift the spirits. In the city of Cuenca, in central Spain, archaeologists have recently documented graffiti in a historical building used by the SIM, the Service of Military Intelligence (*Servicio de Inteligencia Militar*) (Domínguez-Solera et al. 2018). The SIM's mission was to fight against the Fifth Column, the Nationalist sympathizers who were actively undermining the Republic from within (Alía Miranda 2015). However, SIM agents, largely communists, often employed their power to quench all political dissidence. The prison in Cuenca is witness to these repressive activities: in one of the cells there is a graffiti that reads "antifascists coming from the front are detained in Cuenca" and a drawing depicts a fat man with short mustache and the legend "The secret police with the face of a *facha* [fascist]". Indeed, the author has aptly captured the look of a prototypical Nationalist boss (like Franco). Out of seven graffiti with indication of month and year, six are dated in November and December 1938.

Making do in Guadalajara

After the Offensive of the Upper Tajuña River, in the Spring of 1938 (see Chapter 7), the Republicans dug in, excavated trenches and shelters, set up barbed wire fences and machine guns, raided the enemy lines and were raided in turn. Some of the positions retained by the Popular Army after the offensive were very exposed to enemy fire. Those that suffered the most in the sector were Vértice Cerro and Alto de la Casilla, the hills that fell during the first day of the Republican attack. In Alto de la Casilla, the central core of the fortifications is a firing trench that surrounds the hilltop—again, an unfortunate decision in industrialized warfare (González-Ruibal 2013). The

248 *Dead men walking*

difference with Nationalist positions, however, is that Alto de la Casilla is not an isolated stronghold, but part of a continuum of fortifications, connected with a linear trench and extending several kilometers between the municipalities of Abánades and Sotodosos. One of the trenches leaving from Alto de la Casilla leads to a well-camouflaged pillbox that controls access to the road to Sotodosos. The pillbox was meant for a machine gun that would have swept a wide tract of the road, but the Nationalists never launched another offensive through this area. We excavated the pillbox and discovered that it had been transformed into an ordinary shelter, where soldiers ate, rested and got warm: there was a hearth and next to it a knife, a spoon and a large tin can. Quite a lot of ammunition did turn up (up to 60 Mosin cartridges), but not a single spent casing that indicated that soldiers fired from this position. Inside, we also documented fragments of the inscription indicating the unit of engineers in charge of the works.

As in other sites, perhaps more interesting than the Civil War remnants were the pre-war vestiges. When the soldiers excavated the trenches they cut across the remains of a medieval deserted village. The present landscape of the Tajuña Valley is quite different from that of the Spanish Civil War, but it is also very different from the landscape of the fourteenth century, when the now-depopulated rural areas of Guadalajara were brimming with villages. There were fewer trees, roe and deer than today, and more people, roads, sheeps and cultivated fields. We know of at least four abandoned medieval settlements in the region, which we documented during survey, but there are probably more. In the deserted hamlet near Alto de la Casilla we found glazed wares typical of the Late Middle Ages, round stone tokens (whose purpose we do not know) and bones of domestic animals. Behind the trenches, we discovered the foundations of stone houses and even a billon coin with the coat of arms of the Kingdom of Castile. The reason for the abandonment of this and nearby villages was the Black Death. From the mid-fourteenth century, a combination of pests, famine and bad crops produced a steep demographic decline in Castile, from which some areas never recovered. In Guadalajara, we know of several villages that lost their entire population to the bubonic plague.[7] Despite the time distance, the medieval site has something in common with the trenches: both remind us that the four horses of the Apocalypse have ridden across the bucolic landscapes of Spain—time and again.

The main position in this sector was Alto de la Casilla itself (Figure 9.7). From this height, Republicans had perfect visual control of La Nava, the plateau that they conquered with so much sweat and blood during the combats of April 1938 and that they had to surrender just a few days later. Unfortunately for the Republicans, the positions were equally visible for the enemy. The hilltop was the object of several Nationalist assaults after the Republican offensive and suffered intense artillery and aerial bombing. We documented these attacks and documented 32 craters in less than 3,500 square meters. And this does not take in consideration the grenades that exploded over ground level or the impacts of smaller caliber weapons that

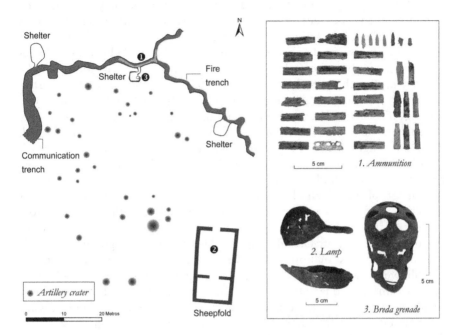

Figure 9.7 Republican position of Alto de la Casilla (Abánades, Guadalajara).
Source: © Manuel Antonio Franco Fernández and the author.

are invisible today. We also have evidence from raids and harassing fire: impacted Mauser bullets from the Nationalist rifles and machine guns, a large number of Mosin Nagant shell casings and stripper clips and numerous Lafitte and Breda grenade fragments. Also two Enfield stripper clips: the old British rifles which had saved Madrid in 1936 (Chapter 3) were still used in secondary frontlines at the end of the war.

Although Alto de la Casilla was a difficult position, soldiers managed to survive. When they were bombed, they took shelter in small dugouts. They could not use the sheepfold that gives its name to the place (*casilla*, "small house"), because it was too exposed to enemy fire. Still, we found a small lamp made with a tin can there, a simple but perfect object. The most surprising find, however, was a small bottle of Martini Rosso, of the Spanish brand Rosita. The same alcoholic drink that the Nationalists were consuming in another line of fire, this time at the University City. As in Madrid, alcohol gave soldiers the extra morale needed to endure life in a very exposed position.

The trench from Alto de la Casilla continues all the way to the limit with Sotodosos. Not far from the municipality's limit we excavated another site, a tract of trench and a dougout, which is named *Posición 64* in the documents.[8] The trench is part of a line extending one kilometer and a half. It was mostly built in dry stone, rather than dug, because it was easier than cutting through the rocky

250   *Dead men walking*

ground. Most parapets are still in place, as if the war had only paused, ready to resume at any moment. The document that describes Position 64 informs us that the trench had 1,675 meters protected by 1,575 meters of barbed wire fence, a stone parapet that was one meter tall, and four shelters. One shelter was mortar-proof, the others were of "flimsy construction" (*endeble construcción*). It is thus possible that the one that we excavated was the mortar-proof, because it is deep, it was excavated in the bedrock and had thick stone parapets. The document also tells us that the entire sector was garrisoned by 115 soldiers—one for each 15 meters of fortification—who were armed with rifles, three light machine guns and one heavy machine gun. The trench furnished very little material, meaning that, unlike Alto de la Casilla, it saw very little action. Still, we know that as late as 19 February 1939, the Nationalists planned a raid here to destroy a light machine gun. The raid was actually carried out a few days later, but on March 4 (only three weeks before the end of the war) a report indicates that it was a failure: the Republicans found out about the attack and escaped, taking the machine gun with them.[9]

The shelter was rich in finds. We found an enormous mallet in the backfill weighing several kilos that was used to break the bedrock. It is hard to imagine one of the short and skinny Spaniards of the time wielding it, but then we cannot forget that most of them were peasants and workers, used to manual labor. Shortly after the war somebody sealed the structure with stones. We know that it had to be early in the postwar period because the layer of rubble preserved in situ the last objects abandoned by the Republicans. On the floor of the shelter there were cartridges, tin cans, Republican coins, a mess tin, an empty Soviet ammunition box and buttons. The box is dated 1927 and was produced in Lugansk, eastern Ukraine. All ammunition found on the floor is Soviet 7.62 mm, except one: a 7 mm cartridge produced in Belgium by the legendary FN Herstal factory (still active today). The coins were of one peseta and 50 cents, all with the effigy of the Republic. The abandonment of Republican coins is frequent in late contexts: after the end of the war, they were worthless and even incriminating evidence. Among the objects found on the floor, the amount of recycled elements is noticeable: a wire was added to the ammunition box to serve as a handle; a tin can was transformed into a small jar and another one into a cooking pot or a container for carrying water. Another tin with a wire handle was found outside the shelter. The Republican trenches speak eloquently about the misery of the later days of the war. Everything was recycled, nothing was wasted. What a different picture to the one we got in El Castillo! If it were not for the ammunition, we would think that the shelter had been used by homeless people. Also, if it were not for two other finds: a complete, but empty, 75 mm shrapnel shell and an unexploded 50 mm Valero round. This trench mortar was probably part of the equipment of the troops stationed in Position 64. As for the shrapnel shell, it was

Position 64 and Alto de la Casilla were in the very line of fire, separated from the enemy by just a few hundred meters. But the situation in the rearguard, though safer, was not substantially better. We excavated the camp of the 138 Mixed Brigade, made up, as we saw in Chapter 6, by Catalans. It was near Canredondo, a village located seven kilometers behind the Republican lines (González-Ruibal 2016a). The military headquarters were originally established inside the village itself, but after several aerial bombings, the Republican command decided to move it elsewhere, with the purpose of making the base less vulnerable and avoiding collateral civilian damage. It was thus taken to a valley some three kilometers to the north of Canredondo, Vallejo del Chulo, which was well protected by hills and trees. The move was a success, as no other bombings are documented and, in fact, we were unable to identify a single fragment of artillery shell or aviation bomb during our work. The camp was established shortly before the Offensive of the Upper Tajuña River that started on 31 March 1938 (see Chapter 7) and was in operation until the end of the war. At its peak, there were 247 men, including the command of the 138 Mixed Brigade and staff from transmissions, engineers, trains, armored cars, munitions and the medical corps. The camp is well-preserved and is made of 32 rectangular or square dry stone structures, hardly different from the typical sheepfolds and shepherd huts of the area (Figure 9.8). The excavation revealed that they all had an earthen floor and often a hearth, sometimes partially excavated in the ground. The longest structures were probably multifunctional spaces and soldiers slept, cook and spent time there. They might look miserable, and indeed they were, but compared to the dugouts that we documented in another Republican position in this sector, Los Castillejos, they were luxurious: in this latter place, the shelters were unipersonal and were a mere hole in the ground surrounded at times by a stone parapet. They are so small that they have no place for a hearth. Surviving in these human burrows was heroic in the winter, when night temperatures can fall to minus 20 degrees.

We conducted a metal detector survey of the camp of Vallejo del Chulo and excavated seven structures. They turned out to be considerably clean: few artefacts were found inside or around them, which shows that the place was thouroughly searched for valuables after the war. The most frequent find was ammunition of the usual types: a total of 101 elements (bullets, casings and cartridges). This is only a third of the ammunition found in the Nationalist position of El Castillo, but still an important quantity. Six complete clips appeared packed together behind a hut, as if they had been hidden for some reason. The ammunition is predominately Soviet 7.62 mm. The contrast with the Nationalist positions in the same area is better seen in two aspects: food and health. Tin cans are scarce—20 items of which seven belonging to condensed milk—and the soldiers were eating very little meat, if at all, since not a single animal bone appeared in the excavations. The diet

252 *Dead men walking*

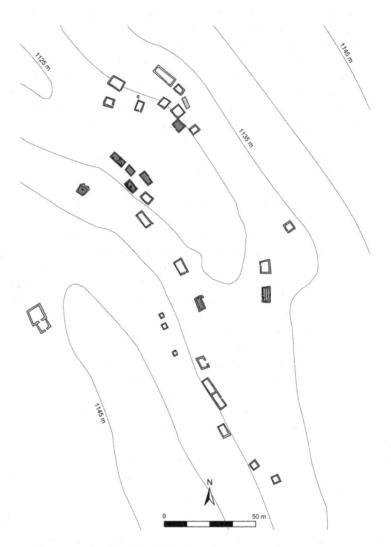

Figure 9.8 The camp of Vallejo del Chulo, Canredondo (Guadalajara).
Notes: In grey, excavated structures.
Source: © Manuel Antonio Franco Fernández and the author.

was supplemented, as elsewhere in the Republican lines, by vitamin and mineral complexes. Thus, we found a tin of the brand Ruamba, a product of the Laboratory of Pedro Viñas y Dordal (Barcelona), which was used as an antianemic and was advertised at the time with the slogan "Regenerates blood plasma. It is the joy of children and a delight for adults". The starving soldiers of Canredondo probably found little joy and delight in consuming Ruamba, instead of fresh meat and vegetables. We also found a few fragmens

Dead men walking 253

of medicine bottles and a free sample of cough drops, but it is little considering that an infirmary was located here according to archival documents. Few of the objects that were carried by the soldiers turned up: only four coins, of which two were not used during the Civil War: a medieval coin and one from the time of Philip IV (r. 1621–1640). The others are one Republican *peseta*, a 50 cent coin of the Revolutionary Period (1868–1873) and, the strangest of all, a French coin of Napoleon III, dated 1855. French coins were used like the Spanish *perras*, the low-value currency, and remained in use until the 1940s. The only personal belonging is a silver watch lost by a soldier, with its name scribbled. The survey also yielded two insignias with the Catalan coat of arms—like the ones we found in the nearby position of Alto del Molino (see Chapter 6). Life for Catalan soldiers was particularly hard: after the fall of Catalonia, many felt there was little reason to fight and Franco's army increased its propaganda campaign dropping pamphlets that encouraged soldiers to desert. One read: "Contribute yourself to the splendorous dawn of the New Spain adding your enthusiasm and effort to the cause of FRANCO".[10] Another one named the Catalan towns that had been captured by the Nationalists in January and February 1939 and asserted triumphantly: "Catalonia is already Spain".[11] Many, indeed, tried to desert, and some never made it. Between October 1938 and February 1939, Nationalist bullets killed five soldiers of the 138 Mixed Brigade stationed in Guadalajara. During this same period, Republican soldiers killed eight of their own that were trying to cross over to the enemy lines (Corral 2006: 54).

The trenches of famine in Madrid

Guadalajara was hard, but Madrid was not an easier frontline. Hunger was perhaps worse in Madrid than elsewhere, because authorities had to feed a starving population and a standing army. At the University City, we know that food was neither abundant nor varied, due to the constant complaints in both official documents and testimonies. Quality and quantity deteriorated through the war: writer Ángel María de Lera remembered that by 1939 food consisted "almost exclusively in two soups—one at midday and one at night— and a ladleful of water blackened with roasted barley, which was served for breakfast" (cit. in Calvo González-Regueral 2012: 405). In contrast to the thousands of animal bones found in the Nationalist lines, we only documented four tiny bones of chicken and cattle in the Republican trenches of the last months of the war, which means that meat consumption was extremely low. Only a dozen tin cans have been retrieved, mostly belonging to sardines and a few cases of Soviet corned beef. Bottles are equally scant in war levels, again in stark contrast with the enemy trenches. The situation in the frontline mirrors that of civilians: in late 1938 milk was no longer available even for children under two years of age. By January 1939, the daily ration consisted in 100 grams of bread and 100 grams of lentils, chickpeas or

254 *Dead men walking*

rice—a third of the food received by prisoners at the Gulag around that time (Snyder 2010: 27). By late February, there was no longer wheat (Campos Posada 2018: 475–476).

Recycling was intense at the University City, perhaps even more than in rural fronts, given the proximity of the factories and the dearth of recyclable materials (metal or glass) found during our fieldwork. In Chapter 4 we saw how the Republican command was issuing orders requesting the collection of spent shell casings as early as May 1937. As the war progressed, the importance of recycling only increased: writer Ángel María de Lera again informs us that during the last months of the war "the company leaders had to account, in the daily report, for the bombs and cartridges that had been spent, because the ammunition pool was exhausted and not a single bullet should be wasted" (cit. in Calvo González-Regueral 2012: 405). Military orders also refer to the collection of condensed milk cans. Meaningfully, we only found a lid of *La Lechera* ("The Milkmaid"), probably from a pre-war stock as this milk was produced in Nationalist-held territory in the north, but not a single can.[12] Along with tins and glass, blankets, cloth and even religious stamps were also recycled. The orders of the 7 Division were printed on them—probably with a desecrating intention. In this context of scarcity, the find of an ammunition box with a scatter of burst cartridges in one of the trenches is bewildering (see Figure 4.6). But there is an explanation to it. Clearly, somebody dumped it there at the end of the war and shot at it to render it useless, just before the trench was backfilled. It is a powerful testimony of the end of the war.

We found a lonely red star insignia in one of the Republican trenches. It does not imply any political affiliation, because it was official with the Popular Army. It might have been lost by a soldier, but it is also plausible that it was wittingly removed from the uniform. On 17 March 1939, scarcely two weeks before the end of the war, the red star was officially eliminated from the uniform (Alía Miranda 2015: 244), in a belated and useless attempt at ingratiating the enemy. The small and broken insignia is perhaps the best metaphor of the vanquished Republic.

That the war was lost was known by many well before March 1939. Soldiers in Madrid, as in Guadalajara, tried to desert. In December 1938, one of the soldiers stationed at the trenches that we excavated at the University City tried to pass over to the enemy. His name was José Torres Ferrer, he was 27 years old and from a village in Granada. But José got lost in the labyrinth of trenches in Puerta de Hierro and ended up returning to his own lines without noticing. The mistake proved to be fatal: he was executed by firing squad (Corral 2006: 58–59).

The southeastern fringe of Madrid had been the scenario of heavy fighting in 1937, during the Battle of Jarama (see Chapter 5). The entire area remained heavily fortified and thousands of toops were stationed there. We know that, at least for the Republican lines, fortification works increased substantially during the last months of the war particularly from October 1938 onwards. Among other things, it is a reflection of the policy of resistance at all costs espoused by President Negrín. It is perhaps to this construction surge that we have to attribute the position of Casas de Murcia, in the neighborhood of Vallecas. This was the first site of the Spanish Civil War to be excavated archaeologically and published, although unfortunately with limited detail (Morín de Pablos et al. 2002, 2003; Pérez-Juez et al. 2002). The hill, which had an Iron Age settlement, was fortified with a linear trench without zigzags but with foxholes or firebays and a central shelter that acted as the command post (Figure 9.9). We ignore its construction date, but, since it was doubtless abandoned at the end of the conflict, we can infer that most of the materials were deposited during late 1938 and early 1939. Ammunition, which is abundant, is massively of the Soviet 7.62 mm caliber, which corroborates a late occupation. Archaeologists recovered a number of glass containers, including four intact inkbottles with remains of blue, black and red ink, gun oil flasks, a bottle of castor oil and a bottle of vitamins. As already mentioned, inkbottles are more abundant in Republican trenches than in Nationalist ones and this might be reflecting the literacy campaign undertaken by the Popular Army. As for the medicines, they are particularly representative of life conditions during the last stage of the war: castor oil was used to treat constipation, which was endemic among Republican soldiers due to a diet that was both scarce and lacking in fresh foodstuffs. Regarding the vitamins, they were replacing the lack of fruits and vegetables.

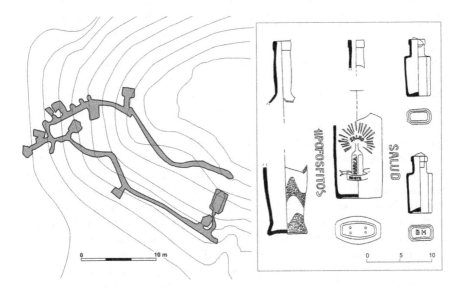

Figure 9.9 The Republican position of Casas de Murcia, that defended the south of the city of Madrid, with vitamins and medicines found at the site.

Source: Author's drawing based on Morín de Pablos et al. (2002).

256 *Dead men walking*

Some 20 kilometers to the east were the trenches of Rivas Vaciamadrid. Here we excavated some late fortifications and trenches that were built near the Valencia road, the main route connecting Madrid and the Republican war-time capital (González-Ruibal and Rodríguez Simón 2018). The excavations centered on two pillboxes excavated (or hewn) in the soft gypsum and a camp with dozens of dugouts. The architecture of the two pillboxes is telling of the difficult conditions of the Popular Army at the end of the war. We know from the available documentation that they had been built from 25 October 1938 onwards.[13] Very little concrete was used and this of very poor quality. It was basically employed in the revetment of the embrasures and, in one case, to prepare a platform to set up the machine gun. The pillboxes were reinforced with stone and in the case of the larger structure, tree trunks. The structures bear a striking resemblance to the vernacular subterranean architecture of the region. The extensive gypsum cliffs that dominate the geography of southern and southeastern Madrid and the poverty of many landless families in the countryside propitiated the emergence of a characteristic hypogeic architecture that lasted until well into the post-war period—in fact, it was revived during the post-war period and used by refugees, homeless people and poor families (Morín de Pablos et al. 2005). It is more than likely that, as in other cases, soldiers were resorting to their prewar experience and skills when constructing the fortifications.

Machine guns were likely never deployed in the nests, as the area was of limited strategic relevance. In fact, it seems that the entire fortification complex, which has a 3-km long trench and at least four machine-gun emplacements, was constructed in anticipation of a Nationalist attack, which never came, not to be actually occupied by troops. Proof of that is the virtual absence of wartime materials found inside or around the trench, both during survey and excavations. Soldiers probably spent their time in the many dugouts. Here we did find artifacts, but not a great quantity of them, compared to other similar late positions, either Republican or Nationalist.

Pillboxes were transformed into residential spaces (as we saw in Alto de la Casilla, in Abánades), which is good indication of the lack of military activity in this frontline. In fact, the poor quality of the constructions had as much to do with scarcity as with lack of strategic relevance, as we know that the Republic was still building sturdy concrete pillboxes in other points. Despite its very short life span (just a few months), one of the pillboxes experienced quite a lot of transformations: the entrance was sealed, a niche with a hearth and a chimney was open near the former door and another shelter was excavated between the trench and the pillbox (Figure 9.10). Evidence of residential use includes buttons and shoes, tin cans (one of them still in situ, over the hearth), a few sheep or goat bones, alcoholic drinks, a perfume bottle, an inkbottle, one Republican *peseta*, and medicines. Yet the proper living space was behind the fortifcations, in a narrow valley. The shelters were dug along the slopes and were very small, like those we saw in Mediana

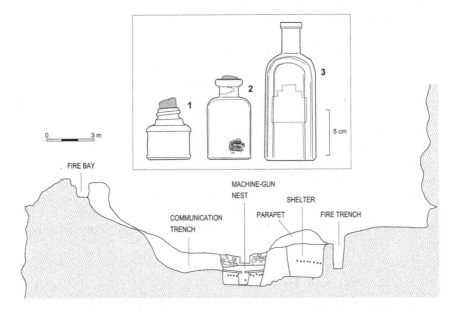

Figure 9.10 Section through a Republican fortification in El Piul (Rivas Vaciamadrid) that watched over one of the main accesses to Madrid, the Valencia road.

Notes: Finds include: 1. Inkbottle; 2. Bottle of perfume; 3. Laxative. The first two appeared in the machine-gun nest transformed into a shelter, the laxant in the proper shelter, adjacent to the nest.

Source: © Author.

(Chapter 6). With a typical surface of three square meters, they probably accommodated two or three soldiers each. Despite their rudimentary look, at least some were equipped with electric light: we found cable and part of a bulb still inserted in its metallic screw. There were 40 lamps and 5,000 meters of cable in this sector, but it was not enough and units in the field were furnished with candles and oil.[14]

As at the University City, faunal remains are all but absent: a dozen sheep bones were found in a total of nine excavated structures. Already in January 1938 the food supply in the sector was eliciting complaints, although it was incomparably better than civilian rations. Soldiers' daily meals included rice with chickpeas or lentils, 300 grams of bread and 80 to 100 grams of Soviet canned meat.[15] The use of canned meat is revelatory of the difficulties found by the Popular Army to provide fresh victuals to their troops and might explain the scarcity of bones in our site—although tins were also very sparse. Undoubtedly, the rations described above declined during the last months of the conflict.

The most abundant finds were, as in other Popular Army positions of the late war period, ammunition-related: Republican soldiers were far better armed than they were fed. In fact, cartridges are suprisingly homogeneous,

258 *Dead men walking*

82% belong to the Soviet 7.62 mm caliber. The medicines again speak eloquently of the soldiers' lot: a bottle of laxative and one with sulphurous mineral water reveal endemic constipation. The mineral water came from Carabaña (a village near Madrid) which has a thermal source exploited commercially since 1864. It was renowned in the 1930s for its laxative properties (Vilar-Rodríguez and Lindoso-Tato 2015: 48). The premises of the company were used as a base by the Republican Army during the war and they might have looked after the production and distribution of the bottled water. Other medicines found in the site include cough syrups and products for the treatment of pulmonary diseases. Personal objects are very infrequent, the most remarkable being a large cruficix found during the survey of a nearby camp. Its big size shows that it was probably worn conspicuously. Being Catholic was definitely not a problem in the Republican lines, once the revolutionary fervor of the early months of the war receded. And then, in 1939 it was only faith—any faith—that could sustain the Republican Army.

The last Republican offensive

The Popular Army launched several attacks in different fronts during the month of January so as to slow down the Nationalist advance in Catalonia. The most ambitious was the Battle of Valsquillo or Peñarroya, in western Andalusia and Extremadura (5 January–4 February). The Republicans, who had mobilized 90,000 men and many guns and tanks, suffered 6,000 casualties and failed to have any effect on the Catalonia front or to cut Nationalist territory into two in Extremadura (Sagarra et al. 2016: Chapter 18).

With combats raging in Catalonia and Andalusia, the Republican command in Madrid decided to launch yet another attack, this time in Brunete, where the Popular Army had already failed in the summer of 1937. This is a virtually unknown operation that lasted only two days (13–14 February 1939) and changed nothing, but ended up with disproportionate losses for the Republic in terms of men and *matériel*. Colonel Martínez Bande only wrote a few lines about this battle in his multivolume history of the Spanish Civil War (Martínez Bande 1985: 81–84). We had the chance to investigate it and threw some light on the episode. It was a chance encounter. Unlike my other projects, this was an assignment from the Heritage Directorate of the Regional Government of Madrid and the intervention was not driven by research but heritage goals and the object was a group of pillboxes around Brunete (González-Ruibal and Franco Fernández 2019). We knew that all the structures were built late in the war, because some had inscriptions with the dates 1938 and 1939. Archival research conducted in parallel to fieldwork confirmed that two units of engineers, the 21 and 22 companies of the 8 Battalion of Engineeres of the 20 Division had been based in the area since October 1938.[16] As a result of the works, the Brunete frontline was solidly fortified with several lines of trenches and eight concrete pillboxes. Five of them belonged to a type known as CGIS, a modular structure whose basic element was a square machine-gun nest (Castellano Ruiz de la Torre and Schnell 2011). Three or four could be combined to make cruciform or T-shaped structures (Figure 9.11). They were well made and capable of sustaining heavy artillery and aerial bombing. Access to the pillboxes was through underground galleries. The units defending the Nationalist line at Brunete were armed with machine guns, mortars and a 37 mm PaK 36, a German anti-tank gun.

The pillbox that we excavated was a T-shaped CGIS structure. We located the underground gallery and cleared the embrasures, which revealed the inscription *Viva la 21ª Cñia 1939* ("Long Live the 21 Company, 1939"). This gave us the date of construction and the unit in charge of the works, which coincided with the archival data. We had low expectations of finding traces of combat, given the very late date of the fortifications. We were surprised: we found lots of spent ammunition everywhere, as well as artillery shell fragments. Our first hypothesis was that the remains were related to the first Brunete offensive of July 1937. Yet the area where the pillbox was located was rather marginal to the line of advance. Also, some of the spent ammunition was dated

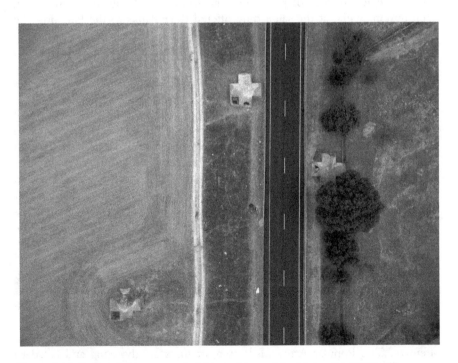

Figure. 9.11 Orthogonal image produced by a drone of the Nationalist CGIS pillboxes protecting the main road leading to Brunete.

Source: © Manuel Antonio Franco Fernández and the author.

260 Dead men walking

1938. Archival documents revealed that the Nationalist units that bore the brunt of the Republican attack on 13 January 1939 were Positions 18 and 19. As it turned out, this was exactly the area where we were excavating.

The Republican offensive was doomed from the beginning, but this does not mean that it was not carefully planned: a special army corps was created for the occasion that was provided with 10 T-26 tanks and as many armored vehicles. The attack began at 7:30 a.m. with the bombing of the Nationalist positions by the Republican 75 mm howitzers. The trouble for the Popular Army seems to have started already at this point, because the fire largely missed the objectives, possibly due to the dense morning fog. In fact, we were unable to discern any impact on any of the concrete pillboxes and large pieces of shrapnel near the Nationalist trenches are scarce. Furthermore, an unexploded 75 mm shell appeared during survey some 300 meters from the pillbox that we were excavating, far from the Nationalist lines.

This was not the only problem that fog would cause. Out of the 10 tanks that participated in the attack, eight advanced through the plain in front of our pillbox. They managed to get close enough to the enemy lines so as to crush the barbed wire at some points; yet they inadvertently deviated from their course due to the poor visibility. This had two fatal implications: they left the infantry devoid of protection and facing the Nationalist positions in open terrain, while at the same time offered their flanks to the PaK 36. The gun was fired by a particularly dexterous gunner, Corporal Elicio Correa Correa, who would be decorated for their actions that day. According to the citation, Corporal Correa, in the absence of the sergeant in charge of the piece, "managed to destroy five Red tanks among the great number employed by the enemy, thanks to his quick and precise fire, thus contributing to prevent the occupation of Position 18 by the enemy, as well as causing the demoralization of the enemy".[17] Three other tanks were destroyed with grenades and flammable bottles.[18] A 37 mm fuse of the gun appeared in the field as well as several fragments of Lafitte grenades that might have been used to destroy the remaining tanks, but we were unable to find traces of shells shot by the T-26, despite the medal citation mentioning the explosion of projectiles around the gun. The reality seems to be a bit less epic: the tanks likely had little opportunity to shoot back at the PaK 36. Republican soldiers, fixed to the ground in a treeless plain, could hardly return the enemy fire either and were ruthlessly annihilated by rifle and machine-gun bullets, until they were able to withdraw during the evening. A GIS analysis of the viewshed from the pillbox that we excavated shows that the area through which the Republicans had to advance was under the visual control of the machine-gun nest almost in its entirety (Figure 9.12).

On January 16, the Republican command communicated the end of the offensive. The Popular Army made two attempts at advancing and failed to occupy a single inch of terrain. It also failed to attract a significant number of troops. It had been a disaster: the Nationalists report 570 enemy dead versus 18 of their own.[19] The difference is so great that Martínez Bande (1985: 84)

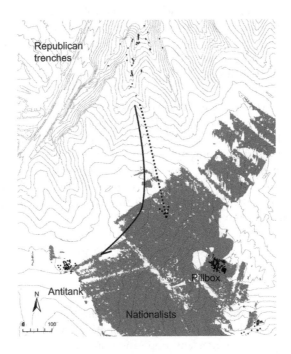

Figure 9.12 Map of the main zone of the Republican attack on Brunete in January 1939, showing the visibility from the pillbox that we excavated.

Notes: The solid arrow indicates the trajectory of the tanks; the dotted arrow, that of the infantry. Points indicate finds.

Source: © Manuel Antonio Franco Fernández and the author.

himself recommends the numbers to be put "in quarantine". Yet Republican casualties are probably not very far from the mark. A commissar's report notes 190 dead and 680 wounded, most of them, if not all, during January 13.[20] Archaeology confirms the disparity in the volume of fire. Spent Mauser shell casings and stripper clips littered the area around the Nationalist pillbox. During our survey and excavation we documented a minimum number of 152 shots by the Nationalists versus only four by the Republicans. Considering the topography of the battlefield and the development of the maneuver, it is surprising that the attacking soldiers had the chance to fire a single shot.

We also surveyed the positions that were the point of departure of the Popular Army, half a kilometer away from the Nationalist lines. Republican soldiers trudged along a narrow creek in front of their parapets to advance into no-man's-land. The dry creek had been altered in some places to prepare parapets and firing positions. We found 7.62 mm cartridges lost by the Republicans, also bullets fired by the Nationalists, mortar fragments and an almost complete 77 mm German howitzer shell. The most remarkable find were three grenades that appeared under a tree next to the point of

262   *Dead men walking*

departure of the Republican attack: two Ferrobellum stick grenades and a Fifth Regiment. They might have been left there by a soldier who perhaps thought them an unnecesary extra load for the battle ahead. If the Republicans lost grenades, the Nationalists did the same with personal items: near the pillbox we found a religious silver medal with depictions of medieval warriors blessed by a saint and the legend: "Labor like a good soldier of Christ" (*Labora sicut bonus miles Christi*[21]). The soldiers of Christ had a good day of killing in the plains of Brunete on January 1939.

The reasons for the defeat were not only bad planning, unfavorable terrain and inexpugnable fortifications. Franco's Army was aware of the Republican intentions, probably because they had been passed on to them. The Nationalists admit that they had information about the attack and therefore decided to reinforce the 20 Division with three infantry battalions, a battalion of machine guns and two mortar sections.[22] The offensive in Brunete was the last serious Republican attack in the Madrid region, but it was not the only major combat to take place before the end of the war, as we will see.

The fall

After so much death and so many great battles the Spanish Civil War ended in an anticlimax. The so-called final offensive was a walkover. The Nationalists did not encounter any opposition and the operation ended up in a five-day promenade (26 March–1 April) through Republican territory (Martínez Bande 1985). During those days, many Republican units destroyed or dumped weapons and supplies and burnt sensitive documents.In Casas de Luján (Cuenca), in the Republican rearguard, archaeologists excavated several pits near an abandoned farmstead that were filled with ashes, dirt and objects from the Spanish Civil War, including an insignia of the medical services. They interpret it as an attempt to erase traces by the Republican military at the end of the conflict (Morín de Pablos 2014). Less ambiguous proof of cleansing activities by the Republicans are the weapons recovered in the Tajuña River near Abánades. Neighbors told us that soldiers threw many weapons into the Tajuña before surrendering and during a metal detector survey of the river we did find an unexploded mortar round and three Republican grenades.

The collapse of the Popular Army had started three weeks before, with the coup of Colonel Segismundo Casado, commander of the Army of the Center, against President Negrín on March 5 (Bahamonde and Cervera 1999). Casado and his supporters wanted to put an end to a war that was already lost and was causing tremendous damage to the civilian population. They also expected to avoid the vengeance after an unconditional surrender. Negrín, who was a socialist, and the communists had no illusions: they defended resistance at all costs, as they feared (with good reason) Franco's revenge: the leader of the Nationalist army had consistently refused any negotiated peace. Negrín expected a great European war to break out soon, which would mean France and Britain supporting the Republic and changing the course of the conflict. Casado's coup in Madrid on March 5 provoked a civil war within the Civil War. It lasted one week and ended with a thousand casualties. The battle pitted all the parties of the Popular Front against the communists and a small faction of the socialist party. Traces of the combats are ubiquitous in central Madrid, mainly in public buildings that were defended by one side or the other: barracks, ministries and military premises. By March 12, Casado was in control of the situation. Negrín fled Spain and the next few weeks were of failed negotiations with Franco, who rejected any concessions and launched his final offensive on March 26. Madrid surrendered without combat on the 28th and the last Republican positions fell three days later. The last stronghold of the Republic was the docks of Alicante, where two thousand Republican refugees were waiting for evacuation in vain, as no ships came to their rescue: many committed suicide during the night of the 31 March to 1 April and on the morning of that day the Nationalists entered the harbor. Republicans were sent to concentration camps (see next chapter), while Franco proclaimed the end of the war. The last month of the conflict, however, saw a surprising but little known defensive victory on the Republican side.

Victory before defeat

During the coup in Madrid, the Nationalists decided to help with an attack on the capital, which the supporters of Casado had been calling for (Bahamonde and Cervera 1999: 397–399). This episode has been recently described in detail by Pedro Corral (2019: 201–218), whom I follow here. The attack started on March 8 at 6 a.m. in three different sectors: to the west, Zarzuela-El Pardo, where the terrible battles of La Coruña road had taken place in December 1936–January 1937; in the center, the University City; to the east, Villaverde, a working-class neighborhood south of Madrid. Thousands of Nationalist troops were involved in the operation, which was a total failure: they suffered 575 casualties in three hours of combat, of which 94 dead; they were unable to capture enemy terrain or to inflict any serious losses on the defendants (around 50 casualties, a dozen dead) and their action did little to help Casado. The sector of the University City comprised two subsectors. One of them, the Moncloa-Arroyo de Pozuelo subsector, lay exactly in front of the Republican trenches that we excavated at the University City (see Chapter 4). According to Republican reports, the Nationalists suffered almost 100 casualties in this part of the frontline. Combats developed in the first line, near the Manzanares River, because the Nationalists were unable to break into the second in this sector. However soldiers in the second and third lines surely provided supporting fire and suffered the enemy attack as well: we might have evidence of it.

In Chapter 4 I described a line of trenches with dugouts at the University City. The trench had been built during the last months of the war, probably

264 *Dead men walking*

around November 1938. The excavation of the largest dugout (Shelter 1) and the metal-detector survey of its immediate surroundings yielded a total of 71 bullets as well as several fragments of artillery shells (Figure 9.13). It is possible that the bullets were aimed at the shelter. The soldiers guarding this sector were unfortunate enough to be in enfilade with the Nationalist stronghold of Cerro del Águila, one of the points of departure of the Nationalist offensive of March 1939. From this heavily fortified hilltop,

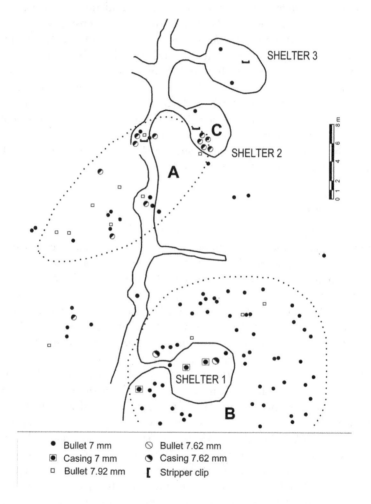

Figure 9.13 Map of trench and dugouts excavated and surveyed in the NW of the University City of Madrid with ballistic evidence most likely related to the Nationalist attack on Madrid in March 1939.

Notes: A. Concentration of 7.92 mm Mauser bullets; B. Concentration of 7 mm bullets probably shot by a Hotchkiss machine gun; C. Spent Mosin Nagant magazine.

Source: © Author.

located 1.2 km from the trench that we excavated, they could easily harass the Republicans. It is impossible to tell with certainty when the bullets were fired. However, the dense concentration seems to indicate two things: first, that most of them were fired in a single event and, second, that they were aimed at that particular spot, where there was nothing before late 1938.

It is highly likely that the bullets were fired by a Hotchkiss machine gun, since 90% of the projectiles are of 7 mm caliber. The caliber, as we know, was shared by the Spanish Mauser and the Hotchkiss. The latter could fire 600 bullets per minute at a distance of almost four kilometers, although its greatest effectivity lay within the 800–2,000 km range (Manrique and Molina 2006: 77). With its rate of fire, the Hotchkiss could have fired the bullets in just 10 seconds (using a 250-round belt or twice if they used the 24-round strip). Our map then probably shows a frozen burst of machine-gun fire.

Republicans did not remain idle. We found several spent casings and Mosin stripper clips in the trench, that could be related to the March offensive, most of them concentratated in two fire bays. As I mentioned, the fortification was constructed in November 1938, so this gives us a postquem date for the traces of combat. There is no documentary evidence of any activity in this sector between November 1938 and 1–3 March 1939, when some light shooting is recorded,[23] or after March 8. So there is a high probability that the traces of combat are related to the last Nationalist offensive in Madrid. Furthermore, part of the casings in the trench appeared on occupation floors, meaning that they had to be fired very late during the war, so as to have escaped maintenance and recycling activities. The clearest context comes from a dugout behind the trench that was used as a firing position. On the floor, we found a Mosin Nagant stripper clip and its five spent shell casings beside: the result of a Republican soldier firing a full magazine against the enemy lines. The Hotchkiss bullets are plausible evidence of the Nationalists providing covering fire to their advancing troops, whereas the Mosin casings show the Republicans stopping the doomed attack.

The offensive itself is a big mystery. Apparently, Franco was not informed. It seems that it was an initiative of General Espinosa de los Monteros, who was in charge of the 1st Army Corps besieging Madrid. Franco just wanted the capital to surrender without fighting, as it eventually did. The Nationalists in Madrid probably thought that the Republican defense would collapse soon, as the soldiers came from levies and there was a steady trickle of desertions coming from the University City. Pedro Corral (2019: 213) believes that the attack was actually a "race between the division commanders of the 1st Army Corps to see who earned the medal of entering in the capital first". The three division commanders, Caso, Losas and Ríos Capapé, had failed to capture Madrid in November 1936 and there existed a manifest rivalry between them. The operation was launched under the banner of "offensive reconnaissance", which was a euphemism to cloak the real intentions. Despite their disaster, they were not punished, or not much: their units were the last to march in the Victory Parade in Madrid one year after the end of the war.

266 *Dead men walking*

Celebrating the end

By late March, some Republican soldiers in Madrid were already abandoning the front and going back home. The surrender of the capital was arranged between both armies and the transfer of power took place near the University Hospital in the morning of March 28 between Colonel Eduardo Losas, commander of the Nationalist 16 Division stationed at the University City, and Colonel Adolfo Prada, on the Republican side. Adolfo Prada, who had supported Casado's coup, had been assigned commander of the Army of the Center on March 12. It was not a coincidence that the hospital was chosen as the place for the surrender. After two and a half years, it had become an iconic landmark for the Nationalists besieging Madrid. It was their most advanced position in the capital and their defense against all odds had caused hundreds of dead.

Yet the surrender did not take place exactly in the ruins of the building, but at its feet: in front of the Asylum of Santa Cristina, and exactly where we conducted our excavations. We know because there is a film capturing the moment: we see the officers meeting, saluting each other, talking briefly and then marching into the Nationalist headquarters at the School of Architecture. We can see part of the facade of the pavilion that we excavated and also a trench from which they leave the frontline. Using military maps of the period and aerial photographs we were able to find the trench, which runs parallel to the laundry that we unearthed (see Chapter 4). It was an ordinary communication trench but also more than that: it was the last trench of the Spanish Civil War, the exact spot where the most important event in Spanish modern history came to an end. And despite that, it was a forgotten place: there was no sign indicating that the war had actually ended there.

The trench turned out to be very well preserved, because it was sealed under two meters of early postwar deposits of sand, clay and rubble: inside, we found a substantial amount of discarded stuff, including remains of uniforms and an unexploded 77 mm German shell. The most interesting evidence, however, came from the entrance to the ditch. Here we found remains of cider bottles lying on the floor, including a complete one. More intact bottles appeared on the floor of the undergound shelter in-between the laundry and the pavilion, the place where we had found an access to a mining gallery (see Chapter 4). They appeared alongside lamb bones and a large amount of unused ammunition and four unexploded mortar grenades (Figure 9.14). As in the case of the trench, the unexploded ordnance proves that the structure had been sealed shortly after the end of the war. There is another element that hints at the early burial of the context. We know that there was rain in Madrid during the days of the surrender. A journalist wrote in the characteristic convoluted rhetoric of the dictatorship: "Today... [March 31] our God in Heaven has sent us, so that peace bears fruit, blessed water from the skies that will bring tomorrow golden spikes".[24] The floor of the shelter was covered in

Figure 9.14 War is over, feast is over: cider bottles and Mauser clips abandoned in a Nationalist shelter at the University City of Madrid.
Source: © Author.

a thin layer of veined silt, in which materials were embedded, as if the place had been waterlogged. Furthermore, one of the bottles was still filled with water. This could only have happened if it had been immersed before the sealing of the deposit. The place, then, was probably backfilled during the last day of March, when the first rains of the spring are recorded, and the early days of April. In fact, there is an order issued by the 16 Division the same day of the surrender, in which the Nationalist command communicated that all entrances to mining galleries had to be closed immediately upon occupation of the Republican positions.[25]

268 *Dead men walking*

The bottles of cider tally well with a celebration. Due to its scarcity (it is only produced in the north of Spain) and low alcoholic content (5–6%), it was an uncommon alcoholic drink in the trenches. But its sweet, fruity taste made it an acceptable substitute for champagne and, for this reason, a typical Christmas drink. And not only in peaceful times: the Nationalist propaganda tempted potential Republican deserters in December 1938 with the gift of a Christmas hamper that included, among other things, a bottle of cider (Corral 2006: 188). It is not difficult to picture the scene: the war is finished; soldiers receive a tasty lamb stew and plenty of cider. They eat and drink, they celebrate, they cheer, they get drunk. They dump all the rubbish into the shelter that had been the entrance to hell only a few hours before. In the moment of bliss they throw away cartridges and grenades, as well. What a better way of symbolizing the end of the war? At least for the victors, because the situation would be very different for the defeated, as we will now see.

Notes

1 http://www.laretirada.com/.
2 The list was published in the official bulletin of Spain (BOE), n° 190, of 9 August 2019.
3 http://www.voluntariosdemadrid.es/primerregimiento.html.
4 http://www.palaciodeoriente.net.
5 http://www.enciclopedia-aragonesa.com/voz.asp?voz_id=7627.
6 The report was prepared by Ricardo Arranz Higuera and Iván García Álvarez.
7 http://www.herreracasado.com/1985/07/05/un-testimonio-de-la-peste-negra-en-berninches/.
8 AGMAV 749Cp.4, D.2.
9 AGMAV C.1822, 11, 1/6 y C. 1822, 11, 1/13.
10 AGMAV 1817.3.4/3.
11 AGMAV 1817.3.4/6.
12 The company had been based in Spain since 1910 and our can probably came from surpluses from before the war, since the province where the factory was located fell into Nationalist hands in September 1937 (see Chapter 5).
13 AGMAV, GC, ZR, L-898, C-4, D-1, H 15 a 36.
14 AGMAV,C.1083,18,1.
15 According to the testimony of three soldiers that deserted to the Nationalists: AGMAV,C.1173,14.
16 AGMAV, C-1672, 11.
17 Boletín Oficial del Estado, 17 May 1939, number 142.
18 98/7-IHCM.
19 97/7-IHCM.
20 193/14-IHCM.
21 Taken from the Bible (2 Timothy 2:3).
22 95/7-IHCM. Most documents of the battle were found by the association "Brunete en la Memoria": http://bruneteenlamemoira.blogspot.com.
23 AGMAV, A.70/L. 1051-1054/R. 155-156/CJ. 881-884.
24 ABC (Madrid), nr. 10.347, 1st April 1939, p. 5.
25 Diary of Operations of the 16 Division. IHCM, DN, A. 10, L.452, C.17. The document was located by Luis Antonio Ruiz Casero, to whom I thank.

10 The never-ending war
April 1939–1952

Did the Spanish Civil War actually end on 1 April 1939? Not really. Historian Jorge Marco (2019) considers that a new phase starts then and lasts until 1952, one of asymmetrical unconventional war. The forces in conflict were the Francoist military and police, on one side, and a series of anti-Francoist guerillas on the other. Spain was enmeshed in a military conflict *de facto*, but also *de iure*, because the state of war was not officially suspended until 1948. Archaeology provides empirical support to the interpretation of a long civil war. If we use the material record to define the conflict, we see that some of the main elements that we associate with the Spanish Civil War also characterize the postwar period: concentration camps, military weaponry, mass graves, and fortifications.

To the camps and weapons I will refer later in this chapter. As for the fortifications, the Franco regime constructed many bunkers, pillboxes, trenches and military camps along its borders, since the possibility of an Allied assault (or an assault of anti-Francoist forces with Allied support) was not discarded until the end of the Second World War. As a matter of fact, the anti-Francoist guerrillas organized a (failed) invasion from France through the Pyrenees in October 1944. Around 6,000 men participated in the attack on the Vall d'Aran, but they could do little against the 50,000 troops swiftly deployed by the dictatorship. Still, combats lasted for a week and both sides sustained over a thousand casualties. The two main lines of fortifications were established along the Pyrenees and in the Gibraltar area (Sáez Rodríguez 2011). The fortification of the border with France started in 1939 in the Basque Country; it became "Line P" in 1944 and until 1950 around 7,000 concrete structures were built, as well as many military camps and trench lines (Sáez García 2005; Zuazúa et al. 2017). The enormous economic investment that these infrastructures implied should not be underestimated: the Spanish economy was bankrupt, there was hunger, and building materials were hard to find. Manpower, instead, was cheap, because the regime could resort to both conscripts and forced labor from political prisoners (Zuazúa et al. 2017: 6–7). The coast was vulnerable to an allied landing, but coastal defenses had been established between 1910 and 1928 and therefore the

270   *The never-ending war*

Franco regime only had to update or expand existing structures. To these structures, aimed at preventing an external invasion, we have to add the hundreds of military and police headquarters that were established throughout the country to fight the internal enemy, as we will see. All in all, the Spanish landscape remained heavily militarized throughout the 1940s.

Regarding mass graves, these were filled both with the corpses of guerrilla fighters, to which I will refer in the next section, and with the bodies of people executed by Franco's justice. As we saw in Chapter 2, the unmarked graves in the cemeteries of San Rafael and Paterna contain the remains of hundreds of individuals killed after 1 April 1939. In Madrid, the Eastern Cemetery was the execution place for over 3,000 people killed in the capital between April 1939 and February 1944 and traces of bullet impacts can still be seen on its brick walls. Many of the killed were thrown into mass graves which were later destroyed, although an ossuary has recently been found with remains that may belong to the victims.[1] Irregular violence continued (or resumed) during the first weeks of the postwar period. In Alcaudete (Toledo), 28 neighbors with ages ranging from14 to 55 were killed 24 days after the end of hostilities and their bodies thrown into a trench (Llave et al. 2010–2011). In Puebla de Alcocer (Extremadura), 42 people were assassinated and their bodies dumped in abandoned trenches in late May 1939 (Muñoz Encinar 2016: 502–508).

The material assemblage of mass graves, internment camps, military weapons and fortifications only disappears in the 1950s. This chronological framework has important political implications, because right-wing revisionism has been defending that the war actually started in 1934 with the October revolution initiated by part of the Left, and ended with Franco's victory in April 1939. By bracketing the war between 1934 and 1939, the Republic and the war are equated, and the Franco regime is separated from the conflict. Apart from the obvious historical flaws of considering 1934 as the beginning of the war—a chronology, by the way, that the Nationalists themselves defended since 1936—there is good material evidence against it. There are abundant archaeological proofs for a war between the 1939 and 1952 period, but virtually none for October 1934 to July 1936.

Guerrilla warfare

The postwar landscape in Spain has two faces: the face of power and the face of resistance. The face of power is that of megalomaniac monuments, memorials, new-built towns and villages, and public buildings in neo-imperial style. Also of concentration camps, prisons and forced labor camps, to which I will refer in the next section. The landscapes of power and violence (physical or symbolic) of the Franco dictatorship are an attempt at imposing a new order, a new discipline and a new subjectivity. Those who resisted created a parallel landscape in the wilderness: a network of camps and shelters in the most isolated and inhospitable lands of Spain. The forests and the mountains became home to a variety of guerrilla groups from the very beginning of the war in 1936 until the 1960s (Serrano 2001). The heyday of the guerrilla, however, spanned between the end of the war and 1948. Shortly after the Second World War finished, it became obvious that the Allies were not interested in overthrowing Franco, and the Communist Party, which backed the partisans, withdrew its support. The last few years of the guerrilla were simply a desperate fight for survival. The last partisan, José Castro Veiga, was killed in Galicia in 1965, after 20 years in the bush.

Absent landscapes

In contrast to the vacuous monumentality of the regime, the landscape of the guerrilla is ephemeral and inconspicuous. Xurxo Ayán Vila (2008) has aptly defined it as an absent landscape: it is there, but invisible to most. There are ideological and material reasons for it. The ideological reasons are obvious: the dictatorship described the partisans as brigands and terrorists, people, or rather vermin, who were both dangerous and expendable. They could—and should—be killed without mercy. This disparaging image has proved to be extremely persistent in collective memory. Those who remembered the truth have remained silent, out of fear or because of the trauma provoked by the violence unleashed by the State. As for the materiality of the landscape, the guerrillas scarcely modified the environment. They reused caves or natural shelters, constructed flimsy structures, moved often, followed routes through the mountains that lay well beyond the everyday space of the peasant (Morín de Pablos et al. 2006). In fact, they occupied a territory which, in the case of Galicia, had been traditionally inhabited by mythical beings—spirits and monsters. Not surprisingly, the guerrillas often acquired a semi-legendary status (Ayán Vila 2008).

One of the best-preserved guerrilla landscapes of Spain is to be found in the southeastern mountains of Galicia. In Casaio (Ourense), there was a place known as *Ciudad de la Selva* ("City of the Forest"), a complex of guerrilla camps that was established by the Federation of Guerrillas León-Galicia. Spanish partisans organized themselves in groups and federations, of which León-Galicia, covering the northwest of Spain, was the oldest: it was founded in April 1942, although its members had been active since the very beginning of the war. At its peak, the Federation had around 100 fighters coming from different parties (the majority were socialist) and relied on a dense network of civilian supporters, who often paid dearly for their commitment to the anti-Francoist struggle. Like other partisans, they sabotaged the economic interests of the State and attacked members of Falange and only secondarily engaged with the armed forces—mainly the Guardia Civil, the rural armed police that was tasked with their liquidation. They were awaiting the allied invasion that would liberate the country from fascism. The organization of the Spanish guerrillas coincides in time with (and often predates) similar movements in

272 *The never-ending war*

France, Belgium, Italy, Greece, the Balkans, and the Soviet Union and can be seen as part of a wider antifascist movement.

The City of the Forest has been the object of three field seasons of survey and excavation (Tejerizo-García et al. forthcoming; Tejerizo-García and Rodríguez Gutiérrez 2019). Researchers have recorded the existence of 18 camps, of which 11 have been documented archaeologically, spanning from 1936 to 1950. They calculate that there were around 23 guerrillas living in the City of the Forest. The camps have three or four small structures, made of dry stone, similar to vernacular buildings known as *chozos* (shepherd huts). At the beginning, the fugitives were simply occupying rock shelters in inaccessible places: in one of them, archaeologists found glazed pottery and tin cans. The remote location and the pottery indicate that it was possibly occupied by somebody from the area. The first proper guerrillas built *chozos* with irregular masonry walls that were occupied sporadically, given the scarcity of finds. The situation changed from 1941–1942 onwards, with the establishment of the Federation. The structures are more substantial, conspicuous and permanent (some even have two stories), they were better made, and had different layouts revealing a diversity of functions. The architectural style of the constructions indicates that there were locals collaborating in the construction. The new *chozos* are the materialization of a well-organized guerrilla group that is actively appropriating the territory— of the kind found in Colombia or in Vietnam during the 1960s–1970s (Tejerizo-García and Rodríguez Gutiérrez 2019).

The materials are also much more abundant. Over a hundred elements of ammunition have been found, half of them belonging to Mausers (7.92 mm and secondarily 7 mm), which were captured to the armed forces. Much of the ammunition came from war stocks, as they have a variety of provenances that are redolent of the heterogeneity that characterized the conflict: Czechoslovakia, Germany, Netherlands, Greece, Belgium, France, Spain and Mexico. All shell casings had been fired, proof that they had all been recycled: obtaining supplies was not easy, as they had to be smuggled or captured. The second most abundant type of ammunition is 9 mm, which can be fired by semi-automatic pistols and sub-machine guns, followed by shotgun cartridges. A few elements of fragmentation grenades were also found. The most extraordinary discovery, however, in terms of weapons was a complete .44 Smith & Wesson with its leather holster. The revolver was produced by the Orbea company in the Basque Country and it became a standard revolver with the Spanish armed forces from 1884 to 1924.

There is plenty of evidence of the guerrilla's diet. The excavation of a warehouse yielded fruit stones (mostly peaches), chickpeas and beans, which were preserved thanks to a fire that destroyed the structure. In the same place archaeologists recovered a significant number of tin cans, mainly of tuna, but also sardines and condensed milk, and 351 faunal remains. The taxonomic analysis identified 56% of sheep or goat bones, 22% of cattle, 11% of goat and 11% of deer or roe deer. Some of the animals were purchased from neighbors, others hunted and still others reared in the camp, as revealed by some goat feces that appeared in the excavation. The guerrillas were well fed, actually better than civilians in the local villages: a man who was a shepherd as a child and visited the camp was struck by the hams, chicken and milk of the partisans: "they had everything". They also had medicines, including what seems to be a bottle of penicillin, which first arrived in Spain, from the US Army in North Africa, in 1944. Around 20% of the finds were of alcoholic drinks. The great majority belongs to local wine bottles, but there was also a complete anisette bottle that appeared next to a bed made of fern. If alcohol is essential in the trenches, it is perhaps more so in the mountains, where boredom was greater as was the sense of uncertainty and isolation.

The work of Carlos Tejerizo-García and his team deconstructs the widely held idea (even on the Left) that the guerrilla was the business of individuals, fighting for their survival. The complexity of the City of the Forest provides a completely different picture: the guerrillas were well organized, often well-supplied, and they posed a real threat to the regime, which had to mobilize immense resources to quench them. In fact, five Guardia Civil headquarters were established around the City of the Forest (Tejerizo-García et al. forthcoming), very close to the camps but invisible to the security forces (Figure 10.1). The Guardia Civil only launched a serious assault in July 1946, when the guerrillas were holding a conference that tried to reunite the federation, at the time split between communists and the rest. The Guardia Civil got wind of the event and attacked the base. They found the huts, looted them and set them on fire—as shown by burnt layers in some of the excavated structures. With the guerrillas dispersed, the civilian liaisons detained or killed, and the allied invasion failing to materialize, the Federation came to an end and so did the City of the Forest.

The Federation of Guerrillas León-Galicia had strong ties with Portugal, from which they obtained supplies and which they used as an escape route. These cross-border networks ended up bringing war to the neighboring country (Coelho and Ayán Vila 2019). On the night of 19 December 1946 three guerrillas, Demetrio García Alvárez, Juan Salgado Ribera and Bernardino García, found shelter in the village of Cambedo, located in the Portuguese region of Tras-ós-Montes, but very close to the Spanish border. The authorities found out and the village was completely surrounded by members of the Portuguese Guarda Nacional Republicana and the Spanish Guardia Civil. One of the guerrillas, Juan, was executed while trying to leave the village; the remaining found refuge in the house of Albertina Tiago after a shootout in which two *guardas* were killed. The Guarda Nacional requested military support. Soldiers from the nearby garrison of Chaves arrived with two mortars and started firing on the village. Two houses were completely destroyed and others showered with fragments. Still, the guerrillas did not die: Demetrio surrendered and Bernardino committed suicide.

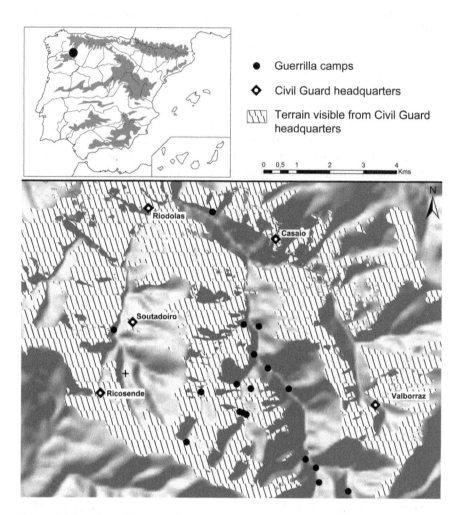

Figure 10.1 Location of the guerrilla camps and Civil Guard headquarters in the Casaio area (Galicia).
Source: © Carlos Tejerizo-García.

Archaeologists excavated the bombed house of Albertina Tiaga, which was never reconstructed. They inferred that the wooden infrastructure of the roof caught fire after being impacted by a mortar round and collapsed, destroying the building. They found a burnt layer over the floor of the ground level. The rich assemblage found by archaeologists testifies to the sudden end of the house and offers a glimpse into a peasant house of the 1940s: there were transferwares, glass bottles, chocolate pots, cooking and storage pots, agricultural implements, a coin from 1921 and many bones of pig from a local race that has disappeared ever since (Figure 10.2). Fragments of the

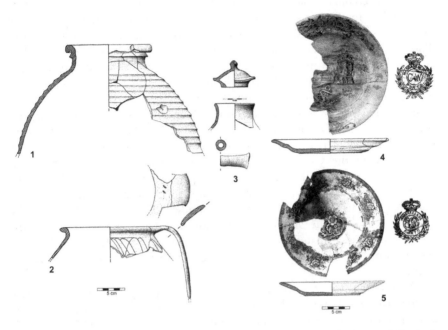

Figure 10.2 A rural world shattered by modern war. Pottery found in the house of Cambedo (NW Portugal) destroyed by the Portuguese Army in 1946.

Notes: 1. Black ware; 2. Burnished jug; 3. Chocolate pot; 4. Transferware (1904–1912); 5. Transferware (1912–1920). Pottery 1–3 coming from the kilns of Vilar de Nantes, located only 22 km from Cambedo; transferwares were produced by Empresa Cerâmica Portuense, based in Oporto, also in NW Portugal.

Source: © Rui Gomes Coelho.

81 mm shells were found around the house. The enormous destruction provoked by the mortars might seem odd, but the Portuguese Army used "granadas de alta potência". This probably refers to the high-capacity 81 mm Stokes-Brandt grenades, which weighed 6.75 kilos and we know the Portuguese military had them in their stores. One of these grenades, known as "trench-busters" during the Great War, was found during our surveys of the University Hospital in Madrid. They are a powerful war weapon, which shows how much was at a stake for the Portuguese dictatorship in this operation.

Coelho and Ayán Vila (2019) argue that the military actions in Cambedo were more than just a matter of anti-guerrilla warfare: they amount to a veritable act of state-building in a yet unruly and permeable borderland, where neighbors from one side and the other of the line sustained illicit relations and networks of solidarity that predated the nation-state. "The nation-state", write the authors, "arrived to Cambedo under the guise of mortar grenades, even before the construction of the first asphalted road" (Coelho and Ayán Vila 2019: 77). The military operation in Cambedo is also

276   *The never-ending war*

redolent of colonial violence: by considering all the inhabitants of the village punishable, the army anticipated the indiscriminate counter-insurgency operations deployed in the African possessions during the 1960s and 1970s. The same premonitory character can be assigned to the violence unleashed against the guerrillas in Spain: it was a prelude to the dirty wars that would devastate Latin America and the colonies, from Africa to South-East Asia, during the second half of the twentieth century.

With the disarray of the Federation of Guerrillas of León-Galicia, a new organization occupied its place: the communist-backed Guerrilla Army of Galicia, created in late 1947. The Second Group of the Army had its base in a house in the village of Repil (Pobra de Brollón, Lugo), which was stormed by the Guardia Civil on 20 April 1949. As in Cambedo, the troops used military weapons—mortars and machine guns. They killed six guerrillas and had nine of their men wounded. The disparity between the casualties on one side and the other indicates that some of the guerrillas were actually assassinated. We know that one of them, Evaristo González Pérez, committed suicide after sustaining a two-hour siege in one of the houses.

The house of the Amaro family was the scenario of much briefer fighting, as the partisans immediately tried to escape. The building was reused as a home during the 1950s, but an archaeological project was able to document several traces of the attack (Ayán Vila 2018, 2019) (Figure 10.3). Near the entrance to the house, archaeologists found Mauser ammunition used by the Guardia Civil against the escaping guerrillas. The main concentration of shell casings pinpointed the place from where the Guardia Civil fired against one of the partisans—Fermín Lada Segura—who fled toward the nearby house of Adela, while shooting desperately with his sub-machine gun. A bullet pierced his jaw, but he managed to walk two kilometers and find sanctuary in the house of a priest.

The house of the Amaro family was a small one-story building, residence at the time of a widowed woman, Teresa, and several children. For two years, the guerrillas, the family and the animals shared the same space. The house testifies to the paramount role of hospitality in the guerrilla war and above all, of women, who have been systematically neglected by narratives that emphasize the figure of the heroic male warrior. Yet women were key to the functioning of the guerrillas and suffered the reprisals: many were imprisoned and some even killed. As Ayán Vila (2019: 53–54) writes, "the true landscape of the guerrilla does not correspond with battlefields, fortified camps or field hospitals, but with the domestic space of a traditional rural society". More important than documenting a combat, continues Ayán, is to document "the humble kitchen with its stone hearth, bench, oven and granary, where Teresa gave shelter, warmth and food to those exhausted men that have been fighting in the mountains for twelve years".

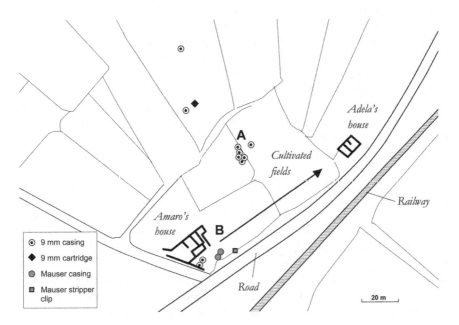

Figure 10.3 Map of the attack on the guerrilla sanctuary in Repil in 1949 based on archaeological evidence and oral accounts.

Notes: The arrow indicates the flight of Fermín Lada Segura (B), under fire from the Civil Guards (A).

Source: Redrawn after Xurxo Ayán Vila (2019).

The graves are not yet full

The most tragic testimony of the struggle of the guerrillas are the mass graves. Members of the security forces, as we have seen, chased and killed members of the guerrillas, including those who surrendered, even those civilians who supported them or who did not denounce them, even civilians who happened to be around: in Gualchos (Granada), the police assassinated 11 people in 1947 after an encounter with a group of partisans. Among the victims there was a pregnant woman (the wife of one of the guerrillas), two teenagers and several farmers who simply looked suspicious. They were all shot in the head and buried.[2] In Pinos del Valle, also in Granada, seven neighbors were detained by the Guardia Civil and assassinated for their supposed relation to the anti-Francoist resistance. It was basically an exemplary punishment: the commander of the region, General Julián Lasierra, told a subordinate: "Take ten and shoot them" (Carrión n.d.: 7). The victims were chosen less for their actual relationship to the guerrillas than for their prewar leftist sympathies. The regime admitted to killing 2,173 partisans between 1939 and 1949 (Moradiellos 2000: 125). That most of the killed were actually murdered in cold blood

278 *The never-ending war*

is demonstrated by the fact that the casualties of the armed forces (Guardia Civil, military and police, in that order) amount to 307 dead. Even if we consider, as it is likely, that the actual figure is closer to 500, the number is still very small in relation to the fallen guerrillas. The truth is that partisans were often captured and then shot in the head under pretext of attempted escape. While the Resistance has become part of the national memory of France, a patriotic example of the war against fascism, in Spain the guerrillas have remained in unmarked graves for decades, the memory of their deeds distorted. The work of archaeologists and physical anthropologists has contributed significantly to change the narrative of the dictatorship, but there is still a long way to go.

Mass graves with the remains of guerrilla fighters and civilians have been dug up virtually all over Spain, from Galicia to Andalusia. The Levante region was one of the first to be systematically searched for killed guerrillas. Up to 2011, seven mass graves were exhumed with the bodies of 44 members of the Levante-Aragón Guerrilla Group or related civilians (Polo Cerdá et al. 2010, 2012). The region where this group operated saw a high increase in State violence from July 1947 onwards, after General Manuel Pizarro Cenjor was nominated as civil governor of Teruel. Pizarro launched a campaign of extermination that left the area filled with corpses. In a mountain next to Alcalá de la Selva (Teruel) researchers exhumed a mass grave with the remains of 11 individuals. The grave had been dug next to the execution place, because three spent shell casings were found among the bones. The executioners fired from a short distance, from the back of the head and through the skull of each victim. Each of the killed shows traces of more than one shot. A 9 mm pistol was used in all cases, which reveals that the crime was carried out by members of the Guardia Civil with their service weapons. Another massacre perpetrated by this paramilitary force was documented in Villarejo de la Peñuela (Cuenca) (Polo Cerdá et al. 2009). Here four people were murdered, again with a 9 mm bullet to the head, but, in this case, death apparently was not enough for the killers. At least two bodies presented clear signals of antemortem violence. Torture in this dirty war was so common and obvious that a military doctor had to complain to a high-ranking officer: "your people [Guardia Civil and police] messed up those they ambushed so much that it doesn't look like they were caught by surprise… We've taken one to the hospital who looked like Christ just after he came down from the cross" (cited in Aguilar and Payne 2016: 163). In the province of Valencia two mass graves yielded 17 bodies: nine guerrillas in Albalat dels Taronjers and eight in Benagéber (Polo Cerdá et al. 2012: 105). In the latter case, half were guerrillas and the other half prisoners from a nearby forced labor camp (Santacreu Soler 2016: 98–105). The majority of the killings throughout Spain were carried out by Guardia Civil and always with the same modus operandi: shots to the head with their standard-issue pistols. In some cases, the victims were also wounded in the thorax or abdomen (Polo Cerdá et al. 2012).

Evidence from the assassination of guerrillas has also been found in Andalusia and Extremadura: to the people killed in Gualchos and Pinos del Valle mentioned above, we can add the exhumations of two individuals in Obejo killed in 1948 and 1949 (Córdoba), three in Adamuz murdered in the same dates (Córdoba) (Baquero 2016: 36–39, 68, 70), four in Marmolejo (Jaén) in 1944 (Baquero 2018: 154–157); five in Pozuelo del Zarzón (Cáceres) in 1946 (Muñoz Encinar 2016: 602–614); three in Castuera (Badajoz), in 1943 (Muñoz Encinar 2016: 615–625), etc. The cases of Pinos del Valle and Gualchos are representative of the strategy of repression: in both cases the victims include guerrillas, supporters and bystanders (Carrión n.d.). The corpses of the guerrillas were often displayed on oxcarts, in the public square or in front of the parochial church, as an example and a warning for the neighbors (Muñoz Encinar 2016: 638). A similar procedure was typical in rural areas until the 1960s with wolves and other wild animals hunted by trappers. Although the guerrilla movement was largely disarticulated by 1948 (thus the official end of the state of war), the killings of partisans continued into the 1950s.

The story told by the exhumations of guerrillas is an important one, because it changes the hegemonic memory of this postwar phenomenon. What we see are not the traces of combat. It is not fugitives who were killed during their escape, as was repeated time and again in the reports of the Guardia Civil. It is disarmed individuals who have been murdered in cold blood, often tortured before being murdered. It was not war, it was a massacre.

Spaces of punishment

The well-known Nazi slogan *Ein Volk, ein Reich, ein Führer* announced the preternatural existence of a people, a state and a leader. In Spain, things were not so clear. Franco never had any illusions as to the loyalty of the Spanish people, which is not surprising, considering that he was the only fascist dictator in Europe who had to attain power through a long and bloody civil war. In January 1942, two and a half years into the postwar period, he proclaimed: "Our Crusade demonstrated that we have the leader and the army: now we need the people and this only exists when unity and discipline are achieved" (Sabín 1997: 409). A people, then, had to be created. The massacres and exiles of the war had gone a long way in achieving the goal, but more work was needed. Such work was trusted to a complex technology of punishment that was materialized in a variety of spaces (Molinero et al. 2003; González-Ruibal 2011b). Like any other technology, it had its own *chaîne operatoire*, in this case with three different stages—classification, disciplining and redemption, each of them characterized by different spaces: concentration camps, prisons and forced labor camps. Each space of internment was tasked with performing a specific transformation of the individual and as such they can be considered machines of subjectivization.

280 *The never-ending war*

The first stage in the operational sequence was represented by the concentration camp (Rodrigo 2005; Hernández de Miguel 2019), which played an apparently contradictory role: camps dehumanized prisoners and transformed them into an undifferentiated mass, but at the same time individualized men: concentration camps were primarily spaces of classification, where the juridical responsibilities of each individual were sorted out. According to the system devised by the dictatorship, prisoners could be categorized as A or *afecto* (conscripts in the Republican Army who were pro-Nationalist); Ad *desafecto dudoso* (Republican conscripts of dubious loyalty): B *desafecto leve* (slightly disloyal, including common soldiers who volunteered); C *desafecto grave* (seriously disloyal: officers and politicians) and D *delicuente común* (common criminals) (Hernández de Miguel 2019: 154–155).

Many were killed or died in the camps. Those who survived were usually sent to prisons, which could mean a transitory space on the way to execution or a longer term of imprisonment—even for life. Life in jail in the 1940s was far from easy: the difference between camp and prison was basically of a legal nature and around 90,000 people died in one kind of detention or the other between 1939 and 1944 (Gómez Bravo 2009: 37). After 1942, the difficult situation in the overcrowded jails (there were over 370,000 individuals incarcerated for political reasons) forced a change in the repressive system. This was also motivated by shifting perceptions of punishment—with a greater weight of the Church and traditional values—and the fate of the Axis in the Second World War, which made Fascism (and therefore Falangism) fall out of favor with the regime. A system of cancellation of penalties by work was thus established, drawing inspiration from the work of Jesuit father José Pérez del Pulgar and ideas of Christian atonement[3] (Gómez Bravo 2009: 53). The space that characterized this third and last stage of the technical sequence was the labor camp, in which prisoners engaged in productive activities while being subjected to indoctrination, before being released into the New Spain (Lafuente 2002).

The concentration camp

The need to build camps started with the collapse of the Northern Front in October 1937. Tens of thousands of Republican soldiers fell into Nationalist hands and had to be interned in improvised detention centers, most of them in Galicia, often in fish canning factories (Costas and Santos 2008). The reuse of spaces for internment camps would be the norm in Spain (González-Ruibal 2011b): monasteries, seminaries, schools, bullrings, factories and almost any other large building. Camps with barracks created *ex novo* also existed but they are scarce: Miranda de Ebro (Burgos), which was operative until 1947 and Castuera (Badajoz) are the best examples. In some cases immediately after the war, camps were but a simple barbed wire fence in the middle of a field or a beach, where prisoners were exposed to the inclemency of the weather.

Between 1937 and 1948 there were in Spain at least 300 concentration camps (Hernández de Miguel 2019)—in comparison, fascist Italy "only" had 135, including those in the colonies (Galluccio 2003). The custom of reusing previous structures that eventually reverted to their original use makes the archaeology of camps more difficult in Spain than in other contexts (Myers and Moshenska 2011; Sturdy Colls 2015; Theune 2018). However, in the town of Castuera (Badajoz), the Franco regime created a camp *ex novo*, which was operative for exactly one year, starting March 1939. Here we have an outstanding and tragic archaeological record, which we had the opportunity to explore in three field seasons (González-Ruibal et al. 2011; Muñoz Encinar et al. 2013) and a rich historical research based on archival and oral evidence, on which the following paragraphs are based (González Cortés 2006; López Rodríguez 2006; López Rodríguez and González Cortés 2019).

The camp of Castuera was established in a remote area, but well-communicated through a railway line that facilitated the transport of prisoners in cattle wagons. The landscape is probably the most dismal in which I have ever had the opportunity to work: a waterless, treeless, eerily silent plain that extends kilometer after kilometer. Through Castuera passed around 20,000 prisoners. The number per day varied, but during the summer of 1939, the average figure was 4,000. Many did not survive. Historian Antonio López Rodríguez (2006) has made an incomplete list of the dead with over 200 names. They died of disease and starvation or were simply murdered. Their bodies ended up in the mine shafts surrounding the camp or in the mass graves of the cemetery of Castuera and other places. The concentration camp had a total surface of around 10 hectares. In this space, 80 prefabricated prisoner barracks were assembled, divided into two groups by a large central square, plus four confinement barracks for especial prisoners. The square, in which inmates were forced to parade, listen to mass and harangues, was dominated by a monumental cross, of which the remains of the concrete and brick pedestal survive to our days. The barracks were located only in the northern half of the main enclosure, which is the earliest. The camp, as it can be clearly seen on the terrain, had to be expanded several times, as the number of prisoners kept growing. These annexes lacked barracks and the inmates were forced to protect themselves with ponchos against the harsh weather (Figure 10.4).

Every enclosure was delimited by ditches flanked on both sides with barbed wire. According to the testimony of a former prisoner, the barbed wire fence was four meters tall (López Rodríguez 2006: 187). Our excavations proved this to be incorrect: in one of our test pits inside a perimeter ditch we found one of the line posts to which barbed wire was fixed. It measured 1.85 m. Stuck into the ground, it could have hardly risen more than 1.70 meters. This speaks not so much about the vagaries of oral recollection, as of the way the material culture of punishment impresses itself upon the minds of its victims. Perimeter ditches, as we could observe, went against Francoist regulations which clearly stated: "Concentration Camps [sic]

282 *The never-ending war*

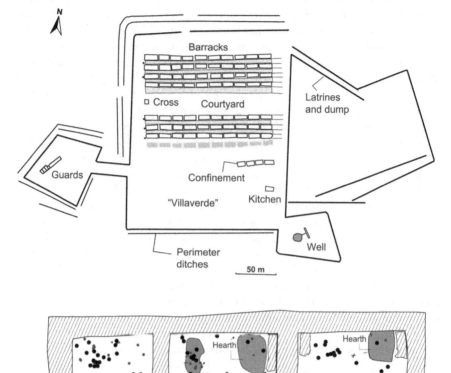

Figure 10.4 Above: Map of the concentration camp of Castuera based on historical aerial photographs and surface survey. Below: guards' barracks with traces of occupation by prisoners engaged in the dismantling of the camp.

Source: © Author and Manuel Antonio Franco Fernández.

will be enclosed by a ditch deep of 1.80 meters and 1.50 meters wide with a double barbed wire fence on both sides".[4] In Castuera, the ditches were rarely more than 0.5 meters deep and in places they hardly attained 0.20 m. The discrepancy indicates that, rather than fulfilling a practical purpose, the role of

The never-ending war   283

the ditches was mainly symbolic: they were separating Spain from the Anti-Spain, the space of everyday life from the space of exception, where life was worthless (Agamben 1995).

The prefabricated barracks were of a type called "Galicia". They were made of wood lined with metallic sheet and had roofs of fiber cement, remains of which appeared during survey and excavation. With such construction materials, the heat in the summer had to be infernal. We can say this, because during our dig in August we endured temperatures of over 42 degrees Celsius in the shade. The barracks had a surface of 70 m^2, in which no fewer than 70 prisoners were crowded. They had five times less space than imprisoned soldiers had in the camps of Germany and the United States during the World Wars (Demuth 2009; Thomas 2011).[5]

The guards lived in a sort of subcamp, also surrounded by ditches and connected to the main enclosure through a corridor. Unlike the inmates, the guards lived in barracks made of dry masonry. The building was divided into four rooms, the first one a latrine; the next two, provided with in-built hearths, probably served as bedrooms, and of the fourth one, which we could not excavate, we ignore the function. The structure had packed-earth floors and there was neither water nor electricity. The first commander of the camp, Ernesto Navarrete, lived in another stone house, located in a prominent place, on the sierra south of the camp. From there, he had perfect visual control over the entire camp and probably enjoyed the sight— he was a known sadist.

We conducted sondages in the perimeter ditches, the latrines and the guards' barracks and found a large number of objects—5,000 in the first field season alone. Most appeared in the latrines, which were used as a dump. Rubbish provides important information about food, hygiene, medical conditions, vigilance, punishment and resistance. Archaeological remains of food can be contrasted with the memories of the prisoners from this and other camps. Former inmates report that meals consisted basically in bread and sardines (Rodrigo 2005: 149–151), but they seldom received a full tin a day. They had to share one among two, three or four people. In our excavations we found a minimum number of 133 tin cans (and fragments of many more). However, we also found a great number of tuna cans: 123 (48% of the total)—which is never reported—as in the trenches. Another kind of container, representing 10% of the total, are large cans with a capacity of one kilo, which might have had legumes: "Food consists this time in a can of lentils for four and the same old fifth of a bread roll" (Guzmán 2001: 242). Meat was virtually absent in the diet: in all test pits together, we only recovered 18 tiny and fragmented bones, which may have been used to prepare a soup. In contrast, in the First World War German camp of Quedlinburg archaeologists found a large number of cattle and pork bones, as well as fish, mostly cod (Demuth 2009: 175). Prisoners were eating their meager lunches in military mess tins, of which we found six. But these were not provided by the camp authorities: some inmates kept them from their

284   *The never-ending war*

time in the army, others requested them from relatives: "see if you can send me a canteen and an aluminum dish for the meals" wrote an inmate, Francisco Quintín, to his mother and sister (López Rodríguez and González Cortés 2019: 130). We also found four spoons and a civilian dish of enameled metal, surely provided by relatives. No forks or knives, because they could have been transformed into weapons. The camp commander, instead, ate on whiteware, which we found around his house.

The diet could be complemented with food and drinks purchased at the commissary, which was available to prisoners depending on their economic means and political classification. They often exchanged personal objects with guards and locals (who overcharged them): as mentioned in the preface to this book, one of the most painful memories of the camp for my wife's grandfather, Francisco, was the exchange of his precious watch—a gift from his father—for a loaf of bread. Those who did not have anything could still make handicrafts, as we will see. Other than barter and ordinary currency, prisoners resorted to the special currency issued by the camps, perhaps the clearest proof that they were total institutions, autonomous universes with their own regulations (Goffman 1968).

The hundreds of glass shards retrieved in the latrines may come from wine bottles purchased at the commissary, but they could also belong to the guards or have been recycled to contain water. More peculiar is the presence of soda water and sarsaparilla. The latter, a soft drink, was common in Spain during the decade of autarky (the 1940s), a (failed) economic model that sought Spain's self-sufficiency in everything, from gasoline to sodas: sarsaparilla was a substitute for Coca-Cola. Most of the prisoners, however, would have rarely tasted anything other than water, which was stored in huge barrels, placed on concrete bases that still exist, at the extreme end of each row of barracks. Prisoners collected water in cans, glass bottles and any other available container. We also found many fragments of *botijo*, a typical Spanish earthenware pitcher and a common find in the trenches, that cools water. Of the camp's kitchen we only have the remains of a stone pavement and drainage ditches, next to which we found tin cans and a small deposit of clams (*Chamelea gallina*). They were probably part of the guards' menu.

The two main and strongly related problems in any concentration camp were health and hygiene. In one of the perimeter ditches we were lucky enough to find a dump of medical materials, including medicine bottles and ampoules. Unfortunately, most of them lack any inscription. Ampoules were used for vaccines, iodine, morphine, anti-diarrheal treatments and bactericides. We do have inscriptions in two bottles of hydrogen peroxide, used for many years as an antiseptic, and in the same dump there was a tube of bactericide ointment. Crowded, dirty and starving, the inmates were easy prey to diseases. In Castuera, as in other camps there was a first aid post and an infirmary outside. Republican medical staff who were imprisoned took care as best as they could of the other inmates. Castuera's infirmary survives: it is an old stable that has partially returned to its original function. When

The never-ending war 285

Nationalist troops captured the place during the offensive of La Serena Pocket, in the summer of 1938, they transformed the farm into a field hospital. Falangist troops covered the walls with graffiti and drawings representing soldiers. The graffiti include personal names and company units ("1st Battalion of the FE de las JONS [Falange] of Badajoz/Mortar Section"). It does not require a great effort of imagination to picture hygienic conditions in an old pigsty. The most visible wall in the room in which the ill were crammed was decorated with an enormous sgraffito with slogans that summarize well the dominant ideology: "Long live the Old Shirts" [the Falangists that have enrolled before the war]. "One, Great and Free" [Spain]. FE [Spanish Falange]. "Glory to the fallen. Long live Franco". From their straw mats, sick prisoners could get acquainted with the New Spain that was waiting for them outside—if they survived. Hundreds of prisoners in Castuera were treated for epidemic typhus, a disease that is transmitted through the fecal matter of an infected louse.

Disease is better known, from an archaeological point of view, in two other places: Valdenoceda (Burgos, Castile) and Fort San Cristóbal (Navarre). Although they were not camps but prisons in juridical terms, life conditions were indistinguishable. Both were in operation during the heyday of the camps (1939–1945) and both reused pre-existing buildings (a textile factory and a late nineteenth-century fortress), overcrowding was the norm and inmates died in scores. In the case of Valdenoceda, the remains of 114 individuals were exhumed who had died of illness and other causes. We know that 61.6% of the 152 deaths registered among the inmates were due to tuberculosis (Ríos et al. 2008). Thirteen of the exhumed skeletons, in fact, show signs of active infection on the ventral surface of the ribs, which is compatible with the advanced stage of this pulmonary disease. Tuberculosis spread in Spain after the war due to malnourishment and overcrowding. In Valdenoceda, the comparison between prisoner and free population shows, however, that mortality owed to the disease was far superior among the inmates: "only" 15.5% of the residents in the village succumbed to tuberculosis in the same time period. Fort San Cristóbal became a prison-hospital to which ill inmates were carried from all over Spain. Around 300 people died of disease or hunger or were simply murdered between 1936 and 1945 (Etxeberria, Pla and Querejeta 2014). Archaeologists and forensic scientists exhumed the remains of 45 individuals who perished between 1942 and 1945. Based on archival documentation, we know that most of the inmates (99%) succumbed to tuberculosis. The disease left traces on the ribs of 29 skeletons. One of them still had the chest drains in place—tuberculosis provokes air or fluid to accumulate in the pleural cavity.

There is a third concentration camp where exhumations have been carried out: the Monastery of Uclés (Cuenca), which was first a Popular Army hospital and then a camp. Archaeological works recovered the remains of 439 individuals, of which 294 died in detention between 1940 and 1942. Unfortunately, little information is available. One hundred and sixty of the

286 *The never-ending war*

dead in the camp are known to have been executed: a forensic study identified 81 individuals with evidence of shot-related trauma (Congram, Passalacqua and Ríos 2014). Many cases of antemortem trauma were identified among the killed, including several fractures and amputations, some healed. These may have occurred during the war, but conditions in the camp prevented them from healing properly (Congram, Flavel and Maeyama 2014: 52–54). Those traumas that remained unhealed might perhaps be related to beatings or torture. A study on 71 individuals who died or were killed in the camp noted that 23 of them had fractured ribs: it is not specified whether these are shot-related or compatible with beatings (Peraza Casajús 2010: 78). The most common scenario was probably of convalescent prisoners from the military hospital being captured at the end of the war and then executed by firing squad or simply with a shot to the head (Congram, Passalacqua and Ríos 2014). Official documents also indicate that 134 prisoners perished of "natural causes"—an unlikely figure in a non-senile adult population, as it amounts to a natural death every six days. More likely they died of hunger, diseases provoked by incarceration and beatings.

Epidemics were strongly related to the lack of hygiene. In the case of Castuera, the internees only had a small pool surrounded by concrete basins (still visible), where they could wash themselves and their clothes. Despite the thousands of items retrieved in the camp, none is related to hygiene—combs, razors, mirrors, toothbrushes. They were scant and therefore treasured: so much so that the prisoners carried these objects with them to their grave, as we will see. In one of the few prisoners' letters preserved, a man asks his wife to send towels and soap (Rodríguez López and González Cortés 2019: 271). I noted how important self-care was for the psychological integrity of the soldiers during the war. The difficulties of performing even a basic grooming surely undermined the inmates' self-esteem. A hygienic measure undertaken by the camp authorities but that further affected the morale of the prisoners was the shaving of their heads: we found a plastic piece from a head shaver in the latrines.

The most insalubrious part of the camp was, in fact, the latrines. They were two 100-meter-long parallel ditches, one of them expressly built as a latrine and the other as a perimeter ditch. The former was not built in one go: our excavations showed that it was being opened as it was needed. When the ditch was full, it was covered with stones, dirt and rubbish from the camp and the original cut extended. References to a similar procedure exist for other camps, such as Rianxo (A Coruña) and Albatera (Alicante) (Costa and Santos 2008: 70; Guzmán 2001: 271). In Castuera, the cut was not deep. Shale appears close to the surface, and the prisoners were forced to hew it, a labor that was surely painful for the weakened prisoners. The irregularity of the ditches indicates that they tried to avoid the hardest veins, because they did not have tools other than picks (one of them we found in one of the perimeter ditches) and their own strength, which was seriously undermined. The latrines were thus very shallow (0.3 to 0.5 meters), too wide (meaning that the surface of evaporation was larger) and very irregular, thus favoring waterlogging and the accumulation of detritus. In addition, since they were dug as pits, rather than a proper linear ditch, they could not drain. The abject filth of the privies surely worked to propagate epidemics (Figure 10.5).

The latrines were not an accident of the system. They were an integral part of it, a tool to further humiliate the prisoners. Defecating together and in public, always with gastrointestinal problems (constipation or diarrhea) made of the ordinary act of going to the toilet an authentic ordeal, both physiological and moral. The prisoners, in fact, could not use the latrines when they needed, but only when they were taken there, in groups, by the guards at specific times. There are some testimonies of this collective humiliation: in Campo de los Almendros (Alicante), a huge camp of 20,000 prisoners that was only operative a few days after the end of the war; a former inmate remembers that they had to relieve themselves in the open, "asses to the wind" (García Corachán 2005: 33). In Albatera, the prisoners defecated in open latrines under the gaze of the guards, who insulted them and played cruel jokes on them: guards rejoiced watching the inmates fall in the ditches, which they often did, as they fainted due to their lack of strength

Figure 10.5 Latrine of the concentration camp of Castuera backfilled with garbage.
Source: © Author.

288 *The never-ending war*

or the pain caused by extreme constipation (Guzmán 2001: 271; Costa and Santos 2008: 68; Lafuente 2002: 148). Eduardo de Guzmán reports that prisoners resorted to can openers to extract the feces, solidified because of chronic constipation, and sometimes provoked hemorrhages themselves. The can openers that we found in the ditches, then, could be more than just rubbish. The latrines are the male equivalent to the castor oil that Republican women were forced to drink. In both cases, the purpose of the perpetrators was to humiliate, by forcing men or women to do in public what should be private and in a pathological way (diarrhea, constipation, vomits). The memory of shame accompanied most former inmates for the rest of their lives (Richards 1998: 165, 191, n.18).

The morphology and location of the privies were not a coincidence. A GIS viewshed analysis reveals that the latrines were perfectly visible from virtually every part of the camp, which was unnecessary: as seen in the GIS map, there were other areas where the inmates would have been hidden from view (Figure 10.6). Furthermore, these zones were further away from the barracks, at a distance that was more in accordance with what the concentration camp norms indicated for waste disposal: 250 meters (López Rodríguez 2006: 193). Camp authorities should have known that latrines and dumps next to the barracks guaranteed epidemics, but they did not care and overlooked the regulations. It could be negligence, a desire to inflict an extra punishment on the prisoners or both. That it was on purpose is demonstrated by the fact that they were also giving less food to the prisoners than was officially stipulated.

Surviving in a concentration camp is not easy, either physically or psychologically. A simple form of psychological survival is engaging in some activity: doing handicrafts, playing games or writing letters— anything that prevents annihilation through anxiety, boredom or fear. We know that the inmates played games because we found two domino pieces in the latrines, one of them made with a shard of glazed tile, the other with a tiny fragment of bone. Thirteen domino pieces inside a fabric bag appeared with one of the killed in the cemetery of San Rafael, in Málaga (Fernández Martín and Espinosa 2019: 340–344). In the camp of San Pedro de Cardeña (Burrgo), international brigaders made a chess game with breadcrumb and soap (Baxell 2012: 368). Francisco Quintín, the prisoner who had asked for a canteen and a dish, sent another letter requesting a ball to play soccer. We do not know whether he received it, most probably not, but we know that it would have had little use: he was sentenced to death and executed for having infiltrated the Falange during the war to provide information to the Republicans (López Rodríguez and González Cortés 2019: 280). Evidence of writing is present in Castuera through two inkbottles and a collection of letters. Most of the prisoners wrote to ask for endorsement letters to be released or at least not killed (López Rodríguez and González Cortes 2019: 272–274). Some never arrived or were in vain.

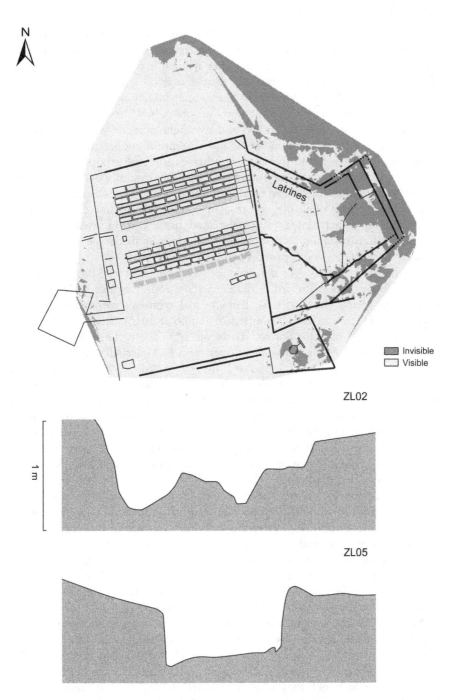

Figure 10.6 Above: a viewshed analysis demonstrates that the latrines were perfectly visible from virtually everywhere in the camp. Below: sections of the latrines showing their irregularity and shallowness, directly contravening concentration camp regulations.

Source: © Pastor Fábrega and author.

290 *The never-ending war*

Handicrafts are perhaps the most common way of maintaining psychological integrity: it is not surprising that in so many prisons inmates paint, do woodwork or engage in other manual activities (Dusselier 2008). The work of professional artists and intellectuals in camps and prisons has been the object of some research in Spain, but virtually no attention has been paid to the handicrafts of anonymous prisoners. Of these we have found some examples in Castuera: an awl and two lighters made with shell casings, the domino pieces mentioned above and a beautiful copper ring, made with coins, of which we found splinters. Another example of prisoners' art are the entrances to the barracks. Some show a remarkably careful work and aesthetic layout. Prisoners selected quartzites of different color so as to create a border that gave the pavement the aspect of a carpet. The desire to appropriate something as impersonal as a prefabricated barrack is in itself a form of resisting dehumanization. It is possible that whoever made the entrance was a mason or a stoneworker, proud of its trade.

Crucial to the survival of the prisoners were the relatives, mostly women. Their collaboration is attested in different ways, some surprising. Thus, a few of the zinc sheets that lined the barracks had women's names inscribed on them. In one we can read "Nati[vidad] Rubio from Abertura" on one side and "Sent by Antonio Rubio, Barracón n°53" on the other. Another inscription reads "María Fernández López from El Helechal", and a third one "Fermina Moyano from..." and on the other side "Moyano 339". On a fourth plaque only the words "Barracón n°9" can be read, alongside an illegible word. These plaques were a form of communication between relatives and inmates. In the case of Rubio and Moyano it is most likely between fathers and daughters or between siblings. In all cases, the relatives lived quite near: Abertura is a village in the province of Cáceres, north of Castuera, and Helechal is in Badajoz, in the same province as the camp. Moyano is a last name typical of Córdoba, a province bordering with Badajoz. It was of course easier for somebody in the region to make a message arrive to the prisoner through acquaintances or personally than for a relative in Madrid or Valencia, hundreds of kilometers away. This communication beyond the barbed wire was essential both from a psychological point of view and for mere physical survival. But it was not without a price: many women were raped or forced to have sex by the guards (Hernández de Miguel 2019: 440–442); others had to practice prostitution to support their families (Casanova 2004: 27).

Mothers, daughters, wives and sisters decisively contributed to prevent the death of their beloved ones by bringing them food. They usually brought them cooked meals (omelets, stews, soups) and bread, which leave no trace in the archaeological record—but are attested in the correspondence. Yet we have the containers in which they were transported. In the zone of the latrines we located a large amount of glazed earthenware sherds, many of them belonging to bowls and pots that may have contained stews (Figure 10.7). The most

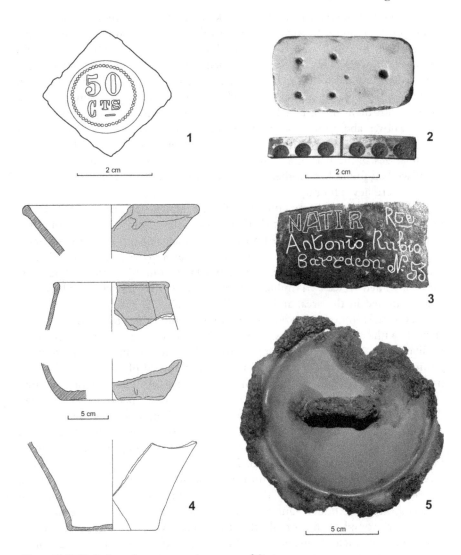

Figure 10.7 Finds from the concentration camp of Castuera.

Notes: 1. Coin issued by the camp authorities and valid within the enclosure; 2. Domino piece made with a tile; 3. Message by a prisoner to a woman relative inscribed in a piece of the metallic sheet that covered the barracks; 4. Glazed and unglazed pottery in which female relatives brought food to the prisoners; 5. Lid of a pot in which food was brought to the camp by a female relative.

Source: © Anxo Rodríguez Paz and Author.

moving find was the lid of a metallic cooking pot, typically used as a lunch box by the working classes in Spain. In 2010, after lecturing about the excavations in the camp to the neighbors in Castuera, an old lady, Aurora Navas, told my colleagues that her mother and father had been executed by the Francoists soon

292   *The never-ending war*

after the end of the war. Her father was killed first and her mother had to rent rooms in their house to survive. Aurora told us that she was unaware of the existence of the camp until late in her adulthood. Or this is what she thought before she saw the pot lid. She then had a flashback: she remembered the women who rented rooms in her mother's house for one or two days and then disappeared. These lonely women, who could be Fermina, Nati or María, carried with them metal pots like the one we found in the camp. Aurora had always known about the concentration camp, but she forgot: the lid awoke her long-repressed memories. For the next couple of years, during the exhumations of the mass graves near the concentration camp, Aurora came to see if we had found her mother. She passed away in 2016. The remains of her parents were never found.

In a concentration camp, under a dictatorship, no form of resistance can prevent a group of men from killing defenseless human beings. In 1979 neighbors and relatives exhumed dozens of human remains from a mass grave related to the concentration camp of Zaldívar (Casas de Don Pedro, Badajoz), which was operative between March and May 1939. The mass grave included at least 31 military from the 109 Mixed Brigade, which had been stationed in the area, and 20 civilians (Muñoz Encinar 2016: 388–390). In Castuera, too, every so often, Falangists and other right-wing militias arrived with a list of names. Ernesto Navarrete, the camp commander, facilitated the delivery; the Falangists took them to the nearby cemetery, or a mine shaft or any other place, shot them and got rid of the corpses. We do not know how many mass graves there are in the surroundings of the camp and we will never know: many of those that existed in the cemetery were destroyed recently due to the construction of new graves. During the exhumations carried out in 2011 and 2012, three graves with a total of 36 individuals were documented, 33 of which were camp inmates (Muñoz Encinar 2013; Muñoz Encinar et al. 2013). The smaller pit had the bodies of three guerrillas. The two others furnished valuable information to reconstruct the history of repression at the camp, despite the very poor state of preservation of the bones. Unfortunately, no identifications could be made, as we lack a complete list of all the murdered. We can, however, return something of their humanity to the dead and offer them a dignified interment: AMECADEC, the local association, took care of the reburial and erected a monument to the memory of the killed.

The largest mass grave was a long and shallow trench containing 22 individuals. They were only a fraction of the total, as the burial had been partially destroyed by the construction of new graves in the 1980s. People were killed in pairs, tied with wire by their hands or arms, in one case by the neck, and the ammunition that was employed indicates that at least six different pistols were used. This means that the killers resorted to personal weapons and that they were right-wing militias, rather than police or soldiers. The presence of shell casings reveals that the killing happened near the mass grave. Nine of the skulls present gunshot impacts (in the frontal or parietal

The never-ending war 293

bone, in the eye socket, in the jaw) and the bullet itself still lodged. Some victims have several traumas, proof of vicious violence and further indication of the work of several killers, some more motivated than others. As mentioned in Chapter 2, a bottle of sherry appeared on the grave's bottom. It is not easy to kill, not even in the name of God and Spain.

The victims were carrying objects related to the concentration camp, like spoons, flea combs, a military canteen and can openers. As often happens in exhumations, religious objects are at odds with Francoist stereotypes of the "Reds"; they include a crucifix, a reliquary, a medal representing Saint Hieronymus on one side and the local Virgin of Guadalupe on the other. The crucifix was issued by the Delegation of Assistance to Fronts and Hospitals, a Nationalist service during the war which reinforces the idea that the prisoners did come from the camp. Those about to be killed had the opportunity of seeing a priest before the execution, so it is possible that the prisoner received the crucifix from a chaplain. He was still clutching it in his hand in the mass grave.

Most of the victims for whom the age could be determined were between 30 and 50 years old (one was over 60), so they were probably individuals with political or military responsibilities during the war or before. It is not unlikely that some were involved in the crimes committed in the Republican zone: the region suffered a wave of revolutionary killings that exterminated entire right-wing families. It is also true that those involved in the crimes were usually the first to escape. In fact, many of the victims were innocent people who had not participated in the violence or even tried to stop it. One of them was José Sayabera Miranda who returned to his village after the war. His crime: belonging to the Communist Party. He was killed, along with his wife, three of his sons and a son-in-law. While in detention, he wrote a letter to a daughter saying "since nobody can honestly accuse me of any crime, as I have the satisfaction of not having committed any, we will be liberated by Franco's justice, in which I trust" (López Rodríguez and González Cortés 2019: 275). A son who survived the killings, Ángel, came regularly to our exhumations, like Aurora, waiting for his parents and his brothers to emerge from the earth. In vain.

Some of the objects that appeared with the human remains tell us about the profession of the killed: one of them was a stationmaster. He was carrying an insignia of the General Association of Employees and Workers of the Spanish Railways, a whistle and a bugle (Muñoz Encinar 2013: 77). Another one was a doctor or a nurse. He had an insignia of the Medical Corps, two syringes, 11 hypodermic needles, a rubber tourniquet, ampoules and remains of medicines (Muñoz Encinar 2013: 94–95). Of other victims we only know their military identity, as reflected in buckles, clasps, leggings and leather boots. There are other objects, some personal: combs and mirrors, pencil leads, lighters, many copper coins, cufflinks, wedding rings, wallets, glasses and even sunglasses. They are an inventory of what the prisoners deemed essential to their survival, physical or psychological. The lenses belonged to somebody suffering hyperopia. The cufflinks and sunglasses (a rarity at the time) evince a certain social status. The wallet had a ticket from the Madrid metro inside: people interned in Castuera came from all over Spain, thus the difficulty of identifying them. The combs and mirrors reveal the inmates' obsession with maintaining their personal appearance.

The other mass grave with victims from the camp appeared in parallel and only a few meters from the former (Alonso Muela et al. 2013). They were surely dug in a short period of time. Unlike in the other mass grave, prisoners here were not killed in couples. The 11 bodies were thrown haphazardly into the grave, one on top of the other, and they appeared in forced postures (Figure 10.8). The form of execution was also different: we found 7 mm Mauser bullets. In this case, it is possible that the prisoners were killed by firing squad at the cemetery wall and then dragged into the mass grave. In fact, the accumulation of bodies is greater in the northern part of the grave, facing the cemetery's entrance, where people were executed. Three individuals had pistol bullets in their heads, two in the skull, one in the jaw, probably the *coups de grâce*. Objects are similar to those found in the other mass grave and are also related to the camp, particularly the many military elements: clasps, the hook of a military canteen, and a buckle with the infantry insignia. We also retrieved lighters, a religious medal (Our Lady of Perpetual Help), pencils, buttons, rings, a wallet... An object unequivocally links grave and camp: a sheet made of zinc of the kind that lined the camp barracks and used by the prisoners to communicate with the outside: it was probably with this purpose that it was kept. These and other artifacts indicate that when the prisoners were summoned in the camp they still had the hope, however weak, of being simply transferred to another camp or prison. This is why they took with them whatever they thought could be useful in their new destination.

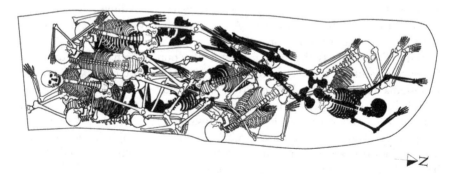

Figure 10.8 Mass grave with the remains of 11 individuals killed at the cemetery of Castuera by firing squad and then dumped into the pit from the left.

Source: © Andrea Alonso Muela, Xurxo Ayán Vila and author.

The never-ending war   295

In general, the victims of this second mass grave did not have as many objects as in the other one. There were two individuals, however, who stood out, whom we named Individual 9 and 10 (Alonso Muela et al. 2013: 136–141). Individual 10 had a Zippo lighter, a mirror and three copper rings. One of the rings he was carrying in his right hand, but the other two were in his pocket at the moment of his death. Individual 9 is the one who appeared with a richer inventory: a flea comb, a mirror, a Bakelite cigarette holder, a couple of decorated cufflinks, a Eureka fountain pen from Birmingham, and the aforementioned infantry buckle and canteen hook. Cufflinks, pen and cigarette holder evince an elegant person of social standing, who might have held positions of responsibility in the Popular Army. Status is also corroborated by two dental prostheses that were outside the reach of most at the time. In his pocket, he was carrying a small leather bag with two copper rings, three complete coins, five in different stages of modification and several copper splinters (Figure 10.9). Individual 9 made rings out of coins: he hammered them laboriously until he obtained small splinters, then he hammered the splinters again until he obtained the desired shape. The rings were similar to those that appeared with his comrade, Individual 10, and to the one that appeared in the latrines of the camp. They were exchanged for food with the guards or in the commissary, as we know from oral testimonies, and they kept him alive a few more days (Lizarriturri 2003: 99; González Cortés 2006: 19). Until they could not help him anymore.

The camp of Castuera was closed at the beginning of April 1940. The dismantling was carried out by a group of 29 prisoners. They were housed in the barracks that had been used by the guards (see figure 10.4, above). On the floor of the barracks we found a hundred can openers. There is little doubt about the menu: sardines and tuna. There were also traces of hearths, around which the prisoners heated their food and warmed up. In some cases, the hearths are delimited with broken iron rods that had been used to support barbed wire. They ate even in the space that their jailers had used a latrine: from the drainage still came a pungent smell of feces. Apart from cans and rods we found little else: a belt buckle, a spoon, an inkbottle, the handle of a mess tin. Poor, anonymous remains for poor, anonymous prisoners. Our excavation did not allow us to return to them this flash of humanity that we can at least capture in the mass graves. But the absence is a realistic testimony of that to which the inmates were reduced: a nameless mass of starving beggars. The Francoist camps, as I noted at the beginning, had a paradoxical double purpose, one explicit, the other implicit. The explicit purpose was to classify the prisoners. The implicit was to punish and humiliate them. The camps acted as a self-fulfilled prophecy: they produced what they wanted to prove: that the "Reds" were inferior beings, degraded humans, less than animals.

Figure 10.9 Objects associated with Individual 10 buried in one of the mass graves of Castuera.

Notes: 1. Comb; 2. mirror; 3. 7 mm bullet used in the execution; 4. Zipper; 5. Hook from a military canteen; 6. Coins modified to make rings; 7. Boot sole; 8. Leggin clasp; 9. Rings made with coins; 10. Cufflins; 11. Cigarette holder; 12. Coins; 13. Dental prosthesis; 14. Military belt buckle.

Source: © Yolanda Porto Tenreiro, Xurxo Ayán Vila and author.

The prison

The camps were a short stop in a long journey of punishment and seclusion. Those convicted by a final judgement were either executed or sent to prison. The archaeological study of Francoist jails is not easy. Most have continued in use until quite recently and the presence of Republican prisoners has been effaced. In this section I am not referring to the varied typology of detention centers, often reusing buildings, that proliferated until 1945, but to prisons proper: spaces that were conceived to incarcerate convicts for their alleged offences or crimes. Most of such prisons had been built between the late nineteenth and early twentieth centuries, in a time of growing social instability and following the then popular radial layout (Bonet Correa 1978): Barcelona, Cáceres, Badajoz, A Coruña, Vigo and Lugo are some typical examples. Between April 1939 and the mid-1940s they became overcrowded with tens of thousands of political prisoners. Many have been abandoned in recent years and some transformed into museums, usually with no reference to their previous role (Sánchez-Carretero 2013: 36–38; Thompson 2017).

Worse was the fate of the prison of Carabanchel (Madrid), which was one of the few actually built by the Franco regime in the 1940s. Construction was carried out by political prisoners between 1940 and 1944 and the complex, which was Spain's largest prison and for a time even Europe's, remained in use until 1998—with no political convicts after 1978. It was demolished in 2008, in the midst of a strong mobilization by neighbors and collectives demanding that part of the building was preserved as a place of memory (Ortiz 2013a and b; González-Ruibal and Ortiz 2015). Thousands of political prisoners spent time there, including some of the most relevant Spanish politicians and intellectuals of the second half of the twentieth century. A year before it was destroyed, my colleagues and I had the chance of studying the site from an ethnographic, historical and archaeological point of view (Ortiz 2012, 2013a and b; González-Ruibal and Falquina 2013; González-Ruibal and Ortiz 2015).

Traces of Republican prisoners could not be documented, as expected. Most of the finds (graffiti, artifacts) were from the 1990s, but the building itself had undergone relatively little modification since 1944 and provided unique material evidence of ideas and practices of punishment prevailing during the dictatorship (Figure 10.10). Punishment in Carabanchel differed from the concentration camps. Wolfgang Sofsky (2013: 47) has written in relation to the Nazi *Lager* that "Absolute power destroys space as a domain for acting and living". In Spain, space was destroyed when prisoners were herded into reused factories or warehouses or in an unregulated or loosely regulated place like Castuera. Lack of order was part of the strategy aimed at demobilizing and demoralizing people, because temporal routines and spatial orientation are crucial to a person's ontological security (Giddens 1984: 60–64). Guards attempted to deprive inmates of their routines in every act of life and regaining them was part of the tactics of resistance deployed by prisoners. Thus, the international brigaders interned in the camp of San Pedro de Cardeña decided at some point to organize queues to receive food as a form of resistance. Before this basic form of social and spatial discipline, the guards enjoyed seeing the prisoners falling on the food like animals, something that reinforced their prejudices about their enemies (Baxell 2012: 362). The lack of time and spatial regulation in the camp meant that prisoners wandered without anything to do. There were no spaces allotted to specific activities (beyond the latrines or the washing area) and no schedule.

Although inmates also experienced beatings, hunger and humiliation in jail, the architecture of the prison was not designed to destroy the spatio-temporal habits, but rather to reshape them. Scenes of disorder are incompatible with

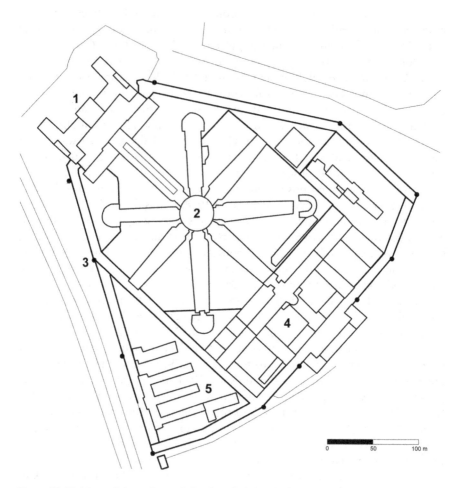

Figure 10.10 Map of the prison of Carabanchel (Madrid) as it was shortly before being demolished in 2008.

Notes: 1. Main entrance; 2. Control center; 3. Sentry boxes; 4. Women's prison; 5. Psychiatric hospital.

Source: © Author.

carceral space; therefore, as opposed to the lack of regulation in the camp, what we have in prisons is an excess. In Carabanchel, the perambulation of the prisoners is strictly patterned, both spatially and temporally (González-Ruibal and Falquina 2013): there was a route to the visiting room, another one to the yard, a space for sleeping, another one for eating, another for working. And each activity had its specific time. Spatial order was also used to impress on the prisoners an awe-inspiring image of power. In the case of Carabanchel, this is attained by means of a very long corridor to access the cells—up to 300 meters from the outside, which is the longest in any radial

The never-ending war   299

jail. Furthermore, the length of the cell corridor looked even greater, because it became thinner toward the end. This also allowed a better control of the cells by the guards watching from the control center and the prisoners to attend mass, which was celebrated there. In fact, the control center worked like the central yard of the concentration camps: it organized space and served to carry out activities of indoctrination. Meaningfully, a statue of the Virgin presided at the entrance to the center. The building was extremely impermeable, in terms of spatial syntax: to reach the least permeable room (the infirmary) from the exterior, 17 steps were necessary (González-Ruibal and Falquina 2013: 104)—in the Argentinian clandestine center of detention Club Atlético, the maximum steps were six (Zarankin and Niro 2006: 177).

The architectural style of Carabanchel is also representative of an idea of punishment. The prison was born outdated. The authorities chose a radial model that had been popular since the construction of the Eastern State Penitentiary in Philadelphia in 1829. The parallelisms between Eastern State and Carabanchel are numerous: both have a central core from which radiate the galleries and the entire complex is in turn surrounded by a high wall with towers (sentry boxes in Carabanchel). Philadelphia's jail has an imposing neo-Gothic facade; in Carabanchel, the facade is neo-Renaissance. As noted above, the radial model was the most popular in Spain in the late nineteenth century. By the beginning of the twentieth, new buildings proliferated in Europe that followed the model of connected pavilions. Why did the Franco regime choose an anachronistic layout? A comment by a North American prison expert who visited Spain in 1959 provides a clue:

> Most Spanish prison directors seem to favour this traditional radial style, feeling that it facilitates circulation of inmates and staff and at the same time permits classification of offenders and allows adequate control over the prisoners' movements. Although this type of layout finds little favour among high-ranking correctional personnel and architects in other countries, the writer has found that, in other countries in Europe and America, custodial personnel generally have been favourably disposed towards it.
>
> (Johnston 1961: 319)

On the one hand, the radial prison becomes the perfect materialization of the classificatory ideal of the Franco regime, which was the rationale behind the camps. This rationale would still be necessary after the properly totalitarian phase of the dictatorship, because Carabanchel would be shared by common criminals, political prisoners and homosexuals. On the other hand, Johnston notes that the radial model is not to the liking of authorities and architects outside Spain, but it is of the guards. In democratic regimes there is a duality between wardens concerned with the practical issues of surveillance and those responsible for the penitentiary system, who are

300   *The never-ending war*

usually of a more liberal persuasion and see in the radial prison an anachronistic form of punishment. In Francoist Spain, there was a perfect match between the warden's and politician's mentality: politicians conceived society with the mindset of a jailer.

The selection of an old model had other reasons as well, equally ideological. Those who backed the coup of 1936 were strongly conservative. Compared to the totalitarian ideologies of Nazism and Italian Fascism, the Franco regime stood out in its mobilization of traditional ideological principles rather than futurist utopias, the more so after the decline of the fascist faction in the regime after 1942. For the military, the references were above all the old prisons of Spain, which had had such a prominent role in the repression of the social movements of the first third of the twentieth century. Many military and police commanders, who were later involved in the 18 July coup, had participated in quenching strikes and riots. Totalitarianism is based in a perpetual movement forward: "Neither National Socialism nor Bolshevism ever proclaimed a new form of government or asserted that their goals had been achieved after attaining power and control over the State machinery" (Arendt 2004: 408). The practical objective of totalitarian movements consists in organizing the People and "maintaining them in motion". In the case of Spain, the "Movement", as the ideology of the regime was known, was basically rhetorical. What Franco pursued was not a perpetual movement forwards, but rather the opposite: the return to a traditional order. This does not mean that the persecution of the enemy was less ruthless or systematic, only that the materialization of the punishment had to find an adequate outlet. It was the nineteenth-century radial prison, rather than the concentration camp, that better fitted the regime.

The forced labor camp

A myriad of infrastructures were built or rebuilt during the 1940s in a Spain devastated by war. Among those who participated in the construction works were huge numbers of Republican prisoners. They toiled in the construction of dams, roads, railways, airports, towns, canals and virtually every other public work. Also the Valley of the Fallen, the monumental mausoleum outside Madrid that Franco built to commemorate the war (Solé 2017). Some of the forced labor camps (*destacamentos penales*) survived until the 1950s and in fact the last one was only closed in 1970 (Lafuente 2002: 235). Labor camps were the last stage in the so-called "penitentiary tourism" suffered by hundreds of thousands of prisoners after the war. Gabriel Saz Urbina's is a paradigmatic case. He was captured at the beginning of 1938 and spent time in the concentration camp of Camposancos (Pontevedra), the prison of San Juan Mozarrifar (Zaragoza), the Monastery of Uclés (Cuenca), the Reformatory for Adults of Ocaña (Toledo), the forced labor camp of Miraflores (Madrid), the provincial prison of Madrid, the Reformatory of Ocaña again and finally the forced labor camp of Colmenar Viejo (Madrid), where he was interned shortly after he was released in February 1946 (Quintero Maqua 2009).

The north of Madrid saw the establishment of several forced labor camps during the 1940s, for the construction of a railway between the capital and Burgos. The line, which was 282 km long, passed through a mountainous region, which explains the many years it took to be completed—between 1926 and 1968. After its inauguration, it was seldom used and was soon abandoned. Several of the forced labor camps related to the works still exist. The best preserved complex is in Bustarviejo, where virtually all structures have survived (Figure 10.11). We conducted archaeological, ethnographic and historical work at the site (Falquina et al. 2008, 2010; Quintero Maqua 2009; Falquina 2012; Marín Suárez et al. 2012), upon which this section is based. The camp of Bustarviejo can be considered representative of the so-called *destacamentos penales* ("penitentiary posts") that proliferated all over Spain in the postwar period.

The camp was operative between 1944 and 1952, first with Republican prisoners who were redeeming penalties and later by common offenders. A graffiti documented on one of the walls dates the completion of the barracks: "YEAR 1945" (Falquina 2012). Prisoners and guards slept in a building with four aisles organized around a central courtyard. The offices, the kitchen, the prison shop and the latrines were also located here. An identical structure has been documented in another labor camp that has been studied archaeologically, the Camp dels Soldats in Artà, Majorca (Suau Mayol and Puig Palerm 2014). This camp was in operation between 1941 and 1942 and occupied by a Disciplinary Battalion of Working Soldiers, another modality of forced labor that involved former Republican military. The barracks at Camp dels Soldats were thatched. In Bustarviejo both inmates and guards were slightly better off, as they slept under a tiled roof. Prisoners

Figure 10.11 The forced labor camp of Bustarviejo. View of the main building with railway works in the background.

Source: © Author.

302   *The never-ending war*

occupied three collective rooms. They slept on straw mattresses lying on the floor and their few belongings were stored on a plaster shelf that surrounded the room. The dormitories in the labor camps of Madrid were typically used by 50, 100 or even more prisoners. Not surprisingly, for many years after the closing of the barracks, the space was used a cow shed. Windows had no bars, but were narrow, horizontal and located very high, so that inmates could not use them to escape. In a time of autarchy, this was probably a practical solution to avoid the use of bars, since steel was very scarce.

The prisoners' latrines were very rudimentary: two rows of concrete toilets (basically a hole in the ground) attached to the wall and with no separation in between. They are redolent of the latrines of Nazi concentration camps, such as Westerbork, Dachau or Auschwitz-Birkenau. Interestingly, in all those cases they were designed to be used while sitting, whereas the Spanish ones are squat toilets. Conditions in the camp were hard due to the lack of privacy, the insufficient food and, in winter, the cold. In the mountains of Madrid, the temperature was usually below zero during large part of the winter and snow was common. Still, the situation had improved significantly in comparison with concentration camps. The privies, for instance, were no longer a mere open space. And the crowding in the dormitories did not reach the levels found at the camps.

The guards belonged to the corps known as *Policía Armada* (Armed Police), which had been created *ex novo* by the dictatorship, and occupied the rooms near the entrance to the compound. They had electricity—porcelain insulators were found on the walls—and the concrete floor was decorated with incisions imitating a tiled pavement. The guards had their own privy, with running water and a shower. During the excavation of its drainage, many artifacts turned up, mostly related to hygiene: a toothbrush, caps of toothpaste, a fragment of a shaving basin and bottles of cologne. A French coin of 5 Francs, dated 1949, appeared mingled with the waste (Falquina 2012). The materiality of the barracks shows that the guards had, as can be expected, a considerably higher standard of living than the prisoners, but this does not mean that their life was easy.

The lieutenant in charge of the detachment of the Armed Police lived in a small hut of 15 square meters attached to a granite outcrop. It lacked water, heating, electricity or toilet. It did have a concrete floor, plastered walls and a tiled roof. On the floor, the excavation documented seven coins dated in the 1940s, a couple of military boots and a child's espadrille—indicating that the lieutenant lived with his family. Poorly paid, in a hostile environment, in remote and isolated outposts, being a guard in Bustarviejo could be a hard job. For the commander of Bustarviejo too hard: according to our informants, he committed suicide by jumping into the railway trench.

Much worse was life for another social group: the inmates' families, of whose presence we have a unique testimony. In some of the camps we have documented their shacks next to the barracks (Figure 10.12). In the case of Bustarviejo it is over 50 huts scattered over several hectares to the west of the

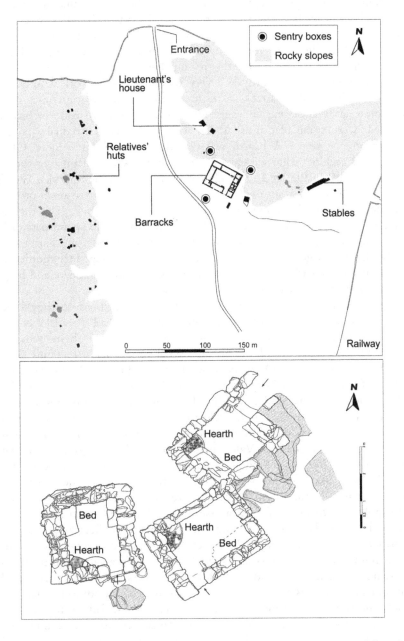

Figure 10.12 Map of the settlement of the prisoners' relatives in Bustarviejo and three huts that were excavated.

Source: © Carlos Marín Suárez, Álvaro Falquina, Jorge Rolland and author.

304   *The never-ending war*

main building. The location is strange, because they were built in a quarry, on top of the heaps of stone that were used as ballast in the railway. Perhaps it was convenient because in this way they had the material ready to build the shacks. With the long working hours, the inmates hardly had any time to construct them. Perhaps also for this reason they are all very small (4–5 m^2). The walls, however, are sturdy and very well made—the work is noticeably better than that of the barracks. The huts had dirt floors, sometimes mixed with some sandy concrete, and very low roofs (ca. 1.5 m) made of brooms. The beds were stone platforms, which would have been originally covered with brooms or straw. A hearth was placed in one of the corners. Of the women and children's life we have evidence in the shape of tin cans, bottles, pottery, remains of footwear, a comb and even a couple of cufflinks. We also found three inkbottles in one the four huts that we excavated, probably indicating that the children were being educated at "home". The diet was miserable. One of our informants, Milagros Montoya, who spend part of her childhood in the camp, remembered going with her mother to the slaughterhouses to get blood that was later boiled as a soup. Her mother also stole from the orchards, but neighbors were usually compassionate and helped prisoners and their relatives (Falquina et al. 2008: 191–192).

Families were often forced to follow the prisoners because they lacked economic resources: it was usually the man who had the salaried job. Inmates received a fraction of the wages that belonged to them, while the rest of the money paid by the companies went to the State (Lafuente 2002). This fraction increased with every dependent. In addition, they received the payment for extra hours in its entirety, which explains their heavy working and obedience: many ended up hired by the same companies that had exploited them. They left good memories in the mountains of Madrid. Some even got married with local women and remained in the region forever. An old woman of Valdemanco, when talking about the inmates said "I do not like to call them prisoners, because they were very good people". Most likely, some were prisoners precisely *because* they were good people. Generally, the camp workers were not remembered as what they were: political prisoners of a dictatorship. The Francoist narrative, as in the case of the guerrilla, had a profound effect in shaping collective perceptions. As happened with the concentration camps, the *destacamentos* left a lasting social stigma in the prisoners and their families. We can imagine the shame of living in shacks around a prison. This was, in fact, part of the punishment. The "Reds" were forced to live in conditions that were widely perceived as primitive and degenerate and this reinforced the stereotypes about them. Francoist propaganda described Republicans as physically degenerate, due to the resentment and bitterness generated by the anti-social behaviour typical of "Marxists" (Richards 1998: 60). By the end of the war, the word "Red" had been equated with "dirty", bearer of a sort of filth that polluted both the soul and the body (Casanova 2004: 25).

The never-ending war   305

Thus, an architect in the Valley of the Fallen, wrote, referring to the forced workers: "It is not that they had a consciousness that they were criminals... They were so, so primitive, that they did things as a simple animal [*bicho*, a pejorative term] could do them, without any consequence whatsoever of what they were doing. Consequence of the war and their very low intellectual condition, of course..." (Lafuente 2002: 122).

According to the testimony of one of the prisoners in Bustarviejo, permission to build huts for relatives was only granted after hard negotiations with the construction company and the guards and even a threat of a strike.[6] Yet we should not see the shacks as a mere act of empowerment. At a time when the dictatorship had all the power, such a workers' victory seems unlikely if there was not something else at stake. In fact, that relatives and inmates were together was to everybody's advantage. The prisoners worked harder, their living with wives and children fit well the nationalist-Catholic ideology of the patriarchal nuclear family as the basic pillar of society, and their presence was in tune with the purposes of redemption and re-evangelization that the labor camp was supposed to fulfill. In addition, families served as a mechanism of surveillance. Something that attracted our attention during our survey in the forced labor camps of Madrid was the absence of barbed wire, fences or walls. In Bustarviejo, surveillance was effected from three sentry boxes, but these were not watching over the space where the inmates worked or lived, but the entrances to the site: a curious prison, indeed, in which it is the outside, and not the inside, that is under surveillance. Yet it makes sense, because the threat did come from the outside, from potential guerrilla raids. In fact, anti-Francoist fighters were active in the Madrid sierra and they even managed to capture a village and raise the Republican flag for a few hours. Inside the compound, families acted as an effective deterrent: who would escape leaving a spouse and children behind? Not many, considering that the regime was keen on taking revenge on relatives, that these usually had no economic resources and that the stay at the labor camp was relatively brief. Still, there were some escapes. We were told of a man, Francisco Bajo Bueno, who left the camp through the main gate, after telling the guards that he had been officially released. Four others simply disappeared "ignoring the way they went, taking their blankets with them", describes a report in characteristic police language.[7] Two men, Julián Navarro Romero and Pedro Arce Rodríguez, were captured during the escape and sent to the infamous prison of Chinchilla (Albacete) in 1945. Yet the lack of fences is ultimately evidence of the absolute control that the dictatorship had achieved over Spain in the 1940s: the whole country was an immense prison (Molinero et al. 2003). It is obvious in the archaeological record that the huts of the relatives (and thus the presence of the families) were subjected to strict regulations by the penitentiary system, because in all the labor camps where they survive they have the same size and shape and are located in the same space—quarries and stone heaps (Figure 10.13).

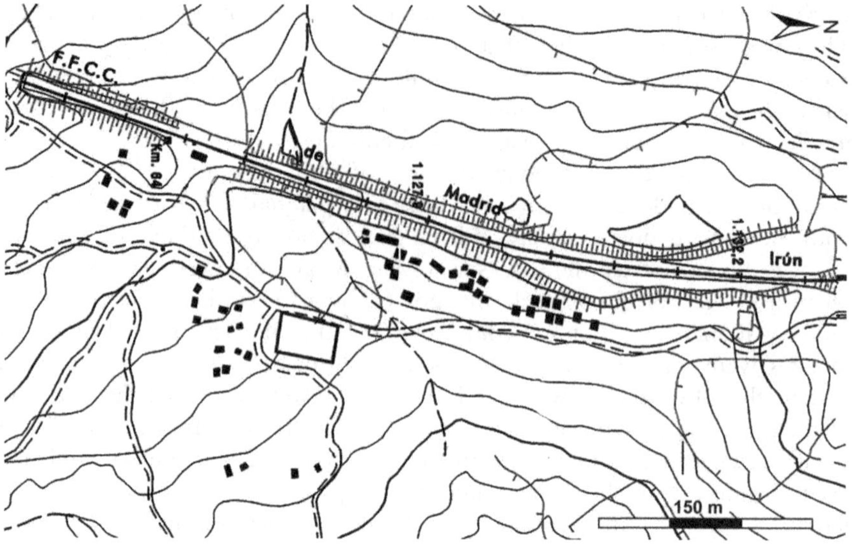

Figure 10.13 Huts of prisoners' relatives built along the Madrid–Burgos railway in Valdemanco.

Source: © Author's illustration based on a topographic map.

The Francoist technology of repression intended to neutralize people, transform them into docile subjects. The regime almost achieved its goals: the absence of physical walls in Bustarviejo also means that they had been displaced inside every individual. Repression is never as effective as when it is assimilated subjectively. But Francoist violence did not manage to completely disarticulate the networks of solidarity among the punished. We found archaeological evidence of these networks: between the 1960s and 1980s, decades after the camp was closed, a group of inmates kept returning to Bustarviejo. In the huts where their relatives once lived, they uncorked bottles of vermouth and sherry, they cooked paella, they ate and drank. They celebrated that they had survived the war, the camps, the prisons, forced labor. That they were alive and well. We found the shells and the glass when we excavated the ruins. And in the distance of time, we rejoiced with them and celebrated their victory.[8]

The vision of the vanquished

It is often said that history is written by the victors. The epic narrative of the dictatorship, however, has a counter-narrative, which is the fragmentary account made up of words, sentences, names and pictures that Republican prisoners left while in captivity. Important collections of prison graffiti from the early Franco dictatorship have survived to our days, mostly from the

The never-ending war   307

north of Spain: Cangas de Narcea (Asturias), Camposancos and Oia (Pontevedra, Galicia) and Fort San Cristóbal (Navarre).

I have already referred to Fort San Cristóbal. The walls of this hospital-prison have preserved hundreds of graffiti left by inmates (Herrasti, Martín and Ferrándiz 2014). Many of them record the names of people and their entrance in prison ("Pamplona, 31 January 1941, detained here. Virgilio"). A prisoner by the name of González de Torrelavega not only inscribed the date: he left us a full calendar covering the months of June and July 1941. The inmates of San Cristóbal came from different social groups, although most belonged to the working classes, as seen in the many spelling errors. Sometimes these errors, which correspond with a faithful transcription of oral discourse, allow us to infer the geographic origin of the prisoners. Thus, a graffiti reads: *El día 6 de disiembre* [diciembre] *del 1941 ingresemo* [ingresamos] *a la 5 de la tarde. Paco, Rafael y Emilio* ("The 6 of December 1936, we entered the prison at 5 in the evening. Paco, Rafael and Emilio"). The spelling errors indicate that the captives came from Andalusia and were only half literate. Most probably, only one of them was able to read and write and left the message in the name of all. A boxer, proud of his trade, wrote *Victoriano Santos de hoficio* [oficio] *boseador* [boxeador] *profesional. M-XXXVIVZ con 23 años de hedad* [edad], "Victoriano Santos, professional boxer by trade, M-XXXVIVZ, 23 years old". The Roman numerals do not mean anything, except an aspiration to literacy. In this context, it is extremely surprising to find a poem in Latin:

> "When the saddest image of that night recurs which was for me the final moment in the city, when I recall the night in which I left behind so much dear to me, a tear now also glides from my eyes".
>
> (trans. Putnam 2010: 83)

It is an elegy from the book *Tristia*, written by Roman poet Ovidius (43 BC–17 AD) in his exile in modern-day Bulgaria. At a time in which Republicans were considered as virtually subhuman, writing in Latin was a powerful form of self-assertion. Several inmates testify to their penitentiary periplus, recording the prison or concentration camp from which they came. Also to life conditions, marked by cold, hunger and physical punishment: "here suffered more cold than a dog. Felipe Pérez Domínguez", "Here spent days an inmate that was transferred from Orduña after 24 months in this despicable fort where hunger forced him to cultivate grasses on the fringes of the courtyard", "15 days punished for refusing to work". It is striking to find some graffiti with the hammer and the sickle and hoorays to the USSR. An atypical inscription, perhaps made by a returned migrant, records several towns in the United States and their baseball teams. Another prisoner wrote "If somebody hears Hooray Spain!/and he does not reply Hooray!/If he is a man he is not Spanish!/And if he is Spanish he is not a man!". This is eloquent testimony that a strong patriotism was definitely not the preserve of the Nationalists.

308   *The never-ending war*

Hundreds of graffiti were also found in Camposancos, a Jesuit seminary reconverted to concentration camp between 1937 and 1939 (Ballesta and Rodríguez Gallardo 2008; Sousa Fernández 2011). Here we found several representations of bombers, which manifest the trauma caused by the continuous bombing undergone by Republican troops on the Northern Front, from where the prisoners came—similar depictions exist in the camp of Cangas de Narcea.[9] As in San Cristóbal, the inmates record their home towns (Gijón, Oviedo, Pontevedra, San Sebastián, Albacete), their dates of entrance and, in some cases, exit from the camp ("José Luís Bau got in 27-1-39, got out 18-5-1939"). Another prisoner simply asks himself in the third voice: "when will he go out" (*cuando saldrá*). Several graffiti convey messages of love, in which the name of the beloved is always absent ("I love you. Jonnas"), surely to avoid reprisals or humiliations. Others preferred to write letters on the walls. One of them reads, in broken, virtually incomprehensible syntax: "Dear friend. I will be happy if upon receipt of this letter you are in good health, well then, myself in good health so far like myself well so far as usual. Enough because I am pissed off with so much..."[10] It is as if the prisoner had made a superhuman effort to write a message that is absolutely conventional and then in the last moment, overwhelm by bitterness, he had fallen apart.

In Oia, about 20 kilometers north of Camposancos along the coast, another camp was operative between 1937 and 1939 (Costas Goberna et al. 2019), which also housed captives from the Northern Front. It reused a building, as well, in this case a twelfth-century Cistercian monastery. Hundreds of graffiti have been preserved here, similar in content to those of Camposancos. There are drawings of combat scenes, women, calendars, many dates of entrance and exit, and even a map showing the route followed by a prisoner from Catalonia to Galicia. One of the most chilling inscriptions reads: "Eugenio Blanco arrived here on 12-2-39 and left" and somebody continued, in a different calligraphy "for the cemetery, on 18-4-1939". An elaborate drawing represents a dining table with all sorts of delicacies: a roasted chicken, fresh fruit, cheese, cake, wine... The artist wrote nearby: "First meal of the day". It is impossible to find a more poignant testimony of the extreme hunger experienced by the inmates. The passing of time, food, women, the hometown, the traumatic memory of combat: these are the concerns of the prisoners. And, above all, there is the obsession with leaving testimony of one's existence: thus the repeated "here was", "here slept", "here was held in detention" (*aquí estuvo, aquí durmió, aquí detenido*) (Ballesta and Rodríguez Gallardo 2008). They were aware that graffiti could be the last and perhaps only proof that somebody, a unique human being, existed and suffered. Totalitarianism intends to make people disappear forever: physically and from human memory, to annihilate their past, their present and their future. The attitude of the man who writes on a wall is that of the one who resists to disappear without a trace.

Notes

1 https://elpais.com/politica/2019/03/01/actualidad/1551468571_037157.html.
2 https://elpais.com/ccaa/2012/08/03/andalucia/1344009656_723083.html.
3 Anarchists had already defended the social value of forced labor and the Republic had institutionalized them before the war (Ledesma 2010: 237).
4 AGMAV. ZN. 24 D. A.41/L.9/C.30, cit. in López Rodríguez (2006: 189).
5 Quedlinburg (First World War, Germany): 2 to 10 m^2 per person. Fort Hood (Second World War, USA), 4.5 m^2.
6 I thank Emilio Silva for sharing the testimony, which was gathered in 2019.
7 AGA 07 15.04, Cj. 4/11988. I would like to thank Alicia Quintero Maqua for the reference.
8 We know from oral testimonies that the inmates of Bustarviejo returned from time to time to commemorate their stay in the camp. There are similar testimonies, including photographs, for the prisoners of other forced labor camps, such as Valborrás (Barco de Valdeorras, Ourense), where the inmates worked in the tungsten mines (García Tato 2016).
9 http://asociacionculturalclio.blogspot.com/2013/09/los-grafitis-y-dibujos-de-la-carcel-de.html.
10 *Querido amigo. Me alegraré que al recibo de esta te encuentres bien de salud, bueno yo asta la fecha bien de saluz como yo asta la fecha bien sin novedad. Sin mas que ya estoy emcabronao de tanta*

11 Aftermath

Heritage and memory

In this book I have proposed an archaeological narrative of the Spanish Civil War based on things, places and landscapes. It is a novel way of telling the conflict, as all previous histories of the war were based on documents or oral testimonies. However, it is not necessarily so new if we go outside academia. Landscapes, places and things (including human remains) have been mobilized to tell the conflict and come to terms with it in a myriad ways since 1936. Remains of the war have been transformed into sacred relics, personal mementos, museum artifacts, collectors' items, memorials and heritage sites in an attempt to make sense of a past seen as traumatic, glorious or both. In this final chapter, I offer a brief overview of the afterlives of material remains—from battlefields to personal objects and from the war period to the present.

Heritage and memory during war and dictatorship

The war was not yet over and it was already being memorialized and transformed into heritage. The most fascinating examples come from the Nationalist side, which is logical: the Nationalists did not see the war as a blight, but as a glorious episode in Spanish history—both a Crusade and a war of liberation. The conflict was the event that would make Spain great again, on a par with the Spanish Empire of the Habsburgs. Memory and heritage took different forms, some grassroots and impromptu, others orchestrated from above. Among the former, we have the case of memorials erected by soldiers to their fallen comrades in the frontlines, at times in the middle of the fray. This is the case with the monument to the fallen brigaders erected during the Battle of the Ebro or the spontaneous memorialization at the University Hospital in Madrid, where the legionnaires erected a monolith to those killed by mines when the war was still raging. Many wartime Republican memorials were destroyed during or after the conflict, but a few have survived. One of the most moving was made near Abánades, the scenario of the forgotten Offensive of the Upper Tajuña River (see Chapter 7). In a place known as Los Castillejos, an anonymous Republican artist sculpted a memorial to the fallen inside a rock shelter, representing two beautiful

Aftermath: heritage and memory 311

effigies of the Republic wearing the Phrygian cap. It had been the icon of the French Revolution, a symbol of freedom and republicanism. Under one of the bas-reliefs an inscription reads: "To the brothers fallen in the fight against Fascism MCMXXXVIII. Sixth Battalion of Engineers" (González-Ruibal 2011a: fig. 14)..

Official memory and heritage in the Nationalist side took different—and often fascinating—forms (see Viejo Rose 2011). One of the first initiatives were the tours through the battlefields of the Northern Front organized by pro-Franco propagandist Luis Bolín (Holguín 2005): international visitors were shown the traces of war, from trenches to pillboxes, in an early case of dark tourism. Already in 1937 and in the northern front, a war museum was planned in Bilbao. Although the exhibition was never opened, the plans were well underway and we even have a list of objects to be displayed, including the underpants of the first Nationalist soldier to cross the Bilbao estuary (Brena Alonso 2016). The project ended up as a temporary exhibition in the Kursaal (casino) of San Sebastián, which displayed basically the weapons captured from the Republican Army during the campaign in the north. Plans for the creation of a "Museum of the Crusade" in Burgos (the Nationalist wartime capital) never came to fruition either (Castro Berrojo 2008: 162–169). The role of a national museum was partially and unsatisfactorily played by the Museum of the Army in Madrid (and now in Toledo), with its fetishistic displays of memorabilia. Other military museums also showcased objects related to the conflict but no museum of the war as such or of any singular battle was ever created. The museum of the Alcázar in Toledo, which was inaugurated as the "Museum of the Siege" in the 1950s, was the closest thing (Castro Berrojo 2008: 169).

There was little interest in creating museums and there was even less interest in turning battlefields into *lieux de mémoire*. Some attempts by the military were soon discouraged. Thus, there was a proposal by a high-ranking army officer to preserve the ruins of the University City of Madrid as they stood at the end of the war and open them to visitors that could be guided by mutilated veterans—a quite dystopic project, but in line with the fascist sensibilities of the period (González-Ruibal 2016b: 82[1]). Although the option was ruled out, the ruins of the university still became a heritage site for a while: signs were installed, reading "Us" and "Them", which explained the front (and the war more generally) to visitors in a brief and bold way (Viejo Rose 2011: 80). The campus, as a prominent battlefield, was also the scenario for parades and Falangist rituals, for which ephemeral stages were built. These were a way of achieving the monumentality so cherished by fascism at a low cost.

Only the ruins of Belchite (see Chapter 5) survived the first phase of commemoration of the regime (Michonneau 2017). Belchite can perhaps be seen as an example of the short-lived influence of fascist ideas of ruination and epic memory. Later, battlefields were, at best, remembered with monoliths or other unimpressive monuments—as we saw in the Ebro

312 *Aftermath: heritage and memory*

(Chapter 8)—often sponsored by veterans, and never became massive destinations of pilgrimage or dark tourism, as the battlefields of the American Civil War or the First World War were to do shortly after the conflict.

More effort was put into memorializing places of revolutionary massacre. Immediately after the war, an ambitious process, known as Causa General, was started to identify mass graves, document episodes of violence and identify culprits. As part of this process, many mass graves were exhumed with the support of the State and the human remains reburied in full honor (Rodrigo 2008). The places of massacre were memorialized with monumental cemeteries and memorials (as in Paracuellos or Aravaca), or crosses and plaques in the case of less prominent killings. The process was largely completed by the mid-1940s. At the same time, virtually every church in Spain had the names of the fallen engraved on its walls, including both soldiers fighting in the Nationalist Army and victims of revolutionary or Republican violence. Inscriptions were crowned by the symbol of Falange, the name of its founder (Primo de Rivera, who had been executed in 1936 by the Republicans), and the slogan *¡Presentes!* (Rodrigo 2008: 200–201). This was very much in line with fascist politics of presence (Peters 2006). Other monuments were erected in places where prominent members of the rebellion had died, such as fascist leader Onésimo Redondo (killed in an act of war by anarchists in Ávila in 1936) or General Mola (who died in an air crash near Burgos in 1937). The landscape was saturated with symbols of Nationalist victory and mourning, every corner inscribed in one way or the other: from monumental crosses to small stencils of Franco on the streets.

The Francoist cult of the dead was epitomized in the Valley of the Fallen near Madrid (Ferrándiz 2011; Solé 2017), a large complex, built between 1940 and 1959, that included a basilica, an abbey, parade grounds and a vast landscaped environment (Figure 11.1). The basilica was conceived as a resting place for the bones of the fallen during the war, which were exhumed from mass graves and military cemeteries all over Spain. Falangist ideologue José Antonio Primo de Rivera was interred in the most prominent place, under the transept, as Franco would be in 1975. At present, the basilica contains the remains of about 33,000 people from both sides. The presence of Republican dead is owed to changes in the meaning of the monument through time. It was originally devised as a monument to the fallen fighting with the Nationalists. But by the late 1950s, the political situation had changed, Spain was no longer fascist and the rhetoric of revenge of the 1940s was attenuated and finally replaced, at least in theory, by one of reconciliation: thus, shortly before the inauguration, the regime decided to incorporate also the remains of some of its enemies. There was a frenzy of exhumations and the bones of Republicans— both soldiers and people murdered in behind-the-lines right-wing violence— were taken to the Valley without the relatives' consent and often against their will (Solé 2009). The work was done carelessly and with no forensic supervision and it is not uncommon in contemporary exhumations to detect disarticulated bones in graves destroyed by the diggers of the 1950s.

Figure 11.1 Entrance to the basilica of the Valley of the Fallen, built 1940–1959.
Source: © Author.

At the time of writing, the Valley of the Fallen remains a highly contested site, particularly in relation to the remains of Franco (Ferrándiz 2019). The remains of the dictator were exhumed in the midst of a huge controversy on 24 October 2019 and transferred to the family mausoleum in Mingorrubio, near Madrid. Despite the fuss, the reinhumation was attended by only a handful of neofascist and die-hard Francoists and the controversy seems to have diminished drastically. Yet the shadow of the Valley still looms large in Spanish society.

That an overtly dictatorial monument like the Valley of the Fallen has not yet been repudiated by Spanish society as a whole has much to do with its reinvention as a center of ecumenical memory in the 1960s. This was, of course, a lie: only Catholics could be buried in the Valley and its totalitarian architecture and message—a celebration of the regime and nationalist-Catholic ideals—was in the antipodes of neutrality. In fact, the monument has always been more than just a burial place: it is a historical narrative. The history of the war (and its outcome) was written through architecture, landscape, symbols and an astute manipulation of the context. The monument was erected next to important landmarks in the history of the Spanish Crown, most notably the monastery of El Escorial, built by Philip II, with the intention of inserting the dictatorship into the long-term history of the Spanish Empire (González-Ruibal 2009; Solé 2017). It is still part of

314 *Aftermath: heritage and memory*

Patrimonio Nacional, "National Heritage", an institution managing only royal sites (despite its name), and the "Imperial Route", a tourist itinerary of royal palaces and monasteries in the Madrid region. From this perspective, the Valley of the Fallen is not radically different from a museum, if we understand by this a device to tell history through a combination of things, images and text.

While the Franco dictatorship commemorated its fallen, relatives of Republican victims were not allowed to mourn their dead in public and were subjected to stigmatization. Republican memory went underground and it was largely repressed (Renshaw 2011; Ferrándiz 2013). Yet not all was oblivion. In some cases, relatives memorialized the dead in subtle ways. They kept the memory of the killing sites and unmarked graves, visited them in secret, looked after them and left flowers. Archaeology bears witness to such practices: in the grave of an anonymous Basque prisoner who had been murdered in Villaverde del Ducado (Guadalajara) in 1937, we found material traces of care: since the moment of the killing, the neighbors looked after the grave, placed religious medals and brought flowers—until the very day we exhumed it, in July 2019. In the cemetery of Granada, relatives and comrades engraved small crosses, names and political acronyms and symbols (including a hammer and a sickle) next to the bullet holes on the execution wall (Barrera Maturana 2011).

A few exhumations were already carried out during the dictatorship in rural areas, of course without any kind of forensic supervision and without publicity, but sometimes with permission from the authorities. In the case of the cemetery of Lleida, the dictatorship allowed the relatives to mark out the graves with the bodies of around 500 victims, as long as the memorials were individual and of a religious nature (Mir 2013: 158). The political rationale was evident: the only public memory that was allowed was that of the victims of revolutionary violence—in the case of Lleida, around 500 as well. Other memories, if allowed at all, had to be private and non-political in nature. Relatives also kept mementos from the killed (Renshaw 2011): photographs, personal objects, such as watches or rings—at times bought back by the killers (Acuña 2007: 90)—and artifacts made in prison. The mother of Galician nationalist and leftist leader Alexandre Bóveda kept until her death bark from the pine tree against which her son had been shot (Acuña 2007: 95). Relatives today collect soil from the mass grave during exhumations, as well as shell casings, bullets, and other elements that were connected to the bodies of the killed (Renshaw 2011: 156–169).

Heritage and memory in democracy

It has become a platitude to say that a pact of oblivion or silence was tacitly accepted during the transition to democracy. The Left had to waive the right to memory and justice in exchange for democracy. This is only partially true. The Spanish Civil War remained very present during the 1980s and 1990s. It

Aftermath: heritage and memory 315

was certainly not concealed. Documentary series were shown on TV in prime time; books on the war and the dictatorship were published and popular during the 1980s and 1990s, and films were made on the topic, some of them highly successful—the most notable example *La Vaquilla* (1985) by Luis Berlanga, which depicts a bunch of apolitical soldiers, both Nationalists and Republicans, only interested in eating, drinking and having fun. What the politicians of the Democratic Transition did was to adopt a historicist perspective on the war in two different ways. On the one hand, the conflict was historicized, in the sense that it was assimilated as yet another episode in Spain's long historical sequence: it was no longer memory and this shift was helped by the death of the majority of the most prominent actors, including Franco himself. On the other hand, the war and the dictatorship were considered done and over, something of the past, not of the present. This was seen as a progressive move by many at the time: the Franco regime had insisted on the perpetual presence of the conflict: through its annual commemorations, its many rituals, its pedagogy and even the motto of the fallen mentioned above: *¡Presentes!* The time of the war was, therefore, the present and there were good reasons for it: Franco based his legitimacy first on his status as the winner of the conflict and then as the only guarantor of peace (Cazorla-Sánchez 2013). The choice of the Democratic Transition, thus, was not so much to erase the war from history but from memory. This came at a cost.

First, those involved in the dictatorship could not be prosecuted—unlike what was to happen in South America—and many made a smooth landing in the new democratic system, retaining positions of prominence in politics, the judicature, academia and the armed and security forces. Some, such as former minister Manuel Fraga, were even hailed as heralds of democracy, thus whitewashing their outstanding role during the dictatorship. Second, the fields of Spain were still filled with corpses: over a hundred thousand bodies lay in unmarked graves and democracy had no plans for them, except more silence. This did not prevent relatives from going and exhuming mass graves, with no scientific supervision and no State support whatsoever (Aguilar 2017, 2018). Hundreds of corpses were thus exhumed and reburied with honors mostly between 1978 and 1980 (Etxeberria and Solé 2019: 409), although some exhumations were still carried out during the 1990s.

Nevertheless, the majority of Republican victims had to wait to the 2000s to be recovered and reburied properly. Many wives, sons and daughters died without being able to find the remains of their relatives. The first scientific exhumation ever to be conducted took place in Priaranza del Bierzo (León) in October 2000 in a mass grave with 13 individuals. It was promoted by the grandson of one of the killed, Emilio Silva, who then became the spearhead of what has been known as the campaign for the recovery of historical memory (Silva and Macías 2003). Despite its strong presence in the media and wide public sympathy, exhumations only enjoyed a measure of support from the government—and quite timid at that—between 2007 and 2011, during the socialist government of President Rodríguez Zapatero, and they

316 *Aftermath: heritage and memory*

have never been considered a State affair. During the aforementioned period, 370 exhumations were carried out with public funding, which recovered the bodies of 6,000 people. Forensic interventions have most of the time depended on grassroots initiatives, but the exhumations themselves have always been coordinated by professionals since 2000 (archaeologists, physical anthropologists, forensic scientists) (Ríos and Etxeberria 2016). The work has been undertaken at the request of relatives and has been conducted mainly by the ARMH (Association for the Recovery of Historical Memory), Sociedad de Ciencias Aranzadi (a Basque research institution), Foro por la Memoria (Forum for Memory, a communist organization) and PREMEX (a project of the autonomous government of Extremadura), with many other exhumations carried out by local chapters of ARMH, Foro por la Memoria or independent NGOs (Ferrándiz 2013, 2016; Muñoz Encinar 2019). Only recently have some regional governments (Catalonia, Navarre, Basque Country and Andalusia) made more serious and coordinated efforts to recover the victims of political violence. The lack of consensus and a common State policy means that such efforts are thwarted whenever there is a shift to the right in a regional government—as happened in Andalusia in 2018.

Monuments and memorials are built to Republican victims, either in the place of assassination or in the new place of burial, when an exhumation has been conducted. But they are a manifestation of the atomized Republican memory: a myriad of individual, unrelated memorials, not linked by any master narrative, any route or any central mnemonic anchor (a national museum or monument). They are tiny, shy memorials: as if afraid to disturb. They are absorbed and neutralized by a landscape already saturated by heritage landmarks, signs, religious and secular monuments (to saints, people killed in car accidents, famous local figures, etc.). At the same time, as these new sites of memory have proliferated, the victims of revolutionary violence have to content themselves with the memory created for them by the Franco regime, which was extremely partial and often distorted: many of the victims in Republican-held territory or fallen soldiers fighting with the Nationalists were far from sympathizers of the extreme right ideology of Franco and his henchmen, but they are forced to lie under memorials that celebrate such ideology—in the Valley of the Fallen, for instance. There has been no attempt at creating a truly democratic and collective memory that repudiates all forms of political violence.

The controversy that arose with the erection of a monument in the cemetery of La Almudena, in Madrid, the scenario of thousands of executions during the Franco regime, manifests the enormous complexity of memorializing a civil war. The monument was to have the names inscribed of every person executed there, but among the 2,934 victims there were around 300 individuals who had been killed allegedly for their participation in revolutionary violence. This was used by the right to discredit the entire idea of commemorating Republican victims and eventually to dismantle it.[2] Some of the supposed criminals had been later demonstrated not to be so,[3]

Aftermath: heritage and memory 317

but others were doubtless perpetrators. Those who defend the monument argue that Republican perpetrators were recorded in the memorial just as persons who had been executed after a fraudulent trial in a dictatorship, but the justification, for me, is not convincing. By including their names, they are somehow transformed from perpetrators into pure victims. The case of criminals who are also victims is ethically obnoxious and cannot be solved in the language of conventional memorials, as was attempted in this case. The arrival of a right-wing government in Madrid in 2019 frustrated the project. With the destruction of the memorial, which was already in place, Republican victims have been, once again, deprived of their right to public memory and their names physically erased—twice in history. At the same time, the victims of revolutionary crimes have only Francoist memorials to remember them. With the growing polarization of Spanish society and the rise of the extreme right, in a global context of rising reactionary populism, the possibility of reaching a minimal democratic consensus seems far away.

The memory of the war under the new democratic regime cannot be restricted to the remains of the killed and the ways to remember them. Other things, apart from bones and memorials, have been the object of contested debates: Francoist monuments, buildings, symbols, prisons, war remains and documents (González-Ruibal 2007; González-Ruibal and Ortiz 2015; Ferrándiz 2011, 2016, 2019; Solé 2017). During the first ten years of the historical memory campaign, Francoist symbols were the object of heated controversies, which somewhat diminished after the so-called Law of Historical Memory of 2007 banned their exhibition and most were removed from public sight. The controversies anticipated those over the Confederate statues in the United States as similar arguments were put forward by those willing to retain them—that they were history, had to be respected as heritage, different perspectives on history have to accepted in the public arena, and so forth. What was debated, however, was not so much whether the Francoist legacy had to be destroyed or maintained as a whole, but which parts could disappear, which should be retained and, if retained, how they should be displayed. More recently, the debate has focused on the Valley of the Fallen and its most uncomfortable resident, Francisco Franco (Ferrándiz 2019), and on the properties acquired irregularly by the dictator and now in the possession of his relatives. The most iconic of such properties is the Pazo de Meirás, a palace in the province of A Coruña (Galicia), which was acquired fraudulently by local authorities and given to the dictator (Babío Urqui and Pérez Lorenzo 2017). The family refuses to return the palace and even to allow visitors in (something to which they are obliged, as the building is listed as cultural property). The Pazo de Meirás and some of the cultural treasures that it contains, are just a symbol of all the wealth acquired by the dictator through corruption. This is estimated in hundreds of millions of euros that the family is still enjoying, along with aristocratic titles and other privileges. Things (palaces, mausoleums, works of art) serve here to make material and intelligible the scale of the larceny and are presented as

318 *Aftermath: heritage and memory*

proof of the persistence of the Franco regime in the present. Therefore, whereas the Democratic Transition tried to change (Francoist) memory into history, the historical memory campaign, by exhuming mass graves, turning prisons and camps into heritage and exposing the perpetuation of Francoist privilege, tries to make history into memory, but one that is critical and democratic. It reminds us that the past is present not because it was glorious and legitimizes the present, but just the opposite: because the past was unjust and it perpetuates and unjust present.

War remains have also been the object of different memory, heritage and historical practices. At some point in the 1970s or early 1980s, some stopped regarding war ruins and military debris as a nuisance or a source of scrap and began seeing them as historical materials. It was usually people living next to the frontlines who started collections, which sometimes developed in amateur museums (Piñol 2011; Juan García 2012; González-Ruibal 2018b). Although they have been essential in raising awareness of war remains as heritage and have an outstanding knowledge of the intricacies of military material culture, they have also contributed much to the destruction of historical landmarks. This was, of course, understandable at a time when the vestiges were not valued as heritage, but unfortunately collecting and metal detecting has grown exponentially precisely after the Spanish Civil War legacy started to be valued by society and legally protected by regional administrations. Trying to establish collaborations with metal detectorists has proved to be extremely difficult in my own experience, although there are some remarkable exceptions. Many detectorists do not abide by any set of ethical rules and have no problem in looting and destroying human remains (Chauton 2016; Ramos 2017). The market of Spanish Civil War militaria is also expanding and many diggers are driven by economic reasons. One of the most tragic cases was the destruction of the mass grave of Monte Sollube (Basque Country), where a looter opened the burial with a bulldozer, destroying the bodies of 30 Italian soldiers so as to rob them of their daggers, which were later sold to antiquarians.[4] The activities of treasure-hunters have in cases such as this hampered the identification of the fallen. Although the suspiciousness of scholars towards metal detectorists, amateur historians and reenactors in some cases can be due to elitism and class-snobbery (Moshenska 2010), the truth is that in my particular experience in Spain, the difficulties of collaboration with amateurs (detectorists or not) have little to do with class and much more with an arrogant and militaristic macho culture, little concern with ethics, disrespect for scientific knowledge and in some cases reactionary ideologies—for a more detailed description see González-Ruibal et al. (2015); González-Ruibal (2017).

In recent years, regional and local administrations have started to manage private collections and to transform them into proper museums. The earliest projects were in the scenarios of the Battle of the Ebro (Piñol 2011). Here, COMEBE (Consorci per la Musealizaciò d'Espais de la Batalla del Ebre) was the institutional response to the growing interest in war remains: a consortium

Aftermath: heritage and memory   319

created to deal with sites and collections associated with the Battle of the Ebro. It was the first of its kind and its establishment dates to 2001. Around the same date, the first publications appeared on war sites in Catalonia (Romero 2001, 2003) and in 2007 the autonomous government of Catalonia founded Memorial Democràtic. The purpose of the Memorial, as its name implies, is to preserve democratic memory in Catalonia, from 1931 to 1980, that is, from the time of the Second Spanish Republic to the Democratic Transition, as well as that of the victims of political violence, irrespective of their ideology. It is also concerned with the repression of Catalan language and culture during Francoism. The memorial documents, manages, protects and disseminates a variety of heritage sites associated with the war and the Franco regime: from mass graves and battlefields to airfields and prisons. It also holds an audio-visual database with testimonies and organizes commemorative acts. In the Basque Country, the autonomous government created Gogora—Institute of Memory, Tolerance (*Convivencia*) and Human Rights in 2014, which is very similar in its design and scope to the Catalan Memorial.[5] Here, the narrative is broader, due to the particular history of the Basque Country, and includes the victims of separatist terrorism and State counterterrorism during the democratic period. In fact, the law establishing Gogora states that its function is "to preserve and transmit the memory of traumatic experiences marked by violence during the last hundred years". As with the Memorial, Gogora is concerned with the conservation and dissemination of the tangible and intangible heritage of the war. In both Catalonia and the Basque Country the influence of peripheral nationalism in institutional initiatives is clear, but the effort to provide an even-handed and respectful account of the war, which incorporates a variety of voices, is praiseworthy.

In Andalusia, Memoria Democrática created by the socialist government in 2017 is inspired by the Catalan Memorial Democràtic, but has a leftist orientation, which is evident in the choice of sites included in the heritage list—mostly related to the Nationalist and later Francoist repression in the region. As the Catalan memorial, it covers the period comprised between the Second Republic and the Democratic Transition. Memoria Democrática lists heritage sites associated with the war and the dictatorship,[6] includes the project *Todo los Nombres*, which records the name of all the killed or disappeared by Nationalist or Francoist violence,[7] and has elaborated a map of mass graves in the region.[8] Most of these initiatives predate the official establishment of Memoria Democrática. Thus, the map of mass graves, *Todos los Nombres* and the list of memory sites was well advanced before 2017. The mapping of graves, for instance, started in 2003. As for places of memory, the list covered 54 sites in 2018. Although most of them are mass graves, killing sites and spaces of repression, the list also includes fortifications (Gibraltar and Cádiz), battlefields (Valsequillo and Lopera), guerrilla landscapes and air raid shelters.

In all cases, the work of grassroots collectives predated institutional intervention, which has largely fed on their initiatives. This is nowhere clearer than in Madrid, which provides a very peculiar form of both

320   *Aftermath: heritage and memory*

grassroots and institutional engagement with the remains of the war and the dictatorship. Here collectives have had a crucial role in developing a heritage sensibility toward the remains of the war. An exhibition on military structures and battlefields in the region was organized as early as 1987 and was sponsored by the then socialist government of Madrid, but the initiative was of a secondary school history teacher (Montero Barrado 1987), who would also be one of the first to understand the archaeological nature of the war remains (Montero Barrado 2001). From the early 2000s onwards different collectives emerged to investigate, protect and disseminate the sites of the Spanish Civil War in and around Madrid (Schnell and Baltuille 2017), mostly concrete fortifications, but also other military and, in some cases, non-military spaces. One of the earliest and most active collectives includes GEFREMA (Group of Studies of the Madrid Front), which was established in 2004 and publishes a journal (*Frente de Madrid*); also important has been the work of Colectivo Guadarrama, which has inventoried the fortifications of several parts of Madrid and neighboring regions (Castellano Ruiz de la Torre and Schnell 2011). Other groups (Tajar, Espacios para la Memoria) and individuals have contributed to raising awareness of the relevance of the Spanish Civil War legacy, by setting up webpages, publishing guides and catalogues (e.g. Arévalo 2008b, 2012) and organizing guided tours. The Madrid administration has been reluctant to create anything that resembles the memorial institutions of other regions, but in 2016 it developed its own initiative, known as the Regional Plan of Fortifications of the Spanish Civil War, for which it set up an advisory board in which representatives from town councils, heritage institutions, grassroots collectives and academia (including myself) are present. Under this plan, the heritage directorate of the regional government has sponsored several archaeological interventions in military remains across Madrid, which are now open to the public. Interestingly, the plan is limited, as the name implies, to fortifications alone (García-Valero et al. 2019).

This is consistent with the right-wing ideology of the regional government. By placing emphasis on military remains, which in the vast majority of cases are related to the period of conventional, symmetrical warfare, they bypass the controversial nature of other vestiges and transform a deeply political conflict into a purely military engagement with two equal sides fighting for reasons that are not made explicit. Conservative politicians and managers insist in that their take on the war is apolitical and only concerned with its historical character and tourist potential. This is surely a smart strategy: they present themselves as opposed to the ideologized, partisan attitudes of peripheral nationalist or left-wing administrations (most notably Madrid's city council between 2015 and 2019), they profit from the growing and cross-ideological appeal of war remains among the population, and they present the sites as an economic asset for local communities. Of course, the non-ideological nature of the plan is questionable. By not explaining the war, they reproduce the conservative account of the conflict as collective madness, in which all sides are to blame equally—although this narrative is now being replaced by the extreme-right view that pins the blame entirely on the Left. By focusing on the military structures, the consequences of the conflict are also left unexplained and particularly the dictatorship—something understandable, as many conservative politicians come from prominent Francoist families. The harshest side of the war—materialized in execution walls and concentration camps—is elided and we are offered instead a sanitized vision of the conflict, with soldiers shooting each other from concrete fortifications. Regional authorities argue that they are promoting a heritage for peace, but it is difficult to understand why showing aesthetically pleasing pillboxes in often picturesque environments would make one value peace or understand the roots of social violence.

Notes

1 AGMAV, C. 2326, L. 50, Cp. 31. This, like all other documents referring to the University City, were located by Alicia Quintero Maqua.
2 https://www.abc.es/espana/madrid/abci-memoria-historica-carmena-homenajeara-335-chequistas-memorial-almudena-201802190059_noticia.html.
3 https://www.nuevatribuna.es/articulo/cultura—ocio/caso-fusilado-saturnino-andres-alba/20190722174903164707.html.
4 http://www.elcorreo.com/vizcaya/pg060115/prensa/noticias/Vizcaya/200601/15/VIZ-VIZ-063.html.
5 http://www.gogora.euskadi.eus/aa82-home/en.
6 https://www.juntadeandalucia.es/organismos/presidenciaadministracionpublicaeinterior/servicios/mapa/lugares-memoria-historica.html.
7 http://www.todoslosnombres.org/.
8 https://www.juntadeandalucia.es/organismos/culturaypatrimoniohistorico/areas/memoria-democratica/fosas/mapas-fosas.html.

Conclusions

In this book, I have tried to offer an account of the Spanish Civil War based primarily on archaeological remains. I have drawn heavily from my own fieldwork, but I have also used the contributions from many colleagues, as more and more archaeological projects, many outstanding from a scientific and ethical point of view, are being developed on the Spanish Civil War and the Franco dictatorship. The account provides an alternative to text-based narratives, but it does not, on the whole, contradict the historians' work—except, perhaps, right-wing revisionists. It was not the objective of the book, in any case. The idea was to cast a different gaze onto a very well-known historical episode, one that transformed Spain and had global repercussions. I have presented a different set of actors: not politicians or military commanders (whose names, as the reader might have noticed, have appeared sparingly in the previous pages), but common soldiers and civilians, often anonymous. This is not just a political, ethical or epistemic choice. It is that archaeology has more to tell about a private in the frontline than about a general in the rearguard, about a woman killed and dumped in a mass grave than about the politician who encouraged or downplayed the killing, about the perpetrator who murdered than about the intellectual who justified the murder. In my work, I have tried to rely as much as possible on material evidence: things found in surveys, exhumations and excavations, in battlefields, besieged cities, concentration camps and unmarked graves. The narrative might have sounded at times monotonous or repetitive, but then the raw material with which I have worked are shell casings, glass shards and bones. It is them that have allowed me to tell a story—a different story.

In our archaeological quest through the landscapes of conflict in Spain, my colleagues and I have found many small stories. Stories that tell about love, fear, courage, hunger, celebration, solidarity and hope. Love is the baby rattle that appeared next to the body of Catalina Muñoz, executed by firing squad. Fear is materialized in the underground shelters in Barcelona or Alicante. Hunger in the absence of animal bones in Republican trenches. Celebration are the bottles of cider drunk by the Nationalists in the last trench of the Spanish Civil War in Madrid. Solidarity and hope, the graffiti left by soldiers on the walls of pillboxes and prisons.

But archaeology is more than a collection of small stories, no matter how powerful. Taken together, archaeological data reveal something about the nature of the war. To start with, they permit a reconsideration of the chronology of the conflict, which does not start in 1931 or 1934, as revisionist historians, keen into blaming the Republic and the Left for the war, assert. It starts in 1936, after the 18 July military coup, which is when a very specific material assemblage made of pillboxes, trenches and mass graves makes its appearance for the first time in the country. And it does not actually end in 1939, inasmuch as that assemblage persists until the early 1950s, blending war and dictatorship together. It is not surprising: after all, a dictatorship is just another form of institutional violence. Archaeology reveals another temporality—a deeper one. Throughout the conflict, the material past was always present: soldiers from both sides mobilized hillforts, castles, palaces and sheepfolds that were hundreds if not thousands of years old. Bases were established in places where guerrillas had taken shelter in the Peninsular War (1808–1814) and soldiers fought and were buried in the same battlefields where the Carlists had fought and been buried a century before. They also built bunkers, trenches and shelters using centuries-old vernacular techniques—the know-how of peasants and shepherds—and put their preindustrial ingenuity at the service of total war—in making improvised weapons and recycling industrial scrap. The deeply historical landscapes of Spain made the Civil War different from other conflicts. The material past determined military tactics and shaped the war experience. By exploring these multiple temporalities, archaeology challenges the flat historicity of conventional military accounts.

Archaeological data speak about time, but also space: they manifest something about the regional diversity of the war. If we were to use material evidence alone, we would conclude that several wars were going on at the same time in the country. This is particularly the case for the isolated Northern Front, where arms, uniforms, insignia and even everyday material culture differed from the rest of Republican Spain. Material culture was not just a reflection of a region that was culturally different from other parts of the country, but it helped to produce—sometimes consciously, sometimes unconsciously—such difference, particularly in the Basque Country.

Archaeology contributes in different ways to military history. Its insight into the mesoscale of the battle is unique. By mesoscale I refer to that level which is not that of the individual soldier, who has a very confusing perspective on the events in which he is participating, nor that of the commanders behind the lines, who follow and coordinate the combats based on often messy and partial information coming from the front. This mesoscale is what has allowed me to propose a complementary narrative of the Battle of Madrid, for instance, by exploring its spatial fringe. And it is also the scale that has enabled the archaeological reconstruction of the forgotten Offensive of the Upper Tajuña. In this book, I have tried to demonstrate that even very well documented events of the contemporary era

324   *Conclusions*

can be rewritten through archaeological evidence. This is also the case with arms suppliers. While it is widely accepted that by the end of the war, Republicans were receiving military support from the USSR equivalent to the fascist counterpart, the truth is that Soviet ammunitions were much older than German ones and therefore potentially more prone to fail than their counterparts. This is knowledge that can only be acquired through archaeological materials, as the dates of the cartridges do not appear on the extant documentation—only the type. In general, archaeology problematizes the widely held assumption that the Spanish Civil War was a prelude to the Second World War. Many of the frontlines and battles that we have seen and many of the weapons and tactics remind us, if anything, of the Great War. But the conflict was not just an iteration of the previous conflict in military terms: it was a hybrid of earlier and new forms of combat, which is also reflected in older and newer weapons: rifles from the 1870s and dive bombers, old cannons from before the First World War and the latest models of tanks. Archaeology also demonstrates in an eloquent way that the armies (particularly the Popular Army) progressively learnt how to fight. Trenches and fortifications were better made, fire more disciplined, resistance stronger.

It is well known through historical documents and oral testimonies that the situation of the Popular Army of the Republic by the end of the war was considerably worse than that of the Nationalists, but archaeology offers powerful, incontrovertible evidence of the great asymmetry between the armies during the last months of the war. Medicines for gastrointestinal diseases, vitamins and nutrition complements are much more abundant in Republican than in Nationalist trenches. Conversely, faunal remains are plentiful in Nationalist positions and virtually absent in Republican ones. Recycling was also much more prevalent among Republicans and Nationalists were shooting more than Republicans did.

Graffiti have proved to be an extremely valuable source of information: the abundance of spelling errors reminds us of the high degree of illiteracy that existed in Spain in the 1930s and they also show how ideologized were many of the soldiers, something that conservatives tend to deny. According to right-wing perspectives, as soldiers massively came from levies (particularly from early 1937 onwards), they had no reason to show allegiance to the side they were forced to fight for. This was surely often the case, but probably not for many, perhaps the majority. In the absence of letters, graffiti reproducing acronyms, symbols and slogans offer a window into the soldiers' political ideas and these remained well-articulated and strong until the end of the conflict—on both sides.

Archaeology, in fact, belies the rhetoric of the war between brothers that transforms social violence into natural catastrophe. Collective craziness or misunderstanding does not explain a bloody war that raged for three years and killed 500,000 people. Political, economic, religious and social issues were at stake. Regarding politics and economy, mass graves are perhaps the best indication of the class nature of the conflict. Contemporary forensic

Conclusions 325

information about revolutionary murders is very limited, but we know who the people were that right-wing militias killed. To put it bluntly, fascists assassinated working-class people and the poor. They were also killing politicians and intellectuals, but the great majority of individuals exhumed in mass graves belonged to the lower classes. We know because they appear with the tools of their trade or with the humble attire of the wage laborer and because their bones bear the mark of extenuating labor: musculoskeletal stress, short stature, chronic malnutrition, disease.

In 2007 I published my first paper on the archaeology of the Spanish Civil War. It was titled "Making things public" and it was a programmatic statement of what my research on the topic intended to be. Since then, I have excavated the war and the dictatorship, literally and metaphorically, to show the relevance of their lessons to contemporary society—in Spain and elsewhere. I believe in the power of things to manifest history and to encourage public reflection. I have talked and written about things in open days, lectures, social media and publications. Talking and writing about the materiality of the past are ways of keeping history open and relevant to the present. This, as I understand it, is the business of archaeology.

References

Acuña, X.E. 2007. *Memorial da liberdade. Represión e resistencia en Galiza 1936–1977.* Santiago de Compostela: Xunta de Galicia.

Adonis. 2010. *Adonis. Selected poems. Translated by Khaled Mattawa.* New Haven, CT: Yale University Press.

Adrada Fernández, R. 1939. *Manual del sargento de zapadores. Especialistas en fortificación.* Zaragoza: Talleres Gráficos El Noticiero.

Agamben, G. 1995. *Homo sacer. Il potere sovrano e la nuda vita.* Torino: Giulio Einaude Editore.

Aguado Benítez, R. 2004. Apuntes para el estudio del cementerio de los italianos de Campillo de Llerena. In F. Mateos and F. Lorenzana (eds.): *Actas de las V Jornadas de historia de Llerena,* 141–158. Llerena: Sociedad Extremeña de Historia.

Aguilar, P. 2017. Las desconocidas fosas abiertas en la transición. *TintaLibre* 47: 28–29.

Aguilar, P. 2018. Memoria y transición en España. Exhumaciones de fusilados republicanos y homenajes en su honor. *Historia y Política: Ideas, Procesos y Movimientos Sociales* 39: 291–325.

Aguilar, P. and Payne, L.A. 2016. Unsettling bones, unsettling accounts: Spanish perpetrators' confessions to violence. In L. Hilbink and O. Ferrán (eds.): *Legacies of Violence in Contemporary Spain,* 166–191. Abingdon: Routledge.

Albir Herrero, C. and Mezquida Fernández, M. 2014. El hospital de sangre de los corrales de Los Garcías, el Collado (Alpuente). *La Linde* 2: 45–59.

Alegre, L. 2018. *La Batalla de Teruel. Guerra total en España.* Madrid: La Esfera de los Libros.

Alexievich, S. 2018 [1985]. *The unwomanly face of war.* London: Penguin.

Alía Miranda, F. 2015. *La agonía de la República. El final de la Guerra Civil Española (1938–1939).* Barcelona: Crítica.

Alonso González, P. 2008. Reflexiones en torno a una Arqueología de la Guerra Civil: El caso de Laciana (León, España). *Munibe Antropologia-Arkeologia* 59: 291–312.

Alonso Muela, A., Ayán Vila, X., Franco, M.A., Martínez Barrio, C. and Porto, Y. 2013. Exhumación en el cementerio de Castuera. Campaña de 2012. In L. Muñoz, X. Ayán Vila and A.D. López Rodríguez (eds.): *De la ocultación de las fosas a las exhumaciones. La represión franquista en el entorno del Campo de Concentración de Castuera,* 116–157. Santiago de Compostela, Incipit-CSIC/AMECADEC.

Alted, A. 2012. *La voz de los vencidos: el exilio republicano de 1939.* Madrid: Taurus.

Álvarez Martínez, V. 2010. ¿ Chatarra o cultura material? a propósito de los restos muebles de la Guerra Civil en el registro arqueológico de la ciudad de Oviedo (Asturias). *Ebre 38: revista internacional de la Guerra Civil, 1936–1939,* 4: 179–201.

References 327

Álvarez Martínez, V., Espósito, D. and González Álvarez, D. 2006. El cementerio moro de Barcia. Breve acercamiento a su estudio. In *I Congreso de Estudios Asturianos (Oviedo 2006)*, 13–50. Oviedo: Real Instituto de Estudios Asturianos.

Álvarez Martínez, V. and Requejo Pagés, O. 2008. El nido de ametralladoras de Fitoria (Oviedo, Asturias). Excavación arqueológica en una fortificación de la Guerra Civil Española. *Complutum* 19(2): 89–101.

Álvarez Martínez, V., Requejo Pagés, O. and Alonso Rodríguez, N. 2009. La arqueología de la Guerra Civil en Asturias. Estado de la cuestión y una propuesta de actuación: el complejo fortificado de Las Matas (Oviedo). *Erada. Revista d'Historia Contemporánea d'Asturies* 2: 79–115.

Amonio, A., Güendis, J., Hoplita, C. and Belenos, J. n.d. Granada de mano FAI "La Imparcial". Available at: http://www.amonio.es/fai.htm.

Antonio A.R., Javier B. de C. and de F. (n.d.). *Las granadas de mano artesanales del Tipo 5º Regimiento* (http://www.amonio.es/otros/Granada_mano_5_regimiento.pdf).

Arendt, H. 2004. *Los orígenes del totalitarismo*. Madrid: Taurus.

Arévalo, J. 2005. La fortificación de campaña en la Guerra Civil española. *Historia Militar* 98: 181–221.

Arévalo, J. 2008a. El Cinturón de Madrid, una fortificación olvidada. *Frente de Madrid* 12: 16–26.

Arévalo, J. 2008b. *Senderos de Guerra. 20 rutas históricas por la sierra de Guadarrama*. Madrid: La Librería.

Arévalo, J. 2012. *Senderos de Guerra 2. Rutas por el frente sur de Madrid*. Madrid: La Librería.

Aróstegui, J., i Morell, J.C. and Calleja, E. G. 2003. *El carlismo y las guerras carlistas: hechos, hombres e ideas*. Madrid: La Esfera de los Libros.

Arthur, M. 2009. *The real band of brothers. First-hand accounts from the last British survivors of the Spanish Civil War*. London: Collins.

Ayán Vila, X.M. 2008. El paisaje ausente: por una arqueología de la guerrilla antifranquista en Galicia. *Complutum* 19(2): 213–237.

Ayán Vila, X.M. 2018. Arqueología de la guerrilla antifranquista en Galicia: el combate de Repil (Chavaga, Monforte de Lemos, Lugo). *Férvedes* 9: 219–228.

Ayán Vila, X.M. 2019. Etnoarqueología de la represión franquista en A Pobra do Brollón (Galicia, España) (1936–1949). *Vestígios* 13(2): 37–61.

Ayán Vila, X.M., Santamarina Otaola, J. and Herrero Acosta, X. 2017. Arqueología, patrimonio y comunidad: el proyecto monte de San Pedro 1937–1937 (Araba, Euskadi). *Trabajos de Arqueología Navarra* 29: 123–147.

Babío Urqui, C. and Pérez Lorenzo, M. 2017. *Meirás. Un pazo, un caudillo, un expolio*. Santiago de Compostela: Galiza Sempre.

Bahamonde, Á. and Cervera, J. 1999. *Así terminó la Guerra de España*. Madrid: Marcial Pons.

Ballesta, J. and Rodríguez Gallardo, Á. 2008. Camposancos: Una 'imprenta' de los presos del franquismo. *Complutum* 19(2): 197–211.

Baquero, J.M. 2016. *Que fuera mi tierra. Anuario 2015. Intervenciones en fosas comunes del franquismo en Andalucía*. Sevilla: Junta de Andalucía.

Baquero, J.M. 2018. *Las huellas en la tierra. Anuario 2016–2017. Intervenciones en fosas comunes del franquismo en Andalucía*. Sevilla: Junta de Andalucía.

Barchino, M. 2013. *Chile y la guerra civil española. La voz de los intelectuales*. Madrid: Calambur.

Barragán, D. and Castro, J.L. 2004. Arqueología de la justicia. Arqueología de las víctimas de la guerra civil española y de la represión franquista. *Revista atlántica–mediterránea de prehistoria y arqueología social* 7: 149–174.

328 References

Barrera Maturana, J.I. 2011. Grafitos y Memoria Histórica: la tapia del Cementerio de Granada. In *XVIIe Colloque International de Glyptographie de Cracovie, 4–10 Juillet 2010*, Centre International de Recherches Glyptographiques (C.I.R.G.).

Baxell, R. 2012. *Unlikely warriors. The British in the Spanish Civil War and the struggle against Fascism*. London: Aurum Press.

Bauman, Z. 1989. *Modernity and the Holocaust*. Cambridge: Polity.

Baxell, R. 2012. *Unlikely warriors. The British in the Spanish Civil War and the struggle against Fascism*. London: Aurum Press.

Beevor, A. 2006. *The Battle for Spain. The Spanish Civil War 1936–1939*. London: Weidenfeld & Nicolson.

Beevor, A. 2011. Total Warfare in the City: Stalingrad, Berlin–and Baghdad. In S. Goebel, ed. *Cities into Battlefields*, 165–176. Abingdon: Routledge.

Bennasar, B. 1996. *Franco*. Madrid: ADF.

Bennett, L. 2011. Bunkerology—a case study in the theory and practice of urban exploration. *Environment and Planning D: Society and Space* 29(3): 421–434.

Besolí, A. 2004. Los refugios antiaéreos de Barcelona: pasado y presente de un patrimonio arcano. *Ebre 38: revista internacional de la Guerra Civil, 1936–1939* 2: 181–202.

Besolí, A., Gesalí, D., Hernàndez Cardona, F.X., Íñiguez, D. and Luque, J.C. 2005. *Ebro 1938*. Barcelona: Inédita.

Besolí, A. and Peinado, J. 2008. El estudio y puesta en valor de los refugios antiaéreos de la guerra civil española: El caso del Refugio–Museo de Cartagena. *Revista ArqueoMurcia: Revista electrónica de arqueología de la Región de Murcia* (3)3. Available at: http://arqueomurcia.es.

Blanco Vázquez, L. and Sierra, G. 2011. *Arquitectura militar española en el Rif. Recintos y fortificaciones*. Málaga: Algazara.

Blanco Gómez, D., Gómez-Bedia Fernández, B., Gutiérrez Cuenca, E. and Hierro Gárate, J.A. 2013. Fortificaciones de la Guerra Civil en la zona oriental de Cantabria: defensas costeras y líneas de contención de los ríos Agüera y Asón. *Castillos de España* 171–172:133–144.

Blanco Rodríguez, J.A. 1993. *El Quinto Regimiento en la política militar del PCE en la Guerra Civil*. Madrid: UNED.

Blanco Rotea, R. 2009. *Memoria del Proyecto del estudio petrológico de las fábricas y el sistema de abastecimiento y evacuación de aguas del Castillo de San Felipe en Ferrol (A Coruña)*. Unpublished Report. Servizo de Arqueoloxía, Xunta de Galicia, Santiago de Compostela.

Boitel, A. 2001. *Le camp de Rivesaltes 1941–1942: du centre d'hébergement au « Drancy de la zone libre »*. Perpignan: Presses Universitaires de Perpignan.

Bolado del Castillo, R., Gómez Castanedo, A., Gutiérrez Cuenca, E. and Hierro Gárate, J.A. 2010. Las fortificaciones de la Guerra Civil y el primer Franquismo en Cantabria. Un patrimonio en peligro. *Actas de las IX Jornadas de Acanto sobre Patrimonio Cultural y Natural de Cantabria*, 43–50. Santander: ACANTO.

Bonet Correa, A. 1978. Arquitectura carcelaria en España. *Historia 16*, Extra VII: 139–144.

Bores, M., Ortega, A. I., Carretero, J. M., Cristobal, E. and Martínez de Pinillos, M. 2007. ¿Quiénes están enterrados en las fosas de Costaján? Descubriendo identidades. Unpublished report. Laboratorio de Evolución Humana. Área de Paleontología. Universidad de Burgos.

Borrás, T. 1963. *Checas de Madrid*. Madrid: Bullón.

Brena Alonso, J.Á. 2016. El Museo de la Guerra de Bilbao (1937–1938). Cinturón de Hierro y turismo bélico al servicio de la propaganda del régimen. *Saibigain* 2: 4–49.

Burström, M. 2013. Fragments as something more. In A. González–Ruibal (ed.):_ *Reclaiming Archaeology: Beyond the Tropes of Modernity*, 311–322. Abingdon: Routledge.

References 329

Busch, J. 1981. An introduction to the tin can. *Historical Archaeology* 15(1): 95–104.

Busquets, C., Ramos, J., Griñó, D., Camarasa, V., Forcades, L. and Moreno, Á. 2015. Arqueologia preventiva en els espais de la Batalla de l'Ebre. De la cultura material d'un camp de batalla de la Guerra Civil a les infraestructures eòliques actuals. In J. Martínez i Tomàs (ed.): *Actes de la I Jornada d'Arqueologia i Patrimoni de la Guerra Civil al front de l'Ebre*, 33–45. Tortosa: COMEBE/Generalitat de Catalunya.

Cabrera Castillo, F. 2002. *Del Ebro a Gandesa: la batalla del Ebro, julio–noviembre 1938*. Madrid: Almena.

Calvo González Regueral, F. 2012. *La Guerra Civil en la Ciudad Universitaria*. Madrid: La Librería.

Campos Posada, A. 2018 Comer o no comer: la cuestión de abastecimiento de Madrid. In G. Gómez Bravo (ed.): *Asedio. Historia de Madrid en la Guerra Civil (1936–1939)*, 441–478. Madrid: Universidad Complutense de Madrid.

Cano, J. J. and Mendoza, Mª.J. 2017. Excavación arqueológica y estudio documental de las estructuras subterráneas localizadas en los terrenos de la c) Raimundo Fernández Villaverde, 50 de Madrid. Unpublished report. Dirección General de Patrimonio Histórico, Comunidad de Madrid, Madrid.

Capa, R. 1999. *Heart of Spain. Robert Capa's photographs of the Spanish Civil War from the collection of the Museo Nacional Centro de Arte Reina Sofía*. New York: Aperture.

Capdevila, J. 1938. *La fortificación de campaña*. Sindicato de la Industria de la Edificación, Madera y Decoración, Barcelona.

Carpentier, V. and Marcigny, C. 2014. *Archéologie du débarquement et de la bataille de Normandie*. Nantes: Éditions Ouest–France.

Carr, G. 2016. Nazi camps on British soil: the excavation of Lager Wick forced labour camp in Jersey, Channel Islands. *Journal of Conflict Archaeology* 11(2–3): 135–157.

Carrandi, F. R. 2004. Los Milagros del Cristo de Limpias. *Los Cántabros* 4: 57–63.

Carrasco, I. 2019. La fosa de la Campana (Sevilla). Un ejemplo de la represión militar tras el golpe de estado de 1936 en Andalucía. In A. Pérez-Juez and J. Morín de Pablos (eds.): *Arqueología de la Guerra Civil Española. La historia NO escrita*. BAR International Series. Oxford: BAR Publishing.

Carrión, F. n.d. Recuperación e identificación de trece víctimas mortales de la postguerra (1947–1951) en el antiguo cementerio parroquial de Pinos del Valle. Fosas comunes de Pinos del Valle. Unpublished report available at: http://granadamemoriahistorica.es/?p=441.

Carrobles, J. and Morín, J. (eds.) 2014. *Los paisajes culturales de la ciudad de Toledo: Los cigarrales. Dehesas, espacios irrigados, torres, cigarrales y trincheras*. BAR International Series 2638. Oxford: Archaeopress.

Casanova, J. 2004 [2002]. Una dictadura de cuarenta años. In J. Espinosa (ed.): *Matar, morir, sobrevivir. La violencia en la dictadura de Franco*, 3–50. Barcelona: Crítica.

Castellano Ruiz de la Torre, R. 2007. *Los restos de la defensa: fortificaciones de la guerra civil en el Frente de Madrid*. Madrid: Almena.

Castellano Ruíz de la Torre, R. 2008. La recuperación de vestigios arqueológicos de la Guerra Civil Española. Experiencia y método: el caso de Guadalajara. *Complutum* 19(2): 33–46.

Castellano Ruiz de la Torre, R. 2014. *Guadalajara y la Guerra Civil. Frente a frente*. Madrid: Colectivo Guadarrama, Grupo de Preservación Histórica.

Castellano Ruiz de la Torre, R. and Schnell, P. 2011. *Arquitectura militar de la Guerra Civil en la Comunidad de Madrid. Sector de la Batalla de Brunete*. Madrid: Comunidad de Madrid.

Castells, A. 2006. *Las Brigadas Internacionales de la guerra de España*. Barcelona: Ariel.

330   References

Castro Berrojo, L. 2008. *Héroes y caídos: políticas de la memoria en la España contemporánea*, Madrid: Los libros de la Catarata.

Cazorla-Sánchez, A. 2013. *Franco: The Biography of the Myth*. Abingdon: Routledge.

Cerrato, M., Torno, J. del and Salguero, J.M. 2002. La casa de la sierra: un episodio de la guerra civil en Extremadura. *Bicel. Boletín Interno del Centro de Estudios Libertarios Anselmo Lorenzo* 12: 25–29.

Chauton, H. 2016. La Guerra Civil en Aragón. Aproximación desde la perspectiva de la arqueología. *La Linde* 6: 136–147.

Chauton, H. 2017. Aragón en guerra. Construyendo memoria desde la arqueología del conflicto. *Trabajos de Arqueología Navarra* 29: 149–168.

Chías, P. 1986. *La Ciudad Universitaria de Madrid. Génesis y realización*. Madrid: Universidad Complutense de Madrid.

Coelho, R.G. and Ayán Vila, X. 2019. Cambedo, 1946: Carta sobre o achamento de Portugal. *Vestígios* 13(2): 63–87.

Collado Lozano, F. 2017. Refugios antiaéreos de la ciudad de Valencia: estudio, propuesta y desarrollo como paisajes culturales urbanos. *Espacio Tiempo y Forma. Serie VI, Geografía* 10: 79–101.

Colodny, R. 2005 [1937]. *El Asedio de Madrid (1936–1937)*. Madrid: Ruedo Ibérico.

Coma Quintana, L. and Rojo Ariza, M. del C. 2010. Arqueología y museografía didáctica en los aeródromos de guerra (1936–1939). *Ebre 38. Revista Internacional de la Guerra Civil, 1936–1939*, 4: 165–177.

Congram, D., Flavel, A. and Maeyama, K. 2014. Ignorance is not bliss: Evidence of human rights violations from Civil War Spain. *Annals of Anthropological Practice*, 38(1),43–64.

Congram, D., Passalacqua, N. and Ríos, L. 2014. Intersite analysis of victims of extra- and judicial execution in Civil War Spain: location and direction of perimortem gunshot trauma. *Annals of Anthropological Practice* 38(1): 81–88.

Cornish, P. 2013. Unlawful wounding. Codifying interactions between bullets and bodies. In P. Cornish and N. Saunders (eds.): *Bodies in Conflict: Corporeality, Materiality, and Transformation*, 9–21. Abingdon: Routledge.

Corral, P. 2004. *Si me quieres escribir. Gloria y castigo de la 84 Brigada Mixta del Ejército Popular*. Madrid: Debate.

Corral, P. 2006. *Desertores*. Madrid: DeBolsillo.

Corral, P. 2019. *Eso no estaba en mi libro de la Guerra Civil*. Madrid: Almuzara.

Costa, X. and Santos, X. 2008. *Galiza na Guerra Civil. Campos de concentración de Muros, Padrón, A Pobra e Rianxo*. Rianxo e A Pobra do Caramiñal, Concellos de Rianxo e A Pobra.

Costas Goberna, J., González Vicente, L. and Álvarez Caeiro, L. 2019. *Con otra mirada. El horror de la Guerra Civil Española en el Monasterio de Oia. 1936–1939*. Oia: Concello de Oia.

Cox, G. 2005 [1937]. *La defensa de Madrid*. Madrid: Oberón.

Crespo Fraguas, A., Díaz Moreno, M.A. and Isabel, S. 2019. Arqueología de la guerra Civil Española en Pinto, Madrid. In A. Pérez-Juez and J. Morín de Pablos (eds.): *Arqueología de la Guerra Civil Española. La historia NO escrita*. BAR International Series. Oxford: BAR Publishing.

Crossland, Z. 2018. Forensic Afterlives. *Signs and Society* 6(3), 622–647.

Demuth, V. 2009. 'Those Who Survived the Battlefields'. Archaeological Investigations in a Prisoner of War Camp Near Quedlinburg (Harz/Germany) from the First World War. *Journal of Conflict Archaeology* 5(1): 163–181.

Díaz i Ortells, J., Piera i Sancerni, J. and Ramos i Ruiz, J. 2008. Els refugis antiaeris de la Guerra Civil espanyola a Terrassa. *Terme* 23: 125–148.

References 331

Diego, M. 2018. Lemoatx, historia de una batalla. In J. Aguirre–Mauleón (ed.): *Lemoatx 1937. La última victoria del Ejército Vasco*, 11–87. Donostia: Sociedad Aranzadi.

De Diego, Quintana and Royo. 1939. *Belchite. Rapsodia Incompleta*. Madrid: Editora Nacional.

Díez de Baldeón, A. 1993. El nacimiento de un barrio burgués: Argüelles en el siglo XIX. *Norba: Revista de Arte* 13: 231–268.

Domanska, E. 2005. Toward the archaeontology of the dead body. *Rethinking History* 9(4): 389–413.

Domínguez, A.J., Fortuna, M., López Rodríguez, A.D. and Sanabria Murillo, D.S. 2017. De fortificación Andalusí a campo de batalla en el frente extremeño durante la Guerra Civil. Exhumación de un soldado en el yacimiento arqueológico de "Castillo de Argallén"(Península Ibérica). *Munibe Antropologia–Arkeologia* 68: 301–325.

Domínguez-Solera, S., Muñoz, M., Pérez, J C. and Peinado, P. 2018. El edificio de la Calle San Juan 10 (Cuenca): Antiguo cuartel del SIM. *Patrimonio, Historia y Humanidades. Revista del Instituto de Estudios Conquenses* 4: 46–56.

Durbán, J.V. and Clemente, E. 2016. Estudio de la planificación defensiva de la 1ª Zona Puig-Rafel Bunyol en la línea de defensa inmediata a Valencia (1938). *La Linde* 7: 70–96.

Dusselier, J.E. 2008. *Artifacts of loss: Crafting survival in Japanese American concentration camps.* New Brunswick, NJ: Rutgers University Press.

Eby, C.D. 2007. *Comrades and Commissars. The Lincoln battalion in the Spanish Civil War.* Philadelphia: Pennsylvania State University Press.

Ellis, J. 1989 [1976]. *Eye-deep in Hell: Trench warfare in World War I*. Baltimore, MD: Johns Hopkins University Press, p. 36.

Espino Navarro, R., Fuertes Santos, Mª. del C. and Rodríguez Ramos, A.M. 2019. Aquí nunca pasó nada. Memoria y ciencia versus amnesia y amnistía. Las fosas de represaliados republicanos de Aguilar de la frontera, Córdoba. In A. Pérez-Juez and J. Morín de Pablos (eds.): *Arqueología de la Guerra Civil Española. La historia NO escrita*. BAR International Series. Oxford: BAR Publishing.

Espinosa, F. 2003. *La columna de la muerte. El avance del ejército franquista de Sevilla a Badajoz.* Barcelona: Crítica.

Espinosa, F. 2010. La represión franquista: un combate por la historia y por la memoria. In F. Espinosa (ed.), *Violencia roja y azul. España, 1936–1950*, 17–78. Barcelona: Crítica.

Espinosa, F. *La columna de la muerte.*

Estado Mayor Central del Ejército. 1948. *Guerra de minas en España (1936–1939). Contribución al estudio de esta modalidad de nuestra Guerra de Liberación*. Madrid: Estado Mayor Central del Ejército. Servicio Histórico Militar.

Etxeberria, F., Herrasti, L. and Ortiz, J. n.d. *Valdediós: la memoria recuperada. Informe relativo a los restos humanos hallados en la fosa de Valdediós (Asturias)*. Unpublished report available at http://www.sc.ehu.es/scrwwwsr/Medicina–Legal/valdedios/Intro.htm.

Etxeberria, F., Herrasti, L. and Jiménez, J. 2011. *Rubielos de Mora (Teruel), dos fosas comunes de la Guerra Civil (1936–1939): exhumación y análisis de los restos*. Bilbao: Sociedad de Ciencias Aranzadi.

Etxeberria, F., Herrasti, L., Pérez de la Iglesia, L., Albisu, C., Jiménez, J., Cardoso, S., Baeta, M., Núlez, C., Palencia, L. and Martínez de Pancorbo, M. 2012. Exhumación, identificación y causa de muerte en la fosa común de AIbra-Oibar (Navarra). *Munibe* 63: 367–377.

Etxeberria, F., Pla, K. and Querejeta, E. (eds.) 2014. *El Fuerte de San Cristóbal en la memoria: de prisión a sanatorio penitenciario*. Arre: Pamiela/Aranzadi/Txinparta.

332 References

Etxeberria, F., Serrulla, F. and Herrasti, L. 2014. Simas, cavernas y pozos para ocultar cadáveres en la Guerra Civil española (1936–1939). Aportaciones desde la Antropología Forense. *Munibe Antropologia-Arkeologia* 65: 269–288.

Etxeberria, F. and Solé, Q. 2019. Fosas comunes de la Guerra Civil en el Siglo XXI: antecedentes, interdisciplinariedad y legislación. *Historia Contemporánea* 60: 401–438.

Fábrega-Álvarez, P. and Parcero-Oubiña, C. 2019. Now you see me. An assessment of the visual recognition and control of individuals in archaeological landscapes. *Journal of Archaeological Science* 104: 56–74.

Falquina, A. 2012. Una arquitectura para la represión. Informe del seguimiento arqueológico en el marco del proyecto *Rehabilitación parcial y musealización del destacamento penal franquista de Bustarviejo (Madrid)*. Unpublished report filed with the Town Council of Bustarviejo.

Falquina, A., Fermín Maguire, P., González Ruibal, A., Marín, C., Quintero, A. and Rolland, J. 2008. Arqueología de los destacamentos penales franquistas en el ferrocarril Madrid-Burgos: El caso de Bustarviejo. *Complutum* 19(2): 175–195.

Falquina, A., Rolland, J., Marín, C. and González Ruibal, A. 2010. De estos cueros sacaré buenos látigos: tecnologías de represión en el destacamento penal franquista de Bustarviejo (Madrid). *Ebre 38: revista internacional de la Guerra Civil, 1936–1939*, 5: 245–271.

Fernández Fernández, J. and Moshenska, G. 2017. Spanish Civil War caves of Asturias in archaeology and memory. *International Journal of Heritage Studies* 23(1): 14–28.

Fernández de Mata, I. 2004. The 'logics' of violence and Franco's mass graves. an ethnohistorical approach. *International Journal of the Humanities* 2(3): 2527–2535.

Fernández de la Reguera, R. 1975. *Cuerpo a tierra*. Madrid: Ediciones G.P.

Fernández Martín, A. n.d. *Recuperación de los restos humanos de la fosa común de la Guerra Civil del cementerio municipal de Teba (Málaga). Memoria*. Unpublished report available at: https://www.juntadeandalucia.es/organismos/culturaypatrimoniohistorico/areas/memoria-democratica/fosas/paginas/informe–actuaciones.html.

Fernández Martín, A. and Espinosa Jiménez, F. 2019. *San Rafael (Málaga). Las fosas: febrero de 1937 – noviembre de 1955*. Junta de Andalucía.

Ferrándiz, F. 2006. The return of Civil War ghosts: The ethnography of exhumations in contemporary Spain. *Anthropology Today* 22(3): 7–12.

Ferrándiz, F. 2009. Fosas comunes, paisajes del terror. *Disparidades. Revista de Antropología*, 64(1): 61–94.

Ferrándiz, F. 2011. Guerras sin fin: guía para descifrar el Valle de los Caídos en la España contemporánea. *Política y sociedad* 48(3): 481–500.

Ferrándiz, F. 2013. Exhuming the defeated: Civil War mass graves in 21st-century Spain. *American Ethnologist* 40(1): 38–54.

Ferrándiz, F. 2014. *El pasado bajo tierra. Exhumaciones contemporáneas de la Guerra Civil*. Barcelona: Anthropos.

Ferrándiz, F. 2016. Afterlives: a social autopsy of mass grave exhumations in Spain. In O. Ferrán and L. Hilbink (eds.): *Legacies of Violence in Contemporary Spain*, 41–61. Abingdon: Routledge.

Ferrándiz, F. 2019. Death on the move: Pantheons and reburials in Spanish Civil War exhumations. In A.C.G. Robben (ed.): *A Companion to the Anthropology of Death*, 189–204. Oxford: Wiley.

Ferrer, J.Á. 2009. Sobre el respeto y el rigor en la rehabilitación de los refugios. *Revista PH* 70: 72–87.

Figuero Maynar, Mª.J., Peral Pacheco, D. and Sánchez Sánchez, J.A. 2010. Estudio paleopatológico y antropológico de los restos óseos. In C. Ibarra (ed.): *Las fosas del Romanzal en Llerena. Historia y Memoria*, 133–233. Badajoz: Diputación de Badajoz,.

References 333

Forensic Architecture. 2014. *Forensis: The architecture of public truth*. Berlin: Sternberg.

Foucault, M. 1975. *Surveiller et punir*. Paris: Gallimard.

Frasquet Carrera, N. 2015. *Inventario y valoración de un patrimonio defensivo en término de Paterna: el caso de las trincheras de la Guerra Civil del frente de Puig-Carassols*. Unpublished Master Thesis. University of Valencia.

Fuertes Palasí, J.F. and Mallench Sanz, C. 2013. *La Batalla Olvidada*. Valencia: Divalentis.

Galdón Casanoves, E. 2010. *La batalla por Valencia, una victoria defensiva*. Valencia: Universitat de Valencia.

Gallego Vila, L. and Solé, Q. 2018. Edificios heridos. Propuesta para una arqueología de los bombardeos de la Guerra Civil Española (1936–1939). *erph_Revista Electrónica de Patrimonio Histórico* 23: 1–26.

Galluccio, F. 2003. *I lager in Italia: la memoria sepolta nei duecento luoghi di deportazione fascisti*. Civezzano: Nonluoghi.

García Corachán, M. 2005. *Memorias de un presidiario (en las cárceles franquistas)*. Valencia: Universidad de Valencia.

García-Rubio, A. 2017. *Identificación de los restos exhumados en el cementerio de La Carcavilla, Palencia*. Unpublished PhD Thesis, Universidad Autónoma de Madrid, Facultad de Ciencias, Departamento de Biología.

García Tato, I. 2016. *El destacamento penal de las minas de wolfram de Valborrás de Casaio (Carballeda de Valdeorras)*. Anejos del Cuaderno de Estudios Gallegos 42. Santiago de Compostela: CSIC.

García Valero, M.Á., Baquedano, I. and Pastor, F.J. (eds.) 2019. *Plan Regional de Fortificaciones de la Guerra Civil (1936–1939) de la Comunidad de Madrid*. Madrid: Comunidad de Madrid.

Garfi, S. 2019a. *Conflict landscapes. An archaeology of the international brigades in the Spanish Civil War*. Oxford: Archaeopress.

Garfi, S. 2019b. Archaeology and memory, and the International Brigades, in a battlescape of the Spanish Civil War. In J. Bessenay-Prolonge, J.-J. Herr and M. Mura (eds.): *Archéologie des conflits/Archéologie en conflit. Documenter la destruction au oyen–Orient et en Asie Centrale*. Actes du Colloque International de Paris. INHA, 2 and 3 Nov. 2017, 145–164. Paris: INHA.

Giddens, A. 1984. *The constitution of society: Outline of the theory of structuration*. Berkeley, CA: University of California Press.

Gil Hernández, E.R. 2017. La fortificación del territorio en el Levante peninsular durante la guerra civil española. *Revista Otarq: Otras arqueologías* 2: 77–90.

Gil Hernández, E.R. 2019. El castillo de Almansa a través de sus graffiti de la la Guerra civil española: una posición estratégica y defensiva. *Revista Otarq: Otras arqueologías* 3: 77–102.

Gil Hernández, E.R. and Galdón Casanoves, E. 2006. *El patrimonio material de la guerra civil en la comunidad Valenciana*. La Guerra Civil en la Comunidad Valenciana, vol. 17. Valencia: Diario Levante.

Giménez Caballero, E. 1944. *Madrid nuestro*. Madrid: Ediciones de la Vicesecretaría de Educación Popular.

Glover, J.A. 1946. Acute rheumatism. *Annals of the Rheumatic Diseases* 5(4): 126–130.

Goffman, E. 1968. *Asylums: Essays on the social situation of mental patients and other inmates*. New York: Doubleday.

Gómez, R. 2011. La intendencia republicana en la ofensiva del Alto Tajuña ¿Qué comían nuestros abuelos en combate? *La Voz del Frente*. Especial nº 1 "Abánades2011", 23–24.

Gómez Bravo, G. 2009. *El exilio interior. Cárcel y represión en la España franquista (1939–1950)*. Madrid: Taurus.

334 References

Gómez Bravo, G. 2018. *Asedio: historia de Madrid en la Guerra Civil (1936–1939).* Madrid: Editorial Complutense.

González Cortés, J.R. 2006. Prisioneros del miedo y control social: El campo de concentración de Castuera. *Hispania Nova* 6. http://hispanianova.rediris.es/.

González García, C. 2014. *Entre Peñagolosa y Espadán. Secretos de un campo de Batalla.* Castellón: Pata Negra.

González García, C. 2015. Prospección arqueológica de un campo de batalla. El vértice Gozalvo, Lucena del Cid, Castellón. *Sagvntvm* 47: 233–248.

González García, C. 2017. Combates en la Serra de la Creu, junio de 1938 (Llucena, Les Useres, Atzeneta del Maestrat). *La Linde* 8: 219–247.

González Gómez de Agüero, E. and Bejega, V. 2015. Arqueología y memoria: la guerra civil en el sector de San Isidro (Puebla de Lillo, León). *Estudios Humanísticos. Historia* 11: 329–350.

González Gómez de Agüero, E., Bejega, V., Ayán, X., Marín, C., Rodríguez González, J., Compañy, G., Álvarez García, J.C., Montoro, J. and González-Ruibal, A. 2017. Castilte-jón, un puesto avanzado republicano en el Frente Norte (Puebla de Lillo, León). *Ebre 38: Revista Internacional de la Guerra Civil, 1936–1939,* 7: 211–238.

González-Ruibal, A. 2007. Making things public: archaeologies of the Spanish Civil War. *Public Archaeology* 6(4): 203–226.

González-Ruibal. A. 2009. Topography of terror or cultural heritage? The monuments of Franco's Spain. In N. Forbes, R. Page and G. Pérez (eds.): *Europe's deadly century. Perspectives on 20th century conflict heritage,* 65–72. Kemble Drive, Swindon: English Heritage.

González-Ruibal, A. 2010. Fascist colonialism: the archaeology of Italian outposts in Western Ethiopia (1936–41). *International Journal of Historical Archaeology* 14(4): 547–574.

González-Ruibal, A. 2011a. Digging Franco's trenches. An archaeological investigation in a Nationalist trench of the Spanish Civil War. *Journal of Conflict Archaeology* 6(2): 97–123.

González-Ruibal, A. 2011b. The archaeology of internment in Francoist Spain (1936–1952). In A. Myers and G. Moshenska (eds.): *Archaeologies of internment.* New York: Springer: 53–73.

González-Ruibal, A. 2012a. Informe de las excavaciones arqueológicas en los restos de la Guerra Civil de Alto del Molino Abánades (Guadalajara). Campaña de 2011. Unpublished report available at https://digital.csic.es/handle/10261/49097.

González-Ruibal, A. 2012b. El último día de la batalla del Ebro. Informe de las excavaciones arqueológicas en los restos de la Guerra Civil de Raïmats, La Fatarella (Tarragona). Unpublished report available at https://digital.csic.es/handle/10261/47780.

González-Ruibal, A. 2013. Arqueología de la Batalla Olvidada. Informe de las excavaciones en los restos de la Guerra Civil de Abánades (Guadalajara). Campaña de 2012. Unpublished report available at https://digital.csic.es/handle/10261/81034.

González-Ruibal, A. 2014. Arqueología de la Guerra Civil en el término municipal de Abánades (Guadalajara). Campaña de 2013: El Castillo y La Enebrá Socarrá. Unpublished report available at https://digital.csic.es/handle/10261/101689.

González-Ruibal, A. 2016a. Arqueología de la Guerra Civil en el Valle del Tajuña (Guadalajara). Campaña de 2014. Memoria científica. Unpublished report available at https://digital.csic.es/handle/10261/129847.

González-Ruibal, A. 2016b. *Volver a las trincheras. Una arqueología de la Guerra Civil.* Madrid: Alianza.

González-Ruibal, A. 2017. Excavating memory, burying history. Lessons from the Spanish Civil War. In R. Bernbeck, K.P. Hofmann and U. Sommer (eds.): *Between memory sites and memory networks. New archaeological and historical perspectives,* 279–302. Berlin: Topoi.

References 335

González-Ruibal, A. 2018a. *Sondeos arqueológicos en los restos de la Guerra Civil en la Ciudad Universitaria de Madrid. Campaña de 2017. Informe preliminar*. Unpublished report available at: https://digital.csic.es/handle/10261/163689.

González-Ruibal, A. 2018b. Museums and material memories of the Spanish Civil War: an archaeological critique. In A.R. de Menezes (ed.): *Public Humanities and the Spanish Civil War*, 93–114. Basingstoke: Palgrave Macmillan.

González-Ruibal, A. and Falquina, Á. 2013. La cárcel de Carabanchel: una aproximación arqueológica. In C. Ortiz (ed.): *Lugares de represión, paisajes de la memoria. La cárcel de Carabanchel*. Madrid: Catarata, 100–121.

González-Ruibal, A. and Franco Fernández, M.A. 2019. *Intervención arqueológica en los fortines de la Guerra Civil de Brunete. Memoria Final*. Unpublished report filed with the General Directorate of Cultural Heritage of the Regional Government of Madrid, Madrid.

González-Ruibal, A. and Ortiz, C. 2015. Carabanchel Prison (Madrid, Spain): A life story. In M.L.S. Sorensen and D. Viejo (eds.): *War and cultural heritage. Biographies of place*, 128–155. Cambridge: Cambridge University Press.

González-Ruibal, A. and Rodríguez Simón, P. 2018. *Intervención arqueológica en restos de la Guerra Civil en el término municipal de Rivas Vaciamadrid y sondeos valorativos en la Casa de Doña Blanca y entorno. Memoria final*. Unpublished report available at: https://digital.csic.es/handle/10261/173699.

González-Ruibal, A., Marín, C., Sánchez-Elipe, M. and Lorente, S. 2010. Guerra en la Universidad: Arqueología del conflicto en la Ciudad Universitaria de Madrid. *Ebre 38: revista internacional de la Guerra Civil, 1936–1939*, 4: 123–143.

González-Ruibal, A., Compañy, G., Franco, A., Laiño, A., Marín, C., Hidalgo, P., Martínez, I, Rodríguez, A. and Güimil, A. 2011. Excavaciones arqueológicas en el campo de concentración de Castuera (Badajoz). Primeros resultados. *Revista de Estudios Extremeños* 67(2): 701–750.

González-Ruibal, A., Vila, X.A. and Caesar, R. 2015. Ethics, archaeology, and civil conflict: the case of Spain. In *Ethics and the Archaeology of Violence* (113–136). New York: Springer.

González-Ruibal, A., Rodríguez Simón, P. and Franco Fernández, M.A. 2017. *Arqueología de la Batalla de Madrid. Parte II. Sondeos arqueológicos en las trincheras republicanas de la Ciudad Universitaria de Madrid. Campaña de 2016. Memoria Final*. Unpublished report available at: https://digital.csic.es/handle/10261/143140.

González-Ruibal, A., Franco, M.A., Rodríguez Simón, P. et al. 2019. No pasaron: arqueología de la Batalla de Madrid (8–23 de noviembre de 1936). In A. Pérez–Juez and J. Morín de Pablos (eds.): *Arqueología de la Guerra Civil Española. La historia NO escrita*. BAR International Series. Oxford: BAR Publishing.

González-Ruibal, A., Rodríguez Simón, P. and Garfi, S. 2015. *Arqueología de la Batalla de Belchite. International Brigades Archaeology Project*. Unpublished report available at: http://digital.csic.es/handle/10261/114184 (2015).

Graham, S. 2004a. Cities as strategic sites: Place annihilation and urban geopolitics. In S. Graham (ed.): *Cities, war, and terrorism: Towards an urban geopolitics*, 31–53. Oxford: Blackwell.

Graham, S. 2004b. Vertical geopolitics: Baghdad and after. *Antipode* 36(1): 12–23.

Grant, J.A. 2018. *Between depression and disarmament: the international armaments business, 1919–1939*. Cambridge: Cambridge University Press.

Grup Búnquers Arenys. 2012. El refugi del Geriàtric. Un refugi antiaeri de la Guerra Civil a Arenys de Mar. *Sessió d'Estudis Mataronins* 28: 39–40.

Guiral Pelegrín, C. 1997. Un basurero romano en Madrid. *Espacio Tiempo y Forma. Serie I Prehistoria y Arqueología* 10: 479–525.

336 References

Guzmán, E. de 2001. *El año de la victoria*. Madrid: Vosa.

Heiberg, M. and Mogens, P. 2005. *Los negocios de la guerra: armas nazis para la República española*, traducción de D. León Gómez. Barcelona: Crítica.

Hernández de Miguel, C. 2019. *Los campos de concentración de Franco. Sometimientos, torturas y muerte tras las alambradas*. Barcelona: Ediciones B.

Hernández Perdomo, G. 2015. *Huellas de guerra: transformaciones urbanas y espaciales durante la Batalla de Madrid en 1936*. Unpublished Master's thesis. Universidad Politétnica de Madrid.

Herrasti, L. and Etxeberria, F. 2017. Dos exhumaciones y una misma metodología en la Ribera de Navarra: de Fustiñana a Urzante. *Trabajos de arqueología Navarra* 29: 15–95.

Herrasti, L. and Etxeberria, F. 2018 Fosas exhumadas en Lemoatx. In J. Aguirre-Mauleón (ed.): *Lemoatx 1937. La última victoria del Ejército Vasco*, 195–223. Donostia: Sociedad Aranzadi.

Herrasti, L. and Jiménez, J. 2012. Excavación arqueológica de los enterramientos colectivos de la Guerra Civil. Boletín Galego de Medicina Legal e Forense 18: 29–45.

Herrasti, L, Exteberria, F., Martínez de Pancorbo, M. and Cardoso, S. 2012. Exhumación y análisis de los restos de la fosa de Ágreda (Soria). *Boletín Galego de Medicina Legal e Forense* 18: 55–70.

Herrasti, L., Martín, C. and Ferrándiz, F. 2014. Escrito en la pared. Mensajes ocultos en los grafitis. In F. Exteberria (ed.): *El fuerte de San Cristóbal en la memoria: de prisión a sanatorio penitenciario*, 265–318. Arre: Pamiela/Aranzadi/Txinparta.

Herrasti, L., Sampedro, A.J., Diéguez, J., et al. 2014. Placas de identificación de combatientes de la Guerra Civil española (1936–1937), recuperadas en exhumaciones de escenarios bélicos en el País Vasco. *Munibe Antropologia-Arkeologia* 65: 289–312.

Herrasti, L., Argote, N., Pérez de la Iglesia, L., Serrulla Rech, F., Jiménez, J. and Etxeberría, F. 2018a. Patología y causa de muerte en dos fosas comunes de Espinosa de Los Monteros (Burgos). *Revista Internacional de Antropología y Odontología Forense* 1(2): 50–98.

Herrasti, L., Jiménez, J. and Etxeberria, F. 2018b. Abordaje integral para el análisis y estudio de una fosa común de la Guerra Civil Española. El caso de la fosa de la Tejera (Araba/Álava). *Romula* 17: 41–57.

Holguín, S. 2005. "National Spain Invites You": battlefield tourism during the Spanish Civil War. *The American Historical Review* 110(5): 1399–1426.

Howson, G. 2000. Armas para España. *La historia no contada de la Guerra Civil Española*. Madrid: Península.

Iniesta Cano, C. 1984. *Memorias y recuerdos: los años que he vivido en el proceso histórico de España*. Barcelona: Planeta.

Izquierdo, A. 2006. *Belchite a sangre y fuego*. Barcelona: RBA.

Jaén, S. 2016. Memoria soterrada: los refugios antiaéreos de la Guerra Civil en Jaén. *Clío. History and History Teaching* 42. Available at http://clio.rediris.es.

Johnston, N. 1961. Recent trends in correctional architecture. *British Journal of Criminology* 1(4): 317–338.

Juan García, N. 2012. Piezas perdidas, objetos encontrados. El valor de los recuerdos convertidos en colección como vía para recuperar la memoria. *ASRI: Arte y Sociedad. Revista de Investigación* 1: 1–16.

Keegan, J. 2000. *The First World War*. London: Vintage.

Kelly, A. 2018. *La Batalla de l'Ebre. Una crítica de la praxi arqueològica*. Unpublished BA thesis. University of Barcelona.

Köhler, A. 2017. *Passing time: An essay in waiting*. New York: Upperwestside Philosophers.

Koltsov, M. 1978. *Diario de la Guerra de España*. Madrid: Akal.

References 337

Kurzman, D. 2006 [1980]. *El asedio de Madrid*. Barcelona: Planeta.

Kuttruff, C. 2009. The Confederate forward line, Battle of Nashville, Tennessee. In D. D. Scott, L. Babits and C. Haecker (eds.): *Fields of conflict. Battlefield archaeology from the Roman Empire to the Korean War*, 294–313. Washington, DC: Potomac Books.

Lachèvre, G.J. 1932. The Stokes-Brandt 81-mm. mortar. *The Military Engineer* 24(136): 370–372.

Lafuente, I. 2002. *Esclavos por la patria. La explotación de los presos bajo el Franquismo*. Madrid: Booket.

Landa, C.G., Montanari, E.G., Romero, F.G., De Rosa, H., Ciarlo, N.C. and Conte, I.C. 2009. Not all were spears and facones: firearms from Otamendi Fortlet (1858–1869), Buenos Aires Province, Argentina. *Journal of Conflict Archaeology* 5(1): 183–200.

Ledesma, J.L. 2010. Una retaguardia al rojo: las violencias en la zona republicana. In F. Espinosa (ed.)· *Violencia roja y azul: España, 1936–1950*, 152–250. Barcelona: Crítica.

Ledesma, J. L. and Rodrigo, J. 2006. Caídos por España, mártires de la libertad. Víctimas y conmemoración de la Guerra Civil en la España posbélica (1939–2006). *Ayer* 63(3): 233–255.

Legendre, J.P. 2018. Vestiges of the Spanish Republican exodus to France. An archaeological study of the Retirada. In J. Driessen (ed.): *An archaeology of forced migration: Crisis-induced mobility and the collapse of the 13th c. BCE Eastern Mediterranean*, 55–74. Aegis 15. Louvain: Presses Universitaires de Louvain.

Leonard, M. 2017. *Beneath the killing fields: exploring the subterranean landscapes of the Western Front*. Barnsley: Pen and Sword.

Levi, P. 1986. *I sommersi ei salvati*. Torino: Einaudi.

Lizarriturri, A. 2003. *Memorias de un combatiente de la Guerra Civil (1936–1939)*. Self-published.

Llave, S. de la, Pacheco, C. and Pérez Conde, J. 2010–2011. Exhumación de la fosa común de Pradera Baja (Alcaudete de la Jara, Toledo). La arqueología de la memoria *Cuaderna* 18–19: 37–50.

Longo, L. 1956. *Le brigate internazionali*. Rome: Editori Riuniti.

Longo, L. 1966 [1956]. *Las brigadas internacionales en España*. México DF: Era.

López Fraile, F., Morín de Pablos, J. and Rodríguez Fernández, A. 2008. La Batalla de Madrid (1936–39). Excavaciones en las defensas de la capital. *Complutum* 19(2): 47–62.

López Jiménez, J., Román Román, J., Parra Moreno, I.Mª. and Gallardo Cano, S. 2008. *Informe preliminar de exhumación de fosa común con víctimas de la Guerra Civil en Grazalema (agosto de 2008)*. Unpublished report available at: http://aricomemoriaaragonesa.files.word press.com/2009/03/informe-preliminar-de-exhumacion-de-la-fosa-comun-en-graza lema.pdf.

López Rodríguez, A.D. 2006. *Cruz, bandera y caudillo: el campo de concentración de Castuera*. Castuera: CEDER La Serena.

López Rodríguez and González Cortés, J.R. 2019. Cartas prisioneras. Vida cotidiana y últimas voluntades en el campo de concentración de Castuera. *Vegueta: Anuario de la Facultad de Geografía e Historia* 19: 255–283.

Lord, F.A. 2013. *Civil War Collector's Encyclopedia: arms, uniforms and equipment of the Union and Confederacy*. North Chelmsforth, MA: Courier Corporation.

Lozano, F. and Lumbreras, M. 2015. Refugios antiaéreos de la Guerra Civil en Alicante: intervenciones arqueológicas en las plazas de Séneca y Dr. Balmis. *Lucentum* 34: 363–400.

McLellan, J. 2006. 'I Wanted to be a Little Lenin': Ideology and the German International Brigade Volunteers. *Journal of Contemporary History* 41(2): 287–304.

338 References

Madrid Ciudadanía y Patromonio. 2016. *El taller de precisión de artillería en la Guerra Civil Española*. Available at: https://madridciudadaniaypatrimonio.org/sites/default/files/blog/2016-0-25._informe_refugio_tpa_definitivo.pdf.

Manrique, J.M. and, Molina, L. 2006. *Las armas de la Guerra Civil Española: el primer estudio global y sistemático del armamento empleado por ambos contendientes*. Madrid: La Esfera de los Libros.

Marco, J. 2019. Rethinking the post-war period in Spain: violence and irregular civil war, 1939–1952. *Journal of Contemporary History*.

Marín Suárez, C., Quintero Maqua, A., Rolland Calvo, J., Fermín Maguire, P., González-Ruibal, A. and Falquina Aparicio, A. 2012. Última estación. Arqueología de los destacamentos de trabajos forzados en el ferrocarril Madrid–Burgos (España). In A. Zarankin, M. A. Salerno and M.C. Perosino (eds.): *Historias desaparecidas: arqueología, memoria y violencia política*, 117–140. Córdoba: Brujas.

Marshall, A. 1920. The invention and development of the shrapnel shell. *Journal of Royal Artillery* 10(1): 12–18.

Martín Aceña, P. and Martín Ruiz, E. 2006. *La economía de la Guerra Civil Española*. Madrid: Marcial Pons.

Martínez Bande, J.M. 1973. *La gran ofensiva sobre Zaragoza*. Madrid: San Martín.

Martínez Bande, J.M. 1978. *La Batalla del Ebro*. Madrid: Editorial San Martín.

Martínez Bande, J.M. 1982. *La marcha sobre Madrid*. Madrid. San Martín.

Martínez Bande, J.M. 1984. *La lucha en torno a Madrid en el invierno 1936–37*. Madrid: San Martín.

Martínez Bande, J.M. 1985. *El final de la Guerra Civil*. Madrid: San Martín.

Martínez Barrio, C. and Alonso Muela, A.L. 2014a. Excavaciones arqueológicas en los restos de la Guerra Civil en Abánades (Guadalajara). Campaña de 2012. Informe Antropológico. Unpublished report available at https://digital.csic.es/handle/10261/95915

Martínez Barrio, C. and Alonso Muela, A.L. 2014b. Arqueología de la Guerra Civil en el término municipal de Abánades (Guadalajara). Campaña de 2013: La Enebrá Socarrá. Informe osteológico de campo y de laboratorio. Unpublished report available at https://digital.csic.es/handle/10261/101748.

Mateo Merino, P. 1982. *Por vuestra libertad y la nuestra. Andanzas y reflexiones de un combatiente republicano, 1936–1939*. Madrid: Disenso.

Matthews, J. 2012. *Reluctant warriors: Republican Popular Army and Nationalist Army conscripts in the Spanish Civil War, 1936–1939*. Oxford: Oxford University Press.

Mazuque Lopez, J. 2009. Línia de trinxeres als boscos del Clot (Renant, Oliola, La Noguera). *Revista de Arqueologia de Ponent* 19: 159–172.

Melguizo Aísa, S. 2018. *Brigadas internacionales en el frente de Caspe. Marzo 1938*. Caspe: Los Libros del Agitador.

Mercaldo, L., Firestone, A. and Vanderlinden, A. 2011. *Allied rifle contracts in America*. Greensboro, NC: Wet Dog Publications.

Mezquida, M. 2014. Arqueología del entramado defensivo republicano al sur del Mijares en Olba (Teruel). Paper presented at the I Congreso Internacional de Arqueología de la Guerra Civil Española, Vitoria-Gasteiz, University of the Basque Country.

Mezquida, M. 2017. Excavaciones y exhumaciones de la Guerra Civil y del franquismo en el País Valenciano. *La Linde* 8: 167–218.

Michonneau, S. 2017. *Fue ayer: Belchite. Un pueblo frente a la cuestión del pasado*. Zaragoza: Universidad de Zaragoza.

Mikelarena Peña, F. 2016. Memoria y relato de la limpieza política de 1936–1939 en Navarra. *Hermes: Pentsamendu eta Historia Aldizkaria= Revista de Pensamiento e Historia* 52: 30–36.

References 339

Miller, G. L., Samford, P., Shlasko, E. and Madsen, A. 2000. Telling time for archaeologists. *Northeast Historical Archaeology* 29(1): 1–22.

Mir, C. 2013. Rememorar a las víctimas: un recorrido por los espacios de duelo de las violencias de la Guerra Civil y la posguerra en Cataluña. In C. Mir and J. Gelonch (eds.): *Duelo y memoria. Espacios para el recuerdo de las víctimas de la represión franquista en la perspectiva comparada*, 139–170. Lleida: Universitat de Lleida.

Mir, M. 2006. *Diario de un pistolero anarquista*. Barcelona: Destino.

Miró, C. 2009. Emprentes de la guerra a la ciutat de Barcelona. In Col.lectiu Desafectos (eds.): *La ciutat i la memoria democràtica*, 21–45. Barcelona: ECOS.

Miró, C. and Ramos, J. 2010. Cronotipologia dels refugis antiaeris de Barcelona. MUHBA *Documents* 6: 54–66.

Miró, C. and Ramos, J. 2011. Els refugis antiaeris de Barcelona (1936–1973). Una nova visió des de l'arqueologia d'intervenció. *Ex Novo: Revista d'Història i Humanitats* 7: 55–79.

Modesto, J. 1978. *Soy del Quinto Regimiento: notas de la Guerra Española*. Barcelona: Laia.

Mohr, C., Rohrenbach, C. M., Landis, T. and Regard, M. 2001. Associations to smell are more pleasant than to sound. *Journal of Clinical and Experimental Neuropsychology* 23(4): 484–489.

Molinero, C., Sala, M. and Sobrequés, J. (eds.) 2003. *Una inmensa prisión. Los campos de concentración y las prisiones durante la guerra civil y el franquismo*. Barcelona: Crítica.

Montero Barrado, S. 1987. *Paisajes de la guerra: nueve itinerarios por los frentes de Madrid*. Madrid: Comunidad de Madrid.

Montero Barrado, S. 2001. Arqueología de la Guerra Civil en Madrid. *Historia y Comunicación Social* 6: 97–122.

Montero Gutiérrez, J. 2009. La visibilidad arqueológica de un conflicto inconcluso: la exhumación de fosas comunes de la Guerra Civil Española a debate. *Munibe Antropologia–Arkeologia* 60: 289–308.

Montero Gutiérrez, J. 2016. Objetos de la memoria colectiva. Descifrando la materialidad de un pasado (des)enterrado. In J.F. Macé and M. Martínez (eds.): *Pasados de violencia política. Memoria, discurso y puesta en escena*, 181–212. Madrid: Anexo.

Montero Gutiérrez, J. and Valdivieso Gutiérrez, E. 2011. Claves metodológicas en el proceso de exhumación e identificación de los restos humanos de la fosa común de la Guerra Civil española de La Granja (Quintanilla de las Viñas, Burgos): aportes desde una perspectiva bio-arqueológica. *Munibe (Antropologia-Arkeologia)* 62: 479–498.

Montero Gutiérrez, J., Alberdi, P., Albo, S. and García Redondo, N. 2017. Aterrados, sacados y (des)enterrados: una mirada arqueológica a los paisajes del terror caliente de 1936 en tierras de Castilla. *Revista Otarq: Otras Arqueologías* 2: 183–204.

Montoliú, P. 1998. *Madrid en la Guerra Civil. La Historia*. Volumen I. Madrid: Sílex.

Montoliú, P. 2000. *Madrid en la Guerra Civil*. Madrid: Sílex.

Moore, P. 2002. *Stamping out the virus: Allied intervention in the Russian Civil War, 1918–1920*. Atgen, PA: Schiffer.

Moradiellos, E. 2000. *La España de Franco, 1939–1975: política y sociedad*. Madrid: Síntesis.

Morcillo, Á. 2007. La posición Jaca. El refugio subterráneo del Parque del Capricho, conocido como "el búnker del General Miaja". *Frente de Madrid* 11: 14–21.

Moreno, R., Castellano, R., Schnell, P., Benayas, D., Rodríguez Pascual, M.A. and Usaola, E. 2006. El refugio antiaéreo del Cuartel General del IV Cuerpo de Ejército de la República española en Alcohete (Guadalajara). *Castillos de España* 142–143:87–91.

Moreno Aurioles, J.M. and García Amodia, D. 2018. Los primeros bombardeos "modernos" sobre una gran ciudad. In G. Gómez Bravo (ed.): *Asedio. Historia de Madrid en la guerra civil (1936–1939)*, 205–232. Madrid: Universidad Complutense.

340 References

Moreno Martín, A. and Muñoz Ballester, À. 2011. Arqueologia de la memòria: els refugis antiaeris a la ciutat de València. *Sagvntvm. Papeles del Laboratorio de Arqueología de Valencia* 43: 177–192.

Morín de Pablos, J. (ed.) 2014. *Excavaciones en Casas de Luján II. El fin de la Guerra Civil Española en la provincia de Cuenca.* Madrid: MArq Audema.

Morín de Pablos, J., Escolá, M., Agustí, E., Barroso, R. and Pérez-Juez, A. 2002. El yacimiento de «Casas de Murcia» (Villa de Vallecas). Excavaciones arqueológicas en un fortín republicano en la segunda línea de defensa de Madrid capital. *Militaria, Revista de Cultura Militar* 16: 139–164.

Morín de Pablos, J., Pérez-Juez, A., Barroso, R. and Escolà, M. 2003. El yacimiento de Casas de Murcia (Villa de Vallecas). Excavaciones arqueológicas en un fortín republicano en la segunda línea de defensa de Madrid capital. *Militaria. Revista de Cultura Militar* 16: 139–164.

Morín de Pablos, J., Díaz, B., Barroso, R., Escolá, M., López, M., Pérez-Juez, A., Recio, A. and Sánchez, F. 2006. Arqueología de la Guerrilla Antifranquista en Toledo. La 14ª. División de la 1ª. Agrupación del Ejército de Extremadura y Centro. *Bolskan* 21: 181–188.

Morín de Pablos, J., Pérez-Juez, A., Barroso, R. and Escolà, M. 2005. La ocupación contemporánea. La guerra civil española y el hábitat en cuevas. In *El Cerro de La Gavia. El Madrid que encontraron los romanos* (Madrid, 14 de junio–25 de septiembre de 2005), 233–254. Madrid: Comunidad de Madrid.

Moshenska, G. 2010. Portable antiquities, pragmatism and the "precious things". *Papers from the Institute of Archaeology* 20: 24–27.

Moshenska, G. 2013. *The archaeology of the Second World War. Uncovering Britain's wartime heritage.* Barnsley: Pen & Sword.

Muñoz Encinar, L. 2013. Exhumación en el cementerio de Castuera. Campaña de 2011. In L. Muñoz, X. Ayán Vila and A.D. López Rodríguez (eds.): *De la ocultación de las fosas a las exhumaciones. La represión franquista en el entorno del Campo de Concentración de Castuera,* 62–115. Santiago de Compostela, Incipit–CSIC/AMECADEC.

Muñoz Encinar, L. 2016. *De la exhumación de los cuerpos al conocimiento histórico. Análisis de la represión irregular franquista a partir de la exhumación de fosas comunes en Extremadura (1936–1948).* Unpublished PhD Thesis. Departamento de Historia, Universidad de Extremadura.

Muñoz Encinar, L. 2019. De la exhumación de cuerpos al conocimiento histórico. Estudio de la represión franquista a partir del caso extremeño. *Historia Contemporánea* 60: 477–508.

Muñoz Encinar, L., Ayán Vila, X. and López Rodríguez, A.D. (eds.) 2013. *De la ocultación de las fosas a las exhumaciones. La represión franquista en lel entorno del Campo de Concentración de Castuera.* Santiago de Compostela, Incipit-CSIC/AMECADEC.

Muñoz Rojas, O. 2011. *Ashes and granite. Destruction and reconstruction in the Spanish Civil War and its aftermath.* Brighton: Sussex University Press.

Myers, A. and Moshenska, G. (eds.) 2011. *Archaeologies of internment.* New York: Springer.

Naval Education and Training Command. 1993. *U.S. Navy Seabee Combat Handbook. Nonresident training course.* Pensacola, FL: United States Navy.

Neitzel, S. and Welzer, H. 2012. *Soldaten. On fighting, killing and dying: the secret Second World War Tapes of German POWs.* New York: Simon and Schuster.

Nerín, G. 2005. *La guerra que vino de África.* Barcelona: Crítica.

Núñez Seixas, X.M. 2006. *Fuera el invasor!: nacionalismos y movilización bélica durante la guerra civil española (1936-1939).* Madrid: Marcial Pons.

References   341

Ortiz, C. 2012. Destrucción, construcción, reconstrucción, abandono. Patrimonio y castigo en la posguerra española. *Hispania Nova* 10. http://hispanianova.rediris.es.

Ortiz, C. 2013a. Patrimonio sin monumentos. Políticas de la memoria y gestión patrimonial de los sitios de represión del franquismo. El caso de la cárcel de Carabanchel. In C. Ortiz (ed.): *Lugares de represión, paisajes de la memoria. La cárcel de Carabanchel*, 42–78. Madrid: Catarata.

Ortiz, C. (ed.) 2013b. *Lugares de represión, paisajes de memoria. La cárcel de Carabanchel.* Madrid: Catarata.

Orwell, G. 1980. *Homage to Catalonia.* New York: Harcourt Brace.

Palomares, J.M. 2000. La Guerra Civil en Valladolid: notas sobre la represión en la ciudad. *Investigaciones Históricas: Época Moderna y Contemporánea* 20: 247–300.

Pascual García, S. 2010. La Guerra Civil Espanyola i el seu patrimoni: exemples de les intervencions arqueològiques a la demarcació de Barcelona i Lleida. *Ebre 38. Revista Internacional de la Guerra Civil, 1936–1938* 4: 145–162.

Peinado, J. 2019. *La defensa de la ciudad de Valencia 1936–1939. Una arqueología de la Guerra Civil Española.* Oxford: Archaeopress.

Penedo, E., Sanguino, J., Rodríguez Morales, J., Marañón, J, Martínez Granero, A. B. and Alonso García, M. 2008. Arqueología de la Batalla del Jarama. *Complutum* 19(2): 63–87.

Penedo, E., Sanguino, J., Etxeberria, F., Herrasti, L., Bandrés, A. and Albisu, C. 2009. Restos humanos del Frente del Jarama en la Guerra Civil 1936-1939. *Munibe Antropologia-Arkeologia* 60: 281–288.

Peña Muñoz, A., Blanco, J., Alonso, E., Jiménez, J. and Aguirre-Mauleón, J. 2018a. Arqueología en las trincheras. In J. Aguirre-Mauleón (ed.): *Lemoatx 1937. La última victoria del Ejército Vasco*, 89–143. Donostia: Sociedad Aranzadi.

Peña Muñoz, A., Blanco, J., Bravo, H., Leizaola, F., Sampedro, J. and Aguirre–Mauleón, J. 2018b. Restos materiales en las trincheras de Lemoatx. In J. Aguirre–Mauleón (ed.): *Lemoatx 1937. La última victoria del Ejército Vasco*, 145–181. Donostia: Sociedad Aranzadi.

Peraza Casajús, J.M. 2010. *Exhumación de la Tahona de Uclés: estudio médico quirúrgico de noventa individuos Madrid.* Unpublished PhD. Universidad Autónoma de Madrid.

Pérez Bowie, J.A. 1988. Retoricismo y estereotipación, rasgos definidores de un discurso ideologizado. El discurso de la derecha durante la Guerra Civil. In *Historia y Memoria de la Guerra Civil. Encuentro en Castilla y León (Septiembre, 1986)*, 353–373. Valladolid: Junta de Castilla y León.

Pérez-Juez, A., Morín, J., Barroso, R. and Escolà, M. Arqueología de la Guerra Civil: Excavaciones arqueológicas en las trincheras. *Revista de Arqueología* 250 (2002): 22–31.

Peters, R. 2006. Actes de présence: presence in fascist political culture. *History and Theory*, 45(3): 362–374.

Piedrafita Soler, J.I. 2010. La loma atrincherada de Fayón (Zaragoza, Aragón). Excavación arqueológica de una posición nacional de la Batalla del Ebro. In *Los años de los que no te hablé. Nueve aproximaciones a la historia social de Caspe y su comarca en el siglo XX.* Caspe: El Sueño Igualitario.

Piñol, C.M. 2011. Los espacios museográficos de la Batalla del Ebro. *Ebre 38: Revista Internacional de la Guerra Civil, 1936–1939,* 6: 159–174.

Polo Cerdá, M., García Prósper, E., Cruz Rico, E., Ruiz Conde, E., Coch Ferriol, C. and Llidó Torrent, S. 2009. Arqueología y antropología forense en territorio AGLA. La fosa común de guerrilleros de Villarejo de la Peñuela (Cuenca). In P. Rodríguez Cortés, M. Isabel Sicluna Lletget and F.J. Casado Arboniés (eds.): *La represión franquista en Levante*, 83–114. Valencia: Eneida.

342 References

Polo Cerdá, M., Cruz Rico, E. and García Prósper, E. 2010. Arqueología y antropología forense de la represión franquista en el territorio de la Agrupación Guerrillera de Levante y Aragón (1947–1948). *Ebre 38 Revista Internacional de la Guerra Civil, 1936–1939*, 4: 203–230.

Polo Cerdá, M, García-Prósper, E., Cruz Rico, E. and Ruiz Conde, H. 2012. Fosas comunes exhumadas en el territorio de la agrupación guerrillera de Levante y Aragón (2005–2011). *Boletín Galego de Medicina Legal e Forense* 18: 99–116.

Preston, P. 1994. *The coming of the Spanish Civil War*. Abingdon: Routledge.

Preston, P. 2012a. *The Spanish Holocaust. Inquisition and extermination in twentieth-century Spain*. London: HarperCollins.

Preston, P. 2012b. *We saw Spain die: foreign correspondents in the Spanish Civil War*. London: Hachette UK.

Proctor, R.L. 1983. *Hitler's Luftwaffe in the Spanish Civil War*. Westport, CT: Greenwood.

Putnam, M.C.J. 2010. Vergil, Ovid, and the poetry of exile. In J. Farrel and M.C.J. Putnam (eds.): *A companion to Vergil's Aeneid and its tradition*, 80–95. Oxford: Blackwell.

Quintero Maqua, A. 2009. El trabajo forzado durante el primer franquismo: destacamentos penales en la construcción del ferrocarril Madrid–Burgos. Paper presented at the *IV Jornadas Archivo y Memoria. La memoria de los conflictos: legados documentales para la Historia*. Madrid, 19–20 febrero, 2009. Available at http://www.archivoymemoria.com.

Radosh, R., Habeck, M.R. and Sevost'ânov, G.N. 2001. *Spain betrayed: The Soviet Union in the Spanish Civil War*. New Haven, CT: Yale University Press.

Raguer, H. 2001. *La pólvora y el incienso. La Iglesia y la Guerra Civil española (1936–1939)*. Barcelona: Península, 119–122.

Ramos, J. 2017. Intervencions arqueològiques a les fosses del front de l'Ebre. Similituds i diferéncies. In J. Martínez i Tomàs and D. Tormo Benavent (eds.): *Actes de la II Jornada d'Arqueologia i Patrimoni de la Guerra Civil al Front de l'Ebre*, 61–78. Tortosa: COMEBE/ Generalitat de Catalunya.

Ramos, J. 2018. La arqueología de la Guerra Civil Española en Cataluña. *Romula* 17: 133–154.

Reibert, T. 2014. *Die Deutschen Minen- und Granatwerfer im Ersten Weltkrieg 1914–1918: Eine Zusammenstellung der ins Feld gegangenen Geräte nebst ihrem Zubehör und ihrer Munition*. Berlin: epubli.

Renn, L. 2016. *La Guerra Civil Española. Crónica de un escritor en las Brigadas Internacionales*. Madrid: Fórcola.

Renshaw, L. 2011. *Exhuming loss: Memory, materiality and mass graves of the Spanish Civil War*. Walnut Creek, CA: LeftCoast.

Reverte, J. 2006 [2003]. *La Batalla del Ebro*. Barcelona: Crítica.

Reverte, J. 2007 [2004]. *La Batalla de Madrid*. Barcelona: Crítica.

Richards, P. 1998. *A time of silence: civil war and the culture of repression in Franco's Spain, 1936–1945*. Cambridge: Cambridge University Press.

Ríos, L. 2011. *Identificación de restos óseos exhumados de fosas comunes y cementerios de presos de la Guerra Civil y primeros años de la dictadura en Burgos (1936–1943)*. Tesis doctoral inédita. Facultad de Ciencias, Departamento de Biología, Universidad Autónoma de Madrid.

Ríos, L. and Etxeberría, F. 2016. The Spanish Civil War forensic labyrinth. In O. Ferrán and L. Hilbink (eds.): *Legacies of Violence in Contemporary Spain*, 62–86. Abingdon: Routledge.

Ríos, L., Martínez Silva, B., García-Rubio, A. and Jiménez, J. 2008. Muertes en cautiverio en el primer Franquismo: exhumación del Cementerio del Penal de Valdenoceda (1938–1943). *Complutum* 19(2):139–160.

Ríos, L., Martínez, B., García-Rubio, A., Herrasti, L. and Etxeberria, F. 2013a. Marks of autopsy and identification of victims of human rights violations exhumed from cemeteries:

the case of the Spanish Civil War (1936–1939). *International Journal of Legal Medicine* 128: 889–895.

Ríos, L., García-Rubio, A., Martínez, B., Herrasti, L. and Etxeberria, F. 2013b. Patterns of peri-mortem trauma in skeletons recovered from mass graves from the Spanish civil war (1936–9). In C. Knüsel and M. Smith (eds.): *The Routledge handbook of the bioarchaeology of human conflict*, 667–686. Abingdon: Routledge.

Robertshaw, A. and Kenyon, D. 2008. *Digging the trenches. The archaeology of the Western Front*. Barnsley: Pen & Sword, 155.

Rodrigo, J. 2005. *Cautivos: Campos de Concentración en la España Franquista, 1936–1947*. Barcelona: Crítica.

Rodrigo, J. 2008. *Hasta la raíz. Violencia durante la Guerra Civil y la dictadura franquista*. Madrid: Alianza.

Rodrigo, J. 2016. *La guerra fascista*. Madrid: Alianza.

Rodríguez Mateos, A. 2009. La publicidad como fenómeno comunicativo durante la Guerra Civil española. *Revista Latina de Comunicación Social* 12(64): 29–42.

Rodríguez Simón, P. and Pérez Esteban, P. 2011. *Vestigios de la Guerra Civil en Aragón*. Teruel. Zaragoza: Gobierno de Aragón.

Rodríguez Simón, P., González-Ruibal, A., Ayán, X., Marín, C., Franco, M.A., Martínez Barrio, C., Laíño, A. and Garfi, S. 2017. Arquelogía de la Guerra Civil en la Batalla de Belchite. International Brigades Archaeology Project. In *Actas del I Congreso de Arqueología y Patrimonio Aragonés*, 671–681. Zaragoza: CAPA.

Rojo Ariza, M.D.C. 2013. ¿ Arqueología y aviación?: la excavación de aerodrómos de campaña en el Penedés. *Revista Universitaria de Historia Militar* 2: 85–108.

Rojo Ariza, M.D.C., Arnabat-Mata, R., Cardona Gómez, G., Íñiguez Gràcia, D. and Fernández-Aubareda, I. 2010. Arqueologia de la Batalla de Catalunya (1939). Excavacions d'un tram de la línea defensiva L-3 a Subirats (Alt Penedès, Barcelona). *Ebre 38. Revista Internacional sobre la Guerra Civil, 1936–1939*, 2: 92–216, p. 205.

Romero, E. 2001. *Itinerarios de la Guerra Civil Española*. Barcelona: Laertes.

Romero, E. 2003. La Guerra Civil en Cataluña y los caminos de la memoria. *Ebre 38. Revista Internacional de la Guerra Civil, 1936–1938*, 2: 77–92.

Romero Serra, M. 2018. Intervenció arqueològica a un refugi de comandament de les Brigades Internacionals durant la Batalla de l'Ebre. Resultats de les excavacions realitzades al Molí de Ferriol (Corbera d'Ebre). *Ebre 38. Revista Internacional de la Guerra Civil, 1936–1938*, 8: 163–176.

Rubia, P. de la and Landera, J.A. n.d. *Informe histórico y antecedentes de la fosa de Valdediós (Asturias)*. http://www.sc.ehu.es/scrwwwsr/Medicina-Legal/valdedios/valdedio.htm.

Rubio-Campillo, X. and Hernàndez, F.X. 2015. Combined arms warfare in the Spanish Civil War: The assault on the Republican defence line at Fatarella Ridge. *Journal of Conflict Archaeology* 10(1): 52–69.

Ruiz, J. 2014. *The "Red Terror" and the Spanish Civil War*. Cambridge: Cambridge.

Ruiz Casero, L.A. 2015. *Más allá del Alcázar. La batalla del sur del Tajo. Toledo y Argés*. Guadalajara: Silente.

Ruiz Casero, L. A. 2017. Patrimonio de la Guerra Civil Española: el Frente Sur del Tajo. *Revista Otarq: Otras arqueologías* 2: 147–167.

Ruiz Casero, L.A. 2019. *El Palacio de Ibarra, marzo de 1937. Reconstruyendo un paisaje bélico efímero*. Madrid: AUDEMA.

Ruiz Casero, L.A. and Vega, C. 2019. Un conflicto moderno en una sociedad tradicional. Materialidad y tácticas militares en Toledo, 1936–1939. In A. Pérez-Juez and J. Morín de

344   References

Pablos (eds.): *Arqueología de la Guerra Civil Española. La historia NO escrita*. BAR International Series. Oxford: BAR Publishing.

Sabín, J.M. 1997. *La dictadura franquista (1936-1975). Textos y documentos*. Madrid: Akal.

Sáez García, J. 2005. La defensa del sector guipuzcoano de la frontera pirenaica durante el franquismo: los campamentos militares en 1951. *Brocar. Cuadernos de Investigación Histórica* 29: 167–204.

Sáez Rodríguez, Á. 2011. España ante la II Guerra Mundial. El sistema defensivo contemporáneo del Campo de Gibraltar. *Historia Actual Online* 24: 29–38.

Sagarra, P., González López, Ó. and Molina Franco, L. 2016. *Grandes batallas de La guerra civil española. 1936–1939*. Madrid: La Esfera de los Libros.

Salaún, S. 1982. *Romancero de la defensa de Madrid*. Paris: Ruedo Ibérico.

Sampedro, A.J., Sardón, A., Sardón, E. and Rodríguez Rebolledo, I. 2018. Material bélico en el campo de batalla de Peña Lemona. In J. Aguirre-Mauleón (ed.): *Lemoatx 1937. La última victoria del Ejército Vasco*, 183–194. Donostia: Sociedad Aranzadi.

Sánchez, P. 2009. *Individuas de dudosa moral: la represión de las mujeres en Andalucía, 1936–1958*. Barcelona: Planeta.

Sánchez-Carretero, C. 2013. Patrimonialización de espacios represivos: en torno a la gestión de patrimonios de los incómodos en España. In C. Ortiz (ed.): *Lugares de represión, paisajes de la memoria. La cárcel de Carabanchel*, 28–41. Madrid: Catarata.

Sánchez Hernández, N. 1997. *Un mexicano en la Guerra Civil Española y otros recuerdos*. Oaxaca: Carteles del Sur.

Sánchez Ruano, F. 2004. *Islam y Guerra Civil: Moros con Franco y con la República*. Madrid: La Esfera de los Libros.

Santacreu Soler, J.M., 2016. Les exhumacions de les fosses communes. In J.M. Santacreu Soler (ed.): *La recuperació de la memoria histórica al País Valencià: reparar i dignificar les víctimes amb subvencions estatals (2006–2011)*, 80–133. Castellón de la Plana: Universitat Jaume I.

Santamarina Otaola, J. 2019. *Segunda campaña de excavaciones en el Monte de San Pedro (Amurrio– Orduña, Araba–Bizkaia). Memoria (Campaña 2017)*. Unpublished report.

Santamarina Otaola, J., Herrero Acosta, X., Ayán Vila, X.M., Rodríguez Simón, P. and Señorán Martín, J.Mª. 2017. Monte de San Pedro. Arqueología de la Guerra Civil. *Arkeoikuska* 2016: 25–35. Vitoria-Gasteiz: Euzko Jaurlaritza-Gobierno Vasco.

Santamarina Otaola, J., Herrero, X., Rodríguez Simón, P. and Señorán, J.M. 2018. Grafitis de guerra. Un estudio arqueológico de los fortines republicanos de Ketura (Araba/Álava). *Ebre 38: Revista Internacional de la Guerra Civil, 1936–1939*, 8.

Santamarina Otaola, J., Pozo Sevilla, K. and Martín Etxebarria, G. 2019. Monte San Pedro. Tercera campaña de Arqueología de la Guerra Civil y socialización del patrimonio. *Arkeoikuska: Investigación arqueológica* 2018, forthcoming.

Saunders, N.J. 2000. Bodies of metal, shells of memory: 'Trench art', and the Great War recycled. *Journal of Material Culture* 5(1): 43–67.

Saunders, N.J. 2009. People in objects: Individuality and the quotidian in the material culture of war. In C. White (ed.): *The Materiality of Individuality*, 37–55. New York: Springer.

Schnell, P. 2012. La arqueología en el estudio de la fortificación de la Guerra Civil Española: Algunos ejemplos. In *Actas del IV Congreso de Castellología: Madrid 7 a 10 de marzo de 2012*, 93–100. Madrid: Asociación Española de Amigos de los Castillos.

Schnell, P. and Baltuille, J.M. 2017. Arqueología de la fortificación de la Guerra Civil y asociacionismo en los frentes de Madrid. *Trabajos de arqueología Navarra* 29: 169–202.

Schnell, P. and Moreno, R. 2010. Refugios antibombardeo de la Guerra Civil Española en el Valle del Henares. *XII Encuentro de Historiadores del Valle de Henares (Alcalá de Henares, Noviembre de 2010)*, 251–264. Alcalá de Henares.

Schnitzler, B. and Landolt, M. (eds.) 2013. À l'Est, du nouveau. *Archéologie de la Grande Guerre*. Strasbourg: Musées de la Ville de Strasbourg.

Schotsmans, E.M., García-Rubio, A., Edwards, H.G., Munshi, T., Wilson, A.S. and Ríos, L. 2017. Analyzing and interpreting lime burials from the Spanish Civil War (1936–1939): A case study from La Carcavilla Cemetery. *Journal of Forensic Sciences* 62(2): 498–510.

Scott, D.D. and McFeaters, A.P. 2011. The archaeology of historic battlefields: a history and theoretical development in conflict archaeology. *Journal of Archaeological Research* 19(1): 103–132.

Scott, D.D., Babits, L. and Haecker, C. (eds.)2009. *Fields of conflict. Battlefield archaeology from the Roman Empire to the Korean War*. Washington, DC: Potomac Books.

Seidman, M. 1999. Quiet fronts in the Spanish Civil War. *The Historian* 61(4): 821–842.

Seidman, M. 2011. *The victorious counterrevolution. The Nationalist effort in the Spanish Civil War*. Madison: University of Wisconsin Press.

Serrano, S. 2001. *Maquis. Historia de la guerrilla antifranquista*. Madrid: Temas de Hoy.

Serrulla, F. 2018. *Antropología forense de la Guerra civil española*. Unpublished PhD Thesis. Universidad de Granada, Facultad de Medicina.

Serrulla, F., Herrasti, L., Navarro, C., Cascallana, J.L., Bermejo, A.M., Márquez-Grant, N. and Etxeberria, F. 2016. Preserved brains from the Spanish Civil War mass grave (1936) at La Pedraja1, Burgos, Spain. *Science & Justice* 56(6): 453–463.

Serrulla, F., Etxeberria, F., Herrasti, L., Cascallana, J. L. and Olmo, J. del. 2017. Saponified brains of the Spanish Civil War. In E.M.J. Schotsmans, N. Márquez-Grant and S.L. Forbes (eds.): *Taphonomy of human remains: forensic analysis of the dead and the depositional environment*, 429–437. Oxford: Wiley.

Shackleford, S. (ed.) 2009. *Blade's guide to knives and their values*, 129–131. Iola: Krause.

Schnell, P. 2012.

Silva, E. and Macías, S. 2003. *Las fosas de Franco: los republicanos que el dictador dejó en las cunetas*. Madrid: Temas de Hoy.

Snyder, T. 2011. *Bloodlands. Europe between Stalin and Hitler*. New York: Random House.

Sociedad Aranzadi. 2008. *Informe de la inspección del pozo-mina de Las Cabezuelas en la localidad de Camuñas (Toledo) con el fin de valorar la posibilidad de recuperar los restos humanos de las personas que fueron arrojadas al mismo durante la Guerra Civil (1936–1939)*. Unpublished report.

Sofsky, W. 2013. *The order of terror: The concentration camp*. Princeton, NJ: Princeton University Press.

Solé. Q. 2009. Inhumados en el Valle de los Caídos. Los primeros traslados desde la provincia de Madrid. *Hispania Nova: Revista de Historia Contemporánea* 9. http://hispanianova.rediris.es/9/index.htm.

Solé, Q. 2016. Executed women, assassinated women: gender repression in the Spanish Civil War and the violence of the rebels. In O. Ferrán and L. Hilbink (eds.): *Legacies of violence in contemporary Spain*, 87–110. Abingdon: Routledge.

Solé, Q. 2017. The Valley of the Fallen: A new El Escorial for Spain. *Human Remains and Violence* 3(1): 3–21.

Solé i Sabaté, J.M. and Villarroya, J. 2003. *España en llamas. La guerra civil desde el aire*. Madrid: Temas de Hoy.

Sousa Fernández, D.R. 2011. Los graffitis verbales en el campo de concentración de Camposancos. In A. Rodríguez Gallardo (ed.): *La escritura cotidiana contemporánea: Análisis lingüístico y discursivo*, 125–150. Vigo: Universidad de Vigo.

Sospedra, R., Feliu, M., Wilson, A.E., Sebares, G. and Hernàndez, M. 2018. La batalla de la Fatarella, 1938. Museografia, iconografia, recreació i memòria. Un model transversal de recerca didàctica. *Ebre 38: revista internacional de la Guerra Civil, 1936–1939*, 8: 229–242.

346 References

Spars, S. 2013. Exposing those who bury the dead. A new perspective in modern conflict archaeology. In P. Cornish and N. Saunders (eds.): *Bodies in conflict. Corporeality, materiality and transformation*, 103–121. Abingdon: Routledge.

Steadman, D.W., Oliart, C., Bauder, J. and Sintes, E. 2007. *Informe del análisis antropológico de veintidós esqueletos de la Guerra Civil Española recuperados de los cementerios de La Guijarrosa y Santaella*. Report available at http://www.todoslosnombres.org/content/materiales/informe-del-analisis-antropologico-veintidos-esqueletos-la-guerra-civil-espanola.

Sturdy Colls, C. 2015. *Holocaust archaeologies. Approaches and future directions*. New York: Springer.

Suau Mayol, T. and Puig Palerm, A. 2014. Arqueologia de la reclusió a Mallorca. El cas del Campament dels Soldats d'Artà. *Afers* 78: 381–396.

Tagüeña Lacorte, M. 1974 *Testimonio de dos guerras*. Mexico, DF: Oasis.

Tejerizo-García, C. and Rodríguez Gutiérrez, A. 2019. Arqueología de la guerra después de la guerra: la organización de la resistencia antifranquista en el noroeste de la península ibérica. *Vestigios* 13(2): 10–35.

Tejerizo-García, C., Rodríguez Gutiérrez, A., Fernández-Pereiro, M., Rodríguez-González, C., Carvalajal-Castro, Á. and Romero Alonso, A. forthcoming. Paisajes de la represión y la resistencia durante la dictadura franquista (1936–1950): la Ciudad de la Selva y la guerrilla antifranquista. In B. Rosignoli, C. Marín Suárez and C. Tejerizo-García (eds.): *Arqueología de las dictaduras políticas de los siglos XX y XXI en Latinoamérica y Europa Occidental. Entre la violencia, la resistencia y la resiliencia*. Oxford: BAR.

Telleria, E. 2011. Sondeos arqueológicos en el poblado de Murugain (Aramaio, Álava). *Estudios de Arqueología Alavesa* 27: 135–216.

Theune, C. 2018. *A shadow of war. Archaeological approaches to uncovering the darker sides of conflict from the 20th century*. Leiden: Sidestone.

Thomas, H. 1994. *The Spanish Civil War*. New York: Simon and Schuster.

Thomas, J. 2011. Archaeological investigations of Second World War prisoner of war camps at Fort Hood, Texas. In A. Myers and G. Moshenska (eds.): *Archaeologies of internment*, 147–169. New York: Springer.

Thomàs, J.M. 1999. *Lo que fue la Falange: La Falange y los falangistas de José Antonio, Hedilla y la Unificación. Franco y el fin de la Falange Española de las JONS*. Barcelona: Plaza & Janés.

Thomàs, J.M. 2011. *Los fascismos españoles*. Barcelona: Planeta.

Thompson, J. 2017. From the Island of Trauma to Fantasy Island: The renovation of San Simón. In B. Sampedro Vizcaya and J.A. Losada Montero (eds.): *Rerouting Galician studies. Multidisciplinary interventions*, 109–126. Basingstoke: Palgrave Macmillan.

Tormo Benavent, D. 2015. Intervencions realitzades pel COMEBE: espais de les Devees i Barrancs, lloc de comandament de la Fatarella, Turó de Valljordà i Puntes de Millet. In J. Martínez i Tomàs (ed.): *Actes de la I Jornada d'Arqueologia i Patrimoni de la Guerra Civil al front de l'Ebre*, 21–31. Tortosa: COMEBE/Generalitat de Catalunya.

Torres Martínez, J.F., Serna Gancedo, A. and Domínguez Solera, S.D. 2011. El ataque y destrucción del oppidvm de Monte Bernorio (Villarén, Palencia) y el establecimiento del "castellvm" romano. *Habis* 42: 127–149.

Torres-Martínez, J.F., Velasco, A.M. and Farraces, C.P. 2013. Los proyectiles de artillería romana en el oppidum de Monte Bernorio (Villarén, Palencia) y las campañas de Augusto en la primera fase de la guerra cantábrica. *Gladius* 33: 57–80.

Torres-Martínez, J. F. and Domínguez Solera, S.D. 2008. Monte Bernorio (Palencia): siglo I aC/1936–1937 dC Arqueología de un campo de batalla. *Complutum* 19(2): 103–117.

References   347

Trapeznik, A. 2009. The State as an agent of industrial development: The Tula Imperial Armaments Factory in Russia. *The Journal of Slavic Military Studies* 22(4): 549–573.

Trias, M.E. 2006. Els refugis antiaeris de la guerra civil a Mollet. *Notes* 21: 107–114.

Valdés, Á. no date. El taller de precisión de artillería de Madrid. Un singular establecimiento industrial militar. Available at: www.arquitecturaviva.com/media/Documentos/3_taller.pdf.

Vallejo, C. 2007. *The complete poetry: a bilingual edition. César Vallejo.* Translated by Clayton Eshelman. Berkeley: University of California Press.

Vicent Cavaller, J.A. and Lengua, E. 2007. Inscripciones y grabados republicanos del chalet de la finca de Gil (la Valld'Uixò): nuevas aportaciones; *ORLEYL:* revista de *l'Associació Arqueològica de la Vall d'Uixò* 4: 105–129.

Vicente Gonzalez, M. de. 2014. *Los combates por Madrid.* Madrid: MKN, Ministerio de Defensa.

Vicente Gonzalez, M. de. 2015. *Los bombardeos y sus consecuencias.* Madrid: MKN, Ministerio de Defensa.

Vicente Gonzales, M. de. 2016. *Las Brigadas Internacionales y las Brigadas Mixtas en la Batalla de Madrid.* Madrid: MKN, Ministerio de Defensa.

Vicente Montoya, L. de. 2016. *Operación Garabitas. La otra batalla de Madrid.* Madrid: La Librería.

Viejo Rose, D. 2011. *Reconstructing Spain: cultural heritage and memory after Civil War,* Brighton: Sussex Academic Press.

Vilar-Rodríguez, M. and Lindoso-Tato, V. 2009. El negocio de la Guerra Civil en Galicia, 1936–1939. *Revista de Historia Industrial* 39(1): 153–192, p. 163.

Vilar-Rodríguez, M. and Lindoso-Tato, E. 2015. La explotación empresarial de las aguas mineromedicinales: la industria del agua embotellada en España (1875–2013). *Agua y Territorio* 6: 44–61.

Viñas, A. 2006. *La soledad de la República. El abandono de las democracias y el viraje hacia la Unión Soviética.* Barcelona: Crítica.

Virilio, P. 2002. *Desert screen. War at the speed of light.* Trans. Michael Degener. London: Continuum.

Webmoor, T. and Witmore, C. L. 2008. Things are us! A commentary on human/things relations under the banner of a "social" archaeology. *Norwegian Archaeological Review* 41(1): 53–70.

Zarankin, A. and Niro, C. 2006. La materialización del sadismo. Arqueología de la arquitectura de los centros clandestinos de detención de la Dictadura militar argentina (1976–1983). In P. Funari and A. Zarankin (eds.): *Arqueología de la represión y la resistencia en América Latina, 1960–1980,* 159–182. Catamarca: Brujas.

Zuazúa Wegener, N., Zuza Astiz, C. and Mendiola Gonzalo, F. 2017. Arqueología y memoria: las fortificaciones de frontera en Navarra bajo el franquismo (Auritz/Burguete y Orreaga/Roncesvalles). *Trabajos de Arqueología Navarra* 29: 97–123.

Annex

Tables

Table 1 Mass graves with remains of women that have been exhumed or where an exhumation has been attempted, based on published information.

	N° women	% women	Region	Found
Puerto Real	2	1	Andalusia	Yes
El Aguaucho	9	100	Andalusia	No
Puebla de los Infantes	2	33	Andalusia	Yes
Guadalcanal	2	33	Andalusia	Yes
Villaverde del Río	1	25	Andalusia	Yes
La Salud	3	20	Andalusia	Yes
San Rafael-Málaga	85	3	Andalusia	Yes
El Madroño	12	34	Andalusia	Yes
Higuera de la Sierra	16	100	Andalusia	Yes
Paterna de Rivera	2	20	Andalusia	Partially
Teba	7	5	Andalusia	Yes
Puebla de Guzmán	15	100	Andalusia	No
Grazalema	14	87	Andalusia	Yes
Gerena	17	100	Andalusia	Yes
Cortijo de Marrufo	5	18	Andalusia	Partially
La Campana	8	25	Andalusia	Partially
Íllora	2	100	Andalusia	Yes
Tubilla del Agua	2	13	Andalusia	Yes
Aguilar de la Frontera	4	6	Andalusia	Yes
Fregenal de la Sierra	7	18	Extremadura	Yes
Llerena	9	35	Extremadura	Yes
Medina de las Torres	14	31	Extremadura	Exhumed 1979
Villasbuenas de Gata	1	8	Extremadura	Yes
El Escurial	3	25	Extremadura	Yes
Izagre	1	10	Castile-León	Yes
Espinosa de los Monteros	4	100	Castile-León	Yes
Medina del Campo	2	5	Castile-León	In process
La Pedraja	1	1	Castile-León	Partially
Lario	1	50	Castile-León	Yes

(Continued)

Table 1 (Cont.)

	N° women	% women	Region	Found
La Carcavilla	1	>1	Castile-León	Partially
Villamediana	3	100	Castile-León	Partially
Gozón	3	100	Asturias	Yes
Valdediós	11	58	Asturias	Yes
Biscarrués	4	100	Aragón	Yes
Calvià	1	?	Balearic Islands	Partially
Flores del Sil	1	50	Galicia	Yes
La Tejera	1	33	Basque Country	Yes

Table 2 Ammunition employed by Republican troops in Casa de Vacas based on shell casings and cartridges found during fieldwork (except those marked * which are bullets). Type refers to the most likely weapon employed, other guns used same calibers.

Caliber	Type of weapon	Provenance of ammunition	Percentage
7 x 57 mm	Mauser 1893/1916 rifle	Mexico, Spain	20
7.92 x 57 mm	Mauser ZB 24 rifle	Germany, Czech Republic	2
7.62 x 54 mm	Winchester 1895 rifle, Maxim 1910 machine gun	USSR	19
0.303	Enfield P14 rifle, Lewis machine gun	United States, Great Britain	57
8 x 50 R*	Mannlicher 1888/95 rifle	Austria-Hungary	>1
8 x 50 R*	Lebel 1886 rifle, Chauchat machine gun?	France	>1
10.4 x 47 R*	Vetterli Vitali 1870/87 rifle	Italy	>1
9 x 23 mm	Semi-automatic pistol	Spain	1
0.25	FN Baby Browning 1906 semi-automatic pistol	United States	>1

Table 3 Explosives found complete or almost complete during excavation or survey in the surroundings of the University Hospital. Sector 1 is the hospice and Sector 2 the area NW of the hospital.

Type	Typology	MNI	Complete	Zone
Mortar	77 mm Erhardt Minenwerfer	1	1	Sector 2
Mortar	81 mm Valero	4	2	Sector 2
Mortar	50 mm Valero	7	3	Sector 1, 2
Mortar	81 mm Stokes Brandt	4	3	Sector 1, 2

(*Continued*)

Table 3 (Cont.)

Type	Typology	MNI	Complete	Zone
Artillery	77 mm FK96	4	4	Sector 1, 2
Bomb launcher (*Granatenwerfer*)	Spanish bomb launcher	4	1	Sector 1, 2, 3
Hand grenade	Lafitte bomb	20	5	Sector 2
Hand grenade	*Tonelete* grenade	1	3	Sector 2
Hand grenade	Fifth Regiment	1	0	Sector 2
Hand grenade	Polish wz. 33	2	0	Sector 1

Table 4 Attacks at the University City, December 1936–May 1937.

Date	Action	Place
10 December 1936	Undetermined	University City
11 December 1936	Republican mine	University Hospital
11 December 1936	Republican mine	University Hospital
15 December 1936	Mine and Republican attack	University Hospital
4 January 1937	Republican attack and Nationalist counterattack	University Hospital
11 January 1937	Nationalist attack	University City
13- 15 January 1937	Republican mine and Nationalist counterattack	University Hospital
17 January 1937	Republican mine and attack and Nationalist counterattack.	University Hospital, Parque del Oeste
19 January 1937	Republican attack	University City
21 January 1937	Republican attack	University City
23 January 1937	Republican attack	University City
25 January 1937	Republican attack	University City
1 February 1937	Intense rifle, howitzer and mortar fire (undetermined)	University City
5 February 1937	Republican attack	University City
7 February 1937	Intense Nationalist firing against Republican positions	University City
11 February 1937	Nationalist attack, Republican counterattack	Parque del Oeste
12 February 1937.	Nationalist attack	School of Philosophy and Letters
15 February 1937	Nationalist attack	University City
23 February 1937	Republican mine and attack, Nationalist counterattack	University City
2 March 1937	Republican mines and Nationalist counterattack	Parque del Oeste

(*Continued*)

Table 4 (Cont.)

Date	Action	Place
11 March 1937	Republican mine and attack	School of Agricultural Engineering
15 March 1937	Republican mine	University Hospital
18 March 1937	Republican mines and attack	University City. General attack
8–20 April 1937.	Republican general offensive	Western Madrid (Casa de Campo, La Coruña Road, University City)
25 May 1937	Nationalist attack	Parque del Oeste

Source: Based on Calvo González–Regueral (2012); Estado Mayor del Ejército (1948), and archival research at Archivo General Militar de Ávila (Spanish General Military Archive) by Alicia Quintero Maqua for this project.bullets). Type refers to the most likely weapon employed, other guns used same calibers.

Table 5 Types of artillery grenades and aviation bombs identified during survey in Lemoatx.

Type	Purpose	Provenance	User
Cannone M13 65/17	High explosive	Italy	Nationalists
Schneider 75/28	Shrapnel	Spain	Both
Schneider 75/28	High explosive	Spain	Both
Schneider 75/28	High explosive	Spain/France	Republicans
Schneider 75/28	Shrapnel	Italy	Nationalists
Krupp/Ansaldo75/27	High explosive	Italy	Nationalists
76.2	High explosive/Shrapnel	Austria	Republican
Krupp 77/24	High explosive	Germany	Republican
Flak 18 88/56	Antiaircraft	Germany	Nationalists
Schneider 105/11	Shrapnel	Spain	Both
Schneider/Vickers 105/11	High explosive	Spain	Both
Schneider/Vickers 105/11 (French fuse)	High explosive	Spain/France	Republican
Schneider 155/13 (Spanish fuse)	High explosive	Spain	Both
Schneider 155/13 (French fuse)	High explosive	Spain/France	Republican

Table 6 Remains of soldiers recovered in the Ebro in the context of archaeological interventions and for which information has been made available.

Place	Municipality	MNI	Context	Side
Mas de la Pila – Cucut	Corbera	35	Open field	Both?
Vall de la Torre	Corbera	5	Open field	?
Barranc de les Vimenoses	Corbera	2	Unknown	?
Coll del Coso	Corbera	14	Trenches	Both?

(Continued)

Table 6 (Cont.)

Place	Municipality	MNI	Context	Side
Parc Eòlic EGC 14	Corbera	2	Trenches	?
Parc Eòlic 2	Corbera	2	Mass grave	?
Vallfogones	Corbera	13	Trenches/open field	Both?
Mas d'en Grau	Gandesa	10	Mass grave	Republican
Pou del Baró	Gandesa	4	Mass grave	Republican
Lo Molló	Pobla de Masaluca	1	Mass grave	Republican
Raïmats	La Fatarella	1	Trench	Republican
Pernafeites	Miravet	106	Mass graves and individual graves	Republican

Index

Page numbers in italics refer to figures. Page numbers in bold refer to tables. Page numbers followed by 'n' refer to notes.

.25 Remington cartridge 216
.44 Smith &Wesson 272
1st Army Corps 265
1st Bandera del Tercio 194
1st Gerona Battalion 171
2 Mixed Brigade 170, 171, 172, 178, 188, 191
2 Navarre Brigade 115, 116
3rd Arapiles Battalion 194
3rd Tabor de Regulares de Alhucemas 194
4 Mountain Battalion of Arapiles 140–141
4 Navarre Division 220
5 Brigade 104
5 Division 170
6 Division 170
6 Navarre Brigade 140–141
7 Division 90–91, 254
XI International Brigade 43, 45, 48, 57, 60, 63, 64, 121, 132, 220
11 Division 213
XII International Brigade 60, 64, 107, 108, 145, 166, 167
13th Division 132
XIII International Brigade 216
XIV International Brigade 166, 167, 168
14 Division 170
XV Army Corps 216, 220, 221, 228
XV International Brigade 104, 121, 131, 132, 165, 166, 167, 216, 220, 221, 231
16 Division 266, 267
17 Burgos Battalion 210
XVIII Army Corps 217
18 Mixed Brigade 104
20 Division 258, 262

20 San Quintín Battalion 189
35 Division 220, 221
39 Mixed Brigade 170, 171–172, 188, 191, 192, 193, 194
42 Division 210, 211
43 Division 213–214
50 Division of the Moroccan Army Corps 216, 220, 225
66 Mixed Brigade 188, 191, 194
70 Mixed Brigade 173
75 Division 170
82 Division 220–221
84 Mixed Brigade 164
95 Mixed Brigade 164
102 Division 210
106 Mixed Brigade 145
109 Mixed Brigade 292
138 Mixed Brigade 146, *146*, 148, 152, 251, 253
152 Moroccan Division 173, 191, 220
226 Mixed Brigade 211
261 Battalion 190, 191
266 Serrallo Battalion 189
267 Cazadores de San Fernando Battalion 178, 189

Abánades 146–147, 149; El Castillo 237–244, *238*, *241*; memorials 310–311; Offensive of the Upper Tajuña 170–176, *172*, *175*, 181, 188, 193, 194
active defense 96–97, *97*
Adonis 73
Adrada, Roque 127, *128*

354 *Index*

aerial bombings: Alto de la Casilla 248; Aragón Offensive 165; Barcelona 205–206; Battle of La Nava 191; Battle of the Ebro 221; Levante Offensive 202–207, *203*, *204*; Madrid 91, 92, 99; Mount Lemoatx 115, **351**; *see also* bombings
africanistas 74
Agramunt (Lleida) 231
Aguilar de la Frontera (Córdoba) 24, 28, 29
airfields 218–219
Albatera concentration camp (Alicante) 287–288
Alberti, Rafael 39, 72
Alcalá de Henares xxiv, 98
Alcalá de la Selva (Teruel) 278
Alcañiz 166
La Alcarria 145
Alcaudete (Toledo) 270
Alcázar castle 40
alcohol 185, 193; bars 244–245; and celebrations 266–268, *267*, 322; and First World War 148; and guerrillas 273; and killings 29–30, 293; and mine warfare 85; in Nationalist lines 242, 244–245; in Republican lines 216, 249; and winter of 1938 148
Alegre, David 102
Alexievich, Svetlana 3
Alfés (Lleida) 218
Algeciras (Cádiz) xx
Alicante 203–204, *204*, 263, 322
Almansa castle 44
Almería 203
La Almudena cemetery 316
Alphonse XII 45, 186
Alphonse XIII 10, 33, 76, 186
Altable (Burgos) 30
Alto de la Casilla 194, 247–249, *249*
Alto del Molino 146, *146*, 147–153, *151*, 170
Álvarez Flórez, Luz 141
American Civil War 48, 60, 147, 312
amputations 214
anarchist grenade 53
Anarchist Iberian Federation (FAI) 16, 103
anarchists 11, 16, 28, 37n2, 52, 57, 65, 102, 103, 170, 171–172, 188, 205
Ancien Regime 9–10, 110
Andalusia 20–21, 316; assassination of guerrillas in 278; Battle of Valsquillo

258; female corpses in 23; mass graves in 20, 23; Memoria Democrática 319
André Marty Battalion 108
Annual, Battle of 23
antemortem trauma 286
anti-aircraft guns 96–97, *97*, 205
anti-modernism 10, 73
anti-tank guns 259, 260
Aragón 6, 9, 102, 130, 231; Aragón Offensive 165, 218, 237; Mediana de Aragón 6, 132–133, 135, 153–157, *155*, 158–160, *158*, *160*, *161*, 162, *163*; retreat 164–165, *166*
Aranda de Duero (Burgos) 34
L'Aranyó (Lleida) 218
Aravaca 32, 49, 100, 101
Arce Rodríguez, Pedro 305
Arenys de Mar (Barcelona) 206
Argüelles (Madrid), bombing of 91, 92, *93*
Army of Africa 11, 12, 21, 23, 40, 143
Army of Andalusia 247
Arroyo del Romanzal (Llerena, Badajoz) 24, 36
artillery 50, 67, 69, 118, 199; Aragón Offensive 165; Battle of the Ebro 221, 222; bombing of Alto de la Casilla 248; bombing of Madrid 91–96, *94*; and distance 96; El Castillo (Abánades) 242; and head protection 138; La Enebrá, siege of 185; Levante Offensive 199; Mediana de Aragón 156; Mount Bernorio 136; Mount Lemoatx **351**; Offensive of the Upper Tajuña 194; Parapet of Death 133, *134*; and trench warfare 171; workshop 98
Association for the Recovery of Historical Memory (ARMH) 22, 316
Astra 400 pistol 30, 176
Astray, Millán 80
Asturias 11, 110, 118, 135, 139–140, 193
Asylum of Santa Cristina 65, 76, 77, 266; canteen 244–245, *245*; drainage system of 80–82; laundry 77, 79, 80; materials excavated in 79, 80, *81*; mine warfare 83; mining tunnels 80; pavilion 77, 78–79, 80; transformation of *78*; trenches/dugouts 79–80; *vaquería* (cowshed) 77–78
Atzeneta del Maestrat (Castellón) 199
Augusto Sacco & Co 240–241
Aurelio Gamir's Bardanol 151
autopsies 13

Aviazone Legionaria 205, 221
Axis, involvement in Spanish Civil War 198, 199
Ayán Vila, Xurxo 228, 271, 275, 276
Azaña, Manuel 13

Badajoz 6; Arroyo del Romanzal 24, 36; Fregenal de la Sierra 24, 36, *37*; incineration of corpses in 26; *see also* Castuera concentration camp (Badajoz)
Bajo Bueno, Francisco 305
Le Barcarés concentration camp 235
Barcelona 27–28, 31, 73, 98, 176, 195, 322; air raids and bomb shelters 205–207; Plaça de Diamant 206; Pujalt boot camp 217–218; Sant Pau d'Ordal 232; Turó de la Rovira 205
Barcia cemetery 140
bars 244–245
bartering: in concentration camps 284; between Spanish and Italian soldiers 243
Bartomeu, Maximino 43
Basque Country 10, 110–113, *111*, 135, 269; common elements 119–121; Gogora 319; Ketura (Zigoitia) 112–113; mass graves in 20; materiality of war in 121; Mount Lemoatx 115–119, *117*, 121, **351**; Mount Murugain (Mondragón) 111–112; Mount San Pedro 113–115, *114*, 121
Basque Nationalist Party (PNV) 110, 115, 119
Battle of Annual 23
Battle of Brunete 121, 132
Battle of Caspe 166–168
Battle of Guadalajara 104, 106–110, 146, 233, 242
Battle of Jarama 104–106, 254
Battle of La Nava 176, 188–189, 248; Republican assault *189*; between stone walls and concrete pillboxes 189–192; Valdelagua sheepfold 192–193
Battle of Madrid 4–5, 39, 71–72, 219, 323; bombing of civilians 91; Casa de Campo, fight in 42–56; Casa de Vacas 45–56; and *sacas* 16; University Hospital 65–71, *66*; *see also* University City
Battle of Peñarroya *see* Battle of Valsquillo
Battle of Santander 135
Battle of Stalingrad 82

Battle of Teruel 6, 102, 153, 164; *see also* Teruel
Battle of the Ebro 6–7, 208–209, 318–319; camps, airfields and downed planes 215–219; Fayón-Mequinenza sector 210–211, *212*; frontline 208; Hill 562 221–223, 224–228, *225*; human remains 212–215, *213*, **351–352**; last day of 219–231; last man standing 228–231, *229*; map *209*; memorials 310; pillboxes, fighting in 222–224, *223*; Terra Alta 208–209; trench, defending 224–228, *225*
Battle of the Segre 214
Battle of Tudela 237
Battle of Valsquillo 258
Battle of Villarreal 110, 113
Bauman, Zygmunt 96
beef 137
Belchite 5–6, 121–123, 165; Church of Saint Augustine *122*, 131; Dehesa de la Villa 124, *125*, *128*; El Saso 126–131, *128*; fortifications around *128*; minor seminary 123–125, *125*; Parapet of Death 132–133, *134*, 135; rubble 131–132; ruins 311
Beretta M1934 233
Berlanga, Luis 315
Berthier rifle 114
Bilbao 110, 119, 311
Bilbao grenade 117, 118
Black Death 248
Blanco Reguero, Hilario 119
blocaos (blockhaus) 42, 74, 124, 237–238
Boer War 198
Bolín, Luis 311
bolt-action rifles 60–61, 112, 193
bombings 231; of cities 73, 74; Durango 111; Gernika 115; impact on buildings 92; Levante Offensive 202–207, *203*, *204*; Madrid 91–99, *93*, *94*; Mount Lemoatx 115, **351**; strategic 202; tactical 202; *see also* aerial bombings
bomb launchers 67, 69
bomb shelters 80, 84, 97–99, 202, 203–205, *204*, 206
boot camps 217
Bordes, Enrique 92
Borriol (Castellón) 200
botijo 284
Bóveda, Alexandre 314
Bram concentration camp 235

356   *Index*

Breda M1930 machine gun 108, 155–156, 190, 211, 225
Breda M35 grenade 182, 242
Brens concentration camp 235
Brigada Político-Social 100
Brihuega 107
Brixia M1935 mortar 108, 155–156, 198
bronchopulmonary diseases 151
Browning M1918 machine gun 186
Brunete: Battle of Brunete 121, 132; Republican offensive (1939) 7, 258–262, *259*, *261*
bullets 159–160; Enfield rifle 62–63, 65, 66; German 7.92 mm bullets 159; lead 127; material of 159; from Mediana de Aragón 159, *160*; Remington 60; rounded bullets 159; Soviet 7.62 mm bullets 159, 182, 192; Spanish 7 mm bullets 61, 159, 175, 294; terminal ballistics 157, 159; Vetterli 52, 60
Burgos, mass graves in 14–16, *15*, 20, 21, 34
burials 145, 174–175, *175*, 292; destruction of 27; with face down 29; shallow graves *28*, 29, 175, 180, 185, 199, 200; types of 31; *see also* cemeteries; mass graves
Bustarviejo (forced labor camp) 8, 301–302, *301*, *303*, 305
Buzanca 105–106

Caballero, Father 244
La Cadellada (Oviedo) 140–141
Calatayud 130
Calvo González-Regueral, F. 64
Cambedo (Portugal) 273–276, *275*
La Campana (Seville) 24, 27
Camp dels Soldats (Artà, Majorca) 301
Campillo de Llerena 145
Campo de los Almendros (Alicante) 287
Camposancos 118, 308
Camuñas (Toledo) 16, 27, 34
canning 193, 240
Canredondo 152, 251
Cantabria 110, 135, 193
Cantabrian Mountains 136, *138*
Cantabrian Wars 136
Capa, Robert 39, 47, 56
El Capricho Park (Madrid) 99
Carabaña 258
Carabanchel prison 7–8, 297–299, *298*
Carabineros 198, 199
La Carcavilla (Palencia) 19–20

Carcedo de Bureba (Burgos) 34
Cárdenas, Lázaro 41
Carlists 10, 11, 110, 111, 123, 124, 131, 167, 178, 323
Carlist Wars 10, 60, 74, 195
Cartagena (Murcia) 98, 203
Casa de Campo 4, 5, 90, 220; artillery bases in 93–94, *94*; fight in 42–56, *44*; *see also* Casa de Vacas
Casa de la Sierra 144
Casa de Vacas 55; ammunition employed by Republican troops in **349**; forgotten battlefield of 55–56; last stand in 45–49; traces of combat 49–55, *51*; trenches 47–52, *47*, 55
Casa de Velázquez 65
Casado, Segismundo 262–263, 266
Casaio (Ourense) 271, *274*
Casas de Luján (Cuenca) 262
Casas de Murcia (Vallecas) 255
Caspe, Battle of 166–168
Castejón, Antonio 43, 210
Castellón 195, 198–199
Castells, Andreu 65
Castile 9, 20, 24
El Castillo (Abánades) 237–244, *238*, *241*
Castiltejón (León) 136–139, *138*
Castro Veiga, José 271
Castuera concentration camp (Badajoz) 7, 280, 281; barracks 281, 283, 295; commissary 284; communication between relatives and inmates 290; drinks 284; finds from *291*; food 283, 284; handicrafts 290; health and hygiene 284–285, 286; latrines 286–287, *287*; map *282*; mass graves 29, 30, 36, 292–295, *294*, *296*; perimeter ditches 281–283; profession of inmates 293; relatives of prisoners 290–292; religious objects 293
Catalonia 10, 11, 13, 165, 211, 258; *cava* 148; defensive lines 232; fall of 253; Lleida province 214–215, 218, 314; Memorial Democràtic 319; national identity 218
Catalonia Offensive 231, 233
Catholic Church 10
Causa General 312
caves 27, 140, 271
cavitation 159
cemeteries 29, 100, 101, 214, 215, 292; Barcia cemetery 140; Cemetery of the Italians 145; Cemetery of the Martyrs

of Aravaca xxii; Eastern Cemetery (Madrid) 270; extrajudicial killings in 31; La Almudena cemetery 316; monuments 316–317; Moorish 140; San Rafael cemetery 17, 18, *18*, 23, 24, 29, 34, 35, 36, 270, 288; urban 17–20, *18*
Cerebrino Mandri 218
Cerrada del Cerrajón 176, 189, *189*, 190
Cerro del Águila 264–265
CGIS pillboxes 259, *259*
checas 99–100
checkers 152
children 235; child soldiers 200; evacuation of 115; graves of 17; of labor camp prisoners 304; and milk products 193, 253
Chinchilla prison (Albacete) 305
chozos 272
Church of Saint Augustine *122*, 131
Church of Saint Felipe Neri 205
Ciempozuelos 104–106
cities 73–74; mass graves in 16–20, *18*, 24; and modernity 73; and war 74–75
Ciudad de la Selva (City of the Forest) 271, 272–273
civilians 4, 19, 23, 74, 76, 91, 201; Battle of the Ebro 215; and bombing of Madrid 91; and bombing over Levant 202–203, 206–207; casualties 12, 91; and Catalonia Offensive 233; and famine 253–254; and guerrillas 277–278; living standards of 32–33; and poverty 256
Clavitam 227
El Clínico *see* University Hospital
Club Atlético (Argentina) 299
cod 149, 246
Coelho, R.G. 275
Colectivo Guadarrama 320
Coll del Moro (Gandesa) 215
collective identities 33, 102, 120
cologne 135, 150
colonial violence 275–276
COMEBE (Consorci per la Musealizació d'Espais de la Batalla del Ebre) 318–319
commissary 284, 295
communication trenches 79, 86, *87*, 113–114, 129, 133, 165, 190, 224, 266
communism 11, 113, 144
communist (Fifth Regiment) grenade 54, *54*, 68, 69, 83
Communist International 140

Compañía de Ferrocarriles del Oeste (Western Railway Company) 34
concentration camps xxii, 123, 140, 263, 280–295; Albatera (Alicante) 287–288; with barracks 280, 281, 283, 295; bartering 284; Campo de los Almendros (Alicante) 287; Camposancos 118, 308; Castuera (Badajoz) 7, 280, 281–285, *282*, 286, *287*, 290–295, *294*, *296*; commissary 284; communication between relatives and inmates 290; drinks 284; first aid post and infirmary 284; food 283, 284, 290; in France 233, 234–236, *234*, *236*; in Germany 233–234; handicrafts 290; head shaving of prisoners 286; health and hygiene 284–285, 286; latrines 286–288, *287*, *289*; mass graves in 292–295, *294*, *296*; Monastery of Uclés (Cuenca) 285–286; in Oia 308; perimeter ditches in 281–283; profession of inmates 293; relatives of prisoners 290–292; religious objects 293; reusing previous structures 280, 281; San Pedro de Cardeña (Burrgo) 288, 297; social status of prisoners 294, 295; survival in 288, 290; Uclés 31; writing in 288
Condor Legion 91, 97, 203, 221
Congram, D. 31
conger eel 130
constipation 255, 258, 288
Corbera d'Ebre 212, 213
Corella, Jesús Moreno 129
El Coronil (Seville) 27
Corpo di Truppe Volontarie (CTV) 106, 107–108, 110, 198, 221, 242, 243
corpses: disposal of 26–27, 29, 100; documentation of 100; incineration of 26–27, 28; rotting 26, 181, 191–192; saponification of 19
Corral, Pedro 263, 265
Correa Correa, Elicio 260
La Coruña road 55, 71, 90, 103, 263
Costaján (Burgos) 32, 33, 34, 36
cough syrups 151, 258
countryside *see* rural environment
coup 10; of Casado (1939) 262–263; of July 1936 3, 12, 74, 99, 110, 300
Cuatro Caminos 64
Cuenca 247
currency/coins xx–xxi, 89, 130, 205, 215, 248, 253, 295, 302

358   *Index*

Dabrowski Battalion 64–65
Deglané, Bobby 246
Degtyarev DP1928 light machine gun
    197, 226
Dehesa de la Villa 124, *125*, *128*
Dehesa de la Villa road 60, 63
De Lera, Ángel María 253, 254
dental prostheses 32
deserters 162–163, 164, 200,
    253, 254, 268
De Sobrón, Luis 92
detention centers 99–100, 280; *see also*
    concentration camps
De Vicente Gonzalez, Manuel 64
Díaz, José 161–162
Díaz Barrasa, Felisa 20
dictablanda 10
diseases 32, 33, 150–152, 258; Black
    Death 248; and civilian casualties 91;
    and concentration camps 281, 284–285;
    epidemics 286, 287, 288; and
    overcrowding in prisons 285; in prisons
    285; trench 88–89, 150; and waste
    management 150
documents, destruction of sensitive 262
Domanska, E. 1
dormitories in forced labor camps 302
Dueñas Méndez, Julián 170
dugouts 48–49, 50, 79–80, *87*, 94–95,
    137, 154, 239, 249, 256, 264, *264*, 265
Durango, bombing of 111
Durruti, Buenaventura 52, 58
Durruti Column 57
dwelling area 160–161, *161*
dynamites 118

Eastern Army 121
Eastern Cemetery (Madrid) 270
Eastern State Penitentiary
    (Philadelphia) 299
Ebro, Battle of *see* Battle of the Ebro
Edgar André Battalion 44–45, 46, 60, 64
Éibar (Navarre) 33
Els Auts (Fayón-Mequinenza sector) 210,
    211, 212
Enciso Column 52, 55, 56
La Enebrá, siege of 176–178, 185–188,
    187; combat-related finds *184*; corral
    fighting in 182–185, *182*, *183*;
    perimeter, defending 178–182,
    179, *181*
Enfield Pattern 14 rifle 47, 51, *51*
Enfield rifles 51–52, 62, 63, 65, 233

epidemics 150, 285, 286, 287, 288
Erhardt *Minenwerfer* 69
El Escorial 313
Espinosa de los Monteros (Burgos) 24, 36
Espinosa de los Monteros (General) 265

Etxaguen 112
Etxeberría, F. 14
Euzkadi (newspaper) 115
Euzko Gudarostea (Basque Army) 110,
    111, 112, 119
extrajudicial violence 13, 14, 19,
    31, 91, 100
Extremadura 6, 7, 270; assassination of
    guerrillas in 278; Battle of Valsquillo
    258; female corpses in 23; idle time in
    143–145; mass graves in 20, 23

F1 grenade 117, 167
FK16 (*Feldkanone* model 1916) 69
FK96 69
Fábrega-Álvarez, P. 133
Falangists xxii, 11, 80, 131, 178,
    240, 285, 292
La Fatarella (Tarragona) 216, 219,
    220–221
Fayón-Mequinenza sector 210–211, *212*
Federation of Guerrillas León-Galicia
    271–272, 273
female identities, artifacts about 36–37, *37*
Ferdinand VII, King 147
Fernández de la Reguera, Ricardo
    181, 243
Fernández García, Genara 25
Ferrándiz, Francisco 14, 26
Ferrobellum grenade 104, 262
fetal remains, in mass graves 24
Fiat CR32 106, 219
field hospitals 90, 131, 214, 285
Fifth Regiment (grenade) 54,
    69–70, 262
Fifth Regiment (military unit) 41–42
Figuerola d'Orcau (Lleida) 214
final offensive 262–263
fire trenches 113, 133, 166, 194, 210, 247
firing squad, execution by 17, 25, 29, 31,
    286, 294
First Regiment of Line Infantry
    Volunteers of Madrid 237
First Spanish Republic 10
First World War 5, 312; alcohol 148;
    amputations 214; concentration camp
    244; fortifications 188; identification

tags 152, 153; tactics 82; trenches 48, 49, 86–87; weapons and ammunitions 50, 51, 52, 60, 69, 70, 108, 114, 116, 186, 324

Fitoria (Oviedo) 139

Flak 18 anti-aircraft gun 97, *97*

fleas 150

Flórez Martínez, Rosa 141

Fomento Street *checa* 99

food 7; Abánades 176; Alto del Molino 148–149; Battle of La Nava 192–193; Casa de Vacas 49, 50; in concentration camps 283, 284, 290, 297; El Castillo 240; El Saso 130; in forced labor camps 304; Guadalajara 247, 251–252; guerrillas 272–273; and hunger xx, 33, 247, 253–258, 285, 286, 307, 308, 322; of Italian soldiers 108; La Enebrá, siege of 179–180, 184–185; Madrid 245–246, 253–254, 257; milk/milk products 78, 148–149, 176, 193, 253, 254; and mine warfare 85; rations 148; University City 78, 88, 257; and winter of 1938 148–149

footwear 36–37, *37*, 49, 89, 118, 137, 185, 187, 228–229, 243–244

forced labor camps 8, 278, 300–306; barracks 301, 302; Bustarviejo 8, 301–302, *301*, 305; Camp dels Soldats (Artà, Majorca) 301; dormitories 302; escapes 305; food 304; guards 302; huts for relatives around 302, *303*, 304, 305, *306*; latrines 302; relatives of prisoners 302, *303*, 304, 305; return of prisoners to 306, 309n8; surveillance 305; wages 304; *see also* concentration camps

Foro por la Memoria 316

Fort San Cristóbal (Navarre) 285, 307

Foucault, M. 26

foxholes 104, 156, 179, 180, *181*, 210–211, 255

Fraga, Manuel 315

France 278; concentration camps in 233, 234–236, *234*, *236*; fortification of border with 269; retreat of Republican soldiers and civilians to 233

Franco, Francisco xxii, 2, 7, 76, 116, 130, 135, 164, 199, 214, 232, 322; Army of Africa 11, 12; and Belchite 5–6, 122, 123, 131; Coll del Moro base (Gandesa) 215; concentration camps 115, 280–295; and criminalization of the political 34; exhumation campaign 13,

16; and Falange Española de las Juntas de Ofensiva Nacional-Sindicalista 178; fortifications 269–270; heritage and memorials 312–314, 315, 316, 317–318, 319; loyalty of Spanish people to 279; military tactics 40, 195; and Nationalist attack of Madrid (1939) 265; and Negrín 262–263; political graffiti 244; prisons 299, 300; propaganda 140, 253, 304; secret police 100; Valley of the Fallen 312–314, *313*, 317; and violence against civilians 23

Franco, Ramón 53

Fregenal de la Sierra (Badajoz) 24, 36, *37*

Freylag, Fritz 44

Fuentes de Ebro 157

Galicia 7, 20, 25, 271, 280

games, playing 152, 288

gangrene 214

García, Bernardino 273

García Alvárez, Demetrio 273

García Gómez, Nicomedes 193

García Rodríguez, Amanda 25

Garibaldi Battalion 108

Garrido M1924 fuse 94

Garrido Valdivia, Antonio 94

garrote vil (garrotte) 17

gas masks 83, 191–192

GEFREMA (Group of Studies of the Madrid Front) 320

gender identities, artifacts about 36–37, *37*

gender violence 22–25

General Workers Union (UGT) 111

geography of mass graves: ambiguity 26; and female victims 23–24; rural environment 20–21, *21*; urban environment 16–20, *18*, 24

geophones 83

Gerena (Seville) 23, 24

German 77 mm gun 69

German Mauser rifles 156, 178, 179, 180, 183, 198, 241

German soldiers 235; Basque Country 129; Casa de Vacas 56; Northern Front 120

Gernika, bombing of 115

Getafe, bombing of 91

Gil Hernández, E.R. 201

global crisis of 1929 11

Gogora 319

Goicoechea, Alejandro 110

360   *Index*

gold teeth 32
González Barros, Alfredo xx
González Barros, Antonio xix, xx
González Barros, Francisco xix, xx
González Barros, Julio xx
González García, C. 199
González Pérez, Evaristo 276
González-Ruibal, A. 318
Göring, Hermann 211
Goya, Francisco 168n8
Gozalvo Hill (Lucena del Cid) 196–197, 197, 199
graffiti 8, 171–172, 306–308, 322, 324; Casa de la Sierra 144–145; in concentration camps 118, 285, 308; El Castillo (Abánades) 244; in forced labor camps 301; and illiteracy 130, 144, 153, 244, 307, 324; of international volunteers 44; of militias 40, 102–103; in monuments 215; in Northern Front 135, 139, 140; with personal names 137, 205, 285; on pillbox walls 112, 190, 192; and political identity 120; in prisons 247, 306–307; propaganda 201–202; trench art 70; underground shelters 205, 206
Graham, Stephen 97
Granada 9, 314
Granatenwerfer 16 69
Gran Vía (Madrid) 92
grassroots collectives 319–320
Grazalema (Cádiz) 23
Great War *see* First World War
Greek Civil War (1946–1950) 1
grenades 53–54, 54, 63, 67–68, 108, 116–118, 133, 134, 190, 230–231; anarchist 53; Breda M35 182, 242; communist (Fifth Regiment) 54, 54, 68, 69, 83; F1 117, 167; Ferrobellum 104, 262; Lafitte 63, 68–69, 83, 85, 116, 121, 154, 155, 156, 180, 182, 184, 189, 189, 190, 197, 212, 223, 226, 260; OTO M35 117; Pera Asturiana (*Asturian pear*) 117, 139; Roma 182; spigot 69–70, 70; *Tonelete* 68, 108, 131, 211; Universal 198, 223–224, 226; wz. 24 offensive grenade 224, 226; wz. 33 defensive grenade 108, 116, 230
Guadalajara 6, 7, 104, 168, 169, 170; Alto de la Casilla 247–249; Alto del Molino 146, 146, 147–153, 151; El Castillo (Abánades) 237–244, 238, 241;

Position 64 249–251; underground cities 98; Vallejo del Chulo (Canredondo) 251–253, 252; *see also* Battle of Guadalajara
Guadalcanal (Seville) 25, 37
Gualchos (Granada) 277
Guangxu, Emperor 205
Guarda Nacional Republicana, Portugal 273
Guardia Civil 271, 273, 274, 276, 277, 278, 279
Guardias de Asalto (Assault Guards) 35, 124
guerra celere (fast war) 106
Guerrilla Army of Galicia 276
guerrilla warfare 7, 269, 270–271; Amaro family 276; Cambedo (Portugal) attack 273–276, 275; camps 273, 274; cross-border networks 273–274; food 272–273; landscape 271–272; mass graves 277–279; medicines and alcohol 273; Repil attack 276, 277; weapons 272
La Guijarrosa (Córdoba) 28
Guipúzcoa 110
Gumiel de Izán (Burgos) 35
Guns of Garabitas 93
Guzmán, Eduardo de 288

handicrafts 290
head shaving of prisoners 286
helmets 138, 184, 242, 243
Hemingway, Ernst 107
heritage: in democracy 314–321; during war and dictatorship 310–314, 313
Hernández, Miguel 144
Hernández Perdomo, Gerardo 74
Hitler, Adolf 144
Holy Year of 1933 185
Hospital Tavera 40
Hotchkiss M1914 machine gun 113, 114, 128, 139, 192, 241, 241, 265
hunger xx, 33, 247, 253–258, 285, 286, 307, 308, 322
hygiene 144, 150; artifacts 118, 124, 161, 217–218, 239, 302; in concentration camps 284–285, 286; and disposal of corpses 27; and epidemics 286, 287, 288; head shaving of prisoners 286
hypoplasia 32

Iberian Anarchist Confederation (CNT) 16, 103, 172, 174
Iberian Anarchist Federation (*Federación Anarquista Ibérica*) 53
Iberian Federation of the Libertarian Youth (FIJL) 103
Iberian Peninsula 9
identification tags 111, 115, 119, 120–121, 145, 152–153, 178, 186, 215
Iglesias, Pablo xxiv
illiteracy 130, 144, 153, 244, 307, 324
incineration of corpses 26–27, 28
Iniesta Cano, Carlos 45
insignias 34, 35, 80, *81*, 89, 120, 129, *151*, 152, *183*, 198, 211, 218, 253, 254, 293
insubordination 164
International Brigades 4, 39, 43, 45, 64–65, 71, 93, 104, 107, 164–165; *see also specific entries*
international volunteers 44–45, 46–47, 55, 56, 168, 216, 220
International Working People's Association (IWPA) 205
internecine conflicts 10
Iron Gate *see* Puerta de Hierro (Iron Gate)
Italian M1915 helmet 242, *243*
Italian soldiers 235; Battle of Guadalajara 106, 107, 108; Northern Front 120, 135–136; *Sacraio Militare Italiano* 136, 145; and Spanish soldiers, bartering between 243

Jaén 203
Jarama 7; Battle of 104–106, 254
Jews 234, 235
Johnston, N. 299
José Barreras 240
Juanola, Manuel 152
Juanola cough pills 152
judicial violence 17, 19, 31; executions of women 25
Junkers JU-52 191

Ketura (Zigoitia) 112–113
Kingdom of Castile 248
Kléber, Emilio 64
Köhler, Andrea 143

labor camps *see* forced labor camps
Lada Segura, Fermín 276
Lamb 130, 266, 268

Lafitte grenade 260; Battle of La Nava 189, *189*, 190; Battle of the Ebro 211, 212, 223, 226; La Enebrá, siege of 180, 182, 184; Levante Offensive 197; Mediana de Aragón 154, *155*, 156; Mount Lemoatx 116; University City 63; University Hospital 68–69, 83, 85; use in underground warfare 83, 85
Lasierra, Julián 277
latrines: in concentration camps 286–288, *287*; in forced labor camps 302
Law of Historical Memory of 2007 317
lead snowstorm 159
Lebel rifles 114, 138, 178
Ledesma Ramos, Ramiro xxii
Lefaucheux, Cassimir 72n9
legionnaires *see* Spanish Legion
leichter Minenwerfer (light mine thrower) 69
Leris, Buenaventura 150
Lesser, Sam 60
letters, writing 130, 135, 152, 247, 286, 288, 293, 308
Levante, guerrillas in 278
Levante-Aragón Guerrilla Group 278
Levante Offensive 6, 169, 195–200; bombing 202–207, *203*, *204*; Gozalvo Hill 196–197, *197*, 199; graves 199–200; involvement of Axis and Soviet Union 198–199; Loma del Morrón sheepfold 198; map *196*; XYZ line 195, 200–202
Levi, Primo 32
El Liberal (newspaper) 119
Lincoln-Washington Battalion 165
Lleida province (Catalonia) 214–215, 218, 314
Llerena 24
logistical warfare 75
Loma de las Ametralladoras (Fayón-Mequinenza sector) 211
Longo, Luigi 93
López Rodríguez, Antonio 281
López Tienda Column 57
Losas, Eduardo 266
Los Castillejos 251, 310–310
L-plan, bomb shelter 98
lung diseases 151–152

M1870/87 Vetterli 52, 60, *61*
M1910 Maxim machine gun 50, 52, 233
M1931 anti-aircraft gun 96, *97*
Macías, Claudio 21, *22*

362 *Index*

Madrid 7, 10, 31, 39, 73, 74–75, 102;
active and passive defense in 96–98, *97*;
barricades 74, *75*; bombing of 91–99,
93, 94; Casas de Murcia (Vallecas) 255;
civilian casualties in 91; extermination
centers in 99–101; fortification of 40,
41–42, *43*; grassroots collectives in
319–320; hideouts 100; last Nationalist
attempts to take 103–110; mass graves
in 99, 101; militarization of 74;
Nationalist attack (1939) 263–265, *264*;
Nationalist frontlines, living conditions
of 244–246; parks 100; Republican
frontlines, living conditions of
253–258; Rivas Vaciamadrid 256–257,
257; *sacas* in 16; surrender of 7, 263,
266–268, *267*; *see also* Battle of Madrid
Madrid Battalion 112, 113, 120
Maestrazgo 195–196
Maeztu, Ramiro de xxii
Magallón (Zaragoza) 20, *21*
makeshift homes 217
Málaga 17–18, *18*, 23, 24, 29, 34,
35, 36, 270, 288
malnutrition 32, 235, 285
Malraux, André 107
Mannlicher-Carcano M1891 108
Mannlicher M1895 rifle 108, 138
Marco, Jorge 269
María Cristina of Habsburg 76
Martínez Bande, J.M. 39, 41, 56, 126,
127, 129, 258, 260–261
masculinity, artifacts about 36
Masquelet, General 42
mass graves 14–22, *15*, 40, 112, 270;
ambiguous space of 26; artifacts 33;
Battle of the Ebro 213–214; Battle of
the Segre 214–215; Caspe 167–168;
Causa General 312; and class conflict
324–325; in concentration camps
292–295, *294, 296*; exhumation of
315–316; female corpses in 22–25; fetal
remains in 24; guerrilla warfare
277–279; hands, tying of 28–29, *28*;
human remains 32–33; identification of
victims 19; La Enebrá 186–187, *187*; in
Madrid 99, 101; massacre, hiding
26–28; and memorials 314; Monte
Sollube 318; *paseos* 15, 16–17, 20;
religious identity in 35–36, *35*; with
remains of women 23, **348–349**; rural
environment 20–21, *21*; *sacas* 14–15,
15, 16, 20, *21*; size of 20, 24; terror-

inspiring efficacy of 26; Teruel 200;
Todos los Nombres project 319; urban
environment 16–20, *18*
Massó Brothers 240
mass rape 141
Matallana de Valmadrigal (León) 34
Las Matas (Oviedo) 139
Mateo Merino, Pedro 221, 223
material culture 34–35, 54, 120, 131–132,
218, 281, 318, 323
Matthews, James 247
Mauser C-96 pistol 198, 233
Mauthausen-Gusen concentration camp
233, 234
Mayorgas, Antonio xx–xxi
meat cans *109*, 192, 240
meat consumption 49, 78, 130, 137, 149,
240, 245, 251, 253, 257, 283
Mediana de Aragón 6, 132–133, 135,
153–157, *155*, 158–160, *158, 160,
161*, 162, *163*
medicines 89, 118, 131, 150–151, 253,
255, 258, 273, 284, 324
Memoria Democrática (Andalusia) 319
Memorial Democràtic (Catalonia) 319
memorials 13; in democracy 314–321;
during war and dictatorship
310–314, *313*
Menéndez Amado, Urbano 141
Mera, Cipriano 170, 172
Mérida 26–27, 35, 192, 240
mess tins 243, 283–284
metal detectorists 318
Mexican Cristero War 168n11
MG08/15 machine gun 116
Miaja, José 99
military courts 25, 178
military museums 311
militias xxii, 2, 3, 51, 102, *103*, 120; left-
wing 4, 16, 34, 40, 41, 52, 57, 118,
119, 140; right-wing 15, 20, 21, 23, 30,
40, 292, 325
milk/milk products 78, 148–149, 176,
193, 253, 254
mineral water 258
miners 34–35
mine shafts 27
mine warfare 82–85, *84*
mining tunnels 80
Miranda de Ebro (Burgos) 280
modernity 10, 73, 123, 131–132, 243
Modesto, Juan 70
Mogrovejo, Manuel *114*, 115

Mola, Emilio 12, 13, 312
El Molar (Tarragona) 219
La Molatilla 194
Molí den Ferriol (Corbera d'Ebre)
   216, *217*
Monastery of Uclés (Cuenca) 285–286
Moncloa-Arroyo de Pozuelo 263
Monte Costaján (Burgos) 29
Monte Sollube 318
Montoya, Milagros 304
Montoya Salamó, Isaac 219
Moorish cemeteries 140
mortars 67, 83, 189, 192, 194; Brixia
   M1935 108, 155–156, 198; Erhardt
   Minenwerfer 69; Spanish spigot 69–70;
   Stokes-Brandt Mle 27/31 50; Stokes-
   Brandt 81 mm 50, 69, 275; trench
   mortars 50, 124, 127, 250; Valero
   M1933 50, 69, 133, 154–155, 183,
   241, 242; Valero 50 mm 63,
   69, 133, 181
Moshenska, Gabriel 207
Mosin Nagant rifles 52, 105, 162, 197,
   198, 224, 231, 265
Mount Bernorio (Palencia) 136–137
Mount Garabitas 43, 90, 93–94
Mount Lemoatx 115–119, 121, 196, **351**
Mount Murugain (Mondragón) 111
Mount San Pedro 113–115, *114*, 121
mourning 13, 27, 175, 314
Muñoz, Catalina 25, 322
Muñoz Encinar, Laura 24
murder, patterns of 14; gender violence
   22–25; massacre, hiding 26–28; mass
   graves 14–22; ways of killing 28–32
Museum of the Army (Madrid) 311
Museum of the Siege (Alcázar,
   Toledo) 311
museums 311, 318
mussel shells 130
Mussolini, Benito 106, 107, 135

Napoleon III 253
La Nava, Battle of *see* Battle of La Nava
Navarre 9, 237; Éibar 33; Fort San
   Cristóbal 285, 307; mass graves
   in 20, 30
Navarre Brigades 111, 115, 116, 140–141
Navarrete, Ernesto 283, 292
Navarro Romero, Julián 305
Navas, Aurora 291–292
Negrín, Juan 220, 255, 262, 263
Neitzel, Sönke 95

newborns, graves of 17
newspapers 115, 119, 161, 206
nits 150
non-professional killers 29–30
Northern Front 5, 21, 103, 280, 308, 323;
   Basque mountains 110–119;
   battlefields, tours through 311;
   Castiltejón (León) 136–139, *138*; end
   of 135–136; Mount Bernorio (Palencia)
   136–137; Oviedo 139–140; Valdediós
   140–141

Offensive of Catalonia 231
Offensive of the Upper Tajuña 6, 169,
   170–173, 247, 251, 310, 323; Abánades
   170–176, *172*, *175*; Battle of La Nava
   188–193; end of 193–194; La Enebrá,
   siege of 176–188
Olba (Teruel) 198, 200
Orwell, George 81, 103, 239
OTO M35 grenade 117
overcrowding in prisons 285, 297
Ovidius 307
Oviedo 139–141
Owen, Wilfred 135

PaK 36 anti-tank gun 259, 260
Palace of Ibarra 107–108, *109*
Palacio de Oriente 240, 241
pamphlets, propaganda campaign 253
Paracuellos 101
Parapet of Death 132–133, *134*, 135
parasites 150–151
Parcero-Oubiña, C. 133
Paredes, Fernando 219
paseos 15, 16–17, 20
Passalacqua, N. 31
passive defense 96, 97–98, *97*, 205–206
Paterna, mass graves in 17, 19, 270
patriarchal ideology 23, 305
Pattern 1914 Enfield 47, 51
Pazo de Meirás 317–318
La Pedraja (Burgos, Castile) 24
Peinado, José 202–203
Peñarroya, Battle of *see* Battle of
   Valsquillo
Peninsular War 147, 237, 323
penitentiary tourism xx, 300
Pera Asturiana grenade 117, 139
Pérez del Pulgar, José 280
perfume 135, 150, 239
perimeter ditches, in concentration
   camps 281–283

364   *Index*

perimortem trauma 28, 30, 31, 154, 180, 200, 213, 214, 215
Pernafeites (Miravet) 213–214
personal weapons, use of 49, 147, 292
Philip II 42, 313
Philip IV 253
physical stress, and living standards 32–33
Picasso, Pablo 115
Piedrafita García, Antonio 141
pillboxes: Alto de la Casilla 248; Battle of La Nava 189–192; Battle of the Ebro 220, 222–224, *223*; CGIS pillboxes 259, *259*; Dehesa de la Villa 124, *125*; Fitoria 139; graffiti 112, 190, 192; as homes 87; Madrid 41–42, *43*; Mount San Pedro 113, *114*; Republican offensive (1939) 258–262; Rivas Vaciamadrid 256; XYZ line 201
Pinos del Río (Granada) 277
Pinos del Valle 279
El Piul (Rivas Vaciamadrid) 256–257, *257*
Pius XI, Pope 186
Pizarro Cenjor, Manuel 278
Plaça de Diamant (Barcelona) 206
planes, downing of 219
Plaza de España (Madrid) 56
Plaza de Séneca (Alicante) 204, *204*
Policía Armada (Armed Police) 302
Polikarpov, Nikolai 219
Polikarpovs I-15 218, 219
Polikarpovs I-16 96, 218, 219
political identity 33–34, 120
political prisoners 7, 297, 304
Popular Army 6–7, 41, 83, 102, 193; Battle of La Nava 188, 191; Battle of Teruel 164; Battle of the Ebro 208, 216; Brunete offensive 121; Castiltejón (León) 137; collapse of 262; Guadalajara 146, 147, 149, 247–253; insignia 254; Levante Offensive 195, 202; Madrid 253–258; Mediana de Aragón 154–155, 162; Offensive of the Upper Tajuña 185, 194; situation at the end of war 324; University city 85–91; Zaragoza offensive 121
Popular Front 11, 13, 99, 162, 263
pork 108, 283
Portugal 273
postcranial traumas 31
postwar period 269; demolition of buildings 77; destruction of burials during 27; forced labor camps 300–306;

fortifications 269–270; irregular violence during 270; prisons 296–300; *see also* concentration camps; guerrilla warfare
poverty 7, 20, 256
Prada, Adolfo 266
pregnant women, killing of 24
Preixens Torebadella, Leandro 215
PREMEX 316
Priaranza del Bierzo (León) 315
Prieto, Indalecio 119
Primo de Rivera, José Antonio 312
Primo de Rivera, Miguel 10
prisons 280, 296–300; Carabanchel 7–8, 297–299, *298*; Fort San Cristóbal (Navarre) 285; overcrowding in 285, 297; radial model 299–300; spatial order 297, 298–299; temporal routines 297; Valdenoceda (Burgos, Castille) 285; *see also* concentration camps
protestants 36
Provincial Committee of Public Investigation 99
Puebla de Alcocer (Extremadura) 270
Puente de los Franceses 44, 55–56
Puente de San Fernando 59
Puerta de Hierro (Iron Gate) 58–65, 62, 90, 254
Puerta del Sol (Madrid) 92
Puerto Real (Cádiz) 24, 25
El Pueyo Hill 165–166, *166*
Pujalt (Barcelona) boot camp 217
punishment 7, 279–280; concentration camps 280–295; forced labor camps 300–306; prisons 296–300
Pyrenees 233, 269

Quedlinburg prisoner-of-war camp (Germany) 244, 283
Quintanilla de las Viñas (Burgos) 30
Quintín, Francisco 284, 288

radial model of prisons 299–300
railway workers 34
Raïmats (Lleida) 220, 221–222, 223, 227
rations 148, 257
Rattenkrieg (rat warfare) 82–85
recycling of materials 7, 90, 137, 250, 254, 324
Redondo, Onésimo 312
Regio Esercito 108
regional identities 9

Regional Plan of Fortifications of the Spanish Civil War (Madrid) 320
regulares 40, 139–140, 194, 215, 246
religious identity 9; artifacts 80, 89, 119, 125–126, *126*, *179*, 185, 258, 293; in mass graves 35–36, *35*
Remington rifles 60, *61*
Renshaw, Layla 14
Repil (Pobra de Brollón, Lugo) 276, *277*
requetés 123, 124, 125
Restoration 10
El Retiro Park (Madrid) 98
Reverte, Jorge M. 39
revolutionary violence 13, 14, 16, 18–19, 27, 36, 100, 103, 293, 314, 316, 317
Rif War 23, 152
Ríos, L. 14, 31
Rivas Vaciamadrid 256–257, *257*
Rivesaltes concentration camp 235, *236*
Rodríguez Ogallar, Francisco xix–xx
Rodríguez Simón, Pedro 165
Rojo, Vicente 231
Roma grenades 182
El Rondal (Abánades) 173, 242
roundabouts, and trenches 104
royal hunting 45–46
Ruiz Casero, Luis Antonio 107–108
rural environment: extrajudicial killings in 31; mass graves in 20–21, *21*; and memorials 314

sacas 14–15, *15*, 16, 20, *21*
Sachsenhausen concentration camp 234
Sacraio Militare Italiano 136, 145
Saint Anthony of Padua (Zaragoza) 136
Saint-Etienne M-1907 machine gun 128–129, 192
Salas Larrazábal, María 68
Salazar, António de Oliveira 1
Salgado Ribera, Juan 273
Sánchez, Néstor 157
Sanctuary of Santísimo Cristo de la Agonía (Holy Christ of Agony) 186
San Felipe castle 25
San Fernando (Cádiz) 35
San Pedro de Cardeña (Burrgo) 288, 297
San Rafael cemetery (Málaga) 17, 18, *18*, 23, 24, 29, 34, 35, 36, 270, 288
Santa Creu mountain range 199
Santamaría, Julián 30
Santander, Battle of 136
Santo Adriano 140
Sant Pau d'Ordal (Barcelona) 232

saponification of corpses 19
sardines 176, 240
Sarrià 37n2
sarsaparilla 284
El Saso 126–131, *128*, *129*
Sayabera Miranda, José 293
Saz Urbina, Gabriel 300–301
Schell, Pablo 92
School of Architecture (University City) 57, 266
School of Medicine (University City) 59, *59*
School of Odontology (University City) 83, 88
School of Philosophy and Letters (University City) 57, 59, 63, 88
Schuh, Philipp 46, 48, 50, 53, 55, 56
SCRM 1935 182
SD 50 bomb 221
Second Spanish Republic 10–11
Second World War 1, 73, 82, 95, 97, 169, 280, 324
Sedano (Burgos) 34
Segre, Battle of 214
La Sendilla (Ciempozuelos) 104, *105*
sensitive documents, destruction of 262
sentinels 85, 156
La Serena Pocket, offensive of 145, 285
Serra del Toro (Castellón) 199–200
Serrano Suñer, Ramón 80
Serrulla, Fernando 14, 27, 30, 32
Service of Military Intelligence (*Servicio de Inteligencia Militar*) 247
sexual violence against women 24
shacks (*chabolas*) 88
shaving razors *15*, 150
sheepfolds: Alto de la Casilla 249; Alto del Molino 146–148, *146*; El Saso 126–127, *129*, 130; La Enebrá, siege of 176–188; Loma del Morrón (Olba) 198; Martín 176, 184; Mediana de Aragón 162, *163*; Offensive of the Upper Tajuña 173–176, *175*; Tío Casto 174, 175; Valdelagua 192–193
shelters *see* bomb shelters underground shelters
ShKas machine gun 218, 219
shot-related trauma 286
shrapnel shells 127
Sierra de Argallén 145
Silva, Emilio 315
Sima de Jinámar 27
skull traumas 30

366   *Index*

slogans 144, 201–202, 206
snipers 53
social class 9, 10, 11, 32, 207, 324–325
Sociedad de Ciencias Aranzadi 316
Sofsky, Wolfgang 297
soft dictatorship 10
Soleràs (Lleida) 214–215
solid waste management 80–82
Soms, Joaquim 152
Soria Division 106
Sotodosos 169, 170, 194, 249
Soviet Union 100, 198; involvement in
    Spanish Civil War 199; military support
    from 49, 52, 108, 219, 324
Spanish Civil War 1, 2; casualties of 2, 12,
    13; fortunes made from 240–241;
    involvement of Axis and Soviet Union
    in 198–199; map of Spain during *4*;
    materiality of 5, 102; material past of
    323; mesocscale of battles 323; and
    nationalisms 9; nature of 323; regional
    diversity of 323; transformation of
    non-conventional to conventional
    war 102; violence, nature of 12–14
Spanish Legion 40, 65, 74, 77, 79, 80, 82,
    85, 152, 192, 210, 310
Spanish Mauser M1893 30, 50, 60, 61,
    113, 162, 198, 241, 265
spigot grenades 69–70, *70*
spondyloarthrosis 32
Stalin, Joseph 219
Stalingrad, Battle of 82
Steel Belt 110
Stellani, Armando 243
Stern, Manfred 48
Stokes-Brandt 81 mm mortar 50, 69, 275
Stokes-Brandt Mle 27/31 mortar 50
strategic bombing 202
strategic warfare 75
surprise attacks 153, 154, 156–157
swastikas 80
Swiss-Army knifes 193
symbolic violence 29

T-26 tanks 49, 107, 108, 169, 182, 185,
    191, 223, 260
tactical bombing 202
tactical warfare 75
Tagüeña, Manuel 216, 221
Tajuña *see* Offensive of the Upper Tajuña
tea 246
Teba (Málaga) 24, 34, 36
La Tejera (Álava, Basque Country) 36

Tejerizo-García, Carlos 273
Tercio de Almogávares 123, 142n3
terminal ballistics 157, 159
Terra Alta 208–209
terra sigillata 131
Teruel 153, 164, 195, 198, 199, 200, 278;
    see also Battle of Teruel
Thirteen Roses 25
Thomas, Hugh xxi, xxii
Tiago, Albertina 273, 274
Todo los Nombres project 319
La Toja 239–240
Toledo 40–41, 311
Tonelete grenade 68, 108, 131, 211
toothbrush 124,161, 184, 230, 302
Torrejón de Velasco 41
Torrelavega, González de 307
Torres Ferrer, José 254
torture 28; centers, in Madrid 99–100; in
    concentration camps 286; of guerrillas
    278; of Republican veterans 233; of
    women 24–25
totalitarian movements 300
training camps 217
tramway drivers 34
trash pits 146, *146*, 149, 150
treason 127, 129–130
treasure-hunters 318
trench art 70, 80
trenches 68; Asylum of Santa Cristina
    79–80, 266; Basque mountains
    111–112, 113, *114*, 116, *117*, 120, 121;
    Battle of La Nava 188, 190; Battle of
    the Ebro 220, 224–231, *225, 229*;
    Belchite 124–125, *126*; Casa de Vacas
    47–52, *47, 51*, 55; communication
    trenches 79, 86, *87*, 113–114, 129, 133,
    165, 190, 224, 266; excavation, during
    winter 146; Fayón-Mequinenza sector
    210, 211; fire trenches 113, 133, 166,
    194, 210, 247; in flood-prone terrain
    88; Guadalajara 237–244, 247–253;
    hollows in 49; isolated trench systems
    188; La Sendilla 104, *105*; Madrid
    244–246, 253–258; Parapet of Death
    133, *134*; trench warfare 54, 68–70,
    171, 239; University City 60, 86–89,
    86, 90, 263–265, *264*; University
    Hospital 68–69
trench fever 150–151
trench mortars 50, 124, 127, 250
Trippe, Gustav 219–220, 231
tuberculosis 285

Tudela, Battle of 237
tuna 240
tunnels 58, 80, 82, 83–84, 85, 159, 224
Turó de la Rovira (Barcelona) 205

Uclés (Cuenca) 31
underground shelters 259, 322; Asylum of
    Santa Cristina 77, 79; Battle of the Ebro
    216, 217; El Castillo (Abánades)
    238–239; El Pueyo Hill 165; El Saso
    127; graffiti 205, 206; Levante
    Offensive 202, 206; Madrid 97–99,
    97, 100
unexploded ordnance 66, 67, 92
Unified Socialist Youth (JSU) 16, 41,
    70, 111
uniforms 34, 123, 141, 152, 162, 163,
    243–244, 254
United Kingdom 206–207, 234
Unite Proletarian Brothers (UHP)
    103, 112
Universal grenade 198, 223–224, 226
University City 4–5, 46, 56–58, 57, 263;
    attacks at 350–351; casualties 58;
    fortifications 86–87, 88; impact of small
    arms fire 59; Iron Gate 58–65; materials
    excavated in 84–85, 88, 89; Nationalist
    frontlines, living conditions 244–246;
    Nationalist lines 76–85; NW corner,
    Nationalist attack through 62;
    Rattenkrieg (rat warfare) 82–85;
    Republican frontlines, living conditions
    253–254; Republican lines 85–91;
    room-by-room fighting 58, 59, 59;
    ruins, as heritage site 311; sewage
    system 83; shelters 87, 88; trenches 60,
    86–89, 86, 90; weapons 60–61, 61,
    62–63
University Hospital 5, 58, 59, 65–71, 66,
    76, 77; artillery/mortars 69–70;
    casualties 68; memorials 310; mine
    warfare 82–85, 84; unexploded
    ordnance 66, 67; unproductive assaults
    68; weapons 65–66, 67–71, 70,
    349–350
U-plan, bomb shelter 98
Upper Tajuña see Offensive of the Upper
    Tajuña
urban environment see cities
urban warfare 68, 73
Urodonal Etach 150
Urra, Father 79
utility knife 167

Vaciamadrid 106
Valdediós 140–141
Valdelagua 191, 192
Valdenoceda (Burgos, Castile) 285
Valencia 195, 200–201; assassination of
    guerrillas in 278; bombing of
    202–203, 203
Valero mortars: 50 mm 63, 69, 133, 181;
    M1933 50, 69, 133, 154–155, 183,
    241, 242
Valladares, Portela xxii
Valladolid 178
Vallbona (Urgell) 232
Vall d'Aran, attack on 269
Vall de Camprodon (Catalonia) 233
La Vall d'Uixó (Castellón) 201
Vallejo, César 139
Vallejo del Chulo (Canredondo) 251, 252
Valley of the Fallen 17, 300, 305,
    312–314, 313, 316, 317
Valsquillo, Battle of 258
La Vaquilla (1985) 315
Vega Sevillano, Luis 22
vertical geopolitics 97
Vértice Cerro 172–173, 194, 247
Vilallonga, José Luis de 29
Villamediana (Palencia, Castile) 24
Villanueva del Duque (Guadalajara) 29
Villar, Fausto 165
Villarreal, Battle of 110, 113
Villarejo de la Peñuela (Cuenca) 278
Villaverde del Ducado (Guadalajara) 314
Viñas, Ángel 89
Virilio, Paul 74–75
Vizcaya 110, 111, 121
Vizuete, Máximo 144

war museums 311
washing 150
waste management 80–82, 150
weapons 30; abandoned by exiling
    Republican soldiers 233; Alto de la
    Casilla 249; Basque mountains, war in
    112, 113–114, 116–118; Battle of
    Jarama 105–106; Battle of La Nava 189,
    190; Battle of the Ebro 211, 212, 218,
    219, 221, 223–224, 225, 226, 230–231;
    Belchite 124–125, 127, 128, 131;
    Brunete, Republican offensive in
    (1939) 259, 260, 261–262; Casa de
    Vacas 47–52, 53–55, 54, 349;
    Castiltejón (León) 138; destroying/
    dumping 262; diversity of 50–51, 118,

368   *Index*

120; El Castillo (Abánades) 241–242, *241*; Guadalajara 147; guerrilla warfare 272; La Enebrá, siege of 178, 179, 180, 182, 183, 186; Levante Offensive 197, 198–199; Mediana de Aragón 154–156, 162; Mount Lemoatx 116–118, **351**; Nationalist attack of Madrid (1939) 265; Offensive of the Upper Tajuña 174, 176; Oviedo 139; Palace of Ibarra attack 108; Position 64 (Guadalajara) 250; quality of 89–90; recycling 90; terminal ballistics 157, 159; University City 60–61, *61*, 62–63, 89–90; University Hospital 65–66, 67–71, *70*, **349–350**

Weltzer, Harald 95

Winchester M1892 233

Winchester M1895 52

winter of 1938 146, 148, 151, 153

women: and guerrilla warfare 276; related to concentration camp prisoners 290; related to labor camp prisoners 304; remains, mass graves with 23, **348–349**; violence against 22–25

work identity, and artifacts 34

World War I *see* First World War

World War II *see* Second World War

wz. 24 offensive grenade 224, 226

wz. 33 defensive grenade 108, 116, 230

XYZ line 195, 200–202

Yagüe, Juan 26, 43, 220

Zaldívar concentration camp 292

Zapatero, Rodríguez 315

Zaragoza 5, 6, 121, 132, 153

ZB-26 machine gun 233

ZB vz. 24 Czech Mauser rifle 112, 113, 114